PRIEST OF NATURE

PRIEST

OF

NATURE

THE RELIGIOUS WORLDS
OF ISAAC NEWTON

ROB ILIFFE

OXFORD
UNIVERSITY PRESS

OXFORD
UNIVERSITY PRESS

Oxford University Press is a department of the University of Oxford.
It furthers the University's objective of excellence in research, scholarship,
and education by publishing worldwide. Oxford is a registered trade mark of
Oxford University Press in the UK and certain other countries.

Published in the United States of America by Oxford University Press
198 Madison Avenue, New York, NY 10016, United States of America.

© Rob Iliffe 2017

Library of Congress Cataloging-in-Publication Data
Iliffe, Rob, author.
Priest of nature : the religious worlds of Isaac Newton / Robert Iliffe.
pages cm
Includes bibliographical references and index.
ISBN 978-0-19-999535-6
1. Newton, Isaac, 1642–1727—Religion. I. Title.
B1299.N34I45 2013
230'.044092—dc23
2013032052

1 3 5 7 9 8 6 4 2
Printed by Edwards Brothers Malloy, United States of America

Contents

Acknowledgements

The roots of this book go back more than three decades to the start of my PhD thesis. Beginning in the spring of 1986, I spent the best part of three years in the Microfilm Reading Room above the Manuscript Room in Cambridge University Library, working my way slowly through six, thick microfilm reels of Newton's theological writings. The microfilm reader had to be turned laboriously by hand, and there was no facility for making copies of the documents. Due to the poor quality of the microfilm copy, the script in the images was often unreadable. When I could read Newton's hand with relative ease, the material often appeared abstruse to the point of being incomprehensible.

The timing was hardly propitious. Although Frank Manuel, Richard Westfall, and David Castillejo had done pioneering work on the subject, scholars no longer appeared to be interested in Newton's theological writings. Indeed, it was becoming increasingly unfashionable to work on the history of early modern science and it seemed unwise and even obtuse to concentrate on the unpublished religious musings of a dead white European male, despite the fact that—or perhaps because—he remained one of the totemic founders of modern science. However, although I was aware that I might wander completely out of the realm of history of science, I chose to study the subject because it concerned what Newton called "difficult things." Rather than simply marvel at the fact that he had spent so much time doing it, I wanted to do justice to the recondite content of Newton's work in this area.

The study of Newton's writings on religion and ancient chronology has moved on dramatically in the last two decades, and there is now a thriving international community of scholars working in the field. This is in part because Newton's life and work remain perennially fascinating. More prosaically, it is due to the fact that almost all of the primary texts are available online as part of the Newton Project, an open access digital edition of Newton's writings in the fields of religion, science, and administration. As a result, it is now possible to search through, read, and annotate digitally in just one hour what took me nearly three years to sift through and record in my own (now indecipherable) handwriting.

From 1998 to 2015, I was the acting director of the Newton Project, overseeing the publication of more than four million words of Newton's theological writings as well as extensive selections from his work on other subjects. This monograph has been immeasurably improved and indeed, made possible by the existence of such resources. While Newton's alchemical interests play only a minor role in this book, I have also benefited from the digital materials available via the Chymistry of Isaac Newton Project directed by Bill Newman at Indiana University. The excellent translations of the Latin texts on the Newton Project produced by Michael Silverthorne have allowed me to check my own earlier versions, and they have enabled many readers to engage with writings by Newton that would otherwise have remained inaccessible.

The Newton Project is indebted to those people who have transcribed and encoded Newton's writings to such a high standard. Of the more than fifty people who have worked on the project I would like to single out for their contributions Dolores Iorizzo, José Manuel Cañas Reíllo, Rebekah Higgitt, Shelley Innes, Raquel Delgado-Moreira, Margarita Fernandez-Chas, Daniele Cassisa, Andy Mansfield, Cesare Pastorino, Janet Yvonne Martin-Portugues, Will Scott, Kees-Jan Schilt, Liz Smith, and Niki Black. Liz and Niki are two of a number of Canadian scholars who have produced high-quality encoded transcriptions of religious documents for Newton Project Canada under the leadership of Steve Snobelen, all of which are now housed on the Newton Project. John Young deserves special praise for the number and outstanding quality of the transcriptions produced over the first decade of the project, and for determining how to create complex XML renderings of heavily rewritten drafts according to the guidelines of the Text Encoding Initiative. Mike Hawkins has been the technical supremo behind the project for almost all of its existence, and it would not exist without his brilliant programming skills. This book is, in an important sense, an homage to their collective labours.

The infrastructure of the Newton Project has been aided by many individuals and organisations. Alongside superb IT staff at Imperial College London and the universities of Sussex and Oxford, Ainslee Rutledge and Fiona Allan provided crucial administrative support for almost its entire duration. The project was underpinned by three consecutive large research grants from the Arts and Humanities Research Council (until 2004 the Arts and Humanities Research Board), two major grants from the Joint Information Systems Committee (JISC), a senior award from the European Union, and substantial funding in 2007–9 from the Royal Society. Generous financial support from the University of Oxford History Faculty, the Dry Family Foundation, Randal Locke and friends, Michael Chowen, and a number of other donors has made possible the transcription of all of Newton's personal papers (including much of his correspondence) and many of his economic and scientific papers.

I was able to carry out much of the research for this book thanks to fellowships at the Dibner Institute (in spring 2004), the Clark Library (in spring 2012), and the Huntington Library (in 2012–13), where Steve Hindle presided over a particularly congenial setting for doing work on Newton. At the same time, I held the Eleanor Searle Professorship in the History of Science at Caltech, a position that gave me the opportunity to develop some of the core ideas in the book. I had many enjoyable and informative conversations with Jed Buchwald and Moti Feingold at a time when their magnum opus on Newton's chronological research was in production, and a number of fruitful discussions with Diana Kormos Buchwald about the digital history of science.

From the beginning, librarians and archivists have offered vital support for my research on Newton-related matters. In particular I would like to thank Orly Simon, Dan Lewis, Peter Jones, Adam Perkins, and Keith Moore for their generous help. Under the excellent leadership of Grant Young, the Cambridge Digital Library has made available images of all the Newton documents in the University Library, and this resource has been exceptionally useful for my work. Newton's key mathematical papers (and the theological writings of his stepfather) were transcribed and published online as part of a JISC-funded project, "Windows on Genius," that involved a productive partnership between the Newton Project and the Digital Library. Godfrey Waller deserves special mention for the unstintingly warm-hearted help he gave me during the years when I worked alone in the Microfilm Reading Room at Cambridge.

The research underpinning this book has been presented in numerous venues over the years, and I have benefited greatly from the feedback given on these occasions. Theologians and historians of religion have offered helpful if usually horrified comments on Newton's take on the early Christian Church, and a number of fundamentalists have remarked with varying degrees of approval on the accuracy of his apocalyptic predictions. Individual scholars, notably Gideon Manning (on Descartes), Michael Stawpert (on the Goths and the Vandals), and Grantley McDonald (on Newton's analysis of scriptural corruptions) have given useful advice on specific areas covered by the book. Any errors of fact are my own.

I have been fortunate to be able to draw upon the skills of the Grantham U3A team that transcribed, encoded, and published the Grantham Hallbook, which sheds a bright light on Cromwellian Grantham and on the activities of William Clarke while Newton lodged with him in the late 1650s. I would like to thank John Down and John Manterfield for their help in bringing this project to fruition, and especially Ruth Crook for sharing her unrivalled knowledge of the life and times of Clarke and his family. The Grantham Gravity Fields Festival ably organized every two years by Rosemary Richards has made it possible to work with local historians at regular intervals.

I have drawn liberally on the work of intellectual historians, historians of philosophy, and historians of political thought, and most notably on the publications of the Churchill College School of Mark Goldie, Justin Champion, and John Marshall. I have also gained numerous insights from the writings of scholars in the history of science, especially Sarah Hutton, Margaret Jacob, John Henry, John Hedley Brooke, Charles Webster, Mario Biagioli, Richard Serjeantson, Dmitri Levitin, Peter Dear, Robert Westman, Sorana Corneanu, and Steven Shapin. In particular, I have stood on the collective shoulders of those historians whose work constitutes the Newton "Industry," most notably Tom Whiteside, Frank Manuel, Alexandre Koyré, Bernard Cohen, Rupert Hall, Richard Westfall, Ted McGuire, Alan Shapiro, Betty Jo Dobbs, George Smith, Bill Newman, Simon Schaffer, Dick Popkin, Moti Feingold, Jed Buchwald, and Niccolò Guicciardini.

The research of Scott Mandelbrote, Jim Force, and Steve Snobelen has been particularly significant for the study of Newton's theology. Jim did pioneering work on Newton's unpublished writings on religion and he gave me vital encouragement early in my career. Scott has written a number of important scholarly articles on Newton's theological writings and has been a supportive co-editorial director of the Newton Project. Steve made extensive and detailed comments on a penultimate version of the book. In doing so, he was typically magnanimous in allowing me to make use of his unrivalled knowledge of early modern anti-Trinitarianism.

Other debts are of a more personal nature. Gerry Martin gave benevolent assistance to my research in its early years, while Martin Beagles, Pete Langman, Pascal Brioist, Iwan Morus, Larry Stewart, and Justin Champion have been excellent friends and colleagues for as long as I can remember. Lisa Jardine gave tremendous backing to the Newton Project and to other aspects of my career, but sadly passed away before this book was finished. Simon Schaffer was my doctoral supervisor and, even earlier, he suggested that I consult Newton's *Principia* papers at Cambridge University Library for an MPhil essay. I have learned far more about the history of science talking with him than from any other source. For what seems like ages, Andy Warwick has encouraged me to complete the tome, and his great book *Masters of Theory* has served as a template for an archivally rich history of science that takes seriously the intellectual content of the documents. Many of the dimly remembered discussions we had in the Eagle and the Hoop and Toy have informed the various approaches taken in the book.

Towards the end of the production process, Tim Miller and Kees-Jan Schilt did important work improving the bibliography and endnotes. Kit Ward was a good-natured and enthusiastic champion of the book from the outset and was instrumental in arranging the contract with Oxford University Press. Tragically, her early death meant that she did not see the project come to fruition. At OUP Alyssa O'Connell, Tim Bent, and Gwen Colvin have seen the book through its final stages with immense skill and great patience, and I am extremely grateful to them for their help. Finally, my family has listened to me talk about the idiosyncrasies of a very strange man for decades. Paul and Cecie Dry have offered constant encouragement throughout the process of writing this book, and my parents, Judy and Ken, deserve special thanks for endorsing my chosen career. Rachel, Samuel, and Jacob were all born after I began working on Newton and have suffered accordingly, though never silently. Finally, Sarah Dry has provided immense and loving support during the life of the book. She has read a number of chapters with a keen eye for sense and tone, and it is dedicated to her.

PRIEST OF NATURE

Introduction

A Rational Christian

In November 1679 the secretary of the Royal Society, Robert Hooke, wrote to Isaac Newton to ask his views on a number of recent scientific theories and discoveries. Newton, the reclusive Lucasian Professor of Mathematics at Cambridge, had been a scientific celebrity since the start of the decade as a result of his extraordinary discovery that white light was compounded of more basic coloured rays. However, a series of disputes about his work had put him off participating in public discussion of scientific issues. He told Hooke that having spent the last few months in the country, he was completely unaware of what natural philosophers in London or anywhere else had been doing. His disillusionment with philosophy had been brewing for some time, he said, and he added that he had been trying for many years to turn away from the natural sciences. Now, he continued, he wanted to concentrate on his "other studies." He had "shook hands" with natural philosophy and was as uninterested in the subject as any rustic was about scholarly pursuits. Instead, he was going to concentrate on research that he enjoyed, or that was of benefit to others.[1]

What was so important that, by comparison, Newton's scientific and mathematical work was an irritating distraction? What, in short, was the content of these "other studies"? Most of his colleagues at Trinity College, Cambridge, were aware that he was devoted to his "chymical" (i.e., chemical and alchemical) investigations, but they also knew that he was an exceptionally serious student of religion. His outward behaviour indicated that he was an "intire"—that is, a devout—Christian, a fine and upstanding member of the Church of England who worshipped regularly and publicly at the college chapel and at the university church, Great St. Mary's. However, by the time Hooke's letter arrived, Newton was harbouring a terrible secret. He believed that the central Christian doctrine of the Trinity was a diabolical fraud, and that all of modern Christianity was tainted by its presence. Jesus Christ, the Son of God, was not equal in any sense to God the Father, although he was divine, and was worthy of being worshipped in his own right. Newton did not arrive at these beliefs as a result of pursuing some dilettantish hobby; nor were they the result of studies he pursued at the end of his life. Instead, they lay at the heart of a massive research programme on prophecy and church history that he carried out early in his career. This was at least as strenuous, and, in his eyes, at least as "rational" as his work on physics and mathematics.[2]

In the century after Newton's death in 1727, information about his real religious opinions was slow to emerge. In Enlightenment Europe, both admirers and detractors became increasingly perplexed by the nature of these studies, and in particular by Newton's dedication to topics such as the meaning and historical identity of the apocalyptic Whore of Babylon. To explain away these interests, they claimed that he had only pursued them when he had moved to London in 1696 to take up the position of Warden of the Royal Mint, or after he had become senile, or even mad. However, Newton produced the monumental and highly original work that is the subject of this book before he left Cambridge in the mid-1690s. Indeed, his deep Christian faith was the most important aspect of his life. His half-niece Catherine Conduitt, who lived with him for much of the London period, related that he often became upset when his acquaintances, in particular the classical scholar Richard Bentley and the astronomer Edmond Halley, spoke "ludicrously" about religion. He cut off all relations with his friend, the chemist Francis Vigani, when the latter told "a loose story" about a nun, a fact that is particularly remarkable when one considers Newton's jaundiced opinion about the monastic orders and Catholics in general. Religion was not an amusing subject, and his successor as Lucasian professor, William Whiston, recalled that Newton often condemned the "wicked behaviour" of modern courtiers, who had "laughed themselves out of religion." Even if he was not a puritan in doctrine, he had a stony-faced earnestness about religion that was widely known. He was no libertine, deist, or atheist, but according to the doctrines of his own church, he was a heretic.[3]

When he died, Newton's friends and relatives outdid themselves in composing hyperbolic statements testifying to his virtue. Catherine's husband, John, who tried to write a biography of Newton soon after the latter had died, recorded a number of instances of his boundless generosity, his "quiet

& meek spirit," and his hatred of cruelty to animals. Bishop Gilbert Burnet, according to Catherine, thought that Newton had the "whitest soul" of anyone he had known, a feature that was more valuable than all of his philosophy. John Conduitt noted that if Newton had been born in a time and place when great inventors were deified, or in a Catholic country where men were canonized, he would have been more deserving of either reward than anyone else. Newton, he stated, lacked any vices at all, while his virtues proved him a saint and his discoveries might well pass for miracles. Conduitt struggled to find the right expression to describe a man who was more than merely human, but whose own religious beliefs were centred on the danger of idolising or deifying any being that was not God. Conduitt was particularly taken with a query allegedly posed by the Marquis de l'Hôpital to the physician John Arbuthnot at the end of the seventeenth century. The Marquis had asked whether Newton was in any sense like other men, but Arbuthnot assured him that Newton put himself on a level with all mankind. At this, a somewhat doubtful Conduitt commented: "Even wee that knew him can hardly think of him without a sort of superstition wch demands all our reason to check." Was he even a man, he asked?[4]

The hagiographical view of Newton was not shared by everyone. After his death, Whiston described him as having the most "prodigiously fearful, cautious and suspicious temper," while the First Astronomer Royal, John Flamsteed, told a correspondent in 1700 that Newton was "through his Naturall temper suspitious" and too liable to see slanders against him in others' comments, especially if they were spiced with levity. Even his friends found him a difficult companion, who had to be treated with extreme care. John Locke told his young relative Peter King, whom he had asked to pay Newton a visit, that Newton was a "very valuable man," not only for his prowess in mathematics, but also for his great knowledge of the Bible, which few people of Locke's acquaintance could equal. When King met him, Locke continued, he should treat Newton "with all the tenderness in the world". He should find out why Newton had kept some of Locke's writings (namely a draft of his Essay on the Corinthians) for so long, but without asking him directly why he had not yet replied, or letting Newton know what he was trying to find out. Locke had "good reasons" to think that Newton was a true friend, but he was "a nice man to deal with, and a little too apt to raise in himself suspicions where there is no ground" (by "nice," Locke meant "prickly"). This widely attested side of Newton's personality is obvious in many of the writings discussed in this book. His distrust of his contemporaries often crossed into overt paranoia, and he "suspected," that is, he was deeply suspicious of their actions and motivations in the same way that he distrusted the actions of those Christians who founded doctrinal orthodoxy over a millennium before him. Indeed, his extensive analysis of the early Christian Church was premised on the view that the greatest and most audacious conspiracy of all time—the joint introduction into Christianity of the doctrine of the Trinity and of various beliefs and practices that would form the basis of Roman Catholicism—had corrupted the true religion to the core. The manner in which he investigated the early church owed much to his underlying character, but this, in turn, was both shaped by his immersion in a bygone textual world and fuelled by his relations with those around him.[5]

Newton's theological research focussed almost exclusively on scriptural exegesis, the history of the early church, and the meaning of prophetic images. Although he was keenly aware of the political and religious issues that concerned English Protestants during his lifetime, his refusal to engage directly with any of them in his private writings is remarkable. Newton felt strongly enough about these issues to take a public stand in the late 1680s against the Catholic king, James II, but his considered opinions about contemporary subjects such as toleration and the proper relations between church and state have to be inferred from his work on the early Christian Church. He hated idolatry, cruelty, and persecution in general, and since he believed that Roman Catholicism embodied all these aspects in their most virulent form, he reserved a particular revulsion for it. He believed that people he took to be the earliest practitioners of Roman Catholicism had been the chief promoters of the Trinitarian abomination that had arisen in the fourth century. As he saw it, Roman Catholicism remained the biggest religious and political threat in his own time. It was the epitome of satanic anti-Christianism, and he understood its nature and historical role through the lens of his study of prophecy. Against this false religion many had borne witness and even died for the cause. Now Newton believed that he was one of the remnant who, as the true saints described in Revelation, would be resurrected to rule over mortals in the millennium.[6]

At the core of Newton's religion was the idea that Christianity was a simple faith. To be a Christian one had to believe only that Christ was the Messiah prophesied in the Hebrew Bible or Old Testament, the Son of God who had died on the Cross and then been resurrected on the third day. A number of things flowed from this minimalist understanding of what was required for salvation. First, Newton believed that being a Christian was not primarily concerned with holding allegedly correct doctrines, and that the main requirement of a godly life was to live according to the practical moral precepts of Christianity. The Christian life was difficult, and it demanded continued vigilance and resistance against the temptations provided both by the outside world and the inner self. Second, although holding these basic opinions was sufficient to be a Christian, more mature, learned Christians like himself were obliged to study Scripture and to discuss more abstruse parts of doctrine with others. Consequently, his own religiosity was characterised by the relentless reading of the Bible and other sacred texts, along with the incessant note-taking and writing of treatises that provide the evidential basis on which this book rests.[7]

As Newton saw it, truly Christian groups and states could be identified by their abhorrence of persecution and by a commitment to toleration of diverse opinions that was consistent with their own security. Like many who had serious doubts about the doctrine of the Trinity, he held that the ideal Christian polity should permit, and actively encourage, a very wide range of religious beliefs (such as his own). He articulated this tolerationist position at length in his later writings, where he repeated the claim that only a few core beliefs about the nature and mission of Jesus Christ were necessary for salvation. These had been expressed in the Primitive Creeds but had been subsequently obfuscated by men who had an interest in making Scripture incomprehensible to ordinary people. Newton asserted that the basic principles of Christian belief were "easy to be understood by the meanest capacities," and on that account, he went on (invoking Hebrews 5:12-14), may "properly <be> compared to milk for babes." These foundational tenets of Christianity were not metaphysically abstruse theories but practical truths. On the other hand, there were "strong meats," truths of great importance but very hard to understand—and not at all necessary for salvation. They were intended for men like Newton of a "full age," whose senses had been trained by experience to discern both good and evil. These generated complex but disputable questions, but they were not things about which Christians should fall out or try to excommunicate one another.[8]

While Christians could discuss such issues, Newton himself showed little inclination to do so. From the start, he preferred to deal only with questions that were susceptible to historical, empirical confirmation in the many editions of early church writings at his disposal. Technical theological subjects whose resolution was not easily accomplished by empirical research, or by his own understanding, were off limits. In keeping with his famous aversion to disputing certain subjects in natural philosophy, he deliberately ignored a series of thorny questions, many of which had caused deep divisions in Protestantism over nearly two centuries. These included the states of nature and grace, original sin, the nature of Christ's atonement for the sins of mankind, what Christ did before his incarnation and between his death and resurrection, the compatibility of free will with God's foreknowledge of future events, the nature of angels, the state and location of souls between death and resurrection, what mortals and saints might do after the Day of Judgement, and forms of church government. Solutions to these problems were neither to be found in Scripture, nor in the history of the transmission of manuscripts of the Greek New Testament. They involved scholastic metaphysics and would lead honest, godly men into barren disputes.[9]

Despite his emphasis on the simplicity of Christian fundamentals, and the requirement that they be based on Scripture, Newton did not evince the antipathy towards the state church that was characteristic of the vast majority of people who shared his anti-Trinitarian views. Nevertheless, he was never entirely comfortable with worshipping according to the doctrine, rites, and ceremonies of the Church of England, and it is telling that in his "Life" of Newton, John Conduitt, who knew him as well as anyone in the last decade of his life, deleted an earlier claim that he was a frequent attender of Anglican services. To some extent Newton had no choice in the matter, and throughout his life as a public official, he was forced to publicly bear witness to his belief in the central doctrines of the Church of England. Privately, he detested many of its tenets, but both private and public writings indicate that he was a sincere member of the national church. His views about his own national church were bound up with his peculiar doctrinal beliefs. If the Church of England were true to its broad founding principles, he claimed in one late text (and the only one in which he ever discussed the subject), it ought to tolerate people like himself as members and allow a great deal of room for frank discussion of abstruse matters. As long as the church did not force certain non-scriptural beliefs and practices on the laity, or proscribe doctrines that were expressly stated in Scripture, it would remain truly Christian.[10]

What Scripture actually *was* became a major research topic for Newton, and ultimately he believed that the authentic word of God could be ascertained only by honest men who were sincere seekers of religious truths.

Determining these truths, which were manifested in Scripture, also placed limits on what Christians should profess in their creeds. Newton believed, for example, that the Apostles' Creed was canonical and that the faith expressed within it should be professed by Anglicans. However, no statement in the two other creeds enjoined by the Church of England (the Nicene and Athanasian) was binding unless it was expressly stated in Scripture. Living by the strictures of the holy text, his religion enjoined a life of positive practical and moral obligations. In addition to practising the Christian virtues, the godly man had to constantly avoid vice and sin, and the latter aspect of his religion also played a central role in his life. In his late essay on the type of worship that ought to be permitted by the Church of England, he argued that it should require only that its members renounce idolatry, ambition, pride, covetousness, and unchastity, and that they keep the Ten Commandments. While these demands were supposed to apply to all Christians, Newton believed that only a select few could ever practise them with regularity. Indeed, earlier in his career, he emphasised a more separatist strain of religiosity as a result of which he identified with a special group of the godly who were set apart even from other Christians. He believed that he existed on a higher moral and religious plane than most of his contemporaries, and that his own righteousness would be proved by being subject to persecution.[11]

Although Newton attacked what he took to be the excessive concentration on doctrinal forms in church matters, he treated the doctrine of the Trinity differently. Over half a century he expended vast energies attempting to understand the nature and origins of what he believed was a diabolical notion. The doctrine lay at the heart of orthodox Christianity and it was the first of the Thirty-Nine Articles of the Church of England. This stated that there was one living and true God, eternal, incorporeal, omnipotent, infinitely wise and good, "the Creator and preserver of all things visible and invisible." This was fine for anti-Trinitarians such as Newton, but less acceptably, the text went on to assert that "in unity of this Godhead" there were three persons, who together made "one substance, power and eternity." In the second article, the Son was identified as the Word of the Father. He was truly begotten ("genitus") of the Father from everlasting, and of the same substance ("consubstantialis") with the Father, though he inherited his human nature from the womb of the Virgin Mary. These two natures were indivisibly united in one person, from which there was one Christ, truly God and truly man. This being really suffered on the Cross, died, and was buried, a sacrifice not merely for original sin but for all the sins of mankind. In the fifth article, the Holy Ghost was asserted to be of the same substance, majesty, and glory as the first two members of the Godhead, although Newton devoted little time to the third person of the Holy Trinity. His own position can thus be characterised by his flat denial of the key features of orthodox Christianity that asserted identity of power and substance between the three persons of the Trinity. He always inveighed against any notion that the members of the Godhead were "coequal," and in particular he condemned as abominations the notions that Jesus Christ was uncreated and was formed of the same substance as God the Father.[12]

For orthodox Anglicans, the doctrine of the Trinity was the foundation of the human relationship with the divine, and of the connection between the supplicant and his or her church. The Trinity linked the visible church to Christ's body and to his continuing presence, which justified and made sacred the central religious and secular institutions in Newton's society. It was on these grounds that denial of the Trinity was a heinous offence that merited the ultimate punishment. In 1612 Bartholomew Legate and Edward Wightman were the last martyrs burned alive for the crime in England, but the death penalty was reasserted in legislation of 1648. Following the publication of a number of anti-Trinitarian texts, the "Ordinance for the punishing of several Blasphemies and Heresies" prescribed capital punishment for those who continued to maintain the "errour." The "Blasphemy Act" was superseded by another act passed just over two years later, which did not carry the threat of capital punishment. However, after the Restoration of Charles II in 1660, the public denial of the Trinity would have meant exclusion from office, social disgrace, and the possibility of prosecution.[13]

Given the nature of Newton's religious views, it is entirely unsurprising that he should have wanted to keep them private. However, he adopted an excessively cautious attitude to publication in every subject. Only a small proportion of the fruits of his pioneering mathematical and optical studies of the mid-1660s appeared in print before 1700, and he believed strongly that the "noble" findings of alchemy should not be revealed to the unworthy. At various junctures after 1690 he was poised to put some of his theological writings into print, but some external circumstance—or private foreboding—always prevented it. As with his work on other subjects, Newton did release some of his religious writings to a handful of trusted readers, a practice known as "scribal publication." Indeed, the very fact that his papers survived his death, that is, the fact that he did not burn the most egregiously heterodox texts, indicates something about his understanding both of their significance and their intended audience. It is probable that he believed that the content of these papers would have some beneficial effect long after he had died, when his work would conceivably form part of the great dispersion of the gospel that would precede Christ's Second Coming.[14]

Newton's extensive writings on the Trinitarian corruption of Christianity are among the most daring works of any writer in the early modern period, and they would merit careful study even if they had not been composed by the author of the *Principia*. As a window into the rich private world of a seventeenth-century English Protestant they stand in comparison with the manuscript remains of other writers such as the great nonconformist Richard Baxter and the puritan craftsman Nehemiah Wallington.[15] However, what marks out Newton's writings are the independence of thought they display. If they had been unveiled to the Republic of Letters when he wrote them, and his authorship revealed, he would now be part of an elite pantheon of original thinkers who are lauded as part of a Radical Reformation or Radical Enlightenment. However, like William Whiston, his successor in the Lucasian chair, he would have been immediately expelled from his college. He would never have had the chance to write the *Principia* or *Opticks*, and much, if not all, of his pioneering work on the calculus might have been lost. He would never have been elected as a Member of Parliament for the University of Cambridge, or elevated to the presidency of the Royal Society, and he would not have been appointed to the positions of warden or master of the Royal Mint. His coffin would not have been carried to Westminster Abbey by eminent lords and grandees, and there would now be no tomb proclaiming his superhuman qualities.[16]

Almost all of the writings discussed in this book have been published only in the last fifteen years. To some extent this is due to the fact that they remain unfinished or unpolished, and to some extent it is due to their heterodox contents. It is also an indirect consequence of Newton's generally jaundiced attitude to publication. His reluctance to reveal the fruits of his labour to the outside world was understood by contemporaries to be decidedly peculiar. In his own time, natural philosophy began to place a heavy emphasis on publication as the best way to standardise research results, reach a sizeable audience, and act as a way of assigning credit. It is partly because authoritative knowledge is held to reside in publicly available, and to a large degree, objective sources, that historians of science have been predominantly concerned with published articles or texts. Similarly, intellectual historians have largely focussed on the canonical published texts of great thinkers that have exerted influence on other writers. In both cases, manuscript writings such as correspondence or drafts are usually seen as being less significant than printed productions, and of interest only because they shed light on the final, published text. Although the predominantly theological writings that form the basis of this book have had to wait until the present century to be published, they are eminently worthy of study. This is not because they shed light on, or are early versions of, some published work, or because they exerted a major influence on his scientific work, or on other authors. Instead, they represent the concerted efforts of the greatest thinker of his age to engage with the biggest questions of his time, and they offer unique, and previously unknown insights into his character.[17]

The belated appearance of these papers on the public stage is also due in part to the pervasive assumptions, engendered in part by the immense success of Newtonian science, that religious belief is by its very nature separate from, or even opposed to the scientific method—and that theology is less intellectually rigorous than scientific research. While it is not difficult for modern readers to accept that Newton was interested in religious issues, it is much harder to accept that the founder of Enlightenment rationality devoted so much time and effort to these topics. Theology, the most significant discipline in early modern intellectual culture, had long attracted the attention of its most talented thinkers and it retained this unrivalled position in Newton's time. By the end of the eighteenth century, however, its disciplinary supremacy was being eroded, and Newton's interest in it became less comprehensible to Enlightenment *philosophes*. The notion that this work was carried out either in his dotage, or for his own amusement, appealed as much to orthodox divines horrified by what little they knew of his ideas, as it did to the growing number of anticlerical commentators. Although there was some interest in his nonscientific papers, the idea that they contained little of "value" underpinned their formal division and physical separation in the late nineteenth century. In 1872 the fifth Earl of Portsmouth generously decided to donate the "scientific" materials to Cambridge University Library, and, following a lackadaisical sifting process that took the best part of two decades, the remainder were returned to him.[18]

Hence, when historians of science investigated the Portsmouth Collection at Cambridge in the 1950s and 1960s, they were confronted only with the papers that revealed the genesis of Newton's great work in mathematics and physics. For a multitude of reasons, almost all of these scholars were predisposed to reject Newton's "nonscientific" research as bizarre, irrelevant to his more significant work, and unbecoming of his genius. However, even if they had been interested in his religious writings, only a fraction of this part of Newton's archive was available for study. Researchers did have access to his alchemical papers, which had been sold off at an auction of the nonscientific residue of Newton's archive at Sotheby's in July 1936. These ended up in King's College, Cambridge, thanks to the farsightedness of the economist John Maynard Keynes, who bought the papers during and after the sale. Nevertheless, with the exception of some records of Newton's experimental researches, historians of science found almost nothing in them to pique their interest. Keynes bought a few theological papers also, which became part of the King's collection, while New College, Oxford, had had custody of a substantial batch of theological manuscripts since the late nineteenth century. However, the bulk of the religious papers were bought up after the Sotheby's sale by the biblical scholar and collector Abraham Shalom Yahuda. After a protracted legal case they arrived in Jerusalem in 1967, where they were made available for study a few years afterwards. They are now housed in the National Library of Israel.[19]

In the 1960s, academic views about the alleged worthlessness of some early modern intellectual pursuits changed in tandem with wider cultural shifts. Newton, it turned out, was a prime candidate for reinterpretation, and the appearance of two works helped change the general picture of his intellectual life. In 1963 Frank Manuel published a book titled *Isaac Newton: Historian*, which was the first modern work to take seriously the content of Newton's researches into chronology. Drawing on papers at King's College and New College, Oxford, Manuel showed that Newton had spent much of the last three decades of his life as a Christian chronologer, attempting to harmonize the histories and genealogies of those civilisations that had left historical records. In pursuing this research, Newton was following in the footsteps of great scholars such as Joseph Scaliger, Samuel Bochart, and Gerard Vossius, but he brought to his task a number of skills (such as his efforts to date historical events by making inferences from the precession of the equinoxes) that they lacked. Nevertheless, even if he used new approaches and techniques from the exact sciences, the general conclusions he reached about the dates of various episodes did not diverge much from those of his contemporaries.[20]

Another stimulus for the study of Newton's nonscientific interests was provided by someone who was not working on Newton at all. Frances

Yates's *Giordano Bruno and the Hermetic Tradition*, which appeared the year after Manuel's monograph, alerted historians to the fact that Renaissance and early modern scholars had believed that a mixture of scientific and religious knowledge—the *prisca sapientia*—had been lost and might now be rediscovered or reconstructed. Inspired by Yates's work, scholars reading the recently published third volume of Newton's correspondence (dealing with the years 1688–94) could see evidence that Newton shared as many intellectual interests with the fifteenth-century Neoplatonist Marsilio Ficino and the sixteenth-century "hermetic philosopher" Giordano Bruno as he did with Galileo Galilei. Placing Newton in the general erudite culture in which he had actually lived and worked, a new generation of historians rushed to condemn the positivist division between his work in the exact sciences, and his writings on religion and alchemy. Emboldened by the discovery and publication of new sources, scholars asserted that there were strong links between all of his writings, and they claimed that his productions had to be connected at some deep level on the grounds that they sprang from a single "mind."[21]

However, the recent publication of his religious, historical, and chronological papers has provided no support for the notion that there is some simple conceptual or methodological coherence to his work. This is not entirely surprising. Trained in the liberal arts, European scholars were conditioned to think, write, and argue in modes that were appropriate to distinct disciplines. Indeed, a key characteristic of Newton's own brilliance was his capacity to study at a level of exceptional technical competence in a wide range of intellectual fields. Moreover, in many places, he himself stipulated that separate forms of enquiry, argument, and demonstration were appropriate for specific subjects. In one passage, he maintained that the force of the demonstrations in his theological writings rested on faith and that men should consider how opposed to God's designs it was that religious truths should be as obvious as mathematical proofs. His own religious arguments, Newton said, would convince only those chosen by God, while the rest could die in their sins.[22]

Newton divided up his intellectual world in other ways, and the most important of these divisions forms the central focus of this book. He repeatedly asserted that scientific enquiry should not be contaminated by the procedures and mores of the legal sphere. He frequently and vigorously condemned the use of hypotheses in natural philosophy because, he claimed, they would lead inevitably to interminable and barren disputes that were essentially litigious. This was not because he was unacquainted with forensic techniques and arguments, and indeed, he made extensive and masterly use of such rhetorical devices in his religious writings. He devoted a large part of his private life to detecting the historical crimes of religious perverts and then prosecuting them for their misdemeanours. However, the judicial style was utterly inappropriate for natural philosophy, and, as he told Edmond Halley in the summer of 1686, its use turned philosophy into a litigious woman who enslaved her suitors. As I show in various parts of this book, the barriers he erected between the separate domains of his thought broke down during times of crisis. At various points in the 1670s and 1680s, he believed that philosophy really had become the litigious arena that he feared. Once others had turned philosophy into a courtroom, Newton was free to treat his contemporaries in the same way that he did the evildoers of yester-year—and he did so with gusto.

Despite these distinctions, general similarities of approach and authorial identity do characterise different domains of his work. His writings in natural philosophy were marked by his strict division between what could be proved with mathematical certainty, and what was merely conjectural or hypothetical. Among the latter he classed the systems of Aristotle and Descartes, as well as any scientific theories that lacked empirical support. Although he denied that religious truths could be proved with mathematical certainty, he drew an almost identical distinction between what was really in Scripture and what was added to it by false traditions or by the artificial productions of the human imagination. Newton's religious values governed his conduct not only in religious study but also in his other intellectual arenas. In the introduction to the same prophetic treatise in which he stated that religious truths could not be mathematically demonstrated, he argued that only a special, select cadre of experts was capable of properly understanding difficult things—the strong "meat" of technically demanding doctrine. Such people were not led "by interest, education, or human authorities," and they "set themselves sincerely & earnestly to search after truth." Avoiding swearing, cheating, lying, stealing, drunkenness, unchastity, pride, and covetousness, they also shunned the opinion of the mob, for most men were led by vanity and worldly ends. Indeed, Newton claimed, one should look upon reproaches from such people as a mark of truth. What was needed was ceaseless, independent erudition, and earnest prayer to God to enlighten one's understanding. He added that there was a moral obligation to profess the truth but one should not be too hasty in becoming a teacher—one needed to be absolutely certain that one was in the right before setting out to instruct others.[23]

Newton's belief that he had a special role to play both in identifying the true religion and restoring its pristine form lay at the heart of his faith. Like many other radical Protestants, he thought that Reformation attempts to cleanse Christianity of its idolatrous and unwanted elements had been only partly successful, and that a more authentic form of religion needed to be reinstated. He argued that this historical dance between corruption and restoration had many precursors, and went back to a time before the Flood. The true religion was always liable to be corrupted by perverted priests and greedy kings, who preyed on the natural tendency of mankind to wallow in idolatry, superstition, and mystery. Periodically, men like Abraham, Moses, and even Jesus Christ himself had come to restore the truth. Sacred history was thus a dialectical process that would close when the world ended with the return of Christ to rule over mortals with his saints. There is a strong sense in Newton's writings—though he never stated it explicitly—that he saw himself as the latest in this line of restorers. Despite the great intellectual courage he showed in going against the religious grain, he was not prepared to put his head above the parapet and spearhead the next stage in the Protestant Reformation in order to reinstate the true religion.[24]

Newton also spent a great deal of time studying ancient Jewish and pagan history. He greatly respected the learning of the ancient priests, whose lost wisdom and scientific knowledge he believed he was resurrecting. In so doing, he was consciously working in the *prisca sapientia* tradition. Natural philosophers created their own specific genealogies of corrupted and regenerated knowledge, and Newton joined a number of illustrious Copernicans who invoked the ancient Greek heliocentrists as authoritative predecessors, whose truths they were now rediscovering. He argued that the Ancients had been Newtonians, and he read his own doctrines into a number of classical sources, whose carefully veiled truths he believed he was uncovering. Newton's highly positive account of the role and capabilities of ancient priests demonstrates that he believed that natural philosophy was to a large extent a religious enterprise through which one could come to an understanding of the way God had created the world. At some deep level he viewed himself as a modern version of these virtuous priests, who had been entrusted with maintaining true heliocentric worship. If the world was the temple of God, then those like Newton who properly studied it were priests of nature. It is in this context that one should place his great work of 1687, the

Principia Mathematica, a text in which he believed that he had resurrected a major component of the *prisca*.[25]

Although he held such priests in high regard, Newton's identity as a layman was essential to his role as a Christian academic. In the mid-1670s he was prepared to give up his fellowship and professorship rather than take holy orders and become a clergyman in the Church of England. After powerful grandees intervened on his behalf, he was given special dispensation by Charles II from the requirement to take orders and hence, by choice, he became one of the very few laymen in the university. The precise reasons for his decision remain unclear, but they are probably connected to his desire to obtain the requisite freedom to pursue his academic research rather than because of any problems with doctrine. Indeed, it was precisely this independent outlook that guided Newton away from orthodoxy. Later on, John Conduitt connected Newton's lay status to his religious opinions, defending him against those "of narrow principles" who might baulk at his "not going into every point of the highest orthodoxy." They should reflect, he continued, on how advantageous it was to Christianity—in such an age of infidelity—"to have a Lay man such a Philosopher &c have spent so much Study upon divinity & so publick ˹&c strenuous˺ an ~~espouser of~~ ˹advocate for˺ it." Like other scholarly laymen— such as his friend John Locke—Newton was a bachelor, and his choice of a life of celibacy was an essential element of his social and religious identity. Revelation 14:4-5 told of how those undefiled by women were the saints who were faultless before the throne of God. He understood this to mean that such people—amongst whom he undoubtedly included himself— were spiritually rather than physically pure, though he did reveal to his physician Richard Mead that he was a virgin.[26]

Newton's strong commitment to independence, which was almost certainly rooted in his religious upbringing, in turn governed his theological studies and religious conduct. In a draft "Memoir" completed soon after his death, Conduitt noted that Newton's view of Christianity was "not founded on so narrow a bottom as to confine it to this or that particular sect, nor his charity & morality so scanty as to ~~allow of persecution~~ show a coldness to those ~~who differed~~ ˹of another opinion˺ in things indifferent much less admit of persecution of wch he always shewed the strongest abhorrence."[27] Like many of Conduitt's insightful comments, this compressed account brings together a number of different aspects of Newton's ethical, intellectual, and political outlook. Apart from confirming Newton's belief that a

Christian society should allow a wide difference of opinion, Conduitt's implicit recognition of Newton's commitment to independent research and to religious eclecticism has implications for how we understand or classify his work. Ever since his death, commentators and historians have sought to claim Newton for this, that, or their own religious camp, but the evidence from his private writings corroborates Conduitt's claim that his views cannot be captured by a single term or label.

Newton had a broad and inveterate commitment to political and religious freedom. Independent enquiry and—within certain limits—respect for others with different views were the foundations of his ideal Christian society, and he contrasted these features with the situation he found in other countries. Conduitt noted, somewhat uneasily, that Newton had been born in a year (1642, the year when the English Civil War started) when "an uncommon spirit of Liberty had taken possession of our forefathers," while in another text he remarked that Newton showed an "inflexible attachment" to liberty. No doubt prompted by many conversations with Newton, Conduitt extolled the daring intellectual path that he had carved out, and remarked that it was surely right to pay "a due homage & reverence to those Great immortal Deliverers who freed mankind from the bondage of Error & Ignorance." Newton, he remarked, was one of the greatest of these supermen, and no one in history matched his intellectual achievements. Born on the auspicious day (25 December) that the whole Christian world celebrated "for having brought a saviour to mankind," he was destined "to introduce a freedom of thinking & to teach men not to give up their reason implicitely to any ~~Hypothesis~~ ⟨System⟩ howsoever dignified or established." Again, this pithy statement bundled together a number of Newton's most strongly held convictions, including his support for religious and intellectual freedom, and his dislike of hypotheses and systems. Conduitt rejoiced that one man had stood tall against the authoritarian tyranny of numerous false ancient and modern worldviews.[28]

Once Newton had the unrestricted time and private space to engage in independent research, he was free to exercise his "understanding." The correct use of reason required a protracted disciplining of the self to avoid the pitfalls provided by the "fancy," which always he associated with irrational private judgement. In his earliest surviving writings, Newton distinguished the functions and capacities of the understanding from those of the imagination, and the division penetrated every facet of his personal and intellectual life. His hostile attitude to the products of the imagination connected his profound scepticism about the role of "hypotheses" in natural philosophy with his hatred of religious "legends" and his pronounced aversion towards literature and poetry. Conduitt recorded that although Newton had dabbled in poetry as a teenager, he often expressed contempt for the practice as he grew older. It was unsurprising that one who had for so long "accustomed/ used his mind to reject all Hypotheses & admitt nothing but truth & demonstration" should come to despise those productions "*whose very essence is of Fancy & Fiction.*" Conduitt added that many of the best philosophers of the age—including Descartes and Halley—had let their imaginations run riot and as a consequence they had invented absurd theoretical systems. Ultimately they had been taken over by what early moderns called "enthusiasm," and even by madness. On the other hand, Sir Isaac had only ever used "patient thought," a phrase that captures the supremacy in Newton's life of the alliance of reason with work, in contrast to the idle deceptions of the imagination. As he wrote in an impassioned essay on the sexual depravity of the first monks (discussed in chapter 5), the effects of the imagination could only be sidestepped by setting the mind to purposeful thought, reading, or other practical engagements. The only way to remain free of its relentless assault was, as he put it, to be never at rest.[29]

Although Newton distrusted the power of the imagination, it came to play a positive and fertile role in his conception of the relationship between humanity and the divine. As we shall see in chapter 3, perhaps the earliest experiment he recorded was an undergraduate effort to test the nature and power of his own imagination, and he never forgot the results of these trials. Many of these researches were performed on the basis that aspects of God were adumbrated in the faculties of the human mind, and arguably his overriding concern in his life was to show in what ways humans had been created in the image of God. In the "Queries" to his *Optice* of 1706, and in the "General Scholium" added to the second edition of the *Principia Mathematica* in 1713, he revealed his belief that the relationship between the human soul and the imagination was analogous to God's relationship with his cosmos. Similarly, the freedom of the will mimicked the creative power of God. While he refused to be drawn into technical theological disputes about free will, in the 1670s, he conducted experimental enquiries to ascertain how it was that humans governed their own bodies by means of their will. For Newton, the existence of freely willed self-motion was a standing refutation of the materialist and allegedly atheistic ideas of Thomas Hobbes and René Descartes.

The third major faculty of the human mind after memory and imagination, the rational intellect, was an inferior, finite representation of the infinite understanding of God, and Newton viewed his scientific and religious re-searches as equally legitimate exercises of his reason. Since the methodology of the sciences now defines what it is to be "rational," few people today would accept that his work on prophecy was as reasonable, objective, or eviden-tially robust as his work in mathematics or physics. However, not only did Newton believe that he could use his understanding to interpret religious passages whose meaning or provenance was doubtful but he also believed that almost all of religion was "rational." Many of his Anglican contempo-raries also argued in favour of a rational religion, by which they meant that there were well-established procedures for reading sacred texts so as to dis-cover the truths they contained, that it was reasonable to believe in revealed religion, and that there were good reasons for adhering to the moral duties demanded of Christians. In claiming that Christian belief was reasonable, they were differentiating their own brand of religion from the sort of inspi-rational or "enthusiastic" type of religion that had allegedly blighted Eng-land during the Commonwealth. Nevertheless, they now had to distinguish themselves from more extreme groups such as Socinians, who claimed that the key doctrine of the Trinity was incomprehensible, unscriptural, and therefore false. Although he differed from them in some points of doctrine, Newton's approach shared a great deal in common with that of contempo-rary Socinians, and he agreed with them regarding the baneful nature of most examples of Christian "mystery."[30]

Although the Socinians claimed that their critique of incomprehensible mysteries was the result of their Protestant values, the orthodox also feared that their approach could be taken up by those who appeared to be no friends of religion at all. The 1680s and 1690s witnessed a profusion of writ-ings from "deists" such as Charles Blount (who largely reproduced the ar-guments of Lord Herbert of Cherbury) and John Toland. These writers, who also claimed that they were acting in keeping with their Protestant con-victions, used many of the sources and analytical tools provided by Socin-ians, though Toland in particular rejected many of their positions as no more comprehensible than those of the orthodox. Although the coherence of these writers' positions has been overstated, in general they suggested that there was a simple "natural" religion common to all mankind that was compre-hensible to all people as a consequence of their natural reason. They set out to explode what they denounced as the false mysteries of institutionalised religions, and thus to liberate common people from the tyranny of priest-craft. Although he never mentioned them, Newton knew their views, and he must have been keenly aware of the much more radical opinions published by the great Jewish philosopher Baruch Spinoza that were being denounced at the same time.[31]

Newton's defence of a rational and comprehensible religion, and in particular, the language he used to discuss priestly corruption, is often indistinguishable from the approach adopted by Cherbury, Blount, and Toland. He may well have thought that the principles of morality could be drawn from nonbiblical sources, and he shared their scepticism and even cynicism both about the existence of religious mysteries, and about the manner in which priests had manipulated false doctrines and practices down the ages to their own advantage. He was highly critical of the morals and actions of orthodox priests in the early Christian Church for, as he saw it, the Roman Catholic clergy had perverted the Christian religion to attract converts, and had played on the tendency of ordinary people to wallow in mystery, idolatry and carnality. However, the millions of words Newton wrote on prophecy show that he had no truck with the deists' dismissal of revealed truths, and he was equally hostile to their attacks on organised religion. Although priests had—throughout history—acted in ways incompatible with their status, Newton did not exhibit the extreme anticlericalism exhibited by many anti-Trinitarians. Indeed, he believed that by depicting the true religious nature of the cosmic temple in which they worshipped, natural philosophers such as himself had some sort of elevated priestly role. Finally, Newton's conception of God drew upon a number of elements within the Judaeo-Christian tradition. His God was a very real Being who had created the universe by an act of will, was intimately connected to it at all times, and occasionally intervened to alter human history and the cosmos at large.

Although he concerned himself almost entirely with events in the early church, when it had all gone wrong, Newton was profoundly engaged with most of the general political and religious questions that concerned his learned contemporaries. His work on the early history of the Christian Church addressed many of the topics that are the subject of Paul Hazard's great 1935 essay on the crisis of late-seventeenth-century European high culture. These include issues of liberty of conscience, the nature and practice of persecution and toleration, relations between church and state, the "Higher Criticism" of Richard Simon, anti-Trinitarianism, deism, the implications of the work of Hobbes and Descartes, the relationship between Judaism and

Christianity, the nature of non-Christian religions both past and present, and the historical and religious status of Roman Catholicism. By the 1670s, these were the purview not only of learned clergymen but also of intelligent laymen. These people had access to a vast array of polyglots, critical editions, encyclopaedias, and other learned writings that constituted a series of resources for conducting intelligent discussion. There were also new journals and other outlets, which filtered these conversations to wider audiences and which allowed both clerics and laymen to make meaningful contributions to the Republic of Letters. Although he was a college don surrounded by people in holy orders, Newton was one of these laypeople with access to these texts and institutions, relatively unconstrained to write and think (if not publish) according to the dictates of reason.[32]

This book is the first extended examination of Newton's early research on these subjects. It takes into account all the millions of his words on religious topics that have recently been published online, including his writings on natural theology, doctrine, prophecy, and church history. By taking seriously what he actually wrote and believed in these many domains, I aim to show that his religious studies were as expansive and technically demanding as any of his investigations in the natural sciences. It can no longer be assumed that these are an embarrassing residue of early modern superstition, or inferior productions of his dotage, which lack any historical or cultural value. Indeed, in contrast to the great Enlightenment myth that Newton only pursued these studies after his creative powers had dried up, it is clear that his most intensive and innovative religious studies took place early in his career, when he was in the prime of his life for pursuing extended and innovative studies in any field that attracted him.

Inevitably there is a question of how his work in religion was related to his work in mathematics and the natural sciences. I say a great deal in this work about connections and interactions between his work in theology and natural philosophy, and I point to common values that underlay his work in each area. However, I also argue that many previous efforts to forge links between his work in these domains have suffered either from using outdated historiographical categories, or from paying insufficient attention to his work in theology. While one can find similarities between his approaches in these intellectual fields, the vast bulk of his writings on church history and prophecy emerged from a parallel intellectual universe to that of his natural philosophy, and they need to be assessed in their own right. This means that his theological researches need to be studied and indeed valued independently from any influence that they may have exerted on his scientific work. Throughout the book I attempt to do this by acknowledging the genuinely novel and innovative features of his achievements, but also by situating his writings within the institutional settings in which he was brought up, and the erudite cultures in which he was trained and immersed.

Finally, Newton's private religious texts are by far the best sources for understanding his personality, and for ascertaining what he took to be his identity and vocation as a godly scholar. He saw himself predominantly as a devout Christian, whose calling was to use his intelligence to discern the truth in whatever field he studied. He repeatedly stated his opinion, and let it be known, that there was nothing more important for a Christian than the study of the Bible, the interpretation of prophecy, and the examination of church history. He also found that he had a particular gift for studying mathematics and natural philosophy to an extraordinarily high level, but most of his working life was spent studying religious topics. He believed that he had a fundamental obligation to use his formidable reasoning powers to divine the truth, and he deployed these faculties as much in his study of the visions of Revelation as he did in creating the theories and techniques underlying calculus and universal gravitation. In so doing, he set out to address the great questions about the origins and nature of the universe, the place of humans within it, and the meaning of their lives, all of which—in his time—were inevitably posed and solved within a religious framework.

I

A Divine Web

Isaac Newton was born on Christmas Day 1642 in a country that had recently descended into a bloody civil war. In April 1640, Charles I had called into being the so-called Short Parliament as a means of raising money to fight a war against the Scots, who had rebelled in reaction to having Anglican forms of worship imposed on them. This Parliament lasted only three weeks, but following defeat by the Scots in the so-called second Bishops War, Charles was forced to summon the "Long" Parliament in November to raise funds to pay for the Scots' expenses. This Parliament was committed to defending its rights against perceived infringements by the Crown, and its leaders also set out to promote a different kind of Protestant religion from that practised within the Church of England. These men were dismayed at the ostensibly Roman Catholic brand of worship promoted by the archbishop of Canterbury, William Laud, which Charles had attempted to impose on the Scots, and indeed, they were sympathetic to the Presbyterian style of worship that most Scots preferred. Over the following year, Parliament made increasing demands for power and autonomy and gradually acquired the means to engage militarily with forces loyal to the king. A civil war between royalists and parliamentarians broke out in August 1642, only months before Newton was born, and the initial conflict was not resolved until 1646. Two years later, a second civil war broke out, and a series of royalist defeats led to Charles's beheading on 30 January 1649.[1]

For almost all of the next decade, England was a republic led by Oliver Cromwell, who took on the title of Lord Protector in 1653. The rituals and ecclesiastical structure of the Church of England were abolished, and a much stricter form of moral discipline was imposed on the populace. We know a surprising amount about the contexts of Newton's life in this period, when he lodged at the house of William Clarke, one of the leading parliamentarians in Grantham. Although Newton's early years were spent in a family environment that worshipped according to the practices of the Church of England, when he lodged with Clarke he was exposed to a different style of worship. What precise influence this exerted on him is hard to determine, but Newton would later exhibit religious sentiments that were characteristic of godly puritans (i.e., those who demanded a "purer" form of Protestantism) who detested "popish" forms of worship. This was the form of worship endorsed by Clarke. It would not be long, however, before the more traditional doctrines, rites, and ceremonies of the Church of England were reinstituted as the state religion. After Cromwell's death in September 1658, his son Richard briefly held the position of Protector, but he was forced to resign the following May. By the end of 1659 a majority of Englishmen were calling for the return of the monarchy, and Charles II was crowned as king in the early summer of 1660.[2]

A week after he was born, Newton was baptised by the rector of Colsterworth, despite (as Newton later claimed) initially being given little chance of surviving more than a few days. His father, Isaac, a yeoman farmer, had died three months earlier, and on 27 January 1646, soon after the younger Isaac's third birthday, his mother, Hannah, married the wealthy local clergyman and recent widower Barnabas Smith. She moved to Smith's rectory at North Witham, which was less than two miles away and on a virtually straight road from Woolsthorpe Manor, leaving young Isaac at home with her mother, Margery Ayscough, and (possibly) her father, James Ayscough Sr. In an affidavit composed in connection with the award of his knighthood in 1705, Newton recorded that he lived with his grandmother until he was about eleven. James Ayscough stated in his 1652 will that he was of Woolsthorpe in the parish of Colsterworth, but since Newton did not mention him in the affidavit, there is no proof that both grandparents lived at Woolsthorpe Manor while Smith was alive. Whatever Barnabas thought of his precocious stepson, it is inconceivable that his mother did not visit him regularly, but either way, Newton was probably deprived of any domestic father figure until he left home to board with Clarke in Grantham in 1655.[3]

Those male figures who were most present in Newton's early life were clergymen. Barnabas Smith had matriculated at Lincoln College, Oxford, in 1597 and had been rector at North Witham since 1610. He was a learned divine, whose more than two hundred volumes of theology passed down to Newton at his death in 1653. Newton left no account of his relations with Smith, though an early confession, in which he recalled (some ten years after the event), "Threatning my father and mother Smith to burne them and the house over them" is indicative of the immense anger and frustration that periodically surfaced throughout his life. He also inherited Smith's gargantuan theological notebook, which contained a number of Smith's theological notes, presumably taken in preparation for sermons. In 1664 Newton titled this tome the "Waste Book," and made a series of mathematical entries that formed the core of his momentous discoveries in the following years. There is no evidence that he read any of Smith's entries.[4]

Hannah's brother William Ayscough brokered her marriage to Smith and he was instrumental in arranging the terms by which Newton inherited property from his mother and stepfather. Ayscough had obtained an MA from Trinity College, Cambridge, in 1637 and five years later was awarded the rectory of Burton Coggles, about four miles east of Colsterworth. In 1644 he must have signed the Solemn League and Covenant, an agreement between the English and Scottish parliaments promising support from the Scottish army provided the English adopted the Scottish Presbyterian system of church government. The agreement called for renunciation of episcopacy and all grades of ecclesiastical office, and the use of the Book of Common Prayer in religious services was abolished by a parliamentary ordinance in January 1645. Ayscough must also have taken the Engagement oath five years later, which required that swearers declare and promise that they would be true and faithful to the Commonwealth of England "as the same is now established, without a King or a House of Lords." It was only thanks to a substantial degree of reconciliation with the parliamentarian regime that Barnabas Smith held on to his living until his death in 1653, and Ayscough must have done the same. Following the Restoration of the monarchy in 1660, he subscribed to the Act of Uniformity on 8 August 1662, and when he died in 1669 he left substantial land and property to his son (also William).[5]

Newton's early life cannot be understood without a grasp of the major religious changes that took place in England between 1630 and 1660. The elevation of Laud in September 1633 to the office of archbishop of Canterbury heralded the return of more traditional forms of worship within the Church of England, and it exacerbated the already substantial rift between traditionalists and those godly Protestants who were deeply disillusioned with allegedly popish developments in the national church. Laud's Arminianism was directly opposed to the Calvinist view, held by most puritans, that human beings were predestined to be either saved or condemned to hell, with no hope of ameliorating their condition through any meritorious deed they committed during their lifetimes. While Calvinists believed that only a small preselected group of individuals would join Christ as saints in heaven, Arminianism held out the hope of salvation for everyone. In opposition to the Calvinist view that God's offer of grace to an elite few (the Elect) was irresistible, Arminians believed that people were free to reject God's offer of grace. Most did so, but some were able to choose to cooperate with this grace through sincere faith and repentance, thus enabling them to have complete free will. In terms of the practice of worship, the Arminian perspective emphasised that only properly adorned priests could administer the holy sacraments that were the most effective means for a believer to acquire divine grace. The celebration of the Eucharist, which was explicitly described as a "sacrifice," was to take place at a stone "altar" at the east end of the chancel, which was to be aligned east-west, railed off, appropriately lit, and perfumed with incense. The language of sacrifice, the emphasis on traditional liturgy, and the stress on the exterior forms of ceremony all reeked of "popery" to many Protestants both within and outside the Church of England.[6]

There were many communities in England who saw themselves as more godly than, and in many cases separate from, the morally lax folk who ordinarily worshipped in the Church of England. Some of these people, who are usually designated as "puritans," decided to remain in the national church. The life of the puritan Nehemiah Wallington, a London turner who wrote a vast amount of religious materials between the 1620s and 1650s, presents a good example of their attitudes and practices. Believing that writing was a form of prayer, Wallington kept a spiritual diary and wrote memoirs, religious reflections, letters, meditations, regimens for a godly life and prayers (and their effects), along with notebooks on Christian doctrine, and accounts of special and general providences. Special providences included numerous examples where drinkers, backsliders, Sabbath-breakers, and scoffers (and during the 1640s, royalists) were summarily (and rightly) dispatched by the Lord for their sinfulness. Wallington saw himself as one of the children or people of God, a born-again (regenerate) community marked out as special thanks to its members' obvious commitment to hard work, the avoidance of sin, and a relentless Christian life. In practice, all fell short of what was required. As we shall see throughout this book, Newton exhibited many puritan characteristics, including the desire to lead an intensely virtuous and godly life, a deadly serious attitude to religion, a detestation of popery, and a belief in a future millennium. However, in other respects, some key features of puritan practice were missing from his daily practice. Belief in special providences, an emotionally charged spirituality, and deep introspection with regard to identifying and repenting his sins, all seem to have been absent from his religious life.[7]

The Lincolnshire of Newton's childhood was a stronghold of puritanism, and there had long been serious tensions between puritan congregations and Church of England authorities. Like many "mainstream" puritans, John Cotton, a graduate of Trinity College, Cambridge, and minister of St. Botolph's Church in Boston, believed that it was better to change the Church of England while remaining within it. However, by 1632, what he saw as the Laudian persecution of his congregation had become intolerable, and the following year he joined Thomas Hooker and like-minded puritans in the New World.[8] The division within the Church of England had repercussions very close to Newton's home. A major argument arose in 1627 over efforts by the traditionalist Peter Titley, vicar of South Grantham, to remove the communion table and erect an altar in the east end of the Church of St. Wulfram and to introduce other Arminian practices such as bowing at the name of Jesus. Titley claimed that parishioners had abused the table by leaning on it and using it as a desk during services. After a showdown between rival groups in Grantham, the anti-Laudian bishop of Lincoln, John Williams, decided that the internal arrangement of the church should be restored to where it had been before Titley had changed it. However, in 1634 Laud ordered that communion tables were to be placed as altars in all churches. These exchanges spilled over into print and the battle between Williams's and Titley's defenders became a national cause célèbre.[9]

In the early 1630s the Alderman's Court (the administrative and governing body of the town) at Grantham approved of regulations that forced parishioners to pay for renovations to the dilapidated church. However, a sizeable faction of worshippers refused to pay, presumably because they believed that the money would be misspent on "popish" paraphernalia such as incense, stained glass windows, and organs. In 1638, despite opposition from many anti-Laudian parishioners, the communion table was moved to the east end of the chancel, and the following year Alderman Alexander More led a renewed attempt to compel Grantham's populace to pay for church renovations. There was unprecedented opposition to this, and as the country headed towards civil war, the situation in Grantham deteriorated. A substantial group within the congregation drew up a petition in April 1640 against the relocation of the communion table and the erection of two organs in the church. They sent their petition to the recently convened Short Parliament, thus bypassing local ecclesiastical authorities such as Robert Sanderson, rector of Boothby Pagnell (about six miles by the shortest roads from both Grantham and Woolsthorpe Manor), and Thomas Hurst, rector of Barrowby (two miles west of Grantham), who supported moving the organs. The advent of the Long Parliament in November doomed the project and the organs would not be replaced until the Restoration.[10]

1. The Religious Locale

Newton's local parish, Colsterworth, was itself heavily affected by the political and religious turmoil of the period. It was the scene of fighting in the civil war and was under parliamentary control thereafter. In 1646 Alexander Hyde, the prebend of South Grantham who had the gift of the Colsterworth living, left to join the king at Oxford. Before leaving, he presented the living to John Castillion, who had only recently obtained his degree of bachelor of divinity from Christ Church, Oxford. Castillion's appointment points to a fascinating, powerful patronage network in the area that links him to Robert Sanderson and his nephew Charles Hoole, a royalist who became one of the most influential educationalists of the seventeenth century. Hoole had himself been the source of a major controversy at Grantham in 1642, following the announcement at a meeting of the Alderman's Court by the master of the Free School that he had decided to retire after forty years in the post. Within minutes of the announcement, Hoole, like Sanderson a graduate of Lincoln College, appeared before the court with numerous testimonials from various knights, gentlemen, and doctors of divinity. The parliamentarians present, soon bolstered by numerous "commoners" who made up the town assembly, succeeded in blocking the appointment. As a consolation prize, Hoole was quickly made rector of Great Ponton, four miles north of Woolsthorpe. He lasted in this post until his ejection in 1646, and thereafter he turned to teaching and pedagogy. Having dedicated his 1660 advice manual for teaching in grammar schools to Sanderson, "his most Reverend, constant, & truly loving Friend," he became Sanderson's chaplain when the latter became bishop of Lincoln in 1661.[11]

Castillion knew Hoole at Oxford and indeed Hoole gave a lengthy encomium to his ability as a classicist in his 1660 handbook. As with Hoole, however, Castillion's accomplishments counted for nothing in the turmoil of the 1640s, and he never took up the official position at Colsterworth.

In February 1646 the Parliamentary Committee for Plundered Ministers sequestered the living for the use of Francis Browne, "a Godly and orthodox Divine." Browne was examined by the committee and told to "officiate the cure there &c. and preach diligently." Despite this, Castillion was apparently appointed as rector in September of that year, which if true, points to Colsterworth being a major point of religious contention in the neighbourhood. In May 1647 Browne complained that he was unable to gain access to the parsonage but whether he ever did so or not, he seems to have remained at the spiritual helm of the church until 1660, when Hyde returned to regain control over the living. Castillion, who had been a tutor to various members of the gentry and aristocracy in the 1650s, successfully petitioned to secure its profits, and he also petitioned for a prebendary stall at Canterbury in June of the same year. Subsequently he rose in the ecclesiastical hierarchy to become dean of Rochester (1676–88).[12]

Following his brief stay at Colsterworth, Castillion was replaced as rector in 1661 by William Walker, who would become the master of Grantham Free School ten years later. Walker, who had entered Trinity College, Cambridge, as a sizar in 1640, wrote a defence of infant baptism in 1677 but was best known for his book on English particles, which was first published in 1655 and which had gone through eight editions by the time of his death in 1684. Newton recorded buying a copy for 3 shillings not long after he arrived at Cambridge in 1661. In his mid-eighteenth-century biography of Newton, the antiquarian William Stukeley—a friend of Newton for his final years—described Walker as "an intimate acquaintance" of Newton, though apart from the plague years in the middle of the 1660s (when Newton was in Lincolnshire) it is difficult to know when they could have known each other. Shortly before his death, Walker recommended his Grantham School pupil Humphrey Newton (no relation) as an amanuensis to Newton, by then the Lucasian professor, and Humphrey would remain with his namesake for five years. Over six decades later Stukeley heard from locals that Newton had been responsible for the joke "Hic jacent Walkeri particulae" "Here lie Walker's particles" that was on Walker's grave in Colsterworth church (see Plate 3), though it would have been a minor miracle if Newton had treated such a serious matter with this degree of impertinence.[13]

The career of Robert Sanderson, rector of Boothby Pagnell between 1619 and 1660, provides the best source for understanding the religious and political tensions in Newton's neighbourhood. Sanderson was no ordinary clergyman and was a fellow of Lincoln College, Oxford, from

1606–19, during which he gained a reputation as a brilliant logician. Indeed, his "Compendium of Logic," which first appeared in 1615 and went through many subsequent editions, was the most popular book on logic in use at Oxford and Cambridge during the seventeenth century. From 1619 until he became bishop of Lincoln at the Restoration, he was rector of Boothby Pagnell. The college connection, as well as the proximity of their parishes and their lengthy tenures, make it certain that Sanderson knew Barnabas Smith. However, there is no evidence that Smith played a key role in Sanderson's intellectual orbit, which by the early 1650s involved most of the senior figures active in the largely underground Church of England.

In his biography of Sanderson, Izaak Walton noted that his diligence and great casuistical learning had drawn him to the attention of Archbishop Laud, who advised Charles to make him a chaplain. Sanderson became a close confidant of the king and was part of a group called by the monarch in 1641 to make some "safe" alterations to the Book of Common Prayer, although its recommendations were never implemented. In 1642 he was named as Regius Professor of Divinity at Oxford, and he delivered lectures on oath-taking and the nature of political obligation. However, he refused to take the Covenant and was soon forced to leave the city, spending two years as a scholar-in-exile in Boothby Pagnell. In 1646 Sanderson returned to Oxford to officially resume his position but two years later he was expelled for a second time. A leading opponent of the regime, he became a prominent figure in a circle of royalist divines that included Henry Hammond, Gilbert Sheldon, and others. It was for both his learning and his loyalty that he was elevated to the bishopric of Lincoln in 1661.[14]

Sanderson pulled off the difficult if not impossible trick of becoming a confidant first of Laud and then of leading figures of the underground Interregnum Church of England, while maintaining overtly anti-Arminian positions in sermons and other writings. Yet despite holding many Calvinist moral, social, and doctrinal positions in common with puritans, he believed that the self-proclaimed godly, such as those in Cotton's congregation, were egregious hypocrites. By the end of the 1650s he had toned down his opposition to Arminianism and he would prove to be a vigorous opponent of comprehension (the effort to change some requirements for membership of the Church of England so that Presbyterians could be included) in the aftermath of the Restoration.[15] Sanderson gained a reputation as a fair judge in local disputes, particularly where they involved property. He assiduously carried out his duties, teaching plain truths from Scripture, reading prayers and sermons, and administering the sacraments. Frequently, in the evenings, he would spend an hour catechising with parents and elders: according to Walton he "grounded them on each point steadfastly, & taught them their duties arising out of each part of Religion profitably."[16]

Although he did not support the imposition of Laudian rituals, Sanderson upset some people by continuing to read from the Book of Common Prayer. In 1650 he subscribed to the Engagement oath but in the same year he was told that Presbyterians in Grantham were upset with his machinations and "refractoriness" in continuing to use the Prayer Book, and was warned that he was in danger of losing his living. He was harassed by soldiers who (according to Walton) sought "to advise him how God was to be served more acceptably, which he not approving, but continuing to observe order and decent behaviour in reading the Church Service," they ripped up his Prayer Book and demanded extempore prayers. Unwilling and indeed unable to preach without notes, Sanderson showed both fortitude and cunning in the face of such provocation and rearranged the elements of his service in order to preserve key features of the traditional liturgy. He kept a lower profile in the remainder of the 1650s, devoting his time to scholarship and basic pastoral duties. He published another edition of his sermons in 1657, this time wisely removing the anti-Arminian passages that had upset Henry Hammond and others. In the last few years of the decade his situation was relieved through the intervention of his friend Thomas Barlow and the generosity of Robert Boyle, who gave him £50 per annum to write up cases of conscience for publication (a text that ultimately appeared in 1660).[17]

Sanderson's successor at Boothby Pagnell, Humphrey Babington, would be a central figure in the first half of Newton's life. Babington went to Trinity in 1634, becoming a fellow in 1640 and college tutor from 1642–47. He was ordained as a priest in 1648 but for reasons that are unclear, he was not ejected as a result of the imposition of the Covenant, a fact that implies that he did sign. However, he was expelled after his refusal to take the Engagement oath in 1650 and spent time in the early 1650s as a minister at Keyworth near Bunny in Nottinghamshire, where his relative, the royalist colonel Isham Parkyns, was Lord of the Manor. In 1654 Babington stayed with Parkyns at Bunny Hall, and in 1655 he was briefly a minister at Stanton-on-the-Wolds in Nottinghamshire, becoming a minister at St. Wulfram's in Grantham for six months in 1656/57. In 1661, following Sanderson's elevation to the see of Lincoln, he became rector of Boothby Pagnell. At the Restoration he also resumed his Trinity fellowship, becoming a senior fellow in 1667. He would divide his time between his parish and his college for the next two decades.[18]

Newton knew Babington at Grantham and was on excellent terms with him at Trinity College, where Babington had become a dominant figure by the 1670s. Stukeley recorded in 1727 that while at Grantham, Newton had begged Babington for a wooden box, from which he had proudly fashioned a waterclock. Although Newton's uncle had graduated from the college, Stukeley mentioned that it was Babington's advice that was the chief reason why Newton went to Trinity; Babington had "a particular kindness for him, which probably was owing to his own ingenuity." As one of the returning exiles in 1660, Babington was already a powerful ally for Newton when he went to the college. Newton stayed with him in Boothby Pagnell for part of the plague years in the mid-1660s, and he benefitted from Babington's patronage as the latter rose through the college ranks. Babington's link to Parkyns is no doubt why Newton owned a copy of Thomas Parkyns's *The Inn-Play, or Cornish-hugg Wrestler* (London, 1713). Parkyns, who intimated that Newton had played a significant hand in allowing him to think of applying mathematics to the art of wrestling, was the grandson of Isham Parkyns and was a fellow-commoner (a wealthy student with similar dining rights to the fellows) at Trinity in the early 1680s.[19]

Babington's only publication, a 1678 sermon on mercy and judgement that was originally delivered at the Lincoln Bench, displays his political and religious views in a particularly clear way. He paid generous respects to his recently deceased predecessor as rector; Sanderson, he said, had been responsible for Babington's appointment at Boothby Pagnell and had given him "many obliging encouragements" while alive—though Babington added modestly that he was obviously unworthy of the support. In his sermon he lauded piety as "the best policy, the great preserver, and surest prop of all Government," but the greatest virtue was mercy. Alluding to the present monarch (Charles II) by way of an account of King David's actions, Babington enjoined both the sovereign and his subjects to be merciful before anything else. Mercy made good laws and kept their number to a minimum; it was an excellent principle for assessing the justice and efficacy of laws that prevented "too many Sutes, Actions, Pleadings; with much strife, debate, contention." Much of this echoes Sanderson's invective against his parishioners' penchant for litigation, although he chose an interesting if apt setting to launch a diatribe against the "subtle delays" and other dark arts of the "perfidious" advocates, whom Babington deemed worse than highwaymen.[20]

Mercy always had to be balanced or reinforced by power. In his account of the virtue of judgement, Babington argued that Christian monarchs had the right to wield the power of the sword, whatever the views of the anarchic libertines and Anabaptists who effectively wanted to bring down all Christian societies. He condemned the "mischievous bloudy Comet" Louis XIV, who lacked either mercy or judgement, but praised divinely ordained monarchy as the best form of government. It was the best defence against the "great furious Bulls of Tyrannical popery, and the lesser giddy cattle of Schismatical Presbytery," both of which had combined during the recent troubles, like Pilate and Herod, with the express intent of bringing down the king. By the end of the printed sermon, Babington was lashing out against present-day enemies, and it is perhaps significant that the dedicatory epistle of the sermon was dated the seventeenth of September 1678, soon after Titus Oates had laid before the magistrate Edmund Berry Godfrey his tales of a Catholic plot against the king. Within a month Godfrey had been murdered, allegedly by Catholics, and the so-called Popish Plot began. Having preached the value of mercy earlier in the piece, Babington now called for action against those "Incendiaries" who hated and persecuted the government. His target was the nonconformists who had suffered under the regime of Charles II but who would cry out "Persecution, Persecution" when just penalties were executed on them. Babington thundered that neither mercy nor judgement could reclaim them and it was, he concluded, the duty of the "Worthies of the Honourable bench" to preserve the foundations of the state against such people.[21]

2. The Apothecary

Newton's early religious instruction was marked by an intense level of discipline. Raised in an environment where clergymen were prominent, he had to take notes on the Bible, and other expository texts, and he had to write down and memorize the content of the sermons that he regularly attended. William Ayscough and Barnabas Smith must have exerted some influence over his education, although it is possible that he was regularly exposed to Francis Browne's puritan sermons at Colsterworth. Newton's grandfather James Ayscough was buried at his son William's church in

Burton Coggles in 1657, which may suggest that Newton's grandmother worshipped there, though as we have seen, James also stated that he was from Woolsthorpe. A third possibility, of course, is that every Sunday one or both grandparents took him on the short trek to the church where his mother resided at North Witham. Like other children, Newton would certainly have been catechised from an early age. At these meetings he would have been introduced, by means of question-and-answer sessions, to basic features of Christianity such as the Creed, the Decalogue (Ten Commandments), the Lord's Prayer, and the sacraments. In preparation for confirmation and beyond, young men and women had to memorise lengthy passages of Scripture, and they were vigorously tested on their understanding of it. Catechising was graduated, that is, there were different levels of doctrinal and textual comprehension expected of catechumens. Newton's tremendous knowledge, not merely of individual passages but of how verses throughout the Bible were interlinked, must have been honed as a result of repeated sessions like this. Outside of the church, there were various catechetical treatises for use in the home, school, and university.[22]

At some point in early 1655 (when he had just turned twelve), Newton began to attend the Free Grammar School at Grantham, lodging with the apothecary William Clarke. Even in 1727, when Stukeley obtained his information about these years of his life, Newton's practical accomplishments seven decades earlier were still fresh in the minds of those who had been his contemporaries. They recalled that he had been inordinately inventive, procuring a "whole shop of tools" with the money his mother gave him. Among the products of his dexterous hands were a model windmill, many clocks, and an extraordinary sundial, many of which were based on drawings and descriptions found in John Bate's *Mysteries of Nature and Art* (probably using the second edition of 1654). As Stukeley pointed out, the apothecary's shop provided sources for Newton's practical knowledge, though he was always drawn back to books. Katherine Vincent (Clarke's stepdaughter) told Stukeley that Newton was "a sober, silent, thinking lad"; after his mother recalled him from the school in the winter of 1659/60, he would go to Grantham on market days, occasionally slipping up to the garret of Clarke's house. Here he read the books of Clarke's brother Joseph, a physician who had tomes on astronomy, physic (i.e., medicine), botany, philosophy, mathematics, and astronomy. Referring to Newton's legendary absentmindedness, Stukeley noted that Clarke's trove of learning "was a feast to him exclusive of any thought of dinner, any regard to market business. there he staid till the servant calld upon him to goe home." These books must have been greatly preferable to the theological tomes bequeathed by his stepfather.[23]

The household in which Newton stayed during the later 1650s was a large and complex unit, but the house itself was easily large enough to accommodate them. Stukeley noted that a major reason for lodging with Clarke was the friendship Hannah Smith enjoyed with Katherine Babington, Clarke's wife and Humphrey's sister. Hannah could have met Katherine at the Skillington dame school that Newton attended as a youth, though by this time Katherine was married to Clarke and living in Grantham. In February 1641, while she was still living at Bunny Hall in Nottinghamshire, the home of her aunt Catherine and her husband, Isham Parkyns, she married Edward Storer (himself recently a widower), who brought with him a young daughter, Ann. Living in Buckminster in Leicestershire, in quick succession Katherine gave birth to Edward Jr., Katherine Jr., and Arthur. Edward Sr. died in June 1644, and in July 1647 Katherine married Clarke at Buckminster, although they quickly moved to his house in Grantham. Clarke himself brought a son and two daughters from a previous marriage, and together he and Catherine had three more children. It was a greatly extended family, whose order was not helped by the presence of the strange village boy who lived in the attic, covered the walls with pictures of animals, and turned his room into a giant sundial.[24]

Of the children, only the Storers feature in the records of Newton's early life. Katherine Storer, who told Stukeley that Newton had written poetry for her (and still remembered the verses), was the most important source for Stukeley regarding Newton's life in Grantham, being the "Mrs. Vincent" whom he met at Grantham in 1727. As she remembered it, she had been the object of Newton's affections when younger, but his devotion to college life had put paid to any thoughts of betrothal. She married the Grantham attorney Francis Bacon in August 1665 at a ceremony officiated by her uncle Humphrey Babington, and Newton (who may have been staying with Babington at Boothby Pagnell at this time) kept in touch with her in the intervening decades. As for the rest of the family, Newton recorded physically beating Arthur Storer in his list of earlier offences, and stealing cherry cobblers from his brother Edward. He also recorded a bout of "peevishness" at William Clarke over a piece of bread and butter, and used the same expression in connection with his mother and one of his sisters. If the latter was the same girl as the one mentioned elsewhere in his list, she was also on the receiving end of a punch from her half-brother. Judging by these entries, and the anecdote about wanting to burn his mother and stepfather, books and mechanical pursuits offered Newton release from an existence marked by frustration and resentment.[25]

The Clarkes were as steeped in learning as the Babingtons. William's brother Joseph had studied with the Cambridge Platonist Henry More at Christ's College, Cambridge, in the late 1640s and would remain on good terms with More for the following decades. Like William, Joseph was closely linked to the parliamentary side during the 1640s and 1650s. On 18 June 1649 he was elected to the position of usher, that is, second master of the Free Grammar School, a post he retained until 1662. More, himself a Grantham Free Schoolboy, stayed at Clarke's Grantham residence in May 1654 and April 1655, the latter occasion probably overlapping with Newton's presence in the town. Joseph Clarke became a trusted physician and in 1674, when More was seeking his advice over a drug for cancer that had been given to him by the chemist Francis Mercury Van Helmont, he referred to Clarke as "a good safe discreet person." Arthur Storer moved to Maryland in the early 1670s and became a merchant. However, he was also an accomplished astronomer, who produced observations that were at least as accurate as those produced by his contemporary Edmond Halley. The earlier contretemps having presumably been forgotten, Storer corresponded with Newton on astronomical matters in the late 1670s and early 1680s, and his observations of the Great Comet of 1680/81 and of Halley's Comet in 1682 were used by Newton in the *Principia*. Edward Storer became a physician and moved to Buckminster, where he fathered four daughters and three sons, all of the boys going on to study at Trinity College, Cambridge.[26]

When Newton moved into the house of William Clarke, he was staying with a man who was twice elected alderman (the equivalent of a mayor) in the 1650s, and who was the most prominent parliamentarian in Grantham. At the outbreak of the civil war he was a member of the corporation (or council) of Grantham and the millmaster of the Well Lane mill. He was not yet a member of the major administrative court of the town, but would thrive when power passed from royalists to the parliamentarians in the early 1640s. An alderman was elected each October by twelve comburgesses (known as the "First" twelve) and twelve burgesses (the "second" twelve). The court (consisting of the twenty-four) met about once a month and it tried offenders and effected punishments, supervised alehouses, administered poor relief, merged the free school, and punished uncivil speech. As the civil war broke out, Parliament took control over most of the county.

Grantham, whose inhabitants had deeply divided allegiances, briefly fell to royalist forces in January 1643 but it was quickly recaptured. In February royalist alderman Robert Colcroft and many other comburgesses were taken prisoner, the town plate was confiscated, and £3,300 demanded by the parliamentary forces for the return of the men and the plate. The town was retaken by the royalists at the end of March, and eighty-six parliamentarians were indicted for high treason at a special sessions court on 11 April 1643. Cromwell arrived in the vicinity in early May, and the town was soon back in parliamentary hands.[27]

At the start of the civil war, Clarke allied himself to the parliamentarian cause, having already made a name for himself as a rabid antimonarchist. As early as June 1642 a series of remarks he made against the king were so troublesome that he was arrested by authorities in Grantham, and his case was even discussed in the House of Commons. According to one report he was overheard saying that Charles should be deposed and one of his sons crowned in his place; according to another, he was said to have denounced a royalist neighbour for being in favour of popery on the grounds that he would support the king in the event of war. The Commons thought Clarke's crimes sufficiently serious to transmit him to King's Bench for trial, presumably for treason, but this never took place—either because he had a highly placed sympathiser, or because the deteriorating political situation made the process impossible. He was one of those indicted in Grantham for high treason the following April, and these events clearly stood him in good stead with the parliamentarian authorities over the following years. As the town lurched into serious financial crisis, his expanding wealth helped his rise. He loaned sums of money to the borough on a number of occasions in the 1640s and was elected treasurer of the corporation in January 1646. In October 1646 he was chief of the "Second" twelve burgesses of the town, and in September 1647, he was made one of the comburgesses.[28]

Clarke predictably made enemies on his climb up the ladder. In November 1646 the royalist Edward Watson was given the standard fine of 3 shillings and threepence (3s. 3d.) for giving "uncivile & unseemlie speeches in open courte" against him, and for calling him a liar. Two months later the court set in motion efforts to fine those "delinquents" who were not well affected to the parliamentary side, including those who had recently prevented Clarke and others from joining the second rank of burgesses. In September 1647 Parliament decreed that no one who had taken up arms against it could have a vote in choosing aldermen, and a few months later Clarke was involved in efforts to raise money for quartering parliamentarian soldiers. In August 1648 he was verbally insulted by one of the churchwardens of St. Wulfram's, a man named Phillip Hollingworth. A disgruntled royalist, Hollingworth had previously doled out anti-parliamentarian abuse, having had to pay the regulation fine of 3 shillings and threepence in November 1647 to the puritan alderman Richard Cony for making "scandalous & un-civill" comments. He directed similar remarks at Clarke, although the court had insufficient time to deal with the case and he escaped the fine.[29]

Clarke, who was by now the leading freeholder in Grantham, was elected alderman in 1650/51 and again in 1656/57. While Newton lodged with him, Clarke's less than harmonious relations with his fellow townsmen took up much of the court's time. At the start of the last court of Alderman Edward Towne in October 1655, a government proclamation was read out reiterating that delinquents could not bear office or have any vote or even say in the election of candidates. Later in the meeting, one member of a prominent local royalist family, Edward Coddington, was censured and fined the usual 3 shillings and threepence for "uncivill speeches" in relation to Clarke, who was a justice of the peace. Remarkably, Coddington said that he did not know whether Clarke meant to kill him or not, but he was afraid of him and "craved the peace ag^t him." Clarke stirred up more resentment in the first court of Alderman Edward Baily, held a few days later. As the previous alderman, Towne apparently demanded that he be accorded seniority above Clarke in the order of comburgesses, and a majority of the court agreed. Since Towne must have been loyal to the protectorate, Clarke was obviously capable of provoking the animosity of people on either side of the political spectrum.[30]

Clarke fell out on a regular basis with other members of the court in the next few years, though such was his political standing that he was elected alderman for a second time in 1656. One long-festering sore concerned a loan to the town of £2000 that Clarke had made in the late 1640s jointly with Thomas Hurst, William Welby, and Robert Trevillian. The town agreed to pay £200 interest on this per annum and in the early 1650s the court determined that this should be funded from profits from the mills. Hurst and Welby agreed to the deal but Clarke and Trevillian did not, leading to a series of bitter disputes in 1656 over the obligations the last two men had to support the upkeep of the work at the mills. Clarke continued to cause trouble during his second tenure as alderman. In April 1657 the court ordered that half of his salary of £10 be taken away since he had "take[n] to himself" many of the fees usually paid to the town clerk and had received many other benefits never before claimed by aldermen. In a fit of pique, Clarke kept the records of the meeting so that the next court session could not take place. At the last full meeting held during his reign, he was granted the right to recover at his own expense all the fees he had expended while executing his duties as alderman, but in an extraordinary show of defiance, the court refused to believe his accounts of his own expenditure over the previous year. The fact that the court continued to press him over the following months for money that he allegedly owed to the town indicates that his standing as a sound Cromwellian could not stop the carping of those who disliked his overbearing and heavy-handed demeanour.[31]

After Clarke's forced resignation from the Corporation in October 1661, he moved to Loughborough in Leicestershire. Over the previous two decades, he had remained hostile to the form of worship practised by the Church of England, and he gave money to support the preaching of the ministers at various points in the 1650s. The religious opening to his will goes beyond the usual platitudes of such a format, indicating that he was a godly man, and it is significant that his stepdaughter Ann (the surviving child from Edward Storer Sr.'s first marriage), married into the influential nonconformist Truman family, immigrating (as Arthur Storer did) to Maryland. One letter from April 1671 that she wrote to a Puritan minister Matthew Sylvester betrays the typical signs of someone brought up in a puritan background. She remarked on the fact that God had been pleased to visit their community with "various providences," which in puritan terms usually referred to sudden deaths (she had lost a baby son at the start of the year), lamented the legislation in England that discriminated so strongly against "so many good people," and congratulated Sylvester for marrying a woman who was a "vertuous branch of very Godly parents." Clarke's relationship with his brother-in-law Humphrey Babington shows that, at times, family connections trumped political and religious divisions. Although he supported the appointment of the puritan Henry Vaughan as public lecturer in the autumn of 1657, he must have had a hand in Babington's brief appointment as minister of St. Wulfram's a year earlier. In Clarke's will of 1671 he twice referred to Babington as his "loving brother" and he made Babington executor of his estate along with his wife and his brother Joseph.[32]

In Clarke, Newton may have had some semblance of a father figure. He was a domineering person who struck fear into his opponents and who remarked at the end of his will that those who did not show the required gratitude for what he had left them would get nothing. The emphasis within his household must have been on a "godly" form of worship, and as we shall see in the following section, some of this style of religiosity may have rubbed off on the boy in the garret. As for Clarke's influence on Newton's political views, it is perhaps telling that Katherine Vincent recalled Newton drawing a number of pictures of kings, including one of Charles I, which he coloured and framed. He wrote down some lines of poetry—which she recalled from memory seven decades after the fact—that were loosely based on the frontispiece of *Eikon Basilike*, the royalist martyrology published in the wake of Charles's death that was allegedly composed by the king himself. If Newton had imbibed Clarke's visceral hatred of monarchy, he did not show it. We do not know whether this episode betrayed his family's political views, or whether it was an act of resistance against Clarke's rule. In any case, the "sober, silent thinking lad" was an independent and private youth, capable of losing himself in textual worlds and of walling himself off from the society in which he lived.[33]

3. Training in Piety

Another key area of religious influence was Newton's school. Following the business with Charles Hoole, the town had sought a new head teacher for the Free School, and Henry Stokes, who had previously been master of Melton School, was selected on 1 February 1650. This was a time of heightened political sensitivity and he must have satisfied the committee as to his religious views, though the language used in the minutes of the Grantham Court to describe the ideal candidate indicates that the town was predominantly concerned with scholarly excellence. Stokes fitted the bill, having been admitted to Pembroke College, Cambridge, in 1638, and Stukeley confirmed that he was "accounted a very good scholar and an excellent schoolm[r]." Stokes noted Newton's great capacity to surpass the other students when he put his mind to it, even though Stokes's own "gentle remonstrances [to Newton] to lay aside his mechanical experiments" were generally ignored. Newton's Grantham idyll ended abruptly when Hannah Smith recalled him from school, probably at the end of 1659, "intending to make him serviceable to her, in management of farming & country business." Stukeley comically understated the issue when he stated that "these employments ill suited Sir Isaac's taste," and despite his mother's stern words, the genius continued to lose himself in his books and his machines.[34]

In Stukeley's beguiling and often perceptive narrative, Stokes emerges as the saviour of Britain's "great glory" of learning. Hannah berated her insufferable son for being useless at managing the family business, and the servants were "not a little offended at his bookishness," calling him "a silly boy [who] w^d never be good for anything." Stokes realised Newton's incomparable talent for inventions along with his precocious penetration: "he never ceasd remonstrating to his mo^r. what a loss it was to mankind, as well as a vain attempt, to bury so ~~extraordinary~~ ⁽uncommon⁾ a talent, in rustic business." Stokes was "sufficiently satisfy'd that he w^d. become a very extraordinary man" and persuaded Hannah to allow Newton to go back to the school and board with him, "that he might perfect his learning & fit him for the University." He soon "compleated" Newton in the learned languages, meaning Latin and Greek. As the story went in Stukeley's 1752 version of events, Stokes lauded Newton in front of the school and moved the other pupils to tears, though the servants at Woolsthorpe Manor declared that Newton was "fit for nothing but the 'Versity."[35]

As Stukeley's remarks indicate, during his last months at Grantham Newton underwent a rigorous training in a large number of Greek and Latin texts, and would have been drilled in their respective grammars. In some schools the New Testament was read in Latin, but in many it was read in Greek, and in some cases this happened as early as the fourth form (when pupils were ten or eleven). It is worth recalling that Newton was a late arrival, going to the school only when he was twelve. He was exposed to a wide variety of classical literary works in his final year at Grantham, but as we shall see in the next chapter, much of his training in the Greek language revolved around the interpretation of passages of the Greek New Testament. It is possible that he was taught some basic Hebrew in order to read the Hebrew Bible, but it is much more likely that he was exposed only to the Septuagint (Greek) version. Like other pupils he was fluent in Latin by the time he arrived at Cambridge and was able to translate from Latin to English and vice versa with ease. In Hoole's *New Discovery of the Old Art of Teaching School*, which might have been the blueprint for teaching Newton if he had been awarded the master's job, he prescribed a detailed outline of religious instruction, which started in the first form and covered every day of the school year. All this built on what most of the students would have learned before they arrived at school, and the repeated exercises continued up to the point when they left, perhaps to go to university. Hoole recommended a daily diet of catechising, sermons, and perhaps most important, note-taking on religious matters, and a passage from the Bible was read every morning and afternoon. Of course, pupils had to do a lot more on Sundays.[36]

Stokes must have installed a pedagogical regime similar to that prescribed by Hoole. As for religious instruction, although Stokes's precise doctrinal beliefs are unknown, there is clear testimony from a near contemporary of Newton's that he ran a pious ship. John Rastrick, who was born in Heckington in Lincolnshire in 1650, was brought up in a godly family and at a very young age gained an excellent knowledge of the Bible. Rastrick was a deeply devout boy who liked nothing better than to immerse himself in books such as Daniel Dyke's *Mystery of Self-Deceiving* and Arthur Dent's *Plaine Man's Path-Way to Heaven*. To a considerable extent, his educational journey resembled the one taken by Newton. Coming from a rural background with a dominant mother, he followed Newton to Grantham Grammar School in 1662 (and entered at the same age), and attended Trinity College, Cambridge, in the later 1660s. Rastrick was at the school in the last year of Stokes's tenure and remembered that it was well governed, the boys being "train[ed] up not only in human learning but in Piety." There were prayers before school every day and Saturday mornings were devoted to catechisms: "All of us that could write were enjoyned to write Sermons in the church." They went back to school on Sundays, when their sermon notes were scrutinised, read aloud, and discussed. Rastrick fell in love with the idea of being a scholar, but his extreme and visible piety left him open to abuse, and he was jeered by other boys for kneeling in the garden and praying to the walls. The great distance from home also caused him to develop "melancholy," and his mother pulled him out of the school at Whitsun in 1663. Echoing Stokes's plea on behalf of Newton, Rastrick recalled that his "Master" at Grantham (Stokes?) feared he would be "spoiled," and his parts "quite buryed," but Mrs. Rastrick was made of sterner stuff than Hannah Smith, and there was no going back.[37]

4. A Godly Boy

Like many other boys who went to university in the Restoration, Newton had to make an abrupt shift from the Presbyterian form of worship he experienced in Grantham to an extreme High Church style. Whatever he thought of the religious rituals in which he had to participate, one piece of evidence indicates that he brought with him a highly private form of religiosity that had existed for many years. On Whitsun (18 May) 1662, almost a year after he had arrived at Trinity College, Cambridge, Newton entered into a small notebook an untitled list of all the faults he could remember having committed. It is possible that some of the episodes he described took place during his early months at university, but a number of explicitly religious sins are interspersed with other events—such as those involving the Storers—that must have occurred in the second half of the 1650s.[38]

Many of Newton's entries in his register of offences do have a distinctly godly flavour. A string of activities entered early in the list were Sabbatarian (i.e., keeping Sunday, the "Lord's Day," as the Sabbath), which itself is indicative of a puritan outlook. Section VIII of chapter 21 of the 1646 Westminster Confession of Faith enjoined the godly to observe a holy rest "from their own works, words, and thoughts about their worldly employments and recreations," and urged them to take up their day in private and public exercises of worship. Referring to sins committed on "Thy Day," Newton included making a feather (presumably a hat), a mousetrap, a clock, and pies; swimming in a bath; squirting water; "idle discourse"; and putting a pin in the hat of John Keys. In the case of the pies, as well as when he was "twisting a cord" and "reading the history of the Christian champions," he explicitly mentioned that the offence took place on a Sunday, and other remarks reveal behaviour that was understood at the time to be characteristic of extreme piety. These include "Using the word God openly," eating an apple at church, and "setting my heart on money learning pleasure more than Thee," a fault into which Newton relapsed twice. The claim that worldly people were more concerned with money, learning, and pleasure rather than attending to God was a central puritan characteristic, and Newton also chided himself for "Caring for worldly things more than God." The fact that the hapless Keys attended the Free School links many of these entries to the Grantham period.[39]

Some entries in the list refer to religious practice—for example, the remark "Carelessly hearing and committing many sermons" shows that Newton was part of a religious community in which sermons played a key role. This appears before his recollection of threatening to burn his mother and stepfather to death, which suggests a memory of events that happened in the early 1650s, but it could equally refer to his time at Grantham. After admonishing himself for "idle discourse" on Sundays and at other times, he also chastised himself for not living strictly according to his own belief. The remaining notes indicate a close, personal relationship with God that is found nowhere else in his writings. Newton confessed that he had not turned closer to God for his affections and had not "loved Thee for Thyself." He had not loved God for his goodness, and crucially, he was a backslider who had not desired God's ordinances. There are no other examples in Newton's writings of the intimacy with God that characterises these notes. Once he became a serious scholar, the religious energy that underpinned this early display of piety would manifest itself in a strictly disciplined religious life and a devotion to study. Central to his studious existence was the scrutiny of the Bible. The strict demarcation between the unadulterated words of divine Scripture and what was merely added to it by vanity of human artifice, would lie at the heart of Newton's approaches to other fields of study.[40]

Some aspects of these entries are indicative of a puritan style of worship, though Newton did not engage in many of the core practices characteristic of the godly. At this early stage, as we have seen, he showed a heightened sensitivity to his conduct on the Sabbath, while his intensive scrutiny of the Bible, and his efforts to live a godly existence would be central features throughout his life. However, he was suspicious of immoderate fasting, and apparently hostile to shibboleths of puritan life such as concern for special providences, psalm-singing, meditation, and the self-examination that would lead to spiritual regeneration. It should be said that the devout bearing that Newton displayed was not exclusive to Puritans. In the wake of the crackdown by Cromwell on traditional rituals in the middle of the 1650s, many members of the outlawed Church of England turned towards a much more intense and personal form of religious existence. Devotional letters, writings, and behaviour made this form of piety much closer in style to that of the godly, and in some cases they were indistinguishable. Whatever the sources of Newton's own form of faith were, by the time he left Grantham for Cambridge in the summer of 1661, he was a God-fearing youth, with an excellent knowledge of Scripture. Once he became obsessed with his studies, he continued to find it hard to maintain regular church attendance, and his notes and essays on theology and natural philosophy would constitute his particular style of worship.[41]

2

A Spiritual Ant

Newton's choice of the college of the "Holy and Undivided Trinity" was determined both by his uncle's connection to the college and also by his links to Humphrey Babington. Despite his mother's substantial wealth, he arrived there in June 1661 at the lowest rung of the college social ladder, being a "subsizar" who was supposed to pay to hear lectures and to wait on the fellows or wealthier students. He may well have avoided some of these impositions through his connections with Babington. He certainly kept in touch with Babington in his first years at the institution, and probably lived with him for various periods at Boothby Pagnell when the plague was raging in 1665–67. In *Never at Rest*, his biography of Newton, Richard Westfall paints an unnecessarily bleak picture of the quality of instruction available at Trinity while he was there. There were brilliant scholars in various fields, and in Isaac Barrow, the first Lucasian Professor of Mathematics, the college boasted someone who was—until Newton's talents blossomed—arguably the best mathematician in the country. Westfall is surely correct, however, to point out that after Newton became famous, not one student or fellow saw fit to leave even the slightest reminiscence of his presence. Even within his college, the independent scholar was also an extreme intellectual hermit.[1]

Newton had lived the first two decades of his life in an environment that was beset by deep tensions between different religious and political groups. When he returned to Grantham in the autumn of 1660, a year before he matriculated at Cambridge, the corporation was in the process of reversing fifteen years of parliamentarian rule. People such as William Clarke lost their power and influence, and alongside the reimposition of traditional religious services at St. Wulfram's, royalists regained control over the town's administrative court. Events at Trinity mirrored those in Grantham, and when Newton arrived there it had recently experienced several major revolutions of its own. However, the reaction to fifteen years of Presbyterian rule was even more radical than it was in Grantham, where the majority of the town leaders had to live on in ignominy. A group of dons with High Church leanings took over in the late summer of 1660, restoring practices that looked decidedly popish to many observers within the college. As a result, a large number of fellows were expelled, the second great exodus from the institution within two decades. These men put up substantial resistance to the vigorous efforts to enforce traditional practices, and when Newton stepped foot in the institution, it had not been fully cleansed of puritan elements.[2]

The college had been a touchstone of divisions within the Church of England for more than a century. During the reign of Elizabeth, Trinity was at the centre of disputes between different Anglican factions, and it was subject to a number of different ecclesiastical orders in the first half of the seventeenth century. In 1613, James I ordered that no one should receive a degree of bachelor of divinity or any doctorate without subscribing to the three Articles in the 36th canon of 1604. These demanded acknowledgement of the sovereign's place as "supreme governor" of England, its dominions, countries, and the Church of England; that the Book of Common Prayer contained nothing contrary to the Word of God, and could be lawfully used; and that the Thirty-Nine Articles of Religion agreed at the London Convocation of 1563 were "agreeable to the Word of God." Six years later, in the face of widespread noncompliance, he further stipulated that all members of the university should kneel and wear surplices and hoods in college chapels during prayer, the sermon, and the administration of the sacrament. Any statements favouring Judaism, popery, or puritanism were to be checked and reformed, and there was also to be catechising between three and four o'clock on Sundays and holy days. The extent to which these injunctions were obeyed differed from one college to another, but they were clearly not generally recognised within Trinity. They would remain a source of contention until after the Restoration.[3]

1. A Divided Trinity

With the rise of Archbishop Laud in the early 1630s, there were decisive moves to rid the university of its blasphemous practices, Calvinist opinions, and puritan forms of worship. Laud was told by his agents that at the university church, Great St. Mary's, the majority of the flock eschewed traditional

liturgical forms of worship, while the church was acting primarily as a
"Lumberhouse" and a storage space for the dry fat used by bookbinders.
Worse still, young scholars were being told to prefer "the private spirit
before yᵉ publick, & their own invented and unaproved prayers before all
the Liturgie of yᵉ Church." Trinity College was singled out for its poor
record in conforming to Laud's policies, and in 1635 Laud received a highly
negative report about the behaviour of its fellows and pupils. The author of
the account alleged that members of the college were neglecting chapel and
the prayers that were held within it, while senior fellows set a terrible
example as a result of their abysmal attendance at chapel and Great St. Mary's.
Fellows and fellow-commoners both seemed to think they had a right to
avoid prayers and the "public table" at the hall, and they were generally to
be found in taverns. The choristers were slovenly, adopting various un-
seemly postures at prayer and neglecting to bow at the name of Jesus, and
when the Creed was repeated many of them "by some men's directions"
turned west instead of to the east of the church. Their surplices and
songbooks were "mean," and they barely used the Litany except at Lent on
Sundays. However, the report noted that the fellows had recently heeded
advice and had begun to rearrange their chapel. In 1636, the communion
table was moved from near the middle of the chapel to the upper (east) end,
the ground was raised, a crucifix placed on the altar, and the chapel adorned
with candlesticks.[4]

The Long Parliament abruptly halted the Laudian revolution, and both
James I's decrees regarding proper worship and Laud's alleged "innovations"
were annulled by the House of Commons in January 1641. Soon afterwards,
heads of colleges were told by Parliament to remove communion tables
from the east end to the middle of the chapel, to lower the chancel (the area
around the altar used by the clergy during services), and to take away the
rails from around the table. "Scandalous pictures" of members of the Holy
Trinity, and all images of the Virgin Mary were also to be taken away and
destroyed. In the following months, as war broke out, the Crown and Parliament vied for support from individual colleges, but with the support of
Cromwell's army Parliament took control of the city in early 1642. On 17
February 1643 the House of Commons ordered that scholars should no
longer be forced to observe traditional ceremonies, and a month later, the
imposition of wearing surplices was also removed. Under pressure from the
troops of William Dowsing, "Commissioner for the destruction of monuments of idolatry and superstition," Trinity complied with the demand to

rearrange the chapel at the end of 1643. The organ and the altar were taken away for safekeeping, "superstitious" figures on the walls were whitewashed, the surplice no longer had to be worn on certain days, and bowing at the name of Jesus (commanded by Philippians 2:10), or to the east end of the church, was prohibited. On 22 January 1644, an ordinance was issued by Parliament for regulating the University of Cambridge, and an order was issued for all fellows who were allegedly ill disposed to Parliament to explain themselves before specially constituted parliamentary committees. Those who did not attend, or who were shown to be "ill-affected to the parliament" were to be summarily ejected from their colleges. The Solemn League and Covenant was tendered on 15 March 1644, effectively outlawing the use of the Book of Prayer and other traditional Anglican practices. As a result of these measures, forty-eight fellows left Trinity College, and their property was confiscated.[5]

Thomas Comber, the master since 1631, made himself technically ineligible for office by refusing to sign the Covenant and was imprisoned for having personally organised the delivery of the college plate to the king. Following the mass exodus of fellows, only one senior fellow of Trinity remained, so the other seven vacant places had to be filled. For some time the college was largely empty, but at the end of 1645 a series of parliamentary appointees duly took up the top positions, and they in turn accepted eight more fellows along with a number of scholars. Thomas Hill, an excellent classicist who had only recently been appointed master of Emmanuel, was announced as the new master. A pronounced Calvinist, he was a member of the Westminster Assembly of Divines and had spent time with John Cotton in Lincolnshire. Hill began his tenure with the aim of reforming the college from the top down, emphasising the importance of faith and scriptural knowledge rather than the pagan, "human" learning that formed the basis of the curriculum. He injected a serious dose of godly discipline into the college (which the young John Dryden likened to that of Sparta's Thebes), but the rise of radical independency in the late 1640s forced him into a position of defending both the traditional curriculum and the importance of academic merit above religious allegiance. This even extended to protecting the interests of the overtly royalist and Arminian scholar Isaac Barrow.[6]

Following the execution of Charles at the end of January 1649, the Cromwellian regime sought to impose its will on the institutions of learning. In October 1649 it ordered that the oath of Engagement to the new republican Commonwealth be subscribed by all members of the university

down to those taking their degrees. In June 1650 Cromwell apparently told
heads of colleges that this did not need to be "pressed," but its implementa-
tion was demanded in November. This resulted in the ejections from the
college of some of the remaining royalists, among whom was Humphrey
Babington.[7] Hill looked on the rise of independency and the wider attack
on universities with dismay, but he did not let up his attack on the traditional
practices of the Church of England. He preached openly against Arminianism
and was quick to stamp out efforts to reintroduce the Book of Common
Prayer at chapel in March 1653, an action that anticipated the law brought
in on New Year's Day 1654 making the use of the Prayer Book by a fellow
subject to expulsion. Later that year the authorities cracked down on major
figures such as James Duport, who was deprived of his position as Regius
Professor of Greek. When Barrow was deemed unsuitable as a replacement
on the grounds of his own Arminian views, he took a four-year sabbatical,
returning only at the eve of the Restoration. Hill died at the end of 1653 and
was replaced as master by John Arrowsmith, the master of St. John's College
since 1644 and Regius Professor of Divinity since 1651. Like Hill, Arrowsmith
had been a member of the Westminster Assembly, and he soon delivered a
series of lectures defending the value for religion of a liberal arts education,
attacking those sectarian "fanatics" who had recently called for the abolition
of the universities.[8]

    The death of Arrowsmith in February 1659 marked the end of official
Presbyterian rule in the college. The fellows petitioned for the appointment
of John Wilkins, the master of Wadham College, Oxford, and leading figure
among the various virtuosi who gathered there in the 1640s and 1650s, and
he assumed the position of master in September 1659. Wilkins instituted more
stringent arrangements for the performance of exercises in the university,
and he won respect for the manner in which he dealt with potentially fractious situations. Over six decades later, Robert Creighton (professor of Greek
from 1666–72) recorded that, while he was a candidate for a fellowship
election held just after Wilkins arrived, he had seen a student hit in the eye
by a tennis ball and had cried out, "Oh God, oh God, the scholar's eye is
struck out!" One of his competitors for the fellowship reported him to the
college authorities for blasphemy and claimed that Creighton was a profane
man who had not attended private prayer meetings. Creighton's tutor, James
Duport (who had replaced Creighton's father as Regius Professor of Greek),
spoke on his behalf and Wilkins confirmed that this was merely an example
of malice on behalf of the accuser. Wilkins justified his decision not to take

the matter further by noting that even if Creighton had not attended private meetings, he always attended chapel and Duport's lectures. As Creighton recalled it, he and his friends were immediately elected to the vacant fellowships.[9]

The universities were pleased when in January 1660, a year before Newton's arrival at Trinity, they heard that a new declaration issued by Parliament proposed to confirm them in their privileges and not subject them to further "reformation." However, the prospect of the return of the monarchy immediately brought about changes in religious practice in many of the colleges. Visiting his alma mater, Magdalene College, Cambridge, in February, Samuel Pepys drank to the king in the Three Tuns (off St. Edward's Passage opposite King's College) and was told that the old puritan "preciseness" in the college discourse had completely disappeared. On 10 May the university was particularly prominent in hailing the return of the king, and an effigy of Cromwell was hanged to great acclaim two days later. As James Mullinger pointed out in his nineteenth-century history of the university, there was no more visibly symbolic event in the academy than the return of the square cap instead of the round pileus favoured by puritans, leading Duport to claim waggishly that royalists had squared the circle.[10]

It was not long before an order came for the reinstatement of ejected heads and fellows. Charles II decided that Henry Ferne had a greater entitlement to the mastership than Wilkins, despite the fact that forty-six members of the college petitioned the new Parliament for Wilkins to continue. The petitioners, who testified to Wilkins's good intentions and resolutions "to promote Religion, Learning and Ingenuity among them," included Duport, Benjamin Pulleyn (soon to be Newton's tutor), the naturalist John Ray, Thomas Bainbrigg, and a number of senior fellows. Ferne was awarded the mastership on 29 April 1660, though Wilkins did not vacate the position until the start of August. Ferne had been elected as a fellow of the college in 1624, gaining various livings in the Church of England before obtaining his degree of doctor of divinity and becoming archdeacon of Leicester in 1641. In the civil war he soon found his way into the ranks of Charles I's chaplains, and rose to become a chaplain-in-ordinary in 1642. He gained a reputation as a brave loyalist, and as an accomplished anti-Catholic and anti-Republican controversialist. Within days of becoming master he set up the mechanisms necessary for restoring the traditional High Church practices. He allowed fellows elected during the Commonwealth to retain their fellowships but permitted only those who fully subscribed to the regulations of

the Church of England to preach at Great St. Mary's. As vice chancellor, a
post he occupied for most of his tenure as college master, he oversaw the
return of older regulations for university business. In 1661, for example, he
prevented about fifty students from taking their BA degrees on the grounds
that they would not subscribe to the three articles in the 36th Canon.[11]

Those opposed to the reimposition of traditional forms of worship could
detect little attempt at moderation in the actions of Ferne and his allies.
Robert Ekins, who had entered Trinity as a sizar in June 1655 and was about
to stand for a fellowship in the 1660 election, recalled over half a century
later that the "Old seniors" had immediately "set up Conformity" when
Ferne arrived in August. They reintroduced the old liturgy and the mandatory wearing of the surplice in chapel, demanding that those who refused
to conform should leave forthwith. Ekins stoutly resisted this pressure, arguing that the new regime did not have the right to eject him, but after protracted resistance he finally left the college "having no prospect of Peace or
Quietness." After the Uniformity Act of August 1662 he was unable to take
up any church living because "he durst not comply with Impositions that
he thought partly needless and partly sinful." Despite being a talented
scholar, John Hutchinson was also forced out. He had been chosen *nem. con.*
as one of four fellows elected from a list of twenty-four candidates under
Wilkins's mastership, but despite contributing to the congratulatory verses
presented to the king by the university, he was compelled to leave. He
settled as a physician in Hitchin and preached gratis in other towns.[12]

2. The Triumph of the Old Gang

The events taking place in the college as Newton arrived there can be seen
most clearly through the eyes of John Ray, who officially resigned his fellowship in August 1662. Ray had arrived at Trinity as an undergraduate in
1646 and was made a minor fellow of the college on the same day as his
friend Isaac Barrow (8 September 1649); like Barrow he was tutored by
James Duport. He was consecutively the college lecturer in Greek (in 1651),
mathematics (in 1653), and humanities (in 1655), and was later appointed
junior dean (in 1658) and steward (in 1659 and 1660). He was an accomplished preacher and was ordained deacon and priest by Robert Sanderson
in London at the end of 1660, the same year that he became a major fellow
of the college. After pupils such as Phillip Skippon, Peter Courthope, and

Timothy Burrell had left his care, he remained in close contact with them. He went on regular research excursions with Skippon and Francis Willughby, the results of which formed the basis of his later eminence in natural history.[13]

Ray told Courthope in January 1659 that his unwillingness to take orders, recently confirmed as a requirement for becoming a fellow at Trinity, derived mainly from his attachment to his studies of the natural world, which were preferable to the study "of that which they call divinity." By autumn of the following year the religious and political landscape had been completely transformed. In September 1660 he told Courthope that Ferne had brought with him "14 or 15 of the old gang," all armed with letters mandated from the king. In jaundiced terms Ray recounted how they had set up a powerful clique among themselves and had readmitted all the new fellows except those who would not conform to the traditional liturgy and practices of the Church of England. Ray warned Courthope that everything had been reset to the status quo of two decades earlier: "service morning and evening, surplice Sundayes, and holy-dayes, and their eves, organs, bowing, going bare, fasting nights." The seniors had heard that Ray would probably refuse to read from the Common Prayer Book, or wear the surplice, but were happy to reserve a place for him in case he promised to conform. There was no chance of that, Ray noted, nor of him taking orders.[14]

Ray was highly respected within the college, and High Churchmen did what they could to change his mind. In early October 1660 he was given two weeks to decide whether to conform to the new requirements and under such pressure he did take orders in December. He continued to tutor students for the remainder of the academic year. As for the new practices, there was vigorous internal debate about whether the college had the right to impose them, and over the following months the institution was profoundly shaken by these religious divisions. In his Worcester House Declaration of 25 October 1660 concerning religious ceremonies, Charles II declared that no one should be compelled to bow at the name of Jesus, nor suffer for doing so, though he noted that bowing was an ancient ceremony of the church. However, wearing the surplice was a different matter; all should be free to wear it or not wear it *except* in the case of colleges, where the statutes and customs related to its use "should be there observed as formerly." This exception was soon invoked by the new High Church regime at Trinity.[15]

By the spring of 1661 Ray was telling his correspondents that he intended to leave at the next possible opportunity. He was ready for the new intake that arrived in June 1661, but was immediately confronted by the horror of student sickness and fatalities. On 5 June (the very day Newton entered the college) Ray told Courthope that a student had recently died of a violent fever, and he was deeply concerned that a serious illness that had afflicted another student, Edward Goring, might be smallpox and might be passed on to other students. On the eleventh Ray passed on the grim news that Goring had died from smallpox three days earlier, having fallen ill only an hour after being dropped off at Cambridge. Concern for his students kept him in Cambridge over the following weeks though Ray was itching to go off on his annual tour with Skippon—a wish he fulfilled at the end of July.[16]

Ferne occupied the college mastership for only a year and a half before being appointed bishop of Chester in February 1662. His successor, John Pearson, was hailed by his admirers as an ardent royalist and one of the best theologians of his age. In 1643 he had come to prominence by preaching against extempore prayer and in defence of the Anglican clergy, and in the 1650s he delivered regular sermons to the parishioners of St. Clement's Eastcheap. In the same decade he was engaged in a number of theological projects, including being the main editor of the Critici Sacri, a collection of learned commentaries on the Bible that appeared in 1660. His famous and influential Exposition of the Creed of 1659 was based on sermons he delivered at St. Clement's, and his loyalty to the Church of England during its troubles was swiftly rewarded with a remarkable accumulation of positions. Having petitioned to be granted the degree of doctor of divinity in 1660, on 4 December of that year Pearson was instituted as master of Jesus College, Cambridge. In the spring of 1661 he was arguably the major representative of the bishops at the Savoy Conference, a gathering set up to consider revisions to the Book of Common Prayer that would make it palatable to Presbyterians. Pearson took a conservative stance, insisting on the retention of practices such as kneeling while receiving the sacrament on Sundays. In June he was appointed Lady Margaret Professor of Divinity, devoting his first lectures to the being and attributes of God. The following April he became the new master of Trinity College, promising a renewed emphasis on scholasticism and the authority of the Church Fathers.[17]

Ray told Courthope at the end of 1661 that there was a fundamental breach between the old and new university, which would "never kindly mingle, or make one piece." His departure was made inevitable by the Act of Uniformity, which effectively annulled what had been demanded in sub-scribing to the Solemn League and Covenant. The Act required that by St. Batholomew's Day 1662, all men in religious or academic authority were to have given their "unfeigned assent, and consent to all, and everything contained, and prescribed in, and by" the Book of Common Prayer. As a consequence, they had to endorse the form of ordaining and consecrating bishops and lower orders as it was traditionally practised in the Church of England, or face ejection. Samuel Dale, who noted that Ray was "very con-scientious [and] entirely scrupulous about Oaths" confirmed that Ray had often declared that the Covenant oath was unlawful and emphasised that he remained a practising member of the Church of England to his death.[18] A month before the Act of Uniformity became law, Ray told Courthope that he had already taken so many oaths and subscriptions "as have taught me to disgust such pills." If he were to "concoct this subscription," he added, "wch I shall hardly prevail with my selfe to doe: it will be certainly contrary to my inclinations & purely out of fear." Ray left the college in early Sep-tember 1662, having been offered the post of tutor by Sir Thomas Bacon to his son Nathaniel.[19]

The revolution overseen by Ferne and Pearson had a profound anti-Calvinist slant, exhibited in the college and university sermons preached by Isaac Barrow who had been awarded the Regius Chair in Greek at the Restoration. As the stars of people like Barrow rose, so others fell, and most collegiate victims of the "Great Ejection" suffered considerable financial repercussions. Ray told Courthope on 13 August 1662 that many ministers in the county would be deprived, adding that they were "the most able and considerable" of the clergy. Upwards of twenty fellows and scholars left the college for reasons of conscience between Ferne's arrival in August 1660 and the Act of Uniformity two years later. Joseph Oddy and Samuel Corbyn (a conduct in the chapel since 1655) became prominent among Cambridgeshire nonconformists and joined a congregation created by Francis Holcroft, a fellow of Clare Hall. Oddy and Holcroft, known jointly in nonconformist historical memory as the "Apostles of Cambridgeshire," held public disputes with Quakers in Cambridge during the early 1660s, and Charles II's spymaster Joseph Williamson heard that Holcroft's meetings at Cambridge attracted as many as three hundred attendees. Oddy, assisted by Corbyn, occasionally preached to hundreds of Independents and Baptists in Cambridgeshire and Bedfordshire and was the dominant nonconformist presence in the area when Holcroft was incarcerated.[20]

3. Godly Discipline

The young Isaac Newton entered Trinity when the institution was in the throes of a profound religious crisis. Although there was an immediate threat from the outbreak of smallpox that had carried off Edward Goring, a more general problem was the growing tension between the dominant High Church group and those fellows who could not accept the imposition of more traditional forms of worship. Entering the college on 5 June, Newton matriculated (i.e., became a member of the university) on 8 July. By this time, he had started to read the basic texts constituting the curriculum and had been inducted into the daily rituals of collegiate existence by his tutor, Benjamin Pulleyn. Frustratingly little is known about Pulleyn, in loco parentis for Newton's early years at Trinity. He entered the college as a sizar in 1650, became a fellow in 1656, and signed for deacon's orders on 5 March 1664. He was an accomplished scholar and in 1674 he was made Regius Professor of Greek, a post he held for twelve years before becoming rector of Southoe in Hampshire. Pulleyn was in charge of a large number of students, and in the early 1660s he took on an average of thirteen pupils a year. For whatever reason, Newton did not distinguish himself early in his academic career and did not receive an exhibition, that is, a form of minor scholarship for academic excellence, in either 1662 or 1663. However, when Pulleyn recognised Newton's aptitude for mathematics, presumably in early 1664 when prestigious scholarship examinations took place, he passed him on to the Lucasian Professor Isaac Barrow to be examined in Euclid.[21]

If Pulleyn was unable to give any useful advice in mathematics and the new philosophy, he must nevertheless have exercised a strong spiritual influence. His role as tutor was to ensure that students obeyed the statutes, particularly the crucial edicts relating to religious practice. Religious duties formed the core of the daily regimen that had changed little since it had been laid down at the college's foundation. The statutes of 1552 and 1560 demanded that Trinity students rise at 4:30 A.M. and attend chapel at 5 having said their private prayers. After this, they had breakfast, during which Scripture was expounded, and from 6 A.M. they were to spend three hours reviewing what they had learned the previous day about logic, mathematics, Latin, and philosophy and preparing for the lectures that were to follow. At 9 A.M. students went to the schools to hear lectures or disputations and returned to these at 1 P.M. having enjoyed two hours for lunch. Private study and leisure activities were supposed to be pursued from 3 P.M. to 6 P.M., when there was supper in the hall. By Newton's time, chapel had slipped to 5:30 A.M. or even 6. Following breakfast, which some scholars consumed in coffeehouses, lectures began at 7 or 8 A.M. and lunch was at noon. The afternoon was devoted to disputations, and evening chapel had by now been brought forward to 5 P.M. After supper, which was usually at 6, most students would retire to spend time with their tutors discussing religious or secular topics.[22]

One student manual that was widely used during Newton's early years at Trinity offers a detailed insight into what was expected of students. This is the booklet written for his students by James Duport, who studied at Trinity College from 1622 and became a fellow in 1627. Despite overtly royalist sympathies, Duport became Lady Margaret preacher in 1646, making it very likely that he subscribed to the Solemn League and Covenant. Between 1645 and 1660 he tutored more than 180 students at Trinity, all of whom must have been given a copy of his "Rules." The chapter headings of the manual are extracted from prescriptions in the college statutes, so the practices enjoined by other college tutors, such as Pulleyn, must have followed Duport's advice very closely. Along with the "Directions" to students written by Richard Holdsworth (master of Emmanuel College, 1637–43), these instructions have been mined by historians for what they say about the humanist curriculum at Cambridge in the mid-seventeenth century. Duport stressed that students should be au fait with a wide range of writings in history and poetry, and in particular, they should know intimately well the works of a handful of great authors. He evinced little interest in natural philosophy or mathematics, except to warn students against infatuation with Cartesianism. However, much less attention has been paid by historians to the religious instructions in Duport's manual, although they were by far the most important obligations mentioned in it. The manual shows that education in Newton's college was marked by a strict religious discipline, which relented little from early in the morning to late at night.[23]

Duport's students were expected to attend chapel on time every morning, being "wholly intent upon ye ordinance at hand." He warned that only the uncouth came "drooping in" to chapel and told students not to engage in the irreligious habit of standing up before a tutor or minister had finished saying prayers. They should go to their tutor's room for prayers in the evening, as soon as the bell had tolled, and when finished they were to retire to their chambers to pray and read the Bible; prayer was the Key of the Day and Lock of the Night ("Clavis diei et sera noctis"). Students had to be in bed by 10 P.M. at the latest, for as Duport cautioned them, there was a time to work and a time to sleep. When senior figures of the college were absent, self-vigilance was obligatory, though God was always watching. Wasting any time at all was to be accounted "the greatest loss in the world," and students should always imagine that every chime of the clock foretold their last hour on Earth: "Repent to day for you know not whether you shal live til to morrow." Duport intoned that students should let their words be few (from Ecclesiastes 5:2), and they were directed to go directly from the chapel to their chambers without engaging in frivolous chatter. They were to mix only with virtuous, studious, and religious companions and were to avoid "rotten" conversation and idleness, which was the Devil's Cushion ("pulvinar Diaboli"). As for common pitfalls, "Customariness & formality" in religious performance was "a canker and a worm" that could cut out the very core of one's religion. Nodding off at prayers and sermons was the "sleep of death," and it provided another open invitation to the devil. Duport warned his students not to swear, lie, or treat the sacred writings with levity ("ludere cum sacris"), for that was "ill medling with edge-tools." Better to be "a young Saint," he thundered, "than to prove an old Devill."[24]

Duport advised students to "be frequent in reading books of good devotions & practicall divinity," such as those by Richard Sibbes, John Preston, Robert Bolton, Thomas Shepard, and Richard Baxter. Above all others, and second only to the Bible itself, Duport recommended *The Temple* by the poet George Herbert, whom he had known when Herbert was a fellow at Trinity. This was a highly popular collection of devotional poems that was regarded as a work of practical divinity by both royalists and parliamentarians in the 1640s and 1650s. Variants of this list of divines were frequently recommended by contemporaries, and they were considered useful, or even mandatory, by tutors with a variety of religious views. Students were exposed on a daily basis to learned sermons, notes on which they were constantly told to insert into various commonplace books. One or two chapters of the Greek Testament were also supposed to be read every day, "besides Chappell time." As for worship in chapel, Duport counselled that one should always take one's Bible or Greek Testament to the service and follow the conduct (chaplain) closely as he expounded the text. The instructions on proper comportment were appropriately different for Sunday worship. Students were to rise earlier, preparing to spend the entire day in religious duties. They were to attend Great St. Mary's church in the mornings and afternoons, taking notes on each sermon; after this, they were supposed to return to their study "& pray for a blessing, upon what you have heard, that the Lord would give you grace to practise it." Conversations on Sundays, if one had to have them, were to be on religious topics only, such as on the sermons or points of doctrine.[25]

Outside overtly religious environments, students were still expected to conduct themselves as good Christians. Holdsworth devoted a section of his handbook to the dangers of general idleness, depraved company, and the neglect of studies, while Duport gave lengthy advice on how to lead a religiously informed life. Walk often in fields, he recommended, and walk alone, "that will put good thoughts in you, and make you retire into your self, and commune with your owne hearts." Wherever they were, students were to abstain from any appearance of evil and to avoid all occasions of sin. At night they were to reflect on the sins that they had committed during the day: "Meditate often on the joye of heaven, & the torments of hell, think continually you have the last trumpet sounding in your eares surgite mortui &c." Duport emphasised that scholarly labour was itself a spiritual activity, and students were to study out of conscience; above all, he cautioned, "let gods glory be your utmost end and aime." Their existence at university was a continuous harvest of godly wisdom: "thinke then you must be as spirituall ants, gathering and laying up food for your soules."[26]

In Duport's Trinity, all superiors had to be respected "submissively and reverently," by "bareing the head, & bowing the body" whenever they were met. Tutors had a specially eminent place in student life. College statutes decreed that they were to be esteemed in loco parentis and, according to Duport, to be treated as an oracle on all occasions, to be consulted "for advice, and directions, as also for resolution of any scruples, or doubt, or difficulty in religion or learning." In their presence, students were to conduct themselves civilly, neither laughing, lolling, leaning, whispering, nor using any other "childish gesture or posture." The roles of the college tutor at Trinity were outlined in a letter written to the seniors of the college by Thomas Hill, prefacing an edition of his 1648 sermon on the character of Paul. Tutors were to encourage general Christian behaviour: piety in the chapel, "industry in the Hall and other exercises, gravitie and civilitie at the Tables, godly sinceritie in all places." Particular attention had to be given to vulnerable new arrivals at the college, who were be monitored with "a vigilant eye." Such youths were especially prone to the snares of "evil companie," and in particular, to the baneful influence of some "ungodly country-man, fellow-pupill, chamber-fellow, or companion."[27]

   Oliver Heywood, who went up to Trinity as a pensioner in 1647, recalled
learning "more of Christ in one year from Mr Hill's plain and precious
Christ-advancing preaching than he had all his time before in the country."
Heywood was directed by his puritan father to be tutored by Alexander
Akehurst, an accomplished natural philosopher and chemist who was then
(as Heywood later remembered) "a flourishing instrument, and was lookt
upon as most pious and laborious in al the college." Heywood's father left
him a number of "serious and grave instructions" for living a godly life at
university, which included noting sermons and writing down his own spiritual meditations. Heywood prospered and interacted with some "ingenious
and gracious schollars with whom I had much familiarity, and was much
furthered by them in the ways of god." However, he noted with regret that
others in the college were tempted by "wicked or idle companions." Such
people arrived at the college with good intentions but were turned away
from the truth; "instructed in artificial contrivances of wickedness," they
ended up neglecting their studies and becoming debauched.[28]
   Although one should not assume that all students were as assiduously
devout as Duport and Holdsworth might have wished, there is no evidence
that the college tolerated general laxity in religious matters either before or
after the Restoration. About three-quarters of the students who obtained
BA degrees from Trinity were destined for the clergy, and the majority
of students had to abide by the statutes. That does not mean, however, that
life was easy for the student who had seriously godly leanings, and John
Rastrick's autobiography provides fascinating evidence of what the new
college regime held in store for an extremely pious student. As we have
seen, Rastrick's early career followed that of Newton's very closely. Like
Newton, Rastrick was forced by his mother to work on country business,
though he sneaked books into the fields with the connivance of his father.
In his quest to acquire the learning that would allow him to become a
scholar, Rastrick enjoyed the latter's support, and in a phrase that echoes
the views of Newton allegedly offered by his servants, he recorded that his
father recognised that he was "fit for nothing else." Against her better judgement, his mother sought out the local minister who tutored Rastrick for a
few months in the spring and summer of 1665. Rastrick's education in the
fundamentals of the classical languages remained decidedly patchy, and it
would prove deeply problematic for him when he went to Cambridge.
In the winter of 1665 he came under the tutorial care of John Walker, curate
of Great Hale. In Walker's rooms Rastrick revelled in the access he enjoyed

to a wealth of books, especially those on the lives of ministers, such as Robert Bolton. Walker prepared him well enough to convince Trinity College to admit him, and Rastrick arrived there on 5 June 1667, six years to the day after Newton had entered.[29]

Rastrick's tutor, Thomas Bainbrigg, quickly set Rastrick on the standard introductory texts of logic and ethics. When the study of technical philosophy proved to be unpalatable, he turned to God for assistance. After a month he wrote to his father, complaining of the lack of preaching, as well as its dubious quality. Rastrick was shocked "that the Nursery of Learning (and piety too it should be) should abound so little with that which I accounted the chief fruits thereof." Equally obnoxious were the "Ceremonys and Formalitys of the Chappell Worship," especially the practice of bowing at the name of Jesus. The Restoration reforms were unbearable for him, as they must have been for other boys brought up in a predominantly puritan culture. Despite this, he settled on a career in the Church of England although he was increasingly beset by melancholy and fears of an early grave. He later recalled that Satan had continued to tempt him throughout his undergraduate days, though he derived comfort from his private meditations and soliloquys with God. With neither the grounding in languages nor the proper method of study for "Academicall Books of Philosophy and humane Learning," he took refuge in tomes of practical divinity such as the copy of Samuel Clarke's *General Martyrologie* that his chamber-fellow borrowed from the college library. Only in the pages of this work, and in some others of Richard Baxter, did he meet with people in a similar state to his own, "the only suitable company the University did afford me."[30]

Rastrick recalled that he was despised by other students whenever he tried to read a chapter of the Greek New Testament or his sermon notes, whether on a Sunday evening or in Bainbrigg's rooms. Pursuing a ministerial vocation, he recalled, had merely left him open to scorn. Comedies and playbooks were in greater repute and of more credit to scholars than divinity books and getting drunk was the only way to insinuate oneself into their company. He told his father in August 1669 that the only benefit he could get from a Cambridge education was to "learn Circumstances and see Fashions." Bainbrigg was distant and only made contact when the quarterly bill was due. Despite his difficulties with the standard Aristotelian curriculum, Rastrick (like Heywood before him) did accept that some scholarly learning was useful and important, and that it could help him properly fulfil his role as a priest. Nevertheless, he turned increasingly to Baxter's works, having initially dismissed him for his lack of a university education. Bainbrigg himself had read *Reasons of the Christian Religion* to his students, and Rastrick had liked it so much he had bought it. Indeed, when he returned to Cambridge in the summer of 1670, Bainbrigg commended Baxter's recently published *Cure of Church Divisions*. By this time, most of the melancholic fumes had dispersed. The scrupulous student had taken his BA in January, happy that the oversight of the presiding scholar had allowed him to proceed to the degree without swearing the usual oaths.[31]

4. A Young Saint

Rastrick's experience of alienation shares many features with what is known of Newton's early years at Trinity. With no record of him having been disciplined for infraction by the college authorities, we must assume that— under the vigilant eyes of Pulleyn and Babington—he followed the obligations placed on him by the statutes. Apart from his daily reading of Scripture he would have read the works of the practical divines and performed catechising in the chapel. Newton would have attended the divinity disputations and must also have heard the often lengthy sermons given both within and outside the college and taken notes on them. He arrived in time to attend (and probably heard) at Great St. Mary's the first sermon ever preached by Barrow on 30 June 1661, which concerned the gratifications of religion. Over the following two years he was almost certainly present at Barrow's thanksgiving sermons, such as the one he gave in defence of the Holy Trinity on Trinity Sunday (14 June) 1663. As Lady Margaret Professor and Moderator of Divinity at Great St. Mary's, John Pearson gave the first oration at commencement on 2 July 1661, and very soon afterwards he gave his inaugural lectures on the being and attributes of God. These dealt with the many defining characteristics of the deity that undergraduates would encounter through their metaphysical study, and they addressed the main ways in which humans might come to a knowledge of God. Whether Newton attended them or not, they provided the sort of comprehensive system of divinity that he would encounter regularly in his undergraduate career.[32]

Compelling evidence indicates that Newton's life at Trinity was saturated with religious study. In his biography *A Portrait of Isaac Newton*, Frank Manuel perceptively noticed that in Newton's jottings from Francis Gregory's *Nomenclatura brevis Anglo-Latino-Græca* (a list of common words and their equivalents in English, Greek, and Latin), he had rearranged Gregory's own order of topics alphabetically and had added a number of his own words in English. In particular, in Newton's notes to chapter 13, which he titled "Of Kindred, & Titles," he added many more terms than can be found in the mundane collection listed under the correlative heading ("Kindred") in Gregory. Manuel argued that Newton—consciously or not—was referring to his mother and stepfather when he added the word *Whoore* to Gregory's *Widow* and *Widower*, and *Wooer*, which appears next to *Wife* and *Wedlock*. Many other emotive terms not in Gregory such as "ffornicator," "Seducer," and "Hypocrite" can be read in a similar way. On the basis that Newton dated his purchase of the book to 1659 (which included all dates up to 24 March 1660), it has been assumed that these entries dated from some time in his last two years in Lincolnshire. However, the list also contains words that clearly date from his time at Trinity, such as *supersedens*, *fellow*, *fellowcommoner*, *Pupill*, *siser*, *Sophister*, M^r *of Arts*, *Schollar*, *Lecturer*, and *pensioner*, and it is therefore certain that they were added after he had arrived at Cambridge.[33]

The additional terms constitute not merely free association but a revelatory word cloud of Newton's at Trinity. It is possible that he drew the extra words from another dictionary, although they are not listed in alphabetical order, as one would expect if he were using the list for writing practice or systematically taking the words directly from a secondary source. Religious terms appear alongside political or other emotive expressions, suggesting that he added the words as they occurred to him. The apparently random character of Newton's own entries is evident from most of the lists he made. Under *H*, *Husband* and *Heir* (from Gregory) are followed by *Heathen*, *Hebrew*, *Hivite*, *Hittite*, *Hungarian*, *Hunn*, *Hermit*, *Hypocrite*, and *Heretyck*; under *I* (= *J*), *Joint-heire* and *Inheritance* (from Gregory) are followed by *Iade*, *Idolater*, *Infidell*, *Iew*, *Israelite*, *Irishman*, *Itallion*, *Iebusite*, *Independent*, *Iustice*, *Iudge*, and *Iesuite*. *S* offered a fascinating combination, arranged like the other lists in no obvious order. To Gregory's banal *Son* and *Sister*, Newton added *Subject*, *Sluggard*, *Swearer*, *Sabbath breaker*, *Slave*, *Sinner*, *Searvant*, *Scold*, *Scoffer*, *Scot*, *Swisser*, *Spaniard*, *Sarazen*, *Saxon*, *Scythian*, *Shuhite*, *Sadducie*, *Sophister*, *Siser*, *Schollar*, *Speaker*, *Sessor*, *Statesman*, *Seducer*, *Seutor*, *Sweetheart*, *Sheriff*, *Schismatick*, *Stoick*, *Sceptick*, and *Sodomite*. It is striking how many of these terms are pejorative or religious, or both, and the text reveals that his mental world, if not the college itself, was populated by a vast array of religious deviants.[34]

The first four headings of Gregory's book were titled "Of the True God,"
"Of God the Son," "Of the Holy Ghost," and "Of Fals Gods & Goddesses."
These subjects would concern Newton for the rest of his life but he did not
incorporate anything under these titles into his undergraduate scheme. He
did copy (with very few additions) those words listed by Gregory under the
title "Of a Church." More significantly, about 60 percent of the additional
terms in his thirteenth chapter have religious connotations. So under *A*
Newton added *Addamite, Ammonite, Ammorite, Assyrian, Arrian, Antichrist,
Anabaptist, Appostle, Alderman, Aerian, Atheist,* and *Apostate;* under *B* (Gregory included *Bastard* in his own list) he added *Blaspheimer, Babler, Babylonian,
Bishop, Brownist,* and *Benjamite;* under *C, Caldeans, Carmelite, Cardinall, Christian,
Clarke, Conduct, Churchwarden, Curate, Canaanite, Calvinist,* and *Celestianan.*
Under *P,* Gregory's *Portion* and *Posteritie* are immediately followed by
Prince, Protestor, Peasant, and *Pirate* and then by a slew of religious expressions: *Pagan, Pope, Preist* [*sic*], *Papist, Protestant, Pharisie, Philistine, Puritan,
Presbyter, Prebune, Patriarch, Pelagian,* and *Priscillianist.* These words betray
the overwhelmingly religious environment in which Newton grew up,
although many of the terms have a more technical bearing that could only
have come from his time at Trinity. They open an extraordinary window
to the world of a youth immersed in Scripture, sermons, prayer, and books
of practical divinity.[35]

Equally telling as evidence of Newton's religiosity at university are the
incidents added after Whitsun 1662 to his list of offences, which tell us a
great deal about his religious practise, and his attitudes to it, while at Trinity.
At one point he noted, "Negligence at chappel," which indicates inattention
to his religious duties rather than failure to attend, while the entry "Sermons at St. Mary's (4)" could mean that his mind was not on the reading
rather than outright avoidance. "Neglecting to pray 3" is unambiguous evidence of backsliding, though we cannot tell how serious this was in relation to the general practice of the other students. The fact that Newton
noted these offences, coupled with his recording of earlier lapses, indicates
that he was a devout young man, but there is little evidence that he was as
dismayed as were Ray and Rastrick by the various High Church forms of
worship that were now de rigueur in chapel. Daily attendance at chapel was
obligatory and closely monitored, and he must have worn his surplice regularly, since he had it washed for 6 shillings in 1662 or 1663. In the early
1690s Newton claimed that he was disillusioned with the formality of college life, though by then he was in the habit of avoiding regular attendance

at chapel. Whatever he thought of the ritual and liturgical practices in which he was forced to engage on a daily basis, he did not believe that they were so redolent of Roman Catholic worship that he should sever his connection with the academic body. Some practices did go too far. At roughly the same time as he wrote down his thoughts on college formality, he composed a short text recommending a new curriculum for university students. In it, he attacked the practice of fasting nights as a hollow, irreligious exercise that gave a licence to youths to indulge in debauched behaviour.[36]

Newton's more general attitude to college discipline can be fruitfully discerned in this draft curriculum, which unsurprisingly gave a central role to mathematics and physics. The scheme enjoined a rigorous work ethic, and Newton included a number of injunctions against idleness, singling out fellow-commoners for their potential to corrode the moral fibre of other students. They were "to perform all exercises in their courses, and to be equally subject to their tutors and Governors with other Scholars and alike punishable by exercises, and those who are resty or idle to be sent away lest they spoil others by their bad example." They were to be treated in exactly the same way as pensioners and sizars, and no student could escape punishment by paying a "mulct," or fine. Instead, Newton demanded that miscreants perform "Exercises," "Admonitions," and "Recantations," according to the nature of the crime. Very occasionally, students could be forced to reach into their pockets. Deans were to visit chambers of all undergraduates at least once a week, on pain of forfeiting 10 shillings to lecturers for every "omission" (presumably of an Act or Exercise). Newton's recommended examination regime was continuous and relentless. In the long vacation, tutors were to make pupils read over all the previous year's lessons, on which they were to be examined at the end of the holiday period. Those who failed the test were to be put down a year. The discipline would continue once a student had gained his BA, and any graduate found in a tavern or other house of ill repute would have his name given to the vice chancellor, who would summon him to answer for it.[37]

When Newton was an undergraduate, college discipline extended to a number of activities that were not strictly religious. However, many of the college rules had implications for religious practice, especially those that related to wasting time in recreational pursuits. Duport suggested that some pastimes were entirely reasonable; bowls, shooting, or "pitching the barre" (akin to tossing the caber) were acceptable "at seasonable times," but football was "a boisterous exercise" more suitable for clowns than scholars.

A small amount of tennis was agreeable, but not immediately after meals, while cards and dice were forbidden by the statutes, except during the twelve days of Christmas. Chess was "ingenious" but time-consuming and even tedious, and Duport warned against it. Ranging more broadly, he admitted that riding out to take the air was a very good thing, although he was ambivalent about angling, being aware that many students went to the alehouse under the pretext, and "there drink like fishes."[38]

Duport admitted that he considered neither wine nor tobacco to be good for young men, and all taverns and inns should be avoided "unless a friend come out of the country and send for you." Indeed, students were not supposed to go into town *at all*, unless to Great St. Mary's, the schools, or a bookseller. Holdsworth railed against the consumption of alcohol: "It is a known, & an ordinarie observation that very few or none that have bin cried up for the greatest wits & parts in the University, have ever come to any considerable preferment, or credible way of living if they were addicted to drinking & Ill companie." Even a single visit to the tavern was a sign that a student was "warping" towards libertinism: "He begins to be out of conceit with a sober, retired way of life and thinks he ought to indulge with Mirth, Pastime & Libertie. He counts constant hard students a kind of flat heads, and fears least he should prove himself an one himself." In 1667 and 1668 Newton visited the tavern on a number of occasions (conceivably to celebrate his election to his minor and major fellowships), but as a freshman he had noted his procurement of beer and China Ale under the heading of "Otiosa & frustra expensa." Indeed, Duport singled out expenses under this exact heading for particular censure, since "ye greatest spenders are ye least students." Despite the concerns of Duport and Holdsworth, the odd pint did not deter Newton from his solitary vocation, and he would waste little time in later years on mirth.[39]

Newton was not interested, as far as we can tell, in football, fishing, or riding. He did pay the regular fee for use of the tennis courts, and one of the first things he purchased while at Cambridge was a chess board (for 2s. 6d.); the entry "Chesse men. Diall" possibly indicates that he was later proficient enough to be in possession of his own pieces. As for other board games, Duport warned that the morning periods in which draughts (Chinese checkers) and other games were played were the "break-necks of studies." Newton's half-niece Catherine Conduitt recalled him telling her much later that he was excellent at draughts and could beat anyone if he was given the first move. He was not so adept at cards, and a few years later he recorded losing twice, uncharacteristic lapses in concentration that cost him the large sum of 15 shillings. As a new fellow and recently appointed master of arts in 1668 he apparently spent some time on the bowling green, though as we have seen, Duport considered this an acceptable pastime.[40]

Duport cautioned that going into the water in general was a terrible idea, and one should never do it, or at least only rarely, since it caused flatulence. In fact, there was widespread concern over the danger posed by bathing in either of the two Cambridge rivers, and in 1572 a (much ignored) decree had been made against any bathing in the county, threatening miscreants with a severe whipping or being put in the stocks, depending on their level of seniority. There is no sense that bathing constituted a form of religious deviance for Duport but in his Whitsun list, Newton recorded squirting water and swimming in a kimnel (a wooden tub) on the Lord's Day, implying that for him it was. These entries presumably date from before he went to Cambridge, but the post-Whitsun entry "Helping Pettit to make his water watch at 12 of the clock on Saturday night" suggests a continuing concern about wasting time on a Sunday—though it may be an admission that both undergraduates should have been tucked up in bed some hours earlier. Otherwise, Newton loaned money to a number of his fellow students, indicating when he was repaid. Like gluttony, it was a religious offence, and it was also against the college statutes. Naturally Duport warned against it. He also recommended that students should be moderate in the weekly expenditure in the buttery, "for he that sizes much studies little." Under the heading "Otiosa et frustra expensa," the Trinity notebook records Newton's purchase of cherries as well as tarts, custards, cakebread, and milk, butter, and cheese. His admission that he had been gluttonous twice since Whitsun 1662 demonstrates a recurring problem, and a repeat of a much earlier misdemeanour recorded as "Gluttony in my sicknesse." The references to pastries and dairy produce smuggled into his rooms is reminiscent of the cherry cobblers stolen from Edward Storer and the plums and sugar robbed from his mother.[41]

It is in the context of the myriad warnings about slacking roommates, given by Hill and others, that we should understand the testimony of John Wickins, who knew Newton far better than anyone else in his formative years at Trinity. In January 1728 his son Nicholas wrote to the Trinity fellow and Plumian Professor of Astronomy Robert Smith giving him what little information Wickins had passed on about "this Great, & Good Man." Wickins, who had entered the college in January 1663 and considered his first

roommate "very disagreeable," had apparently met Newton by chance in
the "walks," finding him "solitary & dejected." They found the cause of their
"retirement" to be the same (though sadly Wickins was not forthcoming
about what this was), "& thereupon agreed to shake off their present disorderly Companions & Chum together, wch they did as soon as conveniently
they could." Like Newton, Wickins was awarded a scholarship in 1664 and
he was elected as a fellow in 1668, becoming vicar of Stoke Edith in Here-
ford from 1675 to his death in 1719. While he was at Trinity, Newton sent
Wickins the dividends and rent for the use of his chamber since like many
fellows, Wickins was frequently absent due to pastoral duties.[42]

One entry from the list of post-Whitsun 1662 offences in the Fitzwilliam
notebook indicates some tension between Newton and his roommate, since
Newton admitted not passing on to him the fact that someone else had
called him a "sot," that is, a drunken fool. Perhaps the chamber-fellow did
not follow Duport's advice that the more experienced student set a good
example to the novice. It is possible that the wonderful line "Using Wilford's
towel to spare my own" is a reference to this individual, presumably the
pensioner Francis Wilford who entered Trinity three weeks after Newton.
However, Wilford is not, on the face of it, a good candidate as the youth in
question, since his father, also Francis, was a chaplain to Charles II and
master of Corpus Christi College, and was made dean of Ely on 20 May
1662 (around the time that Newton wrote his entries). The sons of vicars are
of course not always paragons of virtue or godliness, and if it was Wilford,
the break in their relationship was not bad enough to prevent Newton from
lending him money during their brief return to Trinity in 1666 (in the
middle plague year). Whoever Newton's roommate was, John Wickins's subsequent career as a vicar, and evidence from Nicholas Wickins about
Newton and his father's shared attitude to "disorderly companions," strongly
suggests that Newton found in Wickins a sober, devout spirit who would
not dare to indulge in illicit activities on the Sabbath.[43]

5. Edge-Tools

Although the core curriculum concerned "human learning," the rigorous,
critical examination of Scripture was central to Newton's life at college. If
Duport's notes are an accurate reflection of practise, then Trinity demanded
that students take notes during sermons and regularly scrutinise biblical

chapters. Duport recommended the intense examination of two to three chapters of the Bible every day, in combination with Giovanni Diodati's *Pious and Learned Annotations* or something equivalent. Holdsworth stated that students could get through the Bible in a year if they read three chapters a day (the Psalms could be "dispatch[ed]" in sixteen days), a task that could be done "without prejudice to your other studies" if the reading were spread throughout the day. Duport's recommendation of Diodati shows that the Bible was supposed to be studied in conjunction with supporting textual equipment. The training provided to undergraduates formed the basis of the skills that would be required by learned clergymen in the Church of England, but it also supplied expertise for the heterodox. In time, the availability of editions of the Greek New Testament and of critical tools such as biblical concordances and polyglots would allow readers such as Newton to develop radically unorthodox positions and to question the authority of the Greek text and of specific translations.[44]

This severe training, his excellent memory, and his evident religiosity combined to give Newton an exceptional knowledge of the Bible. Like any learned Protestant he had an advanced understanding of how verses in different parts of Scripture were explicitly or implicitly interconnected and indeed, "interpreted" one another. Few, if any, laymen can have devoted the time to acquire the mastery of the Scriptures that Newton obviously did when he was an established scholar, and few divines had his command of sacred writings. His surviving King James Bible was published in 1660 and bears numerous signs of use, and the intensity of his engagement with the material object is also suggested by the fact that one of his Bibles was rebound in 1668. However, no one copy of the Bible would have survived Newtonian scrutiny for any great length of time and his 1660 Bible, which he gave to the nurse who tended him in his last illness, was not the only one he used.[45]

Although Newton's religiosity at this time was Bible-centred, he needed serious supports in order to help unlock its meaning. He acquired a number of analytic tools during his first year, including the fifth edition of Isaac Fegyverneki's (Feguernekinus's) biblical concordance, and Lucas Trelcatius's list of the most significant places in Scripture, which was composed as a response to the Catholic interpretations of various texts offered by the great scholar (and scourge of Galileo) Cardinal Robert Bellarmine. He also marked his 1561 copy of Calvin's *Institutes* with his name, college, and the date of 1661. The *Institutes* were not explicitly recommended by Duport,

Holdsworth, or (apparently) Bainbrigg, and some of the content would have been unpalatable to High Church scholars. Despite the appearance of the name of the college in Newton's copy, it remains unclear if his use of the text was based on a recommendation from Pulleyn or, which is more likely, it was a gift from William Ayscough. If the latter, it says more about education at the same institution three decades earlier than it does about the religious interests of Newton's tutor.[46]

Exegetes were in particular need of good lexical and contextual tools in order to make proper sense of non-English sources, and Duport cautioned that students could not see clearly into God's word without the "two eyes" of Greek and Hebrew. His handbook shows clearly that at Trinity, the Greek New Testament was to be used not merely as a means of improving one's Greek, but was also supposed to be actively scrutinised in a religious setting. While Holdsworth advised that students should constantly attend to their Greek New Testament throughout their undergraduate degree, Duport's demands were less stringent. He suggested that the mornings of the month of September in the first year should be devoted to its study, and he emphasised the linguistic benefits: "read it with your Lexicon, & pass by no word without full understanding of it giving a mark with your Pen at such words as you doubt you cannot remember." If the handbook is anything to go by, it is hard to see how students could have accomplished everything that Duport and other tutors demanded of them. Nevertheless, the attention to the Greek New Testament and the use of lexical edge-tools constituted part of the core business of university life.[47]

In the spring of 1661, two months before Newton went up to Cambridge, he purchased a Greek-Latin lexicon composed by Georg Pasor, the Herborn Professor of Theology and Hebrew, and a few days later he bought Charles Hoole's popular 1653 edition of the Greek New Testament, whose margins contained the relevant grammatical comments in Pasor's lexicon. Pasor's work was the most widely used of its type in seventeenth-century Cambridge and it was a vital accompaniment to the scrutiny of the Greek New Testament. On the verso of the *Lexicon*'s title page Newton entered the line "Isaac Newton hunc librum possidet, pret: 6^d. Martij 29 1661," later adding his name, college, price, and year of purchase on the flyleaf. Five days after entering the initial comments in the *Lexicon*, he wrote even more proudly "Isaac Newton hujus libri verus est possessor: Pretium £-0-s-3 d-0 Aprilis 3 die A^{no} D^{ni} 1661" on the flyleaf of the New Testament. The timing of these purchases suggests that he acquired them at the end of his schooling at Grantham. Bought on the advice of Stokes or more likely Ayscough, they were clear indications of the sort of study that lay ahead over the following four years.[48]

It may be that once Newton had come under Pulleyn's wing, the latter insisted on his own favourite text, for Newton paid 5 shillings fourpence early in his first year for a copy of Cornelius Schrevelius's Greek-Latin *Lexicon*. We do not know the precise extent to which he used resources like these, but they were essential for many of the linguistic exercises he performed. As his student career progressed, the demands on his Greek increased. An entry in Newton's notebook of accounts for 1667 suggests that he paid 5 shillings and tenpence in connection with reading Greek, though whether this involved special lessons in preparation for a fellowship examination is unclear. Even if he lacked the linguistic skills of Duport or Pulleyn, Newton could read and write Greek to a level that was adequate for his purposes. By comparison, his knowledge of Hebrew, especially while an undergraduate, was almost nonexistent. In the back of the Fitzwilliam notebook in which he listed his early sins, he drew up a table of a number of Hebrew letters, with comments in Latin, though this appears to be a very early encounter with the language. He would never attain any proficiency in it, though much later he would make use of his knowledge of Hebrew letters when considering the Jewish concept of "Makom." Apart from Latin, Greek was by far the most important language that Newton would use in his later theological studies, though he was much more comfortable when dealing with Greek texts that adjoined a Latin translation.[49]

6. Humane Learning

Modern commentators have routinely condemned the value of Newton's undergraduate education for his work in mathematics and physics. This criticism of the predominantly Aristotelian system has a long history, and the ubiquitous denunciations of the traditional curriculum by seventeenth-century proponents of the new philosophy had their own precedents in humanist condemnations of scholastic texts and practices. Newton's recollections of the great work of his student years effectively started with the pioneering mathematical and scientific researches that led to his *annus mirabilis*, and the earlier years of study stood condemned by his silence. Historians have generally lamented that the standard programme was at worst an irrelevant waste of time, and at best a foil for his energies during the marvellous year. As far as his epoch-making contributions to the exact sciences go, this seems a fair comment, for not only did his pioneering research in these areas owe little to the standard curriculum, but his surviving notes on the scholastic set books display only a cursory interest in their content. His serious encounter with "modern" authors constituted a decisive break from this programme, and his engagement with their ideas and texts was evidently the springboard for his later work in the natural sciences.[50]

In seeking to magnify Newton's independence and genius, his immediate intellectual environment at Trinity has been caricatured as being at best sterile, and at worst hostile to the new philosophy. It is true that the general curriculum relied on texts that were expositions of scholastic philosophy, but the college possessed the likes of Ray and Barrow (though the two hardly overlapped), and in the mid- to late 1650s, it had enjoyed the presence of Alexander Akehurst, John Nidd, Francis Willughby, and Walter Needham, who had expertise in medicine and chemistry. There was a broad if qualified interest among college tutors in the new philosophy, and as I show in the next chapter, a number of contemporaries testified to the broad use of Cartesian texts and principles at Cambridge. As an undergraduate, Newton himself had access to almost all the extant works of every major natural philosopher (including Thomas Hobbes), and he must have received some guidance from Barrow. Moreover, the institution provided a setting in which a substantial degree of independent research was possible, and once the standard curriculum had been successfully negotiated, students were able to devote the final year of study to subjects of their own choosing. In one area, however, the standard curriculum was ideal for enhancing the skills that Newton needed for his research. Notwithstanding the fact that it was largely a secular programme of study, it provided the intellectual tools that allowed him to throw himself with his habitual confidence into abstruse theological doctrine and primary writings in early church history.[51]

Instruction in Newton's time was partly by public (college-wide) lectures, but mainly by following set books under the guidance of one's tutor. As the evidence from Duport and Ray shows, the Restoration college student was immediately put in the hands of his tutor and followed the course of learning that the latter laid down. Early in the seventeenth century tutors turned to the numerous introductory texts in ethics, logic, rhetoric, natural philosophy, and metaphysics that were being produced in lucrative numbers by European presses. With these, all the introductions and systematisations necessary for the four-year course were available in a multivolume form. Authors of major works such as the Polish scholar Bartholomew Keckermann, the Sorbonne theologian Eustachius of St. Paul (a Sancto Paulo), and later on the Dutch logician Franco Burgersdijk (Burgersdicius), became famous in European universities. Others, like Johannes Magirus and Robert Sanderson, gained repute from authoring a highly influential volume in just one field of study. The texts prescribed had changed little in the previous decades when Newton entered Trinity College in 1661, and many of the set texts used by students at Christ's College in the 1620s were still being used by first- and second-year undergraduates in the 1660s. However, as we shall see in the next chapter, a number of "modern" texts were being read by tutors and students and were even being prescribed by the former.[52]

The goal of the curriculum, still very much in force in Restoration Cambridge, was to provide a broad introduction to the holistic tradition of learning that had long characterised the university system in the West. The erudition that resulted from engagement with the liberal arts, especially in logic and rhetoric, equipped the student to make his own way, whether in the final year as an undergraduate, going on to postgraduate studies, or moving out into the wider world as a clergyman or gentleman. The capacity to make self-directed progress was central to the pursuit of sacred learning and Holdsworth cautioned that without the maturity to pursue research on their own, students were "Childern yett, & fitter to be under the lash & ferula then in an University." This independent research could include theology, though the subject entered formally into the undergraduate curriculum only in the study of metaphysics and more indirectly, when the Greek Testament was examined. As the testimonies of Rastrick and Heywood indicate, even the most spiritually inclined student recognised that classical learning and proficiency in disputation were essential for the churchman who would need to defend his religion against enthusiasts, papists, Socinians, and others.[53]

The most basic requirement of the scholar was facility in the classical writings. Drilling in classical literature served a number of purposes. On the one hand, it exposed students to the views of the best of the pagan writers, whose ethical recommendations were often deemed on a par with Christian virtues, though Duport warned that pupils should be careful when reading heathen poets, and "take the honey from the flower, & ignore the weeds." Students were supposed to live according to those Roman and

Greek precepts that corresponded to Christian virtues, and it was a mark of learned gentility to embed classical allusions in conversation and writing. Immersion in Greek and Latin writings was also a means of mastering the languages. Students were supposed to be fluent in Latin by the time they reached university, though Duport suggested that they read Greek and Latin texts aloud in order to improve pronunciation. His handbook stipulated that students should speak Latin all the time they were in Hall, and it was the preferred, or obligatory language to be used when practising disputations with chamber-fellows. Latin was required for entering polite society, but Duport believed that excellence in Greek marked out an individual as a real scholar. Translating from Greek to Latin, and Latin to Greek should be frequent, and students were exhorted to write *every day* a short essay, or theme, or epistle, in one of the classical languages. Duport recommended that students read only the best authors (Homer, Aristotle, Virgil, Cicero, Seneca, Plutarch, etc.), and do so in their own tongues.[54]

Despite the emphasis he placed on the natural sciences, Newton's later recommendations for reforming the programme at Cambridge also displayed his commitment to a generalist ideal. Indeed, his advice about the need for students to be grounded in the classical languages exactly mirrored that given by Duport. In Newton's ideal curriculum, the college lecturers in Greek and the *literae humaniores* were to set first-year students tasks in Greek and Latin every day (and this would continue in the long vacation), falling to once a week in later years. Greek lectures were to take place in the mornings, after the tutor's own disquisitions, which were to follow straight after chapel. As with other subjects, students were to be examined diligently and when they fell short, were to be punished with remedial exercises. The earliest of Newton's surviving notes from his time at Cambridge are in Greek, though tellingly, nothing from his undergraduate period survives from the very substantial immersion in (including notes from) the Greek and Roman poets and other classical writers that he must have experienced.[55]

Regulating both speech and thought, logic was held to provide a sure guide to learning in other subjects and was the first subject that students encountered at university. Technically it was concerned with certain demonstrations and with probable arguments, but by Newton's time the subject had become much more closely aligned with the rhetorical arts of persuasion. Holdsworth stipulated that the study of logic should take up the mornings of the first two months at university. This was preferably to be based on a work written by the tutor, since the student would learn from copying out the text and would be able to consult the tutor about difficult passages. Printed volumes were appropriate for riper judgements, when study was to be conducted alone. Holdsworth recommended Burgersdijk's *Idea Philosophiæ Naturalis* since it acquainted the student with Aristotle's terms. To prepare for disputations, which began very early in the degree programme, students were also supposed to read a number of different works, such as Brerewood's *Logic* and Eustachius a Sancto Paulo's *Summa philosophiæ Quadripartita*. After this they could graduate to more difficult texts, such as those by Keckermann and Sanderson. Finally, students would come face-to-face with Aristotle's own logic. Apart from recommending this, Duport also warned students not to follow the method of the logician Petrus Ramus.[56]

At Trinity, Pulleyn evidently considered Sanderson as a beginner's text, though students were probably advised to have acquainted themselves with it by the time they arrived at college. It was not uncommon for pupils to be primed in a standard logic before going to university. The brothers Roger and John North (the latter of whom would be master of Trinity from 1677–83) were given extra lessons in logic before they went to Cambridge, and Newton was advised by his uncle William to read Sanderson's logic before going to Trinity since that would be the set text when he arrived. One presumes that Ayscough had information from Babington or Pulleyn himself about what course would be on offer, though Sanderson's text had been ubiquitous at Cambridge for a number of decades and Newton probably used Ayscough's own copy. According to the account by John Conduitt, "This Sr I. read over by himself & when he came to hear his tutour's lectures upon it found he knew more of it than his tutour." Students were generally encouraged to read more than one logic textbook and at the start of his college notebook there are two references to "Charge for a logick." Newton also bought a work by Burgersdijk, probably the logic, or possibly even the collected texts, at some point early in his career.[57]

Probably the most difficult textual encounter experienced by students during their degree was with the primary texts of Aristotle. Holdsworth and Duport both rated engagement with Aristotle's writings as essential to the life and accomplishments of the true scholar, though it was understood that students could and should only do so with the aid of a commentary. Newton and other Trinity students were introduced to such primary sources much earlier than was recommended by Holdsworth, who held off exposing his students to the original text until the third year. The earliest surviving notes (in Greek) in Newton's undergraduate notebook are from Aristotle's *Organon* (his six works of logic), including brief excerpts from the *Categories* and *de Interpretatione*. From the first, which was an analysis of the various modes in which things existed, Newton made extracts on topics titled "substance," "quantity," "quality," and "passion." As was common with such editions, Aristotle's works were preceded by Porphyry's *Isagoge* (a third-century introduction to logic, treated as an introduction to Aristotle's *Categories*) on which Newton also took notes.[58]

As Rastrick's testimony indicates, the novice at Trinity was usually exposed to teaching in ethics very early on in the first year. Commentators differed regarding the degree to which ethics was linked to religion, not least because almost all the texts devoted purely to morality were composed by heathen writers. That said, most of the classical ethical writers were read through the lens of Christian commentaries, and it was not difficult to point out those few areas where the ancient virtues were deemed to be incompatible with Christian duties. On the other hand, since rhetoric placed a great deal of emphasis on the ethos of the orator or his subject, prolonged acquaintance with the subject was essential for composing a persuasive argument. Holdsworth recommended that students study ethics in the last three months of the first year, the purpose of which was to introduce them to the main doctrines contained in Aristotle's *Nicomachean Ethics*, which they only encountered directly in their third year. Newton, who must have received substantial instruction in the subject, took only very brief notes from the *Ethica* of Eustachius of St. Paul and from Aristotle's *Ethics*, and it is clear that the source of his strong moral sense was derived wholly from his Protestant upbringing.[59]

Newton's grounding in natural philosophy was based on standard Aristotelian texts, though it is interesting that in his first year at Trinity he inscribed his name in a copy of the Spanish author Sebastian Fox Morcillo's sixteenth-century reconciliation of the philosophies of Plato and Aristotle. We do not know whether this was rescued from his stepfather's collection, or was a gift from his uncle, which is probable, but it was unlikely to have been recommended by his tutor. Holdsworth recommended that the study of natural philosophy begin early in year two, either through Eustachius's text or Johannes Magirus's *Physiologiæ Peripitateticæ, Libri Sex, cum Commentariis*. This, along with Keckermann's *Physica*, was commonly taught at Cambridge. Magirus presented both sides of the question in the form of a disputation and was extremely popular at Cambridge, having been used by the Cambridge divine Joseph Mede and many other tutors over the previous half-century, and Pulleyn must have recommended it. Newton took a lengthy set of notes on an encyclopedic range of topics from the 1642 edition of Magirus's work, including issues such as infinity, space and place, and the vacuum (from book 1), and on celestial bodies and comets (from books 2 and 4). He ignored Magirus's sixth and last book (on the faculties of the soul), which covered the faculties of the will, memory and the intellect, and the nature of the imagination and of sleep and dreams. These were standardly dealt with as part of natural philosophy, and although Magirus's treatment was of no interest to him, the subjects would capture Newton's attention for much of his life.[60]

Newton did not ignore the topic of the soul when he took notes on metaphysics. Metaphysics, which was conventionally (if unhelpfully) defined as the science of being qua being, was the last of the four fundamental subjects (along with logic, ethics, and rhetoric) studied by a student. It was the only curricular subject in which students would encounter overtly theological positions. Whatever his early religious studies taught him, Newton encountered his first structured treatment of theology in his metaphysical studies. Apart from addressing the nature of divisibility, intelligibility, and materiality, it dealt with the nature of the soul (as an immaterial substance) and the being and attributes of God. God's existence and attributes were treated as articles of the intellect, not of faith, although whether this division was justifiable was a common topic for disputation. Students were introduced to standard proofs of divine existence, such as variants of the so-called Ontological Argument (which derived the necessity of God's existence from his infinitely perfect nature) and arguments derived from natural theology (i.e., the view that the order and beauty of the world could only have arisen from a wise Creator). As a contemporary (1652) notebook from St. John's College indicates, they were taught that there was some likeness between the Creator and his created world, and also that God was omnipotent, omniscient, ubiquitous, and unchanging, possessing infinite amounts of wisdom, purity, and liberty. These were the subjects addressed in Pearson's inaugural lectures of 1661, and Newton continued to think about them deeply over the next six decades.[61]

Metaphysics was studied by Holdsworth's students towards the end of their second year, and they followed the standard course of progression from tutorial introduction, to set book, and finally to primary source. If the general tenor of the rest of the Trinity curriculum is a guide, then Newton encountered the subject earlier than this. As a mature scholar he would rail against a

scholastic style of metaphysical speculation, as well as the language and concepts of scholastic metaphysics, but early on in his career he was sufficiently
knowledgeable about Aristotelian metaphysics to use and also to criticise its
main tenets. He studied a number of secondary texts on metaphysics and
presumably tried to read Aristotle's *Metaphysics* in Greek. He may have used
Burgersdijk's *Institutionum Metaphysicarum*, if that is what the reference to
"Burgersdicius" indicates in the Trinity notebook, but his surviving metaphysical notes come from the Jena professor Daniel Stahl's *Axiomata Philosophica*. From Stahl Newton took extensive notes inter alia on different kinds of
cause, on actuality and potentiality, the appetites and the will, the notion of
agent and patient, the nature of subject and accident, and on matter and
form—especially on Aristotle's notion of prime matter. Many of these topics,
most of which directly concerned the nature of God, were the focus of the
first notes he took in his undergraduate "Philosophical Questions" research
programme (started in early or mid-1664 and discussed in the following
chapter), but he soon lost interest in the rest, and never studied them again.[62]

The study of history, which formed a major part of the curriculum, went
hand in hand with that of geography. Duport recommended that students
always carry their books on chronology and geography around with them
when they were reading a history book, "else you will miserably loose your
self." Holdsworth's students began immediately with Thomas Godwyn's
English Exposition of the Romane Antiquities in the first two months, followed
by Justinus's *Epitome* of Trogus's world history (in February and March).
Over the next two years they would read the major Greek and Roman historians, again with as firm an eye on linguistic skills as on their content.
Halfway through the first year Holdsworth recommended that students
should read Ovid's *Metamorphoses*, but advised that students first get maps of
Greece and the Roman Empire, along with some other secondary "book of
Mythology." In his proposed curriculum of the 1690s, Newton enjoined
reading the best historians, though tutors were to instill the basics of geography and chronology as preparatory work. Following Duport's advice to
the letter, he recommended that the lecturers in Greek and the humanities
set first years tasks in Latin and Greek authors every day, the frequency falling to once a week in following years. As we have seen, this had the dual
function of improving facility in the classical languages while also exposing
students to the best of ancient textual culture.[63]

With the exception of his rhetorical notes, no trace remains from Newton's
reading in the *literae humaniores*, though he must have been exposed to most of

the works recommended by Holdsworth and Duport. In his Trinity notebook he listed Edward Hall's "Chronicles" as an early purchase, alongside Johann Sleidan's "Four Monarchies." Hall's book listed the major acts passed under the Yorkist and Lancastrian dynasties up to the time of Henry VIII, to whom he devoted a separate, hagiographic, and strongly anti-Catholic work. Newton was possibly referring to the 1631 English translation of Sleidan's *De Quattuor summis imperiis*, but more likely he read the original 1559 Geneva edition. Constituting a lengthy exegesis of the prophecy in Daniel 2 and 7–8, Sleidan traced the *translatio imperii* from the Assyrians (or Babylonians) to the Persians, thence to the Greeks and to the Romans. The work, which was a history of the world from the Flood, culminated in an enthusiastic appreciation of the Germanic Protestant states (and in particular the figures of Charles V and Luther) of the mid-sixteenth century. There is no evidence in Newton's mature historical writing that he was interested in anything from Hall's work, but Sleidan provided an influential Protestant template for thinking about the history of the world that was probably formative for his work in sacred history.[64]

7. Disputing

All students devoted a vast amount of time to rhetorical theory and practice. As theory, it concerned the techniques and arts of persuasion and was distinguished from the discipline that dealt with certain demonstration, and that which concerned merely probable knowledge (dialectics). It demanded knowledge of the different forms of reasoning (logos), the moral character of the speaker (ethos), and the ways in which one could manipulate the passions of the audience (pathos). Rhetorical theory was supposed to be applied in practice, and in terms of the possible careers or social roles that students might have after university, it was the most useful part of their education. Holdsworth's curriculum devoted each afternoon of the four years of study to works in Greek and Latin, rhetoric, history, and poetry. Without Latin and oratory, he cautioned, students would be useless: "you will be bafeld in your disputes, disgraced & vilified in Publike examinations, laught at in speeches, & Declamations. You will never dare to appear in any act of credit in yᵉ university, nor must you look for Preferment by your Learning only." Holdsworth's warnings about how shameful it was to be an inadequate disputant were repeated in a number of rhetorical texts.[65]

The subject was central to undergraduate life in Newton's time. Duport cautioned students to take their rhetorical performances extremely seriously, and he and Holdsworth advised that disputing in a tutor's chambers should continue throughout the student's life at college. Holdsworth was particularly keen to get students reading texts on logical controversy early in their studies, so that they could be acquainted with the sorts of questions that were usually disputed. He also gave instructions for extracting arguments from texts and re-ordering them, warning that students should not try to acquaint themselves with every twist and turn of a controversy for risk of forgetting everything. Once they had learned the rudiments of controversy, they could engage in disputation proper. Nevertheless, despite impressing on pupils about the need to continuously practise their disputational technique throughout their course of study, his students only started serious engagement with the classical texts in rhetoric when they were in the third year of study. This was because they were being prepared for the formal exercises that would take place in the public schools (known as the public acts) during their final year.[66]

Apart from formal examinations, which took place later in a student's career in the chapel or the hall, oral disputation normally took place in a tutor's chamber and was performed either by opposing the tutor or other students. In preparation for these, Duport recommended that students practise logical disputations with a chamber-fellow or acquaintance. Declamations were prepared presentations on a theme made as an exercise for emphasising good style, which included correct grammar and enunciation. Duport advised that they be buttressed with a number of arguments and delivered "thick and threefold," and he warned students not to overload them with classical references. Disputation was an entirely different issue. In the process of disputing, the middle route between faintness and fieriness was to be preferred. Sobriety and calmness were important tactical elements in disputing, but Duport recommended that speakers press their arguments "and then urge them home"; they should call upon their adversary for a response, not leaving off until a satisfactory reply had been received. The disputant should always argue syllogistically or "at least Enthematically" (i.e., by deducing conclusions from widely accepted or probable propositions, or by inviting the listener to do so) and where possible "Categorically" (i.e., by explicitly stating the argument in a standard logical form involving expressions such as "All A are B" or "Some B are not C") and if acting as a respondent, one was to repeat the syllogism before answering. If the respondent were to proceed by breaking down his response into two alternatives, then these should be stated explicitly before choosing one above the other.[67]

Duport told his students that they were to understand that they were not speaking in *genere demonstrative* but in *genere deliberativo* or in *genere judiciali*. These three species of rhetoric formed the basis of the art, canonically laid down in Aristotle's *Rhetorica*. The first, also known as epideictic or ceremonial rhetoric, concerned those actions of an individual that were worthy of praise or blame and it was the only branch of rhetoric not directly aimed at convincing an audience to do or not do something. Deliberative rhetoric was concerned with persuading someone to perform a certain action, or dissuading someone from carrying it out by inquiring whether, given certain ends, courses of action were harmful or beneficial. The goal was to induce hope or fear in the individual as a way of inspiring him to action. Judicial or forensic rhetoric was concerned with accusing or defending individuals for their past actions, and it had particular regard to the moral bearing of the person in question. All types of rhetoric were devised for specific audiences and settings. Ceremonial rhetoric was appropriate for formal occasions, funeral orations, or eulogies while deliberative oratory was designed for public or political speeches addressed to an assembly of citizens. Forensic rhetoric grew out of, and was designed for persuasion in a courtroom, and it was the style of argument that Newton would master in his private writings.[68]

As an undergraduate, and even earlier at Grantham, Newton must have spent a vast amount of time improving his skills in practical disputations. To accompany this, he was required to study Aristotle's *Rhetorica*, and to a lesser extent, exemplary texts by Cicero. Alongside the tuition that was given by Pulleyn, he also had to address the many modern commentaries in existence. Earlier in the century, many at Cambridge had used Keckermann's *Systema Rhetoricæ* and Gerard Vossius's *Rhetorices Contractæ, sive partitionum oratorium*, a compendium of oratorical theory and practice that was a much shorter version of his *Commentariorum Rhetoricum sive Oratorium Institutionum*. Vossius's *Rhetorices Contractæ* placed a great deal of emphasis on the practical functions of the rhetorical arts, and to this end he offered substantial advice on how to manipulate the emotions of the listeners so as to persuade them to perform a particular action. Following Aristotle he presented the three types of rhetorical argument or speech and also analysed the list of emotions treated in Aristotle's canonical text, emphasising the ways that they could best be used to achieve the orator's goal. He wasted little time dealing with deliberative rhetoric, concentrating more on demonstrative and forensic speech.[69]

Pulleyn set Newton to read the *Rhetorices Contractæ*. The surviving excerpts in Newton's notebook are short and represent only a snapshot of the massive study that he must have been obliged to make of rhetorical theory and practice. He noted the standard Aristotelian dictum that rhetoric was the skill of speaking well on any matter so as to persuade, or of finding what is suitable for persuading in any instance. He then wrote down a fourfold division of rhetoric into Invention (the discovery of the best type of speech or argument for the occasion and of the best way to do it, along with the appropriate evidence); Disposition (the arrangement of a speech or argument to best convince an audience); Elocution (style, or the use of tone and figures of speech); and Pronunciation. Vossius omitted the usual fifth branch of memory. Each of these, as was the general way with scholastic texts, was further subdivided into even finer partitions, and so on. Finally, Newton noted down all the emotions that were to be targeted by the speaker—fear, confidence, shame, happiness, kindness, anger, calmness, love, hatred, indignation, envy, pity, emulation, and contempt. In later life he presented written rhetorical cases against religious evildoers with great conviction, immense skill, and even with some panache. While the energy and direction of the critiques came from his deeply rooted religious faith, the techniques he employed were learned and honed in Pulleyn's rooms. One assumes that as a student, he must have been a formidable operator in the cut and thrust of organised college disputation.[70]

Historians who have portrayed the work of Vossius and others as utterly irrelevant to Newton's intellectual education miss the point concerning its significance for his intellectual life as a whole. Like most contemporary natural philosophers, Newton would frequently condemn disputation as irrelevant to demonstration in natural philosophy, but when he wrote on church history, and in particular, when he dealt with the chief corrupters of the faith, the forensic procedures of the law-court were vital. Sermons and disputations were the main arenas in which the various religious differences in doctrine and worship were discussed, and the most significant disputations conducted at university were those performed as part of the divinity acts. These were performed by graduates and fellows, though according to Trinity statutes, undergraduates were supposed to attend these three times a week. With the exception of one incident in the later 1670s, there is no record of Newton participating in such exercises, though he must have attended theological disputations when an undergraduate. In any case, there is no doubt that when he came to write church history, he used sophisticated approaches to evidence and argument that he had learned at school and university. His entire account of Christian past was a giant conspiracy theory, and he put on trial all of the most authoritative architects of modern Protestant and Catholic orthodoxy. In due course, as we shall see later in this book, all those tried in his private court would be found guilty.[71]

3

Infinity and the Imagination

A man may imagin things that are fals but he can only understand things y^t are true for if ye things be fals, the apprehension of them is not understanding.★

At some point in early 1664, Newton began his first active investigations of the natural world. In the same undergraduate notebook in which he took notes from Johannes Magirus, Daniel Stahl, Gerard Vossius, and other scholastic texts, he recorded his first engagement with major works in contemporary natural philosophy under the general heading "Questiones quædam philosophiæ" ("Certain Philosophical Questions"). Now Newton grappled with the ideas of "modern" writers such as Thomas Hobbes, René Descartes, Robert Boyle, Walter Charleton, and Henry More, and he absorbed the factual information that was in their books. These entries show that he was capable of making incisive criticisms of these authors, and also that he was able both to propose tests for deciding between various theories as well as to suggest novel experiments for making discoveries about the natural world. Right from the beginning, Newton was committed to various positions and doctrines that would be cornerstones of his later philosophy. These included the existence of atoms and of vacuous spaces, and the real infinitude of an "absolute" space, which was in turn bound up with his understanding of the nature of God. Virtually all the topics that would interest him later on, such as astronomy, optics, gravity, infinity, and the existence of the aether were present in the "Philosophical Questions" programme.[1]

In this chapter I examine Newton's first account of the nature of the cosmos, and the way in which God was supposed to be present to it. I concentrate on his crucial early encounter with key doctrines in Descartes's

Principia Philosophiæ (1644), which was an essential source for his early metaphysical and scientific thinking. The most important issues Newton gleaned from the *Principia* were Descartes's accounts of infinity and what he termed "indefiniteness," and the extent to which humans were able to understand infinity. Whereas Descartes had argued that only God could be called infinite, and that the size of the universe should be considered "indefinite," Newton responded that there were many really existing things (such as the universe) that were not God but which were infinite. As a result of his analysis, he erected a clear distinction between what the human mind could imagine, compute, or conceive, and what it could understand. Early on in his "Philosophical Questions" writings, he insisted that what could be imagined or conceived should not be taken as a mark of what was real, and that one should not draw inferences about the way the world really was from the limits of human capacities. While the imagination and other human mental operations pertained to what was merely finite, or even false, the trained human understanding could positively grasp what was really infinite, whether it was mathematical, physical, or divine.

Many of the topics covered in the "Philosophical Questions" programme, and in the experimental research he conducted soon afterwards, were very different from those for which he later become famous, though remnants of these interests survived in the later editions of his *Opticks* and *Principia*. These studies were concerned with the nature and power of the soul (in particular, the imagination and the will), and the relationship between the soul and the body. Although Newton was already distrustful of the epistemic reach of the imagination, one of the first serious experiments he ever performed involved an effort to determine the powers of the faculty of the imagination, which despite its imperfections, he understood as possessing a number of significant and positive qualities. Many of these enquiries resulted from his belief that humans were made in the image of God, a view that lay at the heart of his metaphysics. As a result of this, he was committed to the view that one could and should understand various aspects of the being and attributes of the divine through the study of human faculties. Specifically, he argued that the freely acting and effective human will was an undeniable fact of human existence and an adumbration of the voluntary, creative power of God. Consequently, he devised a series of experiments to determine how it was that we moved our own bodies. Although other topics obviously came to the fore in later years, these subjects remained of great interest to him throughout his career.

1. The Cartesian Influence

With the "Philosophical Questions" project, Newton ended any residual interest in Aristotelian doctrines and embraced the delights of the so-called new philosophy. Over the next three years (which included the *annus mirabilis* of 1666) he would make seminal contributions in optics, physics, and mathematics, although none of these achievements would seep out of the walls of the college until the end of the decade, when he was elected to replace Isaac Barrow as Lucasian Professor. More immediately, he was faced with the relatively mundane business of attaining the minimal level of competence in the standard curriculum necessary to keep him at Trinity College after his undergraduate studies. As we saw in the previous chapter, the college held elections for scholarships towards the end of April 1664, and to qualify for one of these Newton was examined on a number of different topics. Mathematics did form part of the test, and according to John Conduitt (who had it from Newton himself), Benjamin Pulleyn sent Newton to be examined by Barrow, who found that he knew depressingly little of Euclid's *Elements* though he was by now a "master" of the contents of René Descartes's *Géometrie*. According to the story, Barrow failed to discuss the Cartesian work, while Newton was too modest to raise the issue. He had presumably been attending Barrow's Lucasian lectures since Barrow had started giving them in the previous month, and he was elected as a scholar despite Barrow allegedly conceiving an "indifferent opinion" of him during the exam. It is inconceivable, however, that he was yet an expert in higher-level mathematics, and much later Newton recalled that he had only began to consult the *Géometrie* in the summer of 1664. Conduitt's account implies either that Newton received some sort of support from Pulleyn, Babington, or even Barrow, or that he knew enough about the scholastic subjects—and Euclid—to convince Barrow. A similar story attends his performance for his bachelor of arts examination early in 1665, which involved participating in disputations on standard scholastic topics in front of other students and fellows. According to his eighteenth-century biographer William Stukeley, this was awarded only after Newton had suffered the disgrace of being "put to a second posing"; given his new obsessions with mathematics and natural philosophy, it is remarkable that he devoted sufficient attention to the curriculum to pass.[2]

The final year of the degree offered students some freedom in the areas that they studied, and it was at this point that many were exposed to the "new philosophy" for the first time. However, Newton was probably already submerged in the new intellectual worlds of natural philosophy and mathematics by the end of his third year. In particular, the sophisticated mechanical philosophy of Descartes's *Principia Philosophiæ* seduced him, just as it did many other students at the time. Descartes's system was designed to replace the Aristotelian philosophy, and he wrote individual works on metaphysics, scientific method, optics, meteorology, and mathematics. He set out to banish opaque scholastic concepts such as "sympathy" and "attraction," and he depicted a universe in which everything operated by contact or impact between bodies. Phenomena such as electricity, magnetism, gravitation, and planetary motion were explained in the *Principia* by appealing to the existence of swirling particles of matter, which Descartes called vortices. His cosmos was full of matter, that is, like the scholastics he was a "plenist" whose world had no empty spaces. Nevertheless, his conception of matter was highly original. He argued that the essential quality of any body (material substance) was its magnitude, or "extension"; according to this extreme view, a body did not occupy space that would otherwise be empty if the body suddenly disappeared, for body and extension were the same thing. The link between mind and body remained obscure in Descartes's system, although in his last book, *Les passions del'Âme* (1649), he argued that the soul was principally situated in (though not completely confined to) the pineal gland. More problematic were the twin issues of how God could be present in the Cartesian universe, and also how human beings could have free will in a world that functioned (and could be explained) on almost entirely mechanistic lines.[3]

The Cartesian system purported to be rigorous, and it explained virtually every natural phenomena, though very quickly critics showed that many of the laws of nature he claimed to have discovered were patently false. In the later seventeenth century it would fall foul both of suspicions concerning Descartes's religious motivations, and also of a general dislike of what critics took to be overly ambitious and ultimately fictitious systems composed by single authors. For English readers, the most significant bridge to Cartesian thought was the work of Henry More, who had immediately been captivated by Descartes's attempt to create a new system of the world and by his emphasis on the *vita contemplativa* as the proper mode of philosophical existence. Through More, scholars at Christ's College were introduced to basic Cartesian doctrines and by the early 1650s a number of students and fellows in Cambridge were engaging with its key tenets. More initially claimed that Descartes was a bulwark against atheism, and he lauded the Cartesian system as a restoration of the true philosophy cultivated by Moses. However, the extreme mechanism of the Frenchman's philosophy, in tandem with his great emphasis on the power of natural reason, soon led to increasing numbers of attacks on his doctrines. Despite this, Cartesian texts continued to be recommended by tutors throughout the 1650s and 1660s, and many of those who detested aspects of his thought greatly admired the brilliance with which he had set about his task. Exposing students to such dangerous ideas may well have been intended as a warning about how to detect and respond to them, but if so the ploy failed, and to the horror of many, Descartes's writings became extremely popular among students.[4]

At the start of his MA oration of 1652, Barrow had offered an extraordinary encomium to Descartes's abilities. Descartes, he said, was the "greatest and most ingenious man, a philosopher in earnest, who is seen to have brought to the contemplation of [the new] philosophy such abilities as perhaps no one else possesses." Free from common prejudice, capable of extended meditation, and blessed with an abundance of leisure, he was "by his own choice free from the reading of useless books and from secular pursuits." However, Barrow identified a number of pernicious consequences of his work. Invoking the arguments of Francis Bacon, Barrow argued that although they seemed plausible, Descartes's theories were the product of a single man's brain, and they remained inventions, "fictious and theatrical worlds." Descartes presumed far too much of the powers of human reason, pretending that by some sort of vain effort, we could understand the causes of phenomena to the same degree that the Creator himself did. Thus, Barrow continued in a Baconian vein, "We would compare the idols of our mind with the ideas of the intellect, ideas which impress their own signatures upon things." Worst of all, the pervasive mechanism of this imaginary system rendered God the maestro of an absurd theatre of mechanical beings, directing "the whole mundane comedy, like a puppeteer or artificer, who repeats and displays his single art *ad nauseam*." Yet even animals displayed desires, and instincts, and signs of will, and Barrow concluded that they showed a care for their own bodies and goal-directed behaviour that could only have arisen as a result of some divine power.[5]

In early 1660s Cambridge the materialist doctrines of Thomas Hobbes were considered as much of a threat to morals and religion as Cartesianism, and by now it was de rigeur to condemn the poisonous consequences of both systems. There was a backlash against the use of Cartesian ideas and language in disputations, and a general agreement that Cartesian had to be refuted. In his 1663 commencement oration, for example, the Christ's student John Covel, later one of Newton's friends, bemoaned the fact that under-graduates were routinely absorbing Cartesian and indeed other dangerous French ideas. Not only were Descartes's doctrines obnoxious, but as Samuel Parker and others noted, the meditative philosophical programme he com-mended actively discouraged students from reading philosophical textbooks or Scripture. Roger North later remembered that a majority of students were positively disposed towards Descartes when he had studied Cartesian texts in 1667, and in the same year, the ex-master of Jesus College, John Worth-ington, asked Henry More to write a textbook of natural philosophy that would rebut and supplant baneful Cartesian doctrines. Worthington selected More on the grounds that he had written so effusively about Cartesianism over the previous two decades, and in a scarcely veiled rebuke, he remarked that More would be particularly aware of this "great evil." He added that Cambridge students idolised the French philosophy, were "enravisht with it, and derive from thence notions of ill consequence to religion," and he lamented that students who had drunk at the Cartesian well would never again pledge allegiance to Aristotle.[6]

2. Some Philosophical Questions

It was in these ambivalent contexts that Newton encountered Descartes's works. Although his notes from the scholastic authors had been almost wholly uncritical, the excerpts from Descartes's writings that he recorded in the "Philosophical Questions" section of the notebook show a serious en-gagement with his ideas. He began with Descartes's metaphysics and natural philosophy, as it was found both in the *Principia* and in his responses to various objections against his *Meditations*. Once Newton started to read Descartes, he was as enraptured by his system as was any other student at Cambridge. Nevertheless, he told the Venetian aristocrat Antonio Conti half a century later that he had soon turned against him; Descartes "was a great man in his time," he admitted, but much of what he had done had been taken without proper attribution from others. He added that Descartes's entire physics was based on the false idea that body was equivalent to extension, and his metaphysics was "nothing but a tapestry of assumptions." Despite these later attacks on the unoriginal and highly fanciful features of Descartes's work, many of the notes taken in his first engagement with Descartes's *Principia* show the great extent to which Newton was initially taken with, and indeed absorbed the latter's physics and metaphysics.[7]

While Newton quickly embraced Cartesian doctrines, he also immersed himself in Descartes's *Géometrie*, a work that would provide him with many of the tools he needed for his pioneering mathematical researches over the following two years. From now on, Cartesianism would play a dual role in almost all his work. On the one hand, its terms and concepts would dominate his early engagement with the new philosophy, and its intellectual DNA would be visible in his mature writings. On the other, his disillusionment with aspects of Cartesian philosophy quickly hardened into outright hostility. Descartes, he charged, offered a portal to atheism for those who— using Cartesian intellectual equipment—could erect a system of the world without including God as the founder and ubiquitous master of the universe. Descartes's work would provide a foil for Newton's own researches, culminating in the deliberate naming of his masterwork as a counterblast to Descartes's *Principia*.[8]

On the recto and verso of the page preceding the first entries in the "Philosophical Questions" programme, Newton took brief notes from the 1656 Amsterdam edition of Descartes's *Opera Omnia* on some of the replies that Descartes had made to various objections to his *Meditations*. The subjects of interest, visible both in his notes and in dog-ears he made to his copy of Descartes's work, concerned the nature and physical reality of ideas; the capacity of the mind to come to term with both finite and infinite beings; the nature of space and place; the mind-body distinction and, most important, the being and nature of God. Newton began by discussing the nature of ideas, noting Descartes's claim that "An Idea as it respects ye object wthout ye mind is but a bare denomination or a mere nothing." However, with respect to the mind itself, Newton commented, "it is objectively in it...'tis a reall entity, viz. a mode of the intellect." He moved on to discuss Descartes's account of whether an infinite being was clearly and distinctly conceivable by a finite mind (in Cartesian terms, by thinking substance). As Newton put it, how could the human mind grasp something so perfect that its only cause could be God?[9]

Many of the features that characterised Newton's mature natural philosophy were present right from the start in the "Philosophical Questions" researches, which collectively constituted his first scientific research programme.

Like a number of his contemporaries, he was attracted to the idea that there was a vacuum because it provided a space, or place, where God could exist in a manner most appropriate to his immaterial nature. In contrast with the scholastic and Cartesian view that the universe was a finite plenum, Newton assumed from the outset that the cosmos was infinite and almost entirely vacuous. In some "Philosophical Questions" entries, he blended scholastic arguments with experimental evidence for a vacuum drawn from the works of Robert Boyle. Newton referred on a number of occasions to Boyle's air-pump experiments, but in keeping with the critical acumen that would become the defining characteristic of his early researches, he proposed a number of new experiments that were designed to test the claims of Boyle, Descartes, and others. For example, he suggested several trials to test whether a number of natural phenomena were caused by an invisible aether, on the grounds that they still occurred in an evacuated (i.e., airless) pump.[10]

For Newton and his contemporaries, the issue of God's creation of, and presence in the universe was closely bound up with the existence of an infinitely extended space. The claim that God was ubiquitously present in the universe, and that he had a determinate relationship with space, had long been a commonplace of natural philosophy. Medieval commentators, who almost all denied that the universe was actually infinite, had distanced themselves from the claim that space was God's body, not least because asserting that God had a body was a particularly pernicious form of materialist heresy. During the seventeenth century, a number of writers began to assert that space was actually infinite, though this raised the problem of how to distinguish the infinitude of space from the infinitude of God. In a number of works of 1671, Henry More, who was reacting to various scholastic, Cartesian, and Hobbesian positions, argued that an infinitely powerful and ubiquitous God required an appropriately large (i.e., infinite) place in which to exist. Against the common view that "spirit" lacked dimensions, More claimed that what was nowhere (i.e., lacked dimensions) was nothing and that immaterial and penetrable "spirit" was extended throughout void space, which existed ad infinitum beyond the finite, material world. By accepting the possibility and reality of empty space, More deliberately broke with the Cartesian equation of matter with extension, while he also denied Hobbes's argument that space was merely an imaginary "phantasm." Extension was a real attribute of a real subject and was independent of our imagination. More wrestled for a number of decades with the nature of the relationship between God and space, and his arguments were of great significance to Newton. In his *Enchiridion Metaphysicum* of 1671, More argued that God and infinite space shared identical characteristics such as being indivisible, omnipresent, incorporeal, uncreated, and incorruptible. This claim made space perilously close to being made a part of God, a notion that Newton would explicitly deny in his metaphysical writings.[11]

Another likely source for Newton's more mature writings about God and space was Isaac Barrow, who in his tenth Lucasian lecture of early 1665, had discussed these topics in the context of Descartes's views. He began by admitting that it was hard to say what space actually was. If it were granted a high degree of independence from the existence of material things so that it were considered to be self-sustaining, then it might also be construed as being independent of God, which was contrary to reason as well as to religion. On the other hand, the "idea" of space seemed to be of something that had "a certain Extension and indefinite Capacity," which was the same definition that applied to things that had magnitude. Citing Aristotle, and presumably with Descartes in mind, Barrow argued that this view made the "bulk" of something indistinguishable from the space it occupied. This notion could be countered by appealing to the fact that all men commonly assumed that space was akin to a vessel that was separate from the things in it. Indeed, this idea of space as a container was "engraven in the Imaginations of all Mortals." As for the nature and extent of the universe, Barrow did not deny that it was in God's power to make matter infinitely large, though Scripture seemed to plainly attest that the amount of matter was finite. The extent of space was a different issue. Turning to Descartes's denial that corporeal substance (considered as equivalent to extension) was infinitely extended, Barrow considered the claim in *Principia Philosophiae* Part 2, Article 21 that corporeal substance was "indefinitely" extended. Descartes had argued that although we could always imagine that there were limits to the size of world, we could "not only imagine but perceive to be imaginable in a true fashion," some indefinitely extended spaces existing beyond these limits. Barrow responded that simply because we could imagine such spaces existing beyond any determinate bounds, did not mean that such spaces really existed: "Imaginability then does at most only prove the Possibility of a real Thing, but nowhere its actual Existence." Descartes's refusal to distinguish between extension and matter meant that his arguments were irrelevant with respect to the extent of vacuous space. However, having appealed to the imagination to defend the existence of vacuous space, Barrow was keen to assert that the same faculty provided no grounds for determining whether space was infinite or not.[12]

Barrow noted that space had its own type of being, existing as a "power" or "capacity" to receive bodies of a certain size. This idea had the advantage that such an entity was dependent on God for its creation and existence. It was neither a "Substance" nor an "Accident" (a non-essential attribute or feature of a substance, such as colour), either of which all real beings had to be according to the scholastic categories that Barrow accepted, but rather, it was a "Mode or Possibility" of both. Barrow's notion was consistent with recent experimental findings about the reality of the vacuum, but was incompatible with Hobbes's subjectivist claim in chapter 7 of *De Corpore* that space was the "Phantasm of a thing existing." Barrow criticised Hobbes's assertion that if all corporeal things in the world were destroyed, which for Hobbes would be everything, the "Phantasm of Space" would still remain in the minds of anyone remaining. Barrow insisted that this was incomprehensible, since "to feign all Things out of the Way, and at the same time to imagine the same Things as existing are direct Contradictions." He concluded that his own account of space was highly agreeable to, and sufficient for mathematicians.[13]

The first entries in Newton's "Philosophical Questions" project predated More's *Enchiridion* by a few years, though they were reliant on his reading of More's *Immortality of the Soul* of 1659. Given the similarity between the topics covered, it is also possible that he discussed these issues with Barrow, or simply developed ideas he heard in Barrow's lectures. These early essays were predominantly scholastic in form and content and concerned the concept of *prima materia*, that is, the "Prime Matter" that Aristotle posited as the formless and unchanging substratum of all formed matter. To determine what this was, Newton proceeded by enumerating a series of possibilities and then eliminating all but one. It must either, he argued, be composed of (a) mathematical "points"; (b) mathematical points and "parts" (i.e., matter divided up into differentiated parts); (c) a simple undifferentiated entity that was "indistinct" before being divided; or (d) "individualls" (i.e., really existing minimal/indivisible parts) such as atoms. Slipping between talking about mathematical and physical infinitesimally small things, he cancelled his initial claim that a mathematical point was "an immaginary entity," but concluded that since such points lacked any real magnitude, an infinite number of them would still only "sinke" into one indivisible point. Quickly dismissing the second option, Newton argued against the third that the Prime

Matter could not have been an homogenous undifferentiated mass at the outset. Newton argued, by begging the question, that a unified whole was a union of more basic parts that were already distinct from each other before they were actually separated. The fact that matter could be rarefied or condensed showed that it was made up of such parts, and he added that these were separated by "vacuities interspersed" between them. In fact, the cosmos was almost wholly composed of these empty spaces. He concluded that there had to be tiny parts of matter that had magnitude but were so little that "theire can ⌜not⌝ be a place too little for y^m to creepe into." Newton decided that these tiny parts, which were either created at the beginning alongside vacuous spaces, or later divided by means of them, were atoms.[14]

Although he developed these arguments in his own idiosyncratic style, Newton's account of the vacuum, parts, and atoms was also heavily indebted to Walter Charleton's *Physiologia-Epicuro-Gassendo-Charletoniana* of 1654. Charleton provided the source for his analysis of mathematical "points," and he had likewise concluded that the *prima materia* must be made up of atoms. Newton added that Henry More had proved beyond any reasonable doubt that matter could be so small as to be "indiscerpible," that is, it could be divided into constituent atomic particles that were so small that they could not be further divided and still exist. However, these minimal "parts," which had dimension or magnitude, could not be *infinitely* small. Using the Cartesian language of extension, but drawing on classical discussions of infinity, Newton argued that although an infinite number of infinitely small, dimensionless things (such as mathematical points) always added up to a finite thing, an infinite number of infinitely small *extended* parts would combine to constitute a thing that was infinitely extended. So a finite portion of matter—indeed, all existing matter—could not by itself be composed of an infinite number of parts, for then it would itself be infinite, which was a contradiction. He added that while matter was not infinitely extended, the vacuum was.[15]

Newton's belief that God's existence was bound up with the existence of void space was demonstrated early on in the "Philosophical Questions" programme in a foundational essay on "violent" motion, that is, on the motion of an object that has been subject to some external force. Against scholastic and Cartesian arguments that motion was impossible unless it took place in a plenum, Newton argued that it was possible and indeed necessary for motion to take place *in vacuo*. Contrary to standard impetus theory, this was, he said, because a plenum would "impede yᵉ motion to be continually thrusting against & resisted by yᵉ body before it but in vacuo it meetes wᵗʰ nothing ⟨impenitrable⟩ to stay it." According to Newton, God existed as far as the vacuum extended, and "being a spirit" he was subtle enough to penetrate all matter and thus could not retard the motion of any material object. Newton's commitment to motion *in vacuo* and the claim that a plenum would impede such motion would be the bedrock of his later physics. Similarly, his view that God was a real ubiquitous and infinite spirit that had an intimate relationship with the vacuous parts of the cosmos would always lie at the core of his metaphysics.[16]

3. Understanding Infinity

In a different section of "Philosophical Questions," Newton addressed the Cartesian concept of "indefiniteness." In the Third Meditation, Descartes had argued that his own faculties might be "indefinitely" perfectible, but no matter how much they were improved they would never be adequate for perceiving the absolute perfection that belonged to God alone. He developed his treatment of infinity and indefiniteness in various sections in Part 1 of the *Principia*, and during his early career Newton seems to have returned to those passages on a number of occasions. In Article 26, Descartes argued that it would be "absurd" for humans to determine anything concerning the infinite, because finite creatures always placed limits on concepts in order to grasp them. Hence, they inevitably became embroiled in tedious arguments when discussing something fundamentally ungraspable such as infinity. Instead, he continued, we should regard as *indefinite* those things "in which, from some point of view, we are unable to discover a limit." All existing extension should be considered "indefinite" because no matter how large was the amount of extension that we might imagine, we could always understand that there could be an even greater amount. Similarly, we could understand that the number of stars God could have created was more than the largest number of stars we could imagine, and so the number of stars should be considered indefinite. In Article 27 Descartes offered a different justification for his use of the term "indefinite," this time on the grounds that the term "infinite" should be reserved for God alone. In the unique case of God's infinitude, our understanding informed us positively that God possessed no limits, that is, our grasp of God's infinitude was not based on merely denying his finitude. By contrast, in cases such as the size of the universe and the number of stars, our understanding could not "positively" grasp that they were infinite and we were forced to fall back on our limited capacities: "we merely acknowledge in a negative way that any limits that they may have cannot be discovered by us."[17]

Newton's response to these obscure but significant passages was premised on a clear distinction between the domains of the imagination and the understanding, and this division would remain at the heart of his work in religion and natural philosophy. His first treatment of the subject occurred under an entry titled "Of Quantity," where the topic was the nature of infinity. Here, in notes that were added some time after the initial entries (and conceivably about the time that Barrow gave his tenth lecture), Newton effectively rejected Descartes's argument for the indefiniteness of all existing extension (which, we should recall, he equated with matter). In this section, Newton stated that a number of different objects of mental operations were all "indefinite" or "undetermined," including the size of the largest sphere that could be constructed; the extent to which matter was divisible; the magnitude of the largest number that could be "recconed"; and the amount of time or extension we could "fansy" (i.e., imagine). Nevertheless, he continued like the number a/o, both eternity and all existing extension were *really* infinite in size. Newton contrasted the number a/o with merely finite numbers, which, he noted, could be called indefinite in relation to the infinitely large number. The term "indefinite," then, could be used to describe both what was really finite and also the human operations of mental conception, computation, and the use of the imagination—all of which, he suggested, pertained to finite things. Only the understanding was capable of grasping what was infinite, and, he implied, what was true and real.[18]

Later in the notebook, under the same heading, Newton developed his attack on the idea that extension should be understood as being really "indefinite" rather than "infinite." To infer that the actual amount of extension in the universe—and not the maximum amount of extension we could "fansy"—was merely "indefinite" on the basis that we could not perceive its limits, was, he said, to make inferences about the real world on the basis of human limitations. Not only were there objections to gauging the true nature of the world, and in particular, the nature of infinity by reference to our limited faculties, but—which was worse—the same argument would apply to our conception of God. In a direct attack on Descartes's argument in *Principia* Part 1, Article 27, Newton argued that if Descartes's use of "indefiniteness" to describe existing reality were legitimate, we would be forced to assert by like reasoning that God was only "indefinitely perfect" merely because we could not grasp his perfection in full. This claim served as a refutation of Descartes's notion of indefiniteness, and also of his claim that although we could understand that God was infinite, we could not understand his infinity. By contrast, Newton believed that God's attributes were both really infinite and positively comprehensible.[19]

In other writings that date from around the time of the "Philosophical Questions" programme, Newton did make inferences about divine powers from limited human capacities. He argued that our capacity to "conceive" an action or state without contradiction showed that it was within the power of God to create it. In this case, he referred to his experience of the powers of his own body, for, as he put it, "I can conceive all my owne powers (knowledge, activating matter, & c.) wthout assigning them any limits." From the knowledge that such powers existed within a finite being, Newton continued, it followed that they could be realised by the deity. Underlying this view was the assumption that anything that was not conceptually contradictory was not physically impossible and could therefore be brought into being by God. On this basis, every feature of this actual world was evidence of a conscious choice by the deity to create one out of a number of possible (i.e., non-contradictory) worlds. With not a little circularity, Newton concluded that the current state of this world, resulting from God's "voluntary & free determination y^t it should be thus" was evidence of both the latter's existence and benevolence.[20]

The relationships between the mind and the body, and between man and God, would become foundational elements of Newton's theological metaphysics. Outlined in his "Philosophical Questions" entries, they were developed to a remarkable extent in an untitled manuscript now known by its first line "De Gravitatione et Aequipondio Fluidorum." The bulk of this essay, which was probably composed in the early 1670s, may well have been inspired by reading More's *Enchiridion*, though Newton diverged from More in many respects. Significantly, it constituted a major and explicit attack on those sections of Descartes's *Principia* that dealt with notions of rest and movement, the nature of extension, the relationship between mind and body, and the relationship between God and extension. Far from being merely a negative critique, Newton developed a highly original, rival account to that of Descartes, according to which God operated with minimal effort on a mathematical substrate to make objects "real" to the senses of human beings. Years later, he would use scientific arguments in Book 2 of the *Principia Mathematica* to show that the Cartesian system of vortices was an unintelligible and incoherent fiction, but in "De Gravitatione" he assailed Cartesianism using a panoply of philosophical, metaphysical, and indeed theological arguments.[21]

"De Gravitatione" did not commence as a metaphysical critique, but as an analysis of fluids that was couched in a mathematical, abstract style of presentation in preference to what he termed a philosophical or physical style. This penchant for mathematicism chimes with the general tenor of his approach in the optical lectures of 1670/71, and with the definition of a light ray he adopted in response to criticisms of his paper on light and colours of February 1672. The use of terms such as "definitions," "axioms," and "scholia" marks it out as part of the same genre as the *Principia Mathematica*, but this was not the only feature that linked the two texts. The opening sections of "De Gravitatione" dealt with Cartesian notions of "rest," "place," and "motion," the basic elements of which Newton had very briefly noted in the "Philosophical Questions" notebook. In Part 2 of his *Principia*, Descartes had radically transformed traditional scholastic categories by defining the place, or "locus" of an object purely by the common surface of the contiguous parts of the object and the surrounding plenum. Motion was defined as "translation" of the object from those parts that were both immediately contiguous to it "and regarded as being at rest." If a body did not move relative to any of these surrounding parts, then, like the earth in its surrounding vortex, it was to be considered wholly at rest. Clearly, in the wake of Galileo's condemnation by the Catholic Church in 1633 for defending the Copernican system, this was designed to be consistent with a geocentric position. Descartes was aware of an objection to this view, namely that following change in the state of the contiguous materials either the object or the relevant parts of the plenum could be considered to be at rest. Accordingly he argued that all motion was "reciprocal," that is, it involved (was a "mode" of) both contiguous elements.[22]

Newton charged that because Descartes gave no reasonable account of how to determine an absolute frame of reference independent of the visible and relative motion of contiguous bodies, real motion from one place to another was unintelligible. "He seems," Newton noted, "to contradict himself when he postulates that to each body corresponds a single motion, according to the nature of things; and yet he asserts that motion to be a product of our imagination" ("tamen motum istum ab imaginatione nostra pendere statuit"). This was because Descartes defined motion as "translation" from surrounding bodies that were not at rest but which only *seemed* to be at rest, even though they might actually be moving. Without being able to pinpoint a precise location in the form of non-relativistic frame of reference for the start and finish of translations, it was impossible to assign any proper or "true" motion to any object. Since the position of each of the bodies that had been contiguous to the object changed throughout the duration of what Descartes termed "real" motion, it would also be impossible to calculate with sufficient precision, "as a geometer would require," the past positions for every element of this (now rearranged) contiguous material. According to Newton, there was no discernible or calculable place, or origin of motion from where any given object could be said to have started, "and if one follows Cartesian doctrine, not even God himself could define the past position of any moving body accurately and geometrically [since the original place] no longer exists in nature." Cartesian motion was therefore merely an imaginary fiction, lacking either a real velocity or a determinable space traversed over a given time.[23]

Newton next proceeded to dismantle Descartes's arguments in favour of identifying body with extension, and for making a radical distinction between thinking and extended substances. It might be assumed, Newton proposed, that extension should be defined either a substance or an accident, or nothing at all. However, it could not be the same as body (i.e., a substance) since although substances were understood to be defined by their capacity to act upon things, extension per se could not "move nor excite in the mind any sensation or perception whatever." Nor was it—as More had implied—an accident "inherent in some subject," because we could clearly conceive extension existing without a subject (e.g., we could not believe that extension would perish with a body if God annihilated it). Yet extension was not nothing, and Newton agreed with Descartes that we had a very clear "idea" of it, which arose from "abstracting the dispositions and properties of a body" so that all that remained were mathematical dimensions of points, lines, and surfaces. As a really existing thing, space had a series of properties including extending infinitely in all directions, being composed of motionless parts, and being "eternal in duration and immutable in nature." Newton argued that these parts were mathematical figures (such as spheres, cubes, etc.), which acted as containers for real bodies. Unlike Barrow, who had asserted their *potential* existence in the tenth Lucasian lecture, Newton claimed that these extended parts of space *actually* existed in their own right, despite being invisible. Space was everywhere spherical, elliptical, and so forth, and when such figures were made visible there was not a new creation of that figure "with respect to space," but merely a "corporeal representation" of it.[24]

The mathematical characteristics of this space were crucial for Newton's discussion of infinity, and he linked his belief in the infinitude of space to the infinite extensibility of some mathematical objects (straight lines, paraboloids, and cylinders) that characterised the proto-space. One could imagine, Newton argued, detaching one side of a triangle from the other at the vertex and rotating it around the point where it joined the base so that it became almost parallel to the other side. At the moment before they became parallel, the lines would meet somewhere that was further away than any assignable distance; however, this was not an *imaginary* infinity but a *real* infinity. Newton rehearsed his earlier claim in the "Philosophical Questions" notebook that although we could not imagine infinite extension, we could understand that extension was infinite. He noted Descartes's statement in the *Principia* to the effect that we can continually imagine greater and greater amounts of extension, but we could understand that there existed greater extension than any we could imagine. Whereas Descartes had been averse from attributing infinity to any existing thing except God, Newton reaffirmed that extension was not to be considered "indefinite," but actually infinite.[25]

Just as in the "Philosophical Questions" account, Newton considered the nature of infinity in "De Gravitatione" in relation to human perceptual and intellectual capacities. By means of his account, he boasted, the faculty of the imagination could be clearly distinguished from that of the understanding. In a compressed argument on the extent to which humans could positively understand the attributes of God, Newton remarked that some might object that it was derogatory to claim that one could only understand what an infinite being (presumably God) was, merely by progressively removing the constraints to the limits of finite being. However, he continued, the more we conceived of those confines being negated, the more we observed something to be attributed to it, and "the more positively we conceived it." By negating all such limits this conception became positive "in the highest degree." Following this process, the term "infinity," though grammatically negative, would become a positive word, again "in the highest degree," with regard to our perception and comprehension. Here Newton appeared to be suggesting, in a manner not that different from Descartes's own claims, that humans could learn to positively understand infinitude, and not merely that some physical and mathematical entities were really infinite. A good example of how humans could know infinity by mastering various procedures was of course ready to hand in the form of mathematics. Geometers, Newton remarked, could accurately know "positive and finite quantities of surfaces infinite in length," and he added that he himself could "positively and accurately determine the solid quantities of many solids infinite in length and breadth, and compare them to given finite solids." He concluded by saying that this was irrelevant to his religious argument, but the comparison between performing operations involving mathematical infinities, and grasping religious infinities, was one that would reappear in his writings.[26]

Newton added that Descartes's use of the term "indefinite" was an affront to good grammar. The term never applied to anything actually existing, he claimed, but "always relates to a future possibility signifying only something which is not yet determined and definite." Before God decreed anything about the world, the amount of matter in the universe and the number of stars in existence was indefinite—but once the world was created they were defined. Similarly, matter was indefinitely divisible, but as a matter of fact it was at any given point in time either divided finitely or infinitely. And by like reasoning, an indefinite space was a space whose future size was yet to be determined, but in fact space was actually finite or infinite and so it was determined and definite. It was also wrong to infer anything about the extent of space from our own fallibility, for even if humans were ignorant of such things, "God at least understands that there are no limits not merely indefinitely but certainly and positively." In any case, rehearsing the point he had made about grasping God's infinitude, he noted that although humans could not imagine space to transcend all limits, they could positively understand that it did so, and know that it was infinite.[27]

A central plank of Newton's theology underlay his account of extension. Although God did not create extension, it was a necessary consequence of his existence. It was neither created by the deity nor was it something that had a separate existence from him. Following More, Newton stressed that all things that existed, even created minds, were extended, and God was no exception. All existing things also existed in time, and God necessarily existed everywhere and always. Yet although God was ubiquitously present in the infinite universe, no one should imagine, Newton wrote, that God was like a body, with divisible parts. Space itself was not divisible into parts, and indeed it had its own manner of existence, being an "emanent effect" of God and a necessary result of God's existence. This meant, contra Descartes, that extension had to be infinitely large. In one rare moment of generosity towards Descartes, Newton remarked that he appreciated that Descartes had feared that by making space infinite, it would perhaps become God, since both shared the perfection of infinity. But this was a mistake, since infinity was not a perfection unless it was an attribute of a perfect thing. Infinity of intellect, power, and happiness was the pinnacle of perfection, but infinity of ignorance, impotence, and wretchedness was the height of imperfection.[28]

Newton developed many of these topics in another text that seems to have been written soon after the first edition of the *Principia* appeared in 1687. This short essay, which reworks sections of "De Gravitatione," is evidently an early version of the "General Scholium," almost certainly composed in the early 1690s in order to be added to a proposed second edition of the *Principia*. In it, he argued that existing in a time and place was the "common affection" of all things. Existing in time and place in a manner appropriate to the being in question did not imply imperfection, since space itself had no parts, that is, it was indivisible. Imperfect things either changed over time or were bounded in time and space, but to be the same always and everywhere was a mark of supreme perfection. Infinite and eternal space was the place of God, and he was the most perfect being both because of that infinity and eternity, and because of the infinite number and eternal succession of his works. It was hard to conceive of an infinite number of things, Newton admitted, but it was not impossible to do so. Mathematicians were used to dealing with aspects concerning infinity that were true, but which the mathematically illiterate considered paradoxical or impossible. Areas of hyperbolas that were infinitely long could be integrated and summed, and approaching bodies could keep halving the distance between them without ever touching (an example he took from the very earliest notes in "Philosophical Questions"). Similarly, whatever was good could become most perfect through "successive improvements," and what was bad could become most evil. On the one hand, Newton argued, this showed that there were many things that were eternal or infinite versions of particular natures that were not God, but also that God was not prevented from exercising his omnipotent creative power by the existence of other infinite things. On the other, this account negated the tendency of humans to hold "nothing quite so holy and perfect as what cannot be understood." In theology this was extremely dangerous, since it led to atheism, and

Newton concluded that his own account was as reasonable as possible, and presumably accessible even to the unlearned.[29]

4. The Human and Divine Wills

Having dismantled the Cartesian conception of extension in "De Gravitatione," Newton turned to the nature of body. Aware that he was possibly veering into the unpleasant realm of speculation, he hedged his account by stating that he was unwilling to positively say what either the nature of bodies or the manner of their creation was. However, he announced that he would describe a sort of being "similar in every way to bodies," and whose creation could not be denied to be within the power of God. To get some grasp of how God may have created the world, Newton pointed out that all people were conscious that they could move their own body at will and believed that others could do the same. Since God's capacity to move bodies via his freely exercised will was infinitely greater and swifter than this, it could not be doubted that God, "by the sole action of thinking and willing," could prevent another body from entering a defined portion of space. Being impenetrable and visible, Newton added, we would call it "body." As the Huguenot scholar Pierre Coste later recalled, Newton's idea that understanding voluntary self-motion was a route towards explaining creation was passed on to John Locke, who repeated the argument in an opaque passage in the second (1694) edition of the *Essay Concerning Human Understanding* (Bk. IV, ch. X, pt. 18). Newton told Coste that God could make determinate portions of space impenetrable and visible in consecutive spaces, thus constituting what would appear to be a moving object. As a number of commentators have pointed out, this idea was more clearly laid out in "De Gravitatione," though aspects of it were obscure.[30]

In keeping with the speculative nature of his account, Newton couched this section as an explicitly imaginary thought-experiment, the likes of which are found nowhere else in his writings. Using the language of "feigning" that he condemned elsewhere, he argued that we could imagine ("fingamur") God endowing a defined empty space with corporeal attributes such as impenetrability and the capacity to be sensed, and we might further imagine, he continued, that this impenetrability could be transported across various spaces. Granted the capacity to be touched and seen, such a body would "operate upon our minds and in turn be operated upon, because it is nothing more than the product of the divine mind realised in a definite quantity of space" ("nihil aliud quam effectus mentis divinæ intra definitam spatij quantitatem elicitus"). It was certain, Newton continued, "that God can stimulate our perception by his own will, and thence apply such power to the effects of his will." A world made up of these sorts of "endowed spaces" would be indistinguishable from the world in which we now live because such spaces would be able to "excite various perceptions of the senses and the fancy in created minds, and conversely be moved by them." These spaces would either be bodies or be like bodies, and if the former, then bodies could be defined as "determined quantities of extension that omnipresent God endows with certain conditions."[31]

Newton claimed that his system had the advantage that there was no need to invoke the scholastic notion of "Prime Matter." Mathematically structured extension now took over the role previously played by the Prime Matter, and he asserted that extension had a much greater reality than Prime Matter, if indeed the latter were anything more than a figment of the scholastic imagination. There was no need, he continued, to postulate some incomprehensible substance that lay behind and underpinned the perceptible qualities of an object, but one should not assume that the entities he had described were any less "real" than bodies, since whatever reality we attributed to bodies came from their sensible qualities. If one quibbled that this creation story left unexplained the precise manner in which God imparted form to space, it was of no moment. Newton had shown that the process of creation had been reduced to the same problem of explaining how we moved our own bodies, and even if we did not know how we moved our own bodies, self-motion achieved by a mere act of will nevertheless remained a fact. His account of creation had the advantage that "God may appear (to our innermost consciousness) to have created the world solely by an act of will, just as we move our bodies by an act of will alone." This paved the way for a possible research programme—if we could discover experimentally how we moved our own bodies, we ought to be able to determine how God moved bodies from one part of the cosmos to the other. I deal with Newton's attempts to do precisely this in the following sections.[32]

Newton added that he had shown that the analogy between humans and the divine was much closer than had previously been realised by philosophers. Noting that the Bible testified that we were created in God's image, he concluded that by granting humans the capacity for free will and self-motion, God had simulated his own creative power in human faculties to the same extent that he had his other attributes (such as reason and goodness). Although the power of *creating* minds and bodies was not available to finite beings, Newton continued, the created mind might—"because it is the image of God"—"eminently" contain body in itself. The relationship between the created world and God's intellect was "delineated" in the human mind, specifically to the extent that we were capable of moving our own bodies. He was not, he said, arguing that humans could create things ex nihilo, and indeed in moving their own bodies humans were subject to the divine laws of nature. Even if humans were unable to truly create anything, it was possible, Newton admitted, that God could create "some intellectual creature so perfect that he could, by divine accord, in turn produce creatures of a lower order." Significantly, however, he did not suggest that Jesus Christ might play such a role and concluded that he did not see why God did not *directly* inform space with bodies by a mere act of divine will.[33]

Newton concluded that his argument provided an idea of body that tied it inextricably to God's existence, an explanation of the distinction between body and extension, and a simple account of mind and body according to which both could combine with each other. On the other hand, the Cartesian view rested on an unintelligible distinction between mind and body and left inexplicable the means by which they might unite in thinking beings. According to Newton, if one stripped away all inessential qualities of bodies, there would remain not merely extension but also the natural faculties "by which [bodies] can stimulate perceptions in the mind and move other bodies." Just like God, the most supreme thinking being, minds had to be extended, for otherwise they would be nowhere and the existence of persons a mere fiction. With his metaphysics, a body could think and a mind could be extended. "De Gravitatione" demonstrates that Newton believed that the nature of the mind was one of the key objects of his researches. Mind itself was in nature, and any plausible metaphysics had to take account of it. It remained to propose and carry out the experiments that would clarify the nature of self-motion and thus provide an inlet into the workings of God.[34]

5. Plastick Souls

In Newton's early researches, as we have seen, he disparaged the value of the imagination as an aid to answering questions about God and the natural world. Nevertheless, even if the "fancy" was not a tool for discovering truth, it had an important function in Newton's system as an object of experimental research. Indeed, it soon played a large role in a much larger programme designed to ascertain the precise roles played by the soul and the external world in contributing to experience and knowledge. In one section titled "Philosophy" he remarked that we could better determine the nature of things from their operations upon one another, than from their operations on our senses. After we had discovered the first, he added, we could perform different experiments to discover the nature of our senses. Yet we could not discover the extent to which an act of sensation proceeded from the soul or the body until we had a better idea of both the soul and the body. These thoughts therefore encouraged a new experimental research programme, which could address the following questions: How did the soul govern human corporeal activity? In which part of the body did it reside? How was it related to the imagination, memory, and the rest of the body?[35]

The origins of Newton's practical investigation of his own brain can be found in his notes from More's *Immortality of the Soul*, a fund of anecdotal information about humans who were either engaged in various routine activities or mired in forms of physical and mental decrepitude. More began with a series of considerations about the state of the soul and the experience of free will on the Hobbesian assumption that perception and consciousness were nothing but "Corporeal Motion and Reaction." This was an interesting if dangerous conceit, he noted, and materialism could not explain phenomena such as freely willed self-motion, or being able to discern morally commendable actions and then perform them. More explained spontaneous action in terms of the continuous movement of "animal spirits" (tenuous particles emanating from the brain) from the seat of common sense to the muscles. The precise manner in which this took place, he stated, "we partly feel and see; that is to say, we find in ourselves a power, at our own pleasure to move this or the other member with very great force, and that the Muscle swells that moves the part." This action clearly showed the influx of spirits directed by the will; the soul moistened the fibrous parts of muscles with "that subtle liquor of the Animal Spirits," and this made them "swell and shrink, like Lute-strings in rainy weather." Spontaneous motion took place because the soul was extended throughout the body and that part of it which was in the muscles guided the animal spirits into their outermost parts.[36]

More spent some time examining the views of other writers on the anatomical location of the soul. He concluded that the Common Sensorium was neither the whole body, the orifice of the stomach, the heart, the brain, the septum lucidum, nor the conarion (i.e., the pineal gland). The latter, favoured by Descartes, appeared to be a region that housed a number of "stones," and More argued that it was "environ'd with a net of veines and arteries which are indications that it is a part assigned for some more inferiour office." The most likely place for the soul was in the fourth "ventricle" of the brain, the place where sensory and other information arrived to be processed. As we have seen, More adhered to the unorthodox view that it was also extended throughout the body; as a result, the movements of the heart and lungs were more than mechanical and were carried out by means of a "plastick power" directed by the soul. This pervasiveness of the soul explained passions, "sympathies," and many other experiences. Whereas Descartes had appealed to phenomena such as a man's involuntary blinking at the shake of another's hand near his face to argue that many human actions were purely corporeal and mechanical, More argued that most responses of this kind could be explained by means of the extended soul.[37]

Newton rejected More's account of an extended soul and indeed, in many of the excerpts in the "Philosophical Questions" notebook, he was evidently taken by the negligible role in experience played by the soul in comparison with that played by education, training, and the body. Under the heading "Sympathie and Antipathie," for example, he recorded that values arising from with the five senses were all dependent on the beholder, and that when it came to music there was no disputing about taste. Under the heading "Of Sensation," he noted from More the fact that "to them of Java Pepper is cold," and he formulated the general principle that it was the bodily constitution of men, along with their culture and education, which gave rise to many of their responses to various objects and situations. Another key source was Joseph Glanvill's *Vanity of Dogmatizing* of 1661. Glanvill emphasised the extent to which philosophers were ignorant both of the physical causes of the union between the soul and the body, and of how self-motion was executed. To determine what actions properly belonged to the soul, it was essential to determine what bodily actions were fundamentally mechanical. In a note titled "Of Motion," Newton took down Glanvill's example of an artist who "plays a lesson not minding a stroke [and] sings neither minding nor missing a note." Continuing the theme of involuntary motion, he noted a passage from More on the visible causes of a snail's motion, in which the Cambridge Platonist had attributed the snail's movement to a perpetual motion of spirits traversing a circuit via the head, back, tail, belly, and thence to the head. Many human and animal actions, Newton decided, such as inducing vomiting by inserting a whalebone down one's throat, were equally mechanical.[38]

Newton's musings on the key role played by the body in human experience are closely related to the highly unorthodox conception of both human and animal souls that he described in another "Philosophical Questions" entry titled "Of ye creation." Although extremely brief, this section is the production of a young man prepared to think innovatively on even the most theologically delicate subjects. He noted that whereas the Hebrew word ברא ("bara," create) used in Genesis 1:1 was conventionally interpreted as meaning creation out of nothing, the same word was used in Genesis 1:21 to describe the creation of great whales and other beasts. However, this could not be an entirely new creation since the matter from which they were produced had existed before, presumably as the Prime Matter. Nor could the term refer to the creation of the soul (or "forme") of a specific creature, such as a whale, since an animal's soul was neither specific to itself nor to its species. Instead, Newton continued, "there may be but one kind of irrationall soule wch joined wth severall kinds of bodys, make severall kinds of beasts." Animals only differed from one another as a result of various contingent features of their bodies, which were their different natural instincts. According to this notion, before the soul of a whale was joined to the whale it could not rightly be termed the soul of a whale, since it was just as much the soul of a horse: "& this creating y^n of whales & severall other creatures must be noe but modifying matter into ye body of a whale & infusing an irrationall soule into it." Underpinning Newton's claim was the assumption, which he expressed in a shorthand interlined comment, that to suppose God created different souls for different beasts was to suppose that he did more than he needed. This appeal to the principle of parsimony, as we shall see later in this book, would play a key role in many of his theological arguments.[39]

Newton did not hesitate to deal with the trickier subject of human souls, emphasising that these too were "of one kind," though of a different type from the irrational soul of animals. While human souls were presumably not identical to one another, he devoted little space to a theological case for their distinctiveness. Indeed, for the most part, humans were very like animals; people varied greatly; they loved, hated, or feared different things and few men, he noted, were "of ye same temper wch diversity arises from theire bodys (for all theire soules are alike)." Newton left no further comment on the topic, and no doubt he did not believe there was one kind of rational soul. However, later he added beneath this account the brief sentence "Eccles: 33 vrs 10 Adam was created of ye Earth," which is a reference to the apocryphal Ecclesiasticus (The Wisdom of Sirach) 33:10. The canonical account of Adam's being formed from dust was Genesis 2:7, and 1 Corinthians 15:46-47 asserted—in the context of Adam—that what was natural came first, and then came the spiritual; the "first man" was from the earth, and "earthy," while the "second man" was the Lord from heaven. For most expositors these passages emphasised the idea that like Adam, human beings were of a corporeal and fallen nature before they were made regenerate. Newton's emphasis on the natural body served a different purpose, and his notes were designed to show that the chief differences between humans, and between animals, lay in their physical characteristics.[40]

Although much of human experience was attributable to actions of the body, Newton drew liberally from More's *Immortality* for evidence that the brain was the command centre for a great deal of corporeal action. He recorded More's various accounts of where the Common Sensorium might be located, but gave no indication that he agreed that the soul was extended throughout the body in the way More described. Under the heading "Of Sensation," he noted that physicians had found that many diseases such as epilepsy were caused by problems with the "Animall functions" in the brain. If a frog's brain were pierced it would lose the capacity to feel anything or to move itself, though it would leap around and retain its sensory faculties if its bowels were removed. Newton offered somewhat contradictory evidence when he recorded that even if cerebral wounds were made deep into the human brain, provided that the same wounds failed to penetrate the four ventricles at its centre, victims could still retain control of their senses and exercise voluntary motion. However, drawing on a typically Morean piece of information, he added that putting weight on a man's brain when he was trepanned (i.e., when a hole had been made in his skull) rendered him incapable of either.[41]

Of greater interest to Newton was the nature and content of dreams, which seemed to occupy the hinterland between body and soul. In a short section titled "Of Sleepe and Dreames" he pointed out that although the memory of dreams was fleeting, the fact that external events could prompt memory of things of which the conscious soul was unaware suggested that the soul might always be actively dreaming while sleeping, and it was certainly capable of producing random images when one was awake. In the section of "Philosophical Questions" titled "Of Memory," he argued that thoughts and the recall of dreams could be triggered by "meeting wth other things of a like nature," while forgetfulness often arose from "ye want of think-ing of things." Dreams and thoughts were more easily remembered than information arriving via the senses: "Meditations remind men of actions, & actions of meditatio[ns]." He concluded the section by arguing that there had to be some dynamic input of the soul in any act of remembering, for even if memory took place by dint of characters or tokens the soul had to remember what those characters meant. In his 1662 list of sins, Newton had mentioned having "uncleane thoughts words and actions and dreams," and he continued to be fascinated by their causes and often baneful effects. As we shall see in the following section, his first research programme was designed in part to discover the causes of dreams and madness.[42]

This view was rehearsed in a section titled "Of ye soule," in which Newton argued that thought could not be mere matter in motion, because then we would never be able to voluntarily recall anything to memory. Memory had to be equated with the *act* of remembering and indeed the dynamic and non-mechanical operation of the faculty of memory was also responsible for instigating the recall of a "phantasme," that is, a specific memory. Newton took an important set of notes from Hobbes's *De Corpore*, commenting that when dreaming, things appeared as vibrant as they did when awake, but that when awake, things experienced in the past seemed more obscure than things perceived in the present. However, if the motion causing past and present "phantasms" were equally strong then we would never forget any-thing, and there would be no difference between what we experienced through "sense," and what we experienced via "phantasie." Although he re-jected Hobbes's extreme materialism, *De Corpore* provided a framework with which Newton could assess the explanatory limits of materialism. In the "Philosophical Questions" notebook he had already determined that natural phenomena that were not merely mechanical could nevertheless be the sub-ject of natural philosophy. His interest soon fell on the faculty of the imagi-nation, which, he believed, mirrored the creative powers of God.[43]

6. Heightening the Imagination

The imagination had a dual role in early modern accounts of the faculties of the soul, being the recipient of images from the senses, which it then stored. Older theories of the imagination held that it passed on images to the faculty of "phantasia" or "fantasy," which combined the images to create "phantasmata." As the active and independent creator of both truthful and fanciful combinations of these images, the imagination also had a reputation for being a powerful source of creativity, though this could make it unruly and even dangerous. Early on in his career, Newton respected the power of the imagination while fearing its baneful religious and philosophical consequences. Some philosophers, including Descartes, accorded a significant role to the imagination in making scientific discoveries but others argued that eradicating its corrupting effects was a necessary prelude to reforming natural philosophy. Although there were many religious and philosophical sources for understanding the workings and dangers of the imaginative faculty, the most influential account of the dangerous effects of the imagination in the context of natural philosophy was to be found in Francis Bacon's *Novum Organum* (1620) and *De Augmentis Scientiarum* (1623). Bacon identified the imagination as a key source of the false "idols" that clouded or corrupted the mind and prevented the philosopher from discovering truths about the natural world. It was the chief source of error, giving rise to the over-hasty and empty speculations, and worse, the vain systems that philosophers were prone to forge. Newton would follow his experimentalist contemporaries in contrasting the good effects of reason, experience, and hard work with the dangerous personal and philosophical consequences that followed when the imagination was allowed to hold sway.[44]

Early on in his studies Newton seems to have valued the imagination as the source of creativity, and his earliest experimental research programme may have been designed to enhance his own powers of creativity. In one entry in the "Philosophical Questions" notebook composed around the middle of 1664, he added the words "& invention" above the line of the title "Immagination. & Phantasie." In this section he noted conventional lore surrounding the best way to promote the workings of the imagination but he also remarked on how to avoid its deleterious effects. As usual, he took some key information from More's *Immortality*:

We can fancie y^e thing wee see in a right posture wth y^e heeles upward. Phantasie is helped by good aire fasting moderate wine but spoiled by drunkenesse. Gluttony, too much study, (whence & from extreame passion cometh madnesse) dizzinesse, commotions of y^e spirits. Meditation heates $y^{<e>}$oun braine in some to distraction in others to an akeing & dizzinesse. The boyling blood of youth puts y^e spirits upon too much motion or else causet[h] too many

spirits, but could [*sic*] age makes yᵉ brain either two dry to move roundly
through or else is defective of spirits yet theire memory is bad.

These notes continued with an excerpt from Glanvill's *Vanity of Dogmatizing*. Glanvill included a chapter in his work that detailed the dangers of the
imagination, a faculty that when unrestrained could lead to the terrors of
enthusiasm and madness. From his chapter on things that were strange but
true, Newton extracted the fact that "a man by heitning his fansie & immagination may bind anothers to thinke what hee thinks as in yᵉ story of yᵉ
Oxford scollar." The imagination was closely related to cognition but it was
also closely connected to memory and the will. Its power could be developed and Newton decided that it could be subjected to experimental
enquiry.[45]

Glanvill's story told of an impoverished student who had left Oxford
University and joined up with some "Vagabond Gypsies," learning their
"Mystery" by insinuating himself into their company. Although he was recognised one day by other students who were passing the entourage, the
scholar convinced them not to reveal his true identity. Taking them to one
side he told them that the gypsies had "a *traditional* kind of *learning*" and
"could do wonders by the power of their *Imagination*." He had learned the
art and even improved it, and to prove this he went into another room for
a few minutes, returning to tell the scholars that he knew what they had
been discussing in his absence because he himself had been responsible
for the content of their conversation. There were "warrantable ways," the
scholar told his friends, "of heightening the *Imagination* to that pitch as to
bind anothers." To explain this Glanvill proposed that the "agitated parts
of the Brain" might instigate motion in the surrounding aether, and this
motion in turn be propagated through bodily fluids. As musical strings
could be made to vibrate in sympathy with one another, so motion could
be conveyed "from the *Brain* of one man to the *Phancy* of another." These
words provoked Newton into action, and soon after reading this section of
The Vanity he devised a series of experiments through which he explored
the nature of the imagination.[46]

Immediately following his notes on Glanvill, Newton entered reports of
an exercise that involved him looking at the sun in order to test whether
external objects or the "fantasy" was responsible for vision. The idea of
looking at the sun almost certainly came from reading Robert Boyle's recently published *Experiments and Considerations Touching Colours*, in which
Boyle reported having looked at the fiery globe through a telescope (with

coloured glass as a protective device). As a result of this, vivid and permanent impressions were made on Boyle's retina and looking at any bright light caused numerous afterimages. Newton performed a similar procedure, after which "all light coloured bodys appeared red & darke coloured bodys appeared red blew." He imported language from Glanvill's *Vanity* into his description of the experiments, showing that the trials were explicitly designed to test the nature and physical limits of the power of the imagination. Newton reported that when the "motion of y^e spirits" in his eye had almost "decayed," so that he "could see all things wth their natur[al] colours," he shut the eye again and "could see noe colour or image till I heightned my fantasie of seeing $\odot$ & y^n began to appeare a blew spot wch grew ligter by degrees in y^e midst until it was white & bright." From all this, he concluded, "I gather my Phantasie & y^e $\odot$ had y^e same operation uppon y^e ~~optick~~ spirits in my optick nerve & y^t y^e same motions are caused in my braine by both." Now when he opened his eyes in the dark exactly the same "phantasms" appeared to him as when his eyes were closed.[47]

In a now lost letter of early 1691, the philosopher John Locke asked Newton about a passage in Boyle's work where Boyle had mentioned a renowned scholar who had ruined his eyes looking at the sun through a telescope without the benefit of a coloured glass. In his reply Newton recalled his undergraduate experiments and noted that whenever he had looked at a bright object, or even a window, the apparition of the sun would reappear. The fact that he could recall the image whenever he concentrated suggested that this involved another problem concerning "the power of phansy" which, he added, was "too hard a knot for me to untye." Such images could not arise from motion alone (this was a familiar argument in the "Philosophical Questions" entries), since then the image of the sun would appear constantly, but they seemed "rather to consist in a disposition of ye sensorium to move ye imagination strongly & to be easily moved both by ye imagination & by ye light as often as bright objects are looked upon." Newton recalled that looking at the sun had seriously compromised his ability to see anything at all, and it had resulted in his confinement to bed for a number of days, during which he did everything he could to divert his imagination from the sun.[48]

Much of Newton's visual and mental damage was caused by the fact that he repeated his experiments. As he recorded in the notebook, having completed a first run of these trials he waited two to three hours until his eye had recovered somewhat and then redid them. Now, he wrote, when he looked at clouds with his good eye, "I could see y^e ⊙ pictured on y^e cloudes or other white objects almost as plaine as if I had looked wth my distempered ey y^e other being shut $^<$& every where about ⊙ appeared a dusky red & blacknesse$^>$." At the end of all this, he could not stop seeing "images" of the sun: "I made such impress on y^e optick nerve y^t let me looke wth wch eye I would ⊙ offered itself to my vew unless I set my fantasie to work on other things wch wth much difficulty I could doe." When the sun's image was not too strongly affecting his vision, he continued, "I could easily imagine severall shapes ~~to be where I usually appre~~ as if I saw y^m in y^e ⊙s place," from which "perhaps may be gathered y^t ye tenderest sight argues ye clearest fantasie of things visible & hence something of ye nature of madnesse & dreames may be gathered." In a final entry, Newton noted that after two days in this state his eyes had been made tender by staying in a dark room for a few hours. His investigations allowed him to explore much broader questions than the merely visual effects that arose from enhancing the power of the fancy.[49] These were seminal experimental enquiries for testing the nature and limits of the power of the imagination. Newton was seeking to bring various natural phenomena and indeed, a number of fundamental human capacities within the purview of natural philosophy. The references to dreams and madness, harking back to the earlier notes from More, and even to his 1662 "confession," provide broader contexts for the programme. As we shall see in chapter 5, this was not the only area where Newton would be concerned about the need to manage the imagination, and his concerns about the fancy had a strong religious foundation.

7. Trepanning the Aether

The analogy between divine and human attributes to which Newton was committed licensed another line of enquiry, and along with attempting to determine experimentally the extent of the power of the imagination, Newton also sought to discover the physiological basis of self-motion. Not long after the "Questiones" researches, his investigations into the nature of the brain, and its role in producing images, took a new turn. He dissected both optic nerves of a sheep, recording that each point in the retina of one eye had a corresponding point in the other, and he noted that from these two points ran "two very slender pipes, filled wth a most lympid liquor... wthout either interruption or any other uneavenesse or irregularity."

These vessels joined up on one side of the brain and according to Newton, they then united into one of two "pipes," continuing deeper into the brain until the two tubes were united. However, the images that came in from each eye could not voyage separately along the unifying pipe to their destination and he suggested that the image "wch is strongest or most helped by fantacy will there prevail and blot out the other." What the physical causes of these images were was also susceptible to experimental investigation. At one point, Newton heated an optic nerve to test whether this would result in the production of an "aery substance" manifested as bubbles, which would indicate the presence of "animal spirits." He found nothing, but reasoned that this was not surprising, since no "aery body" was fine enough to pervade the pores of the brain and nerves "wthout violence." Animal spirits would be a poor way of conducting to the sensorium the very subtle motions caused by vision, and he concluded that it was by means of aetherial vibrations that information travelled along the "pure transparent liquor" filling the pipes.[50]

These early experiments were a significant source for Newton's understanding of the nature and functions of the aether, and also for explaining how the mind moved the body. They would be invoked in different contexts over the next decades, and in his more mature philosophy he argued that explaining freely exercised self-motion was central to understanding how God created the world. As a theological question, the issue of free will was not something on which he expended any significant effort at all, but at some point he decided that experiments on the physiological mechanism by which the soul freely moved the body could provide a means of better grasping the workings of God. As a result of the dissection of the optic nerve and other similar investigations, Newton decided that experiments on the aether were the key to understanding these processes. He presented the results of these enquiries in the "Hypothesis" concerning the causes of light and colours that he sent to Henry Oldenburg, secretary of the Royal Society in December 1675.[51]

The "Hypothesis" explored a large array of subjects concerning the human body and the physical world. At the heart of Newton's exposition lay his understanding of the nature of the aether, and for this he drew from his contemporary alchemical work comparing the way plants, animals, and metals all "vegetated." In a text called "Of Nature's Obvious Laws and processes in vegetation," which dates from the early to mid-1670s, he argued that God formed "protoplasts" at the beginning of time and that nature could only nourish them. However, nature did not only operate in an ordinary "mechanical" way and there was "a more subtile, secret & noble way of working in all vegetation which makes its products distinct from all others." The site of this extraordinary activity was "an exceeding subtile & [‹]inimaginably[›] small portion of matter diffused through the masse, wch if it were seperated, there would remain but a dead & inactive earth." As it was, Newton continued, the earth was alive, resembling "a great animall ‹or rather inanimate vegetable›," which "draws in aetheriall breath for its dayly refreshment ‹and vital ferment› and transpires again wth gross exhalations." This breath was the source of life and growth; the aether itself was "probably a vehicle to some more active sp[irit] & ye bodys may bee concreted of both together." The spirit was "intangled" in the aether and was the "material soule of all matter"—perhaps, Newton added, being light itself. Both the aetherial spirit and light had a "prodigious active principle, ‹both are per-petuall workers›" and "heate exites light & light exites heat, heat excites ye vegetable principle & that ~~excites~~ increaseth heat." Although this text re-mained unpublished, his work on the aether underpinned the argument in the "Hypothesis" and its underlying concepts reappeared four decades later—in different language—in the "Queries" to his 1717 *Opticks*.[52]

In the "Hypothesis" Newton proposed that the aether was like air but much subtler, rarer, and more "elastic." He considered that like air, the aether was a heterogeneous mixture. In a passage that he later asked Oldenburg to insert for publication, he argued that Nature was perhaps composed of "nothing but various Contextures of some certaine aetheriall Spirits or vapours condens'd as it were by praecipitation"—again by analogy with what was discernible in the aerial atmosphere. After being condensed, these "contextures" were "wrought into various forms, at first by the immediate hand of the Creator, and ever since by the power of Nature, wch by virtue of the command Increase & Multiply, became a complete Imitator of the copies sett her by the Protoplast." Newton argued that electrical phenom-ena demonstrated that some quasi-aetherial substance was condensed in bodies, and he claimed that a similar aetherial spirit might be "condensed in fermenting or burning bodies, or otherwise inspissated in ye pores of ye earth to a tender matter wch may be as it were ye succus nutritious of ye earth or primary substance out of wch things generable grow." He repeated the claim from his alchemical text to the effect that nature was a "perpetuall circulatory worker," and also rehearsed the notion that the Earth condensed this aether for its own use.[53]

Newton then discussed the role played by the aether in self-motion, focussing on the mechanism by which the soul might move the muscles. The question of how muscles acted in various states had been the focus of renewed attention by scholars. The physician Thomas Willis outlined an account of muscular contraction using chemical principles in his *Cerebri Anatome* of 1664 and in his *Pathologiæ Cerebri* of 1667. In the former he argued that contraction occurred when animal spirits from the nerves met up with "saline-sulphureous" particles from the arterial blood, whereupon the "copula" formed by the union of the two would break and give rise to an "explosion" when stimulated by the nerves. In *Pathologiæ Cerebri*, this explanatory system changed so that the explosive nature of muscular action was caused by a meeting of "spirituo-saline" particles from the nerves and "nitro-sulphurous" particles from the blood. In another tract of 1670 on the notion of the muscles, Willis paid more attention to the question of how the "tender and immoveable Brain" could bring about muscular contraction by means of the "small and fragile nerves." Since such a situation could not be effected by the brain alone, the cause of violent contraction had to lie in the explosive potential of a meeting between the animal spirits supplied to the tendons or in the muscle itself, and a subtle sulphureous or nitrous liquor derived from the blood. The precise mechanism by which the brain regulated the flow of animal spirits in and out of the tendons was complicated in Willis's scheme, although it was this feature that controlled the extent of contraction.[54]

Newton was clearly aware of the basic doctrines contained in these works but remained wedded to an explanation couched in terms of the aether. In a short, separate text inserted into the text of the "Hypothesis" that he sent to Oldenburg, he argued that a difference in density between the aethers outside and inside the body's muscles might explain what he called "that puzleing Problem"; namely "by what means the Muscles are contracted and dilated to cause Animal motion." Newton hoped that this could "receive greater Light from hence then from any other means men have hitherto been thinking on." If a man could "condense & dilate at will" the aether that pervaded muscle tissue, it would change the force exerted on the muscle by the surrounding aether and make it expand or shrink. This was in principle subject to experimental enquiry; water could not easily be compressed in an air-pump, but Spirit of Wine (i.e., ethanol) and Oil could. Accordingly he suggested that an experiment in which Boyle had caused a tadpole to shrink by attempting to compress the water in which it swam, indicated that it was the creature's "animal juices" that had been compressed. Newton invoked the analogy of Boyle's notion of the Spring of the Air to explain how the muscle would respond to changes in the relative density of the internal and external aethers. Given the exceptional "springiness" of the aether relative to the air, it might not require very much change in the consistency of the "muscular" aether in order to change the shape and texture of the muscle.[55]

This topic had formed the context of a conversation that took place between Newton and Robert Boyle in early 1675, when Newton visited London. In a letter sent to Oldenburg a week after he dispatched the "Hypothesis" (in December 1675), Newton asked him to thank Boyle for the discourse they had had in London, during which they had discussed what Boyle had called Newton's "conceit of trapanning ye common Ether." The sense of this vaguely playful remark is obscure, although the reference to trepanning suggests that the conversation concerned mind-body interaction. In any case, the topic of their talk was clearly related to his project of accounting for the physiology of animal motion in terms of the aether. Newton expressed his hope that when Boyle had "a set of exp^s to try in his air pump, he will make that one to see how ye compression or relaxation of a muscle will shrink or swell, soften or harden, lengthen or shorten it." Although this would have been a relatively easy task with air, Newton evidently hoped that there might be some experimental means of manipulating the aether to see what effect this had on the muscle.[56]

In the "Hypothesis" Newton argued that it was possible that the soul had "an imediate power over the whole aether in any part of the body to Swell or Shrink it at will," but this left unresolved the nature of the dependency of muscular motion on the nerves, which presumably carried the commends from the soul to the muscles. Alternatively, it could be done by means of the soul acting upon the "aetheriall Spirit" in the *Dura Mater* (the outer layer of the three membranes that surround the brain and spinal cord), but, he continued, "still theres a difficulty why this force of the soule upon it does not take off the power of its Springines whereby it should susteyne more or less the force of the Outward Æther." A third possibility was that the soul could *directly* instill this spirit into any muscle by means of the nerves, but this foundered on the difficulty of conceiving how the "tender matter" of the brain and nerves could accomplish "a forcible intending the Spring of the aether in the muscles by pressure." Drawing directly from his earlier researches on the optic nerve, Newton argued that the spirit was so subtle that there appeared to be no good reason why it should not dissipate through the *Dura Mater* and skin.[57]

To solve the problem, Newton invoked the same animal spirits he had been unable to locate almost a decade earlier, but these were now aetherial in nature, and subtle enough to permeate the animal juices in the same manner that magnetic and electric effluvia did glass. There remained the problem of why such subtle spirits did not merely dissipate into the air. To solve this Newton suggested that one could conceive how the coatings of the brain, nerves, and muscles could become "a convenient vessell to hold so subtile a Spirit" by taking into account how some liquors and spirits were disposed to pervade or not pervade boundaries notwithstanding their degree of fineness. Some fluids, like oil and water, were prevented from mixing, Newton claimed, "by some secret principle of unsociablenes." This "unsociablenes" might exist in aetherial substances, acting to keep the solar and terrestrial vortices apart from each other or to keep aether rarer in the pores of bodies than in open spaces. No matter how subtle the aetheriall vital spirit was in man, it could be contained within the coatings of the brain, nerves, and muscles if it was unsociable to them, despite being very sociable to the marrow and juices. To make it suitable for animal motion, Newton argued that some chemical substances that were naturally unsociable could be made sociable by the introduction of a third element:

> in like manner the aethereal Animal Spirit in a man may be a mediator between the common aether & the muscular juices to make them mix more freely; & so by sending a litle of this Spirit into any muscle, though so little as to cause no sensible tension of the muscle of its owne force, yet by rendering the juices more Sociable to the common external aether, it may cause that aether to pervade the muscle of its owne accord in a moment more freely & copiously then it would otherwise do & to recede againe as freely so soon as this Mediator of Sociablenes is retracted.

Since, by hypothesis, the "Spring" of the aether in the muscle was so great, very little of this aetherial animal spirit would have to be introduced into the muscle to effect great alteration in the internal pressure. Newton would speculate no further, and he noted that people were free to offer their own mechanical and non-mechanical accounts of the phenomenon. The difficulty of the topic led to the thought that there was still much to learn about it, but it also suggested that the creator worked in many ways that we had yet to comprehend: "God who gave Animals self motion beyond our understanding is without doubt able to implant other principles of motion in bodies wch we may understand as little."[58]

8. In the Image of God

Although the analysis in the "Hypothesis" ended with an abrupt warning about the limits of human knowledge, the experimental investigation of self-motion continued to beguile Newton. In the "Queries" to the *Optice* of 1706 he asked rhetorically how the faculty of the human will gave rise to the motions of the body, and in a draft passage intended for the same text he classified the indisputable power of self-motion among a series of non-mechanical "active principles." This he described as "the power of life & Will by which animals move their bodies with great and lasting force." On other occasions he seemed to exclude the power of the will from the category of active principles, claiming that "we meet with very little motion on the world besides what is (visibly) owing to these active principles, & the power of the will." As for explaining for this power, he remarked in another draft "Query" that the existence of life and the reality of free will demonstrated that there had to be other (undiscovered) laws of motion. His parting statement in the "General Scholium" appended to the second edition of his *Principia Mathematica* of 1713 was a call to examine the vibrations of a most subtle "electric and elastic spirit" that moved along the solid filaments of the nerves from the sensory organs to the brain, and at the command of the will, from the brain to the muscles. There were insufficient experiments to determine the laws by which this spirit operated, he concluded, and he added that the phenomenon could not be explained in a few words.[59]

The analogy between the human and the divine would remain at the heart of Newton's theological metaphysics. In the essay on God, space, and time that he penned in the early 1690s, the analogy between man and God played a key role. Was it not most agreeable to reason, he asked, that God's creatures shared his attributes as far as possible "as fruit the nature of the tree, and an image the likeness of a man," and by sharing tend towards perfection? Similarly, was it not reasonable to believe that God could be discerned in the more perfect creatures "as in a mirror"? Such a view also enabled humans to understand the being and attributes of the divine. The most perfect idea of God, Newton concluded, and the one that was most easily understood, was that he was a living substance "which by his own presence discerns and rules all things, just as the cognitive part of man perceives the forms of things brought into the brain, and thereby governs his own body." God could enact all possible things with perfect freedom, accomplishing everything that was best and that most accorded with reason. By freely governing one's own actions, human beings thus mimicked the boundless dominance of the *pantokrator* (the Almighty) over his own creation. Newton's voluntaristic conception of God's activity, that is, the idea that God created things and values by mere force of his will, became one of the best-known features of his metaphysical theology, and his accounts of God's creative powers, effected by a mere act of will, were often accompanied by statements about analogous powers in humans. For example, in Query 23 of the *Optice* (Query 31 of the 1717/18 *Opticks*) he noted that God was more able to move bodies in his sensorium by means of his will, and "thereby to form and reform the Parts of the Universe," than humans were able to move parts of their own bodies by their wills.[60]

Newton only published the residue of these experimental enquiries many decades later, in two "Queries" to his *Optice* and in the General Scholium. Although short, they played key roles in his most famous and influential statements about the divine purposes of natural philosophy and the nature of God. In Queries 20 and 23 of the *Optice*, he suggested that the phenomena of the world demonstrated the existence of an incorporeal, living, intelligent, and omnipresent being who "thoroughly perceived" objects by their immediate presence to him. Newton likened all of infinite space to this being's "sensorium," which, he argued, was the location where God was present to his creation. Others, however, charged that Newton had made the world God's sensory organ. This super-sensorium functioned in stark contrast to the restricted domain of the "little sensoriums" of humans whose "thinking substance" merely perceived the images of things and needed organs of sense to do so. As we have seen, he used the human-divine analogy on various occasions to emphasise both similarities and differences between the respective sensoria. In unpublished drafts of the "Queries" for the *Optice* he noted the strong analogy between them, and he emphasised that divine attributes were adumbrated in the human mind. In the *Optice*, he repeated his assertion in "De gravitatione" that the human soul was formed in the Image of God. The very first printed exemplars of the work stated that infinite space *was* the sensorium of God, clearly leaving Newton open to the accusations either that he had committed the materialist heresy of making the world God's body, or worse, that he followed Spinoza in identifying God with Nature. He did his best to suppress these copies and inserted a new version of the passage, in which he argued that God was present to things in his creation *as if* the universe were his sensorium. However, Gottfried Leibniz, the great German philosopher and mathematician who had almost certainly seen the early version, argued that the original text more accurately represented what Newton really believed.[61]

After this, Newton was more careful to emphasise the dis-analogy between the human and the divine. In the General Scholium he protested that God did not possess a body and stressed that the divine mode of being in the world was "not at all human" and "utterly unknown to us." In the second (1717) edition of the English *Opticks*, written in the wake of the correspondence between Leibniz and Samuel Clarke, he deleted altogether the reference to the human soul being made in God's image. To emphasise that he was no materialist, Newton observed that God lacked sensory organs and cautioned that we were "not to consider" the world as his body. However, the similarity between the human and the divine lay at the heart of his religion, and he retained the references to the analogy between divine and human sensoria in the two relevant Queries. In the General Scholium, Newton compared the indivisibility of the human soul throughout an individual's life to the eternal immutability of God, and in a personal note entered into his own interleaved copy of the *Principia*, he connected his own coherent identity throughout his life with the unchanging eternity and ubiquity of God. If theological alarm bells had tinkled with the comments on the divine sensorium in the *Optice*, now they rang out more loudly, and one reader wrote in his own copy of the General Scholium: "Does he not through this definition of persons exclude the Trinity, imagining God as existing in one person, for no other reason than because man exists in one person?" Whether or not this perceptive commentator had independent evidence of Newton's anti-Trinitarian views, he had not only pointed to the key role played by the analogy between the finite and infinite sensoria in Newton's work, but had identified the central question at the heart of Newton's theology.[62]

4

From Liberty to Heresy

After the early 1670s, Newton would never again undertake serious experimental work on the imagination, or indulge in the sort of metaphysical work exemplified in "De Gravitatione." Moreover, by the time he sent his "Hypothesis" on light and colour to the Royal Society at the end of 1675, he had long since tired of his dealings with the Republic of Letters, and even of natural philosophy itself. He had become disillusioned with the scientific community almost immediately after he had published his first article. This paper, an essay on light and colours, was published in the *Philosophical Transactions* in 1672 and proved that white light was heterogeneously composed of more basic, primary rays. However, soon afterwards, Newton was complaining that the need to deal with correspondents was incompatible with the freedom he needed to pursue and discuss his research. The best place to do this, he believed, was in a collegiate environment, where he could work unmolested and converse about his findings with friendly commentators. By the middle of the decade, he was protesting that work in the exact sciences was itself a distraction from more significant pursuits. Although Newton was also working vigorously on "chymistry," the "other studies" to which he often referred increasingly concerned projects in church history and theology. He had different reasons from those relating to his scientific, mathematical, and alchemical researches for being unwilling to release his theological ideas to a wider audience.[1]

This reticence about dealing with the public sphere was obvious even in Newton's first known contact with scholars outside Cambridge. This occurred in the summer of 1669, when he allowed a mathematical work, now known as "De Analysi," to be circulated among London mathematicians. It was with his permission that Isaac Barrow sent it on to the mathematician John Collins, who coordinated a wide range of mathematical activities in London. As a result both of Barrow's decision to resign the Lucasian Professorship and the positive reception of "De Analysi," Newton was elected to the Lucasian Chair on 29 October 1669. A month later he met Collins in a London inn. Since there was at this time no adequate English introduction to algebra, Collins asked him to write one for a Latin version of Gerard Kinckhuysen's *Algebra*. He later told the mathematician John Gregory that although Newton had agreed to do this, he had not pushed Newton for further material, having noticed "a wariness in him to impart, or at least an unwillingness to be at the paines of so doing." Despite having to prepare his first series of Lucasian lectures, Newton worked on his "Observations" on Kinckhuysen in the winter of 1669–70 and he continued to add to them until July 1670 when he sent them to Collins. Collins was sufficiently confident that they would appear in print that he told Gregory on Christmas Eve that the edition of Kinckhuysen, with Newton's notes and additions (made "at the request of Dr Barrow"), was ready for the press.[2]

Newton's apparent reticence about revealing his underlying methods to a wider audience was accompanied by statements that made it clear that he wanted to avoid acquiring a public reputation. In February 1670 he told Collins that publication of one of his solutions to a mathematical problem in the *Philosophical Transactions* "would perhaps increase my acquaintance, ye thing wch I cheifly study to decline... I see not what there is desirable in publick esteeme, were I able to acquire & maintaine it." In July Newton informed Collins that he could print his commentary on Kinckhuysen, adding ominously that he had not written the notes with the intention that they be printed, but only to satisfy Collins's wish to have the book revised. In September he remarked that he had considered writing his own introduction to algebra but had decided against it, worried that "there being severall Introductions to Algebra already published I might thereby gain y^t esteeme of one ambitious among ye croud to have my scribbles printed." This disdain for print culture and public repute was a common rhetorical pose among writers of poetry, but in the new era of scientific journals and institutions, Newton's professed contempt for the public sphere and for print publication was anachronistic and as it turned out, unsustainable.[3]

Partly in homage to Barrow's choice of topics for his Lucasian lectures, Newton chose to make geometrical optics the subject of his own disquisitions when he began giving them in January 1670. Similarly, his confidence in his capacity to mathematize nature was a continuation of the sentiments that Barrow had expressed in the mathematical lectures that Newton had attended many years earlier. By October 1671 a version of Newton's lectures was in an advanced state of preparation for publication, and Barrow told

Collins that it was "one of the greatest performances of Ingenuity this age hath affoarded." At the same time, Newton embarked on substantial revisions of his work on infinite series and fluxions, the latter being the rate of change of any quantity at a given moment (nowadays known as the derivative of a function). His brilliant treatise on the subject, the "Tractatus de Methodis serierum et fluxionum," was a major exposition that, if it had been published at the time, would have put him at the forefront of European mathematics. Snippets from it would form the basis of some of his later work, including the two letters, or "epistolae," sent in 1676 to the secretary of the Royal Society Henry Oldenburg to be passed on to Gottfried Leibniz. By Christmas 1671, Newton had begun a revision of his proposed optical work, and in its finished state the second version (the "Optica") was almost half as long again as the first. More than at any other stage of his life, he was ready and willing to flood the Republic of Letters with his own productions.[4]

However, within weeks Newton had suspended his plans to publish his work. Shortly after Barrow sent Newton's reflecting telescope to the Royal Society at the end of 1671, Newton wrote to Oldenburg to say that he was surprised that the Society had taken so much notice of his instrument, especially given that he himself placed so little value on it. Invoking more rhetorical commonplaces, he added that if the Society had not wanted him to send it, he "might have let it still remained [sic] in private as it hath already done some yeares." He closed by saying that, having been proposed as a candidate to the Society, if he were elected he would show his gratitude by communicating what his "poore & solitary endeavours can effect towards ye promoting your Philosophicall designes." In a much less humble letter sent soon afterwards, Newton told Oldenburg that he wished to send the Society an account of the extraordinarily significant scientific discovery that had induced him to construct the telescope. In his opinion, Newton added, it was "the oddest if not the most considerable detection" that had been made in the history of science.[5]

1. The End of Liberty

The momentous paper Newton sent to Oldenburg on 6 February 1672 was published (with some changes) in the *Philosophical Transactions* and marked his first exposure before a broad audience. He related how in 1666 he had allowed sunlight to pass through a prism onto a wall twenty-two feet away, following the "celebrated *Phænomena* of *Colours*" mentioned in Descartes's *Meteorology*. He was surprised to see an oblong figure instead of the circular shape predicted under the older modification theory (according to which colours were produced when white light was altered in some way), and after carefully measuring the angles involved, resolved the cause of the phenomenon by means of a "crucial experiment" that showed "that *Light* consists of *Rays differently refrangible*." Individual primary rays that together made up white light were associated with specific, immutable colours and each had its own index of refraction.[6] Midway through the narrative, Newton suddenly changed his mode of exposition and broke decisively with the "historical" narrative, arguing that the science of colours could become mathematical with as much certainty in it as in any other field of optics. His doctrine was not a mere hypothesis or conjecture, he urged, but was "evinced by ye mediation of experiments concluding directly & wthout suspicion of doubt."[7]

Some days later, Oldenburg told Newton that the fellows had applauded his "Ingeniosity, as well as [his] high degree of francknesse" in sending them his findings. Newton traded compliments, stating that he took it to be a great privilege "that instead of exposing discourses to a prejudic't and censorious multitude (by wch many truths have been bafled and lost) I may wth freedom apply myself to so judicious & impartiall an assembly." However, he already knew that there was a potential problem with the way he had presented his work. When Oldenburg told him that the Society had voted for his paper to be printed in the *Philosophical Transactions*, Newton replied that he suspected it was "too straight & narrow for publick view," having designed it only for those "that know how to improve upon hints of things." "To shun tediousnesse," he added, he had "omitted many such remarques & experiments." His appeal to a specialist rather than a general audience mimicked his procedure in every other area of his research, but this approach would force him over the following years to continually explain his methods and views for other scholars. Combined with his secrecy about the extensive range of optical experiments he had already performed, this attitude effectively condemned him to participate in the very disputes about intellectual property that he despised.[8]

The revolutionary nature of Newton's work on telescopes, light, and the theory of colours immediately exposed him to a number of comments, criticisms, and queries. The major European natural philosophers Christiaan

Huygens, Jean-Baptiste Denis, and Adrien Auzout requested more information about his reflecting telescope, while other scholars were motivated to
promote the alternative designs for the reflector devised by James Gregory
and the French inventor Laurent Cassegrain. Just over a week after he had
sent the paper on light and colours to Oldenburg, Oldenburg returned a
critique by Robert Hooke—author of *Micrographia* (1665) and the leading
natural philosopher of the Royal Society—which described Newton's
claim that white light was heterogeneous as merely one "hypothesis" among
many. The Jesuit Ignace Pardies wrote at the end of March, arguing that the
oblong image seen by Newton could be explained by assuming that the ray of
light entering the first prism had emanated from different parts of the sun,
while Sir Robert Moray, the first president of the Society, offered a series of
proposals for testing aspects of his theory. Newton was overwhelmed by his
obligation to reply to these comments and criticisms, and he told Collins at
the end of May 1672 that he had decided to scrap the publication of the
optical lectures, "finding already by that little use I have made of the Presse,
that I shall not enjoy my former serene liberty till I have done with it." He
added that he was honoured to be a member of the Royal Society, but was
"a little troubled to find my selfe cut short of that fredome of communication wch I hoped to enjoy, but cannot any longer without giving offence
to some persons whome I have ever respected." Shortly afterwards, he
completed long responses to Pardies and Hooke.[9]

In Newton's reply to Hooke he made the first of what would be oft-
repeated requests to communicate in private. This accompanied his growing
frustration at his obligations to reply to printed criticisms, and his anger at
claims that his theoretical conclusions were merely "hypotheses." In January
1673, Oldenburg passed on a series of critical comments from Christiaan
Huygens on Newton's theory of light, remarking provocatively that Huygens,
like Hooke, had referred to Newton's doctrine as an "hypothesis" or opinion. As we shall see, although many English natural philosophers made a
habit of condemning half-baked and uncorroborated hypotheses and systems, Newton's hatred of both went far beyond the routine dismissal of such
notions expressed by his contemporaries. As a result, the various remarks by
Pardies, Hooke, Huygens, and others about the hypothetical nature of his
theory were bound to trigger the extreme personal response that soon took
place. Newton told Oldenburg that he would permit his correspondence
with Huygens to be published, but he informed the stunned secretary that
he wanted to resign from the Society. He held the body in great honour, he

claimed, but added: "since I see I shall neither profit them, nor (by reason of this distance) can partake of the advantage of their Assemblies, I desire to withdraw." The missive included the £1.6s due and in reply Oldenburg excused him from making any more payments. Later Oldenburg remarked that he had told Newton how surprised he was that Newton had invoked his physical remoteness from London as a reason for his resignation, particularly as he had known this at the time of the election. However, the cultural distance between the friendly collegiate forum at Trinity, and the public sphere constituted by the ignorant and prejudiced readership of print culture, was becoming an insurmountable gulf.[10]

2. Dispensation

Little is known in detail of Newton's movements or intellectual interests for most of 1673 or 1674, although for much of this time he was working intensively on alchemy. To all intents and purposes, he had successfully extricated himself from the demands of responding to printed criticisms, but towards the end of 1674 Oldenburg sent him a letter from the Liège Jesuit Francis Linus. Linus argued that Newton had made a mistake in assuming that the physical source of the rays impinging upon the prism was only as broad as the sun's disk. This essentially rehearsed Pardies's argument from two years earlier except that Linus now claimed that the breadth of the originating arc was caused by the sun's passage through English clouds. In Newton's reply of 5 December, in which he thrice described Linus's claim as a "conjecture," he asked Oldenburg to be excused from his obligation to send in experiments on an annual basis and repeated his claim that he had long since decided to concern himself no further "about ye promotion of Philosophy." He added the rider that if he happened to be in London, he could deliver a paper written some years earlier, but then he apparently dismissed the possibility of travelling to the capital.[11]

A month later, Newton told Oldenburg that he was about to lose his fellowship at Trinity. Since his income would fall precipitously, he repeated the earlier request that he be excused his yearly subscription to the Royal Society. His impending change in status was in connection with the legal requirement that he take holy orders within seven years of becoming a fellow, and there is little doubt that when he wrote to Oldenburg, he genuinely believed that he would have to leave the college by the following autumn. However, after a meeting with senior civil servants in London at the end of February 1675 (presumably on the cards when he wrote to Oldenburg in December), Newton was given dispensation from the requirement to be ordained as a priest in the Church of England. Aside from formally allowing him freedom from various ministerial duties, the granting of this dispensation meant that he would henceforth continue as one of the few lay members of the university.[12]

This was not Newton's first attempt to avoid ordination, since almost two years earlier he had tried to gain a vacant law fellowship within the college. This unsuccessful effort adds weight to the view that he was genuinely concerned with seeking the freedom to pursue his private studies, not least because there was little obligation on the law fellow to lecture on the subject. Robert Uvedale, a horticulturalist who, according to Uvedale family lore, gained the fellowship in preference to Newton, treated the position as a sinecure and spent most of his time running his own boarding school in London. Towards the end of 1674 Newton and his friend Francis Aston were both involved in bids to procure dispensation from taking orders. In a letter to the civil servant Sir Alexander Frazier, who had apparently offered to intercede on Newton's behalf before the rest of the college, he wrote that the college master (Isaac Barrow) had initially received the proposal in a positive light but was much less optimistic about Newton's prospects when he returned after an unexpected three-week break. When Newton spoke personally with the vice-master, the latter's antipathy to it was, he told Frazier, "so much beyond what I could have imagined, that <(considering the Masters indifference & dependence upon ye seniors)> I could not think it would signify any thing to urge it further." Apart from Barrow's lukewarmness, Newton surmised that the reasons against granting the dispensation were threefold: that it would "hinder succession"; allow into these fellowships men who had no skill in medicine or law; and encourage further dispensations by incentivising a flood of applications for the privilege.[13]

Barrow referred only to Aston's petition when he wrote to the government minister Joseph Williamson in early December, laying out the reasons for the college's pronounced opposition to Aston's efforts. He rehearsed many of the arguments against granting dispensation made in Newton's letter to Frazier and emphasised the fact that accepting such a dispensation would run expressly counter to clauses in the oath Aston took when becoming a fellow. It would, he said, "be distasteful, as anything can be, to the College," and many fellows would attempt to block it by reason of its "pernicious consequences." It would also encourage many others to seek a similar exemption and would subvert the main function of the institution, which was to breed divines. For this reason, he added, nothing like it had ever been attempted with any success. It is unclear at what point Newton's own application became separated from that of Aston, but as it turned out, Aston's failure to obtain the dispensation was not a block to Newton's own success in doing the same. Aston's efforts to gain dispensation evidently attracted highly adverse attention from members of the college, and it is unclear how Newton overcame similar obstacles.[14]

A number of historians have suggested that Newton urgently sought dispensation from taking orders because he had already developed serious doubts about the truth of the doctrine of the Trinity. There is no unambiguous evidence for this, and indeed, there are a number of reasons for doubting that this was the chief, or even a single factor in his quest to be relieved from the statutory obligation. The incident concerning the law fellowship strongly suggests that his antipathy to taking orders began some time earlier, and his repeated remarks throughout the 1670s regarding his desire for the freedom to pursue his research suggest that this was the primary motive. Even if he were a committed anti-Trinitarian by this time, it was almost certainly not the reason behind his seeking a dispensation. Harbouring serious doubts about the Trinity did not later prevent him from twice becoming an MP, nor did it stop him from occupying two of the three senior positions in the Royal Mint. All of these appointments required him to publicly swear that he believed in the Thirty-Nine Articles of the Church of England, and indeed he had to do this frequently at Trinity. If Newton was heterodox before 1675, and it was a key factor in his decision to seek the dispensation, then this would be the only point in his career that he found his private beliefs incompatible with making a public profession of his commitment to the liturgy of the national church.

There were many reasons for seeking dispensation that did not involve scruples over conscience. It was possible to make the case that one had no aptitude or vocation for the ministry, or conversely, that one had a special vocation for secular studies such as law and medicine, and that the require-ment to perform religious duties would adversely affect one's ability to pursue these subjects. As it was, Newton had already acquired a substantial reputation in mathematics and natural philosophy, and he made the case that he had a special vocation for the exact sciences. The draft of the letter granting dispensation to the Lucasian Professorship allowing him to keep his fellowship without taking orders was approved by the king on 2 March 1675, and it was made official at the end of April. In the government minister Henry Coventry's accompanying note, he mentioned that the king had justified the terms of the Lucasian Professorship's dispensation on the broad grounds that he was anxious "to give all just encouragement to learned men who are & shall be elected into ye said Professorship."[15]

The outcome of these deliberations must have had the support of Barrow (despite his earlier objections), Babington, and most of the other senior members of the college. All of these men would have sensed any taint of heresy and stamped down on it. Barrow was constantly concerned lest his mathematical studies obstruct his own commitment to the church, and the Aston case shows that had he been minded to block Newton's dispensation he could easily have done so. Newton's appeal specifically concerned the Lucasian Chair and did not create a precedent for other fellows at Trinity. Barrow, who best knew the full range of Newton's achievements in natural philosophy and mathematics, must have accepted the argument that this work would be adversely affected by his other duties. One assumes that he took into account Newton's oft-voiced complaints about being taken away from the "liberty" required to study, while Newton may also have claimed that he had no aptitude for the ministry. He had had many occasions to demonstrate to his friend that he was no scoffer or libertine. If Newton was really pressed by Barrow, he may have proffered the rather ambiguous defence along the lines he gave much later to Archbishop Tenison, namely that he would do the Church of England much more service by *not* being in orders.[16]

Given Newton's known intellectual proclivities at the time, the argument that Barrow helped gain the dispensation for Newton so that he could work on the natural sciences is plausible, but it is striking that it was at this very moment that Newton began to proclaim that he had lost interest in the natural sciences. When he was in London in early 1675, he told Collins that he had no plans to publish anything on optics or mathematics, though over the summer he did communicate with John Smith, a compiler of mathematical tables, regarding the computation of roots. In June 1675 Collins confirmed to James Gregory that Newton had decided to publish nothing further in the exact sciences, although he was prepared to deposit his lectures in the university library, as he was required to do. Instead, Newton was apparently concentrating on his "Chimicall studies and Experiments" (i.e., his alchemical pursuits), a fact that he must have let slip when he was in London.

Collins repeated a similar phrase to Gregory in October, adding that he had not wanted to bother Newton about mathematical concerns for this very reason. He noted that Newton and Barrow had both begun to consider mathematical speculations "to grow at least nice and dry, if not somewhat barren." If Barrow knew of Newton's plans and doubts about the value of these studies, he may have supported the efforts of his friend to procure dispensation from taking orders so that he could pursue his studies in alchemy and, in particular, in theology. Clearly he was not aware of Newton's doubts about the doctrine of the Trinity, if indeed Newton had developed any by this stage.[17]

3. Reading into Heresy

Newton's descent into heterodoxy is shrouded in archival fog. There are no surviving notes on theological matters that demonstrate a clear defence of standard Trinitarian doctrine, which we might assume to predate the heterodox texts. The lack of evidence regarding his early religious research is particularly problematic in the case of his apocalyptic studies, which must have taken up a large portion of his time between 1675 and 1689. His serious study of theology could have been galvanised by efforts to reorder the visions of Revelation, whose importance must have been drummed into him since he was a boy. To understand this in more detail, he would have turned to the 1672 or 1677 editions of the *Works* of Joseph Mede, which provided the sort of systematic general theory of scriptural interpretation that Newton relished. On this showing, having understood these images in detail, Newton would then have delved deeply into historical sources in order to determine how prophecy had been fulfilled in the past. Alternatively, it may be that his visceral anti-Catholicism, or burgeoning doubts about the equality of Jesus Christ and God, prompted him to carry out primary research on the historical origins of these alleged perversions. According to this version of events, he would have brought his prior doctrinal and historical knowledge to his reading of the apocalyptic images and to Mede.[18]

One piece of evidence does provide an unambiguous point at which Newton must have engaged in detail with Socinian positions. Socinians rejected the pre-existence of Christ and denied the existence of original sin. As outlined in the introduction, they believed in the overriding importance of Scripture and strongly emphasised its comprehensibility, claiming that Christianity was a simple religion whose key elements were accessible to all rational people. As part of the recently revived Divinity Act, from the mid-1670s all masters of arts were obliged to propose two questions on theological topics and to read a thesis on the first. Although the speaker could choose his topics, it appears that at least one of them had to be a rebuttal of a Socinian claim. In February 1677, Newton defended the view that the morality of human actions (i.e., that humans were morally responsible for them) did not detract from the fact that God foresaw their certain future existence, a thesis that directly contradicted the Socinian claim that God did not know future contingent events (i.e., events that he did not foreordain). Newton was challenged by three opponents who collectively mounted ten counterarguments, which he would have addressed in a written response before his performance was assessed by Joseph Beaumont, the Regius Professor of Divinity. The text of his reply does not survive, and one wonders whether Newton's lay status forced those present to pay particular attention to his answers. Obviously he could not have betrayed any hint of heterodoxy. He would have required less preparation to answer the second question he proposed for discussion, namely that "the papist cult of the Eucharist is illicit."[19]

Whatever impetus was provided by the Divinity Act requirement, once Newton had escaped from the obligation to answer his critics in the mid-1670s, he immersed himself in church history and apocalyptic studies. During this hermitage he had a physical presence in his seventeenth-century Trinity rooms, but effectively lived out much of his life in the fourth century, when (as he saw it) pristine Christianity was corrupted by the importation of the despicable beliefs and practices that would later constitute the core of the Roman Catholic faith, chief of which was the doctrine of the Trinity. Newton's predilection for the world of the early church was affected by, and had serious implications for, his relations with people in the modern world. As he developed a mastery of the source materials, he acquired a deep and probably unrivalled knowledge of the historical events that constituted what he called the Great Apostasy. Doctrinal amendments and sociopolitical events always went together in his narrative, for the eventual triumph of the Trinitarian abomination required a transformation of both spiritual and secular aspects of the true religion. In terms of his research practice, which was mirrored in every area he studied, his notes and glosses became short essays and then lengthy tracts, none of which seem to have been finished to his satisfaction before he pursued a different project. After devising a general interpretive scheme or framework, he would return to analyse the source materials in more detail, garnering evidence for his case. On numerous occasions, to a bewildering degree, Newton wrote out and copied long quotations from the primary source literature, and often recopied the same sources with no changes. His work was always bolstered by his phenomenal capacity to write down from memory long lists of references to scriptural passages that functioned as glosses to a particular verse.[20]

Although he continually redrafted his history of the events that had taken place in the early church, the core elements and basic shape of his narrative did not change much over the following half century. One early outline of a total history of the rise and fall of Christianity gives an accurate outline of the range of topics that constituted his research programme. This consisted of eight parts: the appearance of the monks ("the authors of all the evils"); the worship of saints, relics, and images; the polytheistic worship of three equal gods, or tritheism; the morals of Athanasius and his followers; the morals and practices of Athanasius's enemies; the nature of the true Christian religion drawn from apostolic writings and very early patristic texts; the decline and fall of the church; and prophetic references to the history of the church and of the General Apostasy. In due course, and backed with a vast range of evidence, he seamlessly incorporated all these topics into a giant history of the corruption of Christianity.[21]

The hideous nature of tritheism, and the radically subordinate status of Jesus Christ relative to the Father, became the dominant doctrinal points in Newton's theology. By the end of the 1670s he had not only developed a sophisticated critique of orthodox Trinitarian doctrine, but had acquired a detailed understanding of the range and credibility of the source materials. Any account of how, and indeed exactly when, Newton arrived at his heterodox position must be conjectural. As we have seen, the "confessional" list from his first year at Cambridge revealed a devout boy in awe of a great deity to whom various duties were owed; later, in his metaphysical and theological writings he accorded absolute primacy to the will, power, and dominion of the Father, saying very little about the salvific role of the Son. Given this emphatic monotheism, a number of historians have emphasised Newton's acquaintance with Jewish sources and his profound knowledge of the Old Testament. Nevertheless, despite his evident interest in and command of Jewish sources, his acquaintance with Jewish literature cannot be considered as the most significant source of his anti-Trinitarianism. He was

much more interested in the typological significance of Jewish ritual practices rather than Jewish thought per se, and his use of the work of the major
Jewish philosopher Maimonides was more concerned with the latter's study
of worship rather than with what it said about Jewish views about the
nature of Yahweh.[22]

If a Judaic source for his views is implausible, so is the idea that he was
influenced by an individual or group. There were no known anti-Trinitarian
family members or cells in Colsterworth, Grantham, or Cambridge when
he was a youth, and his closet acquaintances at Cambridge, such as Henry
More, Isaac Barrow, and John North openly denounced various anti-
Trinitarian positions. In the aftermath of the publication of the *Principia*,
Newton did communicate with the nonconformist mathematician Gilbert
Clerke, who published anonymously the first two tracts of a three-part
anti-Trinitarian work in 1695. Nothing in their correspondence indicates
that either Clerke or Newton was aware of the extent of each other's di-
vergence from orthodox doctrine. His first known personal contact with
anyone known to harbour anti-Trinitarian sympathies occurred when he
met John Locke at some point between the summer of 1689 and early
1690. Another possibility is that his conversion, if there was one, was triggered by coming upon basic mid-seventeenth-century texts of Socinian
writers such as John Bidle and Paul Best, or even the provocative *Nucleus
Historiæ Ecclesiasticæ* (of 1669) of the Arian Sand. Even if they were not easily
accessible, their doctrines were conveniently summarised in Ephraim
Pagitt's *Heresiography* of 1645 and Thomas Edwards's *Gangrena* of 1646.
There is no evidence that he was inspired by reading the works of these
anti-Trinitarians, or that he was taken with the idiosyncratic attack on the
orthodox doctrine of the Trinity mounted by Thomas Hobbes in his *Leviathan*. One must conclude that Newton—with a strong commitment to
independent study—read himself into heresy. Once he had already become
suspicious of the Trinity doctrine, he then went to the source materials,
occasionally making a detour to modern authors such as Bidle and Sand
for further comment and support. It is likely that his inveterate hatred of
idolatry allowed him to make the link between the rise of Roman Catholicism and the unacceptable elevation of the divine status of Jesus Christ.
As he read more deeply in church history, so he identified more and more
with the general position promoted by the early fourth-century presbyter
Arius, which emphasised the omnipotence and dominance of God the
Father.[23]

Arius held that the original form of Christianity had been corrupted by those who wanted to introduce unscriptural terms designed to reinforce the idea that the Father and the Son were "coequal" and "consubstantial." Drawing on tradition, and what they understood to be a reasonable interpretation of scriptural passages, Arians argued that only God the Father was unbegotten, eternal, true, immaterial, omniscient, and sovereign. Arius and his followers held that the Son was the divine *Logos* (or Word), the first of created things, and that therefore "there was a time when he was not." Nevertheless, Arius had also claimed that Christ was "full god, only begotten," a phrase that was criticised by his enemies for endorsing worship of a mere creature. In Newton's time, divines were wary of Arian language or tendencies, and they were constantly afraid that the unwary might tout Arian accounts of the Son. Arianism was closer to orthodox Church of England doctrine than was its twin Socinianism, and for this reason it was held by many to be more dangerous. It was an old heresy, and for most, it was the most pernicious of all those heresies that erupted in the early church. Indeed, it was predominantly Arian positions that were attacked at the great Council of Nicaea called by the emperor Constantine in 325 C.E. to formulate an acceptable account of how the Son was related to the Father. Following Nicaea, architects of orthodoxy such as Athanasius crafted the language and doctrines of orthodoxy to combat the positions they attributed to Arius. In terms of its content, form, and historical development, Arianism was the archetypal heresy for orthodox Christians.[24]

Through his reading of church history, Newton acquired a deep and sophisticated (though of course, heavily biased) understanding of the way aspects of Christ had been discussed in the early ante-Nicene church. He had a vast array of primary and secondary materials at his disposal to gain an understanding of the earliest Christian thinking concerning the doctrine of the Trinity. The most important source on early church dogma was the *Dogmata Theologica* of the Jesuit scholar Denis Petau (Petavius). Although he protested his own orthodoxy against a variety of attacks, Petau published a large number of ante-Nicene texts in the second of his five-volume work that were clearly incompatible with standard Trinitarian beliefs. In part this was designed to undercut Protestant defences of the Trinity from textual witnesses, since like other Catholic scholars, Petau argued that only the tradition of the Catholic Church could act as a witness to the truth of the Trinitarian doctrine. Moreover, his position was compatible with the Catholic claim that tradition had developed and become more refined over time, and that it was the doctrinal stance of later, Latin patristic writers that mattered. Newton evidently found aspects of Petau's approach extremely congenial, as he did the products of many other Roman Catholic writers, and he took extensive notes from his work. He used it repeatedly in his notes on the fourth-century controversies over the status of the Son.[25]

Heterodox writers in Newton's day naturally flocked to Petau's work. The most influential anti-Trinitarian production was Christopher Sand's *Nucleus Historiæ Ecclesiasticæ*, which appeared in an expanded edition in 1676. Sand built on Petau's research to give his own broadly Arian account of the history of the church, according to which the true version of Christianity expounded in the ante-Nicene corpus was corrupted by Trinitarians in the fourth century. As I show later in the book, this work gave rise to a number of impassioned replies, the most important of which were launched by the High Church divines George Bull, William Cave, and Samuel Parker. These scholars found many ante-Nicene references to the Trinity and explained away overly subordinationist passages in these writings by means of a number of common tactics. Yet Sand's work was clearly troublesome to the orthodox, and in his *Defensio Fidei Nicænæ* of 1685, Bull claimed that his friends had importuned him to defend the Nicene faith because of the terrible effects that Sand's work was having on junior scholars. His work was presented as a point by point refutation of Sand's use of given passages from the ante-Nicene patristic literature, and he brought to bear a number of other texts, ignored by Sand, in order to form an antidote to Sand's poison.[26]

Others responded by identifying a pre-Christian, Hellenistic version of the Trinity originating in contact between Greeks and Jews, mediated via the Egyptians. The most important of these was Ralph Cudworth, who argued in his *True Intellectual System* of 1678 that the Christian Trinity had been adumbrated in a number of ancient texts, including many within the Platonic corpus. Cudworth argued that the doctrine had come to Greece when Orpheus, Pythagoras, and Plato had travelled to Egypt and imbibed it from the "Arcane Theology" of the Egyptians. Defending the revealed nature of the mystery, Cudworth emphasised that the Egyptians had themselves received the notion from the Hebrews, but that it became perverted at the hands of many of Plato's followers. To explain its corruption, Cudworth created a learned and complex genealogy that rested on the notion that two streams of Platonism had flowed from the master's teaching: one led to all the subordinationist heresies of the early church, and the other, to the complete and true version of the Trinity divinely revealed to Athanasius and his contemporaries.[27]

The appeal to a pre-Christian Platonic Trinity was fraught with doctrinal danger, not least because there were obvious distinctions of status within the Platonic version. Cudworth claimed that the Platonists who had correctly followed their master affirmed the three hypostases[28] (or, as Cudworth put it, "Subsistences or persons") of the Trinity to be "One Divinity, because they have an essential Dependence and Gradual Subordination in them." He added that the second and third hypostases in the authentic Platonic rendition had not been created from the first ex nihilo (i.e., from nothing) by means of which he hoped to avoid the taint of Arianism, which argued that they had been created in such a way. As for the Christian Trinity, this was a mystery, but not on that account contrary to reason—indeed, having been purified and clarified, Cudworth claimed that it was much more acceptable to reason than the Platonic variety. The second and third persons of the Christian Trinity were not creatures but necessary "Eternal Emana-tions," indestructible, infinite, coeval, and coeternal with the Father. The Father and the Son were two different substances but of one nature and essence. Many of Cudworth's contemporaries, such as the dissenting minis-ter Theophilus Gale, were unconvinced by appeals for doctrinal support from the Greek tradition. In his four-part *Court of the Gentiles*, Gale attacked what he took to be the baneful effects of Neoplatonic Hellenism and set out to show that it was Hebraic language and culture that lay at the source of modern philosophy and religion. Deviant philosophy and religion began with the introduction into Christianity of Greek and particularly Platonic notions, and it was the subordinationist elements within the Platonic Trinity that had led to Arianism.[29]

4. The Problem of Idolatry

Newton believed that the idea that the Father, the Son, and the Holy Ghost were coequal and consubstantial parts of the Godhead had forced adherents to engage in an egregious form of idolatry. The issue of idolatry underlay all of his religious study and he came to understand that the true religion had been repeatedly corrupted by it. Newton's society was saturated with accounts of idolatry, whether it was of newly discovered heathens who indulged in polytheism, or of the descent of the Israelites into false worship, or more commonly, of popish superstitions that (some believed) still contaminated Anglican rituals. Newton frequently noted that there was a natural human tendency to crave superstition, mystery, and other sorts of idolatrous beliefs and practices. This failing was used by crafty priests and kings to turn people away from the true monotheistic faith and to praise and then worship firstly dead men, and after that, animals and the stars. This pattern recurred throughout history, and as result, he argued, the greatest men in the history of the world were those such as Abraham, Moses, and Jesus Christ, who were periodically chosen by God to restore the true religion after it had been perverted by idolaters. There were many sources on ancient idolatry that Newton read directly, while they were conveniently summarised and organised in works by moderns such as Thomas Godwyn, Samuel Bochart, Gerard Vossius, and (after 1685) John Spencer. Nevertheless, he considered the most hideous example of idolatry to be the doctrines and practices of Roman Catholicism.[30]

For many Protestants, the purest form of idolatry was depicted in the experience of the Israelites during their captivity in Egypt. In a short essay titled "Of Idolatry," Newton noted that the Israelites had been unambiguously idolatrous in Egypt and had sacrificed to demons, but even after Moses had returned from the Mount, having delivered his people from Egyptian tyranny, they had still worshipped the molten calf made by Aaron. Many Catholics tried to exonerate Aaron from the charge of idolatry, by claiming that the honour ("dulia") that had been paid to the calf was an acceptable example of veneration, in contrast with the adoration or worship ("latria") that was reserved for God alone. Protestants, who denied that this distinction was supported by Scripture, saw the creation and worship of the calf as a prime example of idolatry. Newton noted that the veneration of the calf had been performed "wth respect to god" since, as they were about to worship it (Exod. 32:5), Aaron said that the following day would be a feast to the Lord. Newton concluded that when the Israelites said "These be this God wch brought the[e] out of the land of Egypt" (Exod. 32:4) the people did not believe that the calf or any other image had done all the things that were attributed to God, but rather they believed that they were worshipping the true God who had earlier told them that he had delivered them from Egypt. However, Newton added, they were mistaken in believing that they could worship God through inanimate objects, and Moses had rightly been angry with Aaron and his flock for their terrible sin. Newton added that Micah (Judges 17) also committed idolatry by worshipping images "wth respect to the true God," notwithstanding the fact that his mother had also dedicated the silver from which they were made to the true God. He concluded his essay by asserting that worshipping God through any inanimate object was idolatry.[31]

At some point, possibly in the 1680s, Newton developed the theme in a sermon. In an exposition of 2 Kings 17:15-16 he discussed how during their capture at the hands of the Assyrians, the Israelites had worshipped the true God via Jeroboam's calves, and at the same time had worshipped the false gods of the Gentiles via their idols. This episode allowed Newton to treat idolatry "in its full latitude & to discourse of its nature in general," and he contrasted false worship with the proper celebration of God. To worship him for his omniscience, eternity, immensity, and omnipotence was appropriately "pious" (Newton deleted the claim that it was "lofty & seraphick worship") and was a Christian duty. However, these aspects of God's glory, which arose from the "necessity of his nature," were almost beyond the comprehension of men and instead he exhorted Christians to praise God on account of his wisdom, power, goodness, and justice. This was the "life and soule" of true worship. Writing self-referentially, or at least aspirationally, Newton added that just as the wisest of men

> delight not so much to be commended for their height or birth, strength of body, bewty, strong memory, large fantasy, or other such gifts of nature as for their wise good & great actions the issues of their will, so ye wisest of beings requires of us to be celebrated ⟨not so much for his essence as⟩ chiefly to be celebrated for ye issues of his will which are ⟨his actions⟩ the creating preserving & governing all things ⟨according to his good will & pleasure⟩.

If this was the best form of worship, then the worst was the veneration of human artefacts. Just as the Israelites and Jews had committed idolatry in ascribing what really applied to God to their own creations, so today, Newton continued, "too many Christians" attributed divine powers to "saints wth their reliques & images." Such people, whose real identity as Roman Catholics was obvious to his audience, were in practically all respects worse than the idolatrous Israelites and Gentiles who had worshipped the true God alongside their false deities. Catholics were by far the most culpable, "for they go a step further out of the way, & double the crime by transmitting their worship first through images to ye soules of dead men & then through ye soules of dead men to God." If there were degrees of idolatry, then the last was among the worst.[32]

5. The *Logos*

For Newton, the most grievous version of idolatry was to turn the Son of God into God himself. His condemnation of this went hand in hand with a strong commitment to the supremacy of God, and in his theological note-book he followed an entry under "Idololatria" with more biblical passages, almost certainly from the 1680s or early 1690s, under the heading "Deus Pater." The first texts in the section were the major anti-Trinitarian proof texts 1 Corinthians 8:4, "We know y^t an Idol is nothing in ye world, & that there is none other God but one," and 1 Corinthians 8:6, "there is but one God the Father." Was it idolatry to worship Christ, he queried? Newton argued that the pre-existent *Logos* had a divine status, but in many places he stated that Christ had been exalted to honour and to dominion both as a result of his taking on the form of a man, and on account of his subsequent sacrificial death. At one point he gave an illuminating exposition of one of his favourite texts, Philippians 2:5-9. In this key passage for anti-Trinitarians, Jesus—although in the form of God—adopted the form of a servant, and being "found in fashion as a man" he humbled himself man, becoming obedient unto death, "even the death of the cross." Newton added that Christ "was a son before his incarnation but now he was made heir." God had determined of Christ that "all should worship him & that he should be as a God over ye whole creation." For, he noted, "Deity & worship are relative terms." Worshipping Jesus Christ *as God* was the highest form of religious perversion but the adoration of the Lamb in Revelation 5:11-14 made it clear that Jesus had earned the right to be worshipped as the Saviour through his obedience, perfection, and suffering.[33]

Newton did not deny that the three persons of God, the Son, and the Holy Ghost (and in particular the first two) existed in some special relation-ship, but he stressed that they were not equal and did not share the same substance. Because God sanctioned it, there was a spiritual union, or union of wills between him and the Son, and for that reason the latter shared many of the Father's perfections. According to Newton, when used with explicit qualification the word *God* in Scripture could refer to any of the three, but it never designated more than one of them at the same time. When "put absolutely," he continued, it denoted God the Father. Christ himself was a special being; Jesus confessed himself in certain places to be inferior to the Father and called him "his God," but at various times he enjoyed the power of the Father, submitting his will to the Father in all things. The Word or

Logos of the Johannine prologue ("In the beginning was the Word"), Newton argued, was conventionally understood in the Platonic or "Arian" sense as an "intelligent being" and so this was the correct meaning. It was this being, and *not* some human soul, who was made incarnate in the Virgin and who experienced temptations and suffered on the cross. The orthodox maintained what, for Newton, was the obscene idea that only a human soul had suffered during the crucifixion. This notion had been introduced by Athanasius as a consequence of his physicalist view that God and the Son were composed of the same substance, and that God would have suffered on the cross without some additional mortal element in the Son. However, Newton argued that this view was based on an inadequate notion of the nature of the *Logos*.[34]

Newton's chief sources of evidence for his radically subordinationist conception of Christ were early versions of Scripture and a vast range of patristic and other texts relating to the early church. Since Catholics did not rest their case for the authenticity of the Trinity entirely on textual witnesses, their editions of the Fathers, the history of dogma, and of variations in manuscripts of the New Testament were particularly useful for anti-Trinitarians such as Newton. Petau's tomes on the history of dogma and Baronius's *Annals* were essential resources for understanding the gradual corruption of the true nature of Jesus Christ, but there were oceans of relevant data in the editions of patristic writings that Newton had in his own rooms and that were available to him in Trinity College Library.[35] On the whole, he consulted Latin translations of original Greek writings but he often pored over Marguerin de la Bigne's *Magna Bibliotheca Veterum Patrum*, and of course, he knew the text of the Greek New Testament extremely well. Occasionally, having cited a Latin text, Newton sensed that it could not be a fair translation of the original Greek and would leave a note to himself to consult the original; the latter might offer evidence of an original subordinationist reading, and thus of likely corruption by Latin translators.[36]

Newton also occasionally drew from modern sources, though typically he often failed to record his debt to them. In one lengthy set of excerpts from the Fathers he listed a series of ante-Nicene passages that indicated or explicitly demonstrated the superiority of the Father. As Scott Mandelbrote has shown, these derive from the 1691 reprinting of John Biddle's *The Faith of One God*. Newton cited a passage from Irenaeus's *Adversus Haereses* to show that God the Father had pre-eminence over the Son in knowing the date of the Day of Judgement, and from later in the source he recorded

Irenaeus's view that the Father was the only true God. After this he wrote down the passage "Christ a God speaking by ye command of y^e *principal* God" from Book 2 of Arnobius's early fourth-century *Adversus Gentes* ("Against the Pagans") and underlined the penultimate word. Other excerpts, all urging the superiority and primacy of the Father, were taken from the early Church Father Tertullian's *Adversus Hermogenem* and his *De Præscriptione Hæreticorum*, and also "in divers places" from the fourth-century *Ecclesiastical History* and other works of Eusebius of Caesarea. All of these early writers entertained some sort of unpalatable belief as far as Newton was concerned but each upheld the unambiguous supremacy of the Father. The list was topped off by a reinterpretation of the original Greek in the Trinitarian proof texts John 20:28 and Hebrews 1:8, and by an examination of all those allegedly pro-Trinitarian passages that had not been mentioned by any of the early Fathers before the Council of Nicaea in 325. Other notes, such as those from the early (c. second century) Christian work *The Shepherd of Hermas*, corroborated Newton's claim that early Christian thought placed Christ far below the Father in terms of supremacy and divinity.[37]

Newton found particular supporting evidence for his view of the subordinate status of the *Logos* in Justin Martyr's second-century *Dialogue* with the Jew Trypho, in which Justin stated that the Son/Word was "voluntarily begotten" by the Father. Justin, a teacher of pagan philosophy as well as a Christian convert, claimed that, as the Word mentioned in John, the *Logos* was the rational force in the universe, but as Jesus Christ he was an angel, apostle, or messenger of God, subordinate and subservient to God though sharing in the divine will. Not everything that Justin claimed for the *Logos* satisfied Newton, but he gave ample evidence that the incarnation of the Word in the Virgin was prophesied in the Old Testament, and that the future event had been revealed to the Jews in a number of different guises. Glossing the central scriptural support for Christ's pre-existence, Proverbs 8:22–31, Newton noted that the statement from Genesis 1:26, "Let *us* make man in o[ur] image" (his italics), "was a praefigurative speech of gods incarnation, for then man was truly in his image. & Gen. 3.22 Behold ye man is becom as own [sic] of us." Newton found further confirmation for the real physical nature of the Word in the early Epistle of St. Ignatius to the Trallians, where Ignatius attacked the docetic position that Christ had merely *seemed* to take on human flesh and suffer. He noted that Ignatius had confirmed that the Word took on a body, since Scripture unambiguously affirmed that it was made flesh, lived among men without sin, and suffered on the cross.

Later he would adduce evidence to show that the Son had a corporeal form after the resurrection as well as before his incarnation.[38]

Newton also took notes from Bishop Dionysius of Alexander's attack on the bishop of Antioch Paul of Samosata's account of the essential humanity of Jesus, written in c. 264. Dionysius defended the divinity of Jesus Christ against Paul's view that Jesus was originally a man into which the divine *Logos* had been infused, residing in him as Reason sits in an ordinary man. Newton observed that Dionysius held that the person of Christ was the *Logos* alone, "& not ye logos & a human soul ⌐together⌐ hypostatically united." Newton remarked that according to Paul, the scriptural reference to Christ taking on the form of a servant in Philippians 2:7 meant that he took on the form of a man, that is, inhabited or dwelt within him. However, Dionysius countered that the *Logos* was made flesh in the same way that a human soul was made flesh when "invested" with a body. As Newton characterised Dionysius's position:

> this is ye form or fashion of a man that his soul by being incarnate sees, heares, & feels, by ye organs of ye body & ye word by being then incarnate take upon him the form of a man; but not ye Hypostasis of a man no more then o[ur] saviour took upon him a new Hypostasis when he was transfigured, or girded himself with a napkin.

In a gloss on this, Newton concurred with Dionysius that if the *Logos* "neither sees with corporall eyes as a man sees nor hears as a man hears nor is subject to ye senses passions & infirmities wch a [man] is subject to it cannot be said to be in ye form or likeness of men." It was one thing to be united to a man, and another to be "formed like a man, so as to become a man," which is what had happened in the case of the *Logos*. Once it had been made incarnate, it was subject to mortal passions and infirmities, and it was the *Logos*, and not God, who had suffered on the cross.[39]

6. Hating the *Homoousion*

Like many of his contemporaries, Newton integrated his account of the true nature of Christ into his history of the early church. Eirenicists cited Constantine the Great's plea, just before the Council of Nicaea in 325, to the effect that disputing over highly recondite issues should not be the cause of a schism in the church. Orthodox theologians pointed to the need at the end of the fourth century for Theodosius and his successors to impose order on a church that was menaced by heretics (especially of the anti-Trinitarian variety), schismatics, and external groups such as the Goths. Orthodox Protestants and Catholics adhered to a basic story that stressed the wisdom and generosity of the emperor Constantine, the man whose conversion to Christianity had resulted in the Roman Empire embracing Christianity as the state religion. He had convened the Council at Nicaea at a moment of crisis in the church, and it had agreed on the formulation that the Son was *homoousios* (for the orthodox, meaning same substance) with the Father. Thereafter, the fates of the diabolical Arius and his malicious followers were contrasted with the miraculous survival and final triumph of Athanasius. Against all odds, the saint had safeguarded the true interpretation of the Nicene Creed during the hard years of his banishment and persecution at the hands of the depraved "Arian" emperors, Constantius II and Valens, and a whole host of tyrannical bishops.[40]

Newton, who disagreed with the orthodox account in every point, devoted a great portion of his theological study to understanding the corruption of original Christian belief during and after Nicaea. Historical study allowed him to uncover the perpetrators of this epoch-making crime, and he made a point of coming to terms with their personalities, actions, and motivations. In terms of the doctrines he attacked and supported, by dint of the language he used, and on the basis of the passion with which he vented his spleen, he clearly aligned himself with the views of Arius and many of his followers. His writings were written in explicit opposition to the orthodox accounts, which traced an unbroken line from Athanasius to modern "orthodox" Christians. For this reason his position is better described as anti-Athanasian rather than pro-Arian. Indeed, although there was substantial disagreement between Anglican clergymen over the nature of the doctrine of the Trinity, it is this explicit and relentless hostility to Athanasius and his core beliefs that marks Newton out as so radical. Like his enemies, he believed that the corruption of doctrine involved a battle between two competing positions or parties, one of which remained true to Christ's word, and the other of which was heretical, being backed by the devil and his allies. Although he overwhelmingly sided with the doctrines and moral bearing of Arius and his followers, he had a detailed grasp of how disputes between the two parties had turned into a polarising and dialectical process in the half-century after the Council of Nicaea. Both sides had forged their own doctrines at least in part to fend off what they saw to be the deleterious implications of the positions of their enemies. This meant that what each side put forward as their own view had to be read with some caution and in its proper context; moreover, it was by no means always a simple battle between good and evil.[41]

To examine these abstruse matters, Newton needed to coordinate the history of doctrine, with secular and church history, and to explain what happened by reference to the Machiavellian machinations of the men who served Satan. Like most anti-Trinitarians, Newton believed that orthodox history and much of the evidence on which it rested was a pack of lies devised by Athanasius and later institutionalized by himself and his corrupt followers. In a short space of time, Newton acquired an extraordinary knowledge of what he took to be uncontaminated information about the rise and spread of the early church. He accepted much of the standard account, especially in terms of the need of the orthodox church to combat a number of terrible early heresies. In 318, the Arian crisis began in Alexandria over the question of whether the Son of God was created or not, and it would become the defining point of doctrine in the formation of what Newton took to be the orthodox position. Alexander, the bishop of the city, decided that the Son was not created and excommunicated Arius and his followers. This action was attacked by the Arian sympathiser Eusebius of Nicomedia, and in response Alexander accused the Arians of believing that there was a time when Christ did not exist, that he was completely dissimilar from the Father, and that he had all the attributes of mortal men. Under the pretext of religion, but as Newton viewed it, actually for maintaining the peace of the state, in 325 Constantine called the Council at Nicaea, which agreed upon the notion that the Son was *homoousion* with the Father. This phrase could denote an identity of nature, essence, or even substance, and efforts to fix its precise meaning would be implicated in most of the contention that followed. From all the clamour surrounding these exchanges, Newton concluded that Arius had numerous supporters, and that the majority of the people opposed what he termed "homousianism."[42]

Newton examined the events before, during, and after Nicaea in intricate detail, repeatedly copying out letters and decrees drawn from the records of the fourth-century historians Tyrranius Rufinus and Eusebius of Caesarea, and the fifth-century historians Socrates Scholasticus, Salminius Sozomenus, Theodoret of Cyrrhus (Cyrus), and, of course, from Athanasius himself. The Council determined that the Son was *homoousios* with the Father, though Newton noted that the exact meaning of the term was ambiguous, and the decision was not unanimous. Indeed, the term had been anathematised when a previous Council had condemned the opinions of Paul of Samosata in 269. The Athanasians, Newton claimed, had deliberately perverted the outcome of Nicaea, and he noted from Sand's *Nucleus* that they had been rendered speechless by the complexity of their own heresy. Their silence, he remarked, "betrayed the enormity of their views." Faced with a potentially disastrous level of disagreement, Constantine now demonstrated his skill in forming a consensus. According to Newton, he acted with great affability in calming the passions that had arisen at the meeting, and cut off potential disputes by having all dissenting opinions burned. The Council excommunicated Arius and soon after this Constantine wielded the sword of his civil power by exiling him, along with his key supporter Eusebius of Nicomedia and two other bishops.[43]

From a number of other primary sources, Newton determined that the Council had concluded that the Father and Son were both substances but not the same *numerical* substance, that is, the Son was not brought into being as a result of God dividing off a part of his own substance. They were therefore similar but not identical in substance. For the truth of the matter Newton turned to the testimony of Philostorgius, the much-despised pro-Arian author known only from the summary of his text made by Photius, the ninth-century Patriarch of Constantinople. Philostorgius claimed that Eusebius of Nicomedia and others had understood *homoousios* as *homoiousios*, that is, they adhered to a similarity of substance between the Son and the Father rather than identity, and according to Newton, those who attended the Council generally believed the same. At one stage he adduced additional testimony from the early fifth-century *Historia Sacra* of Sulpicius Severus to rebut the standard claim that there had been a conspiracy by the Eusebians to pretend that the Council had meant similarity of substance when they subscribed. In any case, as we shall see, he believed that a much greater conspiracy in favour of a consubstantial meaning of *homoousios* had taken place after the Council. As for the evidence from the Church Fathers, it was clear from Petau that many authoritative ante-Nicene Fathers such as Tertullian and Irenaeus believed that the Son was of a more perfect substance than the rest of the creatures, but did *not* believe that the Son was coequal with the Father. Even Alexander, in his Letter to the Council, had agreed that the Son was of an intermediate nature between the Father and the rest of creation. As Newton saw it, in due course the unbiblical term *homoousios* had succeeded precisely because its meaning was opaque. Had co-equality of any kind between the Father and Son been explicitly discussed at the meeting, it would have been rejected.[44]

Newton argued that although ante-Nicene Fathers such as Justin Martyr and Tertullian had believed in Christ's pre-existence, pagan ideas had been imported into Christianity and had given rise to heresies such as the view that the *Logos* was originally immanent in the Father and then later "generated" as the Son. In the last few decades of his life he would concentrate on these early church heresies almost as much as he did on the fourth-century versions, but at the heart of most if not all of these doctrinal perversions was an inappropriately physical understanding of various terms. Indeed, it was the physicalist misrepresentation of the true relationship between the Son and the Father that lay at the heart of homoousianism. Central to Newton's entire theological system was the belief that interpretations of their relationship that asserted identity of substance instead of similarity of nature, or similarity of power and dominion, were diabolical and pagan contaminants. According to Newton (writing in the 1680s or 1690s), the Nicene Council, "in decreing ye Son homousios to ye ffather understood that he & ye father were two substances of one nature or essence," and he claimed that Etienne de Courcelles (Curcellæus) and Cudworth had proved this "beyond all cavils." However, Hosius (bishop of Corduba) and others had translated the Nicene term into Latin *unius substantiae* "to propagate a notion of a singular substance." The orthodox cemented this false understanding of the relationship when they translated the phrase back into Greek, and in 343 the Council of Serdica (modern Sofia), where Hosius presided, "affirmed that there was but one hypostasis of ye ffather son & Holy Ghost." Easterners, who had been sceptical of the term *homoousios* and who detested the notion of a single hypostasis, now thought that the Western church believed in a physical identity of the Son and the Father and thus was irrevocably Sabellian (i.e., the doctrine that the three members of the Godhead were merely modes or perceived aspects of one underlying person). These complex debates continued until 381, when at the Council of Constantinople the emperor Theodosius decreed that doctrine of the *homoousion* was orthodox.[45]

7. Moral Characters

For Newton, the disagreements over abstruse aspects of belief could not be dissociated from events in the political and ecclesiastical spheres. Athanasius, he thought, had cunningly manipulated Alexander throughout the Council of Nicaea, with the "slow old man" trusting the advice of the younger deacon so much that he became a full convert to the Athanasian position. When Alexander died soon after Nicaea, Athanasius took over as bishop of Alexandria, though the Arians accused him of having been improperly elected in secret by a small number of allied bishops. After the council, Constantine sided with the Athanasians, possibly, Newton suggested, because of a letter Arius had written trumpeting the vast numbers of his followers. While Arius and his key supporters were exiled, Athanasius controlled an ecclesiastical power base covering large swathes of Egypt. However, in 330 Eusebius of Nicomedia made an alliance with the Melitians, a group of schismatics who had broken off from taking communion with orthodox Christians after the Diocletian persecution, and who were profoundly opposed to the doctrines and practice of Athanasius. At the same time, Constantine's sister Constantia persuaded the emperor that the Arians should be allowed back from exile, and Arius returned with the priest Euzoius to Constantinople.[46]

Unlike orthodox historians, Newton had a mixed view of Constantine's behaviour. His positive views about the emperor's skill in managing the Council of Nicaea were outweighed by his condemnation of Constantine's personal behaviour, his extreme prejudice against Arius, and by the fact that he had introduced political considerations into religious matters. Newton lambasted Constantine's savage murder of close relatives (including his wife, son, and numerous friends), and his tyrannical bearing towards his subjects: clearly, he lamented at one point, the period could only be described as Neronian. In a remarkable passage he interpreted Constantine's brutality as a result of God's judgement on his hubris at Nicaea. The emperor had lied about his motives in calling the conference, "subverted the truth, [and] oppressed innocent and pious people throughout the entire world." With "reckless blasphemy" he had promoted the unscriptural term *homoousion* as if it were the decree of God himself, "infused into the Fathers by divine inspiration," but in fact he had shaped the decision of the Council and had granted it his own authority. For Newton, he had committed the cardinal sin of mixing religion and politics, seeking at all costs to preserve the integrity of the state under the guise of religion.[47]

Newton's position on Constantine's political interests can be usefully contrasted with that of Thomas Hobbes, who had launched an attack on the conventional understanding of doctrine of the Trinity in chapter 42 of his *Leviathan* of 1651. Having noted that neither the word *person* nor the term

"Trinity" was ascribed to God in the Bible, Hobbes reduced the Trinity to the historical succession of three "persons" (Moses, Jesus Christ, and the Apostles), who were the three representatives of the "person" God. This predictably incurred the wrath of a wide range of commentators, as did the half-hearted defence of his own orthodoxy and commitment to the Nicene Creed that he made in his appendix to the Latin edition of *Leviathan* of 1668. Here, he did retract the claim that Moses was a person in the Trinity, implausibly attributing it to carelessness on his part, and gave a brief account of the Arian controversy in which he attacked the zealous and factious behaviour of Athanasius. He dealt with the subject of the Nicene Creed and the *homoousion* in his *Historical Narration Concerning Heresy*, which appeared in 1680 (shortly after his death), and did so at greater length in his *Historia Ecclesiastica*, which was published in 1688. In the last, he blamed Greek philosophers— drawing on Egyptian precursors—for bringing incomprehensible and unbiblical terms such as the *homoousios* into Christianity. They introduced heresies ("private opinions") into Christianity and created innumerable sects, attempting to create a power structure that would one day overwhelm civil authority. Constantine brought peace and, at least temporarily, the uniformity of religion by smashing pagan temples, but as a result of the efforts of churchmen, the odious distinction between (orthodox) "Catholics" and "heretics" arose in his reign. He should have determined Christian doctrine himself, Hobbes argued, but out of weakness he allowed the clergy's Greek-infected doctrines to become orthodoxy.[48]

There is no evidence that Newton read any of Hobbes's writings on these topics. He would of course have been aghast at the Erastian conceit that civil powers should determine doctrine, but he would have agreed both that Athanasius's obstinate bearing towards Constantine was reprehensible, and that the ultimately successful attempts by priests to acquire political influence and power was a disaster for the church. According to Newton's account, Athanasius built up a substantial track record of sedition in the years following Nicaea, and his influence with Constantine was gradually eroded. In 334 he was ordered to present a defence at the Council of Caesarea against accusations that he had desecrated a sacred place and even murdered a bishop, but he failed to show up. Constantine made an even stronger demand for him to appear at the Council of Tyre, which convened the following year. In one draft Newton admitted that the proceedings were probably prejudiced against Athanasius, but this was because the Fathers present "were intent on restoring the faith that had been altered at the Nicene

Council." They heard various charges of violence and intimidation and set out to locate relevant evidence in order to come to a decision. However, before a verdict could be delivered, Athanasius fled from the chamber and after some delay he was banished to Gaul. The Eastern churches received Arius and his allies into communion, while Athanasius convinced his supporters in the West that Arius had made false accusations. Newton concluded in one draft that because there was corruption on both sides, a final determination of what actually happened would have to wait until the Day of Judgement, "where both sides may be heard impartially." This lukewarm effort at even-handedness is virtually unique among his writings on this subject.[49]

When Constantine died in 337, having been baptised just before his death by Eusebius of Nicomedia, his empire was split into three parts, each ruled by his sons Constantine II, Constantius II, and Constans. Constantine (emperor of Gaul, Britain, and Spain) restored Athanasius to his bishopric but when he died in 340, the Arian sympathiser Constantius forced Athanasius into exile again. Athanasius sent a letter to the Western bishops in his own defence and defied the emperor, fleeing to the West—according to Newton—after his supporters had created havoc. Now he teamed up with Julius, bishop of Rome, who peremptorily summoned Eastern bishops to a Roman council in pursuit, so Newton claimed, of leadership of the entire Christian world. Julius turned the emperor Constans against his brother but in 343 both leaders jointly summoned the conference in Serdica. As Newton saw it, a prejudiced council decided in favour of Athanasius, and the Westerners confirmed their commitment to the Sabellian notion that there was a single hypostasis of the Father and the Son.[50]

In 351 Constantius conquered the usurper Magnentius and became the sole emperor, and in 355 he called a council in Milan, demanding that the Westerners abide by the anti-Athanasian decree made at Tyre. The Westerners agreed to this so long as everyone could agree on the *homoousion*, and to this end Constantius requested that Athanasius explain himself in his presence. According to Newton, Athanasius insolently refused to attend, and his followers rebelled in a bloody campaign against the state troops. In his summary of the episode, Newton told how Athanasius now fled to the desert, "raging and gnashing his teeth against his enemies; celebrating those who had died as a result of the uprising as martyrs...lashing out with mad invective against the Emperor and his ministers as outrageous persecutors, and claiming that Arius had died in a bog-house." What orthodox theologians

depicted as the "blasphemous" "Arian" council at Sirmium (Sremska Mitro-
vica) that met in 357 outlawed all *ousia*-language as unbiblical, and accepted
the so-called anomoean position that the Son was neither identical nor
similar, but unlike the Father. Two years later, another council of Western
bishops was convoked at Ariminum (Rimini). Newton noted that at this
meeting, the *homoousion* was affirmed by the majority though a minority
disagreed. Eastern bishops met at the same time at Seleucia (Silifke), but the
council was irrevocably divided. One group was dismayed by the novelty
and boldness of the term *homoonsios* and asserted that the Son was unlike
the Father, while another group decided in favour of homoousianism.
Constantius died soon after this, and Newton believed that with the advent
of the pagan emperor Julian in 361, the groundwork was laid for the terrible
apostasy that followed. "It is clear," he asserted at one point, that after Ariminum and the death of Constantius, "the Homousian religion flowed forth as
from two fountains, the Pope of Alexandria and the Pope of Rome." As a
result, "the papist church, which survives to this day, arose with its two
horns." Seizing this opportunity to do the devil's bidding, Athanasius hatched
and successfully executed a plan to corrupt the historical record of the early
church along with the Christian religion itself.[51]

In one impassioned and remarkable account of Athanasius's perverted
morals and actions, Newton discussed the conduct of Constantius, reviled
as a persecutor by almost all orthodox historians. Did he persecute the homoousians for their religious opinions? Or for their seditious actions alone?
Newton found the answer both by assessing Athanasius's interests in the
affair and by paying careful attention to clues in his account. In one letter to
his monastic followers, Athanasius had referred to the well-known charges
of fomenting unrest that had been repeatedly raised against him since before
Tyre, and related how his enemies had resorted to forging criminal accusations against his allies. As Newton saw it, various passages in the letter "<suf-
ficiently> shew that the best of Athanasius's martyrs & confessors suffered as
evil doers & seditious persons, & that Constantius & his bishops studiously
avoided punishing them for their faith." Other so-called martyrs had died
for resisting the state, while those who had refused to sign the condemnation
of Athanasius at Milan, including Pope Liberius, were deposed by councils of
their own religion "and suffered not for their faith." According to Newton,
they had sought to "keep up a schism between the eastern & western
Churches, & so were banished as enemies to peace." By refusing to debate
on the issues that Constantius had ordered them to discuss, and by trying to

pervert various councils to their own ends, they had usurped the right of the emperor and so were justly punished as political meddlers.[52]

Newton claimed that after the twin councils of Ariminum and Seleucia, "Athanasius & his friends falling into a rage at the Emperors success, began to write railing books against him; & Athanasius indeed laboured to perswade the Egyptians that the Emperor overcame the western bishops by tyrannical asperity & terror; & yet the contrary is certainly true." Even Hilary of Poitiers, beloved of the orthodox as "The Hammer of the Arians" and "the Athanasius of the West," "in a railing book wch he wrote at that very time against the Emperor, attributes the success [i.e., of Constantius] to his clemency." In the same breath, Newton remarked, Hilary slated Constantius "as the most cruel of persecutors, & yet declare[d] that this consisted in nothing but love & kindness. By this means he had better success then the heathen persecutors by violence, & therefore was in Hilary's opinion more cruel, not to the bodies but to the souls of men." From Baronius, Newton found that Hilary had presented his book to Constantius at Constantinople in 360, hoping to die as a martyr and "fix the name of persecutor" on Constantius. However, he continued, "altho this railery was crimen læsæ majestatis" and thus deserving of capital punishment, Constantius would not be provoked into doing something that might look like religious persecution. Even the theologian Gregory Nazianzen (archbishop of Constantinople during the key years of 379–81), the great defender of Trinitarian orthodoxy, had a good word to say about the emperor, and Newton commented that this testimony "coming freely from the mouth of an enemy & an eye-witness of things, is as great as can be desired."[53]

For Newton, Constantius was exactly the opposite of the negative view of him provided by Hilary and was the antithesis of Athanasius's portrayal of him in his History of the Arians as the persecuting Antichristian emperor who presided over a series of heretical and diabolical councils. Newton outdid himself in an uncharacteristically effusive evaluation of his hero: "the vertues of this Emperor were so illustrious that I do not find a better character given of any Prince for clemency, temperance, chastity, contempt of popular fame, affection to Christianity, justice, prudence, princely carriage & good government, then is given to him even by his very enemies." Constantius retained his imperial dignity but nevertheless "reigned in the hearts of his people, & swayed the world by their love to him, so that no Prince could be farther from deserving the name of a persecutor." It was true that he had slaughtered his uncles and had been uncompromisingly overzealous in pursuing his victory over Magnentius, but he did the first "because they poisoned his father & the last to secure not himself but Christianity from the attempts of the heathens." Apart from these minor blemishes (which had been enough for Newton to condemn Constantine), even his enemies agreed in praising his virtues: "All these witnesses lived in the reign of this Emperor & therefore knew what they wrote, & being his enemies would not favour him. ffor they wrote after his death, & so were at liberty to speak their minds." If any author wrote anything to the contrary, Newton concluded, they should be immediately corrected.[54]

8. Rewriting History

When Julian the Apostate became emperor in 361, he reinstated paganism as the state religion. The re-energised Athanasius returned from his Egyptian exile, intent on introducing yet another conception of the Trinity doctrine in which each member was a separate hypostasis. Newton argued at length that Athanasius and his allies now commenced a vast and diabolical programme that involved corrupting Scripture and undertaking a vast rewriting of the documents from the Council of Nicaea, along with many of the works of the ante-Nicene Fathers. It was for this reason that Newton believed that all patristic texts were to be read with suspicion. One needed to know when, by whom, and for whom they were written. Differences of opinion among the "homoousian" writers were grist to his mill, since he could point to the inherent tensions within the orthodox accounts and select whichever remarks or positions suited his case. He took patristic texts at face value when facts or arguments suited his general approach, and he was particularly partial to the long laments by contemporaries about the abject sinfulness of orthodox Christians. Few of those writings considered heretical by the orthodox Trinitarians had survived the general suppression and destruction and, as Newton saw it, the history of the post-Nicene debates had likewise been perverted by a monumental conspiracy. Orchestrated by Athanasius, this had resulted in the falsification of the history of contemporary events and of the earliest texts of the Fathers, thereby polluting all accounts of the early church that followed. Some authentic texts and doctrines did survive the process, and Newton did have at his disposal sources such as Petau's volumes and the counter-orthodox history of the church composed by Philostorgius, whom he cited whenever he could.[55]

Like other anti-Trinitarian authors, Newton drew comfort from the fact that many of the writings of the earliest Church Fathers, especially Origen, Justin Martyr, and Clement of Alexandria, contained mildly or even strongly subordinationist accounts of the Second Person of the Trinity. However, he also believed that like Scripture itself, these texts had been tampered with by depraved zealots during the fourth and fifth centuries. In one introductory chapter from a proposed treatise on church history, he considered in detail many of the problems associated with determining the authenticity of ante-Nicene documents. Theological disputes often arose from preconceived opinions, he said, and without grasping the nature of these beliefs, one could neither comprehend the disputes themselves nor trust the composition of the texts on which the disputants relied. To serve their own ends, "pious men," a term that for Newton invariably described Roman Catholics, had routinely altered texts when they transcribed or translated them, altering not only Latin translations but also Greek originals. It was obvious, for example, that texts had been corrupted when they contained arguments and concepts that could only have been forged decades or centuries after the event. One needed a great deal of expertise to detect these alterations, and Newton set about identifying fraudulent texts and removing them from the historical record.[56]

The ringleader of this great project was of course his old sparring partner Athanasius. By twisting the words of early Fathers such as Origen, Theognostus, Dionysius of Alexandria, and Dionysius of Rome, Athanasius had "dared anything and everything and got away with it because of his reputation." He made Origen refute notions, such as the Arian staple "There was a time when the son was not" even though the claim was first bruited long after his death in the controversy between Alexander and Arius. Athanasius recast Origen's writings to give them a distinctly Athanasian tinge, and he made Dionysius of Rome attack imaginary precursors of Arius for opinions that Athanasius would later foist—again falsely—on Arius. This sat well with Petau's demonstration that many of the ante-Nicene Fathers had been radically subordinationist, because Newton could assume that the texts that indicated otherwise were later insertions. He also made ample use of the exegetical principle of charity according to which respected authors should be assumed to have written clearly and cogently. On a number of occasions, he argued that a number of normally judicious writers had made such moronically incoherent defences of orthodox positions that key elements of these texts must have been inserted by Athanasius. One woeful example was the ludicrous concoction of an entire letter, supposedly written by Dionysius of Alexandria, which defended the *homoousion* against Paul of Samosata. Other writings, Newton noted contemptuously, showed that Dionysius argued against the notion of the *homoousion*, and anybody with an ounce of learning knew that the orthodox had condemned Paul for holding the same doctrine.[57]

Many, but by no means all, of the arguments Newton deployed in his attack on scriptural corruption were his own. He was not alone in believing that there had been a terrible corruption of religion in the past, and that the conspirators behind this apostasy had gone on to pervert the documents of the early church to defend a false doctrine. Indeed, this particular chapter on church history shows well how, when armed with a series of standard exegetical techniques, and with access to all the core primary documents, his natural propensity to sense conspiracies was used in the service of religious truth. Armed with his own assumptions about what authentic and pre-contaminated Christian doctrine was, and with a detailed grasp of Athanasian doctrine, he sniffed out anachronistic Athanasianisms in ante-Nicene debates and writings. Unsurprisingly, in each case where he "suspected" that there had been some textual malpractice, Athanasius was found guilty of fraud. The Athanasians had made it their business to corrupt these texts and many others, allegedly in order to "eliminate the interpolations of heretics, to restore authors to their pristine state, to protect the chaste ears of readers and the orthodox faith," but it was all an elaborate cover for their own perversions. Their evil plans might still succeed, Newton concluded, but it was up to people such as himself to detect the fraudulent activity and reverse it.[58]

5

Abominable Men

Legends Vide Monks★

Newton's analysis of the early church allowed him to see at firsthand how Roman Catholic doctrine developed in the aftermath of Nicaea. Although much of his work focussed on the introduction into Christianity of what he took to be pernicious doctrines regarding the relationship between the Father and the Son, he also made a detailed study of the incorporation into it of the central doctrines and practices of what would become Roman Catholicism. Indeed, he took the two processes to be closely interlinked. From the late 1670s interaction with Catholics would be largely confined to people who had lived over a millennium before he was born, but in the earlier part of the decade, the publication of his optical work brought him into contact with a group of Jesuits based at Liège. His initial encounter with the members of the order was positive, but he would soon distrust them both individually and as a body. In due course, he would condemn them and their approach to natural philosophy, accusing them of deliberately involving him in interminable public disputes.

In adopting this visceral form of anti-Catholicism, Newton shared the assumptions of many of his countrymen. English Protestants had closely followed their European colleagues in condemning a number of practices such as the granting of indulgences, the use of images in worship, the worship of saints, the doctrine of transubstantiation, the cult of the Virgin, and the doctrine of papal supremacy. Following the work of the mid-sixteenth-century Protestant exiles John Bale, John Foxe, and others, the historical position of the Church of England was set in an apocalyptic framework and contrasted with a sordid history of diabolical attempts by papists on the very fabric of the nation. By the late seventeenth century, English Protestants had memorized the key dates of the various attacks that the ecclesiastical and political beast had mounted against the state. Assaults on Protestantism launched by Queen Mary and later, by the armada of her husband, Philip II, were followed by various efforts, widely believed to have been orchestrated by Jesuits, to undermine the body politic. These included the Gunpowder Plot (1605), the Great Fire of London (1666), and, more latterly, the Popish Plot (1678–81), during which pope-burning ceremonies attracted crowds in the tens of thousands. In the middle of the century, many puritans believed that Charles I and Archbishop Laud were involved in a plot to bring back arbitrary government and the worst aspects of Roman Catholicism. Later, others claimed that the civil wars had been orchestrated by papal agents and, in particular, by sectarians who were Jesuits in disguise.[1]

After the Restoration many nonconformists, and some Anglicans, were again anxious about Catholicising tendencies in religion and politics. Moreover, although the Royalist Cavalier Parliament of 1661–79 was intensely hostile to the aspirations of nonconformists, it looked equally unfavourably on Roman Catholicism. This brought it into confrontation with Charles II and his brother James, Duke of York, both of whom had been brought up in exile during the Commonwealth in a predominantly Roman Catholic environment. Each of them appointed a number of Catholic advisors and had sympathies towards the rights of Catholic subjects. Relations between Parliament and Crown became fraught in the early 1670s. Having recently prorogued (discontinued) Parliament, in March 1672 Charles announced a Declaration of Indulgence (i.e., Toleration), suspending the execution of the penal laws that were in operation against nonconformists and Catholic recusants. However, the following month witnessed the start of the Third Anglo-Dutch War, and within a year he was forced to recall Parliament in order to raise funds for the campaign. In return for this, Parliament forced him to annul the Declaration and to institute the Test Acts, which, under the guise of defending the king from the sinister machinations of Jesuits and Catholic priests, compelled all office-holders to deny transubstantiation and to take Anglican communion.[2]

The Test Acts forced into the open the religious beliefs of James, who had privately taken communion within the Roman Catholic Church for many years. The revelation of his conversion was swiftly followed by his marriage to the Catholic Mary of Modena in late 1673 (his first wife, Anne Hyde, had died in 1671). It was by now obvious that a succession crisis would occur if Charles died, and when alleged the "Popish Plot" was revealed in the autumn of 1678, a new "Whig" grouping led by the Earl of Shaftesbury fanned the flames of prejudice and fraud that fuelled the Plot and vigorously attempted to pass legislation that would exclude James from the throne. After a number of Catholic lords and Jesuit priests were hanged on the say-so of known perjurers, the Stuart monarchy came close to collapse. However, Charles and James were supported by "Tories" who feared that Whig machinations were pretexts to return the nation to the bad days of the Commonwealth, and the Exclusion Crisis petered out in 1681. Charles reasserted control over city corporations and other institutions by supporting a Tory backlash against nonconformists and other Whig supporters that lasted until his death in February 1685.[3]

1. Corporate Cavillers

The Restoration witnessed an outpouring of tracts and books written against idolatry, the vast majority of which were implicitly or explicitly targeted against popery. Catholic doctrines were a regular target in the pulpit and condemnations were routinely rehashed in hundreds of books published during the period. Three future archbishops of Canterbury were also prominent in anti-Catholic polemics. Thomas Tenison's *Of Idolatry*, published in the year that the Popish Plot and the Exclusion Crisis took hold, examined the subject in various forms from the earliest times in the Old Testament, through the advent of Arianism and Islam, to present-day Socinians and Catholics. As the reign of Antichrist in England seemed to loom, John Tillotson preached a sermon on superstition and idolatry in 1687, and William Wake published a number of his writings against idolatry and popery in a collection of 1688. Newton took a keen interest in these arguments, and read widely in scholarly anti-papist literature. He inscribed his name in the copy of Edward Stillingfleet's 1671 *Discourse of Idolatry Practised in the Church of Rome*, one of the most influential of all late-seventeenth-century writings on the subject. He bought this copy from Isaac Barrow's library, and he inscribed his name in Barrow's copy of Stillingfleet's 1673 response to his critics. Newton also owned and dog-eared a copy of Barrow's posthumous 1680 *Treatise on the Pope's Supremacy*, a major assault on every conceivable aspect of the historical and theological underpinnings of papal authority. If the two of them ever discussed religious matters, this was at least one topic on which there would have been vigorous agreement.[4]

It is in the context of this rampant anti-Catholicism that one should examine Newton's increasingly fractious relations with Jesuit natural philosophers

in the mid-1670s. In April 1672 Henry Oldenburg sent Newton the observations on his paper on light and colours that had been made by the French
Jesuit Ignace Gaston Pardies, telling him that he would see "how nimble y^t
sort of men is to animadvert upon new theories." Despite being irked by
Pardies's description of his theory of the heterogeneity of white light as an
"hypothesis," Newton ended the correspondence by thanking him for his
cordiality, ingenuity, and sincerity. His relations with Jesuits would never
again be so cordial.[5] After a gap of more than two years, Oldenburg sent
Newton a set of comments on his theory of light made by the Liégois natural philosopher Francis Linus. Referring to the production of the simple
oblong image, Linus argued that Newton had made a mistake in assuming
that the source of the rays impinging upon the prism was only as broad as
the sun's disk. Instead, when the sun shone through clouds, the clouds created a much larger base for the light that entered through the hole made in
the sheet covering the window. This meant that the ray of light began to
spread before it made contact with the prism, giving rise to the oblong
spectrum. In his reply to Oldenburg, Newton confirmed that he had carried out the experiment on clear days, and that the prism had been placed
right next to the hole in the window so that the light ray had had no room
to diverge. He added that to prevent Linus from "slurring himself in print
wth his wide conjecture," Oldenburg should refer him back to the diagram
of the experimental set-up that had accompanied the published version of
his second answer to Pardies. Oldenburg duly told Linus that Newton's
procedure had been carried out exactly as stated in this response. Linus's
letter appeared in the *Philosophical Transactions* for January 1675, along with
an anonymous truncated version of the reply given by Newton.[6]

On seeing the published version of his text, the slighted Jesuit reiterated
his position in a second letter that Oldenburg passed on to Newton when
the latter visited London in February 1675. When Newton had still not replied by autumn 1675 to this and other criticisms, Linus complained to
Oldenburg that he had expected an answer from Newton, "wch notwithstanding, I could not beleeve, the mistake being to cleare to be any way
defended." Oldenburg passed on the gist of this to Newton who replied in
the middle of November. Although Linus had framed the issue in terms of
his "mistakes," Newton took the point in question to be about his honour.
He reminded Oldenburg that when he had shown Newton the letter in
London, "I told you y^t I thought an answer in writing would be insignificant because ye dispute was not about any ratiocination, but my veracity in

relating an experiment, wch he denies will succeed as it is described in my printed letters." The joint subjects of scientific truth and Newton's integrity were to be determined "not by discourse, but new tryall of ye experiment"— perhaps at the Royal Society. It is now that he began to seriously consider that it was not his own status as a truth-teller, but that of his Roman Catholic critics that was in question.[7]

Newton took Linus's criticism of the crucial experiment to be evidence that Linus had not tried it and he told Oldenburg in November 1675 that "by his denying [it] I know he has not done yet as [it] should be tried." In December, as Newton's "Hypothesis" was being read before the Royal Society, one of Linus's students, John Gascoigne, replied on behalf of his supervisor who had recently died. Gascoigne requested that Oldenburg print Linus's second letter to Newton, since—he alleged—Newton himself had asked Oldenburg not to print the first until his own answer could follow it. Gascoigne said that he accepted Oldenburg's description of Newton's humility and meticulousness, but added that "to think him either more moderate or exact and studious than Mr Line was, will be hard to persuade those, who were acquainted with him." Linus had probably done three experiments for every one that Newton had done, and that in a much clearer sky than one could find in England. Finally, Gascoigne remarked that he hoped the entire correspondence could be printed.[8] In January 1676, Newton told Oldenburg that the Jesuits should send an accurate and precise description of the measurements made in their experiments and clarify their arguments by sending some diagrams. However, he added, there was much to dislike about their behaviour. In particular, he claimed that far from wishing to influence the dispute in print, the publication of his critique of Linus's original letter "made me say to one, that I wish^t they had been suppres^t for I doubted ye printing them would make Mr Linus unquiet & so in ye end create me trouble." As with the immediate response to his initial paper on light and colours, Newton now found it impossible to extricate himself from the demands of print culture.[9]

It was never likely that Newton would be granted his wish for his encounters with Linus and Gascoigne to be consigned to oblivion. Indeed with the publication of these letters in the *Philosophical Transactions*, the disputes with the Jesuits gathered momentum. Linus's second letter of February 1675 appeared in the *Transactions* at the beginning of 1676, followed by his own letter to Oldenburg of November 1675. Newton realised that he had left a hostage to fortune by suggesting that the crucial experiment be determined by the

Society itself, and in February 1676 he told Oldenburg that since the issue had been left unresolved, readers might gain the impression that he had acknowledged that his own claims were unsubstantiated. To correct this, he argued—in a text laced with copious references to Linus's "friends"—that Gascoigne should try to reproduce the crucial experiment. However, the Jesuits had agreed that the experiment be performed before the Royal Society, and in April Newton requested that Oldenburg arrange for this to happen, claiming that Linus's colleagues would not otherwise acquiesce. Such a trial was performed successfully on the following day (27 April 1676), and the Society ordered that Oldenburg inform "those of Liege" about the outcome.[10]

Now that the Society had definitively settled the issue Newton could relax, and he thanked Oldenburg for the work he had done in getting the experiment tried in London. However, in May, he was suddenly faced by new criticisms from yet another Jesuit, Anthony Lucas, whom Gascoigne had asked to take his place in the exchange. Lucas had attempted to perform experiments with much more care than his predecessors and, having praised the ingenuity of Newton, told Oldenburg in May 1676 that he "rejoiced" that the Society's trials "agree soe exactly with ours here, tho in somewhat ours disagree from Mr. Newton." According to Lucas, the length of the image produced by passing sunlight through a prism was never more than three and a half times its breadth, a far cry from the multiple of five claimed by Newton. "Soe much," he wrote, in words that were not forgotten by the Cambridge don, "to the matter of fact." Next Lucas listed a number of different experiments that he had performed, all of which appeared to contradict one or more of Newton's key positions. With a large dose of optimism, Lucas ended by stating that he hoped his findings would not be "unwelcome" to Newton.[11]

A stunned Newton responded in August 1676, specifying more experimental and material protocols for the replication of his work. However, he continued to stress that multiple replicated and publicly witnessed experimental trials alone were useless for validating experimental knowledge. Instead, he pointed Lucas to the authority of the single crucial experiment: "For it is not number of Exp's, but weight to be regarded; & where one will do, what need of many?" Newton told Oldenburg that he had privately performed an extensive number of other unpublished experiments and added that before he had written his first letter to Oldenburg about colours, he had written a major work (the suppressed treatise) on the subject in which he had laid down the underlying principle of the experiments. It was

wholly unnecessary, he added, to release these when the simple trials proposed in his original paper sufficed to make his claim. Four days later he
apologised to Oldenburg for sending something shorter than he had originally
intended, but added that this was "perhaps more to ye purpose considering
who I have to deal wth, whose buisiness it is to cavill."[12]

Lucas remained deeply unsatisfied by Newton's aggressive and unyielding
posture and sent further comments to Oldenburg in October 1676. He
drew Newton's theory into a "close Syllogisticall method" and argued that
unequal refrangibility had still merely been *assumed* by Newton to be "in-
trinsecall" to differently coloured rays. He did not see how, "according to
the received laws of Logick," the crucial experiment could be a demonstrative proof that there was no cause of differential refrangibility *external* to the
light ray. Instead, he proposed a series of experiments in different refractive
media and invoked the practice of Robert Boyle and other members of the
Royal Society to support his claim that theories had to be supported by a
"vast number of new experiments, each wherof, is deservedly conceived to
add new strength to this Theory." He added some experimental data to
make good his case that different colours at the same angle of incidence
suffered the same degree of refraction and asserted that until Newton
showed him what was wrong with these experiments, "his distinction between
number & *weight* of experiments may possibly appear to some more subtill
then weighty."[13]

This accusation that his argument was a mere sleight of hand further increased Newton's blood pressure and intensified his belief that the Jesuits
merely wanted to dispute with him in the barren legal mode of the scholastics. He complained bitterly of the obligation he was under to communicate with them, telling Oldenburg that he had made himself a "slave to
Philosophy." In apocalyptic tones he added that if he could be free of the
entire business, he would "resolutely bid adew to [Philosophy] eternally,
excepting what I doe for my satisfaction or leave to come out after me. For
I see a man must either resolve to put out nothing new or to become a slave
to defend it." As for Lucas's complaints about the length of the oblong
image, Newton again returned him to the crucial experiment, asserting that
anything other than establishing the existence of differential refrangibility
was a "new attempted digression." What mattered was the truth of his experiments, for this was the basis of his theory: "Which is of more consequence," he asked, "ye credit of my being wary, accurate and faithfull in y^e
reports I have made or shall make of experiments in any subject, seeing y^t a

trip in any one will bring all ye rest into suspicion[?]" He did not wish to be "jostled out" by an irrelevant topic and professed himself to be tired of the whole business.[14]

Lucas was more unconvinced than ever by Newton's position. In a letter of January 1677 he told Oldenburg that he *had* examined the crucial experiment and that his previous epistle had *not* been "a jostling out of the point by a new attempted digression.... I having but follow'd the way which he himselfe had track'd out for me." He drew attention to Newton's repeated and unsupported references to his private stock of experiments and argued that Newton himself ought to assume Lucas's own critique was "very rationall."[15] Perhaps as a way of ending these disputes, Newton now revived the plan to publish a substantial work on optics. In mid-December 1677 he told Robert Hooke, newly appointed as a secretary of the Royal Society following the death of Oldenburg, that he planned to publish his optical letters, "amongst some other things wch are going to ye Press." The antiquarian John Aubrey also approached him at the same time with a view to publishing his correspondence with Lucas. However, either because Newton could not get independent testimony for his doctrines, or because he felt it would involve him in disputes, or more likely because he was close to a mental breakdown, the volume did not appear.[16]

At some point in the winter of 1677/78, a fire in Newton's rooms destroyed many of his optical papers and he lost much of his correspondence, including a copy of the second letter written by Lucas in October 1676. Newton wrote directly to Lucas on 2 February 1678, asking about Linus's methods for prosecuting the crucial experiment on a clear day. At the end of February, Lucas forwarded him a copy of his third letter of January 1677 and told Newton that Hooke would send him a copy of his second. Newton, who duly received the latter from Hooke, somehow realised that the new letter was a different version from the one originally sent and noted later that some of the differences between them were "very material." One major addition was the following statement regarding his claim—as Lucas put it—that separate rays of light possessed an *intrinsic* unequal refrangibility that was the cause of the unequal refractions, rather than the shape of the prism, the nature of the glass, or some other cause. Provocatively, Lucas now added that it was this intrinsic refrangibility that Newton "fancys demonstrated from the experimentum crucis. Contrary, say I, this pretended demonstration (if taken singly) is inconclusive." If Newton had so far maintained a thin veneer of politeness in his dealings with Linus, Gascoigne, and Lucas, the explicit reference to the imaginary or fraudulent nature of his demonstrations drove him beyond the bounds of civility.[17]

In a critique of Lucas's first two letters, written on 5 March 1678, Newton described Lucas's missives as making a "stir" about his objections and pointed to a host of "mistakes" allegedly committed by Lucas in trying his own optical experiments. Newton complained that Lucas had treated him with "ill language" for his unwillingness to meddle with the experiments Lucas had proposed and remarked: "if you will not yet freely let us know your mistakes but hope to mend ye matter by new disputes, you are at your liberty." As his ire waxed, he listed a number of complaints about Lucas's behaviour. Lucas had continually tried to distract him from the business at hand and had "pressed" new objections on him. Newton now developed the claim that the Jesuits had mounted a sort of conspiracy against him and he invited Lucas, Gascoigne, "& ye rest of Mr Line's Friends in your Colledge" to "consider how to compose things to your common credit." Linus's friends had been "very zealous in defending him urging Mr Oldenburg to print our Letters & contending y^t Mr Line had tryed ye Experiment often before many witnesses & in clearer days than England doth ordinarily allow." Newton had for some time taken the Jesuits to be corporate and conspiratorial authors and he told Lucas that "what I find don in your Name I must esteem done by them who upon Mr Lines death engaged themselves (as Mr Gascoigne exprest) to pursue this business on & afterwards employed your pen in it." In a thinly disguised threat to Lucas's colleagues, Newton added that his comments were not supposed to "reflect" on them, but to make them "cautious" in how they proceeded.[18]

In an addition to this letter, also dated 5 March 1678, Newton turned even more biliously to the final (third) letter sent by Lucas in January 1677. He railed against Lucas's attempts to "reconcile" him with the truth, and he argued that the language of the law court was completely inappropriate for this kind of affair:

> You endeavour to oblige me into a new dispute wth you by calling me *a Demurrer* & your new objections *your main Debate* &c. And my profer to answer one or two of your objections wch you should recommend for ye best you despise as if it was Illegal (as you term it) if I answer not all. Do men use to press one another into Disputes? Or am I bound to satisfy you?

Instead of being unable to answer his objections, as Lucas had implied, Newton asked him whether his own silence was not due to "think[ing]

them too weak to require an answer"—"How know you but y^t other prudential reasons might make me averse from contending wth you?" In any
case, Newton continued, he did not think optics was a proper subject to
dispute about in public, and he informed Lucas that on these grounds, this
and the accompanying letter were to be judged private. He ended by stating
that he hoped that Lucas would consider how little Newton wanted to
explain Lucas's "proceedings" in public.[19]

The affair did not quite end at this point. In May 1678 Hooke told
Newton that he had seen a copy of yet another production from Lucas and
remarked, "I much admire your patience that you will trouble your self wth
such an extravagantly impertinent—, who will never yeald be the matter
never soe plain." Soon afterwards Newton told somebody (probably Aubrey)
that he had heard rumours that "instead of becoming more moderate
[Lucas] still betakes himself to sharper language than ever." Now Lucas had
received an answer from Newton he was "for contending further," and he
had begun to persuade Aubrey that Newton was "hot & that he gives me all
this time to grow cooler in." For the last time Newton raked up the bones
of the Jesuits' position. They had tried to find new observations to support
Linus "though in candor & aequity they ought to have sent an immediate
acknowledgement to take of those suspicions of error & dishonesty in me."
The supposed reconciliation of Linus with Newton and truth was merely a
trick and the addition of new objections was a ruse to embroil him in more
disputes. On the other hand, Newton had sent his last letter "not to prolong
disputes but to be published wth his letter if he thought that more his interest rather then to keep quiet." However, Lucas had already "arrived to that
degre of sharp language as makes his letters unfit to be further medled
with." Sometime later, when he heard that Aubrey had the letter from Lucas
ready to send on to him, Newton asked him to keep it.[20]

2. Anti-Catholic Prejudice

The "prudential reasons" to which Newton referred in his letter to Lucas
were almost certainly connected to his increasing conviction that Lucas's
co-religionists had been responsible for the worst perversions that Christianity
had ever experienced. Indeed, the exchange with the Jesuits, and with Lucas
in particular, undoubtedly hardened Newton's ingrained anti-Catholicism
and fuelled his investigations into the history of the rise of their religion.

The correspondence with Lucas reached its climax just months before the existence of the Popish Plot was revealed to an anxious nation. About this time, Newton began his research into early church history and embedded it in a Protestant apocalyptic history of the world. He believed that a group of early Christians had created a counter-religion that incorporated the most idolatrous elements of pagan beliefs, while the corrupt and unnatural bodily practices of the most extreme eremites had infiltrated many areas of the Christian practice. In time, as he saw it, Roman Catholics took to rewriting Scripture, inserting texts in support of the Trinity that changed the fundamental evidence relating to Christ's true nature. In the secular realm, popes began to assume an illegitimate power, forming ecclesiastical courts that prosecuted people for their religious views and not for other offences. To their shame, as Newton saw it, many modern Protestants supported the idolatrous and polytheistic doctrine of the triune Godhead, and they endorsed the persecution of those who believed in authentic Christian doctrine.[21]

As we shall see later in this book, all the major works on the Apocalypse that Newton valued identified Roman Catholicism as the epitome of idolatry. For example, Joseph Mede's posthumous *Apostasy of the Latter Times*—available to Newton in the latter's *Works*—provided a detailed demonstration of how the Great Apostasy described in 1 Timothy 4 was fulfilled in Catholic legends, false miracles, saint- and image-worship, and in the rise of the monks. Other works provided more detailed technical and historical arguments about the nature and rise of popery. Few of these notes can be dated with precision, and those that can were composed after 1690. However, many of them, particularly those dealing with the rise of what he understood as the earliest form of Roman Catholicism, must have been composed during the 1680s.[22]

One of Newton's investigations into the historical evolution of Catholicism began with a short excerpt on the objects of Catholic prayer taken from John Jewel's *Defence of the Apologie of the Churche of Englande* (1566). In one undated series of notes he recorded from Jewel the conditions under which Catholics prayed to the Virgin. Despite the fact that Catholics professed that there was only one mediator of salvation, and many mediators of intercession, they still prayed to Mary and even to Thomas Becket; each of these, in Newton's eyes, was a gross act of idolatry. If specific Roman Catholic practices represented the diabolical apex of idolatry, the religion as a whole betrayed characteristics of the more general perversion. After a series of references to occasions where Roman councils had referred to the pope as a God on Earth, Newton gave an account, with many supporting references from the Fathers, of pagan idolatry. However, the doctrine of transubstantiation was much worse than this, since Catholics believed the monstrous doctrine that the Eucharistic wafer and wine were literally transmuted into the blood and body of Christ. Hence, as Newton pronounced, pagan idolatry at its worst was never as bad as papism. In a "note" appended to these points he returned to the question of the worship of the Virgin, claiming that the heathens knew that the souls of departed men that they worshipped were creatures, but were nevertheless considered by all Christians as guilty of idolatry. Just as it failed to excuse them, so Roman Catholics who worshipped dead men and the mother of the saviour were guilty of monumental idolatry.[23]

As Newton warmed to his task, he condemned Roman priests for engaging in numerous pagan ceremonies and for performing a number of alleged miracles merely by saying "this is my body." While celebrating the Mass, they turned the bread into nothing—"or wch is wors into the body of Christ." They contracted Christ's body "into the quantity of ye least crumb of bread" and in an instant multiplied it in a number of different places. He noted that transubstantiation occurred "wthout passing through intermediate places or removing from its own place, or else to be [sc. it is] new produced i.e. created." However depraved the priest, the procedure was accomplished merely by speaking the relevant words, and "then he offers this liveless moveless body of Christ to god the father." Could any man, Newton thundered, believe that the wafer-become-body-of-Christ was in heaven?[24]

Newton drew liberally, though usually without acknowledgement, from the monumental collection of Protestant writings that detailed the history of Catholic idolatry. Many of his own notes rehearsed traditional anti-Catholic positions. For example, he noted that after Gregory the Great, large numbers of popes "were advanced to the popedom by known whores" while sometimes, he continued, "being magitians they advanced themselves to it by their own art...& oftner by murder & poison." These "Villains or as they call them incarnate Devills thronging in by twenties & thirties, ⟨one upon another⟩, & sometimes two or thre together (i.e., collaterally) make up that succession that ye p^{e}sent church of Rome so much stands on." From Jewel's *Defence* Newton detailed the gradual introduction of image-worship into the church, while in the same source he found numerous testimonies that the use of images in worship was not practised in the first ages. From Jewel's account of the "Popish doctors" Alphonso de Castro and Jean Gerson, Newton noted that the use of the cup in the sacrament was withdrawn because of the various filthy and loathsome practises to which it gave rise. He then proceeded to give a very brief history of the rise of the secular power of the pope. In the late medieval period, he noted, the popes gradually acquired more and more temporal power, culminating in 1300 when Boniface VIII "did one day shew himself in his Pontificals as Pope and another in his Imperial Robes as Emperor." This was one of many events that signified the new hold of the Catholic Church over the temporal domain.[25]

In excerpts from the Palestinian historian Sozomen and others, Newton noted that the adoration of images began in the Eastern church in about 380, while the inside of Western churches was being painted in the second decade of the following century. He remarked that Gregory the Great (pope from 590 to 604) was the promoter of many abuses of religion, such as the use of images in temples (especially in Italy and France), indulgences, and purgatory. He also added that the cloistered life of nuns and the ban on their marrying began about the time of Constantine the Great, the same restrictions on monks arriving around 390. Newton drew a number of stories from Antonius Bargensis's mid-fifteenth-century *Chronicle* of the Benedictine monks of the Olivetan Order, including one about the fraudulent means by which an initially incredulous woman had become convinced about transubstantiation, and one about a monk who had reappeared the night after he had died excommunicate, claiming that he had been freed from purgatory after Gregory had forced his absolution to be read over his grave. In time Newton incorporated these pieces of information were into a grand narrative that detailed the central role played by such practices in the Great Apostasy.[26]

As we have seen, Newton decided early in his researches that the perversion of Christianity in the fourth century had been masterminded by Athanasius. This unprecedented abomination took root in Rome and Alexandria and spread into all the neighbouring nations with the help of monks and a depraved clergy. In his historical accounts of the corruption of the church, monks enjoyed starring roles as practitioners and disseminators of abject religious perversions. Even before Nicaea, according to Newton, they had already begun to corrupt religious practice by insisting on deviant ascetic regimes. Under Athanasius, in the hope of acquiring converts, they transformed Christianity into a superstitious cult whose rites resembled the religious practices of pagans. In one version of his history of their rise, which probably dates from the early 1680s, Newton charged them with being the vanguard of the Great Apostasy that ultimately polluted the purity of early Christianity. At times, the analysis was couched in prophetic language. At one point, for example, he claimed that when the Roman Catholic clergy combined with the monks and imbibed their beliefs and practices, they constituted the two-horned beast or false prophet arising from the land (Rev. 13:11–18). However, the essay was supposed to be a straightforward historical account of the rise of the monastic profession, and similar accounts were deliberately shorn of prophetic references.[27]

In another chapter from an early treatise on the rise and true nature of the Apostasy, Newton collected a long series of passages from primary sources demonstrating how the cult of miracle-working relics had taken hold in the Holy Lands. "Were I to bring together everything that exists on the subject," he claimed, "I would need to write a book," and indeed, he spent much of his life trying to write one. Making one of the few (if vague) references in his entire oeuvre to contemporary writings on the issue, Newton remarked that many modern writers had conceded that the Christian Church became idolatrous in the early fifth century, and has noted that few had realised that the origins of its demise had come earlier than this. Indeed, this chronological rearrangement was one of the key innovations in Newton's scheme, and bringing the onset of the Apostasy forward allowed him to connect up the Trinitarian and Roman Catholic abominations he believed were constitutive of the Great Apostasy.[28]

All evidence pointed to key events that took place in the reign of Julian the Apostate (361–63) for the period being what Newton termed "the origin of the evil." Central to the story was what happened to the oracle of Apollo at Daphne. According to Hilary, bishop of Poitiers and, for Newton, one of chief promoters of religious perversion, the oracle refused to answer Julian when he went to consult it in 362 because the remains of Saint Babylas were close by. Justin had the saint's remains exhumed and taken back to where he had originally been buried, whereupon the temple burned down. The faithful started to worship Babylon's bones and Newton concluded that the devil, "despairing of preserving his ancient worship, destroyed it with his own hands, that he might rather attract worship and veneration to the relics of the dead among the Christians." Miracles, which had ceased for three hundred years, were now allegedly performed on an almost daily basis,

Newton complained, but to what purpose? What use were they to the true Church, and what doctrine did they elucidate? Why did God suddenly allow miracles to be performed now rather than before? It could not have been part of God's design, Newton concluded, for it was evident from the mid-fifth-century commentator Salvian's *De Gubernatione Dei* ("The Government of God") that these Christians were the worst who ever lived. Rather, the sheer number of false miracles were intended to ruin true Christianity, masterminded by a dark angel—Satan himself—who had fallen from heaven, and who knew he had little time to play his tricks on Earth (Rev. 12:12).[29]

3. The Rise of the Monks

Newton began another draft chapter with the appearance of the first monks. Antony—the Desert Father known as the "father of all monks"—was credited by Newton with being the founder of the movement since early in the fourth century he made the monastic life attractive to numerous converts. In a synopsis of Athanasius's *Life of Antony*, Newton outlined all the miracles and other deeds allegedly performed by Antony, who had heroically set up the order of monks despite being tormented by demonic beasts in the shape of serpents. Newton told how with the support of Athanasius, Antony trained up monks to combat Arianism, and his student Pachomius created the first *Coenobium* or religious community. Over time these institutions moved from the Egyptian desert into the cities, and Athanasius was able to have members of his own order appointed as regular clergy. When Antony came to Rome in about 340 he gained new acolytes, and the practice quickly spread. One of his disciples, Hilarion, spread it into Syria and Palestine, and later Augustine brought monastic practices with him to Africa. Indeed, as Newton learned from Baronius's *Annals* and other sources, by the end of the century thousands of monks could be found in every part of the Middle East and Europe. In one text, he denounced both Egypt and Italy as the twin spawning grounds of the two-horned beast described in Revelation 13, but the major source for monkish practices remained Egypt, where the clergy was almost wholly monastic and where there was immense popular support for the order.[30]

In various drafts, Newton described the close relationship between Athanasius and the Egyptian monks, then under the leadership of Antony. Here, as in many other places, he had to balance his belief that all the supernatural feats in Athanasius's *Life* of the monk were false, against his need for much of the rest of the narrative to be a true indication of monkish madness and excess. Indeed, he argued against some Protestant historians in favour of the authenticity of the text, though in so doing—not for the last time—he put himself in the same camp as Roman Catholic writers such as Bellarmine and Baronius. It was presumably written by Athanasius in 358 or 359 (soon after Antony's death), Newton argued, since he read in Baronius that Jerome reported a contemporary named Marcella speaking of the book. Some Protestant theologians had thought the text a later forgery on the basis that it made Antony out to be unlearned, but Newton cited a number of historians who confirmed that what Athanasius said of Antony's life was reliable. In addition to this, he brought out independent evidence both from Sozomen and from the spiritual writings of the early fifth-century monk John Cassian proving that Athanasius had given an accurate description of the extreme behaviour of the monks. Most important, although many Protestants thought that such a "pious & judicious" man as Athanasius could not have written a tale with such "monstrous & incredible" events in it, Newton countered that it was precisely because he wrote other things like it that one *should* believe it was a product of his fertile brain his fertile brain.[31]

As Newton saw it, the perverse success of the *Life of Antony* was guaranteed by the devil. The text engendered respect for monasticism and disdain for the godly anti-Trinitarian emperor Constantius in equal measure, and it promoted belief in miracles and in the "magical" use of the sign of the cross. According to Newton, it was not any old legend but it was the original template for all such "Ecclesiastical Romances." It spawned numerous supernatural stories of the same kind, many of which, he noted, were now found in the compilation of lives and sayings (collectively known as the *Vitaspatrum*) of the Desert Fathers to be found in the Dutch Jesuit Heribert Rosweyde's *Acta sanctorum*, but more pertinently it was the "original of those ecclesiastical legends wch are still use[d] in the Church of Rome." The spread of the novel and evil cult by means of this fraudulent biography, according to Newton, represented an astonishing turnaround for Athanasius, who had been at his lowest ebb and "seing no hopes of recovery unlesse by extraordinary practices, set himself upon all kind of sophistry & began with writing this life." Athanasius now began to literally rewrite history and also to nourish what Newton believed to be the satanically inspired monastic orders.[32]

Athanasius elevated members of these orders to the highest levels of the church, and in return, Newton claimed, "there was an extraordinary affection among the monks for Athanasius, their head, and the bond of affection was the Nicene faith, which they had imbibed from Athanasius and Antony their Apostle." This close connection between the two men and their followers was the source of nearly all the calamities and commotions that followed in the church, and the monks played their part by rising to become the most riotous and seditious group within Egypt, which already excelled in that sort of behaviour. While Athanasius waxed lyrical about the crimes of his enemies, he ignored the excesses of his own people. For Newton, compelling evidence presented by the Eastern churches at Serdica (in 343) indicated that Athanasius had "stirred up" his followers, both monks and nuns, to engage in seditious acts against people and property—though other indications suggested that Egyptians needed little encouragement to indulge in violence. Ultimately, Newton surmised, the Athanasians had been rightly punished for rioting rather than being chastised for their religion (as Athanasius had falsely stated). Indeed, the state had been lenient in only flogging the worst of the Athanasians, and the small amount of fatal collateral damage had been due to the unfortunate excesses of over-zealous individuals.[33]

In most of his accounts, Newton assigned to Athanasius sole responsibility for bringing in elements of paganism and superstition into Christian practice. At the heart of this perverse activity, he claimed, Athanasius introduced into the West monastic practices, miracle-working, and the use of the sign of the cross, to which he attributed the power to suppress black magic. Newton argued that when Athanasius was still in Egypt he had claimed that the relics of Christ, or rather the signs of these relics, possessed supernatural power. As a diabolical accompaniment, he had "invented" the practice of miracles in Alexandria at the end of the 350s. When performed without faith in Christ, Newton claimed, what could be more superstitious and hateful than pretending that inanimate objects or the mere speaking of words could perform beneficial effects in the world? At other times, he named Hilary of Poitiers as a chief promoter of the doctrine of miracles and the intercession of saints in the West. The source of some of the worst aspects of Catholicism, Newton suggested, occurred when Hilary returned to the West from Asia Minor in 361, having met with a number of the most extreme monastics. Hilary used his brilliant organisational acumen to influence the councils that reasserted homoousianism (understood by the Latin, Western bishops to mean consubstantiality); following him, the consubstantial Trinity regained its hold in Italian cities, where it had ever since reigned.

However, Newton usually attributed miracle-worship to Athanasius and his party, who "found by experience y^t their opinions were not to be propagated by disputing & arguing, & therefore gave out that their adversaries were crafty people & cunning disputants & their own party ‹simple› well meaning men." They passed a law forbidding monks from disputing about the Trinity, and thus left their cause to succeed by means of the twin perversions of false miracles and "monkery."[34]

Despite having once believed that the relics of true martyrs should be buried underground, Athanasius, who supervised their distribution, now kept the bones (or rather, according to Newton, fake versions thereof) of John the Baptist buried in a wall cavity ready to be shown to the faithful. Once he had convinced people that the relics of saints could perform miracles, the holy remains of saints and martyrs were brought out before the people at regular intervals. Following a long tradition of Protestant attacks on the doctrine of purgatory, Newton mined Baronius's *Annals* to show that the first Christians had buried bodies smeared with unguents in catacombs or sandy crypts, a practice taken from the Jews. Unlike pagans, they feared cremation because they believed that Christians did not die but fell asleep in God before they rose again. This belief was soon corrupted by Roman Catholics, and by the middle of the fourth century it was widely believed by the credulous flock that saints heard their prayers; that they prayed along with ordinary people; and that when uttered, demons feared the form (but not the sense) of the words left by the saints. Such was the astonishing speed at which these pernicious views and practices were propagated, Newton added, that the false religion had become universal by 381.[35]

Newton drew from a wide array of sources to show how quickly the cult of saints and martyrs spread across Europe, the Holy Lands, and North Africa. By the end of the century relics of saints and martyrs had proliferated to an extraordinary degree, and the sale of these items was widespread. Admittedly, Newton claimed, this was done by less scrupulous individuals but their very success was an indication of what the vast majority of people were prepared to believe. Private homes were filled with pious frauds, and Newton used a letter by the presbyter Lucian on the discovery of the martyrs Stephen, Nicodemus, and Gamaliel (the whereabouts of which had apparently been revealed to him in a dream in December 415) as evidence of the pervasiveness of the cult: "from this celebrated revelation of saints, apparently carried out for the necessary benefit of humanity, we can imagine the extraordinary credulity and superstition of the age and the fraud of men and devils in other revelations." As in other areas of his research, he attributed these events not only to the propensity of ordinary people to believe in the ludicrous statements of fraudulent monks but also to the very real machinations of the devil in exciting the dreams in the first place.[36]

As Newton described it, the growth of temples, altars, and other monuments to the dead, dedicated by the relics of martyrs, was the lynchpin of the new pagano-Christianity. Roadside altars proliferated because so many relics were suddenly produced to venerate the exponentially expanding number of martyrs. In addition to spots close to the tombs of earlier, genuine victims of Roman persecutions, monks managed to get altars constructed anywhere they managed to convince ordinary people that the location of a martyr had been revealed to them in their dreams. In a very short time, as pagans themselves had prophesied, they replaced the heathen shrines. With demand so intense, the bodies of martyrs had to be divided up and spread around the known world—"who therefore," Newton complained, "will not admit that the entire country was completely filled with these abominations?" Who could count the incredible amount of places dedicated to the cult? Being Newton, he did try, adducing evidence from Theodoret's *Ecclesiastical History* to show that the Catholic Church could boast tens of thousands of martyrs, but he concluded that given the vast numbers involved, only a rough qualitative assessment was possible.[37]

From the 360s and 370s, the temples were built on a grand scale, and their interiors became much more splendid than before. People competed to outdo one another in magnificence; many buildings were gilded with gold, and their great doors bedecked with ivory, silver, and jewels. After citing contemporary evidence from Pope Damasus, Jerome, and Prosper of Aquitane on the extent of such opulence, Newton commented: "I do not mention these things on the grounds that I would disapprove of expense and magnificence in the true worship of God, but in order to demonstrate the zeal of the century in the false cult of the Saints." Indeed, he argued that the apportioning of saints to a city on the basis of the distribution of relics was a fulfilment of Daniel's prophecy (Dan. 11:38) that land would be divided among the Mahuzzim (guardians) with gold, silver, and precious things. Ordinary people burned with devotion towards the saints, honouring them as guardians and protectors. From the saints they sought health and other blessings, and in return for their beneficence the faithful thanked them, offered them sacrifices, and celebrated them on frequent festival days. Even more loathsome was the development of pilgrimages to Jerusalem,

Alexandria, and Rome, which now became obligatory rites. Newton argued that a previous and harmless custom of visiting shrines as a sort of tourist attraction had "instantly" become a superstition. In particular, the relics of Jesus Christ himself were held to have special powers, and the prayers of the faithful were alleged to restore his actual cross on a daily basis, "as if by vegetation." In line with his general Protestant scepticism about such claims, Newton remarked that he suspected that the cross had never been found but had been fabricated.[38]

4. A Protestant Work Ethic

A key plank of Newton's attack on Roman Catholicism was his accusation that the extreme ascetic bodily practices of the Desert Fathers—which were celebrated within the Catholic faith—were unnatural, irreligious, and directed towards the inflammation of lust. His writings on this subject are particularly interesting because his own existence as a celibate college don, a life he experienced until he moved to London in 1696, was in many respects very similar to the lives of the monks. As far back as the ancient Greeks, philosophers had cultivated different forms of physical and mental ascesis, and the early modern Protestant don was obliged to engage in a specific version of self-discipline. Newton believed that his vocation was a celibate life devoted to intense study, and he understood that continuous immersion in some or other project was the only way to avoid idleness, which led to the demons of viciousness, carnal temptation, and idolatry. It was precisely because of the structural similarities between his own existence and that of the men whose spiritual practices he considered to be utterly perverse, that he had to distinguish between them.[39]

As we have seen in James Duport's advice to young students, scholarly idleness was regularly denounced in the collegiate environment. Perhaps the most protracted campaign at late seventeenth-century Trinity in favour of properly directed industry was conducted by Isaac Barrow, who in a number of sermons encouraged students to work to their utmost. Industry, he noted, was "a serious and steady application of mind, joined with a vigorous exercise of our active faculties, in prosecution of any reasonable, honest, useful design." Although it was difficult and testing, Christian scholars could practise industry, and he pointed out that Scripture variously described it as "agonistic and ascetic exercise," wrestling, running a race, warfare or combat, offering violence, and watching. Industry, coupled with the grace of God, ensured success, while slothfulness and vice guaranteed failure. Perseverance would bring wealth, honour, wisdom, and virtue. Wisdom required pains-taking labour because truth "commonly doth not lie in the surface...but is lodged deep in the bowels of things"; continual exercise "doth render [our mind] capable and patient in thinking upon any object or occasion." The student had to "wade through" a vast compass of learning and could not afford to be ignorant in any one part—otherwise "he will be a lame scholar, who hath not an insight into many kinds of knowledge." "The idle scholar," Barrow concluded, was a "nonsense." The greatest reward of industry was virtue, which required a continual exercise of vigorous self-criticism, carried out by "extirpating rooted prejudices and notions from our understanding, bending a stiff will, and rectifying crooked inclinations," "curbing eager and importune appetites," "taming wild passions," and "struggling with unruly lusts within."[40]

Most people inevitably succumbed to the temptations and pestilences of idleness. Sloth, according to Barrow, was the "nursery of sins" and he asked his listeners to cultivate the requisite "vigilancy of mind," "intention of spirit," "force of resolution," and "command and care over ourselves." Solid hard work left "no room or vacancy for ill thoughts or base designs to creep in," and the senses of the busy man "do not lie open to ensnaring objects." Barrow warned that the slothful were fit for, and merited only, a servile and sordid condition, being prone to delusions that further prevented them from doing their duty. The idle drone was nothing more than "an unnatural excrescence, sucking nutriment" from the common weal, being "very apt to conceit or pretend imaginary difficulties and hazards, and thence to be de-terred from going about his business." Idleness racked souls "with anxious suspense and perplexing distraction" and infested them with "crowds of frivolous, melancholic, troublesome, stinging thoughts." Of course, the devil himself set a typically perverse example, being an inveterate worker and a man of industry, always waiting to ensnare slackers and backsliders. Among the latter, Barrow included those who wasted their time playing sports or hunting and noted ironically that such people exerted their efforts only in corrupting and debauching themselves. The genteel student, who made up much of Barrow's audience, had a special obligation to be diligent. Hard work would equip him to resist the seductions of Satan but without serious business to preoccupy him, time would "lie upon his hands, as a pestering incumbrance." His body would "languish and become destitute of health, of vigour, of activity, for want of due exercise," and ultimately he would be prey to all the mischiefs that sprang from idleness and stupidity.[41]

Newton adhered to Duport's and Barrow's recommendations and his propensity for hard work became legendary amongst his contemporaries. It was central to his research ethic, and indeed, to his notion of what it was to be a godly scholar, and he told Conduitt and others that sustained thought, rather than moments of inspiration or genius, was the secret of his great intellectual achievements. Nevertheless, it was possible to work too hard, and Newton constantly pushed himself to the limits. The fate of his friend John North, Barrow's successor as master of Trinity College between 1677 and 1683, provided a salutary lesson of the consequences of studying oneself to destruction. Roger North recorded that his brother John's "temperature of body and austere course of life were ill matched, and his complexion agreed with neither." His "face was always tincted with a fresh colour, and his looks vegete and sanguine, and as some used to jest, his features were scandalous, as showing rather a *madame en travestie* than a bookworm." In continually aiming at self-improvement, John "kept himself bent with perpetual thinking and study, which manifestly impaired himself." Even conversation, Roger continued, which for others was a source of relief, "was to him an incentive of thought. He was sensible of this, but did not affect any expedients of relief to his mind." Unfortunately, John North had no outlet such as manual exercise to give vent to the pent-up humours and being "abstemious in extremity proved of ill consequence to his health." His body exemplified the hazardous constitution and precarious habitus of the scholar, and ultimately he would sacrifice himself to his vocation.[42]

North suffered from the classic health complaints of sedentary scholars, and he inspected his urine every morning. His main problem was his severe work discipline; as Roger put it, "It is certain that he was overmuch addicted to thinking, or else he performed it with more labour and intenseness than other men ordinarily do, for in the end it will appear that he was a martyr of study." John "scarce ever allowed himself any vacation; what he had was forced upon him [and] was the most intense and passionate thinker that ever lived and was sane." To a man with this temperament, the appointment to the college mastership was deleterious in the extreme. He was now thrust into "an anxious, solitary and pensive" course of life, which, with his austere way of ordering himself, caused the terrible sickness that would ultimately debilitate him. When his friends warned him that his self-denials endangering his health, he would "return a tradition of Bishop Wren, who when he was told he must not keep Lent, his body would not bear it, 'Will it not?' said he, 'then it is no body for me'." Inevitably, North's frail body could not take the strain, and a debilitating stroke was brought on by the necessity of having to discipline some loutish undergraduates. In his last years, John found some solace in collecting spiders and examining their behaviour, and he resorted to drinking large amounts of sherry. He recovered most of his previous power of thought but after his premature death in 1683, Roger wondered whether a wife might not have preserved his brother longer.[43]

A comparison between Newton's and North's care of the self is instructive. The physician and pioneering vegetarian George Cheyne later reported that he had been told that when Newton performed his early work on optics "to quicken his faculties and fix his attention, [he] confined himself to a small quantity of bread…with a little sack and water, of which, *without any regulation*, he took as he found a craving or failure of spirits." The source for this anecdote may have been John Conduitt, who was keen to show that Newton was highly self-disciplined without being a slave to an excessive dietary or corporeal regime. He reported that Newton "had a patience and perseverance in any study he was pursuing [and] was very temperate & sober in his diet tho without ever observing any rules or strict regimen." As a student, Newton had tried to regulate his health—as everyone did—by means of homemade recipes. A number of these are extant, testimony to the care with which he looked after himself while in college. One of them, "Lucatello's Balsam," was of particular importance to him. This was a universal panacea capable of being taken both internally and externally, and the illnesses it purported to treat included measles, plague, and smallpox, for which he recommended "a ¼ of an ounce in a little broth take it warme & sweate after it." It also cured gangrene, though for rabies and poison it had to be taken internally as well as externally. The writer and diarist John Evelyn used it to calm his son Richard when he vomited after choking on a bone and Newton consumed a substantial quantity when he believed he had consumption. John Wickins, who knew Newton better than anyone else did during the 1660s, said that the latter would often make a home brew of the balsam and drink about a quarter of a pint.[44]

Many of Newton's acolytes commented on his healthy and balanced lifestyle. Humphrey Newton told Conduitt that in his rooms Newton "walk'd so very much, y[t] you might have thought him to be educated at Athens among y[e] Aristotelian sect," but added that he was "always thinking with Bishop Sanderson, Temperance to be y[e] best Physick." Conduitt joined with Humphrey in relating Newton's self-discipline to that of the Ancients, recording that "Sir I. resembled Socrates in keeping between the medium of luxury & penury [&] was grave & chearfull." Some emphasised Newton's total lack of physical activity, if only to draw attention to his natural capacities. William Stukeley recalled that partly as a result of his sturdy constitution, and partly by his great prudence, Newton had "preserv'd his health to old age, far beyond what one could have expected in one so intirely immers'd in solitude, inactivity, meditation and study." Others believed that his excessive devotion to work went so far as to threaten his own destruction, a view that was in keeping with the parallel and later legendary discourse that emphasised his neglect of his clothing, sleep, and diet. Roger North recounted that his brother believed that if Newton "had not wrought with his hands in making experiments, he [would have] killed himself with study; a man may so engage his mind as almost to forget he hath a body, which must be waited upon and served." North concluded that John clearly saw in Newton what others plainly witnessed in his own case.[45]

North's testimony concerning Newton's phenomenal work ethic provides good evidence of the extent of his devotion to alchemy and theology in the late 1670s and early 1680s. This had consequences for his public professions of religion. Humphrey Newton told John Conduitt that in the second half of the 1680s, on account of this work, Newton only rarely graced the college chapel with his presence although he frequented Great St. Mary's on Sundays. He supposed that Newton found it difficult to get up in time in the morning, having stayed up working until 2 or 3 A.M. the previous night. Similarly, he noted that Newton's "earnest & indefatigable Studyes" took up his afternoons, "so y^t he scarcely knewe ye Hour of Prayer." He added that Newton had sometimes gone to dine in the hall with his surplice on, a piece of information that was mixed in with other facts in order to attest to Newton's absent-mindedness. When Conduitt wrote to Humphrey again to prompt further memories of Newton's private prayers, Humphrey merely repeated that his intense work practice must have deprived him of the opportunity. Despite Humphrey's reverence for his fellow countryman, and his fixation on Newton's relentless studying, it remained strange to him four decades later that Newton had been so neglectful of worship. In turn, perhaps to remove any taint of irreligion, Conduitt and others argued that the very study that Humphrey saw as a distraction, itself constituted a more significant form of worship.[46]

5. Monsters from the Id

Newton left an extensive account of how one should live a religious and productive scholarly existence, and it was deliberately framed as a contrast with what he took to be the depraved lives of the early monks. His examination focussed on the eremites' vows of self-restraint and chastity, and on the techniques they used to resist (or as Newton suspected, to provoke) the temptations of the imagination. As we noted in chapter 3, the latter was understood to be the typical source of creativity and disorder in the individual, and at the start of his career Newton tried to gauge and even enhance its powers. However, as he noted at the end of the same research programme, it threatened to corrode mental and physical health. As the predominant source of incomplete or false knowledge about the natural world, the imagination was more broadly implicated in melancholy, lustful fantasies, errant dreams, and madness, permanently churning out thoughts and images that tempted the Christian towards idleness and sin. Although Joseph Glanvill treated the faculty from the point of view of natural philosophy in his *Vanity of Dogmatizing* of 1661, he also had something to say about the dangers it posed for religion. Its "evil conduct" was a greater danger to faith than was reason, and, as Henry More had shown in his *Enthusiasmus Triumphatus* of 1656, it was largely responsible for the delusions of the religious enthusiast. Reason, on the other hand, was the friend of faith.[47]

Within the religious sphere, the imagination was most commonly associated with idolatry. When Francis Bacon referred to the idols of the mind, most readers would have thought in the first instance of warnings about the dangers of humans idolatrously devising visions of the divine from their own imaginations. In his *Institutes of the Christian Religion*, Calvin had described human nature as a "permanent factory of idols," noting that the mind conceived them and the hand gave them birth. The Old Testament warned that most men could only be confident that God was near to them if they could obtain a visual reassurance of his presence. Calvin cautioned that although graven idols were an affront to all that was holy, idolatry began in the mind, and one had to renounce, or at least control, the imagination. Yielding to its temptations was to invite the sinner to make the world in his own image, to create a fraudulent and depraved world, and to turn away from God. Idleness allowed the imagination to run riot in undisciplined minds, especially in those of the immoral and slothful rabble, and the best way to control it was to immerse oneself in purposeful work. For many puritans, the imagination could be restrained and limited only by making it regenerate, thus using it in the service of faith. As we have seen, Newton owned the 1561 edition of Calvin's *Institutes* and he signed his name in it when he arrived at Trinity College in 1661. Although he left little record of his engagement with the text, its stark diagnosis of the idolatrous proclivities of the mind must have exercised a powerful influence on to him. In the event, he devised a series of demanding techniques for evading the temptations of imagination, combining a devotion to hard work, a commitment to chastity, and a heightened sensitivity to the dangers of idolatry.[48]

Newton's analysis of chastity and the imagination formed part of a lengthy chapter on the origin and rise of monasticism. While undated, this text is almost certainly from his Cambridge period, when he was immersed in the history of the fourth-century corruption of Christianity. In this extraordinary narrative he argued that although the monastic profession began in Egypt, a parallel perversion had grown up in the West that also forced the clergy into celibacy. At the start of the fourth century, a number of Western church decrees enjoining continence in marriage were promulgated in order that the Christian priests should not be seen by the people to be less pious than the priests of Apollo, Juno, Diana, and Vesta, all of whom were bound to celibacy. In the East it was still possible to retain a wife within one's residence (if not in one's bed) and remain a priest, even as increasing numbers of canons were formulated against allowing other women within priestly homes. By the middle of the century, the complete denial of sexual relations with women was demanded of Western clergy, and in a detailed account Newton listed many examples where the celibate life was required in Gaul, Africa, and Italy. After the Council of Serdica in 343, Athanasius exported the principle of monastic celibacy back to Egypt, "just as he had formerly transferred monasticism from Egypt to the West." This "superstition," Newton went on, was backed by wrongly applying various passages from Scripture, and by the end of the century it was almost universally understood that the priesthood had to be composed of virgins.[49]

In the first few years of their existence, monastic communities were largely composed of married men maintaining sexual self-denial. However, citing Augustine's treatise on marriage and concupiscence (lust), Newton remarked that it had been virtually impossible in the early church to force married clergy to abstain from intercourse. It would have been much better if only celibates had been brought into the priesthood "as the Papists now do," though he added that he did not approve of the Catholic restriction of the priesthood to celibates. Enforcing celibacy on priests, as the "Athanasian doctors" did, ran counter to the marriage vows commanded by Christ under the false appearance of chastity, and effectively forced wives to commit adultery. Indeed, Newton argued, the practice of continence within marriage was doubly dangerous on the grounds that it led both to the violation of the marriage oath and the committal of fornication in one's heart. Unless the temptations had been overcome already, taking a vow was no way to avoid the lustful urges that were liable to overwhelm the unwary. Fighting the beast within would lead to certain defeat, while only by ignoring it or sidestepping it, and incorporating virtuous practices into one's daily life, could its effects be avoided.[50]

Newton's critique of oaths taken by people who were not ready, able, or willing to abide by them was of a piece with his more general Protestant conviction that oaths had to be both sincerely made and undertaken by those with the experience and capacity to be true to them. He argued that in cases where oath-takers were unable to live up to them, it would be better if one did not swear oaths at all, though as we shall see, there must have been many occasions when he himself had to assert his adherence to doctrines that he privately despised. There were specific problems with swearing an oath of abstinence, which, he continued, by itself only increased incontinence, since such a vow would immediately provoke thoughts about how to preserve chastity. From this, struggles with immorality would inevitably ensue, followed by mental torture, and even death. The most angelically virtuous people, he went on with evident self-reference, "never think about chastity and sexual immorality (except in passing), but keep their minds occupied with better things in which their piety is secure." Those who were preoccupied with chastity, and with preserving their vows, would always fail. After these words of wisdom, Newton remarked that because of the offensiveness of the subject he would only give one or two examples of how the monastic vow led to the opposite of what was intended. However, in the following pages he detailed numerous cases of monks who were tormented by their imaginations and dreams over the course of their lives.[51]

Newton drew a number of examples from Palladius of Galatia's early fifth-century *Lausiac History*, available to Newton in Rosweyde's *Vitae Patrum*. One of these was the experience of the Egyptian monk Moses, who was tempted by demons into fornication, having been tormented for many years in his dreams and visions. In fact, Moses was unable to overcome these images and after a series of hideous trials lasting six years, he needed a miracle to extinguish the fires of lust. Primed by his Protestant cynicism about such stories, Newton noted that Moses had probably only pretended to be cured in order to save his reputation. Many other stories of how the early monks had been sorely tried by their own imaginations were readily at hand. Palladius himself admitted in his *History* that he constantly fantasised about women, but was reassured by an elderly monk named Pachon that this was not because he was idle or lacked virtue—indeed, the older man had himself been in his cell in the desert for over forty years and was still tempted. At Pachon's lowest ebb, the devil had transformed himself into an Ethiopian girl whose outlines were dredged up from memories of Pachon's youth, and with whom he dreamt that he had carnal relations. For Newton it was Pachon's very battle with these thoughts that had kept alive the "wild beast" of lust, until old age finally promised to liberate him from the struggle. Both Palladius and Pachon, he noted in an addition to the text, were contemporaries of Athanasius. Even the "great" Jerome was tempted by unbearable thoughts, his mind boiling with desires. As a desert monk, his sun-dried body had become emaciated and virtually useless, but still he had vivid dreams of being surrounded by dancing girls. Again, only old age offered the promise of liberation from the torture. Hagiographers routinely portrayed the monks' struggle with lust as a badge of their virtue, but how, Newton asked, since they brought the battle upon themselves, and the contest reinforced the very images they professed to detest, could they possibly be depicted as heroic?[52]

As Newton saw it, an unbiased researcher such as himself could find countless examples of temptation in such histories, many of them being of the most illustrious members of the monastic order. The founder of the order in Palestine, Hilarion, was also forced to battle with the demons of his imagination, which engulfed him with numerous images of feasts and naked women. At an advanced age, Pachomius himself, the architect of the coenobitic (i.e., monastic) way of life, was provoked by visions of shamelessly nude women; as Newton put it sarcastically: "Fortunate Pachomius, who could see such things, or rather form them by the great force of his imagination, and that frequently and for a very long time, and yet remain unharmed and innocent." Even the arch-monk Antony, as Athanasius related in his *Life*, struggled with the usual problems of sordid daytime thoughts and nocturnal visits from women. If the greatest of them all could not conquer such visions, then who could? Monks held in the highest regard those who struggled most vigorously with such torments, even if they were unsuccessful. It was, Newton admitted, a good thing to have command over one's passions, and one could conquer some of them by sheer willpower. Yet lust was a different matter: fighting against it could only inflame it, and thinking continually of chastity could only lead to a loss of innocence: "The cell, the solitude, the habit, hunger, thirst, vigils, every ascetic practice will constantly bring to mind the reason for these things; and the more effort he puts into them, the more often and more powerfully it will do so." As men grew weary from battling with their sexual demons, so it became easier for the imagination to concoct even more extreme visions.[53]

In his condemnation of monastic ascesis, Newton returned to the notes from his undergraduate experiments on the eye and brain, and on the forms of extreme behaviour that could lead to madness. Lack of sleep, brought on by the battle with thoughts of fornication, would intensify the power of the imagination, a fate that befell madmen, those suffering from fevers, and those with chronic insomnia. Perpetual excess led to "constant dreams at night, frequent fantasies during the day, as vivid as if the things themselves were standing right in front of him." This "beast" or "serpent" of lust could not be overcome by force, but only by evasion and flight. If one dwelt too much on sexual virtue, one would be disturbed with all sorts of mental anguish, and, Newton added, "if a man goes after it and struggles with it, it attacks him in return and fills his breast with poison." The techniques used by the Desert Fathers and their companions to embrace chastity and to destroy its enemy merely inflamed the situation, and the fact that the coenobites (i.e., the non-solitaries) frequently associated with others engaged in similarly perverse quests only made things worse. In old age the battle left the combatant in a terrible condition: "only after a long time and very great hardship, wounded all over, drenched with blood and inevitably oppressed in later life with the stench and pain of his wounds, will he finally, and in a wretched state, overcome the beast." The irony was, Newton marveled, that none of these men realised that their own ascetic practices had given rise to the very visions against which they fought.[54]

In a related analysis, probably from the 1680s or early 1690s, Newton contrasted the balanced, chaste life that conduced towards a healthy and useful body against the sort of "vitious extreames" of existence that produced a perverted and enervated husk. On the one hand, pampering a body

enflames lust & makes it lesse active & fit for use. ⸢And on the other hand⸣ to macerate it ⸢by fasting & watching⸣ beyond measure does ye same thing. It does not only render ye body feeble & unfit for use, but also enflames it

˂& invigorates˃ lustful thoughts: for ~~at length it invigorates~~ yᵉ ~~imagination &~~
~~brings~~ ˂the want of sleep & due refreshment disorders the imagination & at
length brings˃ men to a sort of distraction ˂& madnesse˃ so as to make them
~~think they~~ have visions of weomen conversing with 'em ~~& sitting upon their~~
~~knees~~ & think they really see ˂& touch˃ them & hear them talk.

Newton noted that he had not met with "more uncleannesse & greater
arguments of unchast minds in any sort of people then in the lives of the
first Monks" and their embrace of filthy mental images seemed to be a deliberate strategy: "what else means their doctrine that its better to contend
with & vanquish unchast thoughts then not to have them, their frequent
visions of naked weomen, their digging up the bodies of dead weomen wᵗʰ
wᶜʰ they burned in lust, their lusting even after passive sodomy." To top it
all, he added, the hagiographers related these and many other stories *without
blushing*. It is hardly an exercise in fanciful speculation to read this autobi-
ographically. The passionate anger underlying this much-corrected piece
virtually leaps off the paper, and Newton continually veered between offering self-prescriptions on the godly life, and issuing condemnations of the
depraved practices of the long-dead monks. In these words we can see the
religious and ethical directives that underlay the life—and great productions—
of their author.[55]

6. Monastic Communities

The perils of the monastic life did not merely exist at the individual level.
In further remarks from his essay on early Christian self-discipline, which
closely reflect on his own situation, Newton reported that those who were
sexually abstemious and who did not attempt to battle with lustful thoughts,
but avoided them, were much less stricken with such images than the "impure
mob." However, the monks perversely believed that those plucked from
the general population, or, as Newton put it, the "mass of fornicators," were
capable of doing battle with the devil within. The environment of extreme
physical deprivation in which such novices found themselves rendered even
the most resolute will powerless. Newton claimed that doctors had determined that those whose bodies became debilitated through poor digestion
were more inclined to night-time fantasies and to the "emission of fluids."
How much more then were fasting monks prone to the same complaints?
Their diet, their vows of chastity, the lack of books, their aimless meditations,

the solitude that gave rise to such vivid fantasies, and the excessive vigils that occasioned melancholy and an overactive imagination all led to madness. After spending too much time in a monastic environment, their inflamed imaginations became so powerful that monks could no longer distinguish between fantasy and reality, and some even became unable to stand the sight of real women. One old monk went into town looking for a woman, while another tried to have intercourse with a devil who—as he often did—had taken on the form of a woman. Thus, Newton remarked with a rare poetic flourish, was "the lustful rustic converted into an even more lustful monk."[56]

All of this diabolical behaviour, Newton concluded, "could neither be generated nor survive outside of the sewers of the Egyptian cells, which were seething with a most fetid and putrid mass of filth." In time, such practices were reinforced by the development of communities of monks. Many novices did all they could to escape, "roasted and tormented by the filthy pit of their thoughts," but the older monks voyeuristically exhorted the younger men to reveal their innermost thoughts in exchange for counsel and solace, warning that keeping such notions private would only exacerbate them and give succour to the diabolical enemy. Holy men travelled around the desert giving advice on how to confront temptation, prayers were said for sufferers, and water was sprinkled over those affected. This, Newton concluded, was the origin of the idea in confession that the less serious mental sins could be washed away by blessed water, while more serious offences required penitence. At this point, his fascinating sociology of early monasticism came to an end.[57]

Newton's condemnations of the practices of the self of the Desert Fathers were among the most potent of all his critiques of Roman Catholicism. As he saw it, the monks deliberately inflamed their imaginations and burned in lust, perversely producing the very effects and symptoms that they were seeking to avoid. By contrast, his commitment to chastity and a celibate life lay at the heart of his religious beliefs. His views concerning the proper life of a don can be inferred both by attending to what he said about the perverted practices of the Desert Fathers, and also by looking at his positive statements about what constituted a virtuous existence in a religious environment. His prescriptive accounts regarding the scholarly good life, and his vivid depictions of the baneful effects of the imagination, were autobiographical. They drew both on elements of his religious upbringing and also on more personal experiences of heterosexual daytime fantasies and night-time dreams. In his undergraduate work, he performed extraordinary experiments to understand, control, and enhance the astonishing power of the imagination, all with a view to shedding light on the nature of madness and dreams. The perversions of monkish ascesis, where pervasive dreams of non-existent women drove monks to insanity, were a warning of the dangers to bodily and mental health, as well as to religion, when the imagination ran riot.

Newton's analysis of the dangers and pathologies of the imagination blurred and sometimes eroded the distinction between his own experience and that of the men he hated. The Desert Fathers had suffered from the same sorts of problems he had encountered himself, and there is occasionally a sense that Newton sympathised with them in their suffering. However, their self-produced hardships were more extreme than his, and their deviant religious practices only served to make their situations worse. Newton's own existence was lived out in a quasi-monastic community, and his attitude to the lives of the Desert Fathers had its basis in his personal struggles at the college and in his observations on fellow hermits like John North. Even if he was not a slave to a dietetic regime, he lived according to a rigorous religious regimen that allowed him to escape the worst effects of his imagination. Like the Desert Fathers, he had chosen the life of a celibate, but his existence was crafted in explicit opposition to their appalling practices. Their energies were directed inwardly in an attempt to grapple with a mental force that paradoxically drew strength from their fight against it. Their bodies were not fit for productive work, and enervated by their struggles, they produced no great tributes to their Creator. By contrast, Newton understood that the imagination could only be managed by engaging in a Herculean work ethic that would obviate idleness and lustful thoughts. His commitment to his scholarship was a key part of that work ethic, and the great treatises he wrote in the natural sciences and in theology were the textual residue of this work. These arose from the exercise of a work regime that required the continual refinement of experience and the understanding in the service of producing a godly and productive man.

6

Prisca Newtoniana

Despite expending such an intense effort on the history of the early
Christian Church, Newton also devoted a great deal of time in the
1680s and 1690s to analysing the nature and perversion of pre-Christian religion. In the mid-1680s, in addition to his other work on alchemy and
prophecy, he explored the nature of the original form of worship handed
down to posterity by Noah and his descendants. He argued that this was a
uniquely rational religion, since its reverence for a fire at the centre of the
sacred space (the so-called vestal religion) was based on the heliocentric
system. The manner in which he explained the subsequent corruption of
this religion shared many similarities with the way he accounted for the
corruption of Christianity, but the earlier deviation from religious truth had
naturalistic elements that the later version lacked. Newton was by no means
original in his claim that there had been an unadulterated religion based
on reverence for the cosmos, though his account contained Copernico-
Newtonian elements that were inevitably lacking in other versions. In a
number of ways his approach was more radical than that of some of his
contemporaries, and many claims—notably about the rationality of a proto-
Newtonian religion—would have been completely unacceptable to them.
His paean to the ancient learning of the Egyptians would have been particularly offensive to many, as would his claim that the Noachian religion differed in no major way from the Christian religion. As it turned out, his
writings in this area were made available to only a few trusted confidants,
and potential critics never got the chance to condemn his opinions.[1]

By Newton's time, a wealth of material pertaining to ancient cultures was
available to any erudite scholar who wanted to understand the earliest forms of
religion and achievements of ancient philosophers. Although the Christian
doctrine of the Fall implied that significant forms of knowledge available to
Adam—including natural knowledge—had been lost very early on, many
Christian divines believed that core truths had passed on intact to Noah and

had survived the Flood. A number of classical authors had attributed great learning in this post-diluvian period to the Egyptians, who had allegedly inherited their religious and scientific knowledge from Noah's progeny. From here it passed to other nations, at a time when the cultural attainments of the Israelites were at low ebb. For many scholars, the reasons for the corruption and loss of this wisdom through ignorance or idolatry became as significant as the nature of the ancient learning itself. In the late fifteenth century, as part of a more general humanist interest in determining authentic texts and printing accurate editions of them, Florentine Neoplatonists argued that they were engaged in restoring this wisdom, which they termed the "occult philosophy" (*prisca sapientia* or *philosophia perennis*). This process involved excavating mysterious truths from the texts of numerous classical authors, including poets who had allegedly veiled these mystical truths in allegories. Bolstered by the recovery of long-lost texts such as Lucretius's *De Rerum Natura*, authors could now make available to the public coherent philosophies linked to accounts of ancient beliefs contained in classical doxographies (lists of the religious and philosophical tenets of earlier writers and schools).[2]

The attempt to locate true religion and its corruption in the distant past was a precarious exercise for Christians. It threatened to downgrade the unique significance of Christ's message and risked providing evidence that the corruption of religious practice was so old, that religion had never in fact been untainted. Another dangerous assumption lay at the heart of efforts to resurrect the *prisca*. Although nearly all Christians argued that religious and philosophical truth had originated with the Hebrews, the high praise accorded to Egyptian or Ethiopian learning in many ancient accounts implied that learned Hebrews such as Moses were indebted to Egypt and to key aspects of Egyptian culture. This issue was invigorated by Marsilio Ficino's fifteenth-century translation of the "Pimander," one of the writings of the Egyptian magus Hermes Trismegistus who was widely believed to have predated (or been a contemporary of) Moses. There was good classical warrant for situating the origins of his learning west of the Sinai. Acts 7:21-22 stated that Moses had been brought up by the daughter of the pharaoh and had been trained in the arts of Egyptians, while in his "Life" of Moses, Philo of Alexandria recorded that he had learned Egyptian symbols. More generally, a number of other sources, such as Herodotus and Diodorus Siculus, attested to the great antiquity of Egyptian learning.[3]

Ficino harmonized the writings of Plutarch, Iamblichus, and many other Neoplatonic philosophers with those of the "Corpus Hermeticum," thereby reconstructing a secret but widely dispersed learning that had supposedly been hidden by the cognoscenti and subsequently lost. This theologico-philosophical wisdom had been passed on from its founder Zoroaster to Hermes's contemporary Moses, and then via Orpheus, Aglaophemus, and Pythagoras to Plato. Others embellished the notion of a tradition of lost knowledge that only they themselves could authentically revive. For example, Ficino's student Pico della Mirandola initially gave high praise to the attainments of the Egyptians, drawing supporting evidence from Plutarch's *De Iside et Osiride*, the single most important source of knowledge for the Egyptian religion. Pico argued that their zoolatry (animal-worship) and mythology concealed a deep knowledge about the cosmos, and in his later writings, he recommended a "practical" Cabbala (the ancient Jewish mystical interpretation of the Bible) allegedly known to the ancient Hebrews, which involved uttering words that possessed the power to work natural magic. A century later, Giordano Bruno made the daring claim that the Egyptian religion had been the purest form of the *prisca*, which had thrived before its decline at the hands of Judaism and Christianity. It was for statements like this that he was burned at the stake in 1600.[4]

The history of idolatry and of other corruptions of religion was central to all undertakings concerned with rescuing the true philosophy from the past. The great Dutch scholar and theologian Gerard Vossius's 1641 work on the theology of the Gentiles and the origin of idolatry constituted a virtually limitless database on ancient idolatry as well as a source for those who wanted to find elements of pagan idolatry in Catholic worship. In addition to using sources from the Old Testament, Vossius used a wealth of pagan records (and drew liberally from John Selden's *De Diis Syris*) to offer a global history of the corruption of the true religion. The vestal worship, which involved the use of a perpetual sacred fire, was common to the Hebrews and other nations. However, it had soon descended into solar and astral worship, according to which the pagans had wrongly venerated these heavenly bodies *in their own right* ("*cultus proprius*") rather than using them as "symbolic" worship ("*cultus symbolicus*") to adore the true God. Vossius dealt at length with the cult of the gods, a topic that would lie at the heart of Newton's own critique. He argued that men began to worship the heavenly bodies as "powers of nature," and then, according to what historians termed "euhemerism," to worship their own historical ancestors as stars. There was then a further stage of corruption when the people constructed statues and images of their kings so that they could see them and deify them. At first, the Egyptians treated the statues and images by means of symbolic worship but later the man-made objects came to be worshipped in themselves. Newton took virtually wholesale Vossius's description of solar and astral worship, arguing that in its pristine uncontaminated form, it was neither symbolic worship nor worship of the objects themselves, but a key part of the most ancient religion of all.[5]

As with Vossius's great work, Samuel Bochart's two-part *Geographia Sacra* (1646–51) would be a vital resource for Newton. Part 1 dealt with the growth of human civilisation after the Flood as described in Genesis 10, along with the inexorable dispersion of humans across the known world. In successive books, Bochart examined linguistic transmission, geographical translation, mythological inheritance, and religious practice in order to trace the history of Noah and the fate of the progeny of Shem, Japheth, and Ham. In analyses that were either praised as brilliant or criticised as entirely fanciful by contemporaries, he derived a genealogy of ancient peoples by attending to etymological coincidences in the languages of distinct cultures and dynasties. Although the technique had existed since classical times, Bochart developed more than anyone before him the assumption that individuals worshipped by different mythologies were identical, and were ultimately based on real historical individuals. By demonstrating the consonance between their characteristics, he showed that numerous persons in disparate religions had in fact been the same person. His foundational identification was of Noah with Saturn and from here he showed that a Saturnian figure was worshipped in every religion and was thus understood as the ancestor of all societies. Although Newton was heavily reliant on Bochart, he concentrated on the antiquity and cultural achievements of the Egyptians rather than those of the Chaldeans or Phoenicians, which Bochart emphasised. As with his copy of Vossius, Newton's copy of the 1681 edition of Bochart's work was battered from decades of intensive scrutiny, a quest for knowledge that began in the years before the *Principia* appeared.[6]

1. The New Philosophy and the Prisca

Another related tradition appropriated by Newton came from within the fields of astronomy and natural philosophy. The notion that an ancient pre-Aristotelian knowledge had been lost was eagerly integrated into heliocentric astronomy, and it constituted an important part of attempts to

counter the authority of geocentric passages in the Old Testament. Co-
pernicus himself appealed to the authority of Pythagorean and other
Greek heliocentrists in his *De Revolutionibus* of 1543, and his followers
also described their own work as an exercise in restoration. His devotee
Georg Rheticus went to the lengths of erecting a fifteen-metre obelisk,
crowned by a golden ball, in imitation of the ancient Egyptians and in
praise of Copernicus. In 1576 the English Copernican Thomas Digges
argued that heliocentrism was a revival of Pythagoreanism, but the most
influential defender of a Pythagorean source for heliocentrism was
Johannes Kepler. In his *Mysterium Cosmographicum* of 1596 he claimed
that God had maintained the distances between the planets in light of
geometrical properties of the five regular solids and duly noted that the
mathematical proportion of the heavens had been known to Pythagoras
and Plato. His commitment to the Pythagorean ideal of a mathematically
based harmony in nature was most clearly shown in his *Harmonices Mundi*
of 1619, in which he argued that planets sounded the intervals of the musical
scale while they carved out their elliptical orbits.[7]

As well as astronomers, natural philosophers sought out ancient sources
of authority for their various philosophies. However, at the same time as the
Ancients were praised for being guardians of original philosophico-religious
wisdom, they were also condemned for being the source of its corruption.
These accounts overlapped with the histories of the true religion and their
perverted mirror images that philosophers and other writers were composing at the same time. Like many others, Robert Boyle constructed a complex genealogy of the transmission and corruption of what he took to be
the true philosophy. As was the case with all philosophers who appealed
to an ancient lineage to support their present positions, he invoked a complex series of historical arguments and doctrines to assail what he took to
be deviant modern philosophies. According to Boyle, an authentic ancient
experimental and corpuscular philosophy had degenerated into the barren
speculative philosophy of the Aristotelians. In his *Certain Physiological Essays*
and *The Sceptical Chymist* (both of 1661), and again in his *Excellency of Theology*
of 1674 (written in 1665), he claimed that Moschus (a Phoenician who lived
before the Trojan War) had invented the atomist hypothesis, which had in
turn been advanced by Democritus, Leucippus, and, lately, by Descartes.
The true version of the corpuscular philosophy promoted by Democritus was
valuable for Boyle and other English natural philosophers, not merely because
of its conceptual content, but because Democritus and other right-minded

Ancients had apparently cultivated the correct experimentalist (and non-speculative) approach to understanding nature. Once corrupted by a people known as the Sabians (whom Boyle identified with the Chaldeans), this perverted form of natural philosophy deteriorated still further into the materialist atomism of Epicurus, whose disdain for the use of observations and experiments rendered his philosophy useless if not theologically dangerous.[8]

Boyle analysed the relationship between the cultivation of false philosophy and the practise of an idolatrous religion in his *Free Enquiry into the Vulgarly Receiv'd Notion of Nature* of 1686 (originally composed in 1666). He argued that the earliest form of idolatry and polytheism had been the effect of a deviant understanding of the natural world, which consisted of attributing life, sense, and understanding to corporeal and inanimate objects, and ascribing to Nature things that truly belonged to God. The earliest sort of idolatry was the worship of the celestial lights, especially the sun and the moon, and this was cultivated in the time of Moses by people who had been infected by the astral worship of the Sabians. Boyle cited Maimonides's claim, and referred to supporting evidence from John Selden, that many of the ceremonial laws given to the Jews were designed to combat the magical rites and idolatrous religious practices of these Sabians. However, their ideas spread to China, Greece, and Egypt and they were the source of the Aristotelian doctrine of intelligent celestial orbs. Although Christians had been seduced by such views, they were "Corrected and Master'd by the sound and Orthodox Principles they held together with it." Boyle cautioned that the worship of inanimate objects remained a great danger, and he feared that many learned men might venerate Nature excessively.[9]

The Cambridge scholars Henry More and Ralph Cudworth also portrayed their work as a restoration of an ancient pre-Aristotelian philosophy and linked their histories of philosophy (and its corruption) to their histories of religion. In More's *Conjectura Cabbalistica* of 1653, he referred to the authentic "Tradition of Moses" as the "Jewish Cabbala," whose mysteries were essentially the same as the abstruse doctrines that Plato and Pythagoras brought out of Egypt. The source of their knowledge was Moses himself, a fact confirmed by the mid-second-century Platonist Numenius, who described Plato as Moses Atticus (since he spoke Greek in the Attic dialect). Moses, More claimed, was a "master of the most sublime and generous speculations that are in all natural Philosophy," and much of his book was aimed at articulating or recovering what this exquisite natural knowledge was. By

1662, the task of creating an acceptable genealogy for the history of philosophy was complicated by More's ambivalent relationship with Cartesianism. Still anxious to rescue some elements of Descartes's system from the accusation that it was atheistic, he claimed that the "ancient *Pythagorick* and *Judaick* Cabbala" was a combination of the authentic elements of Platonism and Cartesianism, though in recent times the last two had been tragically broken asunder. Shorn of its more unpalatable mechanical elements, Cartesianism was identical to the philosophy of Democritus and thus to the acceptable "physiological part" of Pythagoreanism; in turn the latter was identical with the Sidonian philosophy, and finally the Sidonian was none other than the "Mosaical" philosophy. As a result, More concluded, the acceptable parts of Cartesian natural philosophy were consonant with the Moschical/Mosaical philosophy.[10]

Cudworth's *True Intellectual System* of 1678 constituted the most sustained exposition and critique of the *prisca* tradition ever to reach publication, and it would be a central source for Newton's work in the same area. He assailed a vast number of "atheisms" and "enthusiasms," praising "Pythagorean monads" as the true continuation of the more ancient oriental wisdom that he designated the "Moschical Philosophy." Like More, Cudworth agreed with the view that Moschus was the Moses of the Old Testament and he praised Descartes for being the first restorer "of the atomical philosophy, agreeably to the most part, to that *Moschical* and *Pythagorick* Form." Descartes had elevated the mechanical part of his system "into an exactness at least equal with the best *Atomologies* of the *Ancients*," but Cudworth still thought that some of its mechanical aspects were obnoxious. Many of the ancient "Religious Atomists" had been "infected with this "Mechanizing Humour," but Descartes had outdone them all in his works, "and even the very Atheists themselves." It followed that there were two separate streams of the atomistic philosophy. The first, immaterial variety, was "the most *Ancient* and *Genuine*, that was religious, called *Moschiacal* (or if you will *Mosaical*) and *Pythagorical*" but in contrast with Boyle—and Newton—he noted that the second adulterated and materialist variety, cultivated by Leucippus, Democritus, and Epicurus, was atheistic. In his own writings, Newton would rely heavily on this account, concerning that the most ancient and true Pythagorean philosophy was both immaterial and atomistic. However, he disagreed with Cudworth over the claim that the doctrines of Epicurus were irreligious.[11]

2. The Problem of Egypt

A key problem for philosophical genealogists was the place in their scheme of the intellectual accomplishments and religious beliefs of the Egyptians. One of the most extensive works on Egyptian learning in the seventeenth century was published by the Jesuit scholar Athanasius Kircher. His multi-volume *Oedipus Ægyptiacus* (1652–54) was a virtuoso interpretation of a vast range of Egyptian sources (many of which were recorded on obelisks that had been brought to Rome), based on over two decades of work and gathered from every conceivable archaeological and textual source. Kircher claimed that the hieroglyphs revealed the Egyptians' self-image as the guardians of true religious and natural knowledge, though he added that their zoolatry was deeply objectionable. Indeed, they had played a major role in the corrosion of the "hierogylphic" theology, which he identified with the hermetic philosophy. Despite the recent proof by Isaac Casaubon that the Hermetic writings were composed after the time of Christ, Kircher placed Hermes Trimegistus at the head of a monotheistic but esoteric religion whose practitioners included Orpheus, Plato, and Pythagoras. Its doctrines included the Cabbala, Persian magic, Chaldean astrology, Pythagorean mathematics, and Phoenician theology. The downfall of the true religion began early after the Flood, being occasioned by the trio of human superstition, crafty priests, and Satan. As a result of these baneful influences, the Egyptians' knowledge of the natural world, made up of their genuine achievements in engineering, mathematics, astrology, and natural magic, had descended into demonic or idolatrous practices. It was for this reason that he had no truck with Bruno's efforts to laud as orthodox the Egyptians' doctrine of magic. As he did with most of his other sources, Newton would forage selectively in Kircher's work for facts about the past, without paying much—or any—attention to the core thesis put forward by the author.[12]

Although their learning had been lauded by the ancient historians and extolled by moderns such as Kircher, there was good reason to believe that these accounts were overblown and worse, that the Egyptians were the originators of idolatry. One of the most sustained attacks on their credibility came in Edward Stillingfleet's *Origines Sacrae* of 1662, which drew from Vossius and Bochart to undercut the claims to religious truth made by the Greeks, Chaldeans, Egyptians, and Phoenicians. The Phoenicians seemed to openly admit to being the originators of idolatry and "turned all the stories of the gods into Allegories and Physical discourses," while the Chaldeans' skill in astronomy had soon dwindled into judicial astrology. The Greeks and Egyptians were even worse; the theology of the latter was so "monstrously ridiculous" that even those "overrun with the height of *Idolatry* themselves, did make it the object of their scorn and laughter." The Greeks introduced poetry to incite the vulgar into idolatry, and the practice was perfected in the time of Orpheus. Using an argument that would later be deployed against orthodox Christianity by deists, Stillingfleet proposed that ancient theology was "a meer fable…and the Governors of the Commonwealth made use of these things the better to awe the silly multitude and to bring them to better order." He reasoned that the heathen priests kept all their records of learning or history in deep obscurity in order to "deceive the silly people and maintain them in an *obsequious Ignorance*, which is never the *Mother* of any true *Devotion*, but of the greatest *Superstition*."[13]

In the second book of his *Origines*, Stillingfleet examined the claims of the Egyptians in more detail. According to Scripture, Solomon's learning was said to have outstripped the Egyptians (1 Kings 4:29–31) and it was probable that Moses, as the third-century B.C.E. historian Manetho and the first-century Jewish historian Josephus both related, was one of the priests at Heliopolis. Although they were able geometers, astronomers, and geographers, the scientific attainments of the Egyptians could not have been great, "because of their Magick and Superstition, whereby they were hindered from all Experiments in those natural things which they attributed a Divinity to." In an obvious attack on Henry More, Stillingfleet argued that most forms of attribution of learning to the Jews (for example, the Mosaick Cabbala, and the identification of Moses with Moschus) were "*fancyes* too extravagant and *Pythagorean* to be easily embraced." Finally, he showed from what he termed "the wonderful agreement of heathen Mythology with the *Scriptures*," that much of the true religion had been widely transmitted. However, many elements of pagan religions, such as that of the Egyptians, were a perversion of what was contained in the Bible.[14]

Cudworth disagreed strongly with these attacks on Egyptian learning, though he was careful not to elevate their cultural achievements above those of the Hebrews. He claimed that there was a "true, real learning and doctrine" beneath the religious rites of the Egyptians, "notwithstanding [their] multifarious Polytheism and Idolatry," and this was precisely why the Greeks had travelled there to draw from their superior learning. Although their scientific expertise vanished, their secret religious knowledge yet remained, for "besides their Vulgar and Fabulous Theology (which is for the most part that which Diodorus describes)" the Egyptians had another recondite scientific knowledge and theology that was concealed from the vulgar, and communicated only to the kings, and learned priests. Similarly, although the Persian magi performed rational religious rites in front of large audiences, the true meaning of their ceremonies was concealed from the vulgar by allegories, fables, and special symbols. Moses, of course, was highly skilled in all this sort of learning. Cudworth maintained this opinion about Egyptian wisdom despite being aware of Casaubon's proof that some of the works attributed to Hermes were later forgeries. Indeed, he claimed that they contained authentic Egyptian knowledge. He accepted the identification of the Egyptian Thoth with both Hermes and the Latin Mercury, and made Thoth the "first inventor of Arts and Sciences...and of the Hieroglyphick Learning." It was the knowledge held by Thoth that Moses had acquired, and in which he had become an adept.[15]

The idea that Egyptian achievements had been systematically underplayed by historians, and that Hebrew learning had been much less than was traditionally claimed, was put forward by scholars working in a very different tradition. In his own works, Newton cited positively the arguments made by John Marsham in his *Canon Chronicus*, and more relevantly, by John Spencer in his *De Legibus Hebraeorum*. Marsham and Spencer held that many of the religious rites and ceremonies of the Old Testament were derived from the customs of the Egyptians, but Spencer went a great deal further than his countryman. Drawing on the approach adopted by Maimonides in his *Guide to the Perplexed*, Spencer claimed that God had allowed the continuation of many harmless customs of the Egyptians with which the Israelites had become familiar through long experience and deemed these to be suitable for "symbolic" worship. For example, building on observations made in Selden's *De Diis Syris*, Spencer argued that the golden calf mentioned in Exodus 32 was constructed in the image of the Apis bull. This served a dual purpose; the Israelites would have lapsed into heathenism if forced to participate in something with which they were completely unfamiliar, while it also made it easier for the gentiles to convert to a form of worship that resembled their own practice. Mosaic ritual laws thus mimicked or mirrored those of the Egyptians, and the latter lay at their very heart. Spencer held little truck with the religious beliefs of the Egyptians, but followed Maimonides in holding that the Mosaic laws had been specifically designed to draw the Israelites away from idolatrous practices, particularly those of the star-worshipping Sabians. On this showing, the introduction of the Mosaic laws was a strategic move, a divine ploy to use the best means possible for dissuading the crude and superstitious Israelites from idolatry.[16]

Many of the orthodox were dismayed at Spencer's views and argued that they were grist to the mill of those who were no friends of religion. He did have some followers. For example, in his *Archaeologiae Philosophicae* of 1692, Thomas Burnet followed Spencer in ridiculing the attainments of the Hebrews. He praised Egyptian and Chaldean learning, holding that there had been a pristine knowledge known to everyone *except* the Jews. In return, John Woodward charged that works like Burnet's were highly corrosive of the Judaeo-Christian tradition. Spencer's project, he complained, created a climate in which "it became a fashion to ridicule the Jews, slight the Mosaic economy, and represent it as only moulded and copied after the pattern of the Gentiles." Attacking the Egyptians' abject immorality, Woodward claimed that the only positive aspects of their life were their agricultural policies, which allowed them time for contemplation and improvement of science and arts, but he could not assent to the "common opinion" that they had ever been in possession of true and robust knowledge. They had no interest in facts, and their hieroglyphics and obelisks were "the fancy of a people infinitely suspicious above other people." The Greeks were "feral" for the duration of the Israelites' stay in Egypt and extolled the wisdom of the Egyptians, unaware that Moses and the Israelites had much improved them. The Egyptians were "sunk in Idolatry" while their zoolatry served to embolden religious scoffers and even atheists. Although some of these authors expressed diametrically opposed views of the merits of the Jews and the Egyptians, there was a great deal of room for manoeuvre between the extremes. By showing that the Jews and Egyptians were both descended from the Noachian religion, Newton occupied this intermediate space.[17]

3. The Newtonian Prisca

Newton threw himself wholeheartedly into the study of the rise and fall of the ancient religion, treating information in many of the above-mentioned tomes as resources for his own account. In the 1680s and early 1690s he developed a highly original account of the nature of an ancient wisdom that had been shared by all the first generations after Noah. Like his other religious writings, the exact date of his earliest forays into this subject may never be known, but the project was certainly well advanced by the middle of 1685. In the summer of 1686 he told Edmond Halley that the previous autumn he had suppressed what was then the second and final book ("liber secundus") of the *Principia* for lack of a good theory of comets. In a brief introduction to this work he extolled the Copernican learning of the Ancients, linking this to the vestal fire-centred religion that he claimed was the most ancient and true. The motivation for Newton's entry into the general area of ancient religion and natural philosophy remains unclear, but it is probable that it originated in an effort to understand the true nature of idolatry by going back into its pre-Christian manifestations. If this is the case, then the Copernico-Newtonian doctrines enunciated in the "liber secundus" may have been grafted on to a pre-existing project on the history of postdiluvian civilisation, rather than the other way round.[18]

Further evidence for dating these interests comes from writings in the hand of Humphrey Newton, Newton's amanuensis between 1684 and 1688, and one such treatise, titled "*Theologiae Gentilis Origines Philosophicae*" ("Philosophical Origins of the Gentile Theology"), can be dated with assurance. There is nothing in this text that betrays any awareness of the doctrines in the *Principia*, while it also omits any reference either to the supra-lunary orbit of comets, or to the Copernican relevance of the vestal religion—both of which are in the introduction to the "liber secundus." For that reason, it seems reasonable to see the "*Origines*" research as a separate but related project to the specifically philosophical programme underpinning the elements in the "liber secundus." During the period that Humphrey served Newton, there seem to have been three separate projects: one dealing with the mystical Egyptian truths about nature brought to Greece by Orpheus and Pythagoras; another that analysed the nature of the ancient heliocentric vestal form of worship; and the last, a Bochartian genealogy of the generations that spanned out across the world after the Flood. Each of these would be developed systematically and largely independently over the next years and decades, but they were occasionally woven together by Newton to tell a complex and wide-reaching history of the fate of ancient wisdom.[19]

Newton remarked in Book 3 of the *Principia* that the "liber secundus" had originally been composed in a "popular method," in contrast with the published version. This, he said later, was couched in a propositional form and was deliberately framed in a forbiddingly recondite style so that Newton could "avoid being baited by little smatterers in Mathematicks." These earlier efforts to embed elements of the *prisca* tradition into his great work were not baroque glosses that were composed simply to make the work more accessible, or to give a superficial aura of authority to the text. They were the tip of an intellectual iceberg in which Newton told the story of the original pristine religion, whose perversion was accompanied by that of the scientific wisdom held by the priesthood. He claimed that before this corruption, only priests were qualified to be proper guardians of true knowledge about the natural world. This priesthood, distributed throughout the world, kept the real content of this learning hidden from the masses though they dropped hints about it in poetry and other texts. Unpicking the history of the corruption required an analysis of a number of its components, including the nature and extent of the original vestal worship, whose placement of the sun at the ritual and physical centre of worship made it, as Newton put it, the most rational religion of all. From a host of primary sources he systematically recovered (that is, he read into them) the Newtonian core of the Pythagorean philosophy, which was the best attested example of the old religion and learning. While he drew a great deal of evidence for the vestal-astral religion from the second book of Vossius's *De Theologia*, much of his energy was devoted to finessing and extending Bochart's ambitious effort to make a coherent account of all known genealogies of ancient peoples.[20]

Although the notion that the Ancients engaged in vestal worship was a commonplace, Newton fully Copernicanised the notion and claimed that it was through the vestal religion that the Ancients worshipped the Temple of the true God. In the introduction to the suppressed "liber secundus," he stated that the Ancients were heliocentrists who worshipped in orbital temples around perpetual fires that—as in the case of Numa Pompilius, the second king of Rome—represented the solar system. The Egyptians were the first astronomers and spread their knowledge abroad while the Greeks, "a people more addicted to the study of philology than of nature," assimilated their soundest knowledge from them. This ancient natural philosophy, he continued, held the cosmos to be almost wholly composed of empty space, and the introduction of solid orbs was a later corruption promoted by Eudoxus, Calippus, and Aristotle. Newton reserved a special place for the ancient cometary theory, since the supra-lunary trajectories of comets made a nonsense of the idea of solid orbs. Indeed, the Chaldeans, he continued, thought that comets were a sort of planet, which had eccentric and even periodic orbits. In addition, he repeated the commonplace view that "in the Vestal ceremonies we can recognize the spirit of the Egyptians who concealed mysteries that were above the capacity of the common herd" under the veil of religious rituals and hieroglyphic symbols.[21]

There was no reference to the Ancients in the *Principia* when it appeared in the summer of 1687 but Newton's commitment to various forms of the *prisca* tradition was not kept secret. In early 1692, he told his friend, the Swiss mathematician Fatio de Duillier, that he was about to add classical allusions (the so-called Classical Scholia) to propositions IV–IX of the third book of a proposed second edition of the *Principia*. Fatio told Christiaan Huygens that Newton believed that he had discovered that Plato and Pythagoras possessed all the demonstrations offered in his "System of the World" (Book 3 of the *Principia*) that were founded on the inverse-square law. They made a great mystery out of their learning, Newton claimed, but if the surviving fragments of their writings were properly reconstructed, they would show that the Ancients had the same ideas as those enunciated in the *Principia*. In turn, Huygens told Fatio that he seriously doubted that the Pythagoreans were sufficiently skilled to have given a demonstration relating to elliptical planetary orbits and attributed Newton's view to a certain degree of modesty. He did not believe, for example, that the fifth-century B.C.E. Greek philosopher Philolaus had offered a fully fledged Copernican system, though along with Galileo and others, he accepted that there may have been an oblique reference to centrifugal force in Plutarch's *de Facie in Orbe lunae*.[22]

This commitment to adding Classical Scholia to a new edition of the *Principia* burned for many years. In conversations conducted with the Scottish mathematician David Gregory in May 1694, Newton mentioned that in the new edition, he would write at length to demonstrate the consonance of his philosophy with that of the Ancients, and principally with that of Thales. Newton also believed that it was clear, Gregory added, that Thoth (the Egyptian Mercury) was a Copernican from the fact that he attributed the names of his illustrious predecessors to the planets. Later in the year, Gregory remarked that—according to Newton—the Ancients were not merely Copernicans but, as Fatio had told Huygens, were bona fide Newtonians, since Plato and others were aware of universal gravitation. Gregory also recorded that Newton believed that Galileo and Plutarch had both referred to Plato's knowledge of universal gravitation, a statement that is backed by citations from both authors among Newton's preferred additions to the Classical Scholia. Like the references to ancient Newtonianism and the vestal religion in the "liber secundus," none of these claims made their way into later editions of the *Principia*. Nevertheless, they did get circulated to a restricted audience, and as a proud Fatio told Huygens, Newton had been far more candid than usual in allowing Fatio to see and disseminate his views to a select few. Indeed, they soon appeared in print. In 1694, Gregory had asked Newton if his own "Notes on the Newtonian Philosophy" could be published, and in return Newton gave Gregory a copy of the proposed Classical Scholia. Gregory duly published them in his 1702 book on the 'elements' of physics, astronomy, and geometry, while leaving their source anonymous.[23]

Gregory was also privy to an even larger enterprise aimed at recovering the knowledge of the Ancients. As early as December 1691 Newton told him that he was to publish something on the geometry of the Ancients, which would accompany another text that he had just completed on the quadrature (integration) of curves. In the summer of 1694 Gregory recorded that Newton would add these two works to the proposed second edition of the *Principia*. Newton would write about the errors of the moderns concerning the intention of the Ancients, and it would be shown "that our specious Algebra is fit enough to find out, but entirely unfit to consign to writing and commit to posterity." In the papers that survive from this project, Newton sought to determine how great Greek mathematicians such as Euclid, Pappus, and Apollonius had in fact made their discoveries, a process that was utterly obscured by the form in which they had demonstrated their proofs. Specifically, Newton set out to reconstruct a number of lost works that allegedly contained a treasury of mathematical techniques, notably three books by Euclid on "Porisms" (either a corollary, or mathematical proposition midway between a theorem and a problem) and some lost books by Apollonius, whose outline had been given by Pappus in a preamble to the seventh book of his *Collections*. Like virtually all of his other projects, this remained unfinished, and certainly unpublished, but in any case Newton gave up the classical veneer part way through the longest draft of the work.[24]

4. Orphic and Pythagorean Truths

Many of the themes of the "Classical Scholia" and "liber secundus" were adumbrated in one Newtonian exposition of the atomistic philosophy that had allegedly been brought from Egypt by Orpheus and Pythagoras. In 1694 Gregory recorded that Newton believed that the atomistic philosophy of Epicurus and Lucretius was the true and ancient one, but had been wrongly interpreted by the Ancients as atheistic. Newton incorporated all the ancient atomists into his version of the authentic *prisca*, and in drafts for the Classical Scholia, he asserted that the Ancients believed that all matter consisted of atoms (thus repeating his claim at the start of the "Philosophical Questions" programme). By propounding the doctrine of universal gravitation, Ionic and Italic philosophers such as Epicurus, Democritus, Pythagoras, and Orpheus were continuing the tradition propagated by the disciples of Thales. In his *True Intellectual System*, Cudworth had argued that the Ancients designated atoms mystically as "monads," and that ancient numerology and hieroglyphics were also drawn from this mystical philosophy. In a fascinating critique of Cudworth's attack on Epicurus's philosophy, Newton denied that the Egyptian theology described in Aristophanes's *Birds*, which was the source of the Orphic, Pythagorean, and Epicurean philosophy, was irreligious. According to the play, "night" was said to have spread her black wings over the chaotic abyss and laid an egg; the chorus proclaimed that the passage of night had given rise to "love," which by "fluttering" on the abyss had created all the animals and gods. Newton claimed that "night" was the invisible deity, and "love" the spirit that moved on the face of the waters in Genesis 1:2. He concluded that Cudworth was deeply mistaken in representing this, and by extension the Epicurean philosophy, as atheistic.[25]

Newton also recorded Cudworth's argument that Pythagoras had been initiated by Aglaophemus in mystical Orphism. In one short but significant essay from this period, he remarked that a key tenet of this mystical philosophy was the notion that the moon was habitable and that single stars were worlds containing land, air, and aether. The Ancients were also aware that the earth was a type of planet.[26] Educated in Egypt, the argonaut Orpheus was the first to bring the true theological and astronomical knowledge from Egypt into Greece, though he "infected all of Greece with fables." Some, such as the second-century writer Lucian of Samosata, had placed the fount of astronomical knowledge in Ethiopia, but based on the analysis in Marsham's *Canon Chronicus*, Newton argued that the place Lucian meant was actually Thebais, which was Upper Egypt. This learning, he claimed, was ultimately lost among the Egyptians due to the repeated incursions of the Babylonians, Persians, and the Greeks, though it was preserved in the sacred and historical books.[27]

Newton repeated the standard claim that Pythagoras had travelled to Egypt and had brought back to Greece the art of speaking allegorically in numbers and symbols. He added that the Egyptians correctly placed the planets in the order Saturn, Jupiter, Mars, Venus, Mercury, the sun, and the moon. To amuse the vulgar, Pythagoras represented the distances of the planets from one another by means of harmonic proportions of tones and semi-tones, and by referring to the music of the spheres. However, amongst his own disciples, he propagated the Copernican astronomy by explaining their true meaning. Relying this time on Plutarch's *Life of Numa Pompilius*, Newton noted that the learned Numa philosophised in the same way, that is to say, in the Pythagorean or Egyptian manner. The Egyptians integrated their philosophy and their religion by building temples in the form of the solar system, and Numa did the same, erecting a circularly shaped vestal temple and consecrating a perpetual fire in its middle for worship.[28]

According to Newton, Pythagoras's disciples learned the truths of the Egyptian philosophy and, as a result, they embraced the existence of many worlds, and, in particular, the mystical significance of the numbers seven and twelve. The Egyptianised Pythagoreans taught that Venus and Mercury orbited around the sun, and they depicted the orbits of the five planets—Saturn, Jupiter, Mars, Venus, and Mercury—as concentric circles, representing the path of the moon separately from these. In astrology they always listed the seven principal heavenly bodies (which did not include the earth) with the sun in the centre; they added fire, air, water, and earth, along with quintessence so as to make the number twelve. Pythagoras himself designated the correct order of the planets by the intervals between the tones, placing the sun in the centre, and he "compelled his disciples to remain silent about the secret lest the true meaning of the allegory should leak out to the vulgar."[29]

Once in Greece, Newton went on, those who had not been taught in the schools of the mystical philosophers began to develop divergent opinions about the meaning of the enigmatic accounts of the mystical philosophers, and philosophy degenerated into competing schools. Here, presumably, was the historical source of the sort of anarchic scientific community into which Newton feared philosophy in his own time might degenerate. Now, as a consequence of general ignorance about the true meaning of philosophical statements, there arose the false conceptions concerning the planets revolving about the earth, solid spheres, and the four elements. The numerous disciples of the Egyptians, from the Chaldeans to the Pythagoreans, had correctly held that comets were a type of planet, but once solid orbs had been introduced by Eudoxus, Calippus, and Aristotle, "comets were thrust down into regions below the moon." This fascinating text appears to be the source of the opening paragraphs to the "liber secundus" and represents Newton's most sustained effort to outline the content of the scientific knowledge known to the Egyptians and their successors.[30]

5. The Classical Scholia

These views underpinned the philosophy expressed in the Classical Scholia. Aside from Cudworth, Newton pillaged compendia such as the *Mythologiae, sive explicationis fabulae* of Natalis Comes (Natale Conti) for information. As in his other studies, he consulted original sources—for this project they included Plutarch's *De facie in Orbe Lunae*, Lucretius's *De Rerum Natura* (of which he had a 1686 edition), and Macrobius's *Commentarium in Somnium Scipionis*. The notion that the Ancients had veiled their truths in mysteries licensed Newton to use his own counter-allegorical hermeneutic procedures in order to decode their alleged meaning. To aid his task, at many points he subtly rephrased original sources in order to give their underlying meaning a decidedly Newtonian slant. Based on Diogenes Laertius's *Life of Anaxagoras*, Newton argued that the latter knew of the mutual attraction of the sun, the moon, and the earth, and believed that the moon was inhabited. His alleged teacher, Anaximenes, believed that each star was a solar system, and so did Democritus. The Classical Scholia drew heavily upon the writings of the ancient atomists and what Newton called "the crowd of philosophers that preceded Aristotle." Prime amongst these was Lucretius, whose vacuist and atomistic philosophy was—at least according to Newton—consonant with universal gravitation. In a proposed addition to Proposition 7 of Book 3, Newton referred approvingly to Lucretius's account of infinite space, which he had allegedly proved from the fact that without it, gravity would cause all the material of the universe to conglomerate in one giant mass. Newton would return to these arguments in his correspondence with Richard Bentley in the winter of 1692/93.[31]

In the text that was intended to appear in the revised Proposition 8, Newton noted that the Ancients had not explained at sufficient length the mathematical relations governing the diminution of gravity away from a centre. They were, however, aware of these relations and hid them from the

vulgar in the usual way. These could now be decoded, and in various references the Ancients seemed to have alluded to an inverse-square law by relating the distances between planets to the relationship between the length
and tension of stretched pieces of organic material. Newton referred to
Macrobius's claim in his commentary on the *Somnium Scipionis* (in Book 2,
ch. 1) that Pythagoras's discovery of the true laws of the heavens came by
experiments using hammers of varying weights hung on sheep intestines
and the tendons of oxen. By these means, Newton claimed, "he learned that
the weights by which all tones on equal chords were heard, were reciprocal
to the squares of the length of the chords by which a musical instrument
emits the same tones." The Newtonised Macrobius also testified that having
found out this ratio by these experiments, Pythagoras then applied it to the
heavens, thereby becoming aware of the inverse-square law.[32]

This account of the Ancients' views provided a useful way for Newton
to discuss both the "causes" of things—forbidden by his professed resolution
not to feign hypotheses—and also the pervasive presence of God. His
proposed scholium to Proposition 9 hinted at the cause of gravity by
describing what the Ancients had thought about it. As he put it in the
opening sentence: "Thus far I have explained the properties of gravity.
I am not considering its cause [but] I will say in what sense the ancients
theorized about it." Thales held that all bodies were animate, inferring
this from magnetic and electrical attractions, and in doing so he taught
that everything was full of gods—by which he meant animate bodies. By
this, Newton claimed, he meant that the Ancients were aware that God
existed everywhere, and they knew that the immediate cause of gravity
was God. Their reference to Pan in the mystical philosophy assumed he
was "supreme divinity inspiring this world with harmonic ratio like a
musical instrument and handling it with modulation." From this conception the Ancients "named harmony God and soul of the world composed
of harmonic numbers" but over time this degenerated into animism and
gave rise to the doctrine of souls moving solid globes. However, such
souls had originally been understood as one and the same God, and all
the Ancients had taught that "a certain infinite spirit pervades all space
into infinity, and contains and vivifies the entire world." By means of certain symbols the Ancients had instructed their disciples that "matter was
moved within that infinite spirit" and was driven from one place to another "not in inconstant leaps but harmonically," according to the mathematically precise laws Newton had expressed in the *Principia*.[33]

6. Scientific Knowledge and Pagan Theology

If the Classical Scholia focussed on atomistic and Pythagorean sources for
Newton's natural philosophy, his tract on the "philosophical origins" of the
gentile theology—despite its title—concentrated almost entirely on an analysis
of the genesis of secular polities. He drew heavily upon Selden, Bochart,
Vossius, and Marsham for his sources of ancient genealogies, although he
was often prepared to wade in to the primary sources.[34] Arguing that the
ur-religion was based on astronomical and scientific knowledge, he claimed
that the twelve gods of the various nations for whom records survived represented the twelve objects of the mystical philosophy, namely the seven
planets (including the sun and moon), the four elements and the quintessence. In the first chapter of the work, Newton argued that the Ancients had
practised a "dual philosophy, sacred and vulgar." The philosophers "handed
down the sacred philosophy by means of types and enigmas, while the
rhetoricians ("orators") wrote down the vulgar version openly and in a
popular style." This sacred philosophy flourished in Egypt and was founded
upon serious astronomical knowledge. Newton drew on the first-hand account given by Clement of Alexandria in his *Stromata* in which he described the sacred procession of the Egyptian priests that was built on their
geographical and astronomical knowledge.[35]

Many of the participants in the Egyptian ceremony had roles that required an understanding of the natural world. As Newton put it, after the
"mystical harmony of the spheres had been signified by the preliminary
hymns," an astronomer proceeded with the sacred books, which contained
their astronomical learning. Following this came the priests' amanuensis
who (unlike Humphrey) knew the truth about the heavens, the earth, and
the stars. The procession was formally closed by the chief priest and the
Overseer of the sacred things, who was well versed in religious rites and
theology. Newton delved into Macrobius's commentary on the *Somnium
Scipionis* to give a gloss on what the details of the procession meant: "By joining their knowledge of the stars and the world to theology, and giving prime
position to astronomy, they were indicating that their theology was directed
towards the stars. And the gods of the Egyptians were certainly the stars and
elements." This could be confirmed by looking at the names of their gods in
all the civilisations that had left records, and Newton agreed with Herodotus
and Lucian that nearly all these had originated in Egypt.[36]

Newton's analysis of the twelve gods was by far the lengthiest element of this project, and he began by arguing that the planets and elements became repositories for the memory of those men most revered after the Flood. Just as Galileo named the satellites of Jupiter after his Medici benefactors, so the Ancients had named the stars and planets after their heroes. All nations preserved similar myths about their earliest ancestors, and so these had to refer to the same people and their deeds. The Chaldeans, Egyptians, and Persians had much older records than the Greeks and at one point Newton stated that if their records could be distinguished from the fictions of the Greeks, then the history of the times immediately after the Flood "could be written up with some degree of truth." Newton took at face value the standard euhemerist equation of Saturn with Noah and the Latin Janus, and noted down Bochart's extensive etymological and typological arguments in favour of the same. From here he proceeded to deduce the one true genealogy underlying the many different histories of the gods recorded in different traditions, a matter seriously complicated by the fact that nations recorded various generations of the earliest men using the same names. All these identifications were detailed at great length, and on one sheet he wrote down the headings of the other chapters of a book that would have constituted a unified history of the nations that peopled the planet after the Flood.[37]

A central chronological aid was the myth of the four ages, and Newton argued that Noah reigned in a quasi-communist paradise in Babylon during the Golden Age. Numerous primary sources were culled from Bochart and Natalis Comes to support his claims though for finer-grained analysis Newton went directly to the primary sources. While Japheth and Shem were given dominion over Europe and Africa, Ham (Cham, or the Egyptian Jupiter Hammon) ruled in Egypt with his son Mizraim (Osiris, Pluto, or Serapis) during the Silver Age. His other progeny Chus (Hercules, Moloch, Jupiter Belus, Pan, or Mars), Phut (Antaeus, Atlas, Typho, or Neptune), and Canaan (Chna, Busiris, Prometheus, or Vulcan) respectively, ruled Arabia, Libya, and Phoenicia in the Bronze Age. Chus ultimately took on and killed his treacherous brother Phut and became the first king of Chaldea; his son Belus II, grandson of Cham, ruled a vast empire in the Iron Age. The opportunity to coordinate a vast range of primary and secondary sources provided by these materials was exactly the sort of herculean analytic challenge to which Newton rose. Building on the account in Bochart, he offered numerous mini-proofs according to which characters in different national genealogies were shown to be identical with individuals in other histories.

This analysis dates from some point in the mid- to late 1680s, but his obsession with the topic never waned. Ultimately it was expanded into a vast project that he termed "The Chronology of Ancient Kingdoms."[38]

7. The Religion of Stonehenge

Newton's analysis of ancient learning was intimately connected to his belief that there had been a foundational ur-religion common to all men. As part of this vestal religion, people had worshipped using open circular structures, and later temples surrounded a perpetual fire that was used for ceremonial sacrifices. In one tract, titled "The Original of Religions," he stated that this religion "was spread over all nations before the first memory of things," and he marshalled a host of evidence to prove its universal presence across the globe. In Italy, for example, it was the Etruscans who had propagated the vestal religion; in their religious rites, the priest laid his hands upon the altar when a sacrifice was ready and gave prayer to the god Janus and the goddess Vesta. Similarly, Dionysius of Halicarnasseus had testified that the Latins had worshipped in an ancient vestal temple more than four hundred years before the founding of Rome. Newton made use of the common theory that posited a difference between native and adventitious gods, concluding that "in Janus its probable they worshipped ⟨their common father as⟩ the supreme God (Iaꟁ-Noah, or Ja-No) in Vesta the frame of Nature." Evidence from the structure of the temples, as well as from the etymological origins of the names of their chief gods, proved that the Ancients worshipped the true God as the *Deus Naturae*, and as a result, they also worshipped him for his power and dominion.[39]

The Egyptians had worshipped according to this religion from their earliest times and vestal fires had existed in the cities of Canaan and Syria long before Moses. Newton claimed that such shrines were called "high places" in Scripture because nations frequently kept them on the tops of mountains. There were many altars with fires in Israel in the times of Abraham, Samuel, and Solomon, and the same fires burned in the "prytanea" (temples) of other nations. The Assyrians and Chaldeans held it to be the most ancient form of worship, and vestal fires were everywhere to be seen across the European continent and far beyond. Newton cited reports from places as far away as China and India, and as close as Ireland and England. The crude features of Stonehenge showed it to be an ancient prytaneum, since it was "an area compassed circularly wth two rows of very great stones wth passages on all sides for people to go in and out at."There were similar pieces of prehistoric architecture in Denmark, and the monks of Kildare conserved a similar sacred site under the name of Briget's fire, their Coenobium being called the house of fire.This conservation of a continuous fire for sacrifice, Newton concluded, was "the most universal as ye most ancient religion of all religions" and no later religion became as general.[40]

Its great age, Newton claimed, proved it to be the religion of Noah and his sons "& tis not to be doubted but that ye religion wch Noah propagated <down> to his posterity was the true religion." It divided up beasts and fowls into clean and unclean, that is, those that were fit for consecration and those that were not, and Newton argued that it was eminently reasonable to believe that Noah's family sacrificed in a sacred place, "& accounted it as irreligious to sacrifice wth strange or prophane fire as to sacrifice an unclean Beast." Wherever they went, they took this fire with them, and by these means the religion was promulgated across the world.The vestal religion also determined the patriarchal structure of ancient polities, since in the true religion it was the father who sacrificed and performed the office of the priest. In the ancient cities the place of the prytaneum was also the court "in which ye Elders of ye City sat <in Council>." Priests were thus given a political role: Egyptian priests were members of the nobility, Abraham was a priest and a prince, Roman emperors were *Pontifices maximi*, and Christ himself was a priest of a higher order even than Aaron—a king as well as a priest.[41]

Moses erected altars of unhewn stones to commemorate the first altars, which preceded knowledge of ironworking. However, even after this, the Israelites continued to use them. The fire was a key feature of scriptural references to worship, being placed in the priests' court and in both the outward court of the people in the Tabernacle and in Solomon's Temple. Other writers, including Macrobius, Clement of Alexandria, and Seneca all attested to the naturalistic features of the original form of worship. According to Newton, making these buildings a "symbol of the world" was thus part of the worship that early nations received from Noah: "The whole heavens they recconed to be the true <& real> Temple of God & therefore that a Prytaneum might deserve the name of his Temple they framed it so <as in the fittest manner to> represent the whole systeme of the heavens." Newton added approvingly that nothing could be more rational than this point of religion. Hence, he concluded, "twas one designe of y^e ~~true systeme of y^e~~ first institution of ye true religion to propose to mankind by ye frame of y^e

ᶜancient⁾ Temples, the Study of the frame of the world as the true Temple of yᵉ l̶i̶v̶i̶n̶g̶ ᶜgreat⁾ God they worshipped."This was a stunning claim, which implied that what the Ancients did was neither an example of "cultus symbolicus" nor of "cultus proprius," and it implicity sacralised the office of the modern natural philosopher.[42]

The fire-religion accorded a primary place to the role of the learned priest, and knowledge of the natural world was a substantial part of their theology. The Indian Brahmans safeguarded the learning of their culture, as did the Persian magi and the Babylonian and Chaldean priests. The Greeks acquired their great knowledge of astronomy and natural philosophy by studying with Egyptian priests, and among the Greeks it was an elite group among the divines who possessed a true understanding of the natural world. As Newton understood it, this was the major reason for believing that this ur-religion "was the most rational of all others ᶜtill the nations corrupted it⁾." There was no way, he wrote, "to come to yᵉ knowledge of a Deity but by the frame of nature" adding the significant rider "wᵗʰout revelation" above the line. From the beginning of time, he wrote, the true system of the world had been adumbrated in the form of a sacred fire, "so that anyone of keen mind, from any people, might gather the truth from it, and thus come to know God from his works." In writing about the learned priesthood in this manner, Newton clearly saw the role of the modern natural philosopher as that of a priest of nature, and outside of organised religion, natural philosophy was the most important way of grasping the nature of God.[43]

8. Corruption

David Gregory observed in May 1694 that Newton believed that religion had always remained the same thing throughout history, but that various nations had polluted what they received from Noah and his sons with their own inventions. Newton, Gregory wrote, believed that Moses had started to reform the religion of the Hebrews but had retained the indifferent elements of the Egyptians. Newton apparently told him that it was the Egyptians who most of all debased religion with superstition and from them it spread to other peoples. Gregory was evidently correct in placing the Mosaic reformation at the heart of Newton's analysis, but for whatever reason, he gave a misleading view of what Newton thought. Newton did think that the Egyptians had been the source of the egregious corruption of religion but he also invoked the authority of Spencer's *De Legibus Hebræorum* to support his claim that Moses had kept what the Egyptians had practised in respect of the true God, while rejecting the worship of their false gods. Indeed, he claimed that Spencer had shown that what there was in the Mosaic religion concerning the true God contained little more than what was originally practised among the Egyptians. Newton showed scant interest in the finer details of Spencer's argument, but in its broad outlines, it served his purpose.[44]

Newton's claim that idolatry had begun through the perverted adoration of heavenly bodies was a commonplace by the time he wrote, but his own use of the notion had a number of idiosyncratic aspects. He argued that idolatry was promoted by the malign self-interest of priests, but that this was aided by the inveterately superstitious character of human beings, a view that he rehearsed in other writings. Most important, the naturalistic tenor of the vestal religion gave its decline a very particular set of characteristics. In "The Original of Religions," he claimed that the prytanea were sacred planetaria: the fires at their centre were a type of the sun and all the elements mirrored different parts of the universe, itself the temple of God. In time, men were "led by degrees" to worship the sensible objects of the heavenly bodies as "the ⟨visible⟩ seats of divinity." Moses and Job, Newton continued, both cautioned against worshipping the heavenly bodies in their own right, but this very early form of idolatry was "more plausible than that of dead men & statues, mankind was more prone to it & hence it spread further." After this initial perversion, there was a general sort of corruption of the vestal religion in which men worshipped false gods and goddesses in their temples. In due course this degenerated further into the belief in the transmigration of the souls of the dead into animals, and, finally, the worst kind of idolatry would reveal itself as the worship of dead men and statues. Although he did not say so explicitly in this text, the last comment obviously referred to Roman Catholicism.[45]

Newton argued that men in the first ages had tried to honour their ancestors by attaching their names to countries, cities, and heavenly bodies, just as Galileo had done in the modern age. These men represented these entities by various hieroglyphical figures and gave them wings like angels to denote the motions of the stars. However, they soon "feigned [that] their Souls or Spirits [were] translated into ye stars & y^t by these spirits & intelligences ye stars were animated & shone & moved in their courses & understood all things below." People then invented stories according to which the astral intelligences were bestowed with the characteristics of famous men and thereby ruled terrestrial events. So Venus was held to govern love, Mars governed war, and Mercury governed commerce and learning. Newton claimed that it was the priests who began to make a more sinister use of these inventions, arrogating to themselves the sole right to interpret celestial signs. Thus, "astrology and the gentile theology were introduced by crafty priests to promote the study of the stars and the expansion of the priesthood, and at length they were propagated throughout the world." It was, he continued, by means of these "fictions" that "yᵉ soules of yᵉ dead grew into veneration wᵗʰ yᵉ stars & by as many as received this kind of theology were taken for yᵉ Gods wᶜʰ governed the world." Since the "nature of Mankind is prone to superstition they began to ~~honour~~ ⁺pay respect to⁺ these Gods in the Prytanea or Temples together wᵗʰ yᵉ true God," and at length they worshipped the false gods with the religious practices that were appropriate only for the true God.[46]

As Gregory noted, Newton held that the original corruption of this kind happened in Egypt, the oldest kingdom of all. He cited Herodotus ("a Greek") and Lucian ("an Assyrian") to show that they were the first to worship the twelve gods and to erect images in their honour. Through the increase in commerce they propagated this form of worship to the Greeks and Assyrians, but it was the Egyptians who had first set up annual ceremonies in honour of their inaugural king and queen, Osiris and Isis. It was not long before the offspring of heroes like Chus were worshipping their great ancestors in their prytanea alongside the true God as part of their sacrificial Bacchanalia.[47] In another version of the text, Newton attributed the promotion of false worship to the machinations of kings rather than priests. It was by playing on the excessive superstition of the common people for their ancestors that they founded the illegal authority of the divine right of kings. This in turn caused the vulgar to believe superstitiously that the rulers were gods—a process that "tended to yᵉ establishment & enlargement of yᵉ Regal authority & dominion." Soon, Newton went on, all kings were named after the greatest gods: "after death to augment & perpetuate their honour, it grew in fashion to consecrate them (as was usually done to yᵉ Roman Emperors) & from that time they were accounted Divi." Thus, he concluded, "was yᵉ world soon filled with Gods." Much later he would rail against courts like that of the first Assyrian king Jupiter Belus for promoting idolatry among the common people.[48]

Like the "Philosophical Origins" tract, the bulk of the English "Original of Religions" treatise soon turned into an extensive attempt to decipher and make coherent the various national genealogies. In a shorter Latin draft of

the treatise Newton devoted more space to the development of the transmigration of souls and of zoolatry. After the names of the venerated dead
were attributed to the stars, he argued, the stars were allocated the characteristics of these dead men, by which they were held to affect lives and
events on Earth. He was careful, however, to note that astro-idolatry was
a perversion of the original religion and was not part of it. In due course
it developed into something far worse. The Egyptians were led to believe
that the soul of Osiris had entered into an ox, and that the souls of others
had entered "cows, oxen, and other animals, and into plants and unformed
stones, and finally into statues and sculptures of all kinds." The priests
feigned that the souls of the dead could be invoked both by the use of
various incantations and by the introduction of oracles, astrology, and
forms of black magic. By means of such necromancy, various spirits could
supposedly be ordered to be present at the behest of the priest. These dark
arts of deception, Newton wrote in a separate draft, were precisely those
"<heathen> superstitions from wch Moses made a reformation." Again, the
reference to the incantations and the intercession of priests to communicate
with the dead clearly marked out these corruptions as precursors of Roman
Catholicism.[49]

The corruption of religion was inevitably accompanied by the complete
loss of true scientific knowledge. This happened because people began to
take literally what the mystical philosophers had only spoken of allegorically.
The ignorant common people took Vesta to be the earth, and they assumed
that the vestal fire signified not the sun but some invisible and fictitious fire
in the centre of the earth. Philosophers began to claim that the heavens
were not composed of some fluid but that the planets and fixed stars in-
hered in solid orbs. After Eudoxus had introduced this corruption, it was a
short step to feigning that the planets were moved along these solid orbs by
intelligences, that is, by the souls of the dead. Because of the solidity of the
spheres, they now believed that comets were a type of meteor that existed
below the sphere of the moon. They also interpreted literally the mystically
arranged order of the planets so that they came to believe that the orbits of
Venus and Mercury lay inside that of the sun. Worst of all, they took the fifth
essence, which for the ancient philosophers had been the incorruptible, immutable and immortal being diffused throughout the heavens, for the incorruptible physical material of the celestial spheres. Thereafter, the Western
world was contaminated by the Aristotelian philosophy and by Trinitarian
anti-Christianism.[50]

9. Reason and Restoration

Newton's understanding of the historical function of Moses's task had interesting consequences. When David Gregory visited him in the spring of
1694, Newton told him that Christ had reformed, that is, restored the religion of Moses—itself a restoration of those true elements of worship that
were embedded within the Egyptian religion. While some aspects of Gregory's accounts of what Newton thought should be treated with scepticism,
this minimalist conception of Christ's historical role is corroborated by the
heading of the final chapter of Newton's early outline of a book on the
topic. This stated explicitly that the Christian religion "became ("evasit") no
more true and no less corrupt than the Noachian." As we have seen, Newton
argued that Moses had retained all of the true elements of the Egyptian religion, purging it of Egyptian idolatry and necromancy. Once this, in turn,
had been predictably corrupted, Christ's mission had essentially the same
function as the Mosaic version, except that Christian depravity would
plumb depths that were much lower than those to which the Jews had sunk.
Christ's reformation of the Mosaic religion was thus *in some sense* nothing
more than a return to the true elements of the rational Noachian-Egyptian
religion, though it was destined to be corrupted to a much greater degree
than the world had previously witnessed.[51]

Newton's researches demonstrated, at least to himself, that the relationship
between the restoration and corruption of the true religion was cyclical. Various forces throughout history were always liable to re-combine, and kings and
priests always tried to take advantage of the predilection of mankind towards
superstition. However, great men, inspired by God, could lead humanity back
to the true religion. The latter, as Newton understood it, had a naturalistic or
scientific component, and the original religion was "rational" precisely because
the Ancients fashioned their temples in recognition that Nature was the temple
of God. According to Newton, they worshipped the true God in and through
his temple, which was made up of the heavens and everything in it. This worship was not the idolatrous worship of God through inanimate things but a
reference to the fact that the true God was the God of the natural world. The
study of nature was the study of God's temple, and the wonders of the universe
were supposed to be the focus of human attention. The ancient religion, which
enjoined the study of the heavens as a truly religious endeavour, was thus restored to some extent in the *Principia*'s revelation of the divine blueprint for the
world.

Newton's account of the way a true, simple, and naturalistic religion became corrupted can be usefully compared with the contemporary works of the "deists" or "freethinkers" Lord Edward Herbert (Herbert of Cherbury) and Charles Blount. In two earlier works, *De Veritate* (1624) and *De Religione Laici* (1645), Herbert had proposed the idea that there were five common "notions" that were the foundations of the true, natural, rational religion. In his posthumous *De Religione Gentilium* of 1663, he drew liberally from Selden's *de Diis Syris* and from Vossius's *De Theologia Gentili* to historicise this idea, finding the origin of religion in the ancient adoration of the stars. Departing from Vossius, who believed that the gentiles had idolatrously worshipped the stars as proper gods in their own right, Cherbury argued that the pagans had anciently worshipped the true God symbolically through their veneration for the stars, and, most important, via their worship of the sun. He went on to examine the progress of idolatry from the first image worship of the Egyptians, who instituted the adoration of their forefathers before tacking on the superstition of zoolatry. No one would deny, he went on, that a "race of crafty priests" had introduced idolatry and polytheistic superstition, adding innumerable gods to the pantheon and then constructing false prophecies and fables to beget respect in the vulgar. They included incomprehensible mysteries and artificial rituals, which perverted the simple, natural religion practised in the earliest times. Cherbury's main theses were rehashed towards the end of the century by Charles Blount, who repeated the charge that it had been the priesthood that had introduced superstitions, rites, and ceremonies and who had corrupted the original religion by playing on the fears of the vulgar.[52]

Newton shared with Cherbury and Blount many convictions about the nature of idolatry and the tendency of the vulgar to believe silly mysteries, and he held similar suspicions about the way devious priests had perverted the true religion for their own ends. The same view can be found in Robert Howard's *History of Religion* of 1694, a copy of which Newton owned. Howard offered a conventional euhemerist account of the origin of pagan religion and rehearsed the standard deist line that religion had early on been corrupted by clerical interference, mystery, and metaphysics. Such criticisms of deviant priestly excess were not simply the preserve of anticlerical writers. It was a common tactic used by many Protestant writers to assail Roman Catholic priests, and it was obligatory to show—not least because they thought Catholicism was essentially pagan—how they were adopting the same tactics as their pagan ancestors. From one perspective Newton's account is an example of exactly this approach, and he was no "deist" insofar as the term denotes support for the

idea of a largely absent divinity or an aversion to revelation or religious ceremony. Nor did he make any criticisms of modern clergymen as a group, claiming at one point that they were more godly than their forbears.[53]

Nevertheless, despite overwhelming evidence of the sincerity of Newton's
Christianity, and the great veneration he entertained for the religious and
moral practices of the ancient Hebrews, his depiction of the vestal religion as
supremely rational would have unnerved many of his contemporaries. Although he believed that the great truths of religion and philosophy were
passed down through the biblical patriarchs to Noah, his emphasis on Egypt
as the central postdiluvian locus of the true religion seriously downgraded
the historical role of the Israelites. There is nothing special in Newton's narrative about the Israelite experience after the Flood, nor is the scriptural account given primary authority above other sources. This is of course unsurprising, since by hypothesis all people on Earth were direct descendants of
Noah, but in many passages he evinced a reverence for certain pagan historians (such as the supposed Phoenician [Beirut] writer Sanchuniathon) that
placed their testimony almost on a par with that of Scripture.

By saying that Christ essentially did nothing more than restore the Noachian religion, Newton implied that nothing much more was required of the
true religion than to recognise the divine origins of the cosmos, to believe
that Christ was the Messiah who was resurrected on the third day after his
death, and to observe the moral obligations of Christianity. In other writings
Newton did attribute more to Christ than is discernible in this statement,
but the general thrust of his writings on the ancient religion is of a piece
with his tendency to downgrade the role of the Son in respect to that of the
Father. The naturalistic focus of the vestal-Noachian religion is also evidence
that he understood the study of the natural world to be a religious office. His
view of the significance of the *Principia* is understood best by realising that
he really did believe that he had uncovered knowledge that had been known
at the beginning of time and then gradually lost. Knowing its principles, one
might go back to the writings of the doxographers and ancient philosopher
and poets, and unravel the truths that lay underneath their mystical utter-
ances. Read in this way, the fact that the most ancient priest–philosophers had
cultivated the Newtonian religion bolstered the credibility of its modern
variety. Like ancient Newtonianism, the modern version was accessible to a
small number of adepts, and by writing the *Principia* in the recondite, technical manner that he did, Newton was effectively behaving in the way
expected of the priestly guardians of scientific knowledge.

7

Methodising the Apocalypse

Newton's work on the *Principia* interrupted what he believed was the most significant form of study that a learned Christian could undertake. At some point in the late 1670s, he began to devote himself to decoding the images in the prophetic books in the Bible, paying particular attention to Revelation. This research captivated him for the last two decades of his life in Cambridge and it would remain his abiding passion for the next half a century. When he complained to correspondents in the later 1670s about being deprived of the freedom to pursue his "other studies" by public disputes over his scientific work, he was referring as much to his historical and apocalyptic researches as to his alchemical endeavours. Newton studied both Old and New Testament prophecies with an intensity that matched the vigour with which he had initially engaged with mathematics and natural philosophy. He situated himself in a tradition of Protestant apocalyptic interpretation whose greatest exponent was the Christ's College fellow Joseph Mede. One of his only known friends from the 1670s, Henry More, was not only a student of Mede but was also the most prolific author of prophetic texts in late-seventeenth-century England. As we shall see in this chapter, Newton acknowledged Mede's work, especially his *Clavis Apocalyptica* of 1627, as the foundational model for his own efforts, and he discussed prophecy on a number of occasions with More in the late 1670s and early 1680s.

All three exegetes believed that Revelation and other prophetic passages identified the onset and character of the Great Apostasy that had befallen Christianity at the end of the fourth century, and they argued that these text depicted the future fate of the godly. Mede, More, and Newton differed over significant aspects of the Great Apostasy, but they agreed that this terrible debasement of the true religion lay at the heart of the religious perversions and persecutory demeanour of the modern Roman Catholic Church.

Although he participated fully in this tradition, Newton's belief in the diabolical origins of Trinitarianism meant that his prophetic scheme emphasised
events in Christian history that his contemporaries either ignored or understood in a completely opposite way. This is most evident in his stunning
prophetically inflected history of heresy and persecution in the Christian
Church. Viewing the events of both political and ecclesiastical history
through the lens of his anti-Trinitarian and anti-Catholic biases, Newton
depicted the saints and martyrs beloved of both Catholic and Protestant
historians as immoral hypocrites, rightly subjected to atrocities by the
Vandals, barbarians, and Goths.[1]

Mede's scholarly identity and exegetical practices provided a significant
model for both More and Newton. Writing in the 1620s and 1630s, Mede
protested that he was a modest and objective scholar, with no political or
religious axes to grind. However, his work was subsequently taken up by
puritans who were fascinated by the possibilities it gave, both for understanding their contemporary situation as the righteous and persecuted
godly and for determining the nature and date of Christ's Second Coming.
After the Restoration, John Worthington's successive editions of Mede's
works reinstated him as a sober and learned interpreter who was not
responsible for the ways in which his work had been taken up by puritan
fanatics. Although Newton thought that Mede had made some mistakes in
his *Clavis*, he believed that it had laid down the true principles of the field,
and he adopted many facets of Mede's authorial identity. However, he did not
call upon his own expertise as a mathematician in his prophetic work. In the
late 1630s, Mede himself had been beguiled by the still-unpublished work
of the inventor Francis Potter on the number 666, but he died before he
could give a measured assessment of Potter's work. Newton shared many
of Mede's assumptions about the Roman Catholic reference of 666, but
placed limits on the extent to which mathematical approaches should be
imported into apocalyptic interpretation. As I show in this chapter, despite
the fact that Newton argued that one could not prove prophetic arguments
with mathematical certainty, More and others believed that his expertise in
the subject might be used to decode the exceptionally recondite numerical mysteries that were found in prophetic texts.[2]

As in other areas of Newton's theological research, there are no clear indications of the early footsteps by which he became immersed in the serious
study of prophecy. There were two elements of prophetic interpretation,
namely the analysis of the so-called internal order of the prophetic images, and

the "application" of these images to historical events. It is not known whether Newton began his apocalyptic studies with a concern for the proper order of the images, or whether this was a consequence of his heavily anti-Trinitarian study of the early church. As other interpreters routinely did, he dutifully stressed that exegetes should arrange the order of prophetic visions prior to determining the way in which they had been fulfilled in history. However, early on in his studies, Newton had settled on a firm view of the logical arrangement of the images, and this must have been tightly bound up with his idiosyncratic view of church history. With these general approaches in place, he spent half a century fine-tuning historical detail and prophetic images so that they harmonised. In terms of the technical intricacy of his work, the range of images he adduced in his analysis, and his use of detailed historical evidence, he went beyond any other interpreter of his age. However, the radical originality of his approach and the sophistication of his work was combined with a pronounced tendency to lift wholesale phrases and arguments from Mede.

There is no way of dating Newton's early apocalyptic writings with precision, but two signposts aid the general task. In the first place, More's references to Newton's views in a letter of 1680 show that by the end of the 1670s at the latest, Newton had developed a sophisticated understanding both of the internal order of apocalyptic visions, and—one may infer—of the historical events that they described. Second, the bulk of one mature apocalyptic treatise must date from the mid- to late 1680s since it is in the hand of Humphrey Newton, his amanuensis during that period. If we assume that the composition of the *Principia* and its drafts took up most of Newton's waking hours between the autumn of 1684 and early 1687, then this tract was presumably written between the summer of 1687 and Humphrey's departure around the winter of 1688/89. It is possible—but far less likely—that they were composed at the same time, and that he relaxed from the rigours of one by turning to the other. As with all other areas of his theological researches, Newton's writings on prophecy are characterised by a lack of reference to, or any engagement with events and texts from his own time. In all his substantial seventeenth-century treatises on prophecy and the history of the church, there is barely any mention of contemporary events, and only very occasionally does one locate a textual source that constitutes a relevant *terminus post quem*. Newton continued to work on prophetic exegesis until the end of his life, although the multiple redraftings from the early eighteenth century show no major differences from the analytic positions at which he had arrived by the end of the 1680s.[3]

1. The Apocalyptic Tradition

The Protestant apocalyptic tradition in which Newton situated himself was created in the middle of the sixteenth century by John Knox, John Bale, and John Foxe. The culmination of this early endeavour was Foxe's *Acts and Monuments* (commonly known as the "Book of Martyrs") of 1563, which contained stories of martyrdoms from the earliest Christian times up to the end of the reign of Henry VIII. In successive editions, he regaled the reader with increasingly detailed accounts of how various prophetic images had been fulfilled by specific historical events.[4] In the fourth (1583) edition of *Acts and Monuments*, he displayed a much greater interest than hitherto in the application of mystical prophetic numbers to historical events. He followed many predecessors in identifying the first ten-horned beast (Rev. 13:1-2) with the Roman Empire, since its seven heads proved it to be the same as the seven-hilled city of pagan Rome. The second, or two-horned beast (Rev. 13:11-12) was to be identified with the papacy since its two horns (like those of a lamb) denoted the twin arms of Roman secular and spiritual power. The visions of the woman who gave birth to a male child and who was subsequently forced into the wilderness by a water-vomitting dragon (Rev. 12) referred to the true Church and its persecution by the pre-Constantinian emperors. Foxe, and later Thomas Brightman, claimed that what they took to be the first millennium began with the rule of Constantine (from 306 to 337), a period when the Satanic dragon was bound for a period that would last a thousand years. Following the suggestion made much earlier by Irenaeus, and in line with many other Protestants, Foxe understood the number 666 (Rev. 13:17-18) to refer to "LATEINOC" ("Romanus," or in English, "A Man of Rome"), all the letters of which—according to the alphanumeric coding technique known as gematria—totalled 666 when assigned their allotted numbers.[5]

Many Protestant writings were inspired to extend this tradition by the attacks on it mounted by Catholics such as Francisco de Ribera and Robert (later Cardinal) Bellarmine. Ribera argued that the first five seals (Rev. chs 5-6) described the history of the church to the time of Trajan (emperor from 98 to 117 C.E.), while the remaining two depicted the last times. This so-called preterite (or "past") position was the most common Roman Catholic approach in the sixteenth and seventeenth centuries and was designed to neutralize the core assumptions of the Protestant claim that key images in Revelation indicated the future downfall of Catholicism and the imminent return of Jesus Christ. In the first two volumes of his *Controversies*, published in 1581 and 1593, Bellarmine argued that the pope could not be Antichrist since the latter had clearly not yet arrived—nor was there any sign of the universal preaching of the Last Times, a necessary precondition of the Second Coming that many Protestants claimed was now taking place. The work of Ribera, Bellarmine, and other Catholic writers provoked the response of many Protestant exegetes such as Brightman, Hugh Broughton, and the Scottish mathematician John Napier.[6]

Alarmed by the threat that had been posed by the Spanish Armada, Napier laid out his views in his *A Plaine Discovery of the Whole Revelation of Saint John* of 1593. In line with the approach adopted by Petrus Ramus, he divided off church history from imperial history and represented both in a tabular form. In his preface to the "Godly and Christian Reader" he argued that he had adopted a twofold method, both "paraphrasticall" (i.e., in the form of a paraphrase) and "historical." Napier offered both an analysis of the internal logic of the images and an account of how the visions had been fulfilled in history, and as befitted his status as the inventor of logarithms, he set out the work in a propositional and quasi-mathematical form, "as neer the analytick or demonstrative manner as the phrase and nature of the holy Scriptures will permit." Where historical interpretations were possible, these appeared in footnotes, while dates corresponding to specific images were given in the margin. By doing this, Napier subjected Revelation to a rigorous "methodising" long before Mede allegedly pioneered the same, and he brought his authority as a lay mathematician to the business of prophetic exegesis.[7]

Napier's propositions, beginning with the statement that prophetic "days" were real years, moved logically from more general to more specific claims. As early as Proposition 2, he made the novel argument that corresponding trumpets and vials of wrath of Revelation *referred to the same event*, an interpretive assumption whose only other serious exponent during the early modern period seems to have been Newton. With such exegetical building blocks, Napier claimed that he could demonstrate the true mystical internal order of Revelation. Proposition 15, based on observations already made by Knox and others, stated that many of the similar measures of time mentioned in Revelation and Daniel—namely, 42 months, 1,260 days, and "time, times and half a time"—all covered the same historical era. The images depicting this period were of the trampling of the Outer Court of the Holy Temple by the Gentiles (Rev. 11:2), the prophesying of the two witnesses in sackcloth (Rev. 11:3-14), and the duration of the exile of the woman (the true Church of God from Prop. 22) in the wilderness (Rev. 12:6, 14). Napier stated that this was no ordinary or arbitrary length of time but was the duration of the reign of Antichrist. Other propositions amounted to definitions or identifications, all of which were based on staples of conventional Protestant exegesis. In Proposition 24, for example, Napier interpreted the ten-horned beast as the Roman Empire since it was evidently equivalent to the ten-headed fourth beast (understood by most interpeters to denote Rome) mentioned by Daniel (Dan. 7:19-26). The pope was the two-horned beast and the false prophet (Rev. 16:13), identified as *the only* Antichrist (in opposition to those who were unsure whether the proper referent was the pope, or the prophet Muhammed, or both) in Propositions 25 and 26. Along with the core doctrines Mede, Brightman, Potter, and the German exegete Johann Heinrich Alsted, Napier's findings would be translated, summarised, and widely distributed in almanacs and other popular writings during the 1640s.[8]

2. Joseph Mede and the Cambridge Tradition

Joseph Mede's approach was heavily indebted to the labours of these writers, though he presented himself rhetorically as a humble and independent author who had made his own findings through diligent study. A Cambridge don with a keen interest in contemporary political events, Mede was an erudite scholar who enjoyed a wide-ranging correspondence with a broad circle of academics, divines, and laymen. His *Clavis Apocalyptica* was published in 1627 and a second edition followed in 1632, along with his much more extensive *Commentary* (*Commentarius Apocalypseos*) on Revelation. His posthumous *Apostasy of the Latter Times* of 1641 was also highly influential as a demonstration that Roman Catholicism was the heathenish and diabolical Great Apostasy. In his correspondence Mede continued to cultivate his reputation for extreme modesty and objectivity, and he eschewed academic fame and institutional awards. This, and his even-handedness regarding the controversies over religious practice in the 1630s, greatly enhanced his scholarly standing among different sorts of Protestant. Nevertheless, the general thrust of his work appealed mainly to those puritans who were demanding a root and branch change in the structure of the Church of England, and to more radical separatists. Mede's relocation of the millennium into the future was deeply problematic for many in the Church of England, who, frightened by the potentially anarchic consequences of belief in an imminent inversion of the social order, maintained a long-standing orthodox suspicion of millenarianism. After the Restoration, John Worthington pleaded that Mede was not guilty of the way his work had been taken up by "Men of wild Principles and Practices."[9]

In the general preface to his 1672 edition of Mede's *Works*, Worthington pointed out that Mede had identified idolatry as the defining characteristic of the Great Apostasy, and he listed a number of the core aspects of Mede's approach. First, Mede had compared various parts of Scripture, showing connections between them and by observing the proper use of words and phrases in the original Hebrew and Greek. Second, he had attained a mastery of the history and customs of ancient nations, especially "Jewish Antiquity," which facilitated a better grasp of the more obscure parts of Scripture. Third, he had noted the "symbols, emblems and hieroglyphicall representations, which were no less familiar to those Eastern Nations than our Poetical Schemes and Pictures are to us." Finally, Mede's momentous discovery of new synchronisms derived from his view that it was a gross error to assume that the order of the prophetic visions in Daniel and Revelation followed a chronological development. Instead, various "scenes" in Revelation provided new descriptions of and perspectives on the same periods of time and the events they contained. According to Worthington, Mede offered a foundation for future interpreters founded on "natural," "obvious," and even "certain" procedures, so that scriptural exegesis might be freed from the "Pile of private Fancies" of those who wished to skew prophecy to their own ends. These prescriptions followed the tenor of Mede's description of his own practice, and they provided the procedural basis for of all those scholars who worked in the Medean tradition.[10]

The discovery of new synchronisms in Daniel and Revelation was perhaps Mede's chief claim to fame, although he was not nearly as original an exegete as his disciples claimed. In "Synchronism 1" of the *Clavis*, he followed Napier and others in making the time of the woman's stay in the wilderness coextensive with the period during which the ten-horned beast was restored, with the destruction of the Outer Court by the Gentiles, and with the time of the two witnesses prophesying in sackcloth. All this, he claimed, was "almost" obvious because of the identity or similarity of the periods of time that were mentioned as part of these images. In the second synchronism, the times of the two-horned beast and ten-horned beast were precisely synchronised, and in the third, the period covered by the great

Whore of Babylon who rode atop the ten-horned beast (Rev. 17:3-6) was synchronised with the time during which the two beasts exercised their power. Mede went on to make the case (by means of anti-typical contrast with the Whore) that the time during which the 144,000 virgins were sealed (Rev. 7:4-5 and 14:1-3) was contemporaneous with the time of the Great Apostasy. Thus, he concluded that these visions were all synchronous, each describing the rise and fall of the Great Apostasy from the true faith.[11]

Mede argued that another major series of visions were coextensive with the time depicted by the first six seals and were chronologically "anterior" to those that depicted the Great Apostasy. These were the measurement of the Interior Court with a reed in Revelation 11:1, the battle in heaven between Michael and the dragon [after which the dragon (i.e., Satan), was cast down to Earth (Rev. 12:7)], and the labouring of the pregnant woman and the consequent birth of her son (Rev. 12:5). Scripture related that all these were immediately antecedent to the woman's flight into the wilderness, and so they had to be mutually synchronal, with the flight of the woman being part of a later period. In Part 2 of the *Clavis*, Mede turned to the vision of the seven seals, the last of which "comprehended" the visions of the trumpets and the vials. Understood historically, the seals dealt with the Roman Empire, which was first pagan, then briefly Christian (under Constantine), and then in the seventh seal, fully Antichristian until its final transformation in the millennium. The fifth seal (Rev. 6:9-11) witnessed terrible cruelties against the godly, who called out for vengeance against their oppressors. The sixth seal (Rev. 6:12-14) described catastrophic events involving a great earthquake, the blackening of the sun (i.e., its eclipse), and the moon turning blood-red. Mede understood these prophetic images to refer to Christianity's extirpation of diabolical pagan worship, whose triumphant climax took place in the reign of Theodosius at the end of the fourth century. However, this victory over heathenism only prepared the way for the terrible events that were to follow.[12]

According to Mede, the main period of the Great Apostasy commenced with the opening of the seventh seal, which was followed after a short break of half an hour's silence (Rev. 8:1) by the sounding of the first trumpet. During the thirty prophetic minutes of respite, four angels held back winds that blew destruction and disaster from each point of the compass (7:1-2); and this period was coextensive or synchronal with the visions of the sealing of the 144,000 elect (Rev. 7:3-8). The four angels let loose the winds successively in each of the first four trumpets, while Mede made the last three trumpets synchronal with the successive "woes" described in Revelation 8:13. Since the period covered by the beasts was coterminous with the mournful prophesying of the two witnesses, and the latter ended at the close of the sixth trumpet, so the major period of the Great Apostasy also ended at this time. Like the vast majority of Protestant exegetes, Mede reserved the pouring of the vials of wrath for a detailed account of recent history. He argued that they depicted the downfall of the Roman beast and so he placed the first six vials in the sixth trumpet. The millennial era that postdated the Great Apostasy was thus begun by the simultaneous commencement of the seventh trumpet and seventh vial.[13]

In Part 2, Synchronism 5, Mede synchronised the thousand-year period of the dragon's binding in the hellish Abyss (Rev. 20:1-3, 10, 14) with the millennium; in Synchronism 6 he made this period coextensive with both the visions of the New Jerusalem and its marriage to the Lamb (Rev. 21), and (in Synchronism 7) with the rejoicing palm-bearing multitude (Rev. 7:9). The sealing of the dragon in the Abyss at the start of the millennium was also synchronised with the casting of the beast and false prophet into the lake of fire (Rev. 19:20). In an attack on those like Brightman who had argued in favour of a Constantinian millennium beginning in the early fourth century, Mede argued that there was no evidence that the agents of the dragon had been in any way constrained during this period. On the contrary, the rampant dragon had been free to perform his evil deeds both before and during the Great Apostasy, first trying to destroy the woman while she was in labour, second trying to drown her with water spewed from his mouth, and finally by making war with the remnant of her seed once she was safely in the wilderness. The millennium had obviously not yet occurred, but at its end, the dragon would be released from the pit to lead the armies of Gog and Magog against the saints. The forces of goodness and truth were destined to prevail, and with his tail between his legs, the dragon would be sent to the lake of fire in order to join his fellow-travellers (the beast and the false prophet) to be tormented for eternity.[14]

In a brief discussion of the foundations of his own work, Mede argued that interpretation needed a sure method or key with which to proceed. In the case of the Apocalypse, there was evidently a true mystical order to the visions that by no means followed the apparent sequence of images in the text. His own synchronisms, he claimed, could rid the whole business of decipherment from personal bias, conjecture, and uncertainty. With their judicious application, he ventured that there would be much less disagreement between interpreters and the remaining doubtful places would be of little consequence. The precise way in which one could develop his synchronic insights was left deliberately obscure in the *Clavis*, but he dealt with many unsolved problems in his *Commentary* of 1632. Not only did Mede respond at length to many queries from interested readers, but as a foundation for his interpretation he turned to the oneirocriticism (dream interpretation) of the medieval "Arab" author Achmet, using the edition published by Nicholas Rigaltius in 1603. Now he argued that prophetic references could be correctly interpreted only by understanding the sacred language of those nations (Egyptian, Persian, and Indian) that bordered the lands of ancient Hebrews. Central to his account was the claim that the religious practices surrounding the placing of the tabernacle in the middle of the camp of Israel were typological adumbrations of the apocalyptic "theatre" outlined at the start of Revelation. As we shall see, Newton followed Mede in all these procedures, relying heavily on his predecessor's guidance in his major treatises.[15]

3. Henry More's Apocalypse

In the 1630s Puritans such as William Twisse, Samuel Hartlib, and John Dury corresponded with Mede concerning various features of the Apocalypse, and a few months before Mede died in 1638 Hartlib drew his attention to a manuscript version of Francis Potter's *Interpretation of the Number 666*. Potter was motivated by the success of previous interpreters in extracting the number of the tribes of Israel (12) from the square root of the first three digits of the sealed 144,000 virgins, and much of his text was an explanation of the significance of the approximate root (25) of the diabolical number. Its inexactitude was a mystery that required exegetical expertise to decode, he argued, but there were ample examples from history to show that the number twenty-five was associated both with Rome and with the dark dealings of the Catholic Church. On reading Potter's work, Mede was suddenly captivated, as Foxe had been, by the potential of mathematics to unfold the mysteries of Revelation. In a letter that was used as a foreword to the published version of Potter's work, Mede noted that Potter had built on a "mathematical ground," and that his procedures would be better understood by those who knew how to extract square roots. Potter's work appeared in print in the politically and religiously charged year of 1642, when the publication of new and popular versions of scholarly texts took place alongside texts expounding pagan oracles and astrological predictions of imminent political upheaval.[16]

A small number of Protestants doubted the identity of the pope with Antichrist and denied that Rome was to be equated with Babylon. In 1640 Hugo Grotius composed a work designed to prove that the pope was not Antichrist, and he followed anti-millennialist exegetes such as the Jesuit Luis del Alcázar in locating the time and place of the Apocalypse in the Holy Lands of the very early church. He interpreted the Man of Sin (2 Thess. 2) as a reference to Caligula, applied the number 666 to Trajan, and concluded (following 1 John 2:18) that there were many antichrists. Grotius assigned all the standard tokens of antichristianism to pagan Rome, and he understood all attacks on idolatry in Revelation as depicting heathen Roman cultism. For his pains in trying to effect an irenic reconciliation between Christians during the Thirty Years War, he was roundly condemned as a Catholic stooge. His most devoted follower in England was Henry Hammond (the confidant of Robert Sanderson), who sought to nullify millenarianism in his 1653 *Paraphrase and Annotation* of the books of the New Testament. He followed Foxe and Brightman in backdating the onset of the millennium to the reign of Constantine and identified the Man of Sin and Antichrist with the gnostic Simon Magus. Like Grotius, he assumed that the central references in Revelation to the beasts and the Whore all referred to heathen Rome and its persecutions of Christians in the pre-Constantinian era.[17]

The Restoration of Charles II in 1660 made many English exegetes think twice about the wisdom of publishing works depicting the impending Second Coming and the prophetic end of the world, conventionally understood as the overthrow of the political order. Because the events of the 1640s and 1650s had (allegedly) been instigated by people fired up by incendiary interpretations of the Apocalypse, many divines shied away from the futurist and predictive elements within prophetic exegesis. However, despite understandable distrust of millenarian theorising, a number of Anglican interpreters continued to use Mede in order to understand prophetic writings and warn of the dangers that threatened their own times. In particular, the work of Newton's friend Henry More shows that it was possible to recast the English apocalyptic tradition so that it was relevant to the new religious conditions of the Restoration. In More's *Explanation of the Grand Mystery of Godliness* of 1660 he followed Mede closely, asserting at the outset that his synchronisms were "apodictically true to any one that has but a competency of wit and patience to peruse them." More argued that Christianity had remained untainted by the Apostasy until about 400 C.E., and he suggested that one should add the stock 1,260 prophetic years/days to this date to get the approximate time at which the corrupt pagano-Christianity would experience its demise. The return of the monarch in the year that the *Explanation* was published was thus not merely a providential event, but was explicitly prophesied in the Apocalypse.[18]

In 1664 More published his *Modest Enquiry into the Mystery of Iniquity*, modelling it on the style of analysis carried out by Mede in his *Apostasy of the Latter Times*. With various scriptural warnings about the depravity of the last ages in mind, he set out to show "that the Antichristianism which they foretel of is a degeneracy or apostasy of the Church still formally professing Christianity." His method involved depicting the "idea" of "Antichristianism" before ascertaining whether it corresponded to any apostasy described in the prophecies. It was, he stated at the outset, "nothing else but real impiety, gross Fraud and Couzenage, and most barbarous and unparallel'd Cruelty against the harmless Members of Christ," all done under the show and pretence of the Christian religion, which greatly aggravated the offence. More rehearsed a familiar Protestant litany of image-worship, superstitious rites, the worship of saints and angels, exorcism, theatrics, false legends, carnality, purgatory, theo-cannibalism, the idolatrous collection and adoration of relics, and infallibility. The demonstrative scheme was of course prefabricated from his prior belief that Roman Catholicism was the Great Apostasy, and his account of idolatry was merely a highly charged redescription of the central elements of that religion.[19]

In the same year More added a "second part" to the *Modest Enquiry*, which he titled *Synopsis Prophetica*. Many interpreters, he claimed, had brought prophecy into disrepute by dint of their shallow reasoning and rabid prejudice against social order: "we know likewise by woeful experience what wild Applications Enthusiasts make of the *Ten Horned Beast* and the *Whore of Babylon*, phansying in their mad mistaken zeal every legitimate Magistrate that *Beast*, and every well ordered Church that *Whore*." Prophecy *was* terribly obscure but it was a mere atheistic conceit to think that the visions could not be decoded. With serious study, and armed with the correct demonstrative method or key, which of course More claimed to offer, its meaning could be found with a very high level of certainty. Indeed, understood properly, it was the most important and useful evidence that the

Christian religion was the one preferred by God. The last concern was the reason that he never let up his attacks on Grotius, Hammond, and the non-conformist Richard Baxter, whose "absurd" interpretations of Revelation gave succour to popery by rendering the Apocalypse impotent for identify-ing the true nature of Antichrist. More's writings were peppered with claims that once the unprejudiced reader read his book, the meaning of the proph-ecies would be clear and simple, and a mathematically certain interpretation could be easily accomplished. Only the enemies of God, who were *sup-posed* to find interpretation difficult, and those who were "grossly preju-diced," "Enthusiastick Freaks," or downright insane, would fail to be satis-fied by his method.[20]

More composed a lengthy taxonomy of rhetorical techniques that were necessary for understanding the intention of the prophet, who had evi-dently used the same methods ("Prophetic figures") to compose and ob-scure the text. He added an even longer "Prophetick alphabet," which was indebted to his idiosyncratic understanding of the Cabbala and particularly to his own reading of Achmet. More cited Mede and Grotius as the pioneers of this style of enquiry but he boasted that he had treated a much greater number of images than had Mede. At the end, he laid out a set of rules for extracting the proper meanings underlying the visions in Daniel and Revelation that were more complex than the vague recommendations given by his predecessor. These rehearsed Mede's warnings that one should keep to the internal order of the visions and stick to robust and well-tested rules and procedures. Rule 1, for example, enjoined the exegete to prefer the in-terpretation "that keeps close to the approved Examples and Analogie of the Prophetick style" above those "framed at pleasure according to the private phancy." Amongst others, More added the stricture that one should not in-terpret the same words in the same vision in different ways, since doing so was a clear demonstration of fraud and interest.[21]

In its broad outlines More's scheme did not differ that much from Mede's (see Plates 9–13). However, he argued that the three and a half days of the witnesses' lying slain, having been killed by the beast from the bottomless pit (Rev. 11:7-9), was not to be identified with three and a half actual (i.e., non-prophetic) years, as the standard rules of procedure re-quired, and as Mede had claimed. This, More asserted, was a mistake "of no small consequence," since the period was obviously equivalent both to the 1,260 days of their prophesying (Rev. 11:3) and to the time, times, and half a time that made up the period of the Great Apostasy. Ergo, the witnesses were prophesying in a sackcloth while they were visibly dead, a point that More admitted was counterintuitive but nevertheless true. Where Mede had placed six of the vials in the sixth trumpet, More placed them all in the seventh (see Plate 12), since, he claimed, the first vial was poured on the enemies of the two witnesses following their ascension to heaven, which had happened at the end of the sixth trumpet. In the *Synopsis*, he complained that he had previously been misled by previous interpreters into thinking that his own period was not yet past the sixth trumpet, but he now recognised that the beginning of the rise of the witnesses was the Protestant Reformation, at which time the woman had begun to return from the wilderness. More placed his own era in the first of the seven thunders (which contained all the vials—see Plate 13) of Revelation 10:1-7, which were all located in the seventh trumpet. With an even greater degree of precision, he claimed that even as he wrote, the third vial was being poured on the two-horned beast or papacy.[22]

More never relaxed his onslaught on popery. In 1668 he published *The Divine Dialogues*, a work directed against "the Pope and his clergie" and he immortalized protégés such as the scholar-diplomat John Finch and his companion, the physician Thomas Baines, by setting the dialogues in the orchard at Christ's College. From 1669 he extended his list of works on prophecy with his *Exposition of the Seven Churches*, to which he added his *Antidote Against Idolatry*, and the *Visionum Apocalypticarum Ratio Synchronisticis* that appeared in his *Opera Theologica* of 1675. The most detailed exposition of More's scheme was presented in the *Visionum Apocalypticarum*, where he included a number of striking images explaining the interrelations between various images. These were particularly enlightening about the prophetic end of the world, which began with the onset of the millennium. The remaining thunders described the successive stages in the growth of the kingdom of God, namely the descent of New Jerusalem (Rev. 21:2, 10) and the appearance of the palm-bearing multitude; the millennial reign of Christ; the loosing of Satan from his prison; the founding of the bejewelled city (Rev. 21:18-21); Judgement Day; and the great conflagration, during which the saints would be made safe to reign forever. Newton spent a great deal of time discussing prophetic images with More, but made scant reference to his works in his own apocalyptic writings. Nevertheless, as we shall see, he did engage with More's work at the height of the Popish Plot, only to dismiss his approach and indeed his system.[23]

4. An Earnest Seeker of Truth

In books, sermons, and conversations, the young Newton must have been exposed on a regular basis to passages and images in Revelation. As we will see in chapter 9, he made some critical observations about the apocalyptic end of the world while still an undergraduate, and, later, he came to see the study of the prophecies as the central duty of a mature Christian. By the end of the 1670s, he had developed a strikingly innovative account of how apocalyptic images had been fulfilled in history. He embraced the appropriate authorial demeanour of a true Medean disciple, and in one revealing preface to an early draft treatise on the Apocalypse he offered a clear account of the ideal godly exegete. In this text he argued that the prophecies had been revealed by God to be understood only by a select band of the church of Christ: "I mean not all that call themselves Christians, but a remnant, a few scattered persons which God hath chosen, such as without being blinded led by interest, education, or humane authorities, can set themselves sincerely and earnestly to search after truth." Members of the remnant were duty bound to use their intelligence to glean important truths, "for as Daniel hath said that ye wise shall understand, so he hath said also that none of ye wicked shall understand." There was no question that we now lived in the latter days, when truths would be revealed to the faithful, and Newton was confident that he could play a key role in understanding them.[24]

The notion that he was one of the godly permeated Newton's early work. He believed that he was a special exegete and that having "searched & by the grace of God obtained ⟨after⟩ knowledg in the prophetique scriptures," he was morally bound to spread the Word for the benefit of others. The irony in this most private of men (and an anti-Trinitarian at that) recommending the dissemination of gospel truth is obvious, and he warned like-minded people not to be "too forward in becoming a teacher, like those men who catch at a few similitudes & scripture phrases, & for want of ⟨further⟩ knowledg make use of them to censure & reproach superiours & rail at all things that displeas them." Instead, he told his (implied) readers to thoroughly instruct themselves both in the prophecies and also in the plain simplicities of Christianity, in order to put them into practice and make them a habit. There was a moral duty, he wrote, to search the Scriptures, and the danger of neglecting them was great. Since God had been so angry with the Jews for rejecting their Messiah through neglectful misinterpretation, how much more—when the signs were so clear—would he punish Christians for not detecting the true Antichrist?[25]

The good Christian was to search the Scriptures by himself, paying no attention to human authorities or to the opinion of the mob. Newton exhorted his audience to engage in frequent reading and to meditate constantly on what they read, giving "earnest prayer to God to enlighten thine understanding if thou desirest to find the truth." If this were done, he continued, "thou wilt value above all other treasures in ye world by reason of ye assurance and vigour it will add to thy faith, and steddy satisfaction to thy mind which he onely <can> know how to estimate who shall experience it." Newton presumably believed that this described his own condition, and he cautioned that there were few others who exhibited the same characteristics:

> where are the men that do never yeild to anger nor seek revenge, nor disobey governours, nor censure & speak evil of them, nor cheat, nor lye, nor swear, nor use God's name idly in their common talk, nor are <proud nor ambitious nor> covetous, nor unchast, nor drink immoderately? Where are they that live like ye primitive Christians, that love God with all their hearts & with all their souls & with all their might, and their neighbour as their selves; & that in what they do well are not rather led by fashions and principles of Gentility then religion?

Others loved to be deceived, he went on, "wholly led by prejudice, interest, the prais of men, and authority of ye Church they live in." Critics might call you a bigot, a fanatic, or a heretic, and claim that your interpretations were uncertain, but the quest for religious truth was far more important than the defence of one's own religion, which in any case was highly likely to be false. Such condemnation from others was to be welcomed: "Be not therefore scandalised at the reproaches of ye world but rather looke upon them as a mark of ye true church." As we will see, these sentiments about the values required for proper religious study resonated with his more general remarks about the sorts of personal and ethical requirements needed for discovering truth in other fields.[26]

5. Rules, Words, and Language

Like other scholarly interpreters, Newton claimed that he adhered to a rigorous method and he drew on a broad array of different sources. His work leaned heavily on that of "the judiciously learned & conscientious"

Mede (though he had apparently made a few mistakes in his *Clavis*), but he went far beyond Mede in many respects. For general rules of interpretation he followed Grotius, Mede, and More in relying on the oneirocriticism of Achmet, while for specific interpretations he occasionally cited the sayings of the Chalde Paraphrast (Aramaic Targums, or explanations of the Hebrew Bible in the form of paraphrases). Newton's scheme was magisterial in scope, and in the late 1680s, he wrote down an outline of a massive tome consisting of five apocalyptic books, the first of which concerned the language of the prophets. Book 2 covered prophesies in Daniel while the third examined the typological foreshadowing of the method and prophetic scenery of Revelation in the law and history of the Jews. Book 4 was a prosopography or list of the major individuals in Revelation, and the last analysed the way that prophecy had been fulfilled in history. As discussed at the start of this chapter, one almost complete book from this period is in the hand of Humphrey Newton, giving it a likely date of 1687/88. Another, from a slightly later period, was titled "The First Book" and concerned the "Language of the Prophets." It may be that his experience of writing the *Principia* (which was made up of three "books") shaped his decision to cast his prophetic works into a multibook format, or perhaps the influence extended in the opposite direction. Either way, long before he wrote his great book on the principles of natural philosophy, he had arrived at his basic conception of how apocalyptic images were ordered "internally," and of how prophecy had been fulfilled in history.[27]

At the outset of his explication of prophetic discourse, Newton composed a dictionary of apocalyptic terms and their meanings that was even longer than the one More had given in his *Synopsis*. Achmet, Newton wrote, had drawn from the "figurative" or "mystical" language that was shared both by the prophets and by the more "understanding sort of men" in India, Persia, and Egypt whose nations (he learned from Mede) had bordered the Hebrews. Newton stressed that it was vital to show that his own interpretations cohered with the hermeneutical procedures of these people, who were men of genuine interpretive skill, and he added that their techniques were the best guides for understanding Scripture. The fact that ancient nations all agreed in the fundamentals of their interpretations gave a firm basis for relying on them, since "there uses not to happen any such consent in doctrines wch severall nations or severall men in ye same nation frame according to their privat imaginations." As Mede and others had argued, Newton noted that it was precisely because one could rely on the ancient interpreters, and on sound principles of interpretation, that one could be sure interpretations were immune from the suggestions of "private Phantasy."[28]

Newton couched his tract as a "guide," without which, he warned, it would be difficult even for the most learned to interpret prophecies correctly. However, it was intended for the unlearned as well as the educated, and if they used it often, with sincerity and with a desire to truly understand the prophecies, then anyone could benefit from it. In the conventional language of the apocalyptic tradition in which he was operating, he announced that he would first account for the natural order or "internal characters" of the prophecies, and then graft the interpretations on to it. To do anything else was to pervert Scripture "out of the vanity of appearing somebody in the world," and few exegetes escaped the charge. Indeed, Newton disparaged every interpreter apart from Mede, claiming that he found it hard to accept that they actually believed their own interpretations. Truth and certainty lay in first reducing the internal order of the visions to simple and harmonious relations, building on the discoveries of Mede, and in following the precepts in Newton's own work. False interpretations that added unnecessary elements to Scripture under the guise of elucidations exposed the unskilful exegete to the plagues described in Revelation 22:18.[29]

At one point Newton claimed that the reasons he had given constituted evidence that would necessarily "move the assent of any humble and indifferent person that shall with sufficient attention peruse them and cordially believes the Scriptures." Nevertheless, the epistemic status of the arguments he offered in his exegetical demonstrations was unclear. Although Mede had been modest in the claims to certainty that he offered for his own work, others such as Napier and More had claimed mathematical certainty for their arguments. Against this, Newton emphasised that scriptural truths were not susceptible to that level or nature of proof. In a striking passage, he assailed those who

> although they have neither better nor other grounds for their faith then the Scribes and Pharisees had for their ~~religion~~ Traditions, yet are so pervers as to call upon other men for such a demonstration of the certainty of faith in the scriptures that a meer naturall man, how wicked soever, who will but read it, may judg of it and perceive the strength of it with as much perspicuity and certainty as he can a demonstration in Euclide. I could wish they would consider how contrary it is to God's purpose that the truth of his religion should be as obvious and perspicuous to all men as a mathematical demonstration.

It was enough, he continued, "that it is able to move the assent of those which he hath chosen; and for the rest who are so incredulous, it is just that they should be permitted to dy in their sins." According to Newton God had divided up Scripture in such a way that its arguments might be a demonstration to the first, and foolishness to the latter.[30]

In his instructions for best exegetical practice, Newton followed the prescriptions of his predecessors extremely closely. He proposed a series of "general Rules of Interpretation" in order to cut off opportunities for rash or subjective judgements; interpreters were to prefer those interpretations that were of most use for the church, those that concerned the most "considerable things," and those that were most conducive to the internal coherence and simplicity of prophecy. His very first rule followed More to the letter in commending the "analogy of the prophetique style," that is, abiding closely by the known typological or mystical denotations of various terms rather than understanding them allegorically (i.e., "spiritually") or literally. For example, according to Newton, to interpret the term "beast" as a great vice savoured of a "luxuriant ungovernable fansy" that "borders on enthusiasm," since in the Apocalypse the word always denoted either a body politic or occasionally a person who headed that institution. One rule, again drawn from previous exegetes, specified that interpreters should use the same figurative meaning for the same word when interpreted as part of the same vision, while another precept recommended treating the logical order of visions in prophecy as equivalent to the order they occupied in the narrative, unless there were counter indications—which of course there often were.[31]

The demand that interpreters follow the literal meaning of scriptural terms was obviously a staple of Protestant hermeneutics but in the case of apocalyptic interpretation it had no import. Newton argued that where there was a literal meaning intended in Scripture it was invariably to hide the more "noble mystical sense as a shell ye kernel from being tasted either by unworthy persons, or until such times as God shall think fit." In Rule 4, he contrasted the "literal" sense with the possible allegorical import of a word or phrase, though he cautioned that the latter should be invoked extremely sparingly. Crucially, neither had any place in understanding prophetic language. Newton noted that the "usually signification" of any prophetic term—what he called its "figurative" meaning—was to be "esteemed ye proper & direct sense of ye place as much as if it had been ye litterall meaning." Thus prophetic expressions could *never* be understood literally, but could only be deciphered using the special figurative language employed by learned men across the ancient Eastern world. As with Mede and More, the grammar and reference of this ancient language would be the key to producing an accurate rendition of the central prophetic passages in the New Testament. Allegorical interpretations (say, a wound as a spiritual wound) were rejected outright in Rule 5 as the result of an overly vivid imagination, or from giving undue allegiance to "human authority" (by which Newton presumably meant the Roman Catholic Church). Indeed, he claimed that the twisting of prophetic passages to some spiritual allegory had been the door through which all ancient heresies had crept in.[32]

In Newton's dictionary the foundation of the figurative language was the reduction of prophetic statements about the natural world to descriptions about the political world, an approach that—in line with the hermeneutical approaches he adopted in Christology and natural philosophy—gave his account a strongly anti-physicalist flavour. Accordingly, he stressed that there were no grounds in the prophetic tradition for understanding *literally or physically* any apocalyptic descriptions of floods, burnings, or smitings. This claim was clarified in an early part of the dictionary headed "Definitions," which was followed by a list of "propositions." This was apparently an attempt to instil some mathematical structure to the performance, but in a later draft, the heading "Propositions" was changed to "Positions," although the structure and content remained the same. Understood figuratively, the prophetic language described social, political, or occasionally religious events. Hence Newton understood the prophetic sun to refer to a supreme magistrate and the moon to refer to a functionary next in dignity; mountains were cities, and dens and rocks buildings within them. The sea and the earth were two different sorts of people, while particular types of creature represented societies or groups of men according to the conventional qualities associated with the animal in question (a "beast" per se was thus usually but not always bad). The darkening or setting of the sun, moon, and stars stood for the end of a kingdom "or desolation of it proportional to ye darknes if it be not total." Falling into water denoted complete ruin, while turning water into blood meant the great slaughter of a people or the end of a kingdom. Burning, scorching, earthquakes, and whirlwinds meant wars of varying destructiveness, but rain signified the blessing of God— unless, Newton added, "it come wth a flood." Other things were clear to everyone, Newton claimed, so an adulterate church was represented by a whore, the destruction of idols and idol-temples by the falling of rocks and mountains, the springing up of new heresies and false cults by the ascension of the beast out of the bottomless pit, and the figurative end of the world by a harvest or vintage. Still others were so obvious, he concluded, that there was no point mentioning them.[33]

In a justification of the definitions titled "The Proof," he argued that the usage of various prophetic terms was consonant with the way it was used in other ancient sources and in other places in Scripture. Bedecking such claims with references to an array of related passages allowed Newton to show off his stunning knowledge of the Bible, though he was occasionally aided by guides like those he had used at Cambridge, which offered sophisticated collocations of relevant verses. With copious references to Scripture, he argued in an Achmetian manner that horns referred to strength and power, sometimes in the case of a kingdom and sometimes a single person. Eyes had a double sense, signifying mundane policy and counsel when used of ordinary animals, but denoting supernatural acuity or the prophetic spirit itself when understood "emphatically" (i.e., for emphasis), such as when John referred to the seven eyes of the lamb at Revelation 5:6. This referred to the capacity to see things both future and past, and hence the little horn in Daniel 7:8 that "had eyes like the eyes of a man" was not merely a politician "but a seer of a higher kind or to speak in ye Jewish language, a prophet"—though in this case, a false one.[34]

In general Newton held that prophecy concerned only "eternal visible actions" and he restricted the meaning of trees and other vegetables to types of men. However, in comments in his own hand that he added to the treatise written out by Humphrey, he argued that "by some peculiar epithet or circumstance," one might occasionally deviate from the strict rules of the figurative language and allow the terms to refer to mental dispositions. For example, when contrasting the tree of life with the tree of knowledge of good and evil (Ezek. 42 and Rev. 22), he explained that the former signified grace and the latter signified death, since to eat of its fruit inevitably brought about some "unhappy knowledge or other." It was hard to say what this knowledge was, Newton admitted, but the trials of Adam and Eve indicated that it was connected with lust. Just as eating fruit from the tree of life signified wisdom or a saving inward grace and faith, so consuming forbidden fruit signified lustful thoughts rather than committing any lustful act. Similarly, references to the devil, or more broadly to good and evil spirits, might denote the "tempers dispositions & persuasions of mens minds." The casting of the devil into the bottomless pit was thus "the spirit of delusion" that had reigned in the hearts of men and women ever since Eve was first tempted and which would reign until the apocalyptic end of the world.[35]

Only a handful of Newton's contemporaries believed that the meaning of "spirit" in Scripture should not be understood in supernatural terms, and, indeed, this view was frequently condemned as a key element of atheism. Most famously, in Part 3, chapter 34 of *Leviathan,* Thomas Hobbes denied that it made sense to talk of immaterial spirits and attributed the belief that the term designated supernatural entities to vulgar delusion and the misuse of language. Few were willing to follow Hobbes's blanket denial of the existence of immaterial spirits, which in his case extended even to the biblical period. However, it was increasingly common to argue that many medical conditions, particularly mental disease, had been wrongly ascribed to demonic spirits. Newton argued that the common view that lunatics were really inhabited by evil spirits was a misinterpretation of the figurative language, and it was a superstitious and false belief that had been abused throughout history by false conjurors. This applied to accounts in Scripture, and when Christ spoke of casting out devils, one should assume that this referred to diseases unless it could be "proved by the circumstances" that they were "substantial spirits." In May 1692 Newton told Locke that this language of casting out demons was conventionally used in the ancient world to refer to the cure of madmen. This analysis also extended to the manic visions of the early Desert Fathers, who wrongly attributed to a real devil what was actually the result of their own depraved mental and physical regimes. Although it followed from his figurative scheme, the extent to which Newton was prepared to reduce spirit-talk to mental dispositions was a potentially dangerous position. Indeed, the claim that talk of the devil referred to mental illness, or to a general "spirit of delusion," was a very different notion from the much more personal view of Satan that he had articulated in his prophetic works of the late 1670s.[36]

6. Scripture and Nature

Newton made a broad use of the notion of a figurative language. He did so in a letter sent to Thomas Burnet in 1681, in which he gave a detailed account of how interpreters should understand the description of Creation in Genesis. Burnet had just published the first part of his *Telluris Theoria Sacra (Sacred Theory of the Earth),* in which he attempted to explain the creation based on known natural processes, and had written to Newton for advice. Although Moses had not given an accurate account of creation, Burnet wrote (in response to a now lost letter from Newton), he was confident that he himself had. According to Burnet, Moses's story concerned the creation of this present world rather than its "primeval" predecessor. Moses's account of the six days of the original creation was not physically true, as Newton had apparently insisted it was in his first letter, and indeed the Mosaic story was largely incoherent when subjected to analysis. Rather, Burnet argued, it was "Ideal" or "moral," appealing to the very limited knowledge that his unlearned audience possessed of the present globe. Moses's "hypothesis," had not been designed to convey an accurate depiction of the creation to his illiterate audience, which would have been a useless and distracting amusement. Instead, he had given a "short ideal draught" couched in such a way that the people could "easily imagine an Omnipotent power might form it, wth respect to conveniency of man & animals." In writing this, Burnet was making use of a standard principle of interpretation according to which God and various biblical figures were held to have "accommo-dated" their discourse to the degraded reasoning and perceptual faculties of the vulgar. Burnet attempted to persuade the obviously sceptical Newton by flattery: if all divines were as "rational and judicious" as Newton was, he stated, his explanation of the physical reality of the creation, and of Moses's non-explanation of it, would not hinder the reception of the book, as Newton feared.[37]

Burnet's overconfident physical explanation of how the current constitu-tion of the earth came into being was always going to grate with Newton. However, in his reply he did essay a heavily qualified alchemical portrayal of how the earth could have been formed by natural forces, and even wrote something "by way of conjecture" on the creation of the universe. More importantly, he directly opposed Burnet's suggestion that Moses's story was a sort of fable, and he was insistent that it was neither "Philosophicall" nor "feigned." Moses had not tried to give an account that was technically accu-rate, and indeed had even left out some information that he could have added, such as the possibility that some of the bodies God created were much larger than this Earth, "& perhaps habitable worlds." However, far from being a fable or hypothesis it was a *true* description of the creation, but presented "in a language artificially adapted to ye sense of ye vulgar." While Burnet appealed to the way Moses had crafted his account to the *imaginations* of the unlearned vulgar, Newton argued that the Mosaic account had been designed to convey what uninformed individuals would actually have *seen* had they been present. On the fourth day, for example, Moses decided to describe the appearance of the sun, moon, and stars in terms of their apparent rather than their real place in the sky. Indeed, Newton explicitly denied that the entire process of creating the heavenly bodies occurred on the fourth day, and added that he did not believe that Moses "mentioned their creation as they were physical ⁀bodies in themselves⁀." Moses had described them "as they were lights to this earth" and as "part of yᵉ sensible creation," bypassing a description of their actual moment of creation in favour of the point at which the atmosphere first became clear enough for them to be visible.[38]

Newton's specific use of accommodationism in the context of the creation story was fashioned in response to Burnet's use of the same principle. In many respects his views were similar to Burnet's, although he relied on an innovative, non-correspondence theory of truth. According to this, what ordinary people *saw* was not false, even though they did not really "see"— because they could not understand—the real entities underlying the various phenomena they experienced. If Moses had described the process of creation in detail as it really happened, Newton claimed, it "would have made yᵉ narration tedious & confused, amused yᵉ vulgar and become a Philosopher more then a Prophet." Instead, speaking in his role as a prophet, Moses related them "as they were phænomena in our firmament, & describes their making only so far & at such a time as they were made such phænomena." According to Newton, no one who actually understood the process of creation (as Moses evidently did), and who was faced with the difficulty of "accommodating" the description of this event to highly unintelligent ordinary people, could have done better. In a potent critique of the epistemic status of fictional narrative, Newton insisted that this sensory or "phenomenalist" description was not "poetical" but was consonant with the many other "figurative expressions" in the Bible that could be found in prophetic language. The things signified by these statements, he claimed, were not "Ideall" or "moral," but true. The description was not "grounded on a fiction," he told an increasingly chastened Burnet. "At least Divines will hardly be perswaded to [be]leive so."[39]

Newton's use of accommodation theory was a more sophisticated version of the technique standardly used in relation to heliocentric passages in Scripture, for example, by Johannes Kepler in the *Astronomia Nova* of 1609, and by Galileo in his *Letter to the Grand Duchess Christina* of 1615. Like these other Copernicans, Newton used accommodationism to explain away geocentric references in the Old Testament. However, the difference between the language requisite for physically true accounts of the world and that used in Scripture played a much broader and richer series of roles in his natural philosophy. In a scholium to the definitions of the proto-*Principia* text "De motu corporum in mediis regulariter cedentibus" (from the winter of 1684/85), he noted that unlike philosophers, common people did not know how to abstract their thoughts from their senses. Speaking always of relative quantities or measures, they were thus unable to discern the true, real world that lay beyond their perceptual cloaks. Consequently, it would be absurd for expert philosophers or ancient prophets to speak otherwise (i.e., about real quantities) to them. In the *Principia Mathematica*, Newton emphasised this distinction, insisting that "common," "sensible," and "relative" quantities were constantly used in ordinary human interaction while scientists were obliged to deal with "true" and "absolute" quantities. In the scholium to Definition VIII, he rehearsed his claim that when interpreting Scripture, readers should take into account the *common* usage of the words *time, space, place,* and *motion,* since they referred to the "sensible measures" of these terms. This link between the "relative" and the (merely) "sensible" implied that the untutored vulgar were not merely imprisoned behind the walls of their senses, but that they lacked sufficient reason to tell which was the real true and absolute motion when faced with simple, apparent relativity of motion.[40]

Newton's claim that Scripture did not say anything about the physical world was consistent with similar claims made by Kepler and by Galileo in his *Letter to the Grand Duchess Christina,* which Newton could have read in Thomas Salusbury's 1661 translation of the work. As Newton put it, any attempts to derive truths about the natural world from either literal or figurative interpretations of biblical passages—even though they were not strictly false—would inevitably lead to incorrect statements or even to disputes. However, it was equally inappropriate to use the incorrect language in natural philosophy. In the *Pincipia,* he argued that while, those who understood biblical references to the natural world to denote real or absolute quantities did "violence to the Scriptures," those who dealt with relative or "common measures" in mathematics and philosophy were bound to corrupt it. For Newton then, there were two sorts of exegete, each with skills appropriate to the domains in which they worked. The properly trained natural philosopher could go beyond mere sensory data to the true system of the world that lay behind them. To do so required hard work, intelligence, and a proper method, the last of which he had provided in the form of the *Principia*. On the other hand, especially if equipped with Newton's interpretive scheme, the scriptural exegete could do justice to the holy writings by knowing when to interpret passages literally, and when to do so figuratively.[41]

In making this clear distinction between the modes appropriate for grasping the meaning of Scripture and for discovering truths about the natural world, Newton arrived at similar conclusions to those Galileo had reached in his *Letter*. However, as Galileo had also noted, there was a fundamental asymmetry in their relationship between the mathematically sophisticated natural philosopher and the uninformed divine. Although the latter had nothing to say about understanding the natural world, the opposite was not true. The philosopher was not only in a better position to detect passages that needed to be understood in a non-literal way, but was also able to offer advice about how they should be understood. This was particularly pertinent in the case of geocentric passages in Scripture, but as we have seen, Newton's exegetical principles covered a much wider range of naturalistic references than those. He was wary of understanding references to natural events in prophecy as physically real and was positively hostile to physico-theological explanations of the genesis of the cosmos, especially when they were supposed to be derived from the Bible. It was not that such accounts should ignore the Bible, but that natural knowledge, and therefore the true history of the creation and its aftermath, could not be read off from it. Newton told Burnet that physico-theological accounts could only be hypothetical or conjectural, though in fact he thought that they were no better than the figments of Cartesianism. While this exchange is indicative of the changing relationship between theology and philosophy during this period, it also points to Newton's and other philosophers' dual identities as interpreters of nature and Scripture. As a natural philosopher, Newton was a priest of nature not least because his work had direct implications for scriptural exegesis, and, in due course, it might be a key resource for telling the true story of the genesis of the universe.[42]

The *Principia* was not merely an aid to scriptural exegesis, but was a vital tool for discovering the nature of God's creation. According to Newton, the task of determining the true system of the world was exceptionally difficult, constrained both by the tremendous complexity of the world and by the limitations of human beings. In a draft of "De Motu," he pointed out that the continuously operating mutual gravitational effects of the vast number of heavenly bodies meant that the precise paths of planets could only be

known "quam proxime" (i.e., approximately) since they never exactly repeated their paths from one orbit to the next. This claim occurred in a passage now known as the "Copernican scholium," so called because Newton
claimed that although the centre of gravity of the solar system was continuously changing, it had to be very near to where the sun was. Considering
the causes of all these motions simultaneously, he pointed out, and defining
them by exact calculation, exceeded the power of the combined human
intellect. If astronomers took only a handful of observations to determine
the orbit of a planet they would be prone to making errors arising from the
contingent gravitational forces exerted on the planet at those moments.
However, Newton concluded, the planet's true orbit could be approximated
as the mean of many "mutually moderating" measurements. In the published *Principia* he repeated this claim, adding that humans possessed the
ability to make inferences about the real world beyond from the "apparent
motions" of objects. The *Principia*, he wrote, was designed to do exactly this,
serving as the only reliable guide for inferring true motions from their
causes, effects, and apparent differences, while using their motions to determine their causes and effects.[43]

7. Logic and Image

Newton had laid down his prophetic "rules of interpretation" some time
before he wrote down similar methodological prescriptions in the *Principia
Mathematica*. In the tenth of these rules he stipulated that the exegete should
"<have little or no> regard to arguments drawn from events of things <becaus
there> can <scarce> be any certainty in historicall interpretations unless the
construction be first determined." This, as we have seen, was a standard
claim in the apocalyptic literature and much of Newton's work on prophecy
was conducted solely on the images and textual material found in Scripture.
However, Rule 14 explicitly urged that the most notable events in history
were to be aligned with the most significant parts of prophecy, and Newton's deep knowledge of the events of the early church would form a key
element of his analysis. Indeed, he came to believe that the most significant
events in the history of religion had not concerned the Protestant Reformation but in fact had taken place in the fourth and fifth centuries after Christ.
This point of view inevitably had repercussions for his interpretive schema,
and while he relied heavily on the Medean arrangement, his radically

heterodox church history framed his highly original account of how the images of prophecy cohered.[44]

Like Mede and More, Newton understood there to be three major periods described by Revelation. The first partition occurred at the start of the seventh seal, which was followed, after the half hour's silence, by the sounding of the first trumpet. The second partition occurred at the start of the seventh trumpet and vial, which ushered in the millennium. In the earliest draft of his "proof" of various synchronisms Newton listed as his first "proposition" the fact that both the seven seals and the seven trumpets in the seventh seal all concerned "distributions of time" that succeeded one another without overlapping. In the second proposition, he noted that the vials of wrath poured out on the wicked in chapters 15 and 16 of Revelation synchronised with the corresponding trumpets described in chapters 8–11—an account that broke with all serious interpreters with the exception of Napier. To demonstrate this, Newton wrote out the verses of the "correspondent" vials and trumpets side by side so as to show their coherence or "congruity." As he put it, "all the descriptions of one & the same thing must be conjoyned that they interpret one another & supply one another's defects & joyntly make one complete description wch cannot be misapplied to history." At one level, this approach was a special application of a more general interpretive procedure since, like other Protestants, Newton considered his Bible to be a sort of divine hypertext in which various texts in different parts of Scripture were related to, or "interpreted" one another. Learning which passages from the New Testament shed light on one another or on sections of the Old Testament was a key part in the education of a Christian. On these grounds, Newton argued that there was "no better way of interpreting scripture then by comparing the parts of it & reconciling all the synchronall & all the analogous parts of prophesy wch can be reconciled without force." These relationships formed a complex pattern, and the basis of his approach was the relationship between Daniel and Revelation. The analogy between these sacred texts he intoned, was the foundation of all prophetic interpretation, and they were not to be understood as inconsistent with one another.[45]

In Newton's scheme, various passages and visions in Scripture commented on and "explained" one another. The trumpets and vials, for example, "both collateral & both together make up one complete prophecy, ye one supplying what is sometimes missing in the other." Indeed, it was an essential element of his hermeneutical approach that the mutual descriptions did not merely repeat what was in the other, and one "rule" adduced in the text pronounced on the need to avoid where possible "those interpretations which make scriptures tautologize."[46] The idea that passages indulged in mutual explanation underlay Newton's generalisation of synchronisms, which went far beyond what Mede had attempted. For example, he claimed that he could shed light on 666, the number of the beast, by synchronising the vision of the seven thunders (Rev. 10:3-4) with those of the vials and trumpets. In Proposition 3 of the early draft of the proof, Newton suggested that the vision of thunders was "most probably" to be synchronised with those of the trumpets and vials but in "Position 2" of a later version he positively asserted that they *did in fact* cover the same periods. Addressing the perplexing issue as to why the vision of the thunders had not been written down in more detail, he argued that it "was introduced to make up a Ternary number with ye Trumpets and Vials that by ye six intervals of each wch ye Beast's reign takes up they might represent ye same mystery with ye number of ye Beast 666 & explicate ye mystery of y^t number by representing it." He also used as supporting evidence the conventional rendering of 666 as LATEINOC, in this case to depict the Antichristian Trinitarian Western Empire that came into being after the death of Constantine.[47]

8. The Great Apostasy

The synchronising of the vials and trumpets formed a dramatic break with Mede's work, and Newton invoked a vast array of new arguments to make his novel system coherent and persuasive. Even so, many of his synchronisms were standard. Propositions 5–7 of the early draft of the proof identified the false prophet with the two-horned beast, the Whore of Babylon (though it took some time for the beast to be transformed into the Whore), and the Man of Sin. In the text from the later 1680s, Newton supported the identity of the false prophet and the Whore by pointing out that both had conducted themselves like harlots, and there was "no reason to suppose more Apocalyptic Whores then one." Similarly, as we have seen, the seven-headed/ ten-horned dragon in Revelation 12:3 was obviously the same as both the ten-horned beast in Revelation 17:3 and the ten-horned fourth beast described in Daniel 7. "Position 3" asserted first, that the woman in travail (Rev. 12:1-2) was the Church of Christ while her anti-type, the dragon, was "the great Heathen Kingdome," and second, that both of these entities were active during the entire duration of the seven seals. In "Position 4" Newton stated that the beast that was wounded and then healed in Revelation 13:3 was the "great Heathenizing Kingdome derived out of the Dragon" and on this basis, he asserted that much of Revelation concerned how, by a process of metamorphosis, the core business of the dragon was subsequently carried out in the form of the beast. The latter rose in the sixth seal, first from the sea, when he gained his temporal power, and then out of Hades or the bottomless pit, when he dragged up with him "a fals infernal religion."[48]

According to Newton, the "setting up" of the religion of the ten-horned beast by his two-horned colleague (Rev. 13:12-15) took up the prophetic break of half an hour from the opening of the seventh seal to the sounding of the first trumpet. In "Position 8," he claimed that the living image of the ten-horned beast that was erected by the two-horned beast at the start of this interval (Rev. 13:14-15) was an "Ecclesiasticall Assembly of men." The holy rites performed in this interval clearly showed that it referred to matters of religion, and the saints offered prayers to God in respect of the "evil times coming on." Those who had so far attained genuine saintliness, described figuratively as virgins undefiled by women (Rev. 14:4), were sealed during the same break, while others anti-typically received the mark of the beast. The "proof" that the prophecy referred to Christianity derived from the fact that the wickedness of the rule of the beast was so severe: "ye worst things require a corruption of ye best to generate them. Sins are ye greatest where they are against ye greatest light, & if Hypocrisy or a corruption of ye meaning of ye Law be added to ye Sin, it is yet a further aggravation." A Christian, Newton pointed out, was "capable of being wors then any other sort of man" and so only the complete perversion of Christianity could match the level of depravity described by the Great Apostasy.[49]

As it was for Mede and More, the Great Apostasy was central to Newton's interpretation. The period from the start of the seventh seal to the beginning of the seventh trumpet and vial, he wrote, was "but one and the same continued Apostacy wch arrives to a greater height at ye beginning of ye fifth Trumpet, & at ye greatest height at ye death of the Witnesses & after their resurrection declines gradually until first ye great city Babylon be ruined." So significant was it that the entire Apocalypse following the fourth chapter had been composed to describe and explain it. There were numerous references in the Bible to this abomination and

Newton listed the central features of the universal church that epitomised the apostasy, proving from Scripture that its members were idolaters, sorcerers, persecutors, and libertines. Like all interpreters working in the Medean tradition, Newton had no doubt that the Roman Catholic Church fitted the description perfectly and was dismayed that any Protestant would concoct arguments against it. In one assault from the late 1680s on the "extravagant & petulant fansy" of Grotius (whom he did not name), he concluded that no one could seriously or rationally deny that the ten-horned beast was the same as Daniel's fourth beast (7:23-24), which also had ten horns and which was conventionally understood to refer to Rome. Nor could any reasonable person doubt that Roman Catholicism was denoted by the Whore or two-horned beast, which was that little horn that Daniel saw rise up and reign a time, times, and half a time (Dan. 7:8, 24-25; 8:9-14).[50]

Aside from synchronising the trumpets and the vials, Newton's major innovation was to stretch out the apostatic period beyond the 1,260 prophetic days accepted by Mede and many of his followers. As a result, the core images relating to the prophetic forty-two months were synchronised only with the fifth and sixth vials and trumpets, with the key embryonic developments of that apostasy taking place in the fourth century. As we have seen, both Mede and More had added 1,260 years to events at the end of the fourth century, thus producing a key date that for Mede lay very near in his future, and, in More's case, was in the very recent past (this was the end point of the rising of the witnesses, though the millennium lay in the future). For Newton there was no major prophetic event associated with the Reformation, the advent of the Church of England, or indeed the early modern period as a whole. Rather, his interest was focussed almost entirely on the terrible events that took place more than a millennium earlier. The fourth century, which had witnessed the triumph of popery, homoousianism, and monasticism, had been diabolical, but the major intensification or maturation of the Great Apostasy had occurred at the start of the fifth trumpet. The forty-two months of the beast's making war, the reign of the Whore, the stay of the woman in the wilderness, the treading underfoot of the holy city by the Gentiles, and the prophesying of the two witnesses, all began at this juncture, that is, at the onset of the first of the three "woe" trumpets, and the period ended at the close of the sixth trumpet with the murder of the witnesses. Ushering in both the beginning of the papal kingdom and the growth of Islam, the first two woe trumpets depicted the triumph of the ecclesiastical empire of the beast over the temporal sphere.[51]

9. The Making of an Apocalyptic Whore

The rich images in Revelation 12 of the pregnant woman and the male child to which she subsequently gave birth, both being persecuted by the great ten-horned and seven-headed red dragon, were central to Newton's scheme, as they were to all interpreters in the tradition. Revelation told how immediately after his birth the child was swept up to heaven, while the woman fled to the wilderness where she remained for 1,260 days. At the same time there was a "very earnest conflict" in heaven between Michael and the dragon, that is, Satan (Rev. 12:7-9). Like Mede, Newton placed all these visions in the fifth and sixth seals, just before the momentous events ushered in by the opening of the seventh. The defeated dragon was exiled to Earth and spewed out waters after the escaping woman so that she could be consumed by the flood (Rev. 12:15-16). However, she was given two wings of a great eagle to escape the oncoming torrent, while the earth swallowed up the waters. The enraged dragon thereupon vowed to make war with the remnant of her seed. For most interpreters these images referred to the providential resistance of the true Church against a succession of heresies and perversions that started with the gnostic Simon Magus, moved on via the variant forms of Arianism, and ended with the rise and fall of popery. Newton's anti-Trinitarian beliefs obviously prevented him from following this account, though by and large he obeyed Mede in his understanding of the order and timing of the visions.[52]

Referring to his definitions, Newton asserted that the waters of the sea were the people who persecuted the members of the true Church, while anti-typically, the earth that helped the woman by swallowing up the flood depicted the godly people of bordering nations. The logic of his exposition, which broke with Mede's equation of the Great Apostasy with the forty-two months, demanded that the flight of the woman be stretched out from the start of the first trumpet to the end of the fourth, right before the start of the 1,260 days. Similarly, the evolution of the various forms adopted by the dragon took some time. Newton argued that the goal of the two-horned beast was to "rise up slowly by policy" until he morphed into the Whore that sat astride the ten-horned beast. The Whore took advantage of the latter's "declining condition" and rode on him when one of his seven heads was wounded to death (Rev. 13:3-4). At the end of the fourth trumpet this fatal wound was somehow healed, and the world gawped in wonder at the

Whore. Once the woman was secure in the desert, the dragon/Whore did battle with the seed of the woman's "remnant" (Rev. 12:16-17), so called because they were "those true Christians wch remained so few & so much dispersed as not to have ye face of a church." This persecution was also described by the image of the holy city being trodden underfoot by the Gentiles (Rev. 11:2), a synchronism that was drawn from Mede and which formed Proposition 16 in Newton's scheme.[53]

A key problem for exegetes was provided by the comment in Revelation 17:3 to the effect that the wilderness to which the woman had fled was also inhabited by the Whore of Babylon. One of Newton's original "definitions" had affirmed that a wilderness was land wasted by a beast for temporal or spiritual matters, and, indeed, he believed that the Whore was responsible for creating the desert in the first place. Over time, he altered his views and in his late 1680s tract he produced a much more radical account of the internal chronological order of these images. In this later work, he argued that the kingdom of the red dragon was split into two, namely the domains of the dragon (i.e., the earth) and the ten-horned beast (i.e., the sea). There was a correlative division of the true Church. The remnant of the woman's seed was left in the kingdom of the dragon and was persecuted by the two-horned beast or false prophet, which first rose in that kingdom. Newton proceeded to distinguish the two-horned beast from the Whore, now identified as the false church of the kingdom of the ten-horned beast (since the wilderness of Revelation 17:3 was in the territory of the beast on whom the Whore sits). The latter had risen in the sea and continued to persecute the true saints who were left in that kingdom. In these two separate territories there were thus two groups of saints, which Newton identified with the two witnesses.[54]

Newton also made the dramatic claim that the flight of the woman from the dragon's lands into the wilderness was not, as virtually all other interpreters had claimed, a description of the true Church for the duration of the Great Apostasy but was in fact a figurative depiction of the gradual degeneration of the woman into the Whore. He adduced nine separate arguments to back this claim, including the physical proximity of the woman and the Whore; the fact that the woman was fed and nourished in the desert, "y^t is, grows rich & wealthy" (since food prophetically signified riches); the fact that John saw only one woman in the wilderness (because apocalyptic whores should not be multiplied unnecessarily); and the claim that flight referred prophetically to the changing of religion, and thus to becoming spiritually barren. Not all of those who had once constituted the true Church had prostituted themselves, but the majority, those who were merely "external professors" of Christianity, had done so. How could such a wonderful woman have become a whore? John himself had been flabbergasted, "wondering with great admiration" (Rev. 17:6) at her fall from grace although he had expressed no such shock at her gaudy apparel ("Such sights are common enough in yᵉ world," Newton lamented) or even at the monstrous seven-headed and ten-horned beast. If her degeneration seemed so extraordinary to the prophet, Newton concluded, then "there is ˂more˃ reason we should think it true because wonderfull, then too wonderfull to be true." Newton's treatment of the two prophetic women was highly innovative, and his identification of the two witnesses with the remnant populations in the territories of the sea and the earth remained a key part of his prophetic account in the early eighteenth century.[55]

10. A Good Serious Man

The understanding of prophecy remained a topic of great significance in Restoration England. While many orthodox members of the Church of England saw it as an increasingly precarious exercise, the godly still saw it as the most important resource for understanding their own condition. As Mede's letters show, it had always been a minority scholarly sport, and if an orthodox Church of England divine wanted to publish on the subject—as More discovered—it could be a precarious exercise. Indeed, if it had not been so obviously heterodox, it would have been easy for Newton to publish his work as a layman with a calling to decipher the meaning of difficult prophetic passages. The decipherment of prophetic images was a "duty of the greatest moment," a holy puzzle that he had an obligation to solve, but he published nothing. He approached it as he did everything else, with great confidence in his rational powers to solve various problems, while remaining attentive to the pitfalls that arose from relying on private fancy or untested (or false) tradition. Although there is no evidence that he revealed his most controversial findings in this area to anyone else in the seventeenth century, in the rest of this chapter I show how he engaged in vigorous discussions over these issues with Henry More, which spilled into the printed sphere.

At the height of the Popish Plot, while Newton was in Lincolnshire putting his affairs in order after the death of his mother, More wrote *Apocalypsis*

Plate I. Map of Grantham and environs. Photograph by the author.

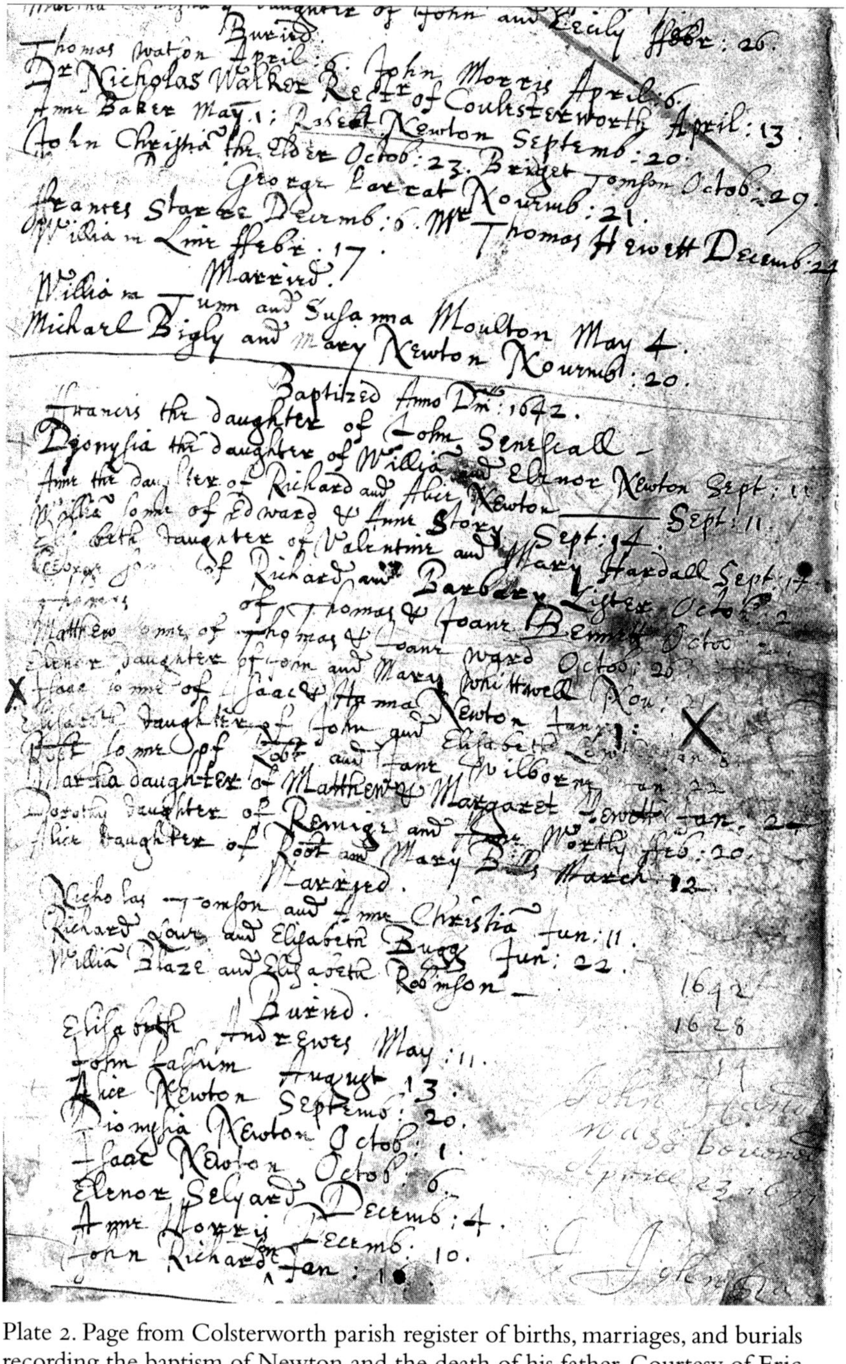

Plate 2. Page from Colsterworth parish register of births, marriages, and burials recording the baptism of Newton and the death of his father. Courtesy of Eric Lomax, Colsterworth Church.

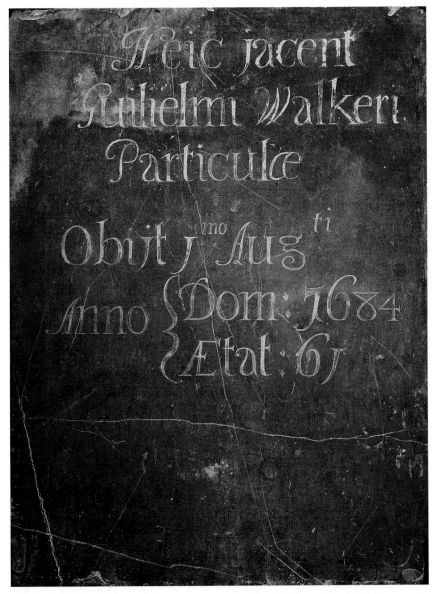

Plate 3. Recently rediscovered gravestone of William Walker, friend of Newton and master of the Grantham Free School, containing an amusing reference to his book on English particles allegedly suggested by Newton. Courtesy of Eric Lomax, Colsterworth Church.

12 Of ye sunn Stars & Plannets & Comets

Whither ☉ move ye vortex about (as Des-Cartes will)
by his beames. pag 54 Princip Philos: partis 3^{ae}
Whither ye vortex can carry a Comet towars y^e
poles & Whence tis y^t y^e ☉ is turned about upon his axis
Whither Cartes his reflexion will will unriddle ye mistery
of a Comets bird.
feb: 1 chap: vers 2 By god made ye worlds by his son 785
αιῶνας. The ☉s spots are coloured some-
times like ye rainebow.
October 16 [618 in Scorpio appeared a comet ye tayle
being extend twixt Spica virginis & Arcturus toward y^e
North pole it passed into libra moveing from ye ye Eclip
tick by^e Tropick of cancer from east to west or Nor-
tharly
On Sathurday, December 10th, 1664. By a slightly
observation I found ye distance of a
Comet from ye center of ye Moone to be 9^d, 18, min.
Its altitude 3^d, 40^m; or 4^d.
The Moons altitude 8^d, 40^m.
The longitude of ye Moone.
On Satturday at 30^{min}: past 4 of ye clock in
ye morning December 17th 1664 A Comet appeard.
Whose distance from Sirius was 30^d, 0^d.
from procion 38^d, 45^d. there was little or noe
difference twixt ye time of its & Sirius his setting
its setting about 2 after him & ye its Right ascention was about 126^d, 32.
& its declinacon Southward 31^d. The Length
of its tayle was about 34^d or 35^d & pointed
toward procion or almost to y^e North
pole, cutting y^e horizon at an angle of about 35?
or 40 & y^e Ecliptick at 47^d.
vide pag 54

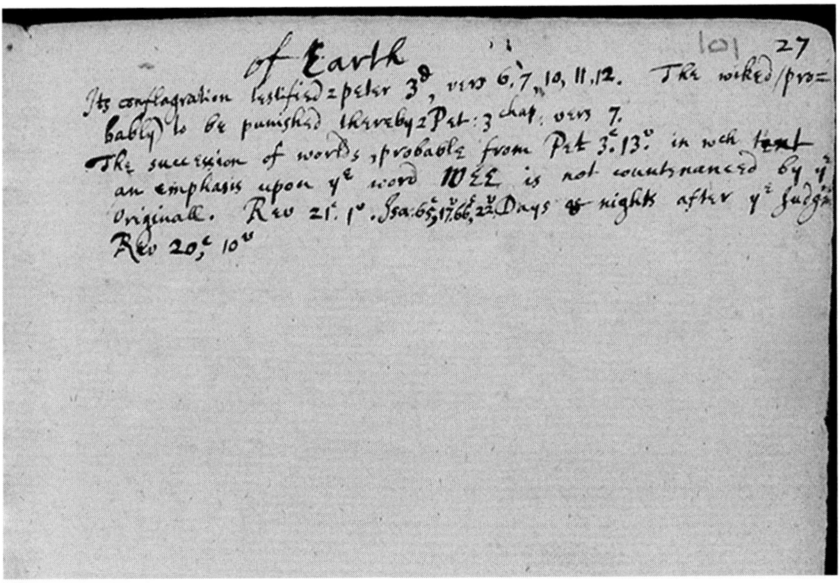

Of Earth

Its conflagration testified 2 peter 3^d, vers 6,7,10,11,12. The wicked prob=
ably to be punished thereby 2 Pet: 3 chap, vers 7.
The succession of worlds probable from Pet 3.13. in wch text
an emphasis upon y^e word WEE is not countenanced by y^e
Originall. Rev 21. 1. Isa:65,17,66. 2 Days & nights after y^e Judga
Rev 20. 10

Plate 5. From the "Philosophical Questions" notebook, showing Newton's early—if guarded—belief in the succession of worlds and the punishment of the wicked in the great conflagration. Courtesy of Cambridge University Library.

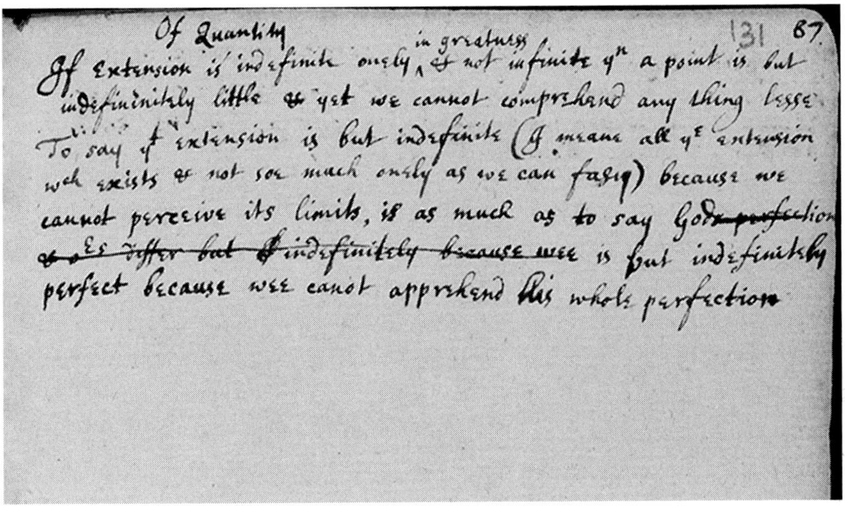

Of Quantity

Of Extension is indefinite onely, & not infinite y^n a point is but
indefinitely little & yet we cannot comprehend any thing lesse
To say y^e extension is but indefinite (I meane all ye extension
wch exists or not soe much onely as we can fasip) because we
cannot perceive its limits, is as much as to say God perfection
or us differ but of indefinitely because wee is but indefinitely
perfect because wee canot apprehend his whole perfection

Plate 6. From the "Philosophical Questions" notebook, showing Newton's early critique of Descartes's notion of "indefiniteness." Courtesy of Cambridge University Library.

The word בָּרָא wᶜʰ Gen i.i. is interpreted to creat
something out of nothing is usd Gen gᵉ 1ˢᵗ v. 21 where
tis saide God creatd greate Whales but yᵉ matter out
of wᶜʰ they were did exist before neither is
it mēant of creating yᵉ soule or forme of yᵉ whale, for yᵗ is
not yᵉ whale alone, as there may be but one kind of irratio=
nall soule wᶜʰ joyned wᵗʰ severall kinds of bodys make
severall kinds of beasts, for setting aside yᵉ different shape
of their body beasts differ from one another but in some
qualitys wᶜʰ are called instincts of nature. now as
in men whose soules are of one kind some love hate
feare &c one thing some another & few men are of
yᵉ same temper wᶜʰ diversity arises from theire body
(for all their soules are alike) so why may not yᵉ se=
verall tempers or instincts of divers kinds of beasts
arise from yᵉ different tempers & modes of theire bodys
they differing one from another more yⁿ one mans body
from anothers. Now yⁿ can yᵗ soule of yᵉ whale
be called yᵉ whales since before it be joyned wᵗʰ yᵉ
whale tis as much yᵉ soule of a horse & this creating
yⁿ of whales & severall other creatures must be not
but modifying matter into yᵉ body of a whale & infus
an irrationall soule into it. Eccles: 33 vis 10 Adam
was created of yᵉ earth.
Whither Moses his saying Gen yᵉ 1 st + yᵉ evening & yᵉ mor
ning were yᵉ first day &c do prove yᵗ God created time.
Coll 1. 16) or Heb 1 ch 2 v Τοὺς αἰῶνας ἐποίησεν expou
ded, he made yᵉ worlds. prove yᵗ God created time

Plate 7. This page from the "Philosophical Questions" notebook, indicating
Newton's interpretation of the word "creation" in Genesis ch. 1., shows his belief
in the existence of one irrational soul "infused" into the bodies of animals, who
are distinct from one another only in terms of the shapes of their bodies and their
natural instincts. He also argued that human souls were alike, and that they
differed chiefly in terms of the constitution of their bodies. Courtesy of
Cambridge University Library.

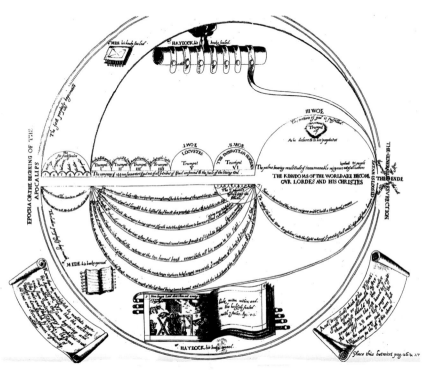

Plate 8. The circular schematic for Mede's system runs chronologically from left to right and comprehends the seven seals. The top half represents the prophecy of the sealed book and the bottom half that of the opened book. Photograph by the author.

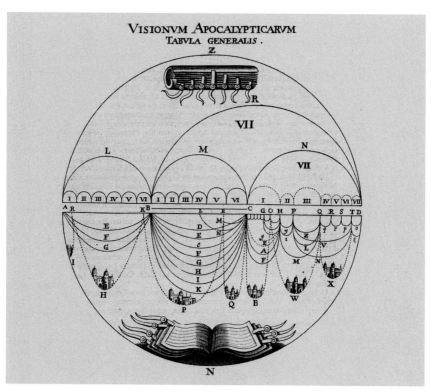

Plate 9. More's "General Table" has a mathematical appearance to it and is indebted to Mede's scheme. The three semicircles L, M, and N, represent the "Antemedial," "Medial," and "Postmedial" visions respectively. R covers the seventh trumpet, while L encompasses the first six seals, M the first six trumpets, and N the seven thunders. The prophecies of the seven churches are represented by the etchings in I to X. Courtesy of the Huntington Library, San Marino, California.

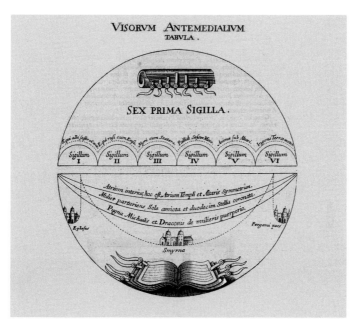

Plate 10. The first six seals, synchronal with the battle between Michael and the Dragon and the woman in travail, and a balance or "symmetry" between the inner and outer courts. Courtesy of the Huntington Library, San Marino, California.

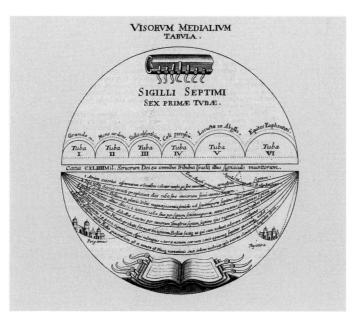

Plate 11. The first six trumpets, coextensive with the 1,260 days of the treading down of the outer court by the Gentiles and the prophesying of the two witnesses; the woman's flight in the wilderness; the instauration of the ten-horned beast; the setting up by the two-horned beast and false prophet of the image of the ten-horned beast; the sealing up of the 144,000 virgins; and the bewitchment of the world by the great Whore of Babylon. Courtesy of the Huntington Library, San Marino, California.

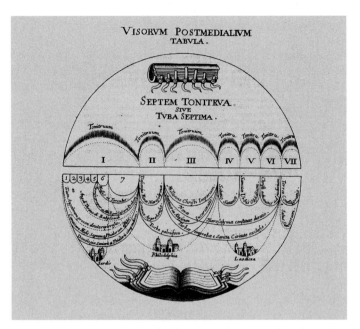

Plate 12. The seventh trumpet is divided amongst the seven thunders. The seven vials are all in the first thunder, after which each thunder contains the descent of New Jerusalem; the millennial reign of Christ; the unbinding of Satan; the blockade of the Holy City; Christ's coming to judgement; the great conflagration. Courtesy of the Huntington Library, San Marino, California.

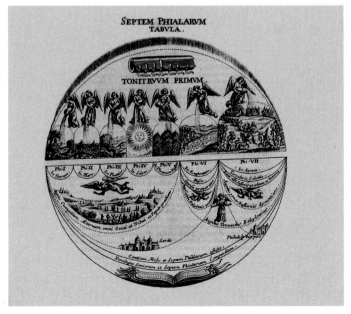

Plate 13. Exploded view of the vials, which are all in the first thunder. Courtesy of the Huntington Library, San Marino, California.

als) I say, if we look closer into them these pretended Synchronizing Congruities will signify no more than thus, and so quite vanish.

For in the first Congruity to say nothing how that [upon the Earth] may have no particular signification Ch. 16. 2. but signify so as [upon the Earth] in the foregoing verse; the Hail cast upon the Earth under the first Trumpet is plainly another thing from the noisome and grievous fore that fell upon men at this rankerous Ulcer most certainly signify quite different things as the Symbols are hugely different. And I must confess I make no question in the world, but that Symbol of an *envious malicious exulcerated mind*, which is the plague of Intoxication or Dementation to them on whom it falls and spoils all their counsels, they being given up to be actuated by evil Angels and the fury of the Devil. This I conceive is a sad plague indeed, and lively set out by the Symbol of a *vexatious Ulcer*. But what an Hail-storm signifies in the Prophetick Style is so well known that I need say nothing of it: Wherefore there is not onely no Congruity betwixt the *first Trumpet* and the *first Vial* to prove they must begin together, but the *Vial* and the things signified by them being so quite different, it is a strong barr against any such presumption.

The second Congruity indeed is more tolerable or passable, if all the rest came to so near an agreement, but in that there is nothing peculiar under the *Second Vial* that answers to the *burning Mountain* cast into the Sea under the *Second Trumpet*, the correspondence betwixt this *Vial* and this *Trumpet* is visibly lame and defectuous.

The

† no. They are ye same See 2 Chron.
6. 28, 29. & Joel,
18, 19, 20.

The third also is a Congruity far more passable than the first, but yet besides the defectuousness in the *third Vial* that has nothing to answer to the falling Lamp or Comet *Lampadias* under the *third Trumpet*; what the Fountains and Rivers suffer under the *third Trumpet*, is a misery to men and bitterness to them, what they suffer under the *third Vial* is a refreshment to men who praise and justify God upon the account.

The fourth Congruity is wonderfully wretched and small. The Sun indeed is smitten under the *fourth Trumpet*, as well as the *fourth Vial* said to be poured upon him, but not the Sun alone under the *fourth Trumpet*, but the Moon also and the Stars; but the Sun alone is mentioned in the *fourth Vial*. Besides, the Sun, Moon and Stars lose their light and the Sun consequently his heat under the fourth Trumpet; but the light and heat of the Sun is so invigorated under the *fourth Vial*, that he scorches men to intolerably that they blaspheme again.

And the fifth Congruity is yet slighter. The *fifth Vial* is poured out upon the Seat of the Beast where by his Kingdome becomes full of darkness. Upon the founding of the *fifth Trumpet*, the Angel of the bottomless Pit, opens the pit and a smoke comes out of it that darkens the Sun and Skie. In eleven large verses wherein the *Vision* of the *fifth Trumpet* is described, there is no more that Symbolizes with the *fifth Vial* than this, that is worth the speaking of. For the gnawing their tongues for pain under the *fifth Vial*, is from their impatiency of that dark inglorious condition they were cast into, not from the sting of any Scorpions. And for the *darkness* arising from the Vial poured on the Seat of the Beast, and that smoak and *darkness* out of the bottomless pit; as the

N n   Seat

Plate 14. In synchronizing the first trumpet and the ulcer in the first vial, Newton attacks More's view that the hailstorm in the first trumpet and the ulcer in the first vial signify different things and events. Newton criticises More's argument that the fourth trumpet and vial cannot be synchronous on the grounds that only the sun is the object of wrath in the fourth vial. The passage shows Newton directly translating the visions into their political referents, thus enabling him to link it to historical events. Courtesy of the Bancroft Library.

Seat of the *Beast* and *bottomless Pit* have no Analogy one to another, so it is incredible that the darknesses themselves should not be quite different things. So small grounds or rather none at all is there for this fifth Congruity.

And as little for the sixth. For there is no correspondency betwixt the *sixth Vial* and the *sixth Trumpet*, but that the great River *Euphrates* is mentioned in them both. For the description of the sixth Vial is comprised within one verse of Ch.16. *viz.* ver.12. But there is a large description of the sixth Trumpet Ch.9. from v.13. to v.20. as there is also of the fifth Trumpet.

II. Which consideration of the descriptions of the *six-first Trumpets*, their being either as large or much larger than the descriptions of the *first six Vials*, is a second argument against the placing of the beginning of the *Vials* with the beginning of the *Trumpets*, as of a partial Vision whose beginning is to be fixt at the *first Joynt* of the foregoing Prophecies of larger extent, to the end that part of the larger extended Prophecies might be more enlarged upon and more copiously described, as it fares with the Vision of the *Ram* and *He-Goat* in *Daniel*. Which partial Vision is annexed to those two more large Visions for a fuller description of the affairs of the *Greek Monarchy*. And therefore this Vision of the *seven* Vials the affixing the beginning of them to the beginning of the *first Trumpet* not serving its due end, it is a sign it is misplaced, and that the beginning thereof is to be placed in the *second Joynt* of those two larger Prophecies [the one comprised in the eleventh Chapter and the other in the three following] and not in the *first Joynt*. These therefore are my two first Arguments against the placing of the *first Vial* with the *first Trumpet*. The

want of a continued *Congruity* betwixt the *Trumpets* and *Vials* all along. And their uselessness for the fuller explaining the affairs of that part of the more universal Visions that they are supposed to Synchronize with. But that there is a part in those more universal Prophecies [Ch.11.] and [Ch.12.and 13.and 14.] that the *Partial* Vision of the Vials will properly serve more copiously to illustrate, I shall note hereafter. I am now onely intent upon the proving that the *Vials* and *Trumpets* do not commence together.

III. Of which I conceive this may be a third Argument, If we do but remember and take notice of the *second* notable *Joynt* in those two more universal Prophecies :(comprised , the one in the eleventh Chapter and the other in the three following] and how in the former that *second* notable *Joynt* is in the con-termination of the sixth Trumpets ending and the beginning of the *Seventh*, where the *Rising* of the *Witnesses* is, and those *Acclamations* in Heaven and *Doxology* of the Elders; And the same *Joynt* in the latter Prophecy at that joyfull *Annunciation* of the Angel, *Babylon is fain is fain* (which *Fall*, as I said above, must needs be the *Rising of the Witnesses*:) The making thus the *six-first* Vials to Synchronize with the *six-first* Trumpets, will leave the *Seventh* Vial alone to possess the whole space of time and affairs from the abovesaid *second Joynt* to the end of those two Visions or Prophecies, whenas in Mr. *Medes* own account, the *seventh* Vial Synchronizes with the Vision of the *Wine-press*; so that in the fourteenth Chapter from verf.9. to verf.17. there is a Chasma of time and affairs which the seventh Vial taketh not in, and so in like manner in the eleventh Chapter, from the same *Joynt* of the Prophecy, to the *seventh* Vial signified

fied

Plate 15. Newton's remark in his copy of More's 1681 book on Daniel repeats the claim that the visions of the vials and trumpets are so different that they cannot describe the same events. Their very variety, Newton argues, is what allows them to describe different aspects of the same historical episodes. Courtesy of the Bancroft Library.

Trumpet, which is but the firſt *Ægyptian* plague of the Myſtical *Ægypt* the *Roman* Empire.

VII. Wherefore ſeventhly, The *ſeven laſt plagues* of the *Vials* ſuppoſing a *Sett* or *Number* of plagues antecedent, and there being no other *Sett* or *Number* of plagues but thoſe of the *ſix Trumpets*, it is manifeſt that that *Sett* or *Number* of plagues of the ſix Trumpets are the antecedent plagues to the ſeven laſt plagues of the Vials, and that theſe ſeven plagues of the Vials follow them, and therefore do not commence with the firſt Trumpet.

VIII. And now in the eighth place, Though all the ſix firſt Trumpets are in the general plagues upon the *Roman* Empire, yet the Wo-Trumpets more eſpecially for their Pagano-Chriſtian Idolatry and perſecution as is expreſly declared *Apoc.* 9. 20. And therefore in reſpect of the fifth and ſixth Trumpets eſpecially, though of all ſix in general, (they being plagues upon *Ægypt* as I noted above) would I have the plagues of the ſeven Vials called the ſeven laſt plagues; and indeed where can the ſeven *laſt plagues* be more properly placed than in the *laſt Wo-Trumpet*, or in the ſeventh or laſt Trumpet, it being a continuation of plagues upon that party of men that did not repent them of the works of their hands, of their worſhipping of *Dæmons* and Idols of Gold and Silver, and of murdering the ſervants of God upon a falſe pretence of their Hereſy, notwithstanding they were forewarned by the plagues of the two firſt *Wo-Trumpets*, the *Locuſts* and *Euphratean* Horſemen. But if the firſt of the ſeven laſt plagues be to be placed in the ſeventh Trumpet, it cannot commence with the firſt.

IX. Ninthly

IX. Ninthly and laſtly, Thoſe plagues that follow a victory over the Beaſt and over his Image and over his Mark and over the number of his name, which certainly ſignifies the two-horned Beaſt, cannot commence with the firſt Trumpet, becauſe this two-horned Beaſt could neither be fought with nor be overcome, before the firſt Trumpet, he having no exiſtence before that Trumpet. But the ſeven laſt plagues of the Vials follow the aboveſaid victory as appears from *Apoc.* 15. and 16. where thoſe that had got the victory over the Beaſt are ſaid to ſtand on the Sea of glaſs, having the Harps of God in their hands, and to ſing the Song of *Moſes* the ſervant of God and of the Lamb, which is a plain *Ænixax*, a *Song of Triumph*, anſwering to that of the Iſraelites upon the overthrow of *Pharaoh* in the red Sea. So that it is a *Triumphal* ſong upon an *actual* victory. This is moſt punctuall and plain, in Chap. 15. and it is ſaid immediately after this ſong, *That the Temple of the Tabernacle of the Teſtimony in Heaven was opened, That the ſeven Angels having the ſeven Plagues came out of it, and that unto them were given ſeven Golden Vials full of the Wrath of God,* and Chap. 16. 1. *they are there commanded to pour them out.* There is no wriggling out of this plain evidence, that the plagues of the ſeven Vials all of them follow the victory over the Beaſt. And therefore it is impoſſible they ſhould commence with the firſt Trumpet.

But it may be you will ſay, what is all this to the purpoſe as to Mr. *Mede,* who does not make the Vials to commence with the *firſt* Trumpet, but rather with the *ſixth?* I grant he does ſo, and yet what I have wrote is much to the purpoſe. Becauſe if once
a man

Plate 16. Newton's remarks on this page make it clear that he assumes from Revelation 15:2 that those of the 144,000 righteous virgins who had not received the mark of the beast (described in Rev. 13 and 14), and who were now singing the triumphant song of Moses, had achieved victory over the beast, presumably the ten-horned version. The comments reveal Newton's belief that the seeds of the Great Apostasy were planted in the middle of the fourth century. Courtesy of the Bancroft Library.

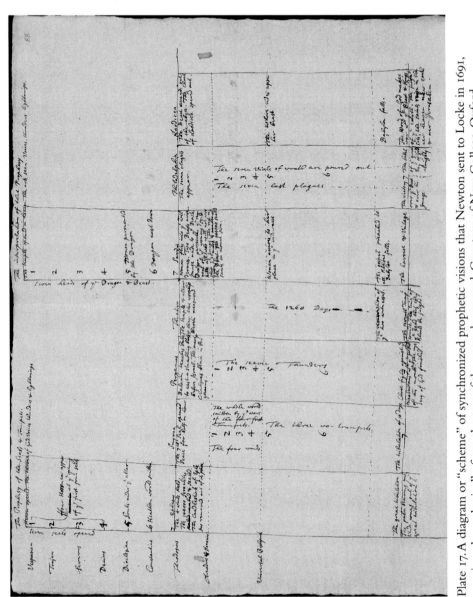

Plate 17. A diagram or "scheme" of synchronized prophetic visions that Newton sent to Locke in 1691, running chronologically from the top of the page downward. Courtesy of New College, Oxford.

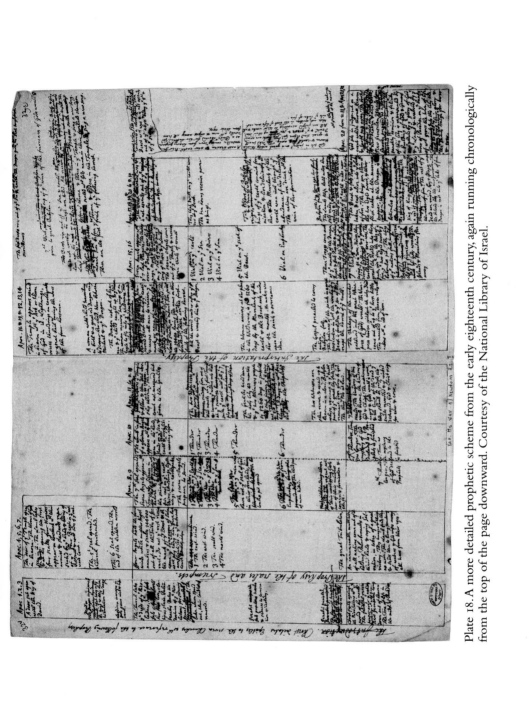

Plate 18. A more detailed prophetic scheme from the early eighteenth century, again running chronologically from the top of the page downward. Courtesy of the National Library of Israel.

	Ultra Euphr.	Cis Euphra-		-sem.
* quàm in Hiſtoria Sara- cen. Elmachini *Siaizarum* dici puto, quomodo apud Benjami- nem Tudelen- ſem *Cæſarea* Palæſtinæ שיריש P.37.	BAGDADI. Togrulbecus Olbarſalanus	*CÆSAREÆ Cappadociæ & ICONII, &c. in Aſia minore.	ALEPI.	DAMASCI.
	Ghelaluddaulas *ann.* 1071. Barkyarucus Muhammedus Mahmudus, *cæ- pit. ann.* 1117. &c.	Sedijduddaulas *cognomine* Cutlumuſus Solimannus Taniſmanius Maſutus Caliſaſtlanus &c.	Sjarfuddulas Roduwanus Tagjuddau- las *fil.* Bulgarus, *cæpit anno* 1117.	Tagjuddaulas Decacus Ababacus, *ad- huc in vivis* anno 1115. ******* ****** Sanguinus Noradinus &c.

Atque iſte rerum Turcicarum ſtatus fuit cùm primùm Euphratem trajecerant, &, quaſi irruptionis in terras Romanas ſpecimine dato, præſtitutis ad Euphratem cat- ceribus coercerentur. Ut ut autem iſte Sultaniarum quaternio ad tempus laxationis

Plate 19. Mede's account of the positions of the four angels at Iconium (modern Konya [or Konieh] in the Central Anatolia region of Turkey), Aleppo, Damascus, and Baghdad prophesied in the sixth trumpet, released with their two million horsemen from their captivity in the river Euphrates to slay a third of mankind. Photograph by the author.

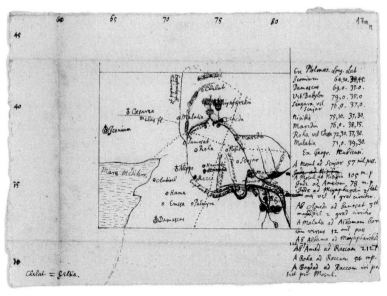

Plate 20. Newton's effort to locate the same positions for the Euphratean tetrarchies that—as he saw it—broke loose in the thirteenth century. The map shows his efforts to locate the four angels in different sultanies, and also to make their centres form a tolerable square. He retains Mede's choices of Damascus and Iconium (i.e., Konieh) but rejects Mede's selection of Baghdad and Aleppo in favour (and backed by substantial evidence) of Mosul and Miyafarekin (modern Silvan), the latter being called "Martyropolis" between the fifth and seventh centuries. Newton argued that Baghdad had ceased to be a major power before the fifth trumpet, while Aleppo was part of the same sultany as Damascus and the latter had always been the capital city of Syria. Newton also argued that although Miyafarekin was more than 100 miles from the Euphrates, one branch of the river—which mingled with the Tigris and flowed on top—passed close to it. Courtesy of the National Library of Israel.

Apocalypseos, a work on Revelation that was published at the start of 1680. His *A Plain and Continued Exposition of Daniel*, which was written in early 1680, appeared a year later. As an ordained minister and accomplished exegete, More was keenly aware of the political and religious issues underlying the crisis. In January 1679, in the wake of the murder of Sir Edmund Berry Godfrey and the incarceration of five Catholic lords in the Tower of London, he wrote to Anne Conway concerning the "dismall plot," which had been "layd deep and reached far." He called on English Protestants to repent their sins in order to avert God's righteous judgement on them: "For the stink and [stench?] of them have too long offended the nostrills of the Almighty so that it may be just with God to cast a dunghill upon a Dunghill and overthrow Protestantism with Poperie." A year later he told Archbishop Sancroft that it was divine providence rather than any prudence on his own part that had led to the timing of the recent publication of his *Apocalypsis Apocalypseos*. Although there was no reference to the contemporary political crisis in this work, the preface to his subsequent book on Daniel displayed a heightened concern with the threat of popery. Emphasising that the Reformed churches were the kingdom of Christ, he warned any "Magistrate spiritual or temporal" against betraying any part of this kingdom to Antichrist, a clear warning to Charles II not to let in popery through the back door. It was the duty of interpreters, he wrote, to warn Protestants about the true character of the terrible plot that had recently been uncovered.[56]

At a time of heightened tension in August 1680, More wrote to John Sharp, a graduate of Christ's College and now a lecturer at St. Lawrence Jewry in London, in an attempt to get John Turner (a fellow of Christ's) a church in London. In this letter, he suddenly veered off onto another topic regarding recent questions that Sharp and Hezekiah Burton (rector of St. George the Martyr in Southwark) had put to him regarding Newton's views on prophecy. Some or all of this group believed that the Lucasian professor had important things to say about the relevance of apocalypse to the present moment. No doubt this was because More had told them of Newton's prophetic interests, but it must also have been because they believed that his numerical ability would be of great help in the business. According to More, soon after he had given Newton a copy of *Apocalypsis Apocalypseos* (presumably at the start of January 1680), Newton had gone to his rooms at Christ's. The latter appeared "not only to approve my Exposition as coherent and perspicuous throughout from the beginning to end, but (by the manner of his countenance which is ordinarily melancholy and thoughtfull,

but then mighty lightsome and cheerfull, and by the free profession of satisfaction he took therein) to be in a maner transported." This account not
only gives us a striking description of Newton's personality, but given the
terrible beliefs that lay behind his peculiar views of the order of apocalyptic
visions, it can also be read as indicative of his standard techniques of dissim-
ulation.[57]

More must have given Newton a copy of his book at the start of January
1680, just over a month after Newton had returned from Woolsthorpe. On
the day after his return at the end of November, he had replied to a letter
from Robert Hooke, remarking that he had been in Lincolnshire over the
previous six months dealing with family matters. As we have seen, during
the ensuing correspondence over the true path of a falling object Newton
informed Hooke that for many years past he had been attempting to "bend"
himself from natural philosophy towards "other studies," so much so that he
had for a long time begrudged the amount of time spent on natural philosophy except when he did so as a diversion "at idle hours." In addition to his
"chymical" researches, his reference to his studies concerned his apocalyptic
researches, which must have begun some time before his departure for Woolsthorpe. More told Sharp that Newton's positive reaction to his book was
evidence that some "peculiar conceits he had of his own, had vanished," but
in a postscript he recounted that Newton had "recoyl[ed] into a former
conceit." These beliefs were thus long-standing, but they were not fatal to
their friendship, since he and Newton continued to remain on good terms
until More's death in 1687.[58]

The Sharp letter provides conclusive evidence concerning the early
chronology of Newton's apocalyptic researches, clearly demonstrating
that he had already developed a well-formed and highly original interpretation of prophetic history by the time More wrote. By the end of the
1670s he had come to the firm belief that each vial and trumpet was synchronous, thus obliterating the very special relevance accorded to the
Protestant Reformation for effecting the downfall of popery that Mede,
More and others attributed to the vials. More was well aware of the implications of Newton's downgrading of the importance of the vials, so
much so that he immediately attacked Newton's position in print. If their
discussion ever broached the historical and doctrinal issues that underpinned Newton's views, then More may have sensed that Newton's approach to prophecy was motivated by an heterodox beliefs. In all other
respects, of course, Newton was in full agreement with Mede and More

about who the guilty party was. Since More did *not* mention the historical referents of prophecies in his letter, and continued his good relations with Newton afterwards, the discussions they conducted must have concerned only the internal relations of the prophetic images.

In his letter to Sharp, More viewed Newton's "conceits" as threefold, namely, "that the seven Vials commence with the seven Trumpets," "that the Epistles to the Seven Churches are [not] a prophecy of the state of the Church from the beginning to the end of the World," and "that the three dayes and a half of the Witnesses lying slain [are] three years and a half after their mournfull witnessing." The last position was the standard view, for which (as we have seen) More had attacked Mede. The first, More said, he had always considered "very extravagant," while as for the second he complained that Newton "pronounces of the seven Churches not having yet read ⟨my⟩ Exposition of them, wch I writ by itself on purpose." One notes with amusement his frustration that Newton pontificated on the topic without having read his work, which constitutes good evidence of Newton's real and professed disregard for contemporary writings (and perhaps More's in particular). More admitted that Newton had "a singular Genius to Mathematicks," and took him "to be a good serious man," but he added that another notable Cambridge mathematician (probably Isaac Barrow) had told him that he had demonstrated his thesis concerning the seven churches "with Mathematicall evidence." Striking his usual confident note, More stated that when Newton had read his three-part appendix to his forthcoming book on Daniel, he would come to More's opinion.[59]

One part of the appendix to More's book on Daniel concerned More's account of the seven churches, while another dealt with his placement of all the vials in the seventh trumpet after the rising of the witnesses. More told Sharp that he found Newton "something inclineable" to the last notion but he added that if they still disagreed after he had read the book it would mean very little to him. The evidence was compelling, he continued, and he did not require anyone else's approval to corroborate his extreme confidence in his own position. The similarities between the parts of the appendix and More's remarks to Sharp about his disagreements with Newton show conclusively that the former were specifically directed against Newton. More made a habit of attacking individuals in appendices; for example, *Apocalypsis Apocalypseos* contained an "epilogue" in which he savagely attacked the positions held by one "R.H." of Salisbury. In 1675 Richard Hayter had claimed that all of the prophecies were "yet to be fulfilled" and had denied most of Mede's most significant synchronisms such as that of the two-horned and ten-horned beasts, and that of the Whore of Babylon with the ten-horned beast. Hayter's exposition was one of many examples of what More took to be exegetical insanity, and like those authors, Newton found himself attacked in print.[60]

The postscript to More's letter to Sharp indicates that yet another meeting had taken place with Newton after More had completed the major part of the letter. In it he alluded to a tantalisingly obscure request from Burton:

> tell him I now understand the meaning of his question touching Mr Newton, but not a word to anyone els. When my Exposition of Daniel comes out with the Appendage, I hope you will easily discerne that Mr. N. was over sudden in his conceits and I have told him myself of this appendage, and that if he be not convinced thereby, he may have leave from me to follow his own opinions. We have a free converse and friendship wch these differences will not disturb. He does still professe my Exposition is a perspicuous and coherent piece.

This text shows that there had been a further series of meetings between More and Newton on the subject of prophecy, while the reference to their friendship and "open" conversation chimes with the form of scholarly intercourse Newton favoured and recommended elsewhere. As it happens, this conversation spilled over into print culture. More titled one appendix "The Authour's Apology for His Placing the Seven Vials Within the Seventh Trumpet after the Rising of the Witnesses, Contrary to the Opinion of Mr. Mede &c." though his arguments were almost entirely taken up with attacking Newton's position, and not Mede's.[61]

11. Exegetical Impertinence

In his "Apology," More began by stating that those of learning, talent, and "sobriety of life" who had diligently applied themselves to the study of prophecy had a right to have their work considered by like-minded men. However, too often people rushed into such things out of mere curiosity, considering neither the difficulty of the task nor what others had said beforehand. Others "out of a fondness towards themselves presume they have more peculiar gifts that way, and by strong prepossession of their private conceits deeply impressed upon their melancholy Imagination render themselves incorrigible and uncapable of the most evident and solid information from others." Another band of expositors were mere fanatics, while a final group had left the byways dug out by previous interpreters merely to serve their own interest. More pleaded that if he had deviated from Mede, it was in the service of the true religion and "by meer force of Reason." Newton read this and must have wondered if any of these rhetorical missiles applied to him. He knew that the arguments were directed against his own positions, and his presentation copy of More's *Exposition* contains his marginal comments on More's arguments against synchronising the trumpets and the vials.[62]

More began by accepting that there was a temptation to affix the start of the vials to what he called the first "joynt" constituted by the start of the first trumpet. This was "because of some specious correspondence betwixt the *Vials* and Trumpets of the same order or numerical denomination," which certainly made a "shew," but this was a gross error and the "pretended synchronising congruities" vanished on closer inspection. At the sounding of the first trumpet, hail and fire mixed with blood was thrown down from the heavens, resulting in the incineration of a third of the earth and trees, and all the grass. The pouring of the first vial caused a "noisome and grievous sore" to fall on the worshippers of the beast and More noted that since the symbols of the hailstorm and the sore were so different, they clearly represented different things. Newton was sufficiently roused to note his objections in the margin (see Plate 14), brusquely dismissing More's argument with the terse statement: "No. They are ye same. See 2 Chron. 6. 28, 29. & Job. 5. 18, 19, 20." These scriptural passages by themselves hardly made the supporting case that Newton demanded of them but it is likely that he simply understood that the referents of the symbols described in his prophetic dictionary were specifically similar. Indeed, he was capable both of interpreting such terms in an Achmetian or figurative manner, and of thinking of these phrases in terms of the historical events they allegedly depicted.[63]

Both More and Newton defended key elements of the Protestant tradition. While More defended the special place of the vials in the standard Protestant apocalyptic interpretation, Newton relied on the standard hermeneutical rule that similar passages should be understood as interpreting each other in a productive and illuminating manner. A note of incredulity was sounded in Newton's response to More's rebuttal of the third synchronism. The third angel poured out his vial of wrath on the rivers and fountains of waters, and they turned into blood. The angel, together with a martyr from the prophetic altar, pronounced this a judgement on all those who had shed the blood of saints and prophets. At the sounding of the third trumpet, a great star fell from heaven, burning like a lamp, and it fell on a third part of the rivers, and on the fountains of waters, while a third of the waters came to taste like bitter wormwood, causing many to die. More claimed that nothing in the third vial corresponded to the falling star in the third trumpet, and asserted that "what the Fountains and Rivers suffer under the *third Trumpet*, is a misery to men and a bitterness to them, what they suffer under the *third Vial* is a refreshment to men who praise and justify God upon the account." In his note on this argument (see Plate 14), Newton found it incomprehensible that More refused to believe that it was the same evildoers who had suffered in both cases, writing, "What? Did ye plague of ye 3^d Vial fall on ye Martyrs of ye Altar who praised God? No they praised God for inflicting it on their persecutors." As we have seen, in Newton's interpretive scheme, the description of the vial enriched that of the accompanying trumpet, and although they were similar, they could not be identical. In one marginal comment (see Plate 15), he put this explicitly: if the synchronisms were as obvious as More wanted, "the Trumpets and Vials would be useless for explaining one another. But now there is such variety, each having what ye other wants & expressing things variously that ye D^r. cannot beleive them ye same."[64]

This view was further articulated in Newton's comments on More's dismissal of the fourth "congruity." In the fourth trumpet, a third part of each of the sun, moon, and stars was smitten, and a third part of the day was left in darkness. The corresponding vial was poured out on the sun, and the latter was given power to burn men with fire; the latter were duly scorched but continued to blaspheme God. More claimed that the alleged synchronism was "wonderfully wretched and small." The sun alone was the subject of the vial, and while in one case the sun's power was diminished, in the other it was substantially invigorated. In his own comments Newton translated the prophetic terms directly into the figurative language and joined the corresponding terms into one richer description. Remarking that "sun" referred to a "king" and that "men" referred to "princes," Newton asked, "did ye King alone without his princes suffer in ye 4th vial?" Even if there were no reference to the suffering of men in the fourth trumpet, the synchronism made sense when both were joined together and interpreted figuratively: "why might not ye Sun loos a 3^d p^t of his light y^t is of his kingdome & at ye same time make war on y^t 3^d p^t, y^t is scorch men wth fire?" More, he continued, "would have ye Vialls no repetition of ye Trumpets unless it be so full y^t every fop may both see it and deride it for an impertinent Tautology." Moreover, this was More's sole argument against synchronising the second, fifth, and sixth congruities. Newton accused More of repeating one argument over and over again merely to "make a shew"—the very phrase that More had himself used against his opponents at the start of his critique.[65]

A number of points arise from this analysis. First, Newton was a deeply committed student of prophecy and had already developed a detailed and systematic understanding of Revelation by 1679. This was not a superficial or ad hoc recasting of Mede's approach since he made major changes to Mede's scheme based on his doctrinal and historical positions. Second, disputes about Revelation could be conducted over the internal order and logic of the Apocalypse without any reference to historical events. The conversation that took place in the margins of Newton's copy of More's book on Daniel must to some extent have replicated the argument of their private discussions, though the latter were conducted with rather more subtlety. Newton must have succeeded in deflecting attention away from the doctrinal implications of his position, though the historical referents of these images lurked only inches below the surface of their discourse. Indeed, it is hard to believe that More, an expert in the Medean apocalyptic tradition and a disciple of the master himself, did not smell something nasty in Newton's complete renunciation of the special position played by the vials in the Protestant tradition. By all accounts, however, Newton's efforts to cover up his true beliefs were a complete success, and More continued to believe that he was a good, serious man. Finally, More's letter and Newton's response to More's attack on him show that Newton was already a confident exegete, whose skills were already rated highly by a small group of interpreters who were eager to understand how the events taking place in England fitted into the prophetic scheme of things.

8

Divine Persecution

Newton's recasting of the Medean approach was derived in large part from the specific rules he composed for interpreting Scripture, and prophecy in particular. However, it also flowed from his very different conception regarding the nature and historical source of the Great Apostasy. He argued that it was bound up with the introduction into Christianity of homousianism and other idolatrous doctrines and practices after the Council of Nicaea, and that it grew in strength in the fifth and the sixth centuries after Christ. It experienced a new burst of life with the advent of Islam and the consolidation of Roman Catholic secular power in the seventh century. Whatever the strength of Newton's claims about the logical priority of his reordering of the prophetic images, doctrinal and historical considerations necessarily shaped much of the core structure of his framework. A number of features characterised his innovative approach. In the first place, he believed that the most serious events in the history of religious corruption occurred during the century following the Council of Nicaea in 325. Second, and as we have seen, by synchronising the visions of the pouring of the vials and the sounding of the trumpets, he downgraded the special significance of the vision of the vials, traditionally understood by Protestants to refer to the recent and future demise of popery. The remarkable historical assumption underlying this approach was that the Reformation provided no historically significant stage in the downfall of Roman Catholicism, a view that says a lot about what Newton thought about the degree to which contemporary Protestant groups had cleansed themselves of the trappings of popery. Finally, his claim that the onset of the fifth trumpet announced a major intensification of the Great Apostasy and the start of the 1,260 prophetic days allowed him to stretch out the central synchronism encompassed by the start of the first and end of the sixth trumpet. Historically this allowed him to escape the problem of locating the onset of the millennium in his own time (since he followed Mede in holding 395 C.E. to be the date of the first trumpet and vial), allowing him to stretch the onset of the millennium some distance into the future.

Like Mede, Newton expressed caution about linking prophecies either to present events or to specific future dates. Restoration interpreters were virtually unanimous in holding that radicals had brought prophecy into disrepute when they made outlandish predictions about events happening in the very near future, which then failed to occur. The standard reasons given by the more "sober" interpreters, which he rehearsed, were that the correct understanding of prophecy could only be done retrospectively, that is, by empirical recourse to history in order to show how prophecies had been fulfilled. Some scholarly interpreters threw this caution to the wind in the later 1680s, when the Roman Catholic king James II threatened the Protestant foundations of the English state, and when William of Orange "miraculously delivered" the English from popery. Yet even though Newton composed a major work on prophecy in the reign of James II, there is no evidence that he saw James's reign as prophetically significant. At the very end of one early treatise on the Apocalypse, he expressly stated that only future events could determine the interpretation of those images describing events associated with the millennial seventh trumpet. Like other more cautious scholarly exegetes, he placed Christ's Second Coming and the start of the millennium (both coextensive with the start of the seventh trumpet and vial) some way into the future.[1]

1. The Logic of Prophetic History

By the time Newton began to apply images to historical events, the Protestant apocalyptic tradition, with the current era at its focus, had been in existence for over a century.[2] Although John Napier synchronised the trumpets and the vials in his *Plaine Discovery* of 1593, he did interpret some of the most important images in his scheme as references to events in the recent Protestant Reformation. In Proposition 5 he argued that momentous historical developments took place about every 245 years, each signalling the sounding of a new trumpet and the pouring of a new vial. In consecutive propositions Napier claimed (with a decidedly loose grasp of dates) that the second trumpet was sounded and the second vial poured in 316 (when Constantine extended the Roman Empire eastwards); the third in 561 (the

Gothic king Totila burned Rome); the fourth in 806 (Charlemagne was made emperor); the fifth in 1051 (Zadok joined the caliph of Egypt and dominated the Turks); the sixth in 1296 (Osman founded the Ottoman state), and the seventh in 1541 (the Reformation). In Proposition 36 Napier stated that Antichrist had begun to reign in about 300, or at the latest 316, notwithstanding the fact that he was bound up for a thousand years at exactly the same time (by Prop. 34). Adding 1,260 years to this, the period of Antichrist's persecution had thus ended in about 1560 when "these papistical policies were destroyed in England, Scotland, and in some parts of Germany, France, & other countries." Propositions 12 to 14 stated that the first three angels with thunders acted every "Jubilee" (or forty-nine years), occurring in 1590, 1639, and 1688. At this point Christ, the fourth angel, would appear with the three last avenging angels to accomplish the Harvest (Rev. 14:16), and it would also be the date at which the Elect would find peace. According to Proposition 10, the Day of Judgement would occur at some point between 1688 and 1700.[3]

Thomas Brightman added substantially more historical detail than Napier in his mammoth *Apocalypsis Apocalypseos* of 1609 (translated as *A Revelation of Revelation* in 1615). He argued at great length that the seven churches in Revelation referred to consecutive stages in the growth of the church; for example, the "dead" church of Sardis (Rev. 3:1-6) depicted the German Reformation, the loyal church of Philadelphia (Rev. 3:7-13) the Genevan churches, and the lukewarm Laodicea (Rev. 3:14-19) the still popishly affected Church of England. More generally, Brightman's historical interpretations of the seals, trumpets, and vials as fulfilments or accomplishments of specific prophecies were highly influential for later exegetes. He claimed that the seventh seal was opened in the reign of Constantine while the first of the trumpets was sounded at the start of the fourth century. The "lesser" trumpets ended with the close of the fourth trumpet in 607, after which Antichrist took control of the church. The "greater" trumpets started in the same year, and they described the apostasy of Muhammed and the decree of the emperor Phocas, which, by giving the pope the title of "Universal Bishop," gave unprecedented temporal power to the new pope, Boniface III. The locusts that swarmed out of the bottomless pit in Revelation 9:2-11 depicted the monks and Saracens in the West and East, respectively, while the sixth trumpet clearly foretold the rise to greatness and subsequent decline of the Turkish Empire. Brightman brought his interpretation up to the present age when the seventh trumpet sounded at the accession of the Virgin Queen Elizabeth in 1558.[4]

Against Napier, Brightman restored the special status of the vials, arguing that the first vial was poured in 1563, when Elizabeth dismissed a large number of Roman Catholic clergy, while further decrees and victories against Catholics comprised the next three. He wrote, as he thought, in the fourth vial. Like Foxe, he believed that an initial one-thousand-year period had started in the reign of Constantine, at the end of which the Turks had been let loose. The preaching of people such as Wyclif represented the onset of another millennium. In the last days, Protestants would defeat the Romish Beast (by 1650), and almost half a century later the Jews would conquer the Great Dragon (the Turk) in the East. The momentous events of previous years—the expansion of learning, the discovery of the New World, the defeat of the Armada, and the general proliferation of Protestantism—convinced Brightman that a golden age was just beginning. Like other Protestant interpreters, he believed that prophetic history could only be understood in the last times (which had arrived), each image being correctly interpreted only when its historical fulfilment had been properly identified and understood.[5]

Outside Britain, a number of authors developed learned prophetic exegeses in the context of the political and religious strife of the Thirty Years War. For example, Johann Heinrich Alsted looked forward to the Edenic time when the conditions outlined in the last chapters of Revelation would be fulfilled, and he defended explicitly millenarian views in his *Diatribe de Milleannis Apocalypticis* of 1627. He pointed to the year 1694 as the moment when the millennium would commence, making this coterminous with the binding of the dragon, and he followed Revelation literally in holding that the war between Gog and Magog would take place a thousand years later. Although he located some central events in the future, he also believed that the trumpets referred to the period between 606 and 1517, while three of the vials had already been poured by 1625. Alsted's views were promoted in England by John Dury, Samuel Hartlib, and John Amos Comenius, and after the *Diatribe* was translated into English in 1642, it became a central resource for astrologers, almanac makers, and many sorts of religious radical.[6]

2. Mede's World

In applying his synchronisms to history, Joseph Mede drew on the work of these writers though he also proclaimed that the interpretations he offered were the fruits of his own labours. In his *Commentary* he argued that the Great Apostasy was set up by the battle in heaven between Michael and the dragon, the latter's defeat, and his subsequent fall to Earth. Immediately after this, the pregnant woman, though menaced by the dragon, at last gave birth to a man-child who was to rule the earth with a rod of iron. Mede understood Michael, who safeguarded the woman during her birth, to be an archangel and not Christ. The man-child was the mystical Christ, whose renewed presence in the secular sphere was represented by means of the victories of Constantine and others over pagans. When the woman fled into the wilderness at the end of this prophetic period, the waters spewed out by the dragon were the pestilent doctrines of the Arian heretics. Orthodox Christians protected her from their filthy beliefs by maintaining the true religion, thus swallowing up (Rev. 12:16) the toxic liquid. In his own "Observations Concerning the Millennium," Mede's editor John Worthington elaborated on this and compared the atrocious behaviour of the Arians against the "faithful Christians" to those of the pagan Roman persecutors. Like Mede and most others, Worthington contrasted the institution of Trinitarianism as the state religion with the baneful actions of the (anti-Trinitarian) barbarians though he also noted Salvian's observations concerning the distinctly ungodly behaviour of many orthodox Christians, which had caused the barbarians to be offended and shamed by their vile lives.[7]

Having fallen to Earth, the dragon now had a short time to do his dirty work, and he passed on various tasks to the ten-horned beast. Mede's analysis of the nature and extent of the latter was rich and extensive. This beast ordered the populace to worship him and was given immense power by the dragon to make war on and to conquer the saints. Mede interpreted the image of the beast as a reference to refer to the secular power of the Roman Empire, which had forced its people to worship images, participate in transubstantiation, and blaspheme saints and angels. The persecution of the saints accelerated in the time of the medieval Waldenses and Albigensians and intensified still further with the brutal suppression of Protestants. This was accomplished with the help of the second beast who had arisen from the earth. This two-horned or "pseudo-prophetical" beast exercised the power of the first, performing miracles and giving life to an image of the ten-horned beast that the population was compelled to worship on pain of death. Mede offered numerous demonstrations that this beast was the pope and his clergy, who presided over Antichristian sacrifices and undertook the spiritual degradation of the faithful. They were the chief performers of those lying wonders that Paul told the Thessalonians would be performed by the Man of Sin.[8]

The sixth seal told of a great earthquake, which was followed by the sun turning black and the moon turning to blood. The darkening of the sun depicted the victory of Christ over the demonic heart of paganism, but the bloody moon depicted the rise to power of the papacy. When the seventh seal was opened, the prophetic half an hour's silence was an allusion to the Jewish practice of remaining silent when incense was being offered. Although the periods depicted by the half hour's silence and the early trumpets would be crucial for Newton, and he would investigate the events they described in great detail, Mede's historical analysis was entirely cursory. In his scheme the first trumpet sounded immediately after the silence ended with the death of Theodosius the Great in 395. At this point the Roman Empire was divided into East and West for the last time, and the Great Apostasy came into being. This was marked by increasing cruelties and savageries meted out on the Roman people by the barbarians, led by the Visigoth Alaric. The Goths, Mede noted, "began in a horrible manner to be stirred up and to fall upon almost the whole Romane Empire by fire and sword continually and cruelly wasting and spoyling it." The Roman general Stilicho briefly checked Alaric's advance but in 404 there were other incursions from more groups of barbarians. Two years later, Vandals, Alani, and many others burst in from the West, destroying whatever stood in their way.[9]

The second trumpet heralded a great blazing mountain being thrown into the sea, after which a third of the sea turned to blood. According to Mede, the vision depicted the sacking of Rome by Alaric in 410 and the consequent slaughter of vast numbers of Roman citizens. Alaric set upon the city in a terrifying blitz and briefly removed the emperor Honorius to insert his own man (Attalus) on the throne, though he quickly put Honorius back in charge. In the following years the Roman Empire was increasingly overrun by Goths and Huns, and its leaders did a deal with the Vandals, giving them entitlement over captured lands provided they resisted the Goths. However, in 455 Rome was captured by the Vandal king Geiseric, leaving the empire divided into the ten kingdoms prophesied in Daniel 7:24 (the kingdoms being the ten horns arising from the head of the dreadful fourth beast in Dan. 7:20). The third trumpet depicted a burning star falling into a third of the rivers. Mede argued that this referred to the extinction of Romulus Augustulus, the last of the Western emperors who was overthrown by the first king of Italy, Odoacer, in 476. The fourth trumpet described how a third of the sun, moon, and stars turned dark, and according to Mede, this sounded in 542, when Totila recaptured much of Italy, thus marking the death knell for the city of Rome. Once the queen of cities, he lamented that she now lacked the power of consuls, senate, and magistrates (the sun, moon, and stars) with which she had once enlightened the world. Now she had fallen "from so great glory into I know not what ignoble dukedome of *Ravenna*, over which in times past shee had commanded, [and] after is constrained to serve under the *Exarchate* (O miserable darknesse) and pay tribute." Newton would radically extend the historical support for this scheme, but when it suited him he retained the general language and even the exact wording of Mede's analysis.[10]

Having conventionally linked the fifth and sixth trumpets to the rise of Islam and the consolidation of Roman Catholic power, Mede placed the first six vials in the sixth trumpet, leaving the onset of the seventh trumpet and vial to be synchronised. In assigning individual vials to historical periods, he varied what was by now a traditional theme: the first vial was the teaching of the medieval heretics; the second referred to the uprising of Luther; and the third was the killing of Roman Catholics by Protestant princes. This was most wonderfully accomplished, Mede thought, in Elizabethan England, when the state instituted the death penalty "for soliciting the Papall cause." The Spanish had sought blood in their Armada but had been thwarted then and afterwards by the English and Dutch, both "abundantly pouring out the Cup of the mightie hand of God." At the start of his *Commentary* Mede claimed that the recent successes of the Protestant prince Gustavus Adolphus constituted the pouring of the fourth vial, although later followers had the luxury of hindsight to help them point out that in doing this, he had perhaps resolved "too hastily."[11] Mede did not give a definitive date for the Second Coming in his published works but interpreters such as Thomas Goodwin added 1,260 years to the date he had given for the sounding of the first trumpet, thus producing the date of 1655. He synchronised the millennium with the Day of Judgement, at the end of which occurred the battle of Gog and Magog and following that, the general resurrection. Newton would follow Mede in his dates for the first five trumpets, but disagreed radically with him over the dating of the vials.[12]

3. The Lamb and the Seals

In one draft of Newton's treatise on Revelation from the late 1670s or early 1680s, he interpreted those images concerning the origins of the Christian

Church in terms of his radically subordinationist view of Christ. He argued that when the Lamb (that is, Christ) took a sealed book from the person who sat on the heavenly throne (that is, God; Rev. 5:6-8), its contents were of "so transcendent excellency that they were fit to be communicated to none but yᵉ Lamb." The information in the book given to the Lamb was not known to the Lamb beforehand, and on these grounds Newton insisted that the whole scene was designed to show that the Christ was not naturally omniscient. This prophetic scene was also an emblem of the uniquely awful apostasy that would start "by corrupting yᵉ truth about yᵉ relation of yᵉ Son to yᵉ Father in putting them equal." The Lamb had earned the right to take the book by his death, an action that made him worthy to receive not only the wisdom of this book but divine power, honour, and other perfections. In due course, Newton claimed, the "orthodox" apostates were to deceive themselves and others by means of a "sophistical distinction" according to which Christ's sufferings were spoken of "in respect of his humane nature & not as he was God." However, the book had been given to the Lamb as he was the *Logos* incarnate, and not to any human soul, and this was why the Lamb was worshipped by the four beasts and twenty-four elders (Rev. 4:4-6; 5:6-14).[13]

As we saw in chapter 4, Christ merited worship according to Newton not because of his nature but because he was obedient and suffered on the cross and hence became "worthy to be exalted & indowed wᵗʰ perfections by yᵉ father." The worship given to the Lamb was ἴσα θεῷ, that is, "as he was a God without all doubt, Divinity & worship being relative terms, & yet it was given to him as he was worthy to take & open yᵉ Book." Although God had decreed in Philippians 2:9 that every knee should bow at the name of Jesus, the worship due to the Lamb and to God was distinct; while the Lamb was *a* God, he was a divinity "inferior to the great God that sate upon the throne." The whole vision, depicting as it did the difference in tenor of the worship offered to the Lamb and God by the beasts and elders, was "no insignificant ceremony but a very weighty passage, a system of yᵉ Christian religion, showing yᵉ relation of yᵉ ffather & Son, & how they are to be worshipped in a general Assembly of yᵉ Church & of yᵉ whole creation." God was the supreme King on his throne and full of perfections, while the Lamb was next in dignity and the only being worthy to receive communication from God. This, Newton thought, was a good place to include an anti-Catholic jibe, and he remarked that in all this description there was "No Holy Ghost, no Angels, no Saints worshipped here: none worshipped but

God & ye Lamb, & these worshipped by all the rest."This hierarchy, outlined at the start of Revelation, was the central core of the religion that was corrupted by the Great Apostasy.[14]

When Newton came to analyse the history of the first seals, he followed the general chronological outlines in Mede's account. The opening of the first four seals referred to the reigns of the heathen emperors before Diocletian (emperor 284–305 C.E.). The conquering white horse of the first seal (Rev. 6:2) was Christ himself, while the rider on the red horse described in the second seal (Rev. 6:3-4) was Trajan, in whose belligerent reign the Roman Empire reached its pinnacle. The third seal (Rev. 6:5-6) depicted a rider on a black horse who held a pair of balances. This referred to the emperor Severus (emperor 193–211 C.E.), who "had a natural affection to judicature from a child [and] was so expert a Lawyer y^t $^<$at y^e age of 32 yeares$^>$ y^e Emperor Marcus designed him Prætor," while the blackness of the horse signified mourning for great men, whose deaths were plentiful in this reign. The fourth seal involved a rider called Death sitting atop a pale horse and accompanied by Hell (Rev. 6:8), and the image described how these ne'er-do-wells were given power to slaughter a quarter of the earth by means of the sword, hunger, death, and "the beasts of the earth." This seal delineated the short reign of Decius (emperor 249–51 C.E.), scarcely notable in itself but significant for the fact that it constituted the start to the astonishing violence, famine, and disease that continued and worsened in the following years. The fourth seal came to an end when Diocletian, having temporarily run out of foreign enemies, began to expand the empire and to persecute the church. Newton commended his own interpretation by remarking: "I have neither forced ye prophesy to history nor history to ye prophesy but taken everything in their natural order according to ye four series of Emperors."[15]

So far the church had experienced only relatively minor persecutions, but in 303 it suffered a major revolution in its fortunes. The fifth seal described the lamentations of those who were murdered for preaching the word of God. Under Diocletian and Galerius (emperor 305–11 C.E.), tens and even hundreds of thousands of Christians were slain, and although Licinius (emperor 308–24 C.E.) initially favoured Christianity, he too became its oppressor. These persecutions ended once Licinius was overthrown by Constantine in 324, but Constantine himself turned persecutor, "siding wth erroneous Christians to oppress ye Church for not admitting new language into their faith; & continued to do so till ye year 328…or 330." Newton variously argued

that the sixth seal (Rev. 6:12–17) began in 312 with the defeat of the emperor
Maxentius (reigning from 306) at the Battle of Milvian Bridge by Constantine,
or in 331 with the demolition of heathen idols by Constantine. Referring to
a wealth of sources available through Baronius and others, Newton initially
settled on the earlier date because it was the end of the ten-year persecution
begun by Diocletian, and he described it as a "most fatall blow" to heathenism. In a different draft he chose the later date on the grounds that although
the sixth seal concerned the destruction of heathen idolatry, Licinius had
resumed his persecution of Christians sometime after his joint rule with
Constantine. Constantine's prohibition against idolatry, which commenced
sometime between 331 and 333 (the precise date "mak[ing] no great difference"), thus marked the start of the seal.[16]

   In the sixth seal, following the darkening of the sun and the reddening of
the moon, "the stars of heaven fell unto the earth…and the heaven departed
as a scroll when it is rolled together; and every mountain and island were
moved out of their places." For Newton this great shaking was the overthrow
of the "Idol kingdom," and he focussed on this period, which followed the
Council of Nicaea, to an extent that none of his contemporaries could have
imagined. The falling stars described the toppled heathen idols, heaven's
departing as a scroll was the demolition of the roofs of heathen temples, and
the removal of mountains and islands were the destruction of altars and
many temples by zealous monks who "swarm[ed] up and down in troops."
The reappearance of Christian emperors after the end of the reign of Julian
the Apostate in 363 caused many "hypocritical heathens" to turn Christian,
thus further diluting the faith. There was little left of paganism by the end
of the century, Newton continued, "so that what Theodosius <& his son's>
did (wch ye Homoüsian Historians keep such a clatter about) was but to cut
<in pieces the carcas of> ye dying Beast wch Constantine & Constantius
<had> set upon in it's full vigour & wounded mortally." However, Newton
noted that Theodosius (emperor 379–95 C.E.) and his trusty monks had
merely exchanged pagan idolatry for a much more diabolical form.[17]

4. The Great Apostasy

In Newton's interpretation of Revelation, all the events of the early church
that he had discussed in a secular mode (as we saw in chs. 4 and 5) were now
understood through the lens of prophecy. In one "Position" he demonstrated

at great length that the division of the Western Empire into ten nations was depicted by the ten-horned beast's rising from the sea (Rev. 13:1), while the Eastern Empire continued in the form of the great red dragon. The following image of the dragon giving the beast his seat (Rev. 13:2) depicted the donation of Rome to the beast but also Constantine's gift of the Western Empire to his sons. When Constans (emperor 337–350 C.E.) became emperor of the West in 340 after the defeat of his brother Constantine II, he was forced—or so Newton claimed—by Athanasius and Pope Julius to take the part of the "Homoüsians." This gave rise to the split in the mid-340s between the Eastern and Western churches. In 353 C.E. the "Arian" emperor of the Eastern Empire, Constantius II (emperor 337–61 C.E.) conquered the "usurper" Magnentius and reunited the Roman Empire. Now in control of the West, he suppressed its Trinitarian religion but always acted, Newton claimed, with virtue and restraint. Newton understood this period as the wounding of the beast (Rev. 13:3) but as the prophecy foretold, it was only temporary. When the wound healed, the beast would experience its political and religious restoration. After Constantius died in 361 there was a brief interlude when Rome was ruled for two years by the pagan Julian and then very briefly by the Christian military commander Jovian. When he died in February 364, the empire was once more split, this time ruled by Valentinian (emperor of the Western Empire from 364–75 C.E.) and Valens (emperor of the Eastern Empire from 364–78). For Newton, Valens followed the godly path of Constantius in attempting to suppress the homoousian religion, but Valentinian tolerated all parties and thus gave an opportunity for the Athanasians to thrive, an event that constituted the ascent of the beast out of the bottomless pit (Rev. 11:7; 13:1).[18]

Newton argued that the expulsion of the dragon from heaven and the gradual ascent of the beast from the pit denoted a change in worship "from a nobler to an ignobler state, from ye stately worship in ye temples of heathen gods to ye sordid worship in sepulchres of ye Christian Divi," and from the worship of kings and heroes "to ye adoration of mean & despicable plebeians in their rotten reliques." Now let loose on Earth, the dragon/devil immediately (Rev. 12:12) began his "new game," allowing Christians to destroy pagan practices as a precondition for the erection of his own religion. As Newton put it,

> The worshiping of Saints & Reliques, & besides that no other worship wch can be accused of Idolatry, began to overspread the world at that very time when ye Idolatry of ye Heathens ceased. ffor their Idol worship (at least among y^e

Romans) ceased at that final universall shutting up of ye Idol-Temples wch was in ye beginning of Gratian's & Theodosius's reign. And then began ye Devil to overspread ye Christian world wth ye worship of S^{ts} & Reliques. In Julian's reign he laid ye bait, wch for a while fermented more secretly, & at length wrought notoriously all ye world over by means of those numberles miracles (whether feigned or diabolical) wch were cryed up in Theodosius's & his sons reigns to be done everywhere by ye reliques & at ye shrines of Saints.[19]

Monks swarmed up and down the empire, recommending relics and selling them to the people. The "gravest Clergy men of that age" Newton be-moaned, began "countenancing ye miracles & looking at them as if ye mi-raculous Apostolic Age itself was revived in & out done by their own." This novel kind of idolatry was masterminded by the devil and put into practice in about the year 360, constituting the inauguration of the Man of Sin prophesied by Paul. These abominations became universal in the reign of Theodosius, Newton continued, and had remained so ever since. All this, as we have seen, was accompanied by the rise of the two-horned beast from the earth. This was the "Ecclesiastical hierarchy of ye triunitarian church," which came to power in Rome and Alexandria (the two horns) after the death of Constantius.[20]

An impassioned Newton wrote of how the godly clergy tried to with-stand the machinations of the monks and the Roman Catholic Church, mounting a brave resistance to their perversions. However, in due course they were heavily outnumbered. The homoousian emperors increased their violence and by such actions "ye Church was dissolved as to its outward form & ye Monkish clergy brought into their room & Monkery every where in-couraged & Hypocrites drawn to that ~~side~~ party." Thus encouraged, the monks "got the opportunity to delude through their feigned stories, lying miracles, garrulity, & formality of godliness, all those that had conscience wthout knowledge." Under Constantine and his successors, the true religion had prospered but soon the Christian world "was grown so full of hypocrites & so cold in devotion that $^⟨$the Empire$^⟩$ deserved y^e plague of those wars w^{ch} $^⟨$God inflicted on it$^⟩$ in y^e reign of Valentinian & ~~Valens~~ Gratian." Newton recommended the *De Gubernatione Dei* of the "sober, cordate & pious" author Salvian as evidence of how quickly the church became corrupted. Earlier historians had borne witness to the shocking immorality of orthodox Christians in this period, but more than any other historian Salvian was able to depict the full range of their depravities, a feature that Newton found extremely helpful. Accordingly, he remarked to his nameless reader:

"To tell you what he says of them [i.e., degenerate Romans] would be to transcribe his book and therefore I had rather send it to you," and he virtually did just that by incorporating extensive citations from Salvian into his own narrative. In each case, Salvian contrasted the Romans unfavourably with the barbarians who were increasingly threatening the integrity of the empire, and he showed how the "lowest ebb" of the true Church occurred towards the end of the reign of Theodosius. As Newton saw it, the visible body of the church was now only present in the barbarian nations while the Trinitarian west was now largely composed of ignorant and hypocritical converts to Christianity.[21]

The death of Valens in 378 put an end to any state support for what Newton believed to be the true religion. The new emperors Gratian and Theodosius were taken up by major wars with European barbarians for the next two years, but a peace treaty with the Goths at the end of 380 left the Roman Empire in relative tranquillity. This, however, set the stage for the decisive opening of the seventh seal, which ushered in events that according to Newton were the most remarkable "of all changes that ever were wrought in yᵉ Christian religion." It combined two features, being "yᵉ foundation ˂& root˃ of all following Apostacy, & in regard of yᵉ unnatural quick & universal propagation, it being wrought by force on a sudden all over yᵉ Empire." All other corruptions Newton could think of had "crept in & spread themselves by almost insensible degree" but the devastating speed at which this one came in was "a most certain demonstration of yᵉ beginning of this seal." At one point he tried to restrain himself by protesting that he would not engage himself in a dispute about whether the seventh seal should be placed at the end of the year 380, but reverting to type he provided a battery of proofs, backed by copious textual evidence, to place the vision to this date. In one draft, which displays his strenuous efforts to find data to support his case, he identified the onset of the Great Apostasy with the peace treaty, the final efforts by monks to overthrow the heathen temples, and the "delivery of yᵉ Churches to yᵉ Homousians," all of which took place in December 380. The fifteen-year period beginning in that dismal year was characterised by a diminution in the number and intensity of wars, and apocalyptically it was marked both by the reference to the holding back of the winds by the four angels, and by the half hour's silence.[22]

Freed from external concerns, Gratian and Theodosius took it upon themselves to spread the hateful religion, and at the Council of Constantinople of 381 the latter banished all bishops who would not accept their diabolical cult. To "put a colour upon these proceedings," Newton raged, these emperors appointed ecclesiastical judges to examine priests and others for orthodoxy. The Council accordingly ratified the doctrine "of ye equality of y^e ⟨divine⟩ persons ⟨& triunity⟩ & of a soule in o^e Saviour besides y^e λόγος or Son & of his Hypostatical union ⟨wth that soule⟩ instead of a true incarnation in ye body." It became orthodox opinion across the Christian world to believe that this soul and not the Son suffered on the cross. This interpretation had previously only been accepted by provincial councils of Western bishops, "being but newly broached by ye Homoüsians," but now it became official and universal. Newton concluded that the year 381 was "wthout all controversy that in wch this strange religion of ye west ~~first~~ wch has reigned ever since first overspread ye world." The earth and all that dwelled in it now began to worship the beast and his image—the wicked church of the West.[23]

5. The Trumpets

What happened during the prophetic half an hour's silence was a crucial part of Newton's entire scheme. The "winds" of barbarian invasions that would constitute just retribution for the unspeakable crimes of Trinitarian Roman Catholicism were briefly held in check while the saints were sealed and numbered (Rev. 7:1-4). Those whose names were to be in the book of life were separated from those who were to worship the image of the beast. Here Newton drew on his experience on the Lincolnshire farm, noting that "when a sheepherd would mark & count ye best sheep of his flock he must separate them from ye rest, so here this sealing & numbring ye saints must be an emblem of a separation then made in ye church between them & ye unfaithfull." Since the sealing of the godly had to refer to later saints such as himself, he noted that the "posterity" of the saints that came after this episode was also sealed, "because all together make but one & ye same church wch was then as it were sealed or by a seale discriminated from ye Apostacy & has ever since continued so." In addition to the 144,000, John also recorded the names of the twelve tribes whose members would make up the total. However, Newton noted, the way in which their names were recounted in Revelation 7:4-8 represented a mystery; they were written down in such an order "as is no where els in scripture to be met with; sons of ye Mistresses & handmaids confusedly intermixed" and "no regard had to ye order of their birth or habitation." He wrote down the Latin meaning of the

names of the tribes alongside the names of their leaders, and the words
made a sentence proclaiming the celebration that was given by the elect to
God through his Son, with the promise of eternal bliss. Newton concluded
that the meaning of this passage was "so plain & apposite that it needs no
comment," yet his argument, like other claims that involved a sophisticated
analysis of Latin words, rather than an assessment of the historical evidence,
was lifted from Mede's *Commentary*.[24]

From Augustine's *City of God* Newton noted that a number of Gentiles
had believed on the basis of a heathen oracle that Christianity would only
last 365 years, and they converted to Christianity when they found this to
be false. This event could be dated precisely to 365 years after Christ's baptism in 30 C.E., and thus to the year 395. The devil, Newton noted, "therefore
plaid a cunning game" by preventing the heathens from converting until
Christianity had reached a serious level of depravity. Newton's disgust with
Trinitarian Roman Catholicism is nowhere better shown than in this analysis. "I know," he said, "they who stand accused hereby will ⟨still⟩ contend
they are yᵉ orthodox Church & yᵉ Barbarians hereticks, & therefore
the Oracle was a lye & my application of these things to them rash & unchar-
itable." It would be impossible to convince such people, since true heretics
were naturally "inconsiderate & therefore confident & obstinate." Newton's
text was not composed for them

> but to make such as already know their backsliding understand how these
> Prophecies are fulfilled in them. Yet for the sake of these men I shall add some-
> thing to shame 'em at least if not convince 'em.... They'll contend yᵉ ~~Trinity~~
> Triunity is no denying yᵉ Father & son, yᵉ Hypostatical Union & impassibility
> of yᵉ son no denying that Jesus Christ came in yᵉ flesh & suffered for us, the
> worshipping of saints & reliques no idolatry; but what will they say of whore-
> dom, murder, ⟨stealing⟩ lying, perjury, perfidy, drunkenness, gluttony, oppres-
> sion, pride, voluptuousness, blasphemies, strifes.

Any of these, Newton continued, was "enough to damn a man as well as
Antichristianism & Idolatry" and warming to his theme, he spluttered that
the Trinitarian Roman church "was yᵉ most wicked kingdom, the worst sort
of men that ever reigned upon the face of yᵉ earth till that time." From the
Annals of "yᵉ great Cardinal Baronius, a man unwilling to confess anything
to yᵉ scandal of his Church wᶜʰ he can decline," the outraged professor read
about the plagues of transvestites that blighted Rome at this time and from
Salvian he recorded pages and pages of evidence about the wickedness of its
citizens. The most serious transgression, he concluded, was "that stupendi-

ous abomination of sodomy" that Salvian condemned for being performed in public.[25]

Worst amongst the idolaters were the clergy, and Newton proceeded to list their crimes. Their sins set a terrible example to their flocks and with the help of Satan they inverted the true tenets of religion, "calling good evil & evil good: I mean their changing y^e doctrine of y^e Church into fables & y^e worship into a heap of supers$^<$ti$^>$tions & making persecution to have y^e name of piety." The entire clergy now started "to be puft up, to set their hearts upon power & greatness more then upon piety & equity, to transgress their Pastoral office & exalt themselves above y^e civil magistrate." Newton again brought out his star witness Salvian, accounting him honest enough not to "mince the matter," in order to provide evidence of the "$^<$almost$^>$ incredible difference of y^e Barbarians & Romans in those principal Christian virtues, Charity, abstinence from pleasures, & Chastity." How senseless were those who, without "considering or going about to inform themselves of what they speak," muddled the godly with the damned and condemned "for hereticks those who lived like true Christians wch hereticks never used to do, & cry up for ye Church a degerate [sic] sort of men wch lived wth hæretical pravity, giving ye best Christians to ye Devil & ye worst to God." This sort of behaviour within the corrupt Roman Empire, coupled with Athanasius's introduction of "abominably superstitious & idolatrous worship… heavily provoked God to send in ye Barbarians to invade & ruin it." Newton concluded that the situation he had depicted was "ye violent & filthy original of the present Roman Church." "Let the world judge," he pronounced, whether the same church had changed any of its ways.[26]

6. The Winds of Wrath

In Newton's account, the holding back of the winds during the prophetic half hour's silence allowed the godly anti-Trinitarians to flee to the safe havens of friendly barbarian nations. Here, they freely preached the authentic Word under the protection of sympathetic rulers and so by means of a divine irony, the Roman persecutions had a wonderful consequence for religion, "for ye Gospel could not but be further propagated among ye Barbarians by those y^t fled & ye affections of ye Barbarians stirred up to favour & patronise those of their own religion & use ye persecutions more sharply." Those who promulgated the uncorruptted religion were supported by the

Ostrogoths and Visigoths, and in his *Chronicle (Epitoma Chronicon)* Prosper of Aquitaine recorded that the army of the heathen Goth king Radagaisus actively supported the true believers.[27]

The godly remnant that remained in the West could only bemoan the arrival of the homoousians with extraordinary groaning and wailing, a feature that was unsurprising to Newton "considering how much they abominated ye religion of ye invaders." They viewed the "coequal trinity as a doctrin of many Gods," as indeed, Newton added, "‹in reality› it is ‹especially according to y^e ~~right meaning of~~ y^e ~~word God~~ language of ye Greeks›." Edicts were approved for confiscating proper places of worship, an action modern Protestant and Roman Catholic apologists defended but which Newton found as sacrilegious as anything perpetrated by Henry VIII. All this showed that the emperor Theodosius "wth his ‹ecclesiastical› Counsellours were as much better skild in ye art of persecuting then Julian ye Apostate as he was then ye other Heathen Emperors." While Theodosius oppressed true Christians with unprecedented fury, he himself lived "in ‹y^t› profuse prodigality & luxury" that justly occasioned his last, fatal illness.[28]

While Mede gave only sketchy descriptions of the barbarian invasions, Newton shone his analytical spotlight on them. Indeed, few historians before him offered anything as richly textured as he did in his unpublished writings on the Gothic invasions, and no one offered the completely sanitised account of Goths' morals and religion that he did. In the case of the first trumpet, Mede only cited two of Jerome's epistles and a brief passage from the Byzantine historian Nicephoras Gregoras, while for the second, which he dated to 410, he merely invited the interested reader to consult books 10 and 11 of Carolus Sigonius's *De Occidentali Imperio*. Similarly, he offered little by way of empirical support for his further argument that the third trumpet was sounded in 476 when the emperor Romulus Augustulus was removed from office by Odoacer. He merely admitted that Odoacer's successor, Theodoric, and those who followed him all administered the Roman Empire in a very wise manner. According to Mede, who dispatched his account in less than a page, the last of the "minor" trumpets sounded in 542, during a campaign in which the Byzantine general Belisarius attempted to recapture lost parts of the Roman Empire from the Ostrogoths. As was prophesied by the reference to the darkening of a third part of the sun and the moon in the fourth trumpet, Rome was burned and a third part of it was demolished. Deprived of glory and consular power, it became an atrophied outpost of the Duchy of Ravenna.[29]

For Newton, the historical referent of the opening trumpet and vial had to be found in the first major invasion that occurred after the start of the seventh seal, and it constituted the violent wind from the east mentioned in the relevant passage. As soon as Theodosius died (in January 395), Ruffin (Rufinus), to whom Theodosius had entrusted the tutelage of his son Arcadius, attempted to acquire the empire for himself and invited in a number of barbarian nations. Based on the short analysis in Mede, Newton argued that the first major incursion was led by Alaric, who in 395 commanded a large army of Goths and reached Athens via Macedonia and Thebes. Simultaneously, a motley crew of Huns, Alans, Ostrogoths, and others approached the Roman Empire from the other side of the Danube and along with Alaric's army they caused immense devastation along the way. These invasions brought to an end the setting up of the ten bestial horns or kingdoms, and Newton struggled to find the right words to describe their admirably vicious exploits. The Roman Empire was left in a "deplorable state" for over a decade, "the ~~enemies~~ invaders ~~acting~~ ⟨proceding⟩ not like generous conquerors but ~~striving by all means to~~ setting themselves ⟨malitiously⟩ to ~~spoil~~ yᵉ lay wast all places & do what misery they could, like ~~wolves~~ ⟨~~ravenous beasts~~⟩ ⟨furies⟩ sent in by Heaven to scourge yᵉ Romans." The astonishing ferocity of these incursions was enough, Newton concluded, "to let you see how universal & wonderfully violent this storm was at yᵉ first irruption." Alaric's army attacked many Greek regions for nearly five years and besieged the emperor Honorius (Western Roman emperor from 393–423), but then Radagaisus prepared an even greater army of Goths, Sarmatans, and Germans. At the start of the fifth century Alaric made peace with Honorius after some setbacks but the army of Radagaisus, having reached as far as Florence, was ravaged by a terrible famine and was subsequently defeated by Honorius's general Stilicho in 406.[30]

Primary sources for Newton's own increasingly global history were available in his well-thumbed copy of Baronius, but for fine-grained analysis he went to many other texts. He plunged into the sixth-century Roman historian Jordanes's *De Getarum, sive Gothorum origine et rebus gestis* to identify the relevant kingdoms that corresponded to the ten horns, along with the precise timing at which they acquired the capacity to wreak destruction on the Christian Romans. He drew extensively from the ecclesiastical history of Socrates Scholasticus, and often compared this with the accounts given by Sozomen (himself reliant in a number of places on Socrates) and Theodoret, whose history was based on a number of other writers. The pagan Greek historian Zosimus provided invaluable evidence from earlier writers about the various campaigns conducted by the Romans against the barbarians. As we have seen, in his *de Gubernatione dei*, Salvian attempted to understand why God had allowed early fifth-century Christians to be subjected to such terrible abuses by the barbarians, while the chronicles of the Byzantine historian Marcellinus Comes described the events in the Eastern Empire after the death of Valens. There was significant historical material in Jerome's *Epistles* and Augustine's *City of God*, while the brief remains of the history written by the Arian historian Philostorgius constituted what for Newton was an objective bulwark against the biases of the orthodox.[31]

The second trumpet was characterised by a western wind, that is, it delineated the terrible invasions of Rome that emanated from Britain, Spain, and France. In this prophecy a great mountain burning with fire was cast into the sea, a vision that was interpreted by Newton (based on his definitions) as "a great city consuming by war to be cast down & sink in ye midst of that people signified by ye sea." According to this trumpet, the third part of the sea became blood, and "the third part of the creatures which were in the sea, and had life, died; and the third part of the ships were destroyed." Newton argued that Rome was the city and the third part of the sea, and the horror that befell it commenced with the new set of incursions that began in 407, around the time that most of the ten kingdoms were given power. Until then there had been an "absolute serenity" to the west of Rome but now what he claimed were the chaste Vandals, Alans, Burgundians, and Alemans, along with a horde of marauding Teutonic tribes, arrived in force to decimate Gallia after being invited in by the treacherous Stilicho. Rampaging through France, the barbarians made their way down to Spain at the same time as the Picts and Scots invaded Britain. Alaric thereupon took his chance to besiege Rome, finally taking it in 410 and setting up Attalus as its emperor. The latter immediately set off to harry Honorius at Ravenna but when Attalus behaved foolishly, Alaric restored Honorius in his place.[32]

Wars raged between the Goths and Romans until 418, when a peace deal was brokered between them. Newton understood the reference in the second vial to every living soul dying in the sea as the political death of the Western Roman Empire, and with not a little *schadenfreude* at Jerome's discomfort following the fall of Rome, he remarked that "the siege of this city was ye nick of time in wch ye empire was slain as to its Monarchical form." In its place came the ten kingdoms, and the term "shipwrack" well described the devastation wreaked by the righteous invaders on the towns and

cities of the Western Roman Empire, "whose houses are analogous to ships."
The contemporary witnesses Augustine, Cassian, Salvian, and Prosper all
remarked on how these devastations had caused Christians of the West to
"murmur against heaven itself & call ⟨Gods⟩ providence & government of
the world in question." However, Newton noted, this was only the start of
the decline and fall of the Roman Empire.[33]

7. Just Torture

The Western Empire had no sooner settled down to the prospect of lasting
peace when a series of major incidents in Africa occurred in the year 427.
The fortunes of the Roman Empire now took a turn for the worse. Drawing together an impressive range of evidence, Newton deviated from Mede
by bringing forward to this year the date of the third trumpet and vial,
which concerned a southern wind. Africa, which had experienced only
minor skirmishes since the death of Theodosius but which was "as big or
almost as big as Gallia & Spain together," now "began to be invaded &
wasted wth most vehement, tedious & universal desolations." That year, the
generals Aetius and Boniface (governor of Africa), came into conflict and
the former put together an Italian army that defeated Boniface in a bloody
battle. Boniface decided to set up an alliance with the Vandals in Spain but
this turned sour when other barbarians invaded Africa and the Vandals
linked up with Alans and others to invade Mauritania. They forced Boniface
to retreat to Hippo and burned the city to a cinder in 431 after a fourteen-
month siege, Augustine himself dying there in August 430. Under Geiseric
the powerful leader of the Vandals and Alans, the Roman Empire in Africa
and in the Mediterranean islands suffered the terrible and incredible desolations detailed in the *Chronicle* of Prosper of Aquitaine. Geiseric took Carthage in 438 and Sicily two years later in a series of what Newton termed
"pyratical incursions," and embarked on what became notoriously despicable actions.[34]

The Vandals' rise to glory—as Newton saw it—culminated in the looting
of Rome and other cities in 455, "carrying into Afric ye whole treasures
thereof & consequently of ye Empire wch ye abstemious Goths had spared, &
captivating ye flower of Italy." Newton noted that they robbed the empire,
in Salvian's words, of its "vital veins and soul" but they also stole its heart,
and even "its marrow too by continually invading & preying upon all places

accessible; there remaind only a trunk wch after a little feeble struggling died of its own accord." The demise of the Western Empire was depicted in the third trumpet by the fall of the great star from heaven burning like a lamp, whose light, Newton argued, was finally extinguished when Odoacer deposed Romulus Augustulus in 476. In the year 500 Theodoric, king of the Ostrogoths, made peace with the emperors of the East and West of the Roman Empire. Although there were other lesser battles in the century, many of which were promoted by Attila the Hun and his sons, it was the Vandals who had unleashed the most havoc on the Roman Empire. For closer inspection of these incidents Newton delved deep into Victor of Vita's *History of the Vandalic Persecutions*, which became a key source of details about the Vandalic atrocities. Victor, Newton noted, added a "short hint of ye sufferings of Europe also by ye Pyratical incursions … after he has been very large in describing ye extreme miseries of Afric by ye banishments, enslavement, various tortures or slaughters of ye natives." The Hunnic wars were severe "ffor while they lasted they were ye most violent of any wars, but ⟨yet⟩ ye Vandalic was much more succesful & fatal to ye Empire." The Vandalic wars were thus those that corresponded best to the description in the third trumpet, where a third part of the waters onto which the star fell became wormwood, and "many men died of their bitterness."[35]

According to Newton's basic principles of exegesis, everything depicted in the third trumpet could be much more readily understood by comparing it with the description in the third vial. After the vial had poured, John heard the angel of the waters give thanks to God for having righteously judged those who had shed the blood of saints and prophets. Newton saw this as a reference to the vengeance exacted on the Trinitarian agents of the beast:

> This affords a third character of these times worthy of yo^e special notice, namely that these wars followed upon a sanguinary persecution of ye Church & were inflicted upon the persecutors as a righteous judgment to shed their blood who had shed the blood of saints & thereby derived upon themselves the blood of all Prop[hets] & Martyrs since ye world began.

This was the start of the Antichristian persecutions of individuals for their religious beliefs that Newton found so deplorable, and he located their origin in the times of Honorius. The persecutions occurred in the context of the Donatist schism, which was the central division within the African church and which had been in existence for about a century. Donatists held it against their opponents that the latter had given up sacred books and vessels when the great persecution of Diocletian and others had taken place. They refused to accept the validity of sacraments other than their own so that orthodox Christians had to be rebaptised when they switched allegiance to them. Honorius had instituted various laws against the African Donatists forcing them to subscribe to his religion, but he repealed these when he feared that they might side with Attalus, whom Alaric had set up against him. Once Attalus was deposed, the repeal allowing freedom of religion was revoked in 411 at a Council of African Bishops that met at Carthage, and Honorius made nonconformity subject to capital punishment.[36]

Theodosius had put out an edict for finding and killing Manichaeans (Persian Gnostics) in 382, but as far as Newton could find, Honorius's dictates were the first for killing true Christians on the grounds of their beliefs. Although they were nominally directed against the Donatists (who, Newton noted, were "Homoüsiani"), Newton argued that they included all others, "& if they were so severe against them of their own faith for disallowing their Baptism only, what would they not do to those whom they thought not only schismaticks & rebaptizers but of an hæretical faith too?" Augustine was initially opposed to the cruel oppression of the Donatists but hardened his attitude, and Newton had evidence that others "wth ye Magistrates were so hard hearted as to murder a few." From this it was "sufficient to derive upon all them that did not abominate their murder, ye blood of all saints & Prophets from ye death of Abel till now"; this was the origin and precedent "to all ye sanguinary persecutions of following ages wch have cut of some hundred thousands." All in all, he concluded, the decrees of Honorius were the first to institute "those bloody persecutions" that had been exercised by Catholics up to the present day.[37]

Newton noted that there was no barbarian nation so domineering and cruel as the Vandals, and the bloody Trinitarian persecutors were dealt a terrible blow: "God shewed his justice in a more especial manner, recompensing them wth persecution for persecution." Newton offered a long description from Victor's *History* of the terrible trials and tribulations suffered by Catholics under the persecution of the Vandals, who used the very same laws enacted by the Roman emperors against the Catholics themselves "professing that they retorted ye Roman laws upon them by way of just retribution." As Newton saw it, the barbarian persecutions enacted by the Huns and others that were so reviled by orthodox historians were seldom enacted for religious reasons and even when they were, there were extenuating circumstances. In any case, he went on, these were "but a flea-biting to what ye Vandals did." Turning the reader's attention to Victor's book, he noted that although the author "hath corrupted ye truth wth some fabulous circumstances after ye manner of ye Monks or rather taken up stories as ye Monks & other hypocritical knaves had corruptly infused them into his credulous party," the substance of his history "ᐸin generalᐳ need not be questioned." The evidence provided by Victor, despite his obvious bias, was grist to Newton's mill and in its own way as important as the immoralities recounted by Salvian. Not for the first time Newton made good use of a writer whom he viewed as a papist; all one had to do was to remove the inevitable legends and take the accounts of orthodox Christian wrongdoing at face value. Having done so, the anti-Trinitarian puritan refused to accept that any of the so-called martyrs and confessors of Victor's narrative had been persecuted for their faith alone.[38]

In justifying some of the worst atrocities against Christians in recorded literature, Newton moved as far away as it was possible to go from the conventional perspectives of both Catholic and Protestant historians. For Newton, Geiseric's half-century reign of terror constituted "one continual lash" to the wicked Catholics, so much so that "some of y^t party have not shrunk to call him Antichrist." However, Newton took his banishment of priests and other actions as a persecution for bad manners and sedition rather than for religion, since Geiseric did not prohibit the practice of their religion by any law. He *was* indeed a hideously cruel tyrant, but the insolence and perversity of the African Catholics, reported by Victor himself, had provoked him unduly and ultimately excused his actions as it did those of all the Vandals. The Africans themselves wrongly believed that they suffered for their religious beliefs and practices, but the fact that they were restrained from practicing their religion was only an unintended consequence of the Vandals' brutal persecution. All this was justice on a cosmic scale and their very real suffering, Newton concluded, "may be ᐸreckonedᐳ a just requital of their persecuting." Geiseric's son and successor Huneric was initially more lenient, calling home all the banished priests and allowing them freedom of worship. However, he soon "purged" his court and army of Homoousians, thereafter "spoiling those he found there ᐸ(on what further motive I know not)ᐳ of their estates & banishing them into Sicily & Sardinia." Worse was to come, and in what followed Newton saw that hand of God in the torture and death of large numbers of men and women in monastic orders.[39]

Under some provocation, according to Newton, Huneric caused the Trinitarians' "sacred Virgins ⟨or Nuns⟩ to be gathered together & searched by Midwives." For their "unchastity" they were strung up, weights applied to their feet "& burnt wth red hot iron plates applyed to their backs bellies paps & sides, & in their torments thus urged to confess their defilers." A number of deaths and deformities resulted from these events, and Newton admitted that the whole business was "very severe," but then one had to consider the "extreme & universal unchastness" of the African Christians. The Vandals were unable to cure this extraordinary immorality by promoting marriage among them, since "prohibition w^thout grace does but inflame ye desire." After due investigation of the nuns, five thousand priests, deacons, bishops, and monks were banished to the desert. Although the details of their crimes were concealed by Victor, Newton concluded that the nuns could not have been punished for their religion:

> I ⟨cannot but⟩ suspect it was ⟨chiefly if not solely⟩ ye result of their confession. The old men among them were once young enough, & though Victor minces ye matter, yet he tells us ye Vandals examined ye Nuns to find occasion of animadverting upon ye Clergy, & amidst so many tortured defiled ones tortured to confess it's impossible but confessions must be made. And why not (some at least) true as well as fals? Yet all are saints wth Victor. Not an ill confession, not a stain to his church, not a crime ⟨particularly⟩ acknowledged ⟨in his own party⟩ in all his history, ~~Nothing there to be met~~ w^th ~~but piety & holiness~~ ⟨Nothing there but Saints,⟩ Not a punishment be it for what it will but makes a martyr or a confessor if inflicted by a Vandal, & it shal [sic] go hard too if his saintship be not recommended by a miracle or two.

Salvian had demonstrated that the African Catholics were the most depraved people "in all ye extremely wicked Empire," being "almost w^thout exception" prone to lechery, lying, deceit, violence, insolence, pride, malice, and injustice. All these "crimes" were enough, Newton thought, to provide the occasion for Victor's martyrs to suffer at the hands of the Vandals, for it was hardly likely that such brutal people would punish only the innocent and spare the guilty.[40]

Huneric gave the remaining clergy a chance to prove their faith from Scripture but "cavilling about superiority & ye language they should dispute in, & urging to have ye multitude brought in, & making tumultuous clamors," they were beaten up and exiled to Corsica and other places. It was at this point that Huneric enacted against their creators the very Roman laws that had been used against the true Church. Newton claimed that these contained no "sanguinary punishment" except against "remiss Judges," but they were strict and involved violent coercion against resisting rebels, even against those who merely used "saucy deriding language, wch they might think religious gallantry." This insolence was not the sort of behaviour tolerated by any conqueror, Newton opined, and it was the Africans' stubborn resistance that gave rise to the Vandals' bloody activities, "seing Victor could produce no law for shedding their blood or tormenting them for their religion." Just as Athanasius and his followers had been properly punished for sedition a century earlier, so the Vandals merely punished the Africans for civil offences. Huneric died but his successors Gundabund and Thrasabund continued to harass the Catholic clergy after initially showing them leniency. Newton again saw the general hand of providence at work in the fact that the Vandals continued to use the Catholics' own laws against them, God "permitting the restaurations of ye Roman African Church, as it were, that they might by iterated persecutions suffer o're & o're what they inflicted once upon the true Church."[41]

The Vandalic Empire was overthrown by the Byzantine general Belisarius in 533 and 534 but Newton followed Mede in locating the onset of the fourth trumpet to the great plague of Rome and the Battle of Mucellium of 542. The main scenes of action were to the north of Rome, and thus it fitted well with the prophecy of the last, northern wind in the fourth trumpet. In this prophecy a third of the sun, moon, and stars was smitten and darkened, "and the day shone not for a third part of it, and the night likewise." For Newton this represented the "utter extinction of the remaining light of ye western Empire" that had been relit under the rule of the Goths and was the beginning of the end of the Evil Empire. God had saved his worst for this occasion and "it was accomplished by ye direst desolations that (I beleive) ever [a] nation felt, God reserving his most grievous scourge for ye fountain of Apostacy & ye most grievous part of that scourge for ye last place to try ye utmost before he would give over an incorrigible insensible people." After a number of incidents, Rome was besieged again by the Lombards in 577 and in terms of sheer wanton destruction they even outdid the Goths: "<partly by> these desolations <but chiefly by storms & fiery meteors> ye city was so wasted y^t ever since it hath scarce been ye 10th part of what it was before." The demise of Rome was now absolute, and Newton repeated Mede's lament about her downfall: "from being Queen of y^e world degraded to I know not what ignoble Dukedome, & compel'd to serve under Ravenna wch formerly served under her, & (O darkness!) even to pay tribute to y\e Exarchs presiding there." By means of a lengthy examination of the period of darkness mentioned in this trumpet, Newton justified the view that its end came in 607, a short time after the Lombardic wars ended, and the year when "that hermaphroditique luminary," the bishop of Rome, professed a universal bishopric.[42]

The fourth vial, whose contents confirmed those of the equivalent trumpet, described men "scorched with great heat" who "blasphemed the name of God" and "repented not to give him glory." Although the barbarians' efforts in the fifth and sixth centuries had practically extinguished the Roman Empire, Newton saw an intensity of Roman Catholic idolatry. Now the Catholic faithful worshipped the saints with even more devotion than before, the increased fervour being promoted by the devotion of Pope Gregory the Great. Gregory, Newton predictably noted, "being a monk was much inclined to superstition," but he was nevertheless a learned, diligent, and skilled man of action, and remodelled Catholic worship into something like its current form. On account of his visible humility and "pretence of miracles," he gained immense credit with his flock. Newton observed that the ten kingdoms that constituted the first trumpet had by this time united in the same faith and held the pope to be the common bishop of their churches: "thus the ten kings began to be of one mind & to agree & give their power & strength & kingdom to the Beast." The church apostate was now vividly painted in Revelation as the filthy whore (Rev. 17:2-4) that was drunk with the blood of saints and "arrayed in purple & scarlet & decked with gemms, who lives deliciously & sits a Queen upon seven mountains & upon the ten horned Beast in spiritually barren wilderness & commits fornication with the kings of the earth & makes the nations drunk with the wine of her fornication." The perversion of the true faith up to this point, Newton cautioned, no matter how bad it was, was nevertheless only a foretaste of what was to come.[43]

8. Creatures from the Pit

For Mede and others, the events portrayed by the first two "woe-trumpets" (i.e., the fifth and sixth) took place on a much grander scale, since they depicted warfare on a global front between Christian and Islamic forces. In the fifth trumpet (Rev. 9:1-11), a star from heaven unlocked the door to the bottomless pit and unleashed smoke that darkened the sun and air. From the

smoke came locusts that were told to hurt no vegetation but only those
without the seal of God on their foreheads. Granted the stinging power of
scorpions, the locusts were given the capacity by Satan to torment these
men for a period of five months. Mede's association of the rise of Islam with
the objects of the fifth and sixth trumpets was a stock interpretation within
the Protestant apocalyptic tradition, and few interpeters disagreed. The
smoke rising from the pit was conventionally associated with the advent of
Islam, the "locusts" with scorpion-like tails being the Saracens. Mede's historical analysis of these periods was more detailed than was the case in the
first four trumpets, and he drew on Elmacinus's (Ibn al-Amid's) *History of the
Saracen Empire* for more accurate dating. Throughout, he justified his interpretations by reference to Achmet, and in the case of the locusts he also
deployed a learned admixture of philological expertise and natural history.
He devoted a number of pages to their life-cycle before concluding that the
core of the period covered by the fifth trumpet lasted from 830 to 980, which
were the prophetic five months (i.e., 150 prophetic days) described in Revelation 9:5 and 10. Since the period of five months was mentioned twice, he
doubled the period and assigned the approximate total period of Saracenical
dominance to the years 750–c. 1055, starting with the Abbasid caliphate and
ending with the moment when Togrul, king of the Turks, captured Baghdad. Almost as an afterthought, and with protestations of exegetical humility,
he brought the start of the trumpet forward to 630, since this was when the
Saracens had begun to extend their empire.[44]

As we saw in the previous chapter, for Newton the woe-trumpets introduced "a new scene of things." Now there was a dramatic escalation of the
apostasy, the rise of a new false religion characterised both by the appearance
of the first woe (Rev. 8:13; 9:12) and by the final ascent of the beast following
his heroic rise from the bottomless pit (Rev. 9:2; 11:7; 17:8). The ancient interpreters recorded by Achmet had concurred that locusts meant soldiers and
by extension armies, while smoke denoted the vast numbers of followers of
this "new" religion. As before, Newton drew the core of his interpretation
from Mede and noted that the doubled reference to the period of five
months made 300 years in real time. He even copied down Mede's observation that he could not remember anywhere else in prophecy where the
Scriptures used the technique of repetition, and that this must therefore
imply some underlying mystery. For dating Newton's writing in this area, it
is surely significant that in 1680 he bought Elmacinus's work on the Sar-
acnes but for supporting evidence he also scoured Gothofredus's notes on

Tertullian, Pococke's translation of Abul Pharaij's life of Muhammed, and Josephus on the genealogy of the Jews.[45]

The Islamic tenor of this prophecy was as obvious to Newton as it was to other Protestant interpreters. Going beyond Mede, he determined that the proper origin of this period was to be found in the year that Muhammed found his "pretended vocation" as a prophet, namely in 609. The prophet was thus the star from heaven who began to open the pit and let out the smoke (in the year 612), while a decade later his arming of his supporters was the appearance of the locusts. Moreover, the fact that he and the ensuing "race" of Caliphs were "Princes both spirituall and temporall in ye strictest sense" pointed to his identity as both the angel of the bottomless pit and king of the locusts. In general, these more recent periods held little interest for Newton, and although his dating differed from Mede's, he relied heavily on Mede's analysis, especially in his treatment of the angel's name, Abaddon in Revelation 9:11. The end of the empire was dated by Newton to 936, when the caliphate lost most of its temporal power. Hence the entire empire lasted 300 years from its inception in Damascus in 635, excepting the last year; this came to twice five months in prophetic terms.[46]

For Mede the sixth trumpet sounded in 1057, the date when Togrul had been given sovereign power by the Abbasid caliph Cajimus Biemrilla (al-Qa'im bi-amri 'llah), and the prophetic text straightforwardly depicted the increasing power of Islam. It described how four angels bound in the river Euphrates were freed so that they could prepare "for an hour, and a day, and a month, and a year, for to slay the third part of men." Horsemen with dazzling breastplates sat on horses whose heads were like lions and whose mouths "issued fire and smoke and brimstone," and set about to slay those who had not repented of their fornications, idolatry, and sorcery (Rev. 9:13-21). In their mode of dress, the horsemen shared certain typological affinities with the locusts while the serpentine tails of their steeds showed their affinity with the old serpent, the devil. Mede followed most of his predecessors in identifying the subject of the trumpet as the Turks. The Turkish Empire subsequently divided into four parts (cf. Rev. 9:15), growing incredibly quickly in the century after the trumpet was sounded. After a prophetic day, month, and a year, or 396 years in real time (Rev. 9:15), the Turks were to destroy other empires, and the prophecy was evidently fulfilled by the sacking of Constantinople in 1453. In an extended interpretation of Revelation 9:18 Mede argued that the fire, smoke, and brimstone referred to the use of gunpowder by Mehmet against Constantinople.[47]

For Newton, the curtailing of the caliphate rule did not constitute the end of the fifth trumpet and vial, and he extended the events described by the vision over two hundred years beyond Mede's date. After the end of the locusts' raging in 936, he wrote, "ye world continued in ye hands of ye Saracens for many yeares though not under ye dominion of ye Chalifa but broken into many temporal kingdoms." Although the Turks now created a number of potent sultanies, the caliphate retained power in Baghdad from the middle of the twelfth century. The origin of the Turkish Empire also agreed with prophecy in arising from "a quaternion of kingdoms seated upon Euphrates ‹in a square position›," since (as Newton learned from Mede) that shape characterised the relative positions of the chief cities in the four sultanies of Baghdad, Mesopotamia (based at Mosul), Maredin, and Syria (based at Aleppo, the previous seat of the dynasty, for the sake of the square). Newton's diagram went beyond Mede's crude tabulation (Plate 19) of the four kingdoms in order to present a detailed representation of the area, though he found it impossible to mould the locations of the cities into a perfect square (Plate 20). The end of the fifth trumpet/vial had to be marked by some major event, and Newton searched for a date around the middle of the thirteenth century. In an earlier draft, he dated the start of the sixth trumpet to 1260 or 1261 but ultimately settled on the year 1258, when Hulacu (Houlagou) the Tartar took Baghdad and ended the rule of the Abbasid caliphate within the city.[48]

It was on the ruins of Constantinople, Newton noted, that the Turks founded the great empire of his own time. Their pillaging of the Byzantine Empire, once a third the size of the entire Christian world, thus corresponded to the "third part of men" killed by the fire, smoke, and brimstone in the sixth trumpet. The rest of the trumpet condemned those who continued to worship ghosts and idols of gold, silver, brass, stone, and wood "which neither can see nor hear nor walk," and who did not repent of their sorceries, fornications, and thefts. Although the primary victims of Ottoman power were the remnants of the old Eastern Empire, Newton claimed that these sinful activities unambiguously referred to the Catholic Church, since over the last few hundred years none but papists had worshipped ghosts and idols in what remained of the Roman Empire. Trotting out the conventional list of popish crimes, he remarked that they were also uniquely murderous, persecuting "those they call heretiques" on a daily basis, and even setting up the "bloody inquisition." Their miracles were mere sorceries "& their *piæ fraudes* but φαρμακείαι inchanted love potions ‹of ye whore› whereby she intoxicates ye understandings of men." As for fornication, Newton pointed to the immoral activities of other

Europeans, particularly papists "who blush not to incourage it by tollerating publiq[ue] stews." Despite this, *all* Christians were guilty of greed and theft since the "heaping up of riches" was the "main designe of almost all men" without caring how they acquired it. Such men were "so universally addicted to overreaching & all kinds of dishonesty" that the Turks believed Christianity to embody greed.[49]

Newton concluded that the reference to the year, month, day, and hour during which the four angels were to "slay" a third part of men in the sixth trumpet depicted the duration of the Turkish Empire and its torment of the Byzantine Empire. The dissolution of this empire could be dated without any trouble to the sacking of its Metropolis in May 1453, and according to prophetic time one should add 391 years to this date to obtain the end of Turkish rule in Constantinople. In the only occasion in his early prophetic writings where Newton essayed a date for some specific future event, he calculated 1844 as the date when the Turkish emperor would lose control over Constantinople and convey his seat to Judæa. This event, he noted, was foretold in the closing verse of Daniel 11, where the prophet stated that a great king "shall plant the tabernacles of his palace between the seas in the glorious holy mountain; yet he shall come to his end, and none shall help him." Newton briefly noted that at the onset of the seventh trumpet and vial, the kingdoms of this Earth would be turned over to God and Christ, the former passing judgement on the good and the evil, and the latter ruling nations with a rod of iron. The little horn of Daniel, and the two-horned beast or false prophet would also be destroyed. This however lay in the future, and he ended his exposition of the sixth vial and trumpet by remarking "since that concerns yᵉ time to come, it will be better to return to yᵉ ⟨Seales &⟩ Trumpets already explained." Although Newton claimed that it would bring prophecy into disrepute to speculate about future events and dates, as I show in the following chapter, he did not shy away from discussing in detail the images in Revelation that referred to future events.[50]

9. The Business of Interpretation

Newton's attempt to understand history through prophecy demanded a thorough knowledge of how the prophetic images cohered, along with a command of large amounts and types of historical data. In accordance with his prophetic "rules," in his exposition he first determined the correct order of the images, and then he "applied" this arrangement to history. In time, as the lower level rules permitted, he aligned the most significant parts of prophecy with the most notable events in history. To what extent, however, was he offering an original account, and to what extent was he basing his analysis on Mede's *Clavis* and his *Commentary*? Newton left few clues to his intellectual debts, though once or twice he explicitly mentioned his dependence on Mede's approach, thereby placing himself within the tradition that Mede had allegedly founded. Accordingly, he based his system on Mede's synchronisms and was heavily reliant on the latter's dates and arguments. Indeed, the extent to which he used Mede's ideas and language, a feature of his work that is only obvious from close scrutiny of the sources, is striking. He copied verbatim sentences and entire paragraphs, complete with Mede's rhetorical ploys and self-conscious admissions of epistemic humility. At times, his texts appear to be a series of unacknowledged excerpts from Mede's works, interspersed with lengthy extracts from primary sources.

To claim that Newton's earliest prophetic work was a glorified series of notes would, however, be to miss the deeply original performance he was undertaking. He made both subtle and substantial changes to Mede's core doctrines, synchronising the vials and trumpets, and breaking the tight link between the forty-two months and the period of the Great Apostasy. He extended and generalised Mede's sketchy rules of procedure, and, based on his rich account of how various "collateral" images might enrich one another, he vastly expanded the range of synchronisms that Mede had offered. In applying these synchronisms to history, he shared many of Mede's assumptions about the unrivalled guilt of Roman Catholicism, but he brought to his task a very different view of what counted as idolatry. Everything of note happened in the fourth and fifth centuries after the birth of Christ, while nothing of any prophetic significance had happened in his own era. These historical views were intimately bound up with, if they did not generate, the major changes that Newton made to Mede's scheme. In line with his reworking of Mede's synchronisms, what strikes the modern reader is the vast evidential support he offered for his interpretations in comparison with Mede and others. All this material was marshalled into an argument to support a general position that by the late 1680s was as radical and complex as anything offered by his contemporaries. In the light of this spectacularly original work, those passages where he simply translated Mede's text and inserted them into his narrative are minor and insignificant.

How did this treatment of theory and evidence tally with his procedures elsewhere? In the *Principia*, Newton separated his problems into mathematical and physical aspects, starting with a series of "definitions" and "axioms" (the Laws of Motion). Using idealised mathematically precise situations involving point masses and different force laws, he dealt first with simple cases and then generalised them to more complicated situations involving two and then many bodies. The assumption of universal attraction meant that no body in this idealised situation could ever move in a perfectly straight line or an exact conic section. However, deviations from these counterfactual situations provided evidence about the magnitude of many the forces acting on any given object at a particular moment. This approach could inform the investigator about forces in the real world, which was the topic of the third book of the *Principia*. Drawing on a number of independent phenomena, such as tides, comets, and the shape of the earth, Newton termed the general force that operated in the universe (the physical manifestation of generalised attraction) "universal gravitation"—though he would not positively say what the physical nature of this force was. As George Smith has pointed out, by producing data that indicated deviations from expected motions, Newton laid down a novel and highly original way of mutually fine-tuning theory and data. Increasingly sophisticated empirical evidence from a host of independent sources could be fed back into the mathematical theory and then tested again against both well-known and unexpected phenomena—thereby corroborating the existence of the general force in question.[51]

Some features of Newton's working practice in prophecy seem to be similar to this approach. The prophetic tradition offered up a ready-made division between the theoretical treatment of the images and the empirical data drawn from history. Newton first construed the "internal order" of prophecy in line with the Medean tradition, and in accordance with his own rules. He began by stating a series of "definitions," "rules," and "propositions" or "positions," from which he derived first simple, and then more complex propositions—all of which built on and enriched his basic synchronisms. This method did not, of course, correspond to the chronological order in which he had originally tackled the subject. Newton did not, that is, deal first with the images and then apply them to "innocent" pre-existing historical data. That said, as we saw in his conversations with More, he was able to deal with the theoretical order of the visions without recourse to empirical data. His system was further revisable and could always be enriched with new ostensibly independent images or passages that refined and bolstered his synchronisms. Indeed, his major treatise of the late 1680s, which differed from his earlier effort in many key respects, contained no historical references but constituted a more complex scheme than that produced by any of his contemporaries.

However, the most significant aspect of Newton's early prophetic research was the "intertwining" of his theoretical structure with his use of data. It is hard to think why he would have initially launched himself into the literature of the early church if he had not already made up his mind that the doctrine of the Trinity lay at the heart of the corruption of Christianity. With these preconceptions, he began to seriously examine the "internal" logical order of the apocalyptic visions, using Mede's scheme as a template. Once he had developed his general prophetic scheme, he foraged in the literature for more detailed evidence that would support it. As we have seen, he amassed a vast amount of often very detailed and exact information, all of which helped him fine-tune his prophetic scheme. Having adduced and possible synchronised another image or two, he would then return to the literature to find supporting information. And so on. Although he was of course working in two entirely separate genres and disciplines, there are prima facie similarities between the way he adduced data in his work on prophecy and the exact sciences. There was no metaphysics, and no contamination by the imagination—just a dynamic interaction between reason and experience, that is, between a continually enriched method and an expanding pile of increasingly detailed empirical data. In each case, his analytical framework guided the collation of special evidence from an ocean of available information—which in turn corroborated and refined a highly original theory that was essentially irrefutable.

9

The End of the World

Although Newton steadfastly refused to relate prophetic visions to events in his own time, the political and religious contexts in which he wrote altered dramatically in the late 1680s. In the early spring of 1685, the Roman Catholic Duke of York became James II of England, and thus chief defender of the Church of England. Later in the year Louis XIV revoked the Edict of Nantes, accelerating the flight of its Protestant Huguenots to a number of neighbouring countries. In Europe, Louis threatened to expand his borders eastwards, though he was thwarted by an alliance (the League of Augsburg) between the Protestant Dutchman William of Orange and the Catholic Holy Roman Emperor, Leopold I. For many Englishmen, James's absolutist tendencies constituted a clear and present threat to the Protestant foundations of the nation. In particular, he made strenuous efforts to impose Roman Catholics into positions in Magdalen College, Oxford, having already attempted to have a Benedictine monk awarded a master of arts degree by Sidney Sussex College, Cambridge. The arrival of William of Orange as a miraculous saviour at the end of 1688, and the ensuing Glorious Revolution seemed to have prophetic significance, and a number of apocalyptical exegetes put pen to paper. For a short period, Revelation became a topic of feverish conversation between senior divines and laymen. Some claimed that the Revolution constituted a partial fulfilment of the rising of the witnesses, while others discussed the likelihood that it was the pouring of one of the vials of wrath on popery. In any case, it seemed to augur bad times ahead for the pope and his religion.[1]

It was now that Newton decided to radically recast his understanding of prophecy although, true to form, he made no reference in these writings to the extraordinary events that were taking place around him. For once, this was not because he had decided to withdraw from society and, indeed, in the spring of 1687, he left the sanctuary of his college rooms and decided to do public battle with Roman Catholicism. Newton's draft notes for his public defence of the rights of Sidney Sussex College show that his own motivation was religious rather than political, although at this point these two facets were as inextricably interlinked for him as they were for many other Protestants. The start of this process overlapped with the completion in the spring of 1687 of Book 3 of the *Principia*, which, to his later chagrin, was dedicated to James II. The immediate cause of Newton's going public, however, was James's efforts to place Catholics into various official positions that they were otherwise prevented from enjoying as a result of the Test Act. To ensure that lay or clergy preachers did not say or write anything that might embarrass James or his religion, he restored the much-hated Ecclesiastical Commission in July 1686. Amongst other things, the Commission claimed the power to alter the statutes of ecclesiastical institutions that it deemed to have contravened the orders of the king. On these grounds, the Commission was given wide-ranging powers to regulate and supervise the universities, and to revise their statutes and even to draw up new ones where they were deemed to be insufficient or non-existent. Although monarchs had traditionally used their power to dispense with college statutes and appoint senior members by mandate, James used his power specifically to place Catholics into key positions, concentrating on Magdalen College.[2]

1. Out of the Closet

On 5 April 1687 James issued a mandamus (a judicial writ from a superior court) on behalf of Anthony Farmer, a graduate of Trinity College, Cambridge, allowing him to assume the presidency of Magdalen College, Oxford. In what was to be the start of active resistance by university members, the college refused to accept the mandamus as legally binding and ten days later they defiantly elected John Hough. Over the next year a number of Catholics became fellows, and in the wake of the Glorious Revolution, the Magdalen College affair became one of the most famous examples of James's abuse of his prerogative. Nevertheless, even before it began, the king had attempted to place a Roman Catholic into a Cambridge college. On 5 November 1686 Edward Spence of Jesus College had given a speech that reflected adversely on the pope and the Catholic Church. He was reported to the authorities by a fellow of Caius College, Joshua Basset, and was forced to publicly retract his comments at the Senate House. Basset, who was described by contemporaries as a "mongrel papist," was rewarded for his loyalty on 3 January 1687 when James issued a mandate to admit him as master of Sidney Sussex College. Having survived an attempt by fellows to force him to swear an oath against popery, heresies, superstition, and error, he convinced the king to issue a mandate for a Benedictine monk, Alban Francis, to be admitted for the degree of master of arts without taking the Oath of Supremacy. Faced with such provocation, representatives from both "houses" of the university senate delivered their view of the affair to the university vice chancellor, John Peachell, on 22 February. When Peachell conveyed the university's opinion that the mandamus was illegal to the king's ministers, it received a stony response. The senate convened again on 11 March, and Newton, who had asked Humphrey Newton to copy out a circulated letter (dated 19 February) raising awareness of the affair, was elected to represent the Non-Regent or "Lower" House (an assembly of senior members of the university) in the business. Along with Humphrey Babington and six other representatives, he was ordered by the Ecclesiastical Commission to appear before them on 21 April.[3]

According to Charles Montagu, Newton's friend and later patron, Spence's recantation caused a great stir at Trinity. Although he was in the throes of finishing Book 3 of the *Principia*, Newton could not have been amused, and he was exercised by the Alban Francis case as soon as it became known. The letter copied by Humphrey called upon stout fellows to be courageous and to rely on the law of the land, for if one papist were permitted to have an MA there would soon be a hundred, and thereafter they could elect the university MPs. While some Trinity fellows like William Lynnet advised that the mandamus not be resisted, Newton and others felt differently. He must have spoken up both at the meeting on 11 March, and at a gathering of the delegates before their appearance on 21 April. At the latter there was apparently a motion to admit Francis to a degree—provided that it did not constitute a precedent—which was put before the delegates to sign. Newton later told John Conduitt that although everyone else agreed to this compromise, it stuck in his craw and he got up from the table. Having walked round it a few times, he turned to the beadle who had been sent by the university to be present at the meeting and said "this is giving up the question, so it is said the Beadle ⟨why do not you⟩ go and speak to it." Newton spoke his mind, desiring that the paper be shown to the university council and then to Heneage Finch, recently dismissed as solicitor-general by James. According to Newton, Finch "was of S^r I's opinion, w^{ch}

the Chancellor of Ely & all the rest then came into." When the delegates
appeared in April before the leader of the Commission, the "hanging
judge" and Lord Chancellor George Jeffreys, the latter harangued Peachell
with typical bluster but allowed the delegates a further six days to prepare
their case.[4]

In one short essay that must have been written in preparation for the
meeting on 21 April, Newton urged his colleagues to respect the laws of the
land guaranteeing the religious statutes of the college and warned them not
to trust to the bare promise of the monarch. This would be even more
unwise than giving up the laws that protected an Englishman's liberty and
property simply because the sovereign desired it and promised to safeguard
them. If they went ahead and removed those laws defending Protestantism
then, Newton said, "tis becaus wee have less zeale for <o^e> God & religion
then for liberty & property o^e civil rights." In being party to abrogating the
obligations of the Test Act, they would absolve the king from his promise to
safeguard the Protestant religion, and it would be an easy matter for him to
revive old laws and customs that would pave the way for the reintroduction
of Catholicism. Newton also noted that the fellows had taken the oaths of
allegiance and supremacy to defend royal authority against foreign power. If
they did anything to dilute this key defence against being enslaved to the
pope, he wrote, "we shall be no truer to <these> o^e oaths then a Dutchman
would be to his who should one day sweare to do his utmost endeavour to
keep out ye sea & ye next day cut ye banks wth his own hands." Some might
have ill-advisedly made promises against these oaths, but Newton reminded
them that they were not binding.[5]

In another important text written on the legal status of the king's dispensing power, Newton reworked a series of notes on arguments made by
counsel in *Godden v. Hales*, a test suit tried at King's Bench in May 1686 on
the legality of the king's dispensing power. Stacked in the monarch's favour,
the judiciary had found in favour of his right to dispense with certain laws
(the Test Act in the case of Hales) in a wide variety of cases. In the first place,
Newton argued that a monarch could never dispense with a law made for
securing the liberty or property of the people. His second, and much more
original argument, concerned the issue of "necessity," recently invoked by
Stuart monarchs on the pretext of defending the interests and security of
the people. Although counsel for the Crown in *Godden v. Hales* had argued
that the king needed to dispense with the effects of the Test Act in order
to create a powerful army, Newton argued that the king could not claim

necessity in cases where the sole basis for the decision was his own "will & contrivance." The king could not be bound by necessity if he could have called a parliament but failed to do so, since Parliament could create a new law to deal with a situation if it saw fit. This came to the crux of the matter, which was that a dispensation based on alleged necessity could not be valid against the will and consent of the people. Newton listed examples of the exercise of arbitrary power by Stuart kings that had been based on alleged necessity, but he concluded that none of these had in fact been legal. In the first place, the king could not be the sole judge of whether an action was necessary, and indeed both the king and the people had to decide that an action was necessary before the operation of a law was suspended. Second, it was necessity itself that justified acting outside the bounds of law, and it ipso facto created dispensation from the law. Hence, the authority to break a law came from the necessity itself rather than from the king's fictitious prerogative in such cases.[6]

At the meeting of 27 April the best argument put forward by the delegates was that the power to confer degrees was not part of the spiritual authority of the university and thus did not concern the Commission. The latter considered this point for some time, and Newton and the others were ordered to return on 7 May. On this occasion, Peachell was asked difficult questions by Jeffreys about a number of previous cases where the institution had awarded an MA despite it not being technically qualified to do so. The delegates returned for the Commission's decision on 12 May and in preparation for the meeting they created their own "Answer" in response to the questions posed to Peachell. Newton had a substantial hand in formulating this document, and in one addition, he emphasised that Peachell and the senate delegates had acted in unison in resisting the mandate. The messengers, he wrote, had felt themselves obliged to contact the vice chancellor out of concern for their religion, which had been "established & supported by ye laws they are commanded to infringe." Papists and Protestants could not "subsist happily nor long together" in the same university, and if the fountains of Protestantism in those institutions dried up, "ye streams hitherto diffused thence throughout ye Nation will must soon fall of." It was their religion and church, and not their preferments that "men of conscience" wished to preserve, Newton stressed, and he added that if that religion "must fall they implore this mercy that it may fall by ye hands of others." A tantalizing reference to the "great wickedness" that the delegates might be forced to commit was broken off in mid-sentence. In the short term, however, their protestations were to no avail, and on 12 May, they were told that the mandate for Alban Francis was legal. Although Peachell suffered personal vilification, they were collectively lambasted for their "sly insinuations" about royal authority. With customary bravado, Jeffreys swept them out of the room with the scriptural warning that they sin no more lest something worse befall them.[7]

2. The Future State

The publication of the *Principia* in the summer of 1687 would soon bring him extraordinary fame, but behind the scenes, Newton was engaged in what he took to be a far more important issue, namely that of thwarting the efforts of James II to subvert the Protestant underpinnings of the two English universities. To some extent, the Oxford and Cambridge cases were intertwined, and in order to help the Magdalen cause, Trinity College, Cambridge, colleagues such as Laughton, Babington, and Pulleyn helpfully testified that while a Fellow of Trinity, Anthony Farmer had acted in a disgraceful manner at a dancing school. Newton may well have helped Laughton provide other information relevant to the Magdalen case. Representatives from Magdalen were ordered to appear before the Commission in June, and although the senior fellow Henry Fairfax attempted to have the college's case taken seriously by the commissioners, Jeffreys treated them with predictable contempt. Nevertheless, as it turned out, the evidence of Farmer's immorality that was sent from Cambridge helped do the trick. At the end of July the Commission decided that he was not fit for office, and Jeffreys lambasted him for being "a very bad man." Newton kept in touch with the Oxford events over the following year and had a number of documents relevant to the case copied by Humphrey.[8]

Not long after his return to Cambridge following his grilling by Jeffries, Newton embarked on a major recasting of his prophetic theory, in which he found new arguments to show that Roman Catholicism was the Great Apostasy. In one lengthy treatise from this period he offered an extended analysis of the prophetic End of the World. However, unlike other interpreters, he did not relate his account to the momentous political events that were then taking place, nor, in keeping with his cautious attitude to prophetic exegesis, did he indulge in speculation about either when, or in exactly what way specific future events would take place. Nevertheless, he did

believe that it was possible to discern from prophecy the general characteristics of the end times, and he had a duty to put the relevant visions in a
logical and chronological order. As before, he was heavily reliant on Joseph
Mede's treatment of prophecy in his *Clavis Apocalyptica* and *Commentarius*,
though as ever he shaped the Medean template in his own way. The basic
chronology of these events was accepted by most Protestant interpreters
working in the millennialist tradition. The Jews would return to Palestine
and convert to Christianity following the general preaching of the gospel.
A great tribulation would ensue, which would involve both a political and
a natural catastrophe, and the Great Apostasy would come to an end. While
the devil was locked up for the millennium, Christ would rule with the
resurrected saints and martyrs in the New Jerusalem. At the end of this
period, the devil would be released to lead the forces of Gog and Magog
against the righteous, but Satan and his entourage would be destroyed by
fire from heaven. Following this there would be the Second Resurrection at
the Day of Judgement.[9]

There were serious problems concerning the order of events around the
millennium, since it was generally accepted that there were two judgements,
two resurrections, and two conflagrations. Revelation 20:4-6 indicated that
there was a judgement at the start of the millennium, after which the godly
martyrs were resurrected and reigned as priests of God and Christ for a
thousand years. Revelation 20:11-15 told how at the end of the millennium,
on Judgement Day, the dead were raised again to be assessed by God according to their works. Those who failed the test were condemned to the
lake of fire to be tormented forever along with the devil, the beast, and the
false prophet. There were also two accounts of destruction by fire. Revelation 20:9 indicated that the forces of Gog and Magog would be devoured
by fire after the millennium, but 2 Peter 3:10 referred to the time of Christ's
Second Coming, when the heavens would pass away, the elements would
melt with fervent heat, and the earth and its works would be burned up.
Numerous other texts throughout the Old and New Testaments could be
interpreted as relevant to these passages.[10]

The apparent redundancy of the two judgements was a perennial problem for exegetes. Mede ruthlessly wielded Occam's razor and reduced them
to a single judgement, a move that required him to extend the judging
process throughout the whole of the thousand years bounded by the first
and last resurrections. Hence the battle of Gog and Magog had to be brought
forward to the end of the millennium, at which time Antichrist would be

released from the pit and then defeated. Mede was not afraid to turn to
Jewish sources for further insight into the chronology of the end times,
though he thought that the Jews were somewhat vague on the fine distinctions between the two different resurrections. To defend his account of the
Day of Judgement, he noted that the rabbi David Kimchi had interpreted
Isaiah 2:12-22 to refer to the days of the Messiah, when the Lord would
pass judgement on the wicked and mete out an appropriate punishment.
Mede also argued there must be two different sorts of people alive in the
millennium, the first group of which would comprise the martyrs and saints
who had shed their blood for God. They would be raised at the First Resurrection and would enjoy a physical existence while ruling in heaven. A
second group of mortals, who had not worshipped the Whore of Babylon,
would be composed of the converted Jews who would survive the initial
conflagration by being raptured up to heaven or into the air (referring to
1 Thess. 4:15-17).[11]

Since the prophetic End of the World appeared to be nigh, or at least not
that far off, it was a good time to put pen to paper in order to account for the
great conflagration that would precede the millennium. In early 1687 Thomas
Burnet began the second volume of his *Telluris Theoria Sacra*, this time dealing with the forthcoming destruction of the globe, and he had finished his
work by May 1688. In it, he attacked those who offered allegorical interpretations of the conflagration and instead he looked for plausible physical
causes by which the event might be accomplished. The existence of volcanoes in Italy offered a gift to those like Burnet who wanted to show that
Rome would be at the epicentre of the conflagration. Years earlier, Mede
had limited the extent of the conflagration to within two hundred miles of
the papal territories, so that the mortals would have a safe abode while the
fires burned. Henry More had pointed to the wide distribution of volcanoes
in Italy and elsewhere and identified vulcanism as one of many probable
natural causes by which the world might be destroyed. Burnet argued that
the terrible fire would begin in Rome in about two centuries' time. Following
the successive explosions of volcanoes and collapse of subterranean caverns,
much of the surface of the planet would be reduced to cinders. This was a
physical melting of the old one in order to prepare the new, the entire process
directed by Providence but achieved by natural causes. In the more prominent religious and political component of the text, he disparaged the spiritual condition of the current world. He decried the lowly state and status of

holy men and looked forward to a new world where procreating saints would rule in the Holy Lands as kings *on Earth*. However, at the end of the millennium there would be a process by which the earth was absorbed into a mass of fire and ultimately turned into a star.[12]

At the same time that Burnet was composing the second part of his text, his friend Drue Cressener was writing what would also be a highly influential apocalyptic treatise. Like Burnet, Cressener had studied under More at Christ's College and in February 1688 he made the stunning prediction that the following year would be a crucial moment in the recovery of the true Church. In the spring of 1688 Cressener had received the second part of Burnet's work in manuscript, but he did not adopt Burnet's physico-theological approach. Indeed, he was more indebted to the work of the exiled French Protestant Pierre Jurieu, whose Francocentric account of the prophetic relevance of the modern age was itself heavily reliant on Mede's scheme. Cressener rehearsed Mede's argument that the three and a half days of the death of the witnesses meant the same number of years and added this figure to the date of the Revocation of the Edict of Nantes (of October 1685), which he took to be the moment when the true religion was suppressed by the popish beast.[13]

For this reason if for nothing else, the Glorious Revolution, which occurred almost exactly three and a half years after the witnesses had been killed, came at a marvellous moment for Cressener. He published his treatise and touted his own interpretive acumen in a dedicatory epistle to the new king at the end of March 1689. He included a number of testimonials from Burnet and others, attesting to the fact that the work had been written long before the miraculous appearance of William of Orange. Cressener now expected William to fulfil his prophetic mission by taking on the Roman Catholic beast in its lair, thereby bringing liberty of worship to oppressed European Protestants. He justified his use of a mathematical framework for his account but cautioned that he did not pretend that his work had the same degree of certainty as a mathematical proof. However, emboldened by his success, in 1690 he published a further "Demonstration" of the mathematical principles underlying his interpretations. Despite the fact that Cressener worked in the Medean tradition, Newton disagreed both with the mathematicism of his approach and with his efforts to understand current events as being of prophetic import. Indeed, as time went on, he placed the end times further and further into the future.[14]

3. Armageddon

Newton's undergraduate notebook demonstrates that even at the dawn of his career, he had not been afraid to subject the topic of the end times to his critical scrutiny. One analysis (Plate 4) was written in the context of his critique of Descartes's claim that his "first element" (the finest matter) could both drive the solar vortex and also continuously expel matter from it to produce light. The thrust of Newton's initial argument against this position, which dates from early 1664, called into question the physical existence and explanatory role of a vortex that appeared (to Newton) to exhaust itself by playing too many roles. He continued on the verso of one page of these astronomical notes under the heading "Of yᵉ Sunn, Starrs and Plannets," possibly adding "& Comets" to the title when he began to view the spectacular comet that appeared at the end of 1664. He queried whether the Cartesian vortex could account for the vertical movement of some comets and asked whether Descartes's approach could really "unriddle yᵉ mistery" of a comet's "bird" (i.e., beard or tail). Later, Newton added notes on the comet of 1618, immediately following them with the start of his own observations of the new comet, which he first tried to spot on 17 December 1664. These entries continued elsewhere in his notebook and he noted that the comet "moved northward against yᵉ streame of yᵉ Vortex cutting it at an angle of 45ᵈ or 46ᵈ." The comet disappeared towards the end of January 1665 and another one (as he saw it) reappeared in April. He took more cursory notes on this, though in the meantime he had immersed himself in the most up-to-date astronomical literature.[15]

Following the reference to the comet's tail, Newton added the reference "Heb 1 chap: vers 2 by God made yᵉ worlds by his son τους αἰῶνας." It is difficult to date this excerpt with precision but it presumably precedes the first entries on the comet of December 1664. In any case, its location in a page on the cosmos is clearly deliberate, and its position in a section on comets implies that he already believed that comets had a profound divine function in the cosmos. Commentators usually invoked Hebrews 1:2 (τους αἰῶνας, literally means "the ages") to shed light on the relationship between God and Christ. Calvin argued that this proved the co-essentiality and co-eternity of God and Christ (as the eternal wisdom of God), and he claimed that the passage showed that scriptural attributions of the creation of the world to either Christ or God were simply different modes of biblical parlance. Newton did not cite the passage for this purpose but did return to it elsewhere in the notebook. At the foot of the page devoted to the creation of animal and human souls discussed in chapter 3, he queried whether the reference to the morning and evening being the "first day" in Genesis 1:5 was evidence that God created time. Following this, he wrote down references to Colossians 1:16 and the Greek passage from Hebrews 1:2 noted above, also querying whether they both proved that God created time. Like the text from Hebrews, the passage from Colossians explicitly stated that it was by Christ that all things were created "that are in heaven, and that are in earth, visible and invisible," but Newton ignored the opportunity to comment on what this said about the relationship between the Son and the Father. There is a possible Trinitarian slant to the way he dealt with the text, though his central interest was in the creation of time—presumably coextensive with the creation of the universe—rather than by whom it was accomplished.[16]

At roughly the same point in his career, Newton made a few provocative entries in the "Philosophical Questions" notebook on the End of the World. Despite its title, the tenor of the remarks he made under the heading "of Earth" (Plate 5) was wholly theological and was completely different from the conventional Cartesian notes he had entered on the topics of water and air in the previous pages. The verses on the End of the World in 2 Peter 3 that Newton cited were central to Christian eschatology, providing an account of the first and last times as well as a way of determining the characteristics of the godly people who would survive the cataclysm. After a description of the demise of the original Earth by means of a torrent of water in 2 Peter 3:5-6, verse 7 referred to the present heavens and earth being kept in store, "reserved unto fire against the day of judgement and perdition of ungodly men." Verse 10 prophesied that when the time came, Christ would arrive as a thief in the night, the heavens would pass away with great noise, the elements would melt with fervent heat, and the earth and the works in it would be burned up. Verses 11-12 questioned what sort of person one should be "in all holy conversation and godliness, Looking for and hasting unto the day of God." The key verse 13 stated that "we" should look for new heavens and a new earth, "wherein dwelleth righteousness."[17]

Referring to 2 Peter 3:6-7, 10-12, Newton noted that the conflagration of the earth was "testified" by such passages, and at this time, he added, the wicked would "probably" be punished. This entry was followed by a reference to the doctrine of the succession of worlds, though Newton again exercised caution in noting that the passage at 2 Peter 3:13 made this merely probable. He added that the reference to the first-person plural in this verse was not justified by the original, but the point of this remains cryptic. Next, he corroborated his note on the succession of worlds by citing Revelation 21:1 and Isaiah 65:17; 66:22 (all of which referred to a new heaven and new earth), and to prove that there would be days and nights after the Day of Judgement, he invoked Revelation 20:10 (which described the eternal post-millennial torment of the beast and false prophet in the lake of fire and brimstone). There is no firm evidence that Newton believed at this stage that the world would be physically destroyed by natural causes, though his insertion of references to apocalyptic texts in sections devoted to natural phenomena obviously suggests that he did so.[18]

In Newton's mature writings on the conflagration, which date from the later 1680s, he understood the descriptions of cataclysmic upheavals to refer to political and religious transformations. As we shall see, his unwillingness to endorse a literal conflagration of the earth was clearly derived from his belief that reference to natural phenomena in the prophetic language signi-fied political or religious upheaval. However, it was also a consequence of his unwillingness, even more pronounced than usual, to speculate about things for which he had no empirical evidence, in this case about future events. In passages of one draft that link his views about the nature of his audience and the epistemic status of his work on prophecy, Newton repeat-edly qualified how much could be known about the fate of souls and bodies in the millennial and postmillennial worlds. In quick succession, he claimed either that such topics were "obscure," that he would not "enter into dis-putes" about them, that it was not his "business" to examine them, or that he would leave it to the reader to consider the matter. In the end, he tried as much as possible to keep to the text but could not resist speculating about life during and after the millennium. As a basis for this work he drew from a vast range of prophetic visions to give a detailed synchronic exposition of various prophecies on the end times.[19]

In his prophetic treatise, Newton argued that future events could only be understood by comparing the prophecies of Daniel and Revelation. He followed Mede in synchronising Christ's Second Coming with the start of the Day of Judgement, and he brought together an array of images (espe-cially that of the seven churches) to shed light on the events during the short but crucial period at the end of the sixth trumpet and vial, which constituted the preconditions of the millennium. As the 1,260 days of the Great Apostasy came to an end, ten kings turned against the Whore, ate her flesh, and burned her (Rev. 17:16), while the two witnesses sprang back into life after their three-and-a-half-day humiliation and ascended to heaven (Rev. 11:11). This, according to Newton and others, was the universal preaching of the gospel (Matt. 24:14). John saw an angel who celebrated the demise of the Whore and sang that Babylon had fallen (Rev. 18:2), while a voice from heaven prophesied the imminent destruction of all those kings and merchants who had fornicated with her. The converted Jews returned from their captivity but three unclean spirits in the shape of frogs suddenly appeared from the mouths of the dragon, beast, and false prophet (Rev. 16:13), making a last-ditch effort to convince undecided Christians to join the battle against the armies of God. Perhaps, Newton conjectured, this was by pretending that the converted Jews were Antichrist, and that the reformed Christians were Antichristians.[20]

These events, according to Newton, were also described in the final chapter of Daniel, which described the events during the Day of Judgement when the dead would be resurrected, some to reward and some to punishment; some to everlasting life and some to contempt (Dan. 12:2). Newton argued that Ezekiel, Joel, Isaiah, and many other Old Testament prophets had described in detail the return of the twelve tribes to Israel at the sounding of the seventh trumpet. On the great day, they would conquer the nations of the four monarchies described in Daniel and set up a righteous and flourishing kingdom. These passages provided a rich commentary on the much shorter text in Revelation, and Newton reproduced them in full, peppered with his own explanatory glosses. They told of the great gathering of the chosen people from among the Greek regions, where they had been dispersed so long before by the armies of Pergamus, the name of the apocalyptic dragon at the time of the Roman Empire (Rev. 2:13).[21]

Revelation 19 promised Christians that a man with no name would return as saviour of the righteous. He would ride a white horse and would rule over nations with a rod of iron, making war against rebellious nations with his sword and his army. Newton understood this description of the rider to refer to a Christian kingdom with its armies rather than to Christ himself. Just before the onset of the millennium, there would be a time of trouble or "great tribulation" described in Daniel, Matthew, and the prophecy of the seven churches. This was the war with the rebellious nations prophesied in numerous places in Scripture (Dan. 9:24-27 and Matt. 24:4-12, 21) and was the battle at Armageddon between the armies of heaven, and the armies of the beast (representing the East and false prophet) and the kings of the earth (from Rev. 19:19 and understood by Newton to represent the dragon, i.e., the devil). According to Newton, the dragon (which he understood to refer to the false religion of the devil or the "spirit of error"), would be supported by the satanic Euphratean horsemen who had last been prophetically active in the sixth vial, but the war would go badly for the forces of evil. At the end of this battle the true Church would be victorious over all the persecuting nations, a triumph that was described figuratively in Matthew and by the Old Testament prophets. When the Euphratean horsemen were slain, the dragon would be separated from his comrades and shut up in a bottomless pit for the duration of the millennium.[22]

Immediately after the destruction of the Whore, the beast and the false prophet would be cast (Rev. 20:20) into a lake of fire burning with brimstone (which for Newton was really hell). The casting down of the beast and false prophet showed they had already been judged and so, Newton surmised, this period had to comprehend the start of the Day of Judgement, the resurrection of the dead, the harvest of the saints, and the consequent vintage of their oppressors' blood. The sealed saints, or palm-bearing multitude resurrected to eternal life, now began their reign with Christ, the sinners were duly slain with Christ's double-edged sword, and the fowls of heaven were authorised to gorge on their flesh (Rev. 19:17-18). The latter event Newton understood "mystically" as the dissolution of evil states and the acquisition of their wealth and dominions by the righteous. The fact that the sword emanated from Christ's mouth, and that the beast and false prophet had been removed, indicated that the preaching of the gospel and the conversion of nations to righteousness would be accelerated.[23]

Central to Newton's eschatological analysis was the fate of souls during the two resurrections described in Revelation 20:4-6, 11-15 and John 5:19-29. Like Mede, Newton's compressing of events into the period around the sounding of the seventh trumpet left him with a problem of accounting for the reference to the second, postmillennial resurrection. He solved this by arguing that there were two deaths, one preceding each resurrection, though he insisted that the resurrection of the dead could not be interpreted allegorically. As the saints and martyrs would be resurrected at the Day of Judgement, so according to the Apocalypse, the rest of the dead would arise at the second resurrection and would be subjected to the Last Judgement. The "first resurrection" would take place at the Day of Judgement and applied to *all* mortals, both those still living and those who had died (that is, "slept in the dust") and gone to the grave. On Judgement Day, meritorious bodies would experience the first resurrection from the grave. However, the "rest of the dead," or the wicked, would never rise again but would die a second death, that is, they would continue in a state of death. As he saw it, the second resurrection referred to immortal bodies. At the end of the millennium, the dragon would be let loose for a short time (Rev. 20:2-3) to lead the satanic armies of Gog and Magog. They would encompass the city of the saints but fire would come down from heaven and devour them (Rev. 20:10). At this, the dragon would be thrown unceremoniously into the lake of fire, to be tormented forever along with his beastly friends.[24]

Elsewhere Newton argued that the idea that the souls of the blessed went immediately to heaven, while those of the wicked went to hell, was yet another fiction devised by Athanasius. In his Life of Antony, he had related Antony's alleged vision of the soul of the hermit Ammon ascending directly to heaven. Like most Protestants, Newton believed that no one could go anywhere before they were judged, and he argued that this particularly pernicious Athanasian fable had been one of the chief means by which heathen demonology had been introduced into Christianity. Ultimately the story gave rise to the doctrines of ghosts, saint-worship, and purgatory, where the majority of those who were neither saintly nor depraved ended up. Before Athanasius, the Greek Church had held no firm view on the state of souls between death and the Day of Judgement, and Newton pointed out that early Christians had originally placed all the dead in Hades, the land of darkness and silence. It was a mistake, he said, to identify Hades with hell, and he frequently rendered references to hell in the King James Version of the Bible as "the grave." According to Newton, until they were resurrected, the dead could not experience any consciousness, being consequently unable to do any good or bad works for which they might be judged before the Day of Judgement. In May 1694 he told David Gregory that religion did not require belief in a separate existence of the soul, but in resurrection with a continuation of memory. Where one remained after death was of less significance than being the same person after resurrection.[25]

4. Living at the End of the World

Revelation 20:11 and 21:1 told of how John saw the old earth, sea, and heaven fleeing from God as he sat on a great white throne, while Revelation

21:2 linked this to the appearance of the New Jerusalem that followed the sounding of the seventh trumpet. Both of these Newton understood to be the founding of a new kingdom of righteousness whose metropolis was the great city. Now God (Rev. 21:3-4) began to dwell amongst mortals and wiped away their tears, feeding them with the tree of life. As we have seen, interpreters usually linked these passages to the Petrine passage that stated that the earth would be destroyed by fire just as it had once been ravaged by water. However, Newton condemned the common belief that there would be a fiery holocaust of the globe as a series of "fansies" brought on by an egregious misunderstanding of prophetic discourse. The physicalist view had been promoted by heathen philosophers who argued that just as the world once perished by water, so it should once again perish by fire. Newton argued that a remnant would survive the figurative conflagration "to re-plenish ye earth a second time," just as Noah had survived the Flood for the same purpose. The fiery annihilation portended no "amendment of the whole frame of nature," but rather the dissolution of kingdoms by war. There were some exceptions to his figurative reading of these passages, and in one version of this text he argued that those thrust into the lake of fire would really be engulfed by flames. Here, up to a point, he followed Mede: such an event would not be a conflagration of a "considerable" part of the habitable world, and thus, Newton concluded, "there is no ground for such a renovation as they suppose." The last claim, with its peculiar reference to unnamed targets, is probably not a dig at his contemporaries but an attack on much earlier writers such as Pliny.[26]

   With Christ's return would come the kingdom of heaven, since he would only judge the quick and the dead when he reappeared with his kingdom (2 Tim. 4:1). According to Newton, the Jews mistakenly believed that the Messiah would come with the outward pomp of earthly regal majesty, but Christ had corrected them. At his first arrival, he had *not* come as a king, and therefore (as it was expressly stated in John 18:36) there was no kingdom of God on Earth except for his command over unspecified "invisible powers." For Newton, Christ would reign at his second coming in a double sense. In the first place he would arrive in person with an innumerable host of angels to do battle with the beast and false prophet (Matt. 13:41). Subsequently Christ and the angels would rule with the resurrected saints over the saved mortals. Second, he was to come in the form of his mystical body or church of mortals led and ruled by a mortal king, who would be his vice-regent on Earth. In Revelation 22:5 and in many other passages it was confirmed that this kingdom, whose centre was the New Jerusalem, would last forever. This is what God had promised Abraham (Rom. 4: 21-22), and Newton urged that Christians should take special heed of the text. Passages from Isaiah confirmed that life would go on as before for these people, but another group of mortals, who had not been deceived by the dragon during the millennium, would decide to join up with the forces of evil at the end of it. Seduced by the dragon into fighting against the righteous in the war of Gog and Magog, they were the rebellious nations outside the city (Rev. 22:15) who would be destroyed by fire in the last battle. As a result, the city would be further extended and righteousness would prevail forever and ever.[27]

The saints did occupy some of the same spiritual space as the mortals and to represent this, Newton conceived of the New Jerusalem as a spiritual city that was shaped like a cube, reaching from Earth to the heavens. How might the saints—the "children of the resurrection"—and angels rule over and communicate with mortal subjects (whom Newton often referred to as the converted Jews)? The nature of their rule would not be carried out in the normal way that individuals reigned over temporal kingdoms, Newton cautioned, but would be carried out in much the same way that angels had exercised their rule over mankind in the past. He suggested to John Conduitt in 1725 that intelligent beings seemed to manage the motions of heavenly bodies under God's direction, but in the apocalyptic text he argued that the idea that heavenly creatures would rule over the surviving mortals as happened in ordinary human societies and converse with ordinary men and women was as "absurd and foolish" as the idea of humans talking to animals. Rather, they would reign invisibly unless they felt like showing themselves on the odd occasion.[28]

The likely postmillennial existence of animals also provoked Newton to comment on God's extraordinary dominion in the world. In the late 1680s treatise, he noted that God was substantially present everywhere, from the lowest hell to the highest heaven and he invoked Isaiah 45:18, in which it is expressly stated that God created the world to be inhabited, to support the claim that no part of the universe should lack inhabitants. Despite likening his knowledge of such things to a blind man talking of colours, Newton speculated that on Christ's return he, his saints, and his angels might move around in space like fishes did in water, moving wherever they pleased. Still more speculatively, he invoked God's immense creative power to envision the range of creatures that could thrive in the millennial world. Just as the present earth was constantly replenished with innumerable animals, some too small to be seen without a magnifying glass, so the millennial universe might be stocked with a variety of beings "whose nature we do not understand": "He y^t shall well consider ye strange & wonderful nature of life & ye frame of Animals will think nothing beyond ye possibility of Nature, nothing too hard for ye omnipotent power of God." In his most fantastic conception, representing the pinnacle of his notion of physical freedom, Newton remarked that the future state might contain "beings who have a sufficient power of self motion" and who could move freely across the entire universe, at the same time making the earth subject to their rule. Pulling himself together after such flights of fancy, he admitted that all these wonderful possibilities would only become clear at the resurrection.[29]

5. Dropping In

Newton's rejection of physical accounts of the End of the World in the realm of prophecy did not mean that he was forbidden from treating the subject in natural philosophy. Indeed, the *Principia* gave him the inspiration—and the tools—to develop a philosophical account of what he called the "revolution" in the cosmos. On a number of occasions he indicated that the earth had only existed for a very short time, and he remarked that life on the earth would be destroyed in the not too distant future. He told Antonio Conti that human existence was of a very short duration, since in recorded history there had been giant forests in what were now hot zones, and various sources recorded that the growth of villages, towns, and cities was relatively recent. Of course, this was consistent with the vast project on the genealogy of the sons of Noah, which, as we have seen, made the Flood a relatively recent event in human history. In March 1725 he told John Conduitt that "the inhabitants of this earth were of a short date" and that all arts had been discovered within historical memory. Conduitt went on to ask how the earth could have been "repeopled" if it had ever suffered from a life-extinguishing catastrophe. Newton told him that the only way a new human population could come into existence was by the power of the creator and, according to the report of the conversation, he did not deny that God might institute a new race of human beings. He said something similar in a letter to Richard Bentley (then preparing sermons for his Boyle Lectures) in a letter of February 1693, though these comments concerned new "systems" rather than new races of men. It was "apparently absurd," he told Bentley, to think that such systems could grow out of old ones "without ye mediation of divine power." With God all things were possible, and he believed that God would not waste the chance to create life in a place where it could be nourished by a local sun.[30]

The doctrines of the *Principia* allowed Newton and his followers to make entirely novel physical and astronomical contributions to the field of natural theology. In a number of places, he paid lip service to conventional accounts of the so-called Argument from Design. As early as the "Philosophical Questions" notebook he had written a very basic statement concerning the impossibility that men and beasts were made merely by "fortuitous jum-blings of attoms," for otherwise, there would be substantial redundancy in the structure of animals, and numerous creatures would be found with one or many eyes. Similarly, he told the physician William Briggs in 1682 that God had done nothing without reason; the fact that all animals had features that were so admirably suited to their capacities would always be the most convincing argument for an intelligent deity and had "convinced mankind in all ages that ye world & all ye species of things therein were originally framed by his power & wisdom." References to divine design permeated his responses to Bentley, whose perceptive comments prompted him to make a series of innovative inferences from his own work. Newton told Bentley that he had written the *Principia* with a view to promoting belief in God among "considering men." The latter should ponder, he continued, the fact that the sun and no other body in the solar system produced heat and light, and indeed, gave out exactly the appropriate light and heat to the six plan-ets, a state of affairs that could only have arisen by design. Moreover, God had ensured that planets travelled at *just* the correct velocities, were at *just* the right distance from the sun (and travelled in just the right orbits), had *just* the right mass (and hence just the right amount of gravitational power), and revolved on their axes at *just* the correct rates. Rehearsing a remark he had made about a perfect (i.e., divine) mechanic in the "Preface to the Reader" of the *Principia*, he insisted that only a being exquisitely skilled in mechanics and geometry could have compared and adjusted all these fea-tures; he might have added that only a great philosopher could have discov-ered the principles underlying their motions.[31]

According to Newton, other considerations flowing from the doctrines of the *Principia* could shed light on God's actions at the time of the creation. In response to a query from Bentley on the long-term effects of universal gravitation on all the matter in the universe, he remarked that provided space were really infinite, matter initially dispersed evenly across the universe would never come together into one mass in its centre, but would make "an infinite number of great masses scattered at great distances from one another throughout all y^t infinite space"—presumably the state of affairs that now existed. Yet this could not explain how the local region of the "chaos" had divided itself up into the solar system as it now was, with a structure that was uniquely suited to life on Earth and perhaps elsewhere. This arrangement could only have arisen, Newton urged, thanks to the "counsel & contrivance of a voluntary Agent." He had changed his mind about the cosmic effects of universal gravitation by the time David Gregory visited him at Cambridge two years later, when he claimed that only through God's continuing intervention (Gregory inaccurately wrote "by a continual miracle") could all the heavenly bodies in the universe be prevented from colliding in their centre of gravity. He used the example for yet another theological purpose in May 1715, when he told Antonio Conti that the sun would have long ago been exhausted if the universe had existed for eternity, and that all the heavenly bodies would by now have piled into one another due to universal gravitation.[32]

Newton also implicitly invoked the principle of parsimony in explaining the amount of work God should be said to have performed in the creative act. When Bentley asked whether the current orbits of the planets could have arisen by the force of gravity alone, Newton considered a situation where the earth was placed with neither gravitational force nor motion in the centre of the *orbis magnus*, that is, at the centre of the present terrestrial orbit around the sun. If it were suddenly endowed with both gravitational attraction towards the sun, and the correct inertial tangential motion, it would then take up its current orbit around the sun. However, Newton added that it would be physically impossible for the earth to acquire these motions by natural causes alone. Nor could God have set up the motions of the planets by creating them very far from their current positions and then letting them fall towards the sun. At some point the deity would have needed to turn the falling motion into a transverse one, since the falling planet would only acquire a stable orbit if the gravitational power of the sun doubled at exactly the moment when the planet arrived at its proper distance from it. As a consequence, God would be required to perform two separate acts, simultaneously turning the motion of the falling planets sideways and doubling the power of the sun. It was far simpler to suppose that God framed the current system of the world in one act.[33]

Newton noted that the motions of the planets were also indicative of a divine hand, though in his correspondence with Bentley, he did not assign a specific role to comets. He told Bentley that unlike comets, which moved in every conceivable plane and direction, the movement of planets in the same direction, and in roughly the same plane, could not have arisen from natural causes, "but were imprest by an intelligent agent." If planets had slightly different velocities and masses, they would not have moved in the elliptical orbits they now had but in hyperbolas and parabolas, or in such eccentric orbits as comets now obeyed. Sometime after 1714, he told his friend William Derham exactly the same thing, and it remained a staple part of his official account of the design argument. In Query 20 of the 1706 *Optice* (Query 28 of the 1717/18 *Opticks*), he posed the question of what the function of comets was, why they moved in such large orbits, and why it was that planets all moved in the same direction. In Query 23 (Query 31 of the 1717/18 *Opticks*), he argued that blind fate could not have made the planets all move in the same direction, though the gravitational influence of comets would in time give rise to various irregularities in this perfect alignment that would increase until the situation required divine intervention.[34]

Although Newton did not discuss the role of comets with Bentley, the nature and role of comets lay at the heart of his cosmological system. He argued in Book 3 of the *Principia* that life on planets was invigorated when it passed through the nourishing residue of comets' tails. In the same way that the water vapour given off by seas was necessary for life on Earth when it fell as rain or was condensed at the top of mountains, so fine material exuded from comets played a similar role on a grander scale. The vapour and "exhalations" from their tails would condense, providing a continual supply of whatever liquid was consumed by vegetation and putrefaction and subsequently turned into "dry" earth. This dry earth would continually increase, Newton continued, and without some external input there would in due course be no revivifying fluids on the planet. Rehearsing the claim in his 1670s alchemical essay on nature's processes in vegetation, he pointed out that comets were the source of that tiny "spirit" that was the "most subtle and excellent" part of the air. This account was repeated in the conversation Newton held with Conduitt in March 1725, in which he noted that, over time, the sun gave off light, "vapours," and other matter, and that this material would congeal into a body. This would eventually attract matter from other planets and became a "secondary" planet or satellite, which in due course, by continuing to acquire more sediment, would graduate to the status of a primary planet. Finally, by attracting even more solar material it would become a comet. After a number of revolutions around the sun, its "volatile parts" would be condensed and become fit to replenish the wasting orb by "dropping" into it. Even at this late stage in life, and in a private conversation, Newton qualified his own comments by emphasising that they were just conjectures. Although they were clearly what he believed, Conduitt recalled that "he would affirm nothing."[35]

When Newton told Gregory in the spring of 1694 that the great eccentricity of cometary orbits indicated that they had some divine function different from that of the planets, he immediately added that the satellites of Jupiter and Saturn could be reserved for a new creation and could take the place of Earth, Venus, and Mars if they were destroyed. Almost a decade later, in the context of discussing the end of the world, Newton repeated his view that the Great Comet of 1680 would sometimes "impinge" on the sun. For the rest of his life, this object would be the most obvious candidate for obliterating the earth, and in his 1725 conversation with Conduitt, he mentioned that the fate of the Great Comet would be "sooner or later" to drop into the sun. This might be after five or six revolutions but when it did make contact, "<this earth would be burnt &> no animals in *this earth* could live." He added that the new stars seen by Hipparchus, Tycho, and Kepler were the results of such an event, and he affirmed that other stars were at the centre of their own solar systems. Since Newton himself had raised the issue of the demise of his own solar system in the context of the Great Comet, Conduitt asked whether he would publish his conjectures as "Queries." After further prompting, Newton opened his *Principia* to the page where there were references to the four previous sightings of the comet, whereupon Conduitt reminded him of a later passage in the book where Newton had referred to the retardation of the 1680 comet by the solar atmosphere, and its probable later descent into the sun. Directly after this, Newton had written about the fact that stars could be recruited or revitalised by this process, and pass for new stars. Were not these passages an oblique reference to everything they had discussed about our own solar system, Conduitt asked? And why could he not admit of the solar system what he had clearly stated of the distant stars? Newton agreed that the fate of the solar system was more relevant to mankind, but with a chuckle added that he had said enough for people to know his meaning.[36]

10

Private Prosecutions

Newton's devotion to the study of prophecy was enabled by the fact that he had extricated himself from what he took to be pointless disputes over his optical experiments. The cavillers who had continually forced him to engage in barren disputes had melted away, and by the late 1670s he was no longer a slave to the Republic of Letters. To all intents and purposes, he had successfully erected a barrier between the external world of print culture and the private domain of his college, where he could pursue his studies of theology and alchemy without interference. However, just when he thought he was out of the fray, he was pulled back into it. In the summer of 1684, Edmond Halley asked him for a demonstration proving that an elliptical orbit was the consequence of an inverse-square law. According to the only evidence relating to this visit, Newton apparently told him that he already had such a proof, but after some searching, he was unable to locate it. He wrote up the demonstration and expanded it in the form of a small treatise titled "De motu corporum in gyrum," which he sent off to the Royal Society in November. By the autumn of 1685 he had completed a two-part work on the motion of bodies, though he apparently suppressed the second part because his theory of comets was inadequate. Within months, he had resolved these problems, and had arrived at the laws of motion and the concepts of force and universal gravitation that would be the linchpins of his *Principia Mathematica*, which was published in the summer of 1687. As it turned out, the *Principia* engaged him in yet another dispute even before it was published.[1]

The strategic retreat into his rooms at Trinity had been the result of Newton's failure to remake the scientific Republic of Letters in his own image. As we saw in chapter 4, the type of doctrinaire mathematical article on light and colours that he published in 1672 ran counter to the generally accepted notion, at least in the Royal Society, that observations and experiments should be clearly described and aimed at a broad audience. The standard line in English experimental philosophy, following the position adopted by Robert Boyle, was that knowledge of the natural world could at best be "probable" and was not capable of being demonstrated to a level of mathematical certainty. Experiments were local trials performed with specialist pieces of equipment in order to produce or analyse specific "matters of fact." As particular events they could not by themselves generate general, universal, and absolutely certain claims about the natural world. To corroborate claims based on such experimental evidence, trials should be conducted many times, in many places, and in front of reliable witnesses, all of which made general claims more probable, but not absolutely certain. This was a far cry from the position adopted in technically forbidding subjects such as the mixed mathematical sciences (for example, optics, statics, or harmonics) or in Aristotelian natural philosophy, where practitioners argued that demonstrations based on syllogisms were absolutely certain.[2]

Newton was hostile to the idea that scientific knowledge could only at best be probable, and he believed that it was capable of the same level of (absolute) certainty as was found in the mathematical sciences. Unlike Boyle and other experimental philosophers, he aimed his work at a narrow audience of technically competent experts, who were supposed to trust his accounts of the experiments he described and understand (and accept) the force of his demonstrations. This is why, in his correspondence with Jesuits in the mid-1670s, he insisted that one "crucial" experiment, rather than many "probable" experiments, was sufficient to convince philosophers who were experts in the field. In turn, this position was attacked by critics from a number of different intellectual traditions, and as we have seen, in 1676 Anthony Lucas complained that both his own practice and that of his Jesuit colleagues was in line with that recommended by Boyle and others.[3]

Boyle's appeal to witnesses and, more broadly, to "testimony" in order to support statements pertaining to facts, drew linguistically and conceptually from English common law. Both humans and subtly varied experiments could provide testimony regarding matters of fact, since many independent pieces of evidence strengthened the degree of probability of a given statement to the extent that it could be "morally" certain. Against this, as I show in this chapter, Newton was deeply opposed to the use of testimony in natural philosophy. In the first place, witnesses were irrelevant because it was the strength of one key experiment that decided between two alternatives, and not, as the Royal Society grandees demanded, the corroborative

support of multiple experiments seen by a large number of people. As the correspondence with the Jesuits showed, when critics could not reproduce Newton's experiments, and claimed that he had not obtained the results that he said
he had, he felt that his honour and his skill as an experimentalist were being
vilified by a group of critics who cited one another as witnesses. Second, and
perhaps more significantly, he believed that witnesses were inappropriate for
scientific enquiry because the type of legalistic support that they gave to statements was inappropriate for confirming statements in natural philosophy.

Although the use of witnesses was at odds with the standards and mores
of natural philosophy, and was always liable to corrupt it, Newton believed
that it was essential for legal trials or situations where the actions and morals
of individuals were in question. As is clear throughout this book, Newton
was adept at prosecuting historical evildoers such as Athanasius, and he was
an expert in adducing relevant documentary testimony to support his arguments in relevant fields. In a number of such texts he reflected on the use of
testimony, and in particular, on the role of such testimony in making legal
cases. In this chapter I examine his analysis of such testimony in his account
of Athanasius's conduct in the immediate aftermath of the Council of Tyre
in 335. He interpreted documents conventionally used by orthodox historians to defend Athanasius from accusations that he was a seducer, a murderer,
and a rabble-rouser, in order to convict him for the same crimes. In doing
so, he argued that Athanasius had perjured witnesses and faked witness testimony to produce his own case, and he gave a detailed account of when
and how the use of witnesses was appropriate. Although the appeal to witnesses was not part of natural philosophy when it ran properly, Newton
made ample use of his forensic skills when questions of intellectual property
and his honour were raised—that is, when natural philosophy had become,
as he put it, a "litigious lady." It is certainly appropriate to attribute his actions in such instances to his underlying personality, which both friends and
enemies took to be characterised by a pronounced prickliness, and even by
varying degrees of paranoia. However, I point to his expert use of standard
forensic techniques in his religious and historical studies, which gave shape
to, and which were in turn fuelled by, his underlying character.

Newton's attack on the use of witnesses in natural philosophy formed
part of a cluster of criticisms of attitudes and practices that he believed were
corrosive of natural philosophy. A potent contaminant of philosophy were
unwarranted "hypotheses," which inevitably forced natural philosophers to
descend into barren but time-consuming disputes. At various junctures he

criticised the use of hypotheses for being irrelevant human artefacts and dangerous figments of the imagination; they were ungrounded in sense-experience and fell a long way short of the level of certainty requisite for scientific knowledge. Ultimately they reduced the arena of natural philosophy to an anarchic disputational forum. Once he had experienced negative responses to his 1672 paper from his critics, his earlier critique of probabilistic statements evolved into a relentless criticism of hypotheses. In attacking the use of hypotheses, and worse, the invocation of "systems" in philosophy, Newton was following a major trend in English natural philosophy practised by Robert Boyle and many others, with Bacon invariably invoked as their patron saint. However, Newton's anti-hypotheticalism was the most extreme of his generation. Long before he made the totemic claim in the "General Scholium" that he did not "feign hypotheses," he denounced the hypotheses put forward by his critics, contrasting these subjective speculations with the authority of his own experiments and the certain statements that could be produced by the mathematical sciences.[4]

Newton's opposition to hypotheses, and indeed to witnesses, cut across the key division in his work between the private and public spheres. In his private writings, and, it should be said, in his own mind, he was committed to the existence and explanatory potential of things like corpuscles, active principles, and aethers. Occasionally Newton did publish hypotheses *as hypotheses* (i.e., statements to which he was, allegedly, uncommitted), such as the "hypothesis" concerning the physical causes of light and colours that he sent to the Royal Society in 1675. He also listed a somewhat inchoate group of propositions under the heading "Hypotheses" in the opening section of Book 3 of the first edition of the *Principia*. However, his public redefinition of the meaning of the term "hypothesis" was so pronounced that soon after he published his 1672 paper on light and colours, he ruled out as hypothetical—and hence inadmissible—any reference to the physical properties of phenomena. Newton's scientific anti-physicalism is clear from his response to the early review of his paper by Robert Hooke, in which Newton exulted that the science of colours relied on no mere hypothesis but was "properly a Mathematicall science." He claimed that he was not prepared to refer to the *physical* basis of a scientific concept such as a "ray" of light, since to do so would be to commit oneself to an as yet experimentally unjustified theoretical entity (such as a "corpuscle"). Instead, he would only speak of light "abstractedly as something or other propagated every way in straight lines from luminous bodies, without determining what that thing is." In his own comments on this text, Hooke perceptively remarked that Newton seemed to be "afraid" of saying what a ray of light was.[5]

Newton's attack on hypotheses was bound up with another aspect of his dislike of litigious practices in natural philosophy. Because hypotheses were artificial and indeed fictional, he claimed, they inevitably generated disputes. They were to be evaded whenever possible but in practice, contention within the Republic of Letters was unavoidable. Indeed, most of Newton's own letters in natural philosophy were composed in the context of disputes in which he was defending not only his honour and the truth of his claims, but also his priority and property rights. Despite his oft-professed hatred of disputes, there was an inevitability about his involvement in these controversies, deriving from his attitudes to scientific demonstration and to the pitfalls of publication. As we have seen, the publication of his theory of the heterogeneity of white light gave rise to disputes in part because of the novelty and implausibility of his claims, in part because his narrative (and the experimentum crucis) was obscure, and in part because he refused to corroborate his statements by appealing to supporting experiments. That is, he deliberately withheld from publication a number of accounts of experiments that could have helped his case, or at least, that were more in keeping with the general practice of contemporary experimental philosophy. The situation was the same in the case of his mathematical work. Although he allowed some acolytes to see and take notes from his manuscript treatises, he refused to print any of these brilliant tracts and relied on dropping obscure hints in letters to people such as Gottfried Leibniz. Such behaviour made it difficult for his critics to believe that he had accomplished what he actually had, and, in turn, it made it virtually impossible for him to convince them of the same. Whether it was unintended, deliberate, careless, or even reckless, this strategy condemned him to engage in the very sort of disputes that he professed to despise. On these occasions, when the order of things had broken down, he prosecuted his opponents for their deviant morals and actions, just as he did the evildoers who had corrupted early Christianity.[6]

In this chapter I show that Newton erected two sorts of boundaries within his natural philosophy, both of which would play a central role in his future work. The first was between public and private knowledge and the second, related barrier, was between certain and hypothetical statements. He experienced his most extreme anxiety when the dividing lines between these domains broke down, and philosophy became "litigious." This happened when philosophers invoked witnesses, or promoted their own "hypotheses," or made unsupportable claims about their own achievements, thereby turning natural philosophy into a forensic dispute about intellectual property. Once public science had become reduced to a law-court, he took great delight in using documentary evidence to convict Hooke, Leibniz, and others of moral debasement, just as he did Athanasius, Jerome, and other religious corrupters. Indeed, his skill in launching private prosecutions against such men provided a significant basis for using the same tactics against his competitors in philosophy and mathematics. Finally, I suggest that the division he maintained between mathematically certain knowledge and uncertain hypotheses was equivalent to the core distinction he maintained between the rational conduct of the understanding and the undisciplined activities of the imagination.

1. Isaac Newton, Litigant

Newton was evidently unprepared for the controversies that followed the news of his reflecting telescope and the publication of his article on light and colours. On a number of occasions in the early 1670s, he told Henry Oldenburg and John Collins that by being dragged into unnecessary disputes, he had sacrificed the precious freedom and tranquillity he enjoyed in his college. Later, when he had become famous, and his doctrines had become accepted as scientific gospel, friends and disciples argued that his dislike of litigiousness was a central part of his unblemished character. Newton's related claims that he did not feign hypotheses, that they led to disputes, and that he hated contention, were all moulded together by followers who argued that his divine methodology flowed from his saintly demeanour. Humphrey Newton, who spent more time with Newton in the late 1680s than anyone else did, recalled after Newton's death that he was "no way litigious, not given to Law or Vexatious suits, taking Patience to be ye best Law, & a good Conscience ye best Divinity." This hyperbolic hymn to Newton's moral comportment was echoed by many throughout the following decades.[7]

The psychological aspect of this hagiography was only partially true, for Newton delighted in the use of forensic, prosecutorial rhetoric. As we saw in chapter 2, his undergraduate education had prepared him with the skills to participate in more formal, intellectual arenas of dispute, while in other areas of his life, especially when it concerned the property at Woolsthorpe, he was used to participating in legal actions. After his mother's death in 1679 he was inevitably dragged into local disputes as a result of having to take a much more active role in the running of the estate. In the early 1680s he won a significant case in Chancery against the local Elston family, who were claiming twenty acres of land at Woolsthorpe on behalf of the rival manor of Colsterworth. At other times he was prepared to go to law to defend members of his family. For example, at roughly the same time as he took on the Elstons, he sued a man named Todd who had claimed that he had not received an order from Newton to pay money on the latter's behalf to his sister Mary. In the letter Newton disparaged Todd as a liar and prevaricator, and at one point Todd received the curt remark: "I shall only tell you in general that I understand your way & therefore sue you."[8]

Newton's propensity to litigate is visible in a number of draft letters relating to his efforts to extract or exact rent from tenants at the manor, although normally he used an agent to deal with more mundane business with the property. At the start of 1688, for example, he sued two of his tenants, a Mr. Storer and his son Oliver, for leaving some of the farm properties in disrepair. This action was connected to a visit Newton had paid to the property the previous March; the case had gone to arbitration in the local parish, and the elder Storer had accused Newton of being rash in bringing the suit against them. Newton defended his actions in a letter to an unknown recipient in which he gave a detailed account of the facts of the case as he saw them. He claimed that when he had visited the property the previous year, Oliver had disparaged it both in his presence and behind his back, and his father had turned an act of generosity by Newton to Newton's disadvantage. He had not started the action against them without justification, he told his correspondent, and he would not end it without satisfaction (which he doubtless obtained). There must have been many other incidents like this; Newton was adept at building up cases against his tenants, and he was happy to take them to court. As we shall see, whether it was Colsterworth locals, counterfeiters, ancient corrupters of the Christian religion, or even natural philosophers, he was truly in his element when he put the morals and actions of his enemies to the test by placing them on trial.[9]

2. Witness Testimony

In the winter of 1675/76, Newton was forced to appeal to the testimony of a handful of fellows of the Royal Society who had been present in London the previous spring, when he had shown them in private how to reproduce the simple oblong image described at the start of his 1672 paper. This would be the only point in the seventeenth century when Newton would endorse the use of witnesses as proper warrantors of scientific claims, though ultimately his efforts to locate the relevant people descended into farce. The immediate impetus for performing this experiment was a series of criticisms made by Francis Linus, who, following his opening letter sent to Henry Oldenburg in the autumn of 1674, had dispatched a second missive to Oldenburg the following February. In this text, as we have seen in chapter 5, he disputed elements of fact in the description of the basic oblong image given by Newton in his original 1672 paper. Newton recalled in January 1676 that when Oldenburg had shown him the second letter, he had mentioned that the affair "being about matter of fact was not proper to be decided by writing but by trying it before competent witnesses." However, the official efforts to reproduce the effect before a wider audience at the Royal Society had come to nothing. Preparations had also been made for a formal performance of the crucial experiment when Newton was in London early in 1675, but the day was cloudy and he had had to return to Cambridge.[10]

In September 1675 Linus complained to Oldenburg that his second letter had not been printed in the *Philosophical Transactions*, and he noted that this might give the appearance to readers that Newton's theory still stood. Oldenburg must have pushed Newton to reply to it, because on 13 November, he told Oldenburg that a few days after the latter had first shown him Linus's letter of February 1675, he had produced the basic image described in his original paper in front of a handful of people that included an unnamed gentleman. Although he could not remember the name of this particular witness, he recalled that Abraham Hill (a merchant and senior member of the Royal Society) had entered the room while the experiment was taking place and that Newton had shown the phenomenon to him. Hill was a close friend of Robert Hooke, and indeed Newton also asked Oldenburg to procure Hooke's testimony on his behalf. Newton reminded Oldenburg that soon after the initial paper on light and colours had been printed in 1672, Hooke "gave testimony not onely to ye Experiments questioned by Mr Line, but to all those set down in my first Letter about Colours, as having tryed them himself." Finally, at the meeting where Linus's second letter had been read, Oldenburg had proposed that Newton try the experiment in front of some members. Newton noted that Hooke had confirmed at the meeting that all the phenomena in his original paper were undeniable.

Newton had promised that if Hooke's testimony were insufficient, he would redo the experiment at a meeting of the Society if he ever happened to attend one again.[11]

Since Newton was not intending to visit London in the near future, he tried another tactic to end the dispute. He told Oldenburg in the same letter that although he found it unpalatable to write any more on the topic, he would send Oldenburg an account of various observations he had mentioned three years previously. A few days later he added that he would send him another "little scrible" to accompany them. Accordingly, in late November and early December 1675, despite his professed aversion to composing a hypothesis on the topic ("fearing it might be a means to ingage me in vain disputes"), he sent Oldenburg a "Discourse of Observations" along with the "Hypothesis" on light and colours discussed in chapter 3. Still interested in locating people who had been present when he had tried the experiment in the spring, Newton referred vaguely to an "Ancient gentleman" who had enquired about an instrument called an ear-trumpet or "otocousticon," though he could not remember his name. The old man was presumably the potential witness described in the previous letter, since Newton also added that if Oldenburg could not remember who it was, Hill might oblige.[12]

Struggling to locate one witness to his own experiment, Newton was forced to confront the collective testimony of the Jesuit order when John Gascoigne wrote from Liège in December 1675. In a text laced with the language of witnessing, Gascoigne requested that Oldenburg print Linus's second letter to Newton, repeating Linus's protest that readers might otherwise think that Newton's account was correct. He added that Newton's accusation that Linus had relied on old experiments without any new trial was "a thing much contrary to Mr Line's humour and practice, and what many here are witnesse of." Linus had repeatedly reproduced his experiments and showed them to anyone who cared to wander into his rooms. The Jesuits, he continued, were awaiting a trial of the crucial experiment before the Society, and before more witnesses, as the only sure way to verify Newton's claims. Since the crucial experiment ran counter to the received laws of refractions, he wrote, it would be difficult "to persuade it as a truth, till it be made so visible to all, as it were a shame to deny it: as indeed it will be when once attested by so renowned a body as that is." Finally, Gascoigne remarked that he hoped the entire correspondence could be printed, with Linus's contribution as the last word.[13]

3. Philosophical Equity

If this were not enough to disturb Newton's fragile peace of mind, he now became embroiled in a highly unpleasant scientific lawsuit with Robert Hooke. When the second part of Newton's "Hypothesis" was read at the Royal Society on 16 December 1675, Hooke remarked that almost all of it had been lifted from his *Micrographia*, which Newton had merely extended in insignificant ways. Hooke had already taken umbrage at the first part of the paper when it had been read at the Society on 9 December, and the next day he had proposed a "New Clubb" at Joe's Coffee house in Mitre Court. Amongst other attendees who met at its inaugural meeting on Saturday the eleventh, Sir John Hoskins, Francis Lodwick, Abraham Hill, and John Aubrey all participated in a discussion about Newton's theory, which, naturally, did not go to the latter's advantage. Soon after Hooke's outburst at the Royal Society, Oldenburg provocatively passed on its gist to Newton, requesting that Newton list the differences between his and Hooke's notions. Newton replied on 21 December, thanking Oldenburg for informing him about Hooke's "insinuation." Telling Oldenburg that he would respond briefly, in order to "avoid ye savour of having done anything unjustifiable or unhandsome to Mr Hooke," he proceeded to defend his own independence while obliterating any credit Hooke believed he merited for the doctrines in his *Micrographia*.[14]

A fascinating draft of this text shows that Newton wrestled for some time with a wide range of issues concerning intellectual property, the sort of behaviour appropriate for scientific discourse, and the freedom he believed he had to draw on whatever sources he felt fit in order to compose a scientific text. He began by stating that, because he knew it was Hooke's "noted humour," he was not concerned at Hooke's claiming the bulk of the doctrines of the "Hypothesis" to himself. Newton protested that he had not presented the "Hypothesis" as an entirely new theory, but only to present a "convenient Hypothesis" to explicate his 1672 paper. He did not know why, in order to make his case, he should not have the freedom to borrow whatever he wanted from any writer, especially when what he had taken was "already secured to y^e Author $^<$& sufficiently known to be his$^>$." However, Hooke had little reason to charge Newton for stealing from him, since "a Cartesian may sooner find y^e sum of Mr Hookes Hypothesis in Des-cartes $^<$then$^>$ M^r $^<$H or any body els$^>$ can find in his Micrographia y^e sum of y^t I sent you, for he has borrowed more from Des-Cartes then I have done from him ~~not to say more~~." Newton proceeded to list all those elements that Hooke had taken from Descartes and remarked that the only difference between them was that Hooke attributed the action of the light medium to a vibrating aether, while Descartes appealed to a "pression or progressive motion ⟨excited by yᵉ action of yᵉ materia subtilis⟩." Since Hooke had so closely modelled his own account on the Cartesian philosophy, "yet cries out at all turns. My Hypothesis, my Hypothesis," he should not criticise others for using the same liberty that he had used himself. The whole business put Newton on an "ill favour'd Dilemma," he continued, "either to contend about meum & tuum in Philosophy or by silence let a slur be put upon me." Although he had always considered it vain to hold on to any doctrine so keenly that he would have to contend for it, where parting with a doctrine brought "a taxation of <having been> disingenuous," it was not vanity to vindicate himself, even if the business were foolish or trifling.[15]

Unsurprisingly, Newton proceeded to defend himself. He had, he wrote, taken less from Hooke than he (Newton) had from Descartes, and less from both combined than Hooke had taken from Descartes. Indeed, Newton listed what he had taken "in general" from both Descartes and Hooke— from the former, that there was such a thing as an aether, and that this body transmitted the action or motion of light most freely in refracting bodies, and from the latter, that aether was a vibrating medium whose vibrations gave rise to the motions in bodies that cause heat. There were other minor observations that Newton had taken from Hooke, but they did not concern the doctrines laid out in the "Hypothesis"; most significantly, in using the notion of the aether, he differed from Hooke "in every thing." After composing a lengthy recital of examples where their accounts were opposed to each other, and where his explanations were superior, Newton added that in terms of explaining colours, the experiments on which his own "Hypothesis" depended (contained in the "Discourse of Observations"), "directly overthr[ew]" all the "hypothetical discours[es]" that Hooke had proffered in *Microgaphia*. The final letter that he sent Oldenburg on 21 December compressed many of the examples of differences between himself and Hooke that he had detailed in the draft, but the antipathy to Hooke was clear. Indeed, in one respect he now went further than in the draft. Having remarked that he accounted for refraction and reflection, and the production of colours in a way utterly unlike Hooke, he added that "in yᵉ colours of thin transparent substances I explain every thing after a way so differing from him yᵗ yᵉ experiments I grownd my discours on destroy all

he has said about them." Although this attack was not read out at the Society's meeting on 30 December, Hooke began another "New Philosophicall
clubb" at the lodging of Christopher Wren on the first day of 1676 and repeated the accusation that Newton had taken his aetherial wave hypothesis
of light from *Micrographia*.[16]

There is no doubt that Oldenburg—undoubtedly acting to generate
copy for the *Philosophical Transactions*—was responsible for much of the hostility that existed between Hooke and Newton. Notwithstanding his claims
to the contrary, Newton himself needed little encouragement to enter the
fray when he felt that his honour and property rights had been infringed.
Nevertheless, in this case, Hooke's behaviour—based on his general resentment at receiving insufficient credit for his discoveries—generated a great
deal of the animosity. Entitlement to his inventions and discoveries was one
of the chief sources of his reputation within the Society, and, indeed, at this
very moment he was engaged in a major priority dispute with Christiaan
Huygens over the invention of a balance-spring watch. Newton thanked
Oldenburg on 10 January 1676 for his "equitable candor" and for passing on
Hooke's "insinuations." It was a "reasonable piece of justice," he wrote, that he
should be given a chance to vindicate himself. He requested that Hooke show
exactly what it was he had taken from *Micrographia*, but gave a number of reasons for thinking that this was impossible. For good measure, he added some
more instances of Hooke's borrowings from Descartes. In the same letter, he
responded to the Jesuit assault on his virtue and competence, and he included
further advice for Gascoigne and others of Linus's "friends." Not only was the
invocation as a witness of the long-dead Kenelm Digby an indication that
Linus relied on old experiments, but Newton was particularly incensed by the
accusation that he had deliberately attempted to manipulate the press.[17]

As it was, Newton's own appeal for witnesses to his reproduction of the
oblong image in London was already running out of steam, not least because his most powerful potential supporter was none other than Hooke.
Accordingly, he added a postscript to the letter to Oldenburg of 10 January,
requesting that when his letter of 13 November 1675 was published in the
Transactions, Oldenburg should either omit any reference to Hooke or Hill,
or put letters for their names, since he now assumed they would rather not
be mentioned. When the letter was published, Hill and Hooke were identified as "A.H. (a member of the *R. Society*)" and "R.H.," respectively, though
this ruse obviously did nothing to hide their identities from the cognoscenti.
To further bait Hooke, Oldenburg allowed the core of Newton's demolition

of him (of 21 December) to be read before the Royal Society on 20 January 1676 and Hooke, shocked by what he heard (and suspecting Oldenburg of stirring the situation by making "fals suggestions" to Newton), immediately decided to de-escalate the situation. From his earlier contretemps with Newton in 1672 he knew that Newton despised public disputes, and within hours he wrote a letter stating that he did not approve of "contention or feuding and proving in print," and would only unwillingly be drawn into a sort of philosophical war. Hooke offered to correspond about natural philosophy by private letter and praised Newton's accomplishments, though in a phrase that Newton later recalled, he added that he would have done something more himself if his "troublesome employments" had not intervened.[18]

In an insincere rhetorical tour de force, Newton replied to "his honoured friend" on 5 February 1676 and acknowledged Hooke's offer of a private correspondence, telling him that what he had done became "a true Philosophical spirit." There was nothing he wanted to avoid more than contention, and above all he wanted to avoid a controversy in print. Next, Newton linked his dim view of print culture with a critique of the epistemic value of testimony: "What's done before many witnesses, is seldome wthout some further concern then that for truth, but what passes between friends in private usually deserves ye name of consultation rather then contest." He had become tired of philosophy, he told Hooke, and would never again take any pleasure spending time on it, but Hooke was the best person he could think of to pass on constructive criticism. This should be done by private letter, and anywhere Hooke felt that Newton had assumed too much, or given him insufficient credit, could also be dealt with by the same medium. Only outside the glare of public dispute could justice truly be done, he said, and on the same theme he added: "I am not so much in love wth philosophical productions but y^t I can make y^m yeild to equity & friendship." Having finished the main business of the letter, he now eulogised Hooke's achievements, famously adding that if he had seen further than Hooke (he knew he had), it was because he was standing on the shoulders of giants. Since Oldenburg was keen to publish the "Hypothesis," Newton quickly told him to omit a passage in which he had unfavourably compared Hooke's contribution to research on diffraction with the work of the Jesuit Francesco Maria Grimaldi. However, allowing the work to be read out in the public forum of the Royal Society had caused the very trouble he feared, and like many of his other works he now stopped its publication in print.[19]

4. Athanasius on Trial

Newton's disparaging remarks to Hooke about witnesses were in part concerned with his jaundiced views about writing for an unlearned and amorphous audience, but his chief bone of contention was that the invocation of witnesses made the discipline inappropriately litigious. No amount of testimony could support the level of certainty that true scientific statements required, and indeed, what was done before witnesses was rarely performed without some reason that had little to do with truth. However, while this sort of evidence was inappropriate in science, Newton was a keen advocate for the use of witnesses in their proper domain. Indeed, in his writings on ecclesiastical history, he wrote at length about how witnesses had been concocted and manipulated in the past, and about the proper use of witness testimony in the analysis of ancient writings. The appeal to both human and textual witnesses formed a key part of the humanist and specifically Protestant apologetics in which he was steeped. Newton had learned from these studies exactly when it was appropriate to make use of witness testimony, and it was inevitable that he would deploy these skills when he became mired in his disputes with Hooke and Leibniz. As we have seen, training in disputation made up much of the practical education in rhetoric that he experienced as an undergraduate, and he was highly skilled in its techniques. Once he turned his attention to the early church, he used copious amounts of judiciously interpreted testimony to find foes such as Athanasius guilty of nefarious crimes and misdemeanours. Other natural philosophers were also capable of switching to the forensic mode, notably Johannes Kepler, who used judicial rhetorical techniques in his defence of the astronomer Tycho Brahe against Ursus—the imperial mathematician at Prague. More significantly, he sifted through and dismantled numerous witness testimonies against his mother when she was charged with witchcraft. However, neither Kepler nor any other philosopher came close to creating the vast edifice of forensic history produced by Newton.[20]

Although Newton's approach to church history was radically heterodox, in his analysis of ancient Christian records he used the same techniques as his orthodox Protestant and Catholic opponents. That is, he examined many different kinds of documentary sources and assessed the credibility and moral demeanour of both godly and (as he saw it) satanic churchmen of the past. His analyses can best be understood by examining the judicial approaches adopted by the orthodox, who acted as targets for his own work. Accordingly, in the following two sections, I look at two major orthodox accounts of the Arian controversy, namely William Cave's *Ecclesiastici* of 1683, and Samuel Parker's *Religion and Loyalty* of 1684. A third work, Nathaniel Bacon's *History of the Life and Actions of St. Athanasius* of 1664 is of interest because the title of his work closely resembles the heading of one extended essay that Newton wrote on the machinations of Athanasius. Nevertheless, Bacon's work was neither as detailed nor as influential as the other two. I then look at how Newton offered a completely different perspective, by showing inconsistencies in the evidence provided by Athanasius, and by making inferences about Athanasius's actions and motivations. Charged with demonstrating the true history of doctrinal and ecclesiastical orthodoxy, Cave and Parker defended Athanasius and violently condemned the doctrines and intrigues of his enemies, namely Arius and his followers (most notably Eusebius of Nicomedia). They both used Christopher Sand's Arian *Nucleus Historiae Ecclesiasticae* and the work of the Arian historian Philostorgius as foils. It is quite possible that Newton had Cave or Parker in mind when he condemned modern historians, although when he did refer to "Homoousian" historians, his target was an entire tradition.[21]

As we have seen, the central fourth-century political and religious disputes over the status of the Son had arisen in the late 310s when Arius had disputed the matter with Alexander, the bishop of Alexandria. The latter had called a synod that had devised a formula to which Arius and others were unable to subscribe, whereupon Arius had fled to Nicomedia, where he met the sympathetic Eusebius of Nicomedia. Eusebius's influence with Constantine (whom he baptized) led ultimately to the creation of the Council of Nicaea in 325.[22] Cave argued that the majority of the council devised the *homoousios* compromise against Arius's "Crafty and Fraudulent shifting" and concluded that as a result of this, Constantine had rightly banished Arius, along with Eusebius of Nicomedia. Given the obnoxious Arian account of the Son, orthodox historians lambasted everything Arius did and stood for. Nevertheless, they spent more time attacking the political machinations of Eusebius and his followers. Parker stressed that Eusebius's followers were actually opposed doctrinally to many positions maintained by Arius and were the true orchestrators of all the "tumults" that followed Nicaea.[23]

Parker and Cave attacked the entire account of "that dull Fanatique *Arian*" Christopher Sand, since he had deliberately misread or invented documents and had placed reliance on the obscure and corrupted writings ("Modern and Barbarous Arabick Pamphlets") constituting the *Annals* of the tenth-century Christian Egyptian writer Eutychius (Sa'id ibn Bitriq) to support his claim that the majority of the two thousand bishops present had voted in favour of Arius. Throughout the text, Parker attacked Sand for his obvious bias and alleged incompetence, though he and Cave protested so much that their works attest to the great significance of Sand's writings in this period. Parker lamented the fact that the "silly Scribler" had been "Canonised among the Wits and the Worthies for his views" and admitted that it was on this account that he had decided to use the history of the Arian controversy to expose Sand's lack of common sense and honesty.[24]

As Parker saw it, the convoluted history of what happened immediately after the great council ended could be resolved by having straightforward recourse to the *Apology* of Athanasius. While Newton accounted this work a devious collection of lies based on fictitious evidence, Parker claimed that the great architect of orthodoxy had been so modest that he had not allowed the force of his narrative to rest on his own authority, "but has justified every part of it by Testimonials from other men, publick Records, and the Letters of his Enemies under their own hands." These texts showed the wicked villainy of Eusebius, who, even after his banishment, had mobilised his great influence with Constantine (he was a trusted advisor to Constantine's sister) and stirred up the Melitians, "old and experienced Plot-makers," against Athanasius. This, Parker noted, was equivalent to Presbyterians making interest with papists against the Church of England, and, indeed, throughout his narrative he equated the plotting of the Eusebians and Melitians with the various conspiracies that had been hatched since the Restoration against Charles II. These had culminated in the Rye House Plot that had been discovered the year before his own book was published.[25]

Thanks to various manoeuvres, Eusebius was readmitted at court in 329 and wrote to Athanasius (who had succeeded Alexander as bishop of Alexandria in 328) asking him to restore Arius. Athanasius predictably refused and continued to promote orthodox Trinitarianism among the faithful. In the meantime Eusebius and the Melitians made various accusations against him, and in 332 he was forced to deal with some business in Mareotis (a town southwest of Alexandria) concerning one Ischyras, who was allegedly acting as a priest without authority. Athanasius sent his presbyter Macarius to deal with the situation but at the same time, Eusebius began to turn Constantine against him; according to Cave, he succeeded "by crafty insinuations" in persuading the emperor to write to Athanasius, requesting

PRIVATE PROSECUTIONS

him "in a positive and peremptory manner" to readmit Arius. Athanasius refused, saying that the Catholic Church could not hold communion with a heretic, whereupon Eusebius resorted to "downright Methods of Fraud and Falshood" in convincing the Melitians to send their own bishops to Constantine's court, armed with grave accusations against Athanasius.[26]

5. Tyrian Convictions

As part of Eusebius's strategy, according to Parker, he now procured the services of Ischyras, "a debauch't pretended Priest" who had allegedly forged his holy orders and subsequently been deposed by Athanasius. Eusebius offered him a bishopric if he would testify against Athanasius, and Ischyras immediately swore both that Athanasius had assaulted his church, and that Macarius had overturned the communion table, breaking the holy cup into pieces and burning his Bibles. The plot thickened, and Ischyras added the much more serious charge that Athanasius had murdered Arsenius, bishop of Hypsele, and had indulged in sorcery using the latter's severed hand. Ischyras brought forward the hand allegedly cut off by Athanasius, and Parker recorded that Arsenius, who was part of the conspiracy, got ready to go into hiding until Athanasius was "dispatched out of the way." However, Athanasius later reported that Ischyras had got cold feet and had confessed the plot in a letter to him subscribed in the presence of a large number of clergy.[27]

Cave argued that Arsenius had originally "fallen under some great Irregularity," had been asked to appear before a court to answer these charges, and had then disappeared. John, the leader of the Melitians, had hidden Arsenius with a presbyter of a monastery in Thebais and then accused Athanasius of his murder. It was at this point that Ischyras had shown off the amputated hand and the news had quickly come to the ear of Constantine who put his nephew Dalmatius on the case. Rehearsing Athanasius's own account in his *Apology Against the Arians*, Cave narrated how Athanasius had later sent one of his deacons to find Arsenius; after some problems, he was located and forced to come out of hiding. Although he initially claimed to be someone else, as a result of pressure from a crowd of witnesses, he was forced to admit his identity along with the details of the plot. Athanasius informed Constantine of the outcome, and the emperor condemned the Melitians for their meddling.[28]

The Eusebians and Melitians did not let up in their attacks on Athanasius. In 334 Constantine convened a council at Caesarea to hear charges of sedition against him but Athanasius wisely refused to attend, forcing Constantine to reconvene the proceedings at Tyre (in modern Lebanon) in 335. While Macarius was forcibly brought to the synod by soldiers, Athanasius again declined to appear, fearing that the gathering was irrevocably prejudiced against him. In the end, according to Cave, he turned up with an entourage of sixty-seven Egyptian bishops "as Witnesses of his Integrity, and Advocates of his Cause." Parker argued that Tyre provided an opportunity to show the "flying Stories" about Athanasius's wrongdoing for the gossip they were, by putting them to "a publick Examination before judges." The council, although it was allegedly managed by Eusebian sympathisers, ultimately failed to produce a sufficiently coherent case against him. Ischyras, who had withdrawn his recantation, rendered his own authority as a witness invalid through repeatedly swearing inconsistent testimony, while Athanasius also survived being accused of immorality by a "common Strumpet." She played her role, as Parker saw it, with some conviction, claiming that Athanasius had caused her to lose her virginity. This attempt to snare him was easily foiled when one of his presbyters, Timotheus, stepped forward and pretended to be Athanasius, whereupon the woman pointed at the presbyter and accused him of the crime. If Athanasius and his allies thought this was the end of the proceedings, they were mistaken, for the Eusebians warned them that there were yet blacker crimes to consider.[29]

The following accusation was potentially the most serious, although Cave termed the whole event a "Tragy-Comick Scene." At Tyre, the accusers of Athanasius produced the hand that had allegedly been cut from Arsenius, believing that Arsenius had fled far away as a result of their threats. However, Athanasius's allies persuaded Arsenius to appear before the council, and it was a simple matter—though not performed without elements of pantomime that orthodox historians loved to repeat—to show that Arsenius was still in possession of all his limbs. Athanasius was still not out of the woods, for his enemies stirred up the local populace against him, alleging that Athanasius had tried to prevent corn shipments from arriving in Constantinople. To keep the peace, the emissaries of Constantine whisked him to Constantinople to see the emperor himself. However, Constantine remained prejudiced against him, and in the meantime the busy Eusebians went to Mareotis to collect what Parker called "Cloak-bags full of fresh Evidence." Athanasius was deposed and excommunicated on the grounds that he was blocking the corn shipments. Cave concluded his account of this episode by pointing out that Arsenius had written to Athanasius after his alleged murder, and before the Tyrian synod, affirming his own orthodoxy and asking to be readmitted into the church. Like almost all contemporary writers on the subject, Parker denounced the Tyrian proceedings as a sham and lambasted Philostorgius and his lackey Sand for inventing fables. They had the gall "to out-face publick and undeniable Records" and were contradicted by the confessions of Ischyras and others, all made "under Hand and Seal." The Arian forgeries were plain for all to see, and all they had on their side was their "incredible confidence."[30]

6. Questions of Evidence

Newton saw the Athanasian account of Nicaea and its aftermath as a tissue of lies, designed to hide the reality of vicious actions perpetrated as the result of a great conspiracy. He focussed on the events at Tyre with an extraordinary intensity and explored the actions and motivations of the participants with a mixture of great brilliance and extreme prejudice. He devoted particular attention to the morals and actions of Athanasius and set out to show that everything said against Athanasius at Tyre and elsewhere by his enemies was based on fact. Athanasius really had cavorted with prostitutes, and he was a liar, a forger, a murderer, and a rabble-rouser. The position taken by Athanasius's accusers was laid out in Athanasius's own writings and in many other documents, and Newton decided that by and large, these accounts—even though chiefly relayed through the writings of Athanasius—could be taken at face value. On the other hand, where Cave and Parker had assumed that the pro-Athanasian documents were authentic and constituted unassailable evidence of Athanasius's innocence, Newton read them either as obvious forgeries or as clear evidence of Athanasius's guilt.[31]

Newton's analysis was rich in the use of standard forensic techniques and language. In one extended examination of Athanasius's actions, he copied down the confessional letter allegedly written by Arsenius to Athanasius and subjected the text to sceptical scrutiny. It did not resemble a freely composed letter, he argued, but rather looked like a "formal covenant of submission drawn up by a Lawyer to be imposed on Arsenius or a recantation imposed on him by a magistrate." If Arsenius had really written the letter, he would have come running to Athanasius, shown himself to the emperor, and put an end to

all the confusion about his fate that was so prevalent in the years that followed Tyre. If he was so well disposed to Athanasius, would he have let the
great man suffer as much as he did? If Arsenius *had* written the letter, in
which he asked Athanasius to reply to him, Athanasius would have known
where he was and would have immediately sent his henchmen to get him.
However, Newton believed that Arsenius really was dead, murdered by the
bishop of Alexandria in a Mafia-style operation.[32]

Throughout his writings on early church history, Newton made extensive use of argument ex silentio, that is, the drawing of conclusions from
absence of evidence. The standard story, as we have seen, was that Athanasius
refuted the accusations of his enemies at Tyre by producing Arsenius alive
and by pulling out his hands for all to see. Newton wrote that he "suspected" this story, primarily because no one mentioned it in the two and a
half decades that followed the alleged events, and he noted that the tale only
emerged among Athanasius's writings when the latter was free to rewrite
history in the late 350s. When Athanasius called a council at Alexandria in
338, he wrote a "large and elaborate" letter to the world defending himself
against the proceedings at Tyre, yet there was nothing of the dead man's
hand nor of Arsenius's appearance in the text. Nor was there any reference
to it in a letter that Pope Julius wrote to the Eastern bishops in 341 defending Athanasius, nor even in the two lengthy letters that he and more than
250 bishops wrote from Serdica in 343. They mentioned that Arsenius was
still alive at the time of writing, but said nothing of his presence at Tyre,
though Newton pointed out that a definitive statement that Arsenius had
been at Tyre would have been "more to ye purpose than all the rest which
they say." "They" neither mentioned nor brought forward witnesses who
could testify to his being alive at Tyre, as they surely would have done if he
had been seen by all the attendees at the council.[33]

Next, Newton demonstrated that the Athanasian argument was inconsistent. Athanasius and his allies had told the story of what had taken place at
Tyre differently in Athanasius's own second *Apology* and in a number of
other letters. The latter related the affair "as if the accusers produced before
ye Council not a dead man's hand but a dead body & Athanasius produced
against them not Arsenius alive but his letter only." Arsenius's alleged letter
to Athanasius was so feeble as a piece of evidence that nearly a decade later
the Council of Serdica still went on to condemn Athanasius for the murder.
That council, in a letter to the church of Alexandria, had related how the
Council of Tyre had commanded the dead body of Arsenius to be laid

before it. From this evidence, Newton argued, it had clearly been this and *not* the magical hand of traditional lore that had been inspected, and he brought his own forensic knowledge into play, arguing that "in cases of murder tis usual to have dead bodies viewed for passing judgement upon them." This must have been done in the council, he continued, so that "by ye features & other marks & wounds & testimony of those who knew Arsenius or had seen his body at ye time of ye murder & buried it & dug it up again the Council might be satisfied whether he was murdered & how." Newton concluded that "to shame ye proceedings of the Council some Jugler (for I will not say sorcerer) has transformed ye whole body into a magical hand."[34]

According to Newton, the Athanasians were forced to exaggerate the evidence conveyed by the letter of Arsenius because it was the only conceivable testimony they could find. He added that they would have produced the said witnesses at the councils they convened in their own favour if any had existed, but they were unable to find a solitary person who could vouch for Arsenius's presence at Tyre. Had such witnesses existed, Newton continued, they would have made a much greater fuss about their testimony "than about a Letter wch no upright Court of Judicature would allow for any evidence at all." In any case, why would Athanasius have been banished if Arsenius had appeared at Tyre? The punishment he was given there was comprehensible only if there really had been a dead body rather than a letter, and the fact that the Tyrian council did condemn Athanasius as a murderer was agreed by the testimony of Athanasius and his friends.[35]

While the Latin clergy betrayed the true state of affairs by their inconsistencies, the Eastern bishops constantly maintained their view that the evil deed had in fact taken place. Their behaviour provided concurrent and independent testimony, and "for my part," Newton wrote, "I can more easily believe what both parties affirmed in that age before newer stories were invented: then that ye Bishops of all ye east should condemn Athanasius for merdering a man who appeared alive before them in ye midst of ye Council <& owned himself to be Arsenius> & was known by many there." Even after Athanasius had appealed to Constantine after Tyre, the decision stood and so, Newton concluded, the entire story about the proceedings at Tyre that the orthodox had handed down to posterity was a fable invented decades after the fact: "I suspect Athanasius to be ye inventor of it because he tells it first of any man in his second Apology written in the Wildernesse at the same time that he broached ye story of ye death." Athanasius was the sole author of the account and had composed it as part of his grand scheme to rewrite history, thus achieving his diabolical goal of neutering the ecclesiastical and political power of the Eusebians. The story was spread around the world by the monks, and it became accepted as gospel.[36]

7. Legal Proceedings

Newton used identical forensic techniques to uncover the truth behind the story of Ischyras, the priest who had accused Athanasius and his presbyter Macarius of extreme violence, recanted his allegations in a confessional letter, and then withdrawn this recantation at Tyre. Cave noted Athanasius's testimony that he had sent Macarius to Mareotis to investigate reports of a disturbance and to summon Ischyras to answer various allegations. Ischyras denied the things he was alleged to have done, and having fled to Nicomedia and been promised a bishopric of his own, he and the Melitians had allegedly devised a plan against Athanasius. In addition to charges of treason and illegality regarding Athanasius's appointment to the bishopric, they accused Athanasius of ordering Macarius to break the communion chalice at Ischyras's church, of overturning the altar, of burning the Bible, and, finally, of burning down his house. As we have seen, Constantine had initially heard these accusations in person in early 332 and had exonerated Athanasius, agreeing that Ischyras could not have been ministering at the altar when Macarius arrived since he was ill in bed, that the place was not a church but a farmhouse, and that catechumens were then in the place so the Eucharist could not have been administered. According to Cave, witnesses confirmed that Macarius had not broken the communion cup, overturned an altar, or burnt a Bible, and they testified that Ischyras's entire story was "forged and fabulous."[37]

To cap it all, Ischyras had then gone on to confess the entire plot in front of six presbyters and eight deacons, whose names were on the deposition but not signed in their own hands. He claimed that he had been physically coerced into doing it by some Melitians, and knew nothing of any wrongdoing by Athanasius, wishing only to be admitted into orthodox communion. Newton "suspected" the truth of Ischyras's confession, this time because "it looks as if contrived rather for the interest of Athanasius then that of Ischyras, & seems more like a formal recantation or certificate then a free Letter, & also conteins a ridiculous story." The Melitians would never have tried to secure false accusers by forcing and beating them, and perjured witnesses were never as enthusiastic as Ischyras had been in listing the accusations against Athanasius; "could a beating bout make Ischyras so hearty in the cause," Newton asked? Why, too, had Athanasius not secured Ischyras's confession in person? "Would Athanasius send up & down ye world to seek Arsenius & not accept of Ischyras when he offered to come in, but content himself wth a bare letter?" These things, Newton claimed, "don't consist." In all respects, he concluded in a different account of the affair, the letter was alien to Ischyras's case, and it was merely an "amateur ruse" that coincided exactly with the designs of Athanasius's friends. When they saw that the letter ascribed to Arsenius had failed to do its work, they thought the letter they concocted as coming from the hand of Ischyras should be confirmed by as many witnesses as possible.[38]

The letter was also rendered absurd, Newton claimed, by the large number of witnesses appended to it. Why invoke the testimony of eleven when two or three would have done? However, the most egregious aspect of the whole case was that the letter contained a reference to witnesses at all, for, he went on, witnesses had no place in ordinary letters but only in certificates or formal documents that were intended to be used as evidence in legal proceedings. The fact that the deacons and presbyters were named in the text as witnesses shows that its author "designed it for evidence." Moreover, in terms of cui bono (the question of who benefitted from the letter), the evidence in it had been designed to support Athanasius and no one else, and so it was fatally tainted. In these statements, Newton revealed quite clearly why witnesses had no place in natural philosophy. Witnesses were used as evidential support when the person marshalling them had to prove a legal or rhetorical case, a purpose that was not necessarily connected to the truth of the matter in question. As Newton would tell Robert Hooke and Edmond Halley, philosophy was not a law-court. Neither the style of legal argument nor the evidence that witnesses provided was relevant to discovering and demonstrating scientific truths.[39]

Newton also drew attention to the fact that the witnesses had been named by the author of the letter but had not actually signed it. If Ischyras had written the letter and had designed it for evidence on his own behalf, he would certainly have caused the witnesses to put their signatures to the text. Newton surmised that it appeared to have been written by somebody else "who had a mind to give credit to it by witnesses, but knew not how either to procure or counterfeit their hands." No witnesses were ever called to prove the truth of the letter at the following councils of Alexandria, Rome, and Serdica. If no effort had been made to get the letter authenticated at

Tyre, then this, Newton claimed, betrayed a guilty conscience and, if such an attempt had been made and the witnesses refused to vouch for its contents, then this also proved the letter false. The whole thing was a farrago and he concluded: "So impudent a case as this was scarce ever brought before a civil Magistrate." Nor had such evidence been taken seriously in ecclesiastical courts until the much later Council of Alexandria in 363, when Athanasius personally presided over the synod.[40]

Newton now concluded by offering his reader what he took to be a much more plausible account of what had actually happened. He argued that Macarius had been sent first to warn Ischyras about his conduct and that when the latter continued his activities, Athanasius had arrived and smashed the place up. Athanasius had claimed that Macarius went alone (without Athanasius) and found Ischyras sick in bed, in a place that was not a church, and on a day that was not the Lord's day, and merely reproved him. However, Newton argued that Athanasius had concocted this story, not at Tyre where the accusation against him had been taken seriously, but much later "amongst y^e <credulous> western Bishops & others of his own party." There were still signs of how Athanasius had suppressed the truth. From records of the Council of Tyre left at Rome, Newton found that the witnesses interviewed by the six representatives sent from Tyre to Mareotis to uncover the truth had told different stories. Some had mentioned that Macarius had indeed found Ischyras sick in bed, as Athanasius had said, but the Greek witness mentioned that Athanasius had discovered him administering the Eucharist. In his deposition to the pope over a decade later, Athanasius had easily suppressed the minority report (since it was written in Greek), and persuaded the pope that, because Ischyras was ill, he could not have been celebrating the Eucharist. For Newton, this was the end of the story: "Now if <Athanasius shuffled in making> this Defense then it's plain that he was gravelled[41] & wanted a just defense." All this, Newton decided in judgement, was sufficient to determine his guilt.[42]

8. Sincerity and Public Profession

Following Athanasius, orthodox historians always disparaged the deliberations at Tyre as less than a full council, but Newton could not let this pass unremarked. Athanasius's "friends" and apologists had attempted to discredit it by making it out to be a mere conventicle but, by assessing the records,

Newton concluded that it was orthodox, authentic, and at least as big as the Council of Nicaea: "the designe of this Council being very great it needed great credit & authority to support it." Constantine had sent out a universal request requiring the attendance of bishops so that it might be full, and Newton pointed out that immediately after the council, Athanasius's supporters had never criticised it for being insufficiently large. On top of this, Athanasians had criticised the council for being one of the "Arian" councils, "and on that account of no authority," but, Newton argued pointedly, the accusation was never proved,

> & an accusation wthout proof is of no credit. The accusation indeed has gained credit among ye followers of Athanasius for a long time, but this makes it no more than popular fame & popular fame <wthout original evidence> thô of five thousand years standing is but popular fame nor can any man take up wth it wthout making himself one of ye giddy mobile. Such fame indeed when ye original of it is forgotten may make a strong presumption, but when we know ye original & y^t it was spread abroad wthout evidence [it] can be of no moment.

"Wise men," he opined, "must look only to ye evidence." The only evidence that the council was "Arian" was that it received Arius into communion and banished Athanasius. It had indeed received Arius but had not condemned Athanasius for subscribing to the Nicene decrees. Moreover, the bishops who made the decision were not "Arian" in any sense of the term, and in almost all of the following councils the same men anathematised those opinions for which Arius had been originally condemned.[43]

If the accusation was that these same bishops dissembled and "were Arian in their heart while they were orthodox in their language," Newton continued, "I must ask you how you or any man else can know that." Such an accusation without independent knowledge of the facts amounted to clamour, calumny, and malice. Had Athanasius and his allies the gift of searching and knowing men's hearts? Evidently not. The only way to know a person's faith was by their public decrees and by the externally visible manner of worship—on these grounds the council was orthodox, constantly condemning Arian positions. In a revealing passage, Newton noted that the Athanasians at the Tyrian council never accused the bishops there of dissembling, and indeed such a charge would have been preposterous:

> Should any Church of our age charge heresy upon any body of men of her own communion, & should the men reply that they always were of ye communion of that Church & always profest her faith & used her worship &

<& that they> still continue in that profession & practise; & should ye accusers grant all this & only reply that notwithstanding their communion profession & practise they were hereticks in their hearts; & should the Judges upon this accusation condemn them to death: I think such proceedings would by all sober men be accounted as malitious & barbarous as any we ever heard of.

The reference to capital punishment for heresy is consistent with Newton's remarks elsewhere on the behaviour of the Roman Catholic Church, but the first part of the passage should surely be read in connection with his own membership of the Church of England. If individuals took communion and worshipped regularly in a properly constituted church, constantly professing the core elements of the faith, then they should be considered bona fide members of that institution. No one had the right or capacity to infer from the public profession of faith offered by other individuals that they were secret heretics, and Newton implied that membership of a church depended more on the continuity of public worship rather than on what individuals sincerely believed.[44]

The relationship between individual sincerity and the public profession of belief was directly raised in a further comment on the case. Newton pointed out that the supporters of Athanasius often complained that the Eusebians dissembled at Nicaea, but even if some of them *were* Arians, he added, this would have made no difference to the authority of the council. Just as the authority of a judge depended "not upon his religion or sincerity but upon his incorporation into ye body politick, & upon his Commission to act," so the authority of a council depended "not upon the secret religion & sincerity of the men but upon their being in external communion wth the Church catholick, & having a legal commission to meet & act in Council." Unless this were so, there was no certain way of determining whether *any* council was authentic. In any case, everyone in this period acknowledged that the council at Tyre *was* authentic: "For Athanasius & his party in that age questioned not ye authority of this Council, but only complained as if they had abused their authority by corrupt judgment." Although contemporaries such as Pope Julius did question the sincerity and integrity of some of its participants, they did not query its authority. Indeed, when the same pope had received Athanasius into communion and absolved him, he had implicitly accepted the sentence of excommunication passed by Tyre.[45]

9. A Litigious Lady

Newton's extensive treatment of what he saw as Athanasius's great perversion of doctrine and history displayed his mastery both of humanist forensic
technique and of the relevant documentary evidence. The language and
style of procedure of the law-court shaped the enquiry and set up a decision
that had never been in doubt. In marshalling evidence in this way, Newton
was doing what was appropriate to, and indeed required by, the intellectual
field in which he worked. He approached his subject using the same tools
with which orthodox divines such as Cave and Parker went about their
own task—with opposite results. Newton's propensity to discern that a situation was appropriate for litigation also says a great deal about his underlying character. Indeed, although the events and the format demanded the
sort of approach he adopted, in these private performances one can discern
the generally "suspicious" nature that was described by both friends and enemies. After some time, his capacity to use these techniques had become
ingrained, informing his pre-existing tendency to suspect and examine the
motivations of others. His litigating skills were used to the full in his responses to his enemies when natural philosophy became disputatious.

The most prominent example of Newton's use of his forensic skills in
natural philosophy is to be found in his relations with Robert Hooke, who
had caused him so many problems in the middle of the 1670s. By 1679
Newton was free to spend most of his time at Trinity College and to work
in the fields of alchemy, prophecy, and early church history. However, as we
have seen, in summer of that year he left Cambridge to tend to his terminally
ill mother and to deal with the more mundane business affairs that arose
from her death. He did not return to the college until the end of November.
Over the following weeks he presumably did alchemy and studied theological
topics, but it was now that Hooke tempted him back into a restricted private correspondence about natural philosophy by assuring Newton that he
could trust Hooke not to reveal any correspondence to a wider audience.
He asked Newton to comment on his own law of the spring and on his
notion that heavenly motions could be analysed in terms of rectilinear inertia
and central attraction.[46]

In reply, Newton politely referred to Oldenburg's "importunity" as the
source of the enmity that had existed between them. He told Hooke that

he had had no time to engage in philosophical meditations, being caught up in "Country affairs." Repeating the protestations of his giants' shoulders letter, he told Hooke that he had been trying to "bend" himself from philosophy to other studies and had long begrudged the time spent on it unless as diversion. "Having thus shook hands wth Philosophy," he added, "& being also at present taken of wth other business, I hope it will not be interpreted out of any unkindness to you or ye R. Society that I am backward in engaging my self in these matters." Newton reassured Hooke that it was not through an excessive reserve or distrust that he had declined correspondence, but he was engaged in other work both for his own satisfaction and the good of others. That said, he included a "fancy" regarding the path taken by a body falling from a tall object to the centre of the earth (on the assumption that the earth offered no resistance) and proposed an empirical test of his notion that such a body would fall to the east of the perpendicular. He concluded offhandedly that if he were ever lucky enough to strike up a regular conversation with Hooke, he would be delighted to communicate anything that he came across.[47]

Hooke replied that he hoped Newton would not desert philosophy at a time when so many others were doing so, and added that he would not demand from Newton anything more than that he occasionally taste the delights of natural philosophy. In a comment aimed at placating his correspondent, he claimed that he hated being a "drudge" at anything and that if Newton was tiring of natural philosophy, then he well understood. However, to Newton's dismay, he revealed that he had read out the part of Newton's letter concerning celestial dynamics at the previous meeting of the Royal Society. Indeed, he had voiced his disagreement with Newton's notion that a body falling to the centre of the earth with no resistance would fall in a constant elliptoid rather than towards the centre in a descending spiral. Newton quickly composed a reply, in which he corrected the "slip" he had made in his original letter. Hooke's response to this elicited no further reaction from Cambridge except for a cursory remark the following December.[48]

More than five years later, as Newton neared the completion of the *Principia*, he was informed by Edmond Halley that Hooke had "some pretensions" towards the discovery of the inverse-square law. Hooke, Halley told Newton, "sais you had the notion from him, though he owns the Demonstration of the Curves generated therby to be wholly your own." Halley suggested that Hooke only seemed to want a mention in the preface and rather hopefully claimed that he was sure Newton, "who of all men has the least need to borrow reputation," would act with the greatest candour. However, enough damage had been done to ensure that there was now no possibility of avoiding a rancorous dispute over intellectual property. Newton immediately responded that he wanted there to be a good understanding between himself and Hooke, but opened with the remark that in the *Principia* material now held by Halley (i.e., what was later published as Book 1), there was not one proposition to which Hooke could "pretend." Rehearsing the demolition of Hooke he had performed just over a decade earlier, he went back over the correspondence of 1679/80, suggesting that Hooke had harassed him into contributing something to the Royal Society and had then made a serious error when he wrote back. Newton had learned nothing new or material from him in the exchange, and for good measure he added that he had discussed the inverse-square law with Christopher Wren in 1677, so that Hooke was the last of them to know it.[49]

Just over a month later, Newton wrote up in more detail what he called the "case" concerning Hooke's morals and actions. Opening with the rhetorical claim that he considered the whole issue entirely frivolous, he immediately revealed just how much energy he had expended on the issue over the preceding weeks. He marshalled a number of different arguments against Hooke, and noted that since they had never discussed the application of the inverse-square law to the heavens, Hooke could not conclude that Newton did not know of it at that time. Newton claimed that even if he *had* received the inverse-square law from Hooke, the latter had lacked any proof that the law held more than *quam proxime* at great distances from the centre of attraction, and the fact that the law did hold was only known because of work Newton had done long after the correspondence. Newton compared the way that Hooke had merely "guessed" at his result with the way that Kepler had guessed at the elliptical shape of planetary orbits, noting that at least Kepler had been correct. Newton's capacity to demonstrate these relations mathematically gave him as much right to the inverse-square law as to the proof of the elliptical orbit of comets.[50]

At the end of the letter, Newton told Halley that he was now going to suppress the third book. Philosophy, he wrote, "is such an *impertinently litigious Lady* that a man had as good be engaged in Law suits as have to do with her. I found it so formerly & now I no sooner come near her again but she gives me warning." In a furious postscript, he added that a friend had revealed that at a recent meeting of the Royal Society, Hooke had "made a great stir pretending I had all from him & desiring they would see that he had justice done him." He told Halley that by way of "justice," he was obliged to tell Halley how Hooke had stolen the Italian Giovanni Borelli's "hypothesis" of planetary motions from its author. As he had done a decade earlier, Newton proceeded to annihilate the credibility of his adversary. Hooke had "done nothing & yet written in such a way as if he knew & had sufficiently hinted all but what remained to be determined by ye drudgery of calculations & observations, excusing himself from that labour by reason of his other business." In fact, Newton thundered, he should have excused himself on the grounds of his incompetence. The profligate sower of "hints," he noted sarcastically, wanted all the credit while "I must now acknowledge in print I had all from him & so did nothing my self but drudge in calculating demonstrating & writing upon ye inventions of this great man." Harking back to the term used by Hooke in their earlier correspondence, Newton composed a riff on the term "drudge," contrasting the achievements of those who did nothing with mathematicians like himself, who actually discovered, confirmed, and did everything.[51]

In the main letter, Newton characteristically shifted the issue onto his home turf of documentary analysis. He referred to three separate writings of his that predated anything written on the subject by Hooke, each of which allegedly gave some sort of proof that Newton had prior knowledge of the inverse-square law. One was an early private effort from the mid-1660s to compare the centripetal force by which the earth attracted the moon with the measure of gravity on the earth's surface. In this now famous calculation, Newton had indeed shown that the attractive force exerted by the earth on the moon was almost exactly consistent with an inverse-square law. The other two alleged references to the law were far more obscure, but they were "public" documents and thus admissible evidence in the case against Hooke. The first was a letter from 1673, directed in the first instance to Oldenburg but intended for Christiaan Huygens, in which Newton had thanked Huygens for his gift of a copy of the *Horologium Oscillatorium*. Although he could not at present locate the document, Newton told Halley that it showed that he then "had [his] eye" on comparing the forces of planets arising from their circular motion and so "understood" the inverse-square law. The second "public" text was the "Hypothesis" of 1675, which had been read at the Society and registered in its books. In this, Newton said, he had "hinted" at a cause of the gravitation towards large celestial bodies and had not expressly stated the inverse-square law because he was only dealing with gravity at the surface of the earth.[52]

In the postscript, Newton explored the possibility that Hooke, in his role as secretary to the Royal Society, and knowing Newton's handwriting, might have derived the idea of how to determine the inverse-square law from his letter to Huygens even though it was not explicitly stated. However, Hooke was a mathematical "bungler" and a sociopath and had misunderstood what he had tried to thieve. So that Halley could be further satisfied in the affair, Newton continued, he should consult the "Hypothesis" that was deposited in the Royal Society. There, if Halley read it properly, he could see that Newton had outlined universal gravitation in vague aetherial terms. Again, he repeated that since it was merely one of his "guesses," he had had no need to expressly state the inverse-square law, though it was implied by his analysis.[53]

Concerned that Newton would keep back the rest of the book dealing with the system of the world, Halley told him on 29 June 1686 that in early 1684 Christopher Wren had promised Hooke a book worth £2 if he could demonstrate that the motions of planets obeyed the inverse-square law. Hooke had said that he had already done so, but that he would conceal it for a limited period of time, "so that others triing and failing, might know how to value it, when he should make it publick." However, Halley added, Hooke had never shown any evidence of this. More recently, an absorbing exchange had taken place in the Royal Society on the occasion of the recent presentation to the Society of the first book of the *Principia*. Hooke's friend Sir John Hoskins had lauded Newton's achievement by saying that Newton had simultaneously invented and perfected the theory, whereupon Hooke had taken umbrage at the fact that Hoskins had not revealed something (presumably a hint relating to the proof) that Hooke had said to him in private. The debate had spilled over into the post-meeting discussion at a coffee house, in which Hooke's claims to some credit to the inverse-square law were dismissed by those present on the grounds that he had left no evidence that he knew of it, either in print, or in the records of the Society. Halley added that the unanimous opinion was that even if Hooke had known of the law, "he ought not to blame any but himself, for having taken no more care to secure a discovery, which he puts so much Value on."[54]

This debate has attracted substantial attention from historians, who have been largely concerned with Hooke's programme for "Compounding Celestiall motions," what he actually knew about the inverse-square law, and whether he received due credit from Newton (and from subsequent commentators). In terms of Newton's own attitude to publication, there is no little irony in Hooke's being convicted for excessive secrecy. Indeed, the news of Hooke's humiliation did give him some cheer, and he admitted to Halley two weeks later that Hooke had "in some respects" been misrepresented to him. However the whole issue still rankled with him and he continued his search for documentary evidence to support his case. At the end of July Newton wrote again; he had "unexpectedly" located the letter to Huygens, allegedly in the hand of his then roommate John Wickins ("& so it is authentick"), which proved that he understood the inverse-square law long before Hooke did. He concluded that he owed Hooke little except "ye diversion he gave me from my other studies to think on these things." This letter has provoked a great deal of comment, not least because the part of the text cited by Newton as evidence of his priority over Hooke was missing from the copy of the letter that Huygens received. The Huygens version of the letter is in the hand of Henry Oldenburg, copied (according to Oldenburg's standard practice) from the original sent by Newton, which was in Newton's hand. The differences between these texts have understandably prompted a number of historians to conclude that at some point, Newton forged the text and had it inserted into the archives of the Royal Society. This inference is by no means unreasonable, though if true, then on this one occasion—and to no great advantage to his case—Newton engaged in exactly the sort of criminal forgery for which he condemned his enemies. In the judicial forum that counted, Hooke was found guilty of trying to steal intellectual property, and his competence and honour were left in shreds.[55]

10. The Master of Testimonies

Hooke never recovered from this humiliation. Although the structure of the dispute resembles the one that had taken place a decade earlier, times had changed; Newton's career was on the ascendant, while Hooke's was waning. He received no "shoulders of giants" reply from his nemesis and lived out the remainder of his life in a somewhat pathetic and embittered state. It is striking that in Newton's treatment of Hooke and, later, of Gottfried Leibniz, the main enemies of the first and second halves of his career, he used the same forensic rhetorical procedures and techniques as he did in his prosecution of ancient corrupters. Both of these disputes, which involved intellectual property rights in the discoveries of universal gravitation and the calculus, concerned significant issues, and he showed that when philosophy

became litigious, he could hold his own with anyone. Outside natural philosophy, these skills were also highly useful. In the case of William Chaloner, the
forger whose plans Newton (as Warden of the Mint) finally defeated in
1699, Newton deployed his analytical expertise in the service of national
security. Whenever he was called to prosecute wrongdoers, he got his man
through the adept use of evidence and the manipulation of witnesses.[56]

When Newton became Warden of the Mint in the spring of 1696 he was
immediately charged with prosecuting counterfeiters, a task that had not
usually been one expected of someone in his role. At the time he took up
his post, the English economy was becoming chronically short of acceptable
silver coin. This was in part because the face value of the coin was worth less
than the silver content, encouraging some people to export silver coin
for its bullion content. Since almost all coin lacked milled edges, "clippers"
simply chopped off bits from the edge of the coin, and by the time Newton
assumed office, about half the coin in circulation was clipped. "Coiners"
took these inferior coins and melted them down to make new coin, with
much less silver content. The job of engaging in legal proceedings against
coiners, who were technically guilty of treason, forced Newton to engage
with a world that existed only a few hundred yards outside his base in the
Tower of London. The business of prosecuting such figures was saturated
with references to witnesses and the "informations" they provided, and
Newton was adept at dealing with such evidence. However, things did not
go well at first. Within a short time of taking up his job he told the Treasury
that juries were sceptical of the witnesses he was using in trials on the
grounds that the latter were eligible for the lucrative reward of £40 for their
testimony. This "vilifying of my Agents & Witnesses," he said, "is a reflexion
on me which has gravelled me & must in time impair & perhaps wear out
& ruin my credit." He complained that prosecuting clippers and coiners was
a "vexatious & dangerous" exercise for which he was unprepared, and in
response he was given more support to improve the quality of the witnesses
and their evidence.[57]

Chaloner came to Newton's attention in 1697 when he informed the
House of Commons in a petition that he was being persecuted for having
previously revealed abuses at the Mint to a Commons committee. Chaloner
stated that numerous witnesses had sworn that key workers at the Mint
were involved in coining, and he claimed that he had invented a more efficient way of producing coin that the highest officials at the Mint were deliberately suppressing. Newton responded with a short account in which he

pointed out that Chaloner's claim to have invented a superior method of minting coins was merely a ruse to gain access to the sophisticated processes that were in use at the Mint. Moreover, there were "divers witnesses" prepared to swear that Chaloner has been making preparations to coin in the first half of 1697. For most of 1698, and into the first weeks of 1699, Newton built a massive case against Chaloner, identifying a vast web of people who had known of, or worked with him since the early 1690s. This involved the use of interrogations and confessions, along with informers and other types of witnesses. Newton travelled widely to interview potential witnesses in inns and prisons, and he paid a number of people to give or procure evidence, amongst whom were a number of spies who prompted Chaloner to sing while he was incarcerated in Newgate gaol. Chaloner was out of his depth against such a skilled and determined prosecutor, and despite heart-rending pleas for mercy, peppered with offers to implicate his colleagues, he was hanged on 22 March 1699.[58]

Newton adopted exactly the same approach in his priority dispute with Leibniz over the invention of the calculus. He made extensive use of his skills in manipulating manuscript testimony, and the most powerful defence of his own priority was based on his capacity to marshal evidence from almost five decades earlier. The dispute involved standard questions of intellectual property, including whether Leibniz's differential calculus was the same as, or relevantly similar to, Newton's method of fluxions; the extent to which Leibniz's invention of the differential calculus was wholly independent of Newton's; and what Leibniz saw or could have gleaned either from Newton's works or from his two visits to London in the 1670s. Leibniz published the basic theorems of the calculus in 1684, and thereafter Newton was content to drop opaque hints concerning his own knowledge of calculus methods, both in his *Principia* and excerpts from the letters to Leibniz (of 1676) that he sent to the Oxford mathematician John Wallis in the early 1690s. Disagreement simmered in the 1690s and the first few years of the eighteenth century, before taking off in a dramatic way thanks to the efforts of various Newtonian and Leibnizian lieutenants such as Fatio de Duillier, John Keill, and Johann Bernoulli. Despite the protests of the two main antagonists that they were above this sort of thing, they pulled the strings of their disciples when it really mattered.[59]

Keill took the lead in drawing Newton's attention to places where Leibniz and his allies had been less than complimentary about Newton's fluxions. He ostentatiously asserted Newton's priority in inventing the calculus in a paper published in the *Philosophical Transactions* of 1708, adding that Leibniz had merely published the same arithmetic in a different notation. In the spring of 1711 Leibniz wrote to the Royal Society requesting that Keill apologise for his insolence, whereupon Newton undertook sterling amounts of investigative research to help Keill with his reply. At the end of the year, Leibniz unwisely appealed to the Society to determine whether or not he had been treated justly in the whole business. Newton (president of the institution) took the opportunity to construct an overwhelming case against Leibniz that was second in size only to the one he mounted against Athanasius. Since insufficient evidence of his seventeenth-century work on calculus had been printed, it became imperative for him to show—using his own papers, those in the Royal Society, and relevant documents (including his own letters) recently found in the archive of John Collins—that his own writings on the subject were much older than anything Leibniz had written. When not working on Mint business or dealing with revisions to the second edition of his *Principia*, Newton spent almost all his time and effort over the following months scouring his own papers for relevant materials. Once located, he treated them as potential items of forensic evidence in the same way that he had dealt with so many other texts.[60]

Leibniz's tactically misguided request that the Society adjudicate the quarrel allowed Newton to bring together an allegedly impartial committee of the Society's fellows, which met for the first time in early March 1712. As Richard Westfall has pointed out, the fact that the committee could identify and organise the vast mass of evidence related to the case, and report its findings all within seven weeks, is a testament to the heroic work that Newton had done over the previous year to assemble the information needed for the committee to make the right decision. Indeed, the extraordinary impact of so many items, in conjunction with Newton's running commentary in the footnotes, produced a predictable verdict. Like Hooke, Leibniz was derided as an inferior scholar whose best work was stolen, or ineptly reverse engineered, from what he had illicitly seen of Newton's work. At the start of 1713 the legal-scientific documents were published under the auspices of the Society in a work now known as the *Commercium Epistolicum*. When the import of this work seemed to have been diluted by a much smaller effort (later termed the "Charta volans") authored by Leibniz and Bernoulli, Newton took it upon himself to write an "Account" of the *Commercium*. This text, the apotheosis of his public forensic rhetoric, took up almost one entire issue of the *Philosophical Transactions* and made it crystal clear that

Leibniz was an inferior mathematician and a plagiarist to boot. He also adopted other stratagems, inviting foreign dignitaries such as Antonio Conti to his home in order to show them that the original manuscripts of his endeavours were extremely old. Like others, Conti was introduced to his early mathematical writings and was given advice by Halley and Newton on how to gauge their great age from the texture of the paper.[61]

Hundreds of pages of Newton's obsessively redrafted writings testify to his historical, forensic approach to the priority dispute. In one commentary he composed on the "Elogium" of Leibniz published by the Académie des Sciences, he noted that in autumn 1714 Leibniz had asked for copies of all the relevant original letters and papers held by the Royal Society so that he could ascertain whether relevant information had been omitted. Newton replied as president that the originals had to be kept safe in the Society archives, and that "he did not print the Commercium himself, nor so much as produce and Letters or Papers which he had then in his own custody." He would not, he said, "make himself a witness in his own cause," a deviant trait he attributed to enemies such as Johann Bernoulli and (as we shall see in the next chapter) Jerome. To prove this, he produced two letters he had received acknowledging the progress he had made as a young man, one by John Wallis, and one—of course—by Leibniz himself. He noted that the scripts had been authenticated by those who knew their handwriting, and added that they "have been seen by forreigners, & nothing material has been found omitted." When Leibniz in turn was invited to submit his own original letters to make good his case, nothing was forthcoming. After his death, Newton quoted exultantly from a letter Leibniz had written to Conti, in which he pointed out that in order to counter the Commercium Epistolicum, he would have had to have produced a work at least as big, recalled a vast number of petty events that happened thirty or forty years earlier, and searched through his old letters, many of which were lost or buried under great piles of papers that he had neither the time nor the inclination to disinter. His adversary had, of course, done precisely this.[62]

11. The Divided Self

At the start of his scientific career, Newton argued that the scientific community would descend into a litigious chaos if it allowed the proliferation of probabilities, hypotheses, and conjectures. Instead, it needed to be "mathematical," that is, it needed to eschew reference to unobserved entities like corpuscles and aspire to be so demonstratively certain that there would be no grounds for disputes. However, his prescriptions had no chance of achieving the sort of compliant audience he wanted, and very quickly after his first paper on light and colours had appeared in print, he was dragged away from his beloved collegiate peace into the cut and thrust of printed exchange. As Newton saw it, the proliferation of uncorroborated hypotheses created an anarchic polity, contaminated by private opinions that could never generate robust scientific knowledge about the natural world. To his dismay, the inability of his colleagues to produce anything more than error-strewn claims or opinionated hypotheses created a litigious society in which he was forced to participate, and from which there was only temporary escape. There is an obvious paradox, or self-fulfilling prophecy, about the way he conducted himself in the Republic of Letters. The combination of his predilection for privacy and his corresponding distaste for print culture, coupled with his abstract, mathematicist approach, which was aimed at a compliant *cognoscenti*, meant that he could neither generate nor bequeath a public record of what he had achieved. In a scientific culture that was increasingly based on public and printed discourse to guarantee the credibility of texts, his entire approach was bound to generate scientific litigation, forcing him to rely upon the very sort of judicial historical enquiry that he claimed had no place in scientific discourse.

Newton's account of the appropriate scientific roles, first of disciplined and rational enquiry, and second, of hypotheses, was an expression of the way that he understood that his scholarly self should best be ordered. As we saw in chapter 5, he argued that the hard work that disciplined the understanding could control the temptations and seductions of the imagination. The triumph of the imagination drew the godly man away from righteousness, just as the introduction of hypotheses into natural philosophy corrupted the pursuit of truth. The use of a proper method would terminate premature and uncorroborated speculation and produce undeniable philosophical truths. His private ascesis formed the basis of his prescriptions for governing the public self, the fruits of which would be an appropriate tribute to God.

In many of his writings, Newton elided the languages of private discipline and scientific method, condemning hypotheses as dreams, fictions, and romances. All were the empty products of an undisciplined imagination and would give rise to anarchy, madness, and falsehood. This claim was prominent in his comments on the third "rule of reasoning" published in the second edition of the *Principia*, where he cautioned that we were "certainly not to relinquish the evidence of experiments for the sake of dreams and vain fictions of our own devising." It also formed the core of the fourth rule that appeared in the third edition of 1726, where Newton argued that propositions collected by general induction from phenomena should be understood to be "very nearly" true—"notwithstanding any hypotheses that may be imagined." The close link between hypotheses and the products of the imagination permeates the voluminous writings related to the priority dispute with Leibniz. The latter should consider, Newton said in one draft, "that Hypotheses are nothing more then imaginations, conjectures & suspicions & ought not to be propounded as Truthe or Opinions nor admitted into Philosophy as such until they are verified & established by experiments." Exceptions to strongly corroborated and inductively derived principles could be admitted, he went on, but they should be grounded in observation and experiment and not be merely hypothetical, for to do otherwise would be "to turn Philosophy into a heap of Hypotheses <which are no better then> a chimerical Romance." Leibniz's system was a fraudulent and even irreligious hypothesis, Newton lectured, and in Samuel Clarke's Fifth Reply to Leibniz, Clarke articulated Newton's view that Leibniz's Harmonia Praestabilita made the whole of the world—and all human experience—into a dream. Turning the created cosmos and even God himself into imaginary objects (as Newton put it in his General Scholium) were the worst forms of sacrilege that one could commit.[63]

The divisions discussed in this chapter also have a major bearing on how we understand the different aspects of Newton's character. Friends saw him as virtuous and rational, but also as inveterately "suspicious," and this second aspect of his personality came to the fore when natural philosophy became litigious. His constant attempts to keep natural philosophy and forensic analysis separate were to some degree an expression of his desire to maintain a separation between the godly, rational aspects of the self, and the wild deceptions of the imagination. On this showing, his oft-repeated wishes to avoid disputation look like desperate and ultimately futile efforts to avoid losing his discipline. As it was, his philosophical angst seems to have been triggered much more by his anxiety over keeping the spheres of philosophy and forensic analysis separate, than it was by philosophy having *actually become* litigious. Once philosophy had become a disputational theatre, he had a series of rhetorical techniques at his disposal for proceeding as that world demanded. As a private prosecutor he could give free rein to his suspicious mind, and although emotion fuelled his performances, there was method in the way that he sifted through the oceans of documentary material to conduct personal vendettas against the living and the dead.[64]

Shortly before Newton's death, he accused Antonio Conti of illicitly handing over a short version of his work on chronology (originally composed for Princess Caroline) to the French, and of fomenting disputes between himself and Leibniz. At the front of the *Philosophical Transactions* for July/August 1725, he set out to destroy Conti's character as he had done so many others, characteristically inventing and imputing various motives to Conti that the latter found bizarre. In a marvellous response, the courtly aristocrat remarked how strange it was that Newton gave up his objective, geometrical reasoning when it came to judging human actions and became a perverse conspiracy theorist. "If he persists in his accusations," Conti noted, "*is he not obliged*, according to his own principle, to prove them, *at the risk of becoming* guilty of calumny? Now how will he demonstrate, as he would a geometric curve... my masquerade of friendship, my clandestine intervention, and other chimeras with which it has suited him to embellish the opinion he has formed of me?" If Conti had known of Newton's long history of treating his enemies in this manner, he would have known the answer to his question.[65]

II

Critical Friends

In the spring of 1687 Newton had publicly and bravely confronted what he saw as a manifestation of diabolical power. Although the efforts to curtail James II's interference with the religious foundations of Cambridge University were ultimately successful, the monarch continued to insert Catholics into all the main institutions of English society as part of his wider plans to mould them in his image. He placed Catholics in powerful positions within the army and completed the formation of a compliant judiciary. Most worryingly, he set in motion mechanisms for "packing" Parliament with his supporters, so that there would be a legal basis for removing the Test Act and penal laws. Such actions increasingly tested the loyalty of all but his most faithful subjects, and two events in June 1688 effectively sealed the fate of his regime. First, on the tenth, James's wife, Mary of Modena, gave birth to a boy, James Francis Edward, who would inherit the Crown and thus continue the Catholic monarchy for the foreseeable future. Second, in April 1688, James republished the Declaration of Indulgence and ordered it to be read in all churches. Supported by dissenters who had not accepted the benefits offered by James under either publication of the Declaration, senior bishops objected to the order and refused to read it. Seven of them, including the archbishop of Canterbury William Sancroft, asserted that the king did not have the power to suspend penal laws and in early June they were put in the Tower of London. They were tried at King's Bench on 29 June and acquitted the next day, being received with hysterical adulation by waiting crowds. It was now only a matter of time before James's position became untenable.[1]

These events provided a pretext and opportunity for William, the Protestant prince of Orange and James's son-in-law by virtue of his marriage to James's daughter Mary, to invade England. From a defensive standpoint, William wanted to forestall any potential alliance between the army of Louis XIV and James's sizeable forces, which included Irish Catholics. On a positive front, he wanted to command those same forces against the French king, and for many within England his religious allegiance made him the most obvious replacement for James. After numerous conversations between William's senior officials and English supporters, an "invitation" was issued to him by a group called "The Immortal Seven" immediately following the release of the bishops.[2] This promised a highly positive reception from the vast majority of Englishmen who were dismayed by the monarch's activities and who would welcome a saviour who would restore their religion, liberties, and properties. In late summer William acquired sufficient financial backing to build a substantial invasion fleet, and at the end of September (10 October [N.S.]), he issued his own "Declaration." After providing a lengthy litany of the abuses committed by James II (though the text was careful to lay chief blame on James's "evil counsellors"), he promised to safeguard free elections and to restore the laws, liberties, customs, and religion of the people. Leaving almost recklessly late in the year, his fleet arrived in Torbay on the auspicious date of 5 November, and just over a month later his army was on the outskirts of London.

As these momentous events unfolded, the author of the *Principia* retreated to his college quarters. He spent some time preparing to publish a major work on optics but devoted a far greater effort to religious issues, dramatically reworking his analysis of Revelation. Despite his retreat from active resistance to James, he was aware of the events that were transforming the political landscape. At some point, he and Humphrey Newton jointly copied a printed translation of a letter sent by James's Jesuit advisor Edward Petre to Louis XIV's confessor, Father La Chaise, on the increasing problems facing the English monarch. The letter discussed Petre's successes in placing Catholics at Magdalen College, Oxford, as well as the possibility that the bishop of Oxford (Samuel Parker, the intruded president of Magdalen) might openly declare himself a Roman Catholic. Another manuscript in Newton's stock of political papers detailed the complaints of the Oxford clergy against the patronizing attitude of their bishop, and he had Humphrey copy out the petition of the Seven Bishops. Whatever else he was doing, he was keeping his eyes firmly on the dangerous encroachments of popery.[3]

1. A Revolutionary Fellow

Even before William arrived on English soil, Newton prepared himself to play a part in the political system. As early as September 1688, soon after it was announced that a parliament would be imminently summoned, it was known that he was standing as an MP for the university, and there was a presumption that he would be elected. There is no doubt that he was prepared to stand as a Whig candidate, ready to do what was necessary to thwart the latest efforts of the king to pervert the true religion. A cooperative Parliament represented James's last great opportunity to influence legislation in his favour, but William's arrival on English soil made it impossible for him to call it. The day after a provisional government was assembled in London on 10 December, the panicked sovereign fled towards France. Anarchy loomed, and in Cambridge a number of students and fellows took up arms as a safeguard against a local "rabble" who were breaking into various houses, ostensibly in search of armed Catholics. Alderman Samuel Newton (no relation) recorded that many of the mob were scholars, noting on 14 December that the whole town "was in uproare and fearfull crying out … arme arme for the Lords sake" to defend themselves against five thousand Irish Catholics allegedly on their way from Bedford. Having been detained by fishermen in Kent as he was about to leave for France, James returned triumphantly to the capital on the sixteenth. He attempted to begin negotiations with the Prince of Orange, but William was no longer prepared to accept any role short of monarch. Under extraordinary pressure, James was forced to leave the country for the second and final time on the twenty-third of December.[4]

At the end of December, having been granted temporary executive responsibilities, William submitted a letter to Cambridge University demanding that it elect representatives in order to constitute a convention "for the Preservation of the Protestant Religion, and restoring the Rights and Libertyes of the Kingdom." Newton, previously ready to stand in more difficult if less tumultuous circumstances, put himself forward as a candidate against Sir Robert Sawyer and Edward Finch, recently appointed under-secretary to his older brother Daniel, the Earl of Nottingham. Sawyer, attorney general for the last four years of Charles's reign, was an archvillain as far as Whigs and dissenters were concerned, not least for having signed more than 120 dispensations in favour of Catholics. In November 1681 he had attempted unsuccessfully to get a grand jury to bring in a bill for treason against Shaftesbury, and following the Rye House Plot he had led prosecutions against leading Whigs. Like many in the last year of James's reign, he made the wise decision to fall out of favour with the king, acting as counsel to the Seven Bishops during their trial in the summer of 1688.[5]

On 15 January 1689, a week before the Parliament was to convene, Newton and Sawyer were elected as the two MPs for Cambridge University. The result was close, with Sawyer receiving 125 votes, Newton 122, and Finch 117. It is extraordinary that Newton defeated Finch, a man with impeccable political connections who had lobbied hard to blacken Sawyer's reputation. The vast majority of those fellows who voted for Finch termed him "praenobilem" or "honorabilem," while two called him "nobilissimum." Sawyer was described by most of his supporters as "dominum" or "militem," but the descriptions of Newton went much further and reflected his standing both as a great scholar and a man of immense virtue. Forty-three slips described him as "praeclarum" (distinguished or illustrious) and twenty as "magistrum," while Henry Jenkes thought Newton was "virum Integerrimum" (a man of the highest integrity). Seven fellows (including Babington) called him "dignissimum" and five "doctissimum." His friends, the university librarian John Laughton, its vice chancellor John Covel, and a number of people who had stood with him in front of Jeffreys, all called him "praeclarum." Perhaps the greatest accolade came from his tutor Benjamin Pulleyn, who wrote that Newton was "summum virum" (a great man). Newton was already the brightest intellectual star in Cambridge, but as much as his eminence in the world of learning, his defence of the university before the commissioners must have played a key role in his election. There was little time to prepare for his role, and he left Cambridge on the eighteenth or nineteenth of January. Having effortlessly shed the identity of a scholarly hermit, he was now thrust into the extraordinary bustle of post-revolutionary politics.[6]

The Convention Parliament was split between a number of different groups, each with differing views on what sort of constitutional settlement was legitimate or even possible. Tories such as Sawyer, along with many senior bishops, felt that James had been harried out of office and denied that his actions in departing the country had left the throne vacant. They argued that the proper order of succession dictated that the Crown should pass to his daughter Mary, with William reigning as a regent. Hard-line Jacobites, who accepted the legitimacy of the birth of James's son, refused to accept that William had any right to become king and called for the return of James, who was the monarch *de iure divino* (by divine right). Many of this group would never swear allegiance to William and they would soon resign their offices as Nonjurors. At the other end of the spectrum stood radical "true" Whigs such as the ex-Leveller John Wildman, his fellow Rye House plotter John Hampden, Thomas Wharton, the cleric Samuel Johnson, and Viscount Charles Mordaunt. This group argued that James—whom they considered a traitor and a tyrant—had abdicated. The Commons debated the status of the throne on 28 January and voted that the throne was vacant, although this formulation was rejected by the Lords when they came to discuss it on 4 February. After William threatened to withdraw completely unless he got his way, both houses agreed on the sixth that James had "withdrawn himself from the kingdom" having "endeavoured to subvert the constitution of the kingdom, by breaking the Original Contract between king and people, and by the advice of Jesuits, and other wicked persons." The throne was deemed to be vacant, and the Convention decided to offer joint sovereignty to William and Mary, with the Dutchman wielding executive authority.[7]

Newton spent most of his initial career as a politician in a committee dealing with the impact of the revolution on the universities. He played a key part in determining the correct way that the university should swear allegiance to the new regime and spent a great deal of time over the following months making recommendations on the rewriting of college statutes so as to remove "what ever favours Popery." Naturally, he was a staunch supporter of the succession and on 12 February he sent his friend John Covel (in his role as university vice chancellor) a copy of the Declaration of Right. This was a statement of what the House of Commons took to be the rights and liberties of the English people, along with the supposed violations of these by James II, and it would form the basis for the Bill of Rights passed at the end of the year. Newton also sent Covel a proclamation affirming William and Mary king and queen. The text gave thanks to God for his use of the Prince of Orange in effecting the miraculous deliverance of England from popery and arbitrary power, and Newton requested that the university read the proclamation "wth a seasonable decorum because I take it to be their interest to set ye best face upon things they can, after ye example of ye London Divines." He gave a number of pieces of advice for Covel to pass on to recalcitrant dons who believed that William was a usurper, and that their previous oaths to James were still in force. Newton argued that Englishmen had a duty to swear allegiance to William as long as he protected them, a fact that was true whether he were king de facto or de iure. Consequently, there was no obligation to be true to an oath of allegiance sworn to James, an absolutist tyrant who had failed to protect, and indeed had utterly subverted, the religious liberties of the people. The university was quick to display its fidelity to the new regime, and on the fourteenth John Laughton gave the institution's thanksgiving sermon at Great St. Mary's. Nevertheless, many dons failed to fall in line with Newton's reasoning, and a number of scholars (including Humphrey Babington) refused to swear allegiance to William and Mary.[8]

One topic more than any other caught Newton's attention in the spring of 1689. William was concerned to promote comprehension in the Church of England, a move that would involve adjusting the terms of membership of the church so that others, particularly Presbyterians (but possibly also Lutherans), might join. A bill for indulgence (toleration) was drawn up by the Earl of Nottingham at the end of February and he produced a bill for comprehension a few days later. On the sixteenth of March, William told both houses of Parliament that he would like to remove the sacramental portion of the Test Act. Despite the fact that the Lords' comprehension bill was extremely narrow in terms of whom it would have permitted to join the Church of England, William's intervention, made at the behest of the dissenting leader Richard Hampden (John's father), deeply concerned many High Church Tories like Sawyer. In the meantime, John Hampden and others drew up a different and much more liberal comprehension bill in the Commons that would allow into the Church of England anyone ordained in a Reformed church. This was soon killed off by Tory Anglicans, but on 9 April a meeting took place between politicians from all parties at the Devil Tavern in Fleet Street, the result of which was that Tories agreed that they would not block a limited bill for indulgence, while the issue of comprehension would be decided by the Church of England Convocation. Newton was part of a Commons committee that met on 16 May to discuss the bill for indulgence, but there is no evidence that he spoke up about the proviso in the bill stating that anyone who denied the Trinity could not benefit from the indulgence.[9]

However, the day before this meeting, John Hampden had bravely objected on the floor of the House to the Trinitarian requirement. Hampden was an extreme Whig throughout the 1680s and early 1690s, but he had also developed radical freethinking opinions when in France during the early 1680s. Here he had met, and indeed sponsored the work of, the great Roman Catholic exegete Richard Simon, and he was soon convinced that many of the historical and textual supports for Protestantism, including much of the text of the Bible itself, were either doubtful or evidently false. Although he had recently renounced his most extreme freethinking views, in his speech of 15 May 1689 he launched into a diatribe against the doctrine of the Trinity. He noted that orthodox Trinitarians had bitterly persecuted the Arians in the early church, thereby laying the ground for the future burning of heretics by Christians. Newton no doubt approved, and from this point in his first parliamentary career, he spent a great deal of time with Hampden. However, the latter's intervention did not prevent the anti-Trinitarian clause from becoming part of the famous "Toleration Act" that was passed into law on 24 May. The freedoms available to dissenters were heavily circumscribed, and all individuals assuming office in church or state still had to receive the sacrament of the Church of England within three months of doing so. Dissenters were only exempted from penalties that otherwise remained in force, and even this concession was denied to Catholics and those who denied the eternity and deity of the Son, and who denied *in preaching or writing* the doctrine of the blessed Trinity.[10]

2. King's and Locke

Over the summer, while Parliament was in recess, Newton turned his attention to natural philosophy and the possibility of acquiring a senior position at Cambridge. He became part of a patronage network that involved John Hampden, the Swiss mathematician Fatio de Duillier, and Christiaan Huygens, whose brother Constantijn was secretary to William of Orange. Hampden and Fatio seem to have been permanently in Newton's company in this period, and they accompanied him to meetings of the Royal Society during the summer. Both were aware of Newton's opposition to a bill aimed at repealing the Act against the Transmutation of Metals (i.e., he was in favour of keeping the Act) originally enacted in the reign of Henry IV, but to Newton's chagrin, it became law just before the end of the session of Parliament on 20 August. Robert Boyle's strong support for the legislation, combined with his previous efforts to publish alchemical secrets, must have been one of the reasons why Newton told Fatio in October that he had refused to "communicate & correspond" with Boyle. Displaying his inveterate dislike of publicity, Newton charged that Boyle had talked to too many people and in his opinion was "too open & too desirous of fame." There was another, more significant reason to feel disillusioned at the end of August. Immediately after the Transmutation Act had been passed, Hampden and Huygens lobbied for Newton (a man "of great and known merit") to gain the support of the government in his efforts to fill the vacant provostship of King's College, Cambridge. George Treby and John Somers, the attorney and solicitor-general, were brought in to support the government case on Newton's behalf, and they obtained the college statutes to prepare their case. They also benefitted, as many others did, from Newton's own forensic preparations, but ultimately all these efforts were to no avail.[11]

In a short but pithy text titled "The Case of King's College," Newton argued that the statutes of the college were technically in possession of the Crown, giving the monarch the authority to interpret, enlarge, overrule, and even revoke their statutes. While they authorised the college fellows "to elect only persons so qualified as they prescribe," Newton continued, they did not bar the king "from ~~nominating~~ authorizing them to elect others." Although the statutes dictated that only college members were eligible for election, Newton cited a number of precedents where this requirement had not been met. When the business was discussed at Hampton Court Palace at the end of August, the college spokesman, George Stanhope, vigorously defended its right to choose its own provost from among its membership and argued that recent appointments by mandate had been illegal. Stanhope had appeared with Newton before Judge Jeffreys, but dug the knife into his erstwhile colleague by pointing out that even those people recently appointed by mandate had "in every other respect" been well qualified. It is of course striking that Newton, who had so bitterly attacked the use of the dispensing power, and who had more recently been involved in restoring the traditional religious liberties back to the colleges, should have supported the right of the Crown to impose a provost by mandate.[12]

In addition to being a member of the college, the successful incumbent of the college rectorship also had to be ordained. Many individuals had been granted divinity degrees as a condition of assuming the post, and the 1689 elections were no exception. Both the ultimately victorious college-backed candidate, Charles Roderick (headmaster of Eton College, King's sister institution), and John Hartcliffe, the person who succeeded Newton as the Crown favourite, had relevant degrees conferred on them at the last moment. Newton made no effort to gain such an award, and for this and other reasons his candidacy quickly fizzled out. Stanhope claimed that the college was an ecclesiastical and spiritual institution whose role was primarily spiritual: the provost was occasionally obliged to officiate at the altar on "certain solemn days," and no layman could possibly perform these functions. One wonders whether these comments hid deeper concerns over Newton's religious beliefs, or at the very least, over his active efforts to avoid taking orders.

It remains deeply perplexing—and at face value, inexplicable—that Newton should have been prepared to take on a position that required the incumbent to exercise the office of a priest. For a number of reasons, of course, he was an excellent candidate. The college had been hostile to James II, so his confrontation with Jeffreys, along with his great academic reputation and his position as a sitting Member of Parliament would have been in his favour. Although his lay status was deeply problematic, he was ostensibly disqualified on the grounds that he was not a member of the college. Above all, the college was in no mood to accept yet another intruded leader.[13]

The parliamentary session that convened towards the end of October 1689 was exceptionally divisive, as radical Whigs did their best to indict senior officials who had worked against them in the previous reigns. In November, a "murder committee" was set up in the Lords to investigate who was involved in prosecuting and then executing the Rye House "plotters," while in the Commons, Whigs repeatedly attacked those who had aided James's regime. In a Grand Committee on the State of the Nation on 14 December, Hampden intemperately referred to the senior ministers the Marquis of Halifax, the Earl of Nottingham, and Lord Godolphin as enemies of William and favourers of popery, since they had represented James at negotiations a year earlier and had retained their positions after the Glorious Revolution. He was one of the prime movers in procuring the expulsion of Sawyer from the house on 20 January 1690 but a week later William ended the Parliament, dismayed by these events. Fatio told Newton on 24 February that the king had arranged with Richard Hampden to prevent his son from standing at the next election, and indeed John Hampden's meteoric political career had effectively come to an end. That Newton should have chosen to spend a large amount of time in public with such a loose cannon is conclusive evidence of his radical Whig convictions, and at many points they must have broached their mutual interest in, and shared opinions on various religious topics. It is almost certainly for his proximity to people like Hampden that Robert Hooke (not, of course, an unbiased observer) noted that Charles Hickman told him in February 1690 that Newton was "the veryest Knave in all the Ho[use]." Hampden would soon be dropped from Newton's list of acquaintances, but the Lucasian professor had already acquired a new set of equally radical friends.[14]

After a few weeks in Cambridge, Newton left for London on 10 March 1690, where he stayed for over a month. Much of that time was spent with Fatio, discussing the latter's theory of gravitation, reading over Huygens's recently published *Traité de la Lumière* (since Newton could not read French), and listing corrections to the *Principia*. More significantly, he now developed a close intellectual relationship with the philosopher John Locke, and they would remain close friends—with the odd hiatus—for the next decade and a half. Locke, who had reviewed the *Principia* for the *Bibliothèque Universelle*, doubtless valued Newton for his intellectual accomplishments, but at this point his standing as a politician with Whig sympathies must have weighed equally heavily in Locke's mind. Secretary to the Earl of Shaftesbury, Locke had been deemed a subversive by the government in the aftermath of the Rye House Plot and had fled into Dutch exile in September 1683. Here he met scholars such as Jean Le Clerc and Philipp Van Limborch, who argued in favour of a polity that permitted a wide range of political and religious views. Locke also had time to work on his three great texts on religious toleration, representative government, and philosophy, all of which were published within a year of his return to England in February 1689 in the entourage of Princess Mary.[15]

At the end of May 1689 Locke was staying in a "philosophical apartment" at the fabulous twenty-acre rural retreat of the Earl of Monmouth and his wife, Carey, in what was then the leafy village of Parsons Green. Locke would soon bring Newton within the orbit of Monmouth, who was his own chief patron. As Viscount Mordaunt, Monmouth had been closely linked to Shaftesbury during the Exclusion Crisis and was a visible opponent of James II, criss-crossing the Channel in 1686 and 1687 to work with Williamite supporters. A man of action, Mordaunt recommended that William invade England as early as the summer of 1687, and he led a cavalry regiment into Exeter in November 1688. Although William considered him "ungovernable," Mordaunt was a trusted confidant in the early months of the revolution and he was rewarded with membership of the Privy Council and promotion to the earldom of Monmouth. His star waned somewhat towards the end of 1689 as he and other Whigs became visibly frustrated with the results of the revolution, and, in particular, with William's reliance on Tory ministers. He was made part of the advisory council of nine following William's departure for Ireland in June 1690, though in her memoirs Queen Mary described him as insane. In the following months she chastised him for trying to usurp the role of the monarchs in appointing ministers, and for promising large sums of money to help the war effort only on condition that William called a new parliament.[16]

In March 1690, Newton and Locke discussed a number of topics, one of which was the issue of finding a senior government place for Newton. At

some point he sent Locke a copy of a proof that planets could orbit in el-
lipses, almost certainly to show Locke exactly what was involved in performing mathematical demonstrations. Locke knew the gist of the *Principia*
well, and having consulted Huygens concerning the trustworthiness of the
mathematical proofs, his laudatory review of the work in the *Bibliothèque
Universelle* had concentrated on Newton's notion of attraction and his
dismantling of the Cartesian system. He praised the "incomparable Mr.
Newton" in the first edition of the *Essay Concerning Human Understanding*,
and indeed his understanding of Newton's achievement changed his view
about the potential of natural philosophy to progress beyond its current
limits. Because he believed that natural history was the dominant disciplinary framework in which experimental philosophy should be pursued,
Locke claimed in the *Essay* that a proper *science* or demonstrative knowledge
of natural objects, which required knowledge of the real essences of things,
was impossible. However, he believed that the *Principia* had provided absolutely certain principles that were the basis of robust knowledge about
significant aspects of the cosmos. In his essay on education of 1693, he
argued that if others followed Newton's lead in applying mathematics to
nature, there would be "more true and certain Knowledge" of the natural
world than could have been expected.[17]

Although Locke thought that natural philosophy might thereby be placed
on a more robust footing, Newton's work rocked his belief that one could
actually discover the principles that would form the basis for a demonstrative science of morality. In the first edition of the *Essay*, he had claimed that
moral philosophy might be capable of being demonstrated by necessary
consequences built on principles that were "as incontestable as those of the
Mathematicks." However, whether he or anyone else could discover those
principles was doubtful. In the summer of 1690, soon after discussing the
nature of mathematical demonstrations with Newton, he tetchily told James
Tyrrell that the purpose of the *Essay* was not to provide demonstrations of
various claims but to analyse how individuals actually went about comparing
their actions to a rule. He told Tyrrell that although demonstrations in morality and religion could progress further than they had done so far, there were
numerous demonstrable propositions in mathematics that neither himself,
Tyrrell, nor anyone else could demonstrate. Two years later, when William
Molyneux asked him to compose a book demonstrating the first principles of
morals "according to the Mathematical Method," Locke replied that he had
once believed that morality could be demonstrated from first principles, but he

was no longer so sure. Newton's procedures had shown that such a proof might be possible in mathematics, but whether Locke or anyone else could do it in the sphere of morality was another question. With something of an understatement, he noted that not everyone could have proved in mathematics what Newton had shown to be demonstrable.[18]

3. Trinitarian Debate

At a critical juncture in their conversations, the doctrine of the Trinity and scriptural evidence concerning the status of Jesus Christ suddenly became the most pressing subject. By this time these abstruse issues were no longer merely the province of scholarly divines but were dominating learned public debate in England. The discussion of the topic in the Republic of Letters had been prompted four years earlier, by the Declaration of Indulgence issued by James in April 1687. For anti-Trinitarians, the temporary liberation of the press created an opportunity to reprint pamphlets and books from earlier in the century. The first to take advantage of the opportunity provided by James's declaration was Stephen Nye in his *Brief History of the Unitarians* of 1687, and Nye's work triggered a number of defences and attacks over the following years. Most importantly, the notion that there was firm manuscript support for Trinitarian proof-texts was deeply shaken in 1689 when Richard Simon published his *Critical History of the Text of the New Testament*. By 1691, the inability of clergymen to formulate a coherent response to attacks on the orthodox conception of the Trinity, often mounted by erudite laymen, exposed major doctrinal fault lines in the Anglican Church. To complicate matters, provocative authors such as Charles Blount and John Toland, who denied all Christian mysteries and revealed truths, entered the fray. These men used many of the same textual and analytic resources as anti-Trinitarians, and the two groups were often lumped together, such as in the 1698 act against blasphemy and profanity.[19]

Nye, rector of Little Hormead in Hertfordshire, published his *Brief History* anonymously in the form of four letters to a "Friend," that is, the merchant Thomas Firmin. Firmin, a great philanthropist and sponsor of anti-Trinitarian productions, had allegedly left the letters with another anti-Trinitarian, Henry Hedworth, who in turn composed a positive response to Nye's texts. In his first letter, Nye recounted traditional anti-Trinitarian arguments from Scripture against the deity of the Son and he outlined a history of general

"Unitarian" belief. Nye claimed that many early Christian and Jewish groups were precursors of modern Socinians, and he described the ways in which authentic Christianity had been perverted by Trinitarians. On a political front, Trinitarian Catholics had frequently used persecution to achieve their ecclesiastical ends. Nye added that the glosses of many modern interpreters (Erasmus, Grotius, Petau, and Episcopius) supported the Unitarian case and adduced as his main source of inspiration Christopher Sand, who had provided a coherent history of Athanasian malfeasance in his *Nucleus*. In the fourth letter he examined a litany of allegedly pro-Trinitarian passages, which he either reinterpreted, so as to make more sense, or rejected as later additions. Hedworth's appended contribution emphasised that the doctrine of the Trinity was not, or ought not to be, an essential article of belief for Christians, and he pointed out that Unitarians had always shown themselves to be loyal subjects.[20]

Nye dealt with the two most significant texts singled out by Socinians as having been corrupted. He claimed that the entire verse of 1 John 5:7 (containing the so-called Johannine Comma), which ostensibly offered heavenly attestation for the doctrine of the Trinity, was an addition to the original text of the Bible. Drawing on Bryan Walton's *Biblia Sacra Polyglotta*, he showed that the passage was found neither in the most ancient Greek manuscripts, nor in the Coptic, Arabic, Syriac, Ethiopic, or "most ancient Latin" Bibles. It was never cited by the Fathers, nor did the "most learned Criticks and Interpreters" acknowledge it as genuine. On the other hand, even if it were accepted as genuine, Desiderius Erasmus, Theodore Beza, and John Calvin all interpreted the final words as denoting agreement in testimony rather than unity of essence or substance—an alternative interpretation that was also conventionally offered by Socinian exegetes. According to Nye, the text in 1 Timothy 3:16 on the "Great Mystery of Godliness," which affirmed God's manifestation in the flesh, was likewise corrupted, since the word *God* appeared neither in the ancient texts of the Bible nor in patristic citations of the passage. Without the spurious word, the phrase referred to the gospel of Christ that had been hidden for so long before being "made manifest" by Christ and the Apostles and proved by miracles, disposing those who would listen to "godliness." Nye added that the corruption had been made by Macedonius, patriarch of Constantinople, and for this and other actions he had been banished by the Byzantine emperor Anastasius in 512. Even if the text were retained, it only meant that God's nature and will were manifested to the Gentiles by Jesus and his Apostles.[21]

Nye's text caused some consternation amongst the orthodox, but it was three years before there was a full-blown controversy on the topic. Although the Toleration Act had exempted anti-Trinitarians from its benefits, in September 1689 William III announced that he wished to set up an ecclesiastical commission to investigate the possibility of altering the liturgy and canons of the Anglican Church in order to facilitate the comprehension of dissenters. This would then go before the Convocation with the prospect of it being passed as law by Parliament. As a result of one proposal to make the reading of the Athanasian Creed optional, Arthur Bury, rector of Exeter College, Oxford, published his irenicist *Naked Gospel* in early 1690 in support of a much simpler creedal form. In his short history of the doctrine of the Trinity, Bury cited Constantine's warning before Nicaea that it was not worth disputing over the nature of the Godhead, and he argued that belief in the triune Godhead had not been demanded of Christians in the time of Justin Martyr. Bury attributed the authority of all orthodox doctrine since Nicaea to the unlawful usurpation of ecclesiastical power by Catholics, the Athanasian doctrine being a Roman notion that was as unworthy of modern attention as the Arian. Unlike Nye, Bury's authorship was known almost immediately but he must have been aware that his intervention would end in tears. His text was condemned as Socinian and was ordered to be burned by the university's Convocation in August 1690. As a consequence, he was hounded out of office.[22]

Nye's *Brief History* was reprinted in the summer of 1690, along with a short tract titled *Brief Notes on the Creed of St. Athanasius*. In response, the Nonjuror William Sherlock suggested that the anonymous author of *Brief Notes* was opposed to all the central doctrines of Christianity and that, in any case, the Trinity was not so difficult to grasp. To the horror of his colleagues, Sherlock developed the idea that the three persons of the Trinity made up a union of people who were conscious of one another's thoughts. In turn, Nye expanded the *Brief Notes* into a work titled *The Acts of the Great Athanasius*. His demolition of Sherlock's arguments, along with his condemnation of the morals and actions of Athanasius and his "Homoousian" lackeys, was short but it constituted the most serious published critique of Athanasius's demeanour in English up to that point. Nye argued that Athanasius set up popery and Trinitarianism at the same time; he was a fornicator, a crafty politician, a seditious rabble-rouser, and a diabolical anti-Christian who devised the doctrine of the Trinity to promote his own ends. Newton almost certainly used one or more of these texts as a crib, and indeed he would have been remiss not to do so, though no evidence of any specific debt to these works survives. He hardly needed Nye's assessment of Athanasius's depravity as an inspiration, but even if he did, he went far beyond Nye in terms of the detail of his exposition.[23]

4. English Books

From the start, these exchanges engaged Locke, who had already shown an intense interest in anti-Trinitarian and, in particular, in Socinian doctrines and beliefs. As John Marshall has shown, numerous passages in Locke's writing from the Socinian corpus survive both in his notebooks and in the margins of the books themselves, and he owned nearly a hundred anti-Trinitarian books or tracts at his death. During his sojourn in France during the late 1670s, and throughout the following decade, he read numerous Socinian works. In his Dutch exile, he began to immerse himself thoroughly in much of the available literature of Socinian doctrinal theology and scriptural exegesis. Locke also maintained a close contact with Jean Le Clerc, the Remonstrant theologian and editor of the *Bibliothèque Universelle*, who followed closely the debates in England and elsewhere on the authenticity of the doctrine of the Trinity and on the issue of religious toleration. As we will see, he would also play a central role in the fate of Newton's writings on the two most notorious Trinitarian proof-texts.[24]

In the mid-1680s Locke took copious notes on the English translation of Richard Simon's *Histoire Critique du Vieux Testament*, and he became fascinated by the issue of textual support for passages relating to the status of Christ. He told Philipp Van Limborch in June 1688 that Simon's *Critical History of the Text of the New Testament* was in press, and he referred to the work on a number of occasions over the following months. Simon's work appeared in the Netherlands at the end of October, but as excitement grew in Locke's intellectual circle over its contents, his close contact with Charles and Carey Mordaunt thrust him back into English politics. This did not end his interest in the subject, and in March 1689 he told Van Limborch that he would send Le Clerc a copy of Nye's *Brief History*. Le Clerc was more interested in the theoretical and practical issues of religious toleration, though these were obviously bound up with the question of the freedom to express heterodox religious opinions. The publication of Locke's *Epistola de Tolerantia* in the summer gave him the opportunity to display his great skill in hiding his authorship of the work, and he made the acquaintance of the Unitarian merchant William Popple, who translated the *Epistola* as the *Letter on Toleration* over the summer.[25]

Tyrrell informed Locke in February 1690 about the publication of Bury's *Naked Gospel* but reported in March that the book had been suppressed by the author "upon some of the Clergyes muttering against it." It had apparently never been on sale, though he himself had read it and pronounced it "ingeniously written." Locke was seriously ill in the weeks after his encounter with Newton, and he recuperated with the Monmouths at Parsons Green from the middle of May until the end of June. By August he was at Oates (near Harlow in Essex) at the country home of Sir Francis and Lady Damaris Cudworth Masham, and he would make this his main academic retreat for the rest of his life. During his stay with the Monmouths he was presumably composing the reply to Jonas Proast's critique of his *Letter on Toleration*, since his response to Proast appeared in print at the end of June. Locke went to London between 17 September and 14 October, after which he returned to Oates for nearly a fortnight. On 16 October he received a letter from the Quaker Benjamin Furly discussing a number of books recently sent to him by Popple, including Proast's response to Locke's *Letter* and Locke's "Ingenious" reply, as well as Sherlock's *Vindication*. Furly also mentioned that Le Clerc was trying to get hold of Bury's *Naked Gospel*, whose consignment to flames had already made it an exceptionally rare work.[26]

Less than a week later, Le Clerc confirmed to Locke that Furly had sent him a few English books on the subject of toleration, which he would use against those he termed "our persecutors." In the volume of the *Bibliothèque universelle* for October 1690 he published notices of a series of works relating to the Unitarian controversy in England under the heading "Livres anglois touchant la Tolerance." Given the hostile reception accorded to Bury's *Naked Gospel*, and the pamphlet war that ensued, the subject of toleration was defined broadly enough to include a lengthy account of Bury's work, a defence of it by his colleague James Parkinson, the university decree calling for the book to be burned, as well as Proast's *Argument* and Locke's *Second Letter*. Le Clerc obtained a copy of Bury's work from Locke in December, and he published a "vindication" of the text the following year. It was in this feverish intellectual context that Locke received a response from Newton on 28 October to a now lost letter, saying that he was revising some "papers" that Locke had requested, and that these would have to wait another week.[27]

5. Learning and Caution

Newton's "Historical Account of Two Notable Corruptions in Scripture," which he finally sent to Locke in the middle of November, was a masterful blend of impassioned analysis and exquisitely crafted, scholarly argument. Addressed "To a Friend," the corrupted passages in question were 1 John 5:7 and 1 Timothy 3:16. A so-called Third Letter is extant in draft, dealing with further examples of what Newton took to be attempted pervisions of Scripture, all of which concerned the humanity or inferiority of the Son. Aside from its radical contents, the most fascinating aspect of the "Historical Account" is the fact that Newton now sent it to Locke on the understanding that Locke would get the tract on the Johannine Comma—and possibly the second passage on 1 Timothy—translated into French *and then printed*. Against type, a newly emboldened Newton now seemed intent on releasing to a European audience a heterodox discourse on the two most disputed biblical passages on the Trinity. Had the "Letters" been published, they would have been anonymous and their authorship untraceable, though in the end, the whole translation process took so long that he came to his senses and suppressed them. As with so many of his writings, the content and (limited) circulation of his missive raise complex issues about its intended audience. It was not printed until 1754, although Newton had tried once more to have it published. In 1709 he authorised his friend and Mint colleague Hopton Haynes to produce a Latin translation of the text on 1 John 5:7, but this was an even less propitious time to publish the work and it too was held back.[28]

The opening sentence from Newton's main discourse of 14 November 1690 reveals that Locke's curiosity about the authenticity of 1 John 5:7 had apparently been provoked by some recent writings, amongst which the works by Bury, Nye, and Simon were presumably the most significant. In his covering letter, Newton apologised for having made Locke wait but told him that he had come across new evidence concerning 1 Timothy 3:16 "wch I thought would be as acceptable to inquisitive men, & might be set down in a little room." By the time Newton sent his text to Locke, the whole thing had now become extremely large, so he now believed that it would be better if only the text relating to 1 John were translated into French. Evidently, Locke had raised the possibility of Le Clerc or somebody else translating the text, a prospect that may have come up in conversation with

Newton a prospect that earlier in the year. Newton was an old hand at authorial caution but in Locke he was dealing with another master of secretiveness and anonymity. By his own standards Newton was wildly enthusiastic about the venture and even raised the possibility of publishing it in English "after it has gone abroad long enough in French."[29]

Newton was already a member of a group of scholars who were deeply interested in the manuscript witnesses for the Greek New Testament. This included John Mill, principal of St. Edmund's Hall, Oxford, since 1685, and John Covel. Covel, as we saw earlier, was vice chancellor of the university having previously been chaplain to Princess Mary and then master of Christ's College, Cambridge. He possessed a number of Greek New Testament manuscripts brought back from his earlier sojourn in the Ottoman Empire, and he made these and other sources available to Newton. From 1678 Mill was encouraged by John Fell, the great editor of classical and patristic writings, and dean of Christ Church, Oxford. Mill had worked on Fell's 1675 edition of the Greek New Testament and now sought to create a new edition with variants that would supersede all those before it. He worked closely in the following decades with scholars such as Covel, John Laughton, Mill's own protégé Richard Bentley, and Newton himself. At the start of 1687 Mill wrote to Covel about readings in the latter's manuscripts and asked him to present his services to "Dr. Montague, Mr Professor Newton, and Mr. Laughton." John Montagu followed John North as master of Trinity College, Cambridge, from 1683 to 1700, when he was replaced as master by Bentley, and Laughton was one of Newton's few known friends in the period. Although Mill's edition had been printed up to Galatians in June 1689, the publication of Simon's *Critical History* forced him to undertake a mammoth re-analysis of patristic citations of Scripture, effectively stopping the production of the work in its tracks. The connection with Mill raises fascinating questions about the extent to which Newton was reliant on others for his research into theology. He consulted Laughton's books in the latter's extensive library, and he scrutinised a number of manuscripts that Covel had brought back from the Middle East. Mill gave advice on readings in the Codex Alexandrinus (the fifth-century manuscript of the Greek Bible now in the British Library), but was more reliant on Newton for help in his great enterprise than Newton was on him.[30]

Newton had probably not read Simon's work when he sent the initial version to Locke, but there was a surfeit of other textual resources at his disposal. The analyses of Erasmus, Grotius, and others, many of which were consonant with Socinian positions, were readily available in the variant readings scattered in the appendix to Walton's *Biblia Sacra Polyglotta* and also in Matthew Poole's 5 volume *Synopsis Criticorum*. Fell's *New Testament* of 1675, which contained readings from Curcellaeus's anti-Trinitarian slanted edition of 1658, presented these and a small number of others in a truncated but assimilable way. A more selective and pointed presentation of radical information was available in Socinian texts such as the Racovian Catechism or in Christopher Sand's *Appendix*, the last of which Newton cited in his own account. Other works, especially those of Nye, had brought the issue of textual indeterminacy to a wider audience. Virtually every relevant edition of the Greek New Testament, as well as all the original patristic works, were available to Newton either in the Trinity College Library, or in the "Public" (i.e., University) Library, though it is possible that he borrowed one of Locke's three copies of the Racovian Catechism. At various points in his career he owned a number of Greek New Testaments, and he scoured patristic literature to find out for himself how various Fathers had cited disputable texts.[31]

Alongside the Syriac, Ethiopic, and Arabic versions of the Bible (all three of which were translated into Latin) and the Vulgate, Walton reproduced in the *Polyglot* a slightly altered version of Robert Stephens's 1550 folio edition of the New Testament, which contained variant readings from manuscripts collated by his son Henry Stephens. Beneath the Greek text, which was also translated into Latin, Walton added variant readings from the Codex Alexandrinus, which had been presented to Charles I thirty years earlier by the patriarch of Constantinople. In an appendix to the *Polyglot*, Walton gave variant readings compiled by Archbishop Ussher and added others from a host of authors, including Stephens, Grotius, and Lucas Brugensis. He added an erudite essay, which, with other additions in the appendix, attempted to situate the writing of the different Bibles in their historical contexts. *The Racovian Catechism* dealt in detail with the most significant Trinitarian prooftexts. In the 1680 edition, many more authorities were cited to show that the Johannine Comma was absent from the oldest Bibles and manuscripts. By the 1680s, the Catechism was the latest in a long line of texts that built upon previous analyses and added new patristic or manuscript evidence that could be mined by readers and future editors. All these works were to be significant analytic resources for Newton in the extraordinary burst of research he undertook in late 1690.[32]

6. The Comma

By far the most controversial passage for exegetes was the Johannine Comma. Many scholars travelling through Europe sought out ancient manuscripts to check whether the passage was present, and during his exile from James II, Gilbert Burnet made it his business to check the existence of that "doubted passage" in all the old manuscripts of the New Testament he could find. In Zurich he consulted the ancient manuscript in which Heinrich Bullinger had said he had failed to find the comma. However, Burnet claimed—in a text that Newton read and cited after he had sent the initial version of his own exegesis to Locke—that while Bullinger was correct, this must have been the fault of the original copyist since the text did contain Jerome's preface to the Epistles in the Vulgate, in which he had claimed that the Arians had "struck out" the comma in numerous manuscripts. Burnet could not understand why Erasmus had omitted the preface from his own edition, given that it was in all the other manuscripts Burnet had consulted. Erasmus's sincerity was not to be "rashly cenured," he claimed, but the preface was in "all the Manuscripts, ancient or modern, of those Bibles that have the other Prefaces in them that ever I saw." As for the comma itself, it was either attached to Latin versions with a "sicut," as it was in a manuscript consulted in Venice, or entirely missing, as it was in a number of documents in Basel. In Strasbourg, the comma had been added to the foot of the relevant page of the oldest manuscript he examined, while in two other copies, the preface was attached but there was no comma. Burnet, who ended his account with the observation that the comma was missing from the Codex Vaticanus (the fourth-century manuscript of the Greek Bible in the Vatican), was criticised for giving ammunition to anti-Trinitarians, but he reaffirmed his support for the passage in a letter to Jean Le Clerc.[33]

A short draft essay on the topic formed part of a notebook that Newton used when he met Locke in early 1690. A reference to Locke's Oates address, probably noted in connection with the visit that Newton made there at the start of 1691, appears at the front of the document and there are other internal clues that date entries to this period. Like other anti-Trinitarians, Newton argued that the account of the unity of the three in heaven in the disputed verse had been introduced by later scribes. They had been influenced by the Trinitarian gloss on the terrestrial unity of the water, blood, and spirit (in what is now verse 8) that they found in the margins of the texts they were copying, and they gradually incorporated the gloss into the text to form a new verse. Many before him, Newton said, had struggled with the authenticity of the text; as he put it, "Those of greater note learning & caution as Grotius, Erasmus & Luther ⟨in his editions of yᵉ new testament⟩ &c reade this place thus There are three that beare record the spirit yᵉ water & yᵉ blood & these thre [*sic*] are one (or into one thing.)" He remarked that this was the correct rendition read in most of the Greek manuscripts and especially in the oldest, such as the Codex Alexandrinus; "the capital letters tis wrote in ⟨& other signes⟩," he added, were evidence of its great antiquity. He also recorded that the passage was missing in a copy seen by Grotius and "supposed by him to be of a thousand years antiquity" and that it was absent from the Syriac, Ethiopic, and Arabic Bibles, and from all the Latin versions of Jerome's time, as the latter himself had noted.[34]

Newton referred to a host of patristic sources that lacked the text, and he drew supporting evidence from the appendix to Sand's *Interpretationes paradoxæ* in which Sand had claimed that he had seen a comma-less Armenian codex at Amsterdam that was more than four hundred years old. Next, he took copious notes on the disputes between Erasmus and his critics Edward Lee and Jacob Lopez de Stunica (Zuñiga), a senior editor of the "Complutensian" Polyglot edition of the Bible published in 1520 under the direction of de Stunica and Cardinal Ximenes (Jiménez de Cisneros). Against Erasmus, Stunica insisted on the authenticity of Jerome's preface to the Canonical Epistles, and indeed, on this issue Newton would side with Stunica and other orthodox critics against Erasmus, Simon, and the majority of Socinian writers. Newton recorded the well-known tale of Erasmus omitting the comma from the first two editions on the basis of being unable to locate it in any manuscripts he consulted, and then retaining it when told that a manuscript containing it had been miraculously discovered by Lee. Erasmus included the text in the third edition but noted that it had been accommodated to the Vulgate and so was not independent from it. Newton would expand this section in the letter to Locke with more detailed material taken from Stunica and others, contained in the ninth volume of John Pearson's *Critici Sacri*.[35]

A final set of notes evinced the manner with which Newton marshalled information, as well as the broad confessional range of works that he consulted. One source was Thomas Smith's printed sermon on the mysteries of the Christian religion, which had appeared in 1675. Smith, dean of Magdalen College, Oxford, discussed 1 Timothy 3:16 and ridiculed the Socinian interpretation, which decried as fraudulent the standard reading according to which God was manifested in the flesh. Towards the end of the sermon he turned his attention to 1 John 5:7, which, along with the affirmation of the Trinity in baptism, was the clearest statement of the doctrine of the Trinity. The comma was too big—or too abstruse—a topic to be consigned to a few minutes in a sermon and Smith devoted an appendix to it in the printed version. He noted its absence from both the codices Alexandrinus and Vaticanus, and he admitted that it was lacking in the codex at Magdalen. However, while Socinus had claimed that the text had been inserted by Catholics, Smith asked how plausible this was given the early adherence to the Trinity within the church. It was much more likely, he claimed (following Jerome, Aquinas, and numerous others), that Arians had been able to "raze this Text, with which they were so oppressed, out of several Copies, from which by Transcripts it might easily be propagated into others." As we shall see, Newton would address this last claim with dripping sarcasm in his letter to Locke.[36]

7. The Rules of Criticism

Although variant readings of doctrinally significant texts created major problems for most orthodox Protestants, Catholic critics like Richard Simon could embrace such disagreements between texts and interpretations, and instead appeal to the overriding authority of textual tradition. When his *Histoire Critique du Vieux Testament* was printed in 1678, Simon created shockwaves in Anglican circles by destabilising the authority of ancient manuscripts. Given that only copies survived, he argued that the task of the critic was to restore or "repair" a text by so-called Rules of Criticism. An "authentic" version could be established by applying these same rules and by appealing to the *public* authority of the church. The effect of all this was at its most potent in Simon's critique of Protestant claims to have access to a pristine text of the Bible, and also in his ridicule of Protestant (and especially Socinian) stipulations that the meaning of Scripture was plain and simple, readily determinable by means of a theologically unbiased application of grammatical rules. Without a well-grounded understanding of how Scripture had been composed and how the writings had fared over the past centuries, Simon coolly noted, Protestants had no independent means of establishing an authentic text that could *then* be interpreted.[37]

An English translation of Simon's work on the manuscripts of the New Testament appeared as the *Critical History of the Text of the New Testament* in

1689. It is possible that Newton read it in order to produce his initial analysis for Locke, though he made no reference to it. In any case, it was the most thorough piece of textual scholarship on such sources available to Newton, and he definitely consulted it when he was asked to amend his text. Simon placed himself amongst those "Learned Men" who from earliest times had set out to purge the Scriptures of manifest faults: "this kind of Labour, which requires an exact knowledge of Books, joyned with a strict enquiry into the Manuscripts, is termed *Critical*; in as much as it judges and Determines the most Authentick Readings, which ought to be inserted into the Text." The goal of critics like himself was "not to destroy, but to establish" and he professed allegiance to no party except Truth. He set out to justify the fact that Jerome, who had translated the accepted (or "Old") Latin text of the Bible into Latin at the end of the fourth century, had "corrected" the "Ancient" Greek and Latin copies "according to the strictest Rules of Criticism." Simon performed a rigorous scrutiny of manuscripts and patristic sources, and from the outset he dismantled a key shibboleth of Protestant research by stating that the oldest Greek manuscripts now extant were not necessarily the most authentic. Although they offered different readings from the Vulgate and from many other copies and editions, he argued that these writings were based on inferior Latin translations of much earlier and now lost Greek originals. Even so, the ancient records, understood according to the "Rules of Criticism," were of more help in understanding the textual and doctrinal basis of the Christian religion than all the subtleties of divines unacquainted with antiquity.[38]

According to Simon, the fact that no "originals" now remained of texts from the apostolic times had allowed numerous heretics to rise up in the early ages, each proclaiming as true their own version of Christianity, and all others false. Great disputes arose over whether certain books or epistles were inspired or canonical but over time, Christian authority had come to reside in the rightly established public authority of the church. For Simon, "private Spirit," or an appeal to the "inward testimony of the Holy Ghost" had no part to play in determining the true meaning of scriptural passages, but the individual *critic* had the right and duty to employ the Rules of Criticism in order to establish the authentic text. Although he agreed that the critic had to proceed by reasonable arguments, he condemned Socinians for adding "Ratiocination" as a medium between tradition and the Scriptures, thereby paving the way to introducing what Simon condemned as subjective interpretations and religious innovations. The Catholic Church, on the other hand, could rely upon "good Acts and Records," and an unbroken activity that constituted a well-founded tradition.[39]

Central to Simon's approach was the notion that there were two types of ancient Greek "Copy." The first composed the original and now lost versions consulted by Jerome, while the second was exemplified by the diglot (Greek/Latin) codices Bezæ and Claromontanus, composed by Latin writers whose Greek was relatively poor and who had produced their Greek texts from the "Ancient Latin Vulgar." This was the common Old Latin version of the Bible that was used publicly in Western churches before Jerome "corrected" it from the oldest and most exact Greek copies to produce the Vulgate. Simon argued that the Codex Bezæ was the first part of a more complete version of the New Testament, of which the Codex Claromontanus (by now in the French Royal Library) and the similar text owned by the Benedictine monks of St. Germain, were the second. The diglot, he noted, constituted excellent evidence of the impoverished state of the unreformed Old Latin.[40]

Simon devoted a great deal of space to proving that, in the vast majority of cases where heretics had been accused of corrupting the New Testament, the charge was groundless. Most changes to Scripture had either been harmless transcription errors, or sincere efforts to shed light on passages in Scripture. Only very rarely were they dastardly efforts to corrupt the Bible, and none of these had succeeded. However, the belief that most changes had been made for nefarious purposes was ubiquitous and he criticised "School Divines" and "Canonists" for assuming that any difference between today's Greek copies and Latin ones should be adjudicated in favour of the latter. Truth, according to Simon, had not simply remained in the Roman church, for it could easily be shown that many Latin patristic writings contained doctrines that were consistent with those condemned in the modern period. Moreover, where there were apparently heterodox passages in Scripture or in the patristic writings, this was not due to devious corrupters. This "most unjust Accusation" had a lengthy pedigree: "So soon as ever there is a difference perceived in Copies, if this difference do favour the Opinions of some Party, they will be sure to accuse that Party of corrupting the Sacred Writings, although that difference does for the most part come from the Transcribers." This was the case even with the Johannine comma, where it was the accepted and orthodox view that the Arians had erased the text. For Simon this was an unwarranted conjecture, founded on insufficient examination of the manuscripts.[41]

In turning to the authenticity of the comma, Simon stated that he had looked at the question afresh, on the basis of as many Greek and Latin manuscripts as he could find. Along with the Catholic Church, the Greek Church now read, "For there are three that bear witness in heaven, the Father, the Word and the Holy Ghost, and these three are one," but it was hard to find *any* Greek manuscripts clearly containing the expression. The passage was completely lacking in seven copies in the King's Library, either in the main textual body or in marginal notes, and the same was true for five examples he saw in Colbert's library. However, in some cases there were "small notes" next to the original passage that *interpreted* the Father, the Word, and the Holy Ghost as a the true referent of the unity of the water, blood, and spirit mentioned in the following verse. In time, he concluded, "'tis much more probable, that that Doctrinal Point was formerly written [in] the Margin, by way of Scholium or Note, but afterward inserted in the Text by those who transcribed the Copies." However, against Erasmus and a number of anti-Trinitarians, Simon denied that Jerome was the author of the comma.[42]

As we have seen, the standard defence of the comma's authenticity relied heavily on taking at face value the passage in Jerome's preface to the Epistles, in which he had argued that "unfaithful Translators" had erroneously excluded the passage from their copies. Simon contended that the preface was spurious, although many contemporaries, both Catholic and Protestant, did take it to be genuine, not least because it gave excellent grounds for believing that the comma was authentic. The preface was also supported by other testimony. In John Fell's comments on Cyprian's third-century *De Unitate Ecclesiae* (in Fell's edition of the latter's *Works*), he had asserted that all men of good judgement were obliged to accept its authenticity on the grounds that Cyprian had made unambiguous reference to the comma. However, Simon pointed out that Jerome's name was not attached to the preface where it was found in older documents, and, indeed, the oldest manuscripts lacked the text entirely. He concluded that the twin facts (a) that the comma was missing in many copies of the Vulgate in which the preface was present, and (b) that where the comma was present, it only existed in the margins of some manuscripts, were conclusive evidence that the preface was not authentic. Moreover, if Jerome had been the author of the preface *and* the comma, the latter would have been in all copies that contained the preface (which condemned others for omitting it), but it was not.[43]

Simon now moved on to deal with the central patristic testimony in support of the comma, namely, the reference in Cyprian. Modern authors of all confessions admitted that the comma was not referred to in any patristic text except that of Cyprian, but this was strange; if the comma had been available to Augustine, for example, would he not have cited it against the Arians? After further investigation Simon concluded that Cyprian *had* applied what was said about the unity of the spirit, water, and blood in the following verse to the Father, Son, and Holy Ghost, but that this was not "an express quotation of those Words, as if they were in the Text itself." Hence the crucial question of whether it was a gloss or a citation was resolved in favour of the former. Simon was supported by the testimony of the sixth-century African bishop Facundus, who in his account of the Trinity cited Cyprian's interpretation, explaining that the three persons of the Godhead were *denoted by* the three witnesses mentioned in what was now the eighth verse.[44]

For Simon, any dispute about the authenticity of the passage was pointless, since the passage could not *by itself* establish a doctrine that was so strongly supported both by tradition and by other passages. Simon lashed Sand for compiling a lengthy list of Bibles that had been printed without the comma, since they were essentially reprints of previous Bibles with no recourse to manuscripts beyond what had been used in the early printed Greek New Testaments. He defended Luther for having initially left out the passage on the grounds that it was doubtful, but argued that its reinclusion by Lutherans as a bulwark against the anti-Trinitarians gave their enemies "the fairest occasion imaginable of Triumphing over them." For Simon, both Lutherans and Calvinists came close to giving anti-Trinitarians a gift by including the passage in their Bibles while offering good reasons for doubting it. Whatever the current manuscript evidence, the present Greek and Latin churches agreed that only "the bare Authority of the Church" obliged Christians to accept the passage as authentic. Thus, for reasons that made no sense to Scripturalist anti-Trinitarians like Newton, who respected the authority of the oldest documents, Simon concluded that the passage *was* authentic.[45]

8. Crafty Knaves

Given the noise it made on its publication, Simon's book must have been a topic of conversation between Locke and Newton early in 1690, although the initial analysis that Newton sent to Locke bore no overt signs of Simon's treatment. In the November 1690 letter to Locke, Newton greatly expanded the short essay in his notebook, and Bullinger and others were added to the trinity of Erasmus, Grotius, and Luther who were praised for their recognition of the truth about the text. Sadly, Newton noted, the majority of Protestants as well as Catholics still cited the place against heresy; truth, however, had to be "purged" of such falsehoods: "whilst we exclaim against the pious frauds of yᵉ Roman Church, & make it a part of our religion to detect & renounce all things of that kind: we must acknowledge it a greater crime in us to favour such practices, then in the Papists we so much blame on that account." By promoting such actions, Newton claimed, Catholics acted in accordance with their own religious precepts, but by endorsing them, Protestants acted against theirs. The true faith had thrived without the text for many centuries, and it was now a danger to religion to allow it to rest on such a frail foundation. The contents of the letter clearly marked out Newton as hostile to the central scriptural supports of the doctrine of the Trinity. He cast the text as a mere piece of textual criticism that involved "no article of faith, no point of discipline" but the net effect of this and the additional examination of the authenticity of 1 Timothy 3:16 was to leave no doubt regarding his anti-Trinitarian leanings. This was a letter, Newton remarked, that was aimed at someone who was capable of being swayed by the evidence alone, and he told Locke who was keenly aware of the latter's "prudence & calmnesse of temper." In an explicit use of *parrhesia* or courageous and frank speech, he added that he was confident he would not offend him by speaking plainly.[46]

Contra Simon, Newton argued that Jerome's preface *was* genuine, though he concurred with Simon regarding the status of the alleged Cyprianic reference to the comma. He criticised Socinians for dealing "too injuriously" with Cyprian in holding that the patristic passage in question was corrupt, for the Church Father had asserted the unity of the Trinity elsewhere. Appealing to the same argument ex silentio that Simon had used, and which he himself used frequently in his historical writings, Newton pointed out that no author in the next centuries mentioned it, even when "all the world was engaged in disputing about the Trinity & all the arguments that could be thought of were diligently sought out & daily brought upon the stage." Given the immense significance of the preface for supporting the doctrine of the Trinity, this was preposterous. He concluded that the unity of the spirit, water, and blood had been routinely understood to refer to the Trinity by commentators such as Cyprian, Eucherius, and Augustine, and that the words *hi tres unum sunt* had been taken from that verse as a warrant for the Trinity. Indeed, the fact that the gloss was needed showed that the "expresse words" of the testimony of the three in heaven "was not yet crept into their books." Like Simon, Newton referred to the testimony of Facundus to support his case.[47]

Simon strove to uphold the integrity of Jerome at every opportunity, an approach that led him to attack Fell's belief that the preface was authentic. However, Newton accepted the authenticity of the text precisely because, as an inveterate conspiracy theorist, he believed that Jerome and his contemporaries had engaged in a wholesale perversion of Scripture. Newton now put Jerome on trial, deploying the forensic techniques and language that he used against Athanasius, Hooke, and others. He pointed out that in the preface, Jerome had admitted that he was correcting the Old Latin by reference to earlier Greek manuscripts, and that he was restoring the comma on the basis of these texts. Jerome had complained that by doing this he had been accused by contemporaries of falsifying Scripture, but he had responded that previous translators had erred by "omitting the testimony of the three in heaven whereby the Catholick faith is established." For Newton, the fact that Jerome admitted (a) that it was not in the Old Latin, (b) that he admitted that he had been accused by others of falsifying the Scriptures, and (c) that he had changed the reading to confirm the true faith, constituted sufficient confirmation that he had perverted the accepted public reading. Jerome would not have been charged with falsifying Scripture if the original reading had been merely doubtful, and he had betrayed his guilt by confessing the Catholic rationale behind his action.[48]

Naturally, judicial language permeated Newton's analysis. The preface by itself was inadequate for determining Jerome's guilt or innocence, he stated, and in castigating Jerome's defence he wheeled out one of his favourite phrases—"no man is a witnesse in his own cause." Instead, Newton decreed, "laying aside all prejudice we ought according to the ordinary rules of justice to examin the businesse between him & his accusers by other witnesses." As an author, Jerome lacked sufficient credibility to be believed in this instance. Others had accused him of writing fanciful histories, while Erasmus had mentioned in his notes on the comma that Jerome was "frequently violent & impudent & often contrary to himself." Newton swiftly advanced to the definitive textual evidence against him. First, by Jerome's own admission, the passage was lacking in the Old Latin. Second, Walton had shown in his *Polyglot* that the Syriac and Ethiopic Bibles, which lacked the text, predated the Vulgate. For supporting testimony Newton also pointed to its absence in the Egyptian Arabic Bible, Sand's reference to the Armenian version in his *Interpretationes paradoxæ*, as well as the Slavonic Bible—a 1581 edition of which Newton had personally seen. From this and other evidence, and "by the unanimous consent of all the ancient & faithful Interpreters" he concluded that the comma was lacking in the ancient Greek version.[49]

The passage was not in venerably ancient Bibles, nor was there any reference to it in any patristic text before the fifth century. Throughout "that vehement universal & lasting controversy about the Trinity in Jeromes time & both before & long enough after it," Newton thundered it had never even been "thought of." It was now "in every bodies mouth," but no trace of it existed "till at length when the ignorant ages came on it began by degrees to creep into the Latine copies out of Jerome's Version." To prove it Newton appealed to the records of councils and a string of sometimes obscure patristic sources. For example, it was simply absent from sources such as the Tenth Epistle of the fifth-century pope Leo the Great ("if," as Newton put it, "the authority of Popes be valuable") and from any of the copies of the Greek Fathers. In a short but brilliantly original piece of analysis, he took great relish in describing all those places where the Greeks could or should have invoked the text but did not do so. For example, Basil failed to cite the place against the (Arian) Eunomians when the latter claimed that Scripture did not support the "conjoining" of the Father, Son, and Holy Ghost. Basil was very diligent in returning an answer to them, Newton claimed, but "perplexes himself in citing places wch are nothing to ye purpose" and so knew nothing of it. After an exhaustive search of the patristic literature, he concluded that it contained no references to the passage.[50]

Like Simon, Newton attacked the view that the Arians had excised the passage from all the copies cited by Augustine and others. Simon had invoked the baneful influence of the false Jeromian preface to explain why this apparently ludicrous story had gained currency, and Newton agreed that the story was preposterous:

> Yes truly those Arians were crafty Knaves that could conspire so cunningly & slyly all the world over at once (as at the word of Mithridates) in the latter end of the reign of the Emperor Constantius to get all men's books into their hands & correct them without being perceived: Ay & Conjurers too, to do it without leaving any blot or chasm in the books, whereby the knavery might be suspected & discovered; & to wipe even the memory of it out of all men's

brains, so that neither Athanasius nor any body else could afterwards remember that they had even seen it in their books before.

How then had the reading been inserted into the text, and by what means had it gained authority? While Simon merely noted that the perpetrators of the interpolation were pious or superstitious men, Newton argued that those who had carried out the corruption were part of the great Athanasian conspiracy. They made false accusations against others but this was merely a ruse to cover up their own crimes: "they that w^{th}out proof accuse hereticks of corrupting books, & upon that pretense correct them at their pleasure without the authority of ancient manuscripts, (as some learned men in the fourth & fifth Centuries used to do) are Falsaries by their own confession." This statement not only damned those who had lived over a millennium before Newton but it also condemned the majority of his contemporaries.[51]

It was clear to Newton that no sixteenth-century editor had personally set eyes on an ancient text with the full seventh verse. Beza came in for particular invective for his cavalier attitude to textual testimony, not least for claiming in his *Annotations on the New Testament* that he had seen manuscripts with his very own eyes (a statement, Newton noted, that he corrected in subsequent editions), when in fact he was merely citing from collations published by Robert Stephens in 1550. Moreover, Beza, Lucas Brugensis, and others following him wrongly inferred from Stephens's claim that he had not found the comma in seven out of fifteen manuscripts consulted, that the passage was extant in the rest. However, Newton remarked, it was clear that he had consulted no more than these seven, and in a later addition to his text, he noted that the passage was missing from all the manuscripts Simon had consulted in France. "Pull[ing] off ye vizzard," Newton complained to Locke, as if there were any semblance of a mask remaining, he said that he wanted to "extreamly complain of Beza's want of modesty & caution in expressing himself." The only manuscript that could possibly have been seen by contemporaries was that "Phœnix" which came to light in the controversy between Erasmus and Lee. Newton doubted its authenticity, suspecting that it was "nothing but a trick put upon him [i.e., Erasmus] by some of the Popish Clergy," to test whether Erasmus would make good his promise of inserting the comma into a subsequent edition if one authoritative example were found. Greek manuscripts were things of immense value and were not simply thrown away: had there been such a manuscript it "would have made a much greater noise than the rest have done against it." "Let those who have such a manuscript," Newton lectured, "at length tell us where it is." As for the great Complutensian edition, this had appealed to the authority of Aquinas, who had claimed not only that the Arians had eradicated the seventh verse but they had inserted "and these three are one" in the *eighth*. "To us," he told Locke, Aquinas was no Apostle. What mattered was the authority of the Greek manuscripts.[52]

At the end of the analysis Newton followed standard anti-Trinitarian practice in asserting that the passage made more sense if it was interpreted as unity of testimony. This was in many ways the most radical part of the dissertation, for it was no longer merely an historical, critical investigation of the text's corruption. The most comprehensible interpretation of the de-Trinitised text, that is, what was now 1 John 5:8 (the agreement "in earth" of the spirit, water, and blood), was that Jesus came first in a mortal body by baptism of water, and then in an immortal one as a result of shedding his blood on the cross and rising from the dead. The three terrestrial witnesses were more than sufficient testimony to warrant the truth of the story, while the testimony in heaven was both redundant and incomprehensible. In few other places did Newton so clearly express his belief that comprehensibility was a central criterion of correct interpretation of a biblical passage. This did not mean that he thought that individuals had a blanket license to determine what Scripture was by their unfettered private judgements, but "in disputable places," he told Locke, "I love to take up wth what I can best understand." Accordingly, he contrasted the free exercise of his own learned understanding, which could shed light on the true meaning of the text, with the ignorant predilection for mystery displayed by most of humanity: "'Tis the temper of the hot and superstitious part of mankind in matters of religion ever to be fond of mysteries, & for that reason to like best what they understand least." The Apostle was an inspired and intelligent man who had written good sense, and as a "considering man" himself, Newton was licensed to use his own intellect to decipher John's meaning.[53]

Even if his work drew from the findings and interpretations of modern commentators, which it did, Newton was by no means wholly reliant upon them. In many places he offered a more substantial analysis than could be found in Nye, Sand, or even Simon, and he located sources that were not standardly available in the critical literature. When he came to write up his work for Locke, he cited a large number of modern authors, though it is likely that he consulted other secondary sources such as Nye and even

Simon himself, which—again following his normal practice—he neglected to mention. It seems likely that he procured help from one or more of his learned friends, though one assumes that they had no idea about the project they were supporting. Locke sent the "Historical Account" to Le Clerc towards the end of December, along with a number of texts on toleration and the Trinity. These included the books noticed by Le Clerc in the *Bibliothèque Universelle*, and he sent a similar collection of works to Newton. Their contents must have taken up much of the conversation that Newton enjoyed with Locke when he made the surprising decision to venture to Oates in the new year, though they must also have discussed the issue of getting Newton a plumb job at the Mint, in which he was now greatly interested.[54]

9. The Great Mystery of Godliness

In his covering letter of 14 November 1690, Newton told Locke that on looking back over what he had written about 1 John 5:7, he had found new evidence concerning 1 Timothy 3:16 ("And without controversy great is the mystery of godliness: God was manifest in the flesh, justified in the Spirit, seen of angels, preached unto the Gentiles, believed on in the world, received up into glory" in the King James Bible). The phrasing of Newton's letter suggests that he and Locke had also discussed this passage at their March meeting, and indeed some brief remarks on the text in his notebook probably date from this time.[55] Newton's short essay on the text shows how, in a relatively short space of time, he could scour secondary texts, mine standard and rare patristic materials, and then present a coherent, learned, and original argument. From numerous sources, he understood that the text was never cited against the Arians in the early church. The earliest extant manuscripts and Bibles (including Jerome's Vulgate) lacked the Trinitarian slant to the passage, instead rendering it in a form whose English translation was "Great is the mystery of godliness which was manifested in the flesh." The lack of early textual warrant for the Trinitarian version of the passage had always caused serious problems for orthodox interpreters, and it was a favourite target of the Socinians, most of whom referred to Erasmus for a favourable scholarly gloss. The *Racovian Catechism* had noted that the word $\theta\epsilon\grave{o}s$ (God) was lacking in many ancient copies, which read the more simple $\mathring{o}$ ("which"), and both Andrei Wissowatius and his nephew Benedict had added further authorities to the non-Trinitarian reading of this passage in their notes to the 1680 edition of the *Catechism*.[56]

In his *Annotations*, Grotius proffered the same variant reading on the grounds that it made "good sense," not on the basis of any Greek manuscripts, but rather on the authority of the Vulgate and the Ethiopic, Syriac, and Arabic Bibles. Newton noted that although the Arabic version of the New Testament did not refer to God, the *Egyptian* Arabic edition cited in the *Polyglot* did; nevertheless, like the Slavonic Bible (which also contained the word), the latter was of a later date and had been contaminated by other texts. The churches of the time, Newton claimed, were "absolute strangers" to the Trinitarian rendition of the passage, and they routinely cited the relative clause when they did refer to it. As for the Greeks, during the fifth-century Nestorian controversy concerning the nature of Christ all sides read the text with relative pronouns ὅ or ὅς, and at no point did Trinitarians accuse those who read the passage in this way of having changed it. Hence the corrupt text was "foisted in" after this. As Nye had earlier affirmed, the true author of the corruption was Macedonius II, the early sixth-century patriarch of Constantinople, who had made miniscule but far-reaching changes to the text with one stroke of the pen. This alteration was made to defend the orthodox decision made at the Council of Chalcedon in 451, which had asserted that Jesus Christ had two natures, one fully divine and one fully human, which nevertheless existed indivisibly as one hypostasis.[57]

Like Simon, Newton cited the authority of Hincmarus, who argued that Macedonius had been banished in a council set up in Constantinople to examine claims against him for changing *O* or *OΣ* into *ΘΣ*. This corruption had been much more easily done than the comma, since it involved the change of one letter by one tiny stroke of the pen. According to Newton, "footprints" of the old reading nevertheless could be seen in some ancient manuscripts, as in the Claromontanus, a Spanish copy seen by Velesius (i.e., from the so-called Velesian readings compiled by Peter Faxard, Marquis of Velez), and the Lincoln College codex ("yᵉ oldest of the Oxford MSS") recorded by Fell. In the case of Beza, although he had indicated that all the oldest Greek texts read "θεὸς," Newton remarked, "I must tell Beza's Readers that his MSS read ὅ." Evidence from other sources, including a text in Colbert's library (the Colbertinus) and, most important, the Alexandrinus which (Newton learned from Mill) gave evidence of an initial reading of *OΣ*; all empirical evidence thus militated against an early reading of θεὸς. As with the comma, Newton concluded by suggesting that his preferred version of the text was far more comprehensible. The insertion of the word *God* made no sense, for how could it be said that God was justified in the spirit? But if the relative clause were accepted as referring to Christ, then it made the meaning "very easy." The "promised & long expected" Messiah, the hope of Israel, was that great mystery of godliness that was manifested to the Jews from his baptism onwards and thus proved to them that he was the person they longed for.[58]

At some point after the dispatch of these dissertations, Newton found time to go over the background to many more corruptions of Scripture. All had been performed to exaggerate the divinity of Christ, and all were staples of anti-Trinitarian criticism. The central perversions of Scripture, Newton concluded, had all been performed in the fourth century, and to the eternal dishonour of all Christians, Catholics had perpetrated many more corruptions than the heretics. In the earliest stages of Christianity the Gnostics had been accused of corrupting Scripture "& seem to have been guilty," Newton claimed, "& yet the catholicks were not then wholly innocent." Later on, Catholics were responsible for all the falsifications of Scripture, but to justify and spread their insertions they simply condemned their enemies, who included ancient interpreters, as arch-corrupters. At every point Catholics inverted the truth, and if they could do this to the Fathers and the Scriptures, what other horrors might they accomplish? "Such was the liberty of that age," Newton raged, "that learned men blushed not in translating Authors to correct them at their pleasure & confess openly y^t they did so as if it were a crime to translate them faithfully." He retained sufficient composure to tell Locke that his analysis was aimed as a general warning, motivated by "the great hatred I have to pious frauds, & to shame Christians out of these practises." Time was short, and accepted interpretations of fraudulent Trinitarian proof-texts had to be "exploded" before manuscripts became too faded.[59]

10. A Friendship in Study

Newton's claim that his account was only a piece of textual criticism conditioned by his own understanding was meant to imply that it was merely a rational exercise. That is, his comments implied that his analysis was the result of the sort of routine and unbiased textual enquiry in which learned Christians such as himself were supposed to engage. In claiming that the relentless study of Scripture performed according to rational principles was a central facet of a godly life, he was, not coincidentally, in harmony with Locke. In his short essay "Of Study," written in May 1677, Locke had asserted that the goal of study was knowledge and "the end of knowledge practice or communication." Life was too short to waste on other men's books and opinions, and in order to discover the most important truths, it was best to use one's independent reason in the form of private study. Locke did accept that languages and critical learning were valuable for understanding the Bible, and "studious men" could study history and antiquity as a means to the same end. Conversation with "an ingenious friend" on profitable subjects might be as fruitful as "settled, solemn poring on books," and it was equally important to study and practice good conduct, which outside the Scriptures was exemplified in pagan writings of Cicero. In the latter, Locke read of the key roles played by temperance, honesty, modesty, self-control, and practical wisdom, all of which aided study.[60]

According to Locke, the great duty was to make Truth the object of study and to seek it impartially, yet the prejudices that were implanted in people from an early age made this almost impossible. The cultures and beliefs in which men grew up were usually erroneous, and only self-sustained study could correct the epistemic fallibility of humanity. At one level, the study of the Bible itself, just as much as the use of the works of "Criticks," was subordinate to attaining the prudence and moral knowledge that would allow one to lead a virtuous, good life. False opinions imbibed from birth, Locke claimed, "put a man quite out of the way in the whole course of his studies" while later "the things he meets with in other men's writings or discourses [are] received or rejected as they hold proportion with those anticipations which before have taken possession of his mind." This was the problem for Catholics and indeed for all those of "corrupted appetites." To make us interrogate errors that might reside in our own "party," Locke claimed, "we had need of all our force and all our sincerity; and here "tis we have use of the assistance of a serious and sober friend who may help us sedately to examine these our received and beloved opinions."[61]

By these terms, Newton's and Locke's interactions constituted an ideal intellectual friendship. Locke had only just published the definitive work on the subject of the understanding, and the topic must have been one of the major foci of their conversations. The "Historical Account" was highly consonant with the strictures for study promoted by Locke, and with many of the values that were independently promoted by Newton. These ethical and religious injunctions were also accepted by many of their contemporaries.

Independent study strengthened the intellect, and it was a virtuous and practical solution to finding oneself surrounded by error and duplicity. In the conclusion to his analysis of 1 Timothy 3:16, Newton confessed to Locke that he had had insufficient time to consult further authors, thus underlining the notion that he had scrutinised the original texts directly rather than relying on modern authorities. Even so, he said, it was more than Locke had so far encountered in other commentators. As he had stated in the introduction to his analysis of the comma, he reminded Locke that he had used a great deal of freedom in writing and sending the discourse, and he invited Locke to interpret it "candidly." He supposed this would be all the more acceptable having been sent to someone with such integrity. An honest man was invariably pleased at the "detection of frauds," while a "man of interest" was troubled by it.[62]

Newton's analysis of the two "corruptions" is unique among his theological writings, both because it had an identifiable recipient, and also because he was initially enthusiastic about allowing his work to be printed. Nevertheless, it displays a number of features common to all his religious activity. It was a technically demanding and brilliant rhetorical performance, which combined a veneer of objectivity with an overt hostility to Trinitarian corruptions and their authors. Newton took whatever evidence was available to make his case, and benefitted from contemporary criticism, whether it was Socinian, Anglican, or Roman Catholic. He presented his findings as the result of intelligent, strenuous, and innovative research, and, indeed, much of his approach was original even if he was heavily reliant on other authors. Newton's lay status underpinned much of the way in which he understood his authorial self. He was, he said, a learned person engaging in a legitimate and rational piece of criticism, who was sending his private text to an honest and inquisitive man of a similar capacity and status. However, when he sent the text to Locke he was also aiming at a much broader readership within the Republic of Letters, and these conflicting demands set up what was ultimately an irreconcilable tension. Just over a year after its composition, he decided to suppress it. As much as his fear that his authorship of an overtly anti-Trinitarian text might be revealed, his customary preference for the more restricted sphere of private correspondence once more predominated. It was, after all, merely a letter to a friend.[63]

12

A Particle of Divinity

An unnatural and short-lived serenity descended over Newton in the winter of 1690/91. Having dispatched the analyses of the two corruptions of Scripture, he was sufficiently inspired to visit Locke in the new year at Oates, in the darkest corners of Essex. He thanked Locke on 7 February 1691 for his and Damaris Masham's "civilities" and also for speaking to Newton's London allies about his future employment prospects. At the start of April, Jean Le Clerc wrote to Locke informing him that when he had time, he would translate the dissertation on 1 John 5:7 into Latin or French, since it was eminently worthy of being published. Surprised that the author showed no signs of having read Simon's *Critical History of the New Testament*, Le Clerc suggested that his views be taken into account. Locke passed on the advice and Newton duly read, or at least cited, the work, adducing additional evidence from Simon and Gilbert Burnet about the absence of the Johannine comma from early manuscripts. He and Locke continued to correspond about theological matters and in June, he told Locke that if the paper on the corruption of Scripture was not imminently forthcoming, they could discuss what to do about it at their next meeting. Soon afterwards, Locke received a letter from Le Clerc stating that he still intended to translate the text, although it would have to appear with other tracts since it was too small to publish alone.[1]

1. A Sad though Great Scholar

Aside from his theological research, Newton continued to work on alchemy, physics, optics, and mathematics in the aftermath of his year-long stint as an MP. He met David Gregory in the summer of 1691 and spent a great deal of time with him; Gregory was rewarded by winning Newton's support for his successful application to become Savilian Professor of Astronomy at

Oxford. When Fatio de Duillier returned in September 1691 from a lengthy period in the Netherlands, he resumed his position as Newton's chief confidant. Fatio's offer to edit a second edition of the *Principia* galvanised Newton into making a series of changes and corrections to the first edition, including the production of the Classical Scholia. However, in the end, neither Newton's nor Fatio's efforts, which were partly inspired by his hope that Newton would include his theory of gravity in the new edition, came to anything. Mathematics was a different issue, and towards the end of 1691, Newton was provoked by both Fatio and Gregory into writing a supreme exposition of his method of fluxions, which he titled "De quadratura curvarum" ("On the quadrature, or integration of curves"). The treatise was also an exercise in staking a priority claim over a raft of calculus techniques and as such, it was predominantly addressed towards Leibniz, who had published the algorithms of his version of the calculus in the mid-1680s. In what is a familiar pattern, Newton must have told Gregory, Fatio, and others in December that he intended to publish the work, along with a tract on the Geometry of the Ancients, but "De quadratura" was published only in 1704 as an appendage to his *Opticks*, while the work on ancient geometry did not appear in his lifetime.[2]

By the start of 1692, the strenuous burst of work on "De quadratura" and his interest in other projects may have started to exert a negative influence on Newton's well-being, and he must have been brooding over Fatio's frequent reminders of the need to assert his mathematical property rights in the face of competition from Leibniz. Newton's increasing anxiety over his lack of appointment in London had also become intertwined with a change of heart regarding the publication of the "Two Corruptions" text. From the heady days in the summer of 1691, when he had believed that he was being set up by Locke and others for the comptrollership of the Mint, his patrons were now offering only insignificant positions. In December 1691 he told Locke that he was not interested in the mastership of Charterhouse, remarking that £200 p.a. and a coach were hardly adequate recompense. He added that he was averse to "confinement to ye London air & a formal way of life," though of course he had sought the latter two years earlier when he applied to become the head of a major academic institution. He had no desire, he told Locke, to sing a new song "to ye tune of King's College."[3]

Robert Boyle's death on the last day of 1691 drew him to London in order to attend the funeral. He stayed there for three weeks but the trip did not go well. On 4 January 1692 Humphrey Babington passed away, and on the sixteenth, Locke's friend Robert Pawling told Locke that he had just seen Newton up two flights of stairs in a "pittifull room" in Suffolk Street. Newton had evidently displayed a pronounced degree of paranoia, and Pawling reported that Newton had claimed that a "great man" (Monmouth) had made some odd remark to him and he was "puzzled to know whether it was a reflection on him or designed for good advice." Newton had also claimed that Locke had made some reference to the incident afterwards but, Pawling remarked, he was unsure how Locke had learned about it. Pawling added that he had suggested that Newton be more frank with Locke and had told Newton that he should not doubt that Locke was a true friend.[4]

Monmouth was not the only patron to be the subject of Newton's height-ened suspicion, and he told Pawling that another great man, undoubtedly Charles Montagu, had let him down. This can only be because he had prom-ised Newton a major position in London that had not materialised, although it is not clear how Montagu, who was only appointed to the Treasury Board two months after the meeting between Newton and Pawling, was in a position to influence events in his favour. Pawling emphasised that Newton had done a fine job of hiding the real reason for his distress, and trying to ascer-tain what his problem was would require the skills of a master cryptog-rapher. When Newton had first raised the topic with him, a shy young man professing his love for a woman could not have been more bashful; it was a sad thing, he noted, "to be a meer, though a great scholar." Whatever the underlying causes of his problem, Newton wrote to Locke just over a week later, repeating his comment about the perfidy of Montagu while probing the degree of support he might expect from Monmouth. He invited Locke to Cambridge and requested that Locke either send the "Two Corruptions" documents to him or bring them with him if he came, both of which im-plied that he no longer wanted the papers to be published. However, a letter written by Le Clerc a fortnight earlier shows that Locke had sent him the additions Newton had culled from Simon and Burnet, and that Le Clerc was about to translate the additional text on 1 Timothy 3:16 into Latin so that the two texts could appear together.[5]

Newton's concerns about the impact of publishing his essay on the comma, and his failure to acquire a major position in London must have both contrib-uted to his malaise. He told Locke in a terse letter of mid-February 1692 that he had assumed that the translation and publication process had been put on hold, and he now begged Locke to put an end to both. He told Locke that he was sorry for "pressing" into Monmouth's company when he had last seen him, but this had been due to the fact that Pawling had "prest" him into the room. Locke must have quickly acceded to Newton's request to prevent the appearance of the "Two Corruptions" text since Le Clerc wrote to him at the start of April saying that he was disappointed that the edition had been stopped. In early May, having been told that the edition had been killed off, Newton repeated his request that Locke pay him a visit, and this time Locke obliged. While Locke was in Cambridge, he met Newton and checked the status of Luke 22:16-20 in the Codex Bezae following a request by Benjamin Furly. Later, he told his friend Edward Clarke that his host (presumably Newton) had "importuned" him to stay, but Lady Masham had wanted him back at Oates and he could not refuse. In July he asked Newton to comment on the eighth chapter of his forthcoming *A Third Letter on Toleration*, promising to send further chapters for Newton to read, correct, and censure.[6]

For some time, alchemy became Newton and Locke's chief topic of conversation, since soon after Boyle's death, Locke had sent Newton some "red earth" that Boyle had left him. Even by his own standards, Newton's ensuing efforts to discuss the sense in which Locke might be obliged to pass on some of Boyle's recipes in connection with this material were tortuous. Indeed, they say as much about Newton's idiosyncratic attitude to publication as they do about the complex codes that governed communication of alchemical processes. In essence, Newton was doubtful that Boyle had produced any of this substance himself, but thought that some of the recipes for the process that Boyle possessed might contain something of significance. As with his letter to Oldenburg of 1676, where he had recommended that Boyle go no further in revealing the process that underlay the production of a special mercury that would "grow hot" when mixed with gold, Newton professed ambivalence about whether the recipes in Locke's possession should be taken seriously. At this time he also discussed alchemy with Fatio de Duillier, who provided him with regular reports about his own ailing health and his friends' success in producing a powerful alchemical mercury. Fatio now found it a good time to dabble in biblical exegesis, and in January 1693 he suggested to Newton that many passages in the Old Testament were actually prophecies of events in his own time and in times to come. Newton commended the fact that Fatio had begun to take the prophecies into consideration, but in a brutal put-down, expressed his view that Fatio had "indulged too much in fansy" in a number of places.[7]

Undeterred, in early May 1693 Fatio tempted him with news of experiments he had conducted with a new friend regarding the purification of mercury, which, when mixed with gold filings and placed in a sealed egg, produced a heap of colour-shifting alchemical trees. There was evidently a "life and ferment" in the composition, Fatio told him, and it had been digesting fruitfully for many months. His friend had already cured many of consumption (tuberculosis) by means of a remedy based on his special mercury, and Fatio was about to take it as part of a course of alchemotherapy. Two weeks later, he asked Newton to fund him for four years in order to develop the mercury into a universal panacea. Newton appears to have been decidedly sceptical about the chances of success, but at the start of June, Fatio's invitation to visit him was enough to tempt him to London. While there, he purchased quicksilver, ammonium chloride, and nitric acid from a druggist on Bow Street, and when he returned to Cambridge on 8 June he immediately entered new alchemical experiments in his notebook. He received an emotional letter towards the end of August from his half-sister Hannah, telling Newton of her husband's imminent death, but by this time he was in no fit state of mind to deal with it.[8]

2. A Derangement of the Intellect

Newton wrote an extraordinary letter to Samuel Pepys on 13 September 1693, saying that Pepys's friend John Millington (a fellow at Magdalene College) had delivered a strange message to him. Using his standard term to indicate his sense of being harassed, he twice mentioned that Millington had "pressed" him to visit Pepys the next time he was in London and added that he had consented to this without realising what he was doing. His odd behaviour was because he was still in an "embroilment" and he had lost his "former consistency of mind," having neither slept nor eaten properly for a whole year. Newton told Pepys pointedly that he had "never designed to get anything by your interest, nor by King James' favour," but he now had to withdraw from Pepys's acquaintance and, indeed, had to break off contact with all of his friends. In his role as president of the Royal Society, Pepys's name had appeared alongside Newton's at the front of the *Principia*. He had remained close to James when, as Duke of York, the latter had been forced to resign from the Admiralty after the passing of the Test Act. Pepys was accused by his many enemies of being a crypto-Catholic at key moments in the 1670s and 1680s, and he refused to take the oath of allegiance to William and Mary. Accusations of complicity in James's alleged tyranny had recently been levelled against him by radical

Whigs, and now Newton was trying to extricate himself from any suggestion that he had tried to benefit from the patronage of Pepys or the discredited monarch.[9]

Pepys told Millington at the end of September that he feared Newton's behaviour had arisen from "a discomposure in head, or mind, or both" and asked Millington what on earth had taken place when they had met. Millington replied that he had never passed on any message to Newton from Pepys, and on hearing about Newton's claim that he had done so, he had immediately set off to see Newton in person. He had finally met up with him in Huntingdon, whereupon an unprompted Newton admitted that he had written Pepys an extremely odd letter, which had caused him a great deal of concern. He attributed this to some "distemper" of the head that had kept him up for five nights, though he was now much better. Millington reported that Newton had apologised profusely for his behaviour and added—as if Newton had intimated that this was the key issue underlying the whole episode—that England must care little for learning or honour when those in power neglected someone of Newton's stature.[10]

About the time Newton sent Pepys his bizarre note, he wrote an equally paranoid letter to Locke signed off "At the Bull in Shoreditch." Newton apologised for believing that Locke had "endeavoured to embroil [him] wth weomen & by other means," and also for saying that it would be better if Locke had died when told that he was ill. He also begged Locke's pardon for taking him for a "Hobbist" (i.e., a materialist), and for saying that he had "struck at ye root of morality in a principle you laid down in your book of Ideas & designed to pursue in another book." He concluded this extraordinary performance by apologising for "saying or thinking that there was a designe to sell me an office" and signed it "your most humble & most unfortunate servant." Like Pepys, this was the first Locke had heard of these accusations. Newton's statement about being embroiled with women certainly raises questions about what event (if any)—or indeed who—might have fuelled the specific allegation. Moreover, his complaint that there was a design to sell him an office must relate to his anxieties about obtaining a position in London, and chimes both with Pawling's earlier remarks and the comments in the Pepys letter. Although Newton seems to have invented certain recent events, such as the message allegedly delivered by Millington, other references do not seem to be completely delusional. In the case of being embroiled with women, it may be that Newton believed that his rigorous techniques for ensuring chastity were being undermined—perhaps because the imminent end of his fellowship and his move to London would provide new temptations. As for the selling of offices, it could be that it was not Newton's failure to obtain a senior position in London, but rather what he might have had to do to acquire it, that fuelled the strange comments exhibited in the letters.[11]

Locke was as shocked as Pepys by Newtons' remarks, and desperate to confirm his friendship with Newton, responded with great magnanimity. He reassured Newton that from their first meeting he had been "intirely & sincerely" Newton's friend and had thought that Newton felt the same way—to such an extent that he would not have believed the sentiments in Newton's letter if they had been relayed to him by someone else. Using the strongest possible terms of affection for a male friend, he added that he took Newton's regret for having voiced such opinions to be evidence that their relationship was still intact. Indeed, Locke continued to believe that this was the case, for just before he died in 1704, he recorded in his copy of *Opticks* that he had received it from the most erudite, honourable, and friendly of men ("Viri Doctissimi, Intigerrimi [*sic*], amicissimi"). Newton's accusation that he had undercut the basis for morality rankled most. This presumably concerned his appeal to ethical hedonism in Book 2, chapter 17, §5 of the *Essay Concerning Human Understanding*, in which he stated that good and evil were nothing but pleasure or pain, "or that which procures Pleasure or Pain to us." Since the second edition was ready for the press, Locke urged Newton to point out other places in his work that had given rise to the remarks, so that he might avoid being seen as doing prejudice to truth or virtue.[12]

News of Newton's troubles spread abroad, and Continental philosophers discussed the possibility that Newton had suffered a "derangement of the intellect." At the end of May 1694, Christiaan Huygens was told that Newton had been suffering from a kind of madness for a year and a half, caused either by overworking or by a fire that had destroyed a great deal of his philosophical material. Newton, he wrote, had betrayed a degree of insanity in a conversation with the archbishop of Canterbury: at this his friends took him in hand, kept him under a sort of house arrest, and administered appropriate medicines. He had now recovered his health to such an extent that he could once more understand his *Principia*. Huygens told his brother that the English were vainly trying to hide the fact that Newton was lost to learning and indeed were covering up the whole business. Although some of this is garbled, or patently false, the idea that Newton was unwell for a longer period of time is not entirely implausible. It is corroborated by Newton himself, by the incident with Pawling, and by evidence from the diary of the student Abraham de la Pryme. The latter recorded in February 1692 that he had just heard that Newton had completed a book on optics, when it was burned to cinders while he was at chapel. When he returned to his rooms, de la Pryme recorded, "Every one thought he would have run mad, he was so troubled thereat that he was not himself for a month after." Historians have located this incident in another stressful period in Newton's life, namely the winter of 1677/78, when he undoubtedly lost optical papers on account of a fire. Nevertheless, given that de la Pryme's anecdote was written in the early 1690s immediately after a known crisis in Newton's life, and since it stated that Newton's book had been in gestation for two decades, it is more consistent with the later period.[13]

After composing his "odd letters" to his friends, Newton went back to his studies with remarkable swiftness and performed these duties with too much efficiency for his temporary "derangement" to be attributed (as some have done) to prolong mercury poisoning. In a brief note to Locke, Newton told him that he could not remember what he had written to Locke, but if Locke wished to send him a copy of the offending passage in his letter, he would attempt to explain it. The very next day, he composed what looks at first glance like a generous letter to Leibniz, in which he remarked that he did his best to avoid philosophical and mathematical correspondence because he feared that he would be pressed into disputes by ignorant people. Responding to a much earlier missive from Leibniz, Newton stated that he was Leibniz's "most sincere friend" and added that he valued friends more highly than mathematical discoveries. Despite these protestations, however, the letter was in part designed to forewarn Leibniz that elements from Newton's earlier 1676 letters to him were about to appear in John Wallis's *Opera*. In a move that foreshadowed the great dispute to come, Newton, who had been primed by Fatio about Leibniz's claims to priority over the integral calculus, was already marshalling evidence to defend his rights in the business.[14]

The following months were partly taken up with the collation of manuscripts and printed sources of Revelation, though Newton must have found the odd moment—or month—to produce the stunning "Geometria" that was the topic of conversations between Gregory and himself in 1694. As for theology, John Mill had visited Newton at Cambridge earlier in 1693, most probably in May, since at the end of that month Newton had mentioned

Mill's forthcoming edition of the Greek New Testament to the philosopher Otto Mencke. In November, Mill reminded Newton about his kind promise to send some comments on variant readings in various manuscript and printed texts of the Apocalypse. In a revealing show of faith, Mill had lent Newton his main copy of his work with variants of New Testament passages, along with a small notebook in which Newton was to note the new readings, and he now asked for them to be returned. Since, he suggested, "wee cannot be not be too carefull in a matter of this Consequence," Newton should get his servant to ensure that the tome was put in the carrier's bag. Mill sent his best wishes to John Covel and John Laughton, thereby confirming the fact that he and Newton were part of a well-defined group of exegetes. After two months of concentrated endeavour, Newton sent back the materials along with new readings from the Fathers, from the Codex Bezae, and from Covel's two New Testament manuscripts— the latter checked by Laughton. Mill thanked him for his "Singular Care and pains" and included many of Newton's readings when his edition appeared in 1707.[15]

3. The Perfect Understanding

The fact that Newton could undertake the activities that Mill requested, along with all the other intellectual researches that obsessed him, was definitive evidence that his intellectual faculties had been fully restored. The hard-won collations he sent to Mill were just as much the products of his reason as were his mathematical work, or his investigations of the natural world. Even if they were not identical, he used broadly similar investigative procedures in his religious studies to those he employed in his work in natural philosophy. One had to first understand the language and concepts in which one was operating and then proceed according to accepted forms of argument. Different styles of demonstration might vary in form, but all employed rational proofs carried out according to the technical requirements of the genre. Along with this, it was vital to adduce appropriate forms of empirical evidence. There were numerous ways in which philosophers and interpreters could fall into error; many people wrongly introduced hypotheses and systems into natural philosophy, relying on inadequate textual authorities or their own imaginings. Similarly, many religious interpretations were the uncertain results either of mere human authority, or of self-interest, or of fancy.

Newton's use of his intellect, and the moral and religious values he attributed to it, were central to his life and work. Like the imagination and the will, the understanding had been forged in the image of God, and one had a duty to use it. Not only could one discern important truths about Scripture and Nature, but by using the intellect properly one could see exactly how attributes of the divine being were adumbrated in mere mortals. In the language of the Cartesian texts that he studied so early in his career, all of his work can be seen as the outcome of his own finite mind seeking to know the infinite and the divine. Contemporaries understood this, revering Newton and his achievement precisely because he had shown that mortals were capable of grasping the ordered structure of the divinely created cosmos. The claims that the *Principia* had revealed the language and blueprint of the divine creation, and that (in Halley's famous words) no mortal could approach the gods more closely, should not be read as mere hyperbole. If Newton's achievements said a great deal about the human intellect, so they said much about the mind of God. God had the capacity to calculate and effect all the infinite motions and their causes that constituted the universe from one moment to the next, but armed with the *Principia*, humans created in the Image of God had the equipment to do something similar.[16]

Newton had high confidence in the extent of his understanding, and contemporaries were fascinated by it. The correspondence between Pepys and Millington is highly revealing in this regard. After his meeting with Newton in the autumn of 1693, Millington reassured Pepys that the "small degree of melancholy" under which Newton was labouring had not affected his understanding, whereupon Pepys replied that such an "evil" befalling Newton was "what every good man must feel for his own sake as well as his." Only a select few possessed similar intellectual gifts along with the virtue and the drive to put them to good use. The legendary difficulty of the *Principia* was couched in terms of the inability of the vast majority of his contemporaries to comprehend it, and Newton proudly recalled at the end of his life that Humphrey Babington said that it would take seven years to understand any of it. At this time he also related—presumably in a humorous vein—the story of a student who reported that the work was so difficult that not even its author understood it. However, ambitious disciples, such as Fatio de Duillier and Abraham de la Pryme, believed (or hoped) that they were sufficiently worthy to undertake the same intellectual journey as Newton, and they devoted themselves to mastering the *Principia*. As a result they entered the elite priesthood of which he was the founding member.[17]

Newton believed that the perfection of the understanding involved the relentless study of sacred texts and the rational examination of the cosmos. His preface to his early treatise on the Apocalypse was saturated with scriptural references to the understanding, for he believed that God had given his people prophesies so that they might be understood in the latter times. Daniel had foretold (12:4, 9-10) that at the end of time, the wise, and not the wicked, would understand, and from this Newton inferred that true understanding could only be achieved by the pure of heart who had attained real wisdom. The godly, he said, should engage in the constant study of Scripture in order to fully understand their faith, so that they might choose and profess that religion they judged to be the most true. Acquiring a mature and more perfect understanding through constant reading and meditation would add assurance and vigour to faith. This work was a necessary but not sufficient condition for grasping core truths, since human wisdom was ineffective without God's help. As Newton put it, it was difficult for the wise to understand the truths of religion, given that they were so "prepossest" with their own imaginations and too engrossed with worldly designs. Ultimately, true understanding of prophecy was a gift of God; if the wise were to understand, they had to purify themselves from sin before they could accept God's offer.[18]

In a unique excursus on the nature of sin, Newton claimed that a sinner did evil not because he could not do what he wished, but because he would not do what he could. He was not condemned to sin by "the blind impuls of his nature" and in principle, he could freely choose not to do evil. However, the extent to which any man could do this was dependent on the degree to which he had improved his understanding. For Newton, the intellect was central to the life of a godly man, because only by perfecting it could he acquire a will that was sufficiently free to choose good over evil. He explicitly equated evil with folly, and he noted that the latter was always avoided by having a perfect understanding. The will was most free where the understanding was most perfect, and so its sincere and painstaking cultivation was the highest Christian duty. Christ himself had admitted that he could have sinned by not fulfilling the prophesies relating to him, but the fact he had not sinned, Newton concluded, was due to his perfect understanding guiding his actions. Newton's hymn to the will reached its zenith in his early text "De Gravitatione" and, in particular, in the General Scholium, where the intelligent designs of God were held to be the result of his supreme will.[19]

Ultimately, Newton's early life (to say nothing of his last three decades) was suffused with an overriding religious purpose. Convinced that he had been created in the Image of God, his scholarly life was in part an exercise in examining how he measured up to his maker. As such, it focussed both on perfecting himself and on understanding the works of God. Accordingly, he strove to make his life that of a godly man, avoiding the temptations of the imagination and its chief effects, idolatry, idleness, and lust. He condemned the imaginary products of human artifice and instead nurtured his understanding so that he could dedicate himself to studying the divine truths of Scripture and Nature. The relentless cultivation of his own intellect was the precondition for gaining a mature wisdom, along with a purified will that could make the correct choice between good and evil, and between true and false religion. It was also this heroic intellectual labour that produced the monumental works in theology, natural philosophy, and mathematics that survive today.

Notes

INTRODUCTION

1. Hooke to Newton, 24 November 1679 and Newton to Hooke, 28 November 1679, in *The Correspondence of Isaac Newton*, 7 vols., ed. H. W. Turnbull et al. (London, 1959–77), 2:297–98, 300–302. I refer throughout this work to "natural philosophy" (and occasionally to its shorter form "philosophy"), which was the term used in Newton's time to describe the study of nature.

2. William Stukeley referred to Newton's "intire" Christianity in his 1752 "Life" of Newton; see Royal Society Ms. 142 fol. 65ʳ. Newton's posthumous works were *The Chronology of Ancient Kingdoms Amended* (London, 1728) and *Observations on the Prophecies of Daniel and St. John* (London, 1733). I refer occasionally in this work to "Anglican" as shorthand for the doctrines and practices of the Church of England, though technically the term is anachronistic.

3. King's College, Cambridge, Keynes Ms. 130.7 fols. 1ʳ⁻ᵛ, 3ʳ; W. Whiston, *A Collection of Authentick Records* (London, 1728), 1074. The fact that Newton had "early and thoroughly" examined the doctrine and records of Christianity in the fourth and fifth centuries after the birth of Christ (hereafter C.E.) was first noted by Whiston in *Authentick Records*, 1076–77. Whiston was a known heretic who had been ousted from the Lucasian Professorship for holding very similar views to those he attributed to Newton. This, and the possibility that his account might be accurate, made it highly problematic for contemporaries.

4. Keynes Mss. 130.7 fols. 1ʳ, 3ʳ and 130.14 fols. 1ʳ–2ʳ. For the source of the Arbuthnot anecdote, see Keynes Ms. 130.5 fols. 4ʳ–5ʳ, though Newton probably regaled his friends with the tale on a number of occasions; see Fatio de Duillier to Conduitt, 8 August 1730, Keynes Ms. 96(F), fol. 1ʳ.

5. John Flamsteed to John Lowthorp, 10 May 1700, in *The Correspondence of John Flamsteed, the First Astronomer Royal*, 3 vols., ed. F. Willmoth et al. (London, 1995), 2:817–18; W. Whiston, *Authentic Records*, 1077; Locke to Peter King, late April 1703 in *The Correspondence of John Locke*, 8 vols., ed. E. S. de Beer (Oxford, 1976–89), 7:772–73. Newton believed that he and others like him were the truly orthodox (i.e., that they held "correct opinion or belief") though like many, he used the term to depict those traditional institutions that wielded political, ecclesiastical, and interpretive authority. For difficulties in defining "orthodoxy," "heterodoxy," and "heresy," and for the breadth of opinions held by the "orthodox,"

see R. Lund, *The Margins of Orthodoxy: Heterodox Writing and Cultural Response, 1660–1750* (Cambridge, 1995), 3–16.

6. Strictly speaking, most of Newton's writings come under the heading of "theology"—that is, the study of the nature of God and of Christian (and occasionally Jewish) doctrine through its canonical works, carried out via specific technical procedures and practices. "Religion" is a more nebulous category related to spiritual aspects of faith, including piety, belief in the supernatural, and the social conditions of various forms of worship. I use the term "religion" loosely in this book to cover a broad range of Newton's faith-based research, and refer to "theology" only when the topic concerns technical matters concerning doctrine. Nevertheless, it is clear that Newton's engagement with both sacred and allegedly non-inspired texts was the core part of his worship.

7. For Conduitt's comments on Newton's relentless commitment to reading and writing, see Keynes Mss. 129.1 fol. 8^v and 129.2 fol. 4^r. More generally, see A. Cambers, *Godly Reading: Print, Manuscript and Puritanism in England, 1580–1720* (Cambridge, 2011).

8. National Library of Israel, Yahuda Ms. 15.7 fol. 134^{r-v}; see also Yahuda Mss. 15.4 fols. 67^r–68^v, 15.5, fols. 98^v–99^v, and 15.6, fols. 100^r–102^v.

9. See, for example, the list of disputable topics at Yahuda Ms. 15.7 fol. 134^{r-v} and more broadly, R. Iliffe, "The Religion of Isaac Newton," in *The Cambridge Companion to Newton*, 2nd ed., ed. R. Iliffe and G. Smith (Cambridge, 2016), 485–523. It is revealing that in his theological notebook, a series of pages on many of these topics are empty; see Keynes Ms. 2, part 1, fols. 18^r–21^r; 32^r–43^r.

10. Keynes Ms. 129.2 fol. 9^v and Keynes Ms. 3 passim. For Newton's efforts to disguise his real opinions, see S. Snobelen, "Isaac Newton, Heretic: The Strategies of a Nicodemite," *British Journal for the History of Science* 32 (1999): 381–419.

11. Keynes Ms. 3 fols. 51^r–52^r. This text was Newton's only explicit discussion of any aspect of the doctrines of the Church of England.

12. See E. C. S. Gibson, *The Thirty-Nine Articles of the Church of England*, 5th ed. (London, 1906), 90–157. The comments in the second article on the Son's being begotten from everlasting of the Father, along with his consubstantiality with the Father, was added in the 1563 edition of the Articles to combat the heresy of Arianism, which had allegedly been revived by Anabaptists; see Gibson, ibid., 120.

13. For anti-Trinitarianism in seventeenth-century England, see H. J. McLachlan, *Socinianism in Seventeenth-Century England* (Cambridge, 1951); P. Dixon, *Nice and Hot Disputes: The Doctrine of the Trinity in the Seventeenth Century* (London, 2003), 98–137; S. Mortimer, *Reason and Religion in the English Revolution: The Challenge of Socinianism* (Cambridge, 2010); and P. Lim, *Mystery Unveiled: The Crisis of the Trinity in Early Modern England* (Oxford, 2012), 69–123. The brutal treatment of Quakers, Baptists, and heterodox thinkers during this period is discussed in J. Coffey, *Persecution and Toleration in Protestant England, 1558–1689* (London, 2000).

14. Keynes Ms. 129.2 fol. 4^{r-v}; for concerns about revealing alchemical secrets, see Newton to Henry Oldenburg, 26 April 1676, in H. W. Turnbull et al.,

Correspondence, 2:1–2. Elsewhere Conduitt recorded that the "boxfuls of informations in his own handwriting" he and Newton consigned to flames were all connected to Newton's work prosecuting clippers and coiners in the late 1690s; see Keynes Ms. 130.7 fol. 3ʳ. For scribal publication, see H. Love, *Scribal Publication in Seventeenth-Century England* (Oxford, 1993); and for the restricted or unauthorised circulation of Newton's mathematical manuscripts, see N. Guicciardini, *Isaac Newton on Mathematical Certainty and Method* (London, 2009), 339–64.

15. See W. Lamont, *Richard Baxter and the Millennium: Protestant Imperialism and the English Revolution* (London, 1979); and P. Seaver, *Wallington's World: A Puritan Artisan in Seventeenth-Century London* (Stanford, 1988).

16. See G. H. Williams, *The Radical Reformation*, 3rd ed. (Kirksville, 1992); and J. Israel, *The Radical Enlightenment: Philosophy and the Making of Modernity* (New York, 2002).

17. Newton's religious, political, and historical writings are all available at www.newtonproject.ox.ac.uk, while his alchemical writings are accessible at http://webapp1.dlib.indiana.edu/newton/.

18. See Sarah Dry, *The Newton Papers: The Strange and True Odyssey of Newton's Manuscripts* (New York, 2014), 80–111.

19. See ibid., passim. H. McLachlan published a small selection of Newton's religious writings from the Keynes collection in *Sir Isaac Newton: Theological Manuscripts* (Liverpool, 1950).

20. F. Manuel, *Isaac Newton: Historian* (Cambridge, 1963); and J. Z. Buchwald and M. Feingold, *Newton and the Origin of Civilization* (Princeton, 2013).

21. See J. E. McGuire and P. Rattansi, "Newton and the Pipes of Pan," *Notes and Records of the Royal Society* 21 (1966): 108–43; D. C. Kubrin, "Newton and the Cyclical Cosmos: Providence and the Mechanical Philosophy," *Journal of the History of Ideas* 28 (1967): 325–46. For various claims that Newton's work was unified in some way, see Frank Manuel, *The Religion of Isaac Newton* (Oxford, 1974), 39–40, 97, 98, 103; B. J. T. Dobbs, *The Janus Faces of Genius: The Role of Alchemy in Newton's Thought* (Cambridge, 1992), 5–15; and J. Force, "Newton's God of Dominion: The Unity of Newton's Theological, Scientific and Political Thought," in *Essays on the Context, Nature, and Influence of Isaac Newton's Theology*, ed. J. E. Force and R. Popkin (London, 1990), 76–102.

22. Yahuda Ms. 1.1 fols. 18ʳ–19ʳ. See R. Iliffe, "'Making a Shew': Apocalyptic Hermeneutics and Christian Idolatry in the Work of Isaac Newton and Henry More," in *The Books of Nature and Scripture: Recent Essays on Natural Philosophy, Theology, and Biblical Criticism in the Netherlands of Spinoza's Time and the British Isles of Newton's Time*, ed. J. E. Force and R. Popkin (Dordrecht, 1994), 55–88.

23. Yahuda Ms. 1.1 fols. 1ʳ–2ʳ, 5ʳ–7ʳ, 18ʳ.

24. The most detailed summary of Newton's views about the restorations that had taken place in human history is at Keynes Ms. 3 fol. 35ʳ.

25. See H. Frisch, "The Scientist as Priest: A Note on Robert Boyle's Natural Theology," *Isis* 44 (1953): 252–65; and R. Iliffe, "Is He Like Other Men? The

Meaning of the *Principia Mathematica* and the Author as Idol," in *Culture and Society in the Stuart Restoration*, ed. G. Maclean (Cambridge, 1995), 159–76.

26. Keynes Ms. 130.7 fol. 4ʳ;Voltaire, *Letters Concerning the English Nation* (London, 1778), 100. Shortly before Locke's death, Anthony Collins called him the "Great Lay Priest" of the age; see E. S. de Beer, *Correspondence of John Locke*, 8:304.

27. Keynes Ms. 129.2 fols. 9ᵛ–10ʳ (later version at Keynes Ms. 129.1 fol. 12ᵛ).

28. Keynes Mss. 130.3 fol. 2ʳ–ᵛ, 130.7 fol. 5ʳ, 129.2 fol. 5ʳ (cf. Keynes Ms. 129.1 fol. 10ᵛ).

29. John Conduitt, draft account of Newton's early life; Keynes Mss. 130.3 fols. 21ᵛ–22ʳ (based on notes from a conversation with Newton in August 1726), 130.10 fols. 1ᵛ–2ʳ, 130.7 fol. 7ʳ. Newton also told Conduitt that he had assumed that mathematics and poetry were so opposed to each other that poets would have a complete antipathy towards him. The phrase "never at rest" is drawn from Newton's 25 May 1694 letter to Nathaniel Hawes in H. W. Turnbull et al., *Correspondence*, 3:360. For the faculty of the intellect, see G. Hatfield, "The Cognitive Faculties," in *The Cambridge History of Seventeenth-Century Philosophy*, vol. 2, ed. D. Garber and M. Ayers (Cambridge, 1998), 953–1002.

30. See J. Spurr, "'Rational Religion' in Restoration England," *Journal for the History of Ideas* 49 (1988): 563–85, esp. 564–65, 568, 577, 581–84; and G. Reedy, *The Bible and Reason: Anglicans and Scripture in Late Seventeenth-Century England* (Philadelphia, 1985), 119–39. Socinianism was named after the Italian theologian Fausto Sozzini (1539–1604). For similarities between Newton's theological positions and those of the Socinians, see S. Snobelen, "Isaac Newton, Socinianism and 'the One Supreme God,'" in *Socinianism and Cultural Exchange: The European Dimension of Antitrinitarian and Arminian Networks, 1650–1720*, ed. M. Mulsow and J. Rohls (Leiden, 2005), 241–93.

31. The key works are Blount, *Great Is Diana of the Ephesians* (London, 1680); Blount, *The Oracles of Reason* (London, 1683); and Toland, *Christianity Not Mysterious* (London 1696). More generally, see J. Champion, *Republican Learning: John Toland and the Crisis of Christian Culture, 1696–1722* (Manchester, 2003); and D. Lucci, *Scripture and Deism: The Biblical Criticism of the Eighteenth-Century British Deists* (Bern, 2008).

32. See P. Hazard, *The Crisis of the European Mind, 1680–1715*, orig. 1935 (New York, 2013).

CHAPTER I

1. The "Long" Parliament was so called because it technically sat until 16 March 1660.

2. Newton's date of birth (which he used) is given according to the Julian calendar, whereas according to the Gregorian calendar then in use in Catholic countries, Newton was born on 4 January 1643. In early modern England, the new

year began on 25 March and most Englishmen and-women would have placed the first three months of his life in 1642 (or alternatively, represented the period between 1 January and 25 March as 1642/43). By the early eighteenth century this situation had become as confusing to his contemporaries as it is to us.

3. King's College Cambridge, Keynes Ms. 130.10; Fitzwilliam Museum, Newton Notebook, fol. 3ʳ. More generally, see C. W. Foster, "Sir Isaac Newton's Family," *Reports and Papers of the Architectural Societies of the County of Lincoln etc.* 39 (pt. 1) (1928), 4–56; G. Christianson, *In the Presence of the Creator: Isaac Newton and His Times* (New York, 1984), 5–6; R. S. Westfall, *Never at Rest: A Biography of Isaac Newton* (Cambridge, 1980), 48–53; and K. Baird, "Some Influences upon the Young Isaac Newton," *Notes and Records of the Royal Society* 41 (1987): 169–79.

4. William Stukeley recorded the existence of Smith's volumes in his 1752 biography of Newton; see Royal Society Library, Ms. 142 fol. 11ʳ. The "Waste Book" is now Cambridge University Library (CUL) Add. Ms. 4004.

5. R. S. Westfall, *Never at Rest*, 45; CCEd ID: 32896; K. Baird, "Influences," 171; Keynes Ms. 125; J. Spurr, *The Restoration Church of England, 1646–1689* (New Haven, 1991). Little is known of Newton's other maternal uncle, also James; see K. Baird, "Influences," 179.

6. See N. Tyacke, *Anti-Calvinists: The Rise of English Arminianism, c.1590–1640* (Oxford, 1987); and for differing attitudes towards ceremonies, see K. Fincham and N. Tyacke, *Altars Restored: The Changing Face of English Religious Worship, 1547–c.1700* (Oxford, 2007), 159–64. Arminianism was named after Jacobus Arminius (Jakob Hermanszoon, 1560–1609), the Dutch theologian whose religious views triggered a violent response from Calvinists in the first two decades of the seventeenth century.

7. P. Seaver, *Wallington's World: A Puritan Artisan in Seventeenth-Century London* (Stanford, 1985), 1–13, 143–52. For various aspects of puritanism in the period 1560–1660, including lengthy assessments of the meaning of the term, see W. Lamont, *Godly Rule, Politics and Religion, 1603–60* (London, 1969); P. Collinson, *The English Puritan Movement* (Clarendon, 1990); P. Lake, *The Boxmaker's Revenge: "Orthodoxy," "Heterodoxy," and the Politics of the Parish in Early Stuart London* (Stanford, 2002); and J. Coffey and P. Lim, eds., *The Cambridge Companion to Puritanism* (Cambridge, 2008).

8. See J. Morrill, "The Church in England, 1642–9" in J. Morrill, ed., *Reactions to the English Civil War, 1642–9* (London, 1982), 89–114. For Cotton, see L. Ziff, *The Career of John Cotton: Puritanism and the American Experience* (Princeton, 1962).

9. B. Couth, *"Crocadiles, French Flies and Other Animalls": Grantham at Peace and War 1633–1649* (Nottingham, 1995), 16, 26–29, 58–59, 71–72. St. Wulfram's had two vicars because of the size of the parish. See C. Holmes, *Seventeenth-Century Lincolnshire* (Lincoln, 1980), 114–21; Fincham and Tyacke, "Altars Restored," 152–59, 177–81, 196–97, and esp. 207–9; and E. Venables, "The Altar Controversy at Grantham in the Seventeenth Century," *Associated Architectural Societies: Reports and Papers* 13 (1875–76): 46–60.

10. B. Couth, *Crocadiles*, 78–79, 88–89, 101–9; *Proceedings in the Opening Session of the Long Parliament*, vol. 1, 3 November–19 December 1640, ed. M. Jansson (Rochester, N.Y., 2000), 156–57. More was the father of the Cambridge Platonist Henry More. The latter, a pronounced anti-Calvinist, remembered that his father had for a long time leaned towards Calvin but towards the end of his life turned away from him; see R. Ward, *Life of the Learned and Pious Henry More* (London, 1710), 8, 22.

11. W. E. Foster, *The Committee of Plundered Ministers of Lincolnshire; Being Extracts from the Minutes of the Committee of Plundered Ministers* (Guildford, 1891), 29–30; A. G. Matthews, *Walker Revised: Being a Revision of John Walker's Sufferings of the Clergy During the Grand Rebellion, 1642–60* (Oxford, 1948), 248–49; B. Couth, *Crocadiles*, 113–17; C. Hoole, *A New Discovery of the Old Art of Teaching Schoole in Four Small Treatises…* (London, 1660).

12. A. G. Matthews, *Walker Revised*, 248; C. Hoole, *New Discovery*, 176; K. Baird, "Influences," 172–74.

13. CSPD 1660–61: 85; E. Turnor, *Collections for the History of the Town and Soke of Grantham* (London, 1806), 153–55; B. Couth, *Grantham During the Interregnum: The Hallbook, 1641–1649* (Woodbridge, 1995), 5; Trinity notebook, vii; J. Venn, and J. A. Venn, eds. *Alumni Cantabrigienses: A Biographical List of All known Students, Graduates and Holders of Office at the University of Cambridge, from the Earliest Times to 1900*. 4 vols. (Cambridge, 1922–53), 4:318–19; RS Ms. 142 fols. 32^r–33^r; K. Baird, "Influences," 177. Thomas Syston became master of the Free School on 8 December 1663, and Walker occupied the post on 14 July 1671.

14. W. Jacobson, ed., *The Works of Robert Sanderson*, 6 vols. (Oxford, 1854), 6:281–315 (for Walton's biography, being the text of the second edition of 1681), 295–96, 300; M. Feingold, ed. *Before Newton, The Life and Times of Isaac Barrow* (Cambridge, 1990), 22–24; and P. Lake, "Serving God and the Times: The Calvinist Conformity of Robert Sanderson," *J. Brit. Studs* 27 (1988): 81–116.

15. W. Jacobson, *Works*, 2:154–59, 161–67; P. Lake, "Serving God," 87–89, 91–93, 96–97, 101–2.

16. W. Jacobson, *Works*, 6:291–95, 364.

17. W. Jacobson, *Works*, 5:20–36 (his defence of his subscribing to the Engagement), 38–41, 55–57, 289; 6:310–12, 379–80; Barlow to Boyle, 13 September 1659 and 30 January 1660 in *The Correspondence of Robert Boyle*, 6 vols., ed. M. Hunter et al. (London, 2001), 1:370, 400–402; J. Walker, *An Attempt Towards Recovering an Account of the Numbers and Sufferings of the Clergy of the Church of England Etc.* (London, 1714), 104. See also P. Lake, "Serving God," 110–12; and M. Hunter, *Robert Boyle: Scrupulosity and Science* (Woodbridge, 2000), 61–64, 74–75. More generally, see V. Kahn, *Wayward Contracts: The Crisis of Political Obligation in England, 1640–1674* (Princeton, 2004); and E. Vallance, *Revolutionary England and the National Covenant: State Oaths, Protestantism and the Political Nation, 1553–1682* (Woodbridge, 2005).

18. See Jon Parkin, "Humphrey Babington," New DNB; CCEd ID: 85773; Bodleian Library, Tanner Ms. 54 fol. 77ʳ; A. G. Matthews, *Walker Revised*, 291.

19. Stukeley to Richard Mead, 26 June 1727, Keynes Ms. 136.3 fols. 4ʳ, 7ʳ; J. B. Mullinger, *The University of Cambridge*, 3 vols. (1873–1911), 3:385–87; and J. Twigg, *The University of Cambridge in the English Revolution* (Cambridge, 1990), 155–63. For Parkyns's book on Cornish wrestling, see J. Harrison, *The Library of Isaac Newton* (Cambridge, 1978), 73–74, H1258. The other students known to have come under Newton's care while at Trinity were all from the local gentry.

20. H. Babington, *Mercy and Judgment: A Sermon* (London, 1678), sigs. A3ᵛ–A4ʳ, 1, 3, 11–12, 26–28. The sermon was originally delivered at the Lincoln Assizes on 15 July 1678.

21. H. Babington, *Mercy and Judgment*, 26–28, 30–31.

22. K. Baird, "Some Influences Upon the Young Newton," 173–74. See also I. Green, *The Christian's ABC: Catechisms and Catechizing in England, c. 1530–1740* (Oxford, 1996), 14–15, 26–27, 64–72, 93–129, 172–73; and F. Watson, *English Grammar Schools to 1660* (Cambridge, 1908), 81–82.

23. Keynes Ms. 130.10 fol. 1ᵛ; Royal Society Library Ms. 142 fols. 33ʳ–44ʳ, 47ʳ–8ʳ; for the dates of his attendance at the school, see R. S. Westfall, *Never at Rest*, 55. The best account of Clarke's life is R. Crook, *Arthur Storer's World: Family, Medicine and Astronomy in Seventeenth-Century Lincolnshire and Maryland* (Grantham, 2014), 9–18.

24. Keynes Ms. 136.3 fol. 5ʳ; "Fitzwilliam Notebook," 3ʳ⁻ᵛ. For further details, see J. Trabue, "Ann and Arthur Storer of Calvert County, Maryland, Friends of Sir Isaac Newton," *The American Genealogist* 79 (2004): 13–27, 15nn17–19, 16n23; R. Crook, *Arthur Storer's World*, 13, 21–23; and P. Broughton, "Arthur Storer of Maryland," *Journal for the History of Astronomy* 19 (1988): 77–96, esp. 79.

25. P. Broughton, "Arthur Storer," 81, 91–93; "Fitzwilliam Notebook," 3ʳ⁻ᵛ.

26. See M. H. Nicolson and S. Hutton, eds., *The Conway Letters: The Correspondence of Anne Finch, Countess of Conway, Henry More, and their Friends* (Oxford, 1992), 97, 393–95; B. Couth, *Hallbook*, 131; King's College, Cambridge, Keynes Ms. 136.03 fol. 4ʳ; Venn, "Alumni," 1:344 and 4:170.

27. B. Couth, *Grantham*, 4–5; B. Couth, *Crocadiles*, 128–35; Turnor, "Grantham," 42–43; C. Holmes, *Seventeenth-Century Lincolnshire* (Lincoln, 1980), 159–66.

28. Couth, *Grantham*, 45, 56, 65; *The Private Journals of the Long Parliament, 2 June to 17 September 1642*, 3 vols, ed. V. F. Snow and A. S. Young (New Haven, 1982–92), 3:136–37; and Commons Journal for 27 June 1642 (http://www.british-history.ac.uk/report.aspx?compid=3891). I am grateful to Ruth Crook for bringing Clarke's interrogation and arrest to my attention.

29. B. Couth, *Grantham*, 69, 73, 74, 77, 93, 110, 119.

30. Grantham Hallbook, fols. 246ʳ, 247ᵛ, 249ʳ, 284ʳ, 286ʳ, 288ʳ⁻ᵛ, 292ʳ; for Towne, see B. Couth, *Crocadiles*, 76–77, 182.

31. Grantham Hallbook, fols. 293ʳ, 295ʳ⁻ᵛ, 297ʳ, 299ʳ, 303ᵛ⁻4ᵛ, 306ᵛ⁻7ᵛ; for the original agreement with Hurst, Welby, and Trevillian, see B. Couth, *Crocadiles*, 220–21.

I am extremely grateful to members of the Grantham U3A, and particularly to John Down, for providing me with prepublication transcriptions of the Hall-book minutes from the 1650s.

32. Grantham Hallbook, fols. 296^v, 302^v, 303^v, 307^r; Turnor, "Grantham," 47. Clarke's will is available at http://www.horry.org/clarke/williamclarke.html. For Ann Storer's letter, see Crook, *Arthur Storer's World*, 58; the original letter is in Dr. Williams Library, Baxter correspondence, vol. 4, fols. 24–25. For comments on non-conformist elements in Newton's early religious upbringing, see S. Mandelbrote, "'A Duty of the Greatest Moment': Isaac Newton and the Writing of Biblical Criticism," *British Journal for the History of Science* 26 (1992): 281–302.

33. Stukeley to Richard Mead, 26 June 1727, Keynes Ms. 136.3 fol. 5^r; and Stukeley, "Life of Newton," RS Ms. 142 fol. 41^r—assuming, of course, that Mrs. Vincent remembered them exactly.

34. Venn, "Alumni," 4:166; B. Couth, *Crocadiles*, 219–20; RS Ms. 142 fols. 33^r, 37^r–38^r, 44^r–45^r. Stukeley claimed that Stokes was rector of Colsterworth when Newton returned to Woolsthorpe, but he transposed onto Stokes what was by now dimly remembered of William Walker; ibid., fol. 48^r. The original account given to Mead by Stukeley in June 1727 for Conduitt's intended "Life" justified Hannah Smith's recall of Newton from his school in financial terms; Keynes Ms. 136.3 fol. 6^r.

35. RS Ms. 142 fols. 48^r–49^r. In his original account of Stokes's intervention, given in a letter to Mead of 1 July 1727, Stukeley recorded that Stokes "often & strongly solicited his mother to return him to learning," seeing that rustic employment was "notorriously opposite to his temper." He noted in the original draft of 1727 that the tears occasioned by Stokes's encomium to Newton were Stokes's own; Keynes Ms. 136.3 fol. 7^r.

36. F. Watson, *Grammar Schools*, 61–66. The Septuagint (named after the seventy Jewish scholars who translated it) was the pre-Christian translation of the Hebrew Bible (Old Testament) into Greek.

37. A. Cambers, ed., *The Life of John Rastrick, 1650–1727* (Cambridge, 2010), 33–36; Hoole gave detailed instructions for managing a school like Grantham in his *New Discovery*.

38. Fitzwilliam Museum, Newton Notebook, fol. 3^{r-v}.

39. Fitzwilliam Notebook, fol. 3^{r-v}. The book Newton read was one of the many editions of Richard Johnson's two-part chivalric romance (originally published in two parts, 1596–97) *The Famous History of the Seven Champions of Christendom: Saint George of England, Saint Denis of France, Saint James of Spain, Saint Anthony of Italy, Saint Andrew of Scotland, Saint Patrick of Ireland, and Saint David of Wales Etc.* (London, 1660).

40. Fitzwilliam Notebook, fol. 3^{r-v}.

41. Fitzwilliam Museum Cambridge, "Fitzwilliam Notebook," fol. 3^{r-v}; F. Manuel, *A Portrait of Isaac Newton* (Cambridge, Mass., 1968), 61–63; R. S. Westfall, *Never at Rest*, 77–78; Spurr, "Restoration Church of England," 22–23.

CHAPTER 2

1. R. S. Westfall, *Never at Rest*, 66–104, esp. 70–74, for an excellent discussion of Newton's social status.

2. C. H. Cooper, *Annals of Cambridge*, 4 vols. (Cambridge, 1842–53), 2:217–23.

3. W. W. Rouse Ball, *Trinity College, Cambridge* (London, 1906), 52–57; M. Curtis, *Oxford and Cambridge in Transition, 1558–1642* (Oxford, 1959), 172–73; J. Heywood and T. Wright, eds., *Cambridge University Transactions During the Puritan Controversies of the Sixteenth and Seventeenth Centuries*, 2 vols. (London, 1854), 1:vii–xii, 39–40; 2:253, 273; C. H. Cooper, *Annals*, 3:129–31; J. O. Halliwell, ed., *The Autobiography and Correspondence of Sir Simonds d'Ewes, Bart. During the Reigns of James 1 and Charles I*, 2 vols. (London, 1845), 1:142.

4. J. Heywood and T. Wright, *Transactions*, 2:392–403; W. W. Rouse Ball, *Cambridge Papers* (London, 1918), 93–95; The horror expressed by Laudian sympathisers at the use of extempore prayers at Great St. Mary's is noted in W. T. Costello, *The Scholastic Curriculum at Seventeenth-Century Cambridge* (Cambridge, Mass., 1958), 125–26. Laud entered into a protracted dispute with the university regarding whether the institution fell within the orbit of his visitational powers; see J. Heywood and T. Wright, *Transactions*, 2:407–9.

5. J. Heywood and T. Wright, *Transactions*, 2:438; C. H. Cooper, *Annals*, 3:316, 320–30, 336, 338–44, 364–79 (esp. 378–79); J. B. Mullinger, *The University of Cambridge*, 3:219–21, 235, 243–44, 266–80, 308, 358–86; A. G. Matthews, *Walker Revised* (Oxford, 1948), 40–41; J. Gascoigne, "Barrow's Academic Milieu," in Feingold, *Before Newton*, 255–58; P. Hammond, "Dryden and Trinity," *Review of English Studies* 36 (1985): 35–57, esp. 42; Trinity College Muniments, "Conclusions and Admonitions, 1607–73," 184.

6. J. B. Mullinger, *The University of Cambridge*, 3:311–13, 333–34, 472–74; P. Hammond, "Dryden and Trinity," 42; Feingold, *Before Newton*, 5–7. For puritan attitudes to learning, see J. Morgan, *Godly Learning: Puritan Attitudes Towards Reason, Learning and Education, 1560–1640* (Cambridge, 1988).

7. J. B. Mullinger, *The University of Cambridge*, 3:369, 375, 385–86, 448–60; J. Heywood and T. Wright, *Transactions*, 2:531.

8. J. B. Mullinger, *The University of Cambridge*, 3:475–77; P. Hammond, "Dryden and Trinity," 48–49.

9. J. B. Mullinger, *The University of Cambridge*, 3:546–47; W. W. Rouse Ball, *Cambridge Papers* (London, 1918); C. H. Cooper, *Annals*, 3:474. Creighton followed in the footsteps of his father who having been Regius Professor Greek in the 1620s, and a member of the exiled court of Charles II, became bishop of Bath and Wells in 1670; Venn, "Alumni," 1:416.

10. J. B. Mullinger, *The University of Cambridge*, 3:549–56.

11. L. Howard, *A Collection of Letters, from the Original Manuscripts of Many Princes Great Personages and Statesmen* (London, 1753), 558–59; J. B. Mullinger, *The*

University of Cambridge, 3:579–82, 574–76; B. Quintrell, "Henry Ferne," New DNB. Ferne was in possession of a patent for the mastership of the college given him by Charles I whenever the position should prove void; see J. B. Mullinger, *The University of Cambridge*, 3:580–81.

12. C. H. Cooper, *Annals*, 3:491; E. Calamy, *An Account of the Ministers, Lecturers, Masters and Fellows of Colleges and Schoolmasters, Who Were Ejected or Silenced After the Restoration in 1660, by or Before the Act for Uniformity; Design'd for the Preserving to Posterity the Memory of Their Names, Characters, Writings and Sufferings*, 2 vols., 2nd ed. (London, 1713), 2:88–89; for Hutchinson, see E. Calamy, *A Continuation of the Account...* (London, 1727), 124–25.

13. Biographical details are from W. Derham, "Select Remains and the Life of John Ray," in *Memorials of John Ray*, ed. E. Lankester (London, 1846), 8–9; and C. Raven, *John Ray: Naturalist* (Cambridge, 1986), 51–52.

14. W. Derham, "Select Remains," 6–7; Ray to Courthope, 3 January 1658/59 and 26 September 1660; R. W. T. Gunther, *The Further Correspondence of John Ray* (London, 1928), 16–18; C. Raven, *Ray*, 57–58 (for the renewed requirement to take orders). For the rearrangement of sacred spaces in the Restoration, see K. Fincham, "'According to Ancient Custom': The Return of the Altars in the Restoration Church of England," *Transactions of the Royal Historical Society*, 6th series, 13 (2003), 29–30.

15. Ray to Courthope, 12 February 1661; R. Thompson, "Some Newly Discovered Letters of John Ray," *J. Society of Bibliography of Natural History* 7 (1974): 114; J. Heywood and T. Wright, *Transactions*, 2:543; A.G. Matthews, *Calamy Revised: Being a Revision of Edward Calamy's Account of the Ministers and Others ejected and silenced, 1660–2* (Oxford, 1934), 405; C. H. Cooper, *Annals*, 3:485 (for his appointment as lecturer); C. Raven, *Ray*, 59–61; Venn, "Alumni," 4:43; and Feingold, *Before Newton*, 32.

16. Ray to Courthope, 12 February 1660/61, 5 June 1661, 11 June 1661, and c. 20 July 1661; R. Thompson, "Letters," 111–23, esp. 114–16; and R. W. T. Gunther, *Further Correspondence*, 19.

17. J. B. Mullinger, *A History of the University of Cambridge from the earliest Times...* 3 vols. (Cambridge, 1873–1911), 3:249; E. Churton, "Memoir of Bishop Pearson," in *The Minor Theological Works of Bishop Pearson*, 2 vols., ed. E. Churton (Oxford, 1844), 1: xxi–xxii, xxxvii–xlvii, l–lvii, lxiv–lxvii.

18. W. Derham, "Select Remains," 15–16; S. Dale, "Life of John Ray," in R. W. T. Gunther, *Further Correspondence*, 29. The Act of Uniformity became law on St. Bartholomew's Day 1662 (24 August) and was known as Black Bartholomew's Day by non-conformists in reference to the fact that it was enacted on the anniversary of the notorious massacre in Paris of Protestants by Catholics in 1572.

19. Ray to Courthope, 24 July 1662, 13 August 1662, 4 September 1662; R. Thompson, "Letters," 119; and Dale, "Life of John Ray," in Gunther, *Further Correspondence*, 25–26, 29–32. Ray noted that Nathaniel Bacon had already been pulled out

of Cambridge, having "broken out into some extravagancies"; in 1675–76 he would lead (and perish in) the Virginia rebellion named after him.

20. Ray to Courthope, 13 August 1662; Gunther, *Further Correspondence*, 25; E. Calamy, *Account*, 2:83–88; J. Greaves, *John Bunyan and English Nonconformity* (London, 1992), 90–96; and G. Lyon Turner, "Williamson's Spy Book," *Transactions of the Congregational Historical Society* 5 (1912): 245–50.

21. Venn, "Alumni," 3:406; R. S. Westfall, *Never at Rest*, 73, 100–103; Keynes Ms. 116; Feingold, *Before Newton*, 65–71.

22. W. W. Rouse Ball, *Notes on the History of Trinity College Cambridge* (London, 1899), 51–52, 78–79; J. H. Monk, ed., *The Life of Richard Bentley, D.D.*, 2 vols., 2nd ed. (London, 1833), 2:242. The statutes are reproduced in *Fourth Report from the Select Committee on Education* (London, 1818); see also G. Peacock, *Observations on the Statutes of the University of Cambridge* (London, 1861), esp. 5–8.

23. See Feingold, *Before Newton*, 10–14; and R. O'Day, "James Duport," New DNB. One Ms. of Duport's text now at Trinity, "Rules to Be Observed by Young Pupils and Schollers in the University" (which lacks pp. 5–6), is internally dated to 1660; see Ms. O.10A.33, p. 15. There is another copy at Cambridge University Library, Add. Ms. 6986, which is slightly different in places from the Trinity Ms. and which does not lack any pages. For an edition with commentary, see A. Preston and P. H. Oswald, "James Duport's Rules for His Tutorial Pupils: A Comparison of Two Surviving Manuscripts," *Transactions of the Cambridge Bibliographical Society* 14 (2011): 317–63.

24. J. Duport, "Rules," ch. 1, "De Pietate, et cultu Dei, et religionis artibus"; Trinity College Ms. O.10A.33 (hereafter "Rules"), 1–2, 7, 13, 15; CUL Add. Ms. 6986 ch. 2 sects 16, 27, 28, 32–35.

25. J. Duport, "Rules," 2–3, 13. For note-taking, see H. F. Fletcher, *The Intellectual Development of John Milton*, 2 vols. (Urbana, Ill., 1956–61), 2:640, 652; and W. T. Costello, *Scholastic Curriculum*, 111–12. Duport named Baxter's *Saints Everlasting Rest: or, a Treatise of the Blessed State of the Saints in Their Enjoyment of God in Glory, Etc.* (orig. London 1650), which had already gone through eight editions by 1660. For Duport's other encomia to *The Temple*, and its later influence, see T. Prancic and J. Doelman," 'Ora pro me, sancte Herberte': James Duport and the Reputation of George Herbert," *George Herbert Journal* 24 (2000/2001): 35–55.

26. H. F. Fletcher, *Intellectual Development*, 2:652–54; J. Duport, "Rules," 3–4, 7–8.

27. J. Duport, "Rules," 7; T. Hill, "Letter to the *Seniors* of Trinitie-Colledg in Cambridge," prefacing "The best and the worst of Paul," in T. Hill, *Six Sermons* (Cambridge, 1649), sigs A2^{r-v}, A3^v–A4^v, a^{r-v}.

28. J. Hunter, *The Rise of the Old Dissent Exemplified in the Life of Oliver Heywood* (London, 1842), 44; J. Horsfall Turner, ed., *The Rev. Oliver Heywood B.A, 1630–1702: His Autobiography, Diaries, Anecdote and Event Books....* 4 vols. (Brighouse, 1881–85), 1:159–60, 162; P. Hammond, "Dryden and Trinity," 49; and Feingold, "Barrow and Newton," 23–24.

29. A. Cambers, "Life of Rastrick," 37–44; R. S. Westfall, *Never at Rest*, 78–79. For apt comments on the extent to which religious discipline was observed at Trinity in the early seventeenth century, see Rouse Ball, *Notes on the History of Trinity College, Cambridge*, 81.

30. A. Cambers, "Life of Rastrick," 45–51. Bainbrigg was a fellow in 1656, ordained deacon and priest in March 1664, and appointed vicar of Barrington in the same year. Much later, he would appear with Newton in front of Judge Jeffreys.

31. A. Cambers, "Life of Rastrick," 51–68. A coffeehouse first appeared at Cambridge in 1664, and plays were resurrected at the college at the same time; see R. S. Westfall, *Never at Rest*, 79–80. Rastrick became an Anglican minister in 1671, but left the Church of England in November 1687 over his refusal to wear the surplice and over what many of his parishioners took to be too much "preciseness" regarding rituals such as baptism.

32. See A. Napier, ed., *The Theological Works of Isaac Barrow*, 9 vols. (Cambridge, 1859), 1:lxxxii, 151–73, 338–66, 4:492–593; E. Churton, ed., *The Minor Theological Works of John Pearson*, D.D., 2 vols. (Oxford, 1844), 1:lvii, lxii–lxiii, 1–269 (for the lectures on God), 398, 399–405.

33. Pierpont Morgan Library Notebook fols. 46^v, 47^r, 48^{r-v}, and 51^v (for "supersedens"); F. Gregory, *Onomasticon Brachy sive Nomenclatura brevis Anglo-Latino-Græca. In Usum Scholæ Westmonasteriensis* (London, 1660), 18–19, 27–28; see further F. Manuel, *Portrait*, 27–28; and R. S. Westfall, *Never at Rest*, 61n54, who also dates them to the Grantham-Woolsthorpe period. Newton used the term "supersedens" in his Trinity notebook, indicating that on a number of occasions he paid to sit with pensioners at Hall.

34. Pierpont Morgan Library Notebook fols. 46^r–48^v passim; F. Gregory, *Nomenclatura*, 18–19.

35. Pierpont Morgan Library Notebook fols. 34^v–35^r (for the entries under the heading "Of a Church"), 46^r–48^v passim.

36. Fitzwilliam Museum, Newton Notebook, fols. 3^v–4^v; his dismissive remarks on a "formal way of life" were made in a draft letter to John Locke in 1691; see H. W. Turnbull et al., *Correspondence*, 3:184. For the draft curriculum, see A. R. Hall and M. B. Hall, *Unpublished Scientific Papers of Isaac Newton* (Cambridge, 1962), 373.

37. A. R. Hall and M. B. Hall, *Unpublished Scientific Papers*, 373. The course of study followed by fellow-commoners is discussed by Moti Feingold in "The Humanities," *The History of the University of Oxford*, vol. 4, *The Seventeenth Century*, ed. N. Tyacke (Oxford, 1997), 217–18, 230–34.

38. J. Duport, "Rules," 14–15 (the comment about drinking like a fish was about the only occasion in the text where Duport displayed his legendary wit). For the acceptability of bowls and chess as academic recreations see the proposed curriculum sent by Evelyn to Boyle in September 1659 in Hunter et al., *Correspondence*, 1:368. In 1580 scholars had been told that they could play football on the green area between the college and the river, but only with other college members; see Rouse Ball, *Notes on the History of Trinity College*, 71.

39. CUL Add. Ms. 6986 secs. 38, 40, 41; Fitzwilliam Notebook, fol. 6ᵛ, 7ʳ⁻ᵛ; H. F. Fletcher, *Intellectual Development*, 2:653–54, 655. Newton's fellowship elections took place on 1 October 1667 and 16 March 1667/68.

40. Trinity College Library Ms. R.4.48c, pp. i and x; CUL Add. Ms. 6986 sec. 47; Keynes Ms. 130.6 (Bk. 2); Fitzwilliam Notebook, fols. 6ᵛ and 7ᵛ.

41. Trinity College Library Ms. R.4.48c, pp. i, ix, xi; and Fitzwilliam Museum notebook, 3ʳ⁻ᵛ; J. Duport, "Rules," 8, 15; J. Heywood and T. Wright, *Transactions*, 1:56 and Rouse Ball, *Notes on the History of Trinity College*, 68. For contemporary religious attitudes to gluttony, see M. Todd, "Puritan Self-fashioning: The Diary of Samuel Ward," *Journal of British Studies* 31 (1992): 236–64, esp. 247–49. Todd points out that gluttony was at the head of Ward's list of sins; like Newton, and others since, he was a repeat offender. Sizing, the etymological root of "sizar," refers to portions of food.

42. Nicholas Wickins to Robert Smith, 16 January 1727/28, Keynes Ms. 137. Note also Trinity College Library Ms. R.4.48c, p. viii, for Newton's removal to another chamber, which possibly refers to his moving in with Wickins.

43. Fitzwilliam Museum, Newton notebook fols. 4ᵛ, 5ʳ; J. Duport, "Rules," 7; Venn, "Alumni," 4:399, 409; Keynes Ms. 137. R. Holdsworth warned that the scholar who neglected his studies would become a "Sott & Clown" and, ultimately, a sectary; H. F. Fletcher, *Intellectual Development*, 2:652.

44. W. T. Costello, *Scholastic Curriculum*, 110–112; H. F. Fletcher, *Intellectual Development*, 2:640. Duport mentioned Diodati, *Pious and Learned Annotations on the Bible: Plainly Expounding the Most Difficult Places Thereof* (the second and third editions of which had appeared in London in 1648 and 1651); see J. Duport, "Rules," 2.

45. *The Holy Bible Containing the Old Testament and the New* (London, 1660); J. Harrison, *Library*, H188. For the rebound Bible, see Fitzwilliam Museum notebook fol. 7ᵛ.

46. The books in question, all marked with Newton's name, college, and the date of 1661 were Isaac Feguernekinus, *Enchiridii locorum communium theologicorum, rerum, exemplorum, atq; phrasium sacrarum...Ed. 5ᵃ.* (Basel, 1604); L. Trelcatius, *Locorum communium S. Theologiæ Institutio per epitomem...12°* (London, 1608); and Calvin, *Institutio Christianæ Religionis, in libros quatuor nunc primum digesta* (Geneva, 1561); J. Harrison, *Library*, H609, H1640, and H335.

47. J. Duport, "Rules," 2–3; R. Holdsworth, *Intellectual Development*, 2:639–40 (in Holdsworth's scheme the year started in January).

48. C. Hoole, *He Kaine Diatheke. Novum Testamentum. Huic editioni omnia difficiliorum vocabulorum themata, quæ in G. Pasoris Lexico grammaticè resolvuntur, in margine apposuit C. Hoole* (Londini, 1653); and G. Pasor, *Lexicon Græco-Latinum in Novum Domini Nostri Jesu Christi Testamentum...* (3 pts.) (London, 1649–50); J. Harrison, *Library*, H199, H1264. See H. F. Fletcher, *Intellectual Development*, 2:276–77; F. Watson, *Grammar Schools*, 507–8.

49. Fitzwilliam Notebook, fol. 7ᵛ. The text by Schrevelius was presumably *Lexicon Manuale Græco-Latinum et Latino-Græcum, Editio secunda auctior multo & emendatior* (Lugduni Batavorum, 1657); see Trinity College Library, Ms. R.4.48c, f.v. For

the utility of Schrevelius in grammar schools (and by extension in universities), see F. Watson, *Grammar Schools* (who draws on Hoole's *New Discovery*), 517.

50. For possible scholastic sources of Newton's later work in natural philosophy, see S. Ducheyne, *The Main Business of Natural Philosophy: Isaac Newton's Natural Philosophical Methodology* (Dordrecht, 2012). Feingold, "Humanities," passim offers an extensive treatment of the curriculum at seventeenth-century Oxford, which applies in a large part to Cambridge.

51. For the existence of a vibrant culture of medical and philosophical study at Trinity in the 1650s and 1660s, correcting earlier declinist accounts, see J. Gascoigne, "The Universities and the Scientific Revolution: The Case of Restoration Cambridge," *History of Science* 23 (1985): 391–434; and Feingold, *Before Newton*, 33–37.

52. Feingold, *Before Newton*, 7–10; W. T. Costello, *Scholastic Curriculum*, 41–42; H. F. Fletcher, *Intellectual Development*, 2:165–66, 650; P. Hammond, "Dryden and Trinity," 42–45; W. S. Howell, *Logic and Rhetoric in England, 1550–1700* (Princeton, 1956). For Francis Willughby's educational experience at Trinity in the decade before Newton arrived, see R. Serjeantson, "The Education of Francis Willughby," in *Virtuoso by Nature: The Scientific Worlds of Francis Willughby FRS (1635–1672)*, ed. T. Birkhead (Leiden, 2016), 44–98.

53. H. F. Fletcher, *Intellectual Development*, 2:653; M. Curtis, *Oxford and Cambridge*, 173–77; Feingold, "Humanities," 219–22, 227–31, 264–65.

54. J. Duport, "Rules," 9–14, esp. 12 and 13; H. F. Fletcher, *Intellectual Development*, 2:275–88; Feingold, *Before Newton*, 16–17; and Feingold, "Humanities," 242–45, 256–69.

55. A. R. Hall and M. B. Hall, *Unpublished Scientific Papers*, 370; Keynes Ms. 130.10 fols. 1^v–2^r. For Barrow's early acquaintance with Greek poets and historians, see Feingold, *Before Newton*, 15–16. Newton's copy of Seneca's *Tragedies* was probably acquired in the early 1660s; see J. Harrison, *Library*, H1489.

56. A. R. Hall and M. B. Hall, *Unpublished Scientific Papers*, 370; H. F. Fletcher, *Intellectual Development*, 2:144–50, 161–66, 626, 634–37, 643; J. Duport, "Rules," 14. More generally, see Feingold, "Humanities," 276–306, esp. 276–81, 286, and 295–96; W. S. Howell, *Logic and Rhetoric*; and W. T. Costello, *Scholastic Curriculum*. When Newton arrived at Cambridge, Sanderson's *Logicae Artis Compendia* (originally published in 1615) was into its fifth edition. See W. T. Costello, *Scholastic Curriculum*, 45, 78, 95, 98, 101; and E. J. Ashworth, introduction to the 1618 edition of Sanderson's *Compendium* (Bologna, 1985).

57. R. North, *General Preface and Life of Dr. John North*, ed. P. Millard (Toronto, 1984), 101; King's College, Cambridge, Keynes Ms. 130.04 fol. 1^r; Trinity College Library Ms. R.4.48c, i, v. For the preparatory study that took place just before a student went to university, see W. T. Costello, *Scholastic Curriculum*, 43–45. Newton wrote the name "Burgersdicius" on the same line in his Trinity notebook as the title of Homer's *Odyssey*, and his copy of the latter (now in Trinity College Library) is inscribed with his name and the date of 1661; see Trinity College

Library Ms. R.4.48c p.x; and J. Harrison, *Library*, H793. Nevertheless, if the entries in the notebook are sequential, the works noted therein are unlikely to have been purchased in 1661. Newton's own copy of Sanderson, inscribed "Isaac Newton Trin. Coll. Cant. 1661," was the third edition of 1631; see J. Harrison, *Library*, H1442. The story of Newton's reading of Sanderson's *Logic* is variously recorded in the Conduitt papers; see Keynes Mss. 129.2 fol. 1ᵛ and 130.10 fol. 2ʳ.

58. CUL Add. Ms. 3996, fols. 3ʳ–10ᵛ. Newton's source text was G. du Val, ed., *Aristotelis Opera Omnia, quæ extant, Graece et Latine* (Paris, 1654). See also J. E. McGuire and M. Tamny, *Certain Philosophical Questions: Newton's Trinity Notebook* (Cambridge, 1983), 15; H. F. Fletcher, *Intellectual Development*, 2:643; Feingold, "Humanities," 298–304.

59. H. F. Fletcher, *Intellectual Development*, 2:157–66, 627, 636–37, 641; CUL Add. Ms. 3996, 34ʳ–36ʳ, 38ʳ–40ʳ. See also N. Fiering, *Moral Philosophy at Seventeenth-Century Harvard* (Chapel Hill, 1981); W.T. Costello, *Scholastic Curriculum*, 64–69 (esp. 66 on the importance of justice); and Feingold, "Humanities," 306–27.

60. CUL Add. Ms. 3996 fols. 16ʳ–26ʳ. See W.T. Costello, *Scholastic Curriculum*, 93–101; J. E. McGuire and M. Tamny, *Philosophical Questions*, 15–17; and R. S. Westfall, *Never at Rest*, 84. Newton's unloved copy of Fox Morcillo, *De naturæ philosophia, seu de Platonis, & Aristotelis consensione, libri V . . .* (Paris, 1560) was later presented to the college library (probably in the early 1680s) by its librarian John Laughton; see J. Harrison, *Library*, H629.

61. W.T. Costello, *Scholastic Curriculum*, 2:71–82, esp. 80–81 for evidence from St. John's College, Cambridge, Ms. K.38. Ontological arguments, which effectively derive their force from definitions or ideas of God, can be divided into two: (i) that an infinitely perfect being must contain existence as one of its perfections; (ii) that the only possible cause of mental conceptions of an infinitely perfect being (than whom no greater being can be conceived) must be that being.

62. H. F. Fletcher, *Intellectual Development*, 2:182–94; CUL Add. Ms. 3996 fols. 43ʳ–71ᵛ. Newton's source was Stahl, *Axiomata Philosophica, sub titulis XX* (Cambridge, 1645); see also J. E. McGuire and M. Tamny, *Philosophical Questions*, 17–18; R. Serjeantson, "The Education of Francis Willughby," 68–69; and S. Ducheyne, *Main Business*, 10–12.

63. J. Duport, "Rules," 13; H. F. Fletcher, *Intellectual Development*, 2:627, 637–38; Feingold, *Before Newton*, 18–19; A. R. Hall and M. B. Hall, *Unpublished Scientific Papers*, 370.

64. Trinity College, Ms. 4.48c, 1, v.

65. Feingold, "Humanities," 223–26, 246–50, 281, 300–306; H. F. Fletcher, *Intellectual Development*, 2:201–18, and (for disputation) 2:219–22; M. Curtis, *Oxford and Cambridge*, 109–11. See also B. Vickers, *In Defence of Rhetoric* (Oxford, 1988); and R. Serjeantson, "Proof and Persuasion," in *The Cambridge History of Early Modern Science*, ed. K. Park and L. Daston (Cambridge, 2006), 132–75, esp. 145–49.

66. J. Duport, "Rules," 8–11; W.T. Costello, *Scholastic Curriculum*, 14–31, 55–64 H. F. Fletcher, *Intellectual Development*, 2:243–61, 635–37. For Hoole's recommendation that Friday afternoons at school be devoted to disputation, see F. Watson, *Grammar Schools*, 95–96.

67. J. Duport, "Rules," 8–11; Fletcher, *Intellectual Development*, 2: 212–13, 240, 251–52. For declamations, see Costello, *Scholastic Curriculum*, 31–34.

68. H. F. Fletcher, *Intellectual Development*, 2:203–4, 219–21; J. Duport, "Rules," 10–11; Feingold, "Humanities," 223–26; G. Peacock, *Observations on the Statutes of the University of Cambridge* (London, 1861), 5.

69. H. F. Fletcher, *Intellectual Development*, 2:217–18, 258–59. More generally, see G. Kennedy, *Classical Rhetoric and Its Christian and Secular Tradition from Ancient to Modern Times* (Chapel Hill, 1980).

70. CUL Add. Ms. 3996 fols. 77^r–80^r; Newton took notes from Vossius's *Rhetorices Contractae, sive partitionum oratorium, Libri V* (Oxford, 1631). Possibly this was Ayscough's copy.

71. See in particular W. T. Costello, *Scholastic Curriculum*, 110–14.

CHAPTER 3

★ Keynes Ms. 2, Part 1, flyleaf.

1. Duport had advised his students to carry around with them their notebooks on philosophical questions wherever they went, so they could consult them whenever they felt like it; J. Duport, "Rules," 12.

2. See Keynes Ms. 130.10 fol. 2^v; W. Stukeley, "Memoirs of Sir Isaac Newton's Life," RS Ms. 142, fols. 50^r–51^r. Newton's own account (from 1699) of his encounter with the *Géometrie* is at CUL Add. Ms. 4000 fol. 14^v. Stukeley possibly conflated the different stories about the scholarship and bachelor's acts; see also R. S. Westfall, *Never at Rest*, 86, 98–103 (esp. 101), 140. Antonio Conti gave an independent account (presumably from Newton himself) of Newton's examination by Barrow, which tallies with what Conduitt later heard; see R. Iliffe, *Early Biographies of Isaac Newton*, vol. 1 of *Early Biographies of Isaac Newton, 1660–1885*, ed. R. Higgitt, R. Iliffe, and M. Keynes (London, 2006), 1:238–39.

3. For Descartes's natural philosophy, see, amongst others, D. Garber, *Descartes' Metaphysical Physics* (Chicago, 1992); D. Des Chene, *Physiologia: Natural Philosophy in Late Aristotelian and Cartesian Thought* (Ithaca, N.Y., 1996); and R. Ariew, *Descartes Among the Scholastics* (Leiden, 2011).

4. See R. Serjeantson, "Willughby," 75 and 77; and J. Gascoigne, "Isaac Barrow's Academic Milieu," in *Before Newton*, ed. M. Feingold, 264–67, 277–78. For More, see C. Webster, "Henry More and Descartes: Some New Sources," *British Journal for the History of Science* 4 (1969): 359–77; and A. Gabbey, "Philosophia Cartesiana Triumphata: Henry More (1646–71)," in *Problems of Cartesianism*, ed. T. Lennon et al. (Kingston, Ont., 1982), 171–250.

5. For the contexts of Barrow's oration and a translation of the text of the performance, see M. Feingold, "Isaac Barrow: Divine, Scholar, Mathematician," in

Before Newton, 1–104 (esp. 24–29); I. Stewart, " 'Fleshy Books': Isaac Barrow and the Oratorical Critique of Cartesian Natural Philosophy," in *History of the Universities* 16 (2000): 35–102 (esp. 69–70, 73, 75–76).

6. M. Feingold, "Barrow" (citing BL Add. Ms. 22,910 fols. 13ʳ–15ʳ); R. North, *The Lives of the Norths*, 3 vols., ed. A. Jessopp (London, 1890), 3:15; Worthington to More, 29 November 1667, in *The Diary and Correspondence of John Worthington*, 3 vols., ed. J. E. Crossley and R. C. Christie (Manchester, 1846–86), 2, pt. 2:254. For anti-Hobbism in Restoration Cambridge, see J. Parkin, "Hobbism in the Later 1660s," *Historical Journal* (1999): 85–108.

7. R. Iliffe, *Early Biographies*, 1:240–41; Newton also recounted the anti-Cartesian motivation underlying his early work to John Craig; see Craig to Conduitt, 7 April 1727; Keynes Ms. 132 fol. 3ʳ.

8. For the inspiration provided by *Géometrie*, see N. Guicciardini, *Newton on Mathematical Certainty*, 61–135.

9. CUL Add. Ms. 3996 fol. 83ʳ⁻ᵛ; see also J. E. McGuire and M. Tamny, *Philosophical Questions*, 127–39.

10. CUL Add. Ms. 3996 fols. 99ʳ (for refraction being caused by "subtile matter" in an evacuated pump), 106ʳ (but sound is not), and 117ʳ; see also J. E. McGuire and M. Tamny, *Philosophical Questions*, 26–27. There is no evidence that Newton had an air-pump of his own, but it is probable that he performed experiments at this time with an air-pump at Christ's College; see Newton to Oldenburg, 7 December 1675, in H. W. Turnbull et al., *Correspondence*, 1:361. For Boyle's experimental program, see S. Shapin and S. Schaffer, *Leviathan and the Air-Pump: Hobbes, Boyle, and the Experimental Life* (Princeton, 1985).

11. H. More, Enchiridion Metaphysicum (1671), 69–70. More generally, see A. Funkenstein, *Theology and the Scientific Imagination from the Middle Ages to the Seventeenth Century* (Princeton, 1986), 24–49, 73–96; E. Grant, *Much Ado About Nothing: Theories of Space and Vacuum from the Middle Ages to the Scientific Revolution* (Cambridge, 1981), 103–81, 221–30; and A. Koyré, *Newtonian Studies* (Chicago, 1965), 192–94.

12. I. Barrow, *The Usefulness of Mathematical Learning Explained and Demonstrated: Being Mathematical Lectures Read in the Publick Schools at the University of Cambridge* (London, 1734), 163–69. See Descartes, *Principles of Philosophy*, in J. Cottingham, R. Stoothoff, and D. Murdoch, eds., *The Philosophical Writings of Descartes*, 3 vols. (Cambridge, 1985), 1: 232.

13. I. Barrow, *Usefulness*, 176–83 (inc. 179–80 for the vacuum); T. Hobbes, *Leviathan: Or the Matter, Forme and Power of a Commonwealth, Ecclesiastical and Civil*, ed. N. Malcolm, 3 vols. (Oxford, 2012). Barrow's critique of the Cartesian notion of extension developed the earlier treatment in his 1652 oration.

14. CUL Add. Ms. 3996 fol. 88ʳ⁻ᵛ and 90ᵛ ("Of yᵉ first mater"). Barrow had invoked the example of rarefaction and condensation as evidence for a vacuum in his 1652 oration; see I. Stewart, "Fleshly Books," 80–81. When it suited Newton to remember the fact during his dispute with Gottfried Leibniz, he recalled attending the lectures Barrow gave in 1664–65; see CUL Add. Ms. 3968.41 fols 84ʳ and 86ᵛ.

15. CUL Add. Ms. 3996 fols. 89ʳ, 119ʳ–120ʳ ("Of Attomes"); J. E. McGuire and M. Tamny, *Philosophical Questions*, 40–42, 50–60, and esp. 115–21 for the influence of Newton's reading of Epicurus.

16. CUL Add. Ms. 3996 fol. 98ʳ⁻ᵛ, 113ʳ–14ʳ. See also R. Ariew, *Descartes*, 248–50.

17. J. Cottingham, R. Stoothoff, and D. Murdoch, *Philosophical Writings of Descartes*, 1:201–2. For Descartes's view of the relationship between infinity and indefiniteness, see R. Ariew, *Descartes*, 241–65, esp. 264; R. Ariew, "The Infinite in Descartes's Conversation with Burman," *Archiv für Geschichte der Philosophie* 69 (1987): 140–63, esp. 148–50; D. Garber, *Descartes' Metaphysical Physics*, 125–26, 328–29, 339–41.

18. CUL Add. Ms. 3996 fol. 90ʳ. See also J. E. McGuire and M. Tamny, *Philosophical Questions*, 114–16.

19. CUL Add. Ms. 3996 fol. 131ʳ.

20. "Of God"—Smithsonian Institute, Dibner Ms. 1031B fol. 4ᵛ (compare with comments on "infinitely swift" motion at CUL Add. Ms. 3996 fol. 89ᵛ).

21. "De Gravitatione" is bound as a small notebook and is designated CUL Add. Ms. 4003. For transcription and translation see A. R. and M. B. Hall, *Unpublished Scientific Papers*, 90–156, esp. 121–24, 141. See A. Koyré, *Newtonian Studies*, 53–114; and J. E. McGuire, "Space, Infinity and Indivisibility: Newton on the Creation of Matter," in *Contemporary Newtonian Research*, ed. Z. Bechler (Cambridge, 1982), 145–90.

22. A. R. Hall and M. B. Hall, *Unpublished Scientific Papers*, 121–24, esp. 122; R. Descartes, *Principia*, Part 2, sects 15, 27, 28. For comments on Descartes's account of motion, see D. Garber, *Descartes's Metaphysical Physics*, 172ff.; and D. Des Chene, *Physiologia*, 255–341. Descartes had suppressed his Copernican book, *Le Monde*, in the wake of Galileo's arrest and condemnation.

23. A. R. Hall and M. B. Hall, *Unpublished Scientific Papers*, 124, 125, 127–28, 129–30.

24. Ibid., 131–38, esp. 132–34; and J. E. McGuire, "Space, Infinity and Indivisibility," 156–68.

25. A. R. Hall and M. B. Hall, *Unpublished Scientific Papers*, 134.

26. Ibid., 134–35.

27. Ibid., 134–36; compare with CUL Add. Ms. 3996 fols. 90ʳ and 131ʳ.

28. Ibid., 136–38.

29. J. E. McGuire, "Newton on Space, Time and God: An Unpublished Source," *British Journal for the History of Science* 11 (1978): 115–28, esp. 117–23.

30. A. R. Hall and M. B. Hall, *Unpublished Scientific Papers*, 138–39; J. Locke, *An Essay Concerning Human Understanding*, ed. P. Nidditch (Oxford, 1975), 628–29; and J. Locke, *Essai philosophique concernant l'etendement humain*, trans. P. Coste, 3rd ed. (Amsterdam, 1735), 521.

31. A. R. Hall and M. B. Hall, *Unpublished Scientific Papers*, 139–40.

32. Ibid., 140–41.

33. Ibid., 141–42. The canonical sources for the claim that humans were created in the image of God are Genesis 1:27; 5:1; and 9:6. A number of places in the

New Testament refer to it, including 1 Corinthians 11:7; Ephesians 4:24; and Colossians 3:10.

34. A. R. Hall and M. B. Hall, *Unpublished Scientific Papers*, 142–44, 146.

35. CUL Add. Ms. 3996 fol. 101^v.

36. H. More, *The Immortality of the Soul, so farre forth as it is demonstrable from the Knowledge of Nature and the Light of Reason* (London, 1659), 134, 151–52, 231–33, 234, 255–56. For the contexts of More's work on the soul, see John Henry, "A Cambridge Platonist's Materialism: Henry More and the Concept of Soul," *Journal of the Warburg and Courtauld Institutes* 49 (1986): 172–95.

37. H. More, ibid., 217–18, 219, 220, 223–24.

38. CUL Add. Ms. 3996 fols. 104^r, 109^v, 117^r; J. Glanvill, *The Vanity of Dogmatizing: Or Confidence in Opinions Manifested in a Discourse of the Shortnes and Uncertainty of Our Knowledge and Its Causes; with Some Reflexions on Peripateticism; and An Apology for Philosophy* (London, 1661), 26, 31–32, 54–55; H. More, *Immortality*, 199–208.

39. CUL Add. Ms. 3996 fol. 129^r. See J. E. McGuire and M. Tamny, *Philosophical Questions*, 315–17, 448, where the shorthand entry is transliterated. Genesis 1:21 reads: "And God created great whales, and every living creature that moveth, which the waters brought forth abundantly, after their kind, and every winged fowl after his kind: and God saw that *it was* good."

40. CUL Add. Ms. 3996 fol. 129^r. Genesis 2:7 (KJV) reads: "And the Lord God formed man of the dust of the ground, and breathed into his nostrils the breath of life; and man became a living soul." I am very grateful to Stephen Snobelen for pointing out that the source of the passage on Adam is from Ecclesiasticus, which in full reads: "And all men are from the ground, and Adam was created of earth." In Job 33:6 Elihu pleaded that he was formed from clay, recalling Job's comment (Job 10:9) that God had fashioned him from clay and might return him to dust.

41. CUL Add. Ms. 3996 fol. 104^r; H. More, *Immortality*, 154–60, 190, 191, 195–96, 197; see also J. Glanvill, *Vanity*, 18–25.

42. CUL Add. Ms. 3996 fols. 108^r, 130^v, 132^r; Fitzwilliam Notebook, fol. 3^{r-v}; H. More, *Immortality*, 255–56.

43. CUL Add. Ms. 3996 fol. 130^{r-v}, 132^r.

44. The fertility of the imagination is discussed in M. H. Huet, *Monstrous Imagination* (Cambridge, Mass., 1993), ch. 1; and for the Reformation assault on idolatry and idols, see C. M. N. Eire, *War Against the Idols: The Reformation of Worship from Erasmus to Calvin* (Cambridge, 1989). For Bacon's influential treatment of the deceits of the imagination, see K. Park, "Bacon's Enchanted Glass," *Isis* 75 (1984): 290–302; S. Corneanu, *Regimens of the Mind: Boyle, Locke, and the Early Modern Cultura Animi Tradition* (Chicago, 2011), 14–35, 90–92; and S. Corneanu and K. Vermeir, "Idols of the Imagination: Francis Bacon on the Imagination and the Medicine of the Mind," *Perspectives on Science* 20 (2012): 183–206. For Descartes and Hobbes on the imagination, see D. L. Sepper,

Descartes's Imagination: Proportion, Images, and the Activity of Thinking (Berkeley, 1996) and Q. Skinner, *Reason and Rhetoric in the Philosophy of Hobbes* (Cambridge, 1996), 363–75.

45. CUL Add. Ms. 3996 fol. 109ʳ; H. More, *Immortality*, 228–29, 231–32; J. Glanvill, *Vanity*, 95–106.

46. J. Glanvill, *Vanity*, 195–201.

47. CUL Add. Ms. 3996 fols. 109ʳ, 125ʳ. R. Boyle, *Experiments and Considerations Touching Colours* (London, 1664), 15–17. See also the pioneering treatment of these passages in M. Tamny, "Newton, Creation, and Perception," *Isis* 70 (1979): 48–59, esp. 52.

48. Newton to Locke, 30 June 1691, in H. W. Turnbull et al., *Correspondence*, 3:153–54; R. Boyle, *Experiments*, 19–20. Newton, who told Locke that he had used a looking glass to look at the sun, possibly consulted the "Philosophical Questions" notebook before writing to him. Sixty years after the initial events, the same experiment was recounted to John Conduitt; see King's College, Cambridge, Keynes Ms. 130.15.

49. CUL Add. Ms. 3996 fol. 125ʳ⁻ᵛ. For the relationship between sensitivity and madness, see G. Speak, "'An Odd Kind of Melancholy': Reflections on the Glass Delusion in Europe (1440–1680)," *History of Psychiatry* 1 (1990): 191–206.

50. CUL Add. Mss. 3975 fols. 17ʳ–20ʳ and 3970 fol. 233ʳ, and for the final version in the 1717/18 edition, see *Opticks*, 346–47, 353–54. For later accounts of the issue of binocular vision, see Newton to William Briggs, 12 September 1682 and 25 April 1685, in H. W. Turnbull et al., *Correspondence*, 2:383–85, 415–17.

51. Collins to Gregory, 19 October 1675, in H. W. Turnbull et al., *Correspondence*, 2:355–56; and cf. Collins to Gregory, 29 June 1675 in ibid., 2:345.

52. Smithsonian Institute, Dibner Mss. 1031B, fols. 1ʳ, 3ᵛ, and 5ᵛ.

53. H. W. Turnbull et al., *Correspondence*, 1:362–86, esp. 364–67.

54. See T. Willis, *Cerebri Anatome* (1664); *Pathologiæ cerebri et nervosus generus specimen* (London, 1667); T. Willis, *Affectionum quae dicuntur hystericæ et hypochondriacæ pathologia spasmodica vindicata contra responsionem epistolarem Nathanael Highmori. M.D. Cui accesserunt exercitationes medico-physicæ duæ. 1. De sanguinis accessione. 2. De motu musculari* (London, 1670), 40–44. See more generally R. Frank, *Harvey and the Oxford Physiologists: Scientific Ideas and Social Interaction* (London, 1980), 222–23, 230–34.

55. H. W. Turnbull et al., *Correspondence*, 1:367–68. The references to self-motion are absent from a short draft of the "Hypothesis" at CUL Add. Ms. 3970 fols. 475ʳ–476ᵛ, but occur in a second draft of the text at fol. 535ʳ⁻ᵛ. In the original autographed letter sent to Oldenburg (CUL Add. Ms. 3970 fols. 538ʳ–547ʳ) the section on self-motion (fols. 540ʳ–541ʳ) is clearly considered to be a separate project and is marked for insertion in a different text. The passage is also missing from John Wickins's later copy of the letter (fols. 573ʳ–581ʳ). Boyle's experiments, actually carried out between August 1662 and May 1663, were initially published in "New Pneumatical Experiments Concerning Respiration," *Philosophical Transactions* 5 (1670), 2011–31, 2035–56 (esp. 2041–43).

56. H. W. Turnbull et al., *Correspondence*, 1:393.

57. Ibid., 1:368.

58. Ibid., 1:368–70.

59. CUL Add. Ms. 3970 fols. 241^{r-v}, 244^r, 252^r, 255^r–56^r, 620^r, 619^r; *Optice*, 343, 346.

60. J. E. McGuire, "Newton on Space, Time and God," 123; *Opticks*, 344–45, 379; see also R. Iliffe, "Isaac Newton and the Political Physiology of Self," *Medical History* 39 (1995): 433–58. For Newton's attack on Leibniz via Clarke, see *The Leibniz-Clarke Correspondence*, ed. H. G. Alexander (Manchester, 1965), 13, 21, 34, 51, 98; Newton to Conti, 26 February 1716, in H. W. Turnbull et al., *Correspondence*, 6:285; CUL Add. Ms. 3968 fols. 41^v, 587^r.

61. Original and revised impression of *Optice. Sive De Reflexionibus, Refractionibus, Inflexionibus & Coloribus Lucis. Libri Tres* (London, 1706), 315, 346–47 (with drafts of related passages at CUL Add. Ms. 3970 fols. 241^v, 242^v, 243^r, 247^r); and *Opticks*, 344–45, 379. See also W. Hiscock, *David Gregory, Isaac Newton, and Their Circle: Extracts from David Gregory's Memoranda, 1677–1708* (Oxford, 1937), 30; and for the original impression of *Optice*, see A. Koyré and I. B. Cohen, "The Case of the Missing Tanquam," *Isis* 52 (1961): 555–66.

62. *Opticks*, 345, 379; A. Koyré and I. B. Cohen, eds. (with the assistance of A. Whitman), *Isaac Newton's Philosophiæ Naturalis Principia Mathematica, the Third Edition (1726) with Variant Readings*, 2 vols. (Cambridge, Mass., 1972), 2:762. The marginal comment on p. 482 in the copy of the second edition of *Principia Mathematica*, now at the University of Toronto Library, is cited in L. Stewart, "Seeing Through the Scholium: Religion and Reading Newton in the Eighteenth Century," *History of Science* 34 (1996): 123–65, esp. 135.

CHAPTER 4

1. Newton's restrictive attitude towards the publication of serious alchemical work can be found in his letters to Oldenburg in 26 April 1676 and to Locke in July and August 1692; see H. W. Turnbull et al., *Correspondence*, 2:1–2; 3:215–19.

2. Collins to Gregory, 24 December 1670, in ibid., *Correspondence*, 1:53–55; D. T. Whiteside, ed., *The Mathematical Papers of Isaac Newton*, 8 vols. (Cambridge, 1967–81), 2:206–47, 364–447; I. B. Cohen, *Introduction to Newton's "Principia"* (Cambridge, 1971); A. E. Shapiro, ed., *The Optical Papers of Isaac Newton*, vol. 1: *The Optical Lectures 1670–1672* (Cambridge, 1984); I. B. Cohen, *The Newtonian Revolution, with Illustrations of the Transformation of Scientific Ideas* (Cambridge, 1980).

3. Newton to Collins, 18 February 1670 and 11 July 1670; Collins to Newton, 13 July 1670 and Newton to Collins, 27 September 1670, in H. W. Turnbull et al., *Correspondence*, 1:27, 30–31, 33, 43. On the preference for manuscript circulation as a way of disseminating works, see H. Woudhuysen, *Sir Philip Sidney and the Circulation of Manuscripts, 1548–1640* (Oxford, 1996) and H. Love, *The Culture and Commerce of Texts: Scribal Publication in Seventeenth-Century*

England (Amherst, 1998). For Newton's secretive attitude to the publication of his mathematical works, see N. Guicciardini, *Newton on Mathematical Certainty*, ch. 16.

4. Newton to Collins, 20 July 1671, in H. W. Turnbull et al., *Correspondence*, 1:68. See A. E. Shapiro, *Optical Papers*, 1:46–279 ("Lectiones Opticae") and 280–603 ("Optica"). The "Lectiones Opticae" and "Optica" are now CUL Add. Ms. 4002 and Ms. Dd. 9.67 (deposited in the University Library as his 1674 professorial lectures), respectively. For "De Methodis," see Whiteside, *Mathematical Papers*, 3:28–31, 32–353; and N. Guicciardini, *Newton on Mathematical Certainty*, 179–202.

5. A. E. Shapiro, *Optical Lectures*, 1:87–89, 439; Newton to Oldenburg, 6 January 1672 and 18 January 1672, in H. W. Turnbull et al., *Correspondence*, 1:79–80, 82–83.

6. Newton to Oldenburg, 6 February 1672, in H. W. Turnbull et al., *Correspondence*, 1:92, 95. A. E. Shapiro, "The Evolving Theory of Newton's Theory of White Light and Colour," *Isis* 71 (1980): 211–35; S. Schaffer, "'Glass Works': Newton's Prisms and the Uses of Experiment," in *The Uses of Experiment: Studies in the Natural Sciences*, ed. D. Gooding, T. Pinch, and S. Schaffer (Cambridge, 1989), 67–104; and A. E. Shapiro, "The Gradual Acceptance of Newton's Theory of Light and Color, 1672–1727," *Perspectives in Science* 4 (1996): 59–139.

7. Newton to Oldenburg, 6 February 1672, in H. W. Turnbull et al., *Correspondence*, 1:96, 100–102.

8. Oldenburg to Newton, 8 February 1672, Newton to Oldenburg, 10 February 1672, Oldenburg to Newton, 9 April 1672, ibid., 1:107–9, 130–33, 135, 144. See also N. Guicciardini, *Newton on Mathematical Certainty*, 193.

9. Huygens to Oldenburg, 3 February 1672, Oldenburg to Newton (with Hooke's comment enclosed in a letter of 15 February), c. 15 February 1672, Pardies to Oldenburg, 30 March 1672, Newton to Oldenburg, 30 March 1672, 13 April (two letters) 1672, 4 May 1672, 10 and 11 June 1672, Newton to Collins, 25 May 1672, in H. W. Turnbull et al., *Correspondence*, 1:89–91, 110–14, 126–33, 136–44, 147, 153–55, 161, 163–68, 171–88.

10. Huygens to Oldenburg, 14 January 1673 (N.S.), Oldenburg to Newton, 18 January 1672/73, Newton to Oldenburg, 8 March 1672/73, in ibid., 1:255–56, 262–63.

11. Newton to Collins, 17 September 1673, 20 June 1674, and 17 November 1674, Newton to Dary, 6 October 1674, Linus to Oldenburg, 26 September 1674, Newton to Oldenburg, 5 December 1674, in H. W. Turnbull et al., *Correspondence* 1:307, 309–11, 317–20, 327–29.

12. Newton to Oldenburg, 5 December 1675 and c. 22 January 1676, Newton to Dary, 22 January 1675, in ibid., 1:328, 332–33 and 7 387. The "Exit" and "Redit" book in Trinity College records that Newton was absent from the college from

9 February to 19 March 1675; see J. Edleston, ed., *Correspondence of Sir Isaac Newton and Professor Cotes* (London, 1850), lxxxv.

13. Newton to [Frazier?], n.d., in H.W.Turnbull et al., *Correspondence*, 3:146, original at King's College, Keynes Ms. 108B. See also R. S.Westfall, *Never at Rest*, 331–33; and J. Edleston, *Correspondence*, xlviii–xlix. The relationship between Aston and Newton's quests for dispensation is opaque, though Newton's expression of gratitude to Frazier for including him in the proposal suggests that his name was added to Aston's in a joint petition.

14. Barrow to Williamson, 3 December 1674; CSPD (1674–75), 443–44.

15. For Newton's letter of dispensation, see J. Edleston, *Correspondence*, xlix–l; and for the Lucasian statutes, see I. Stewart, "The Statutes of the Lucasian Professorship: A Translation," in *From Newton to Hawking: A History of Cambridge University's Lucasian Professors of Mathematics*, ed. K. Knox and R. Noakes (Cambridge, 2003), 461–74. See also M. Feingold, "Science as a Calling? The Early Modern Dilemma," *Science in Context* 15 (2002): 79–119, esp. 93–99, 104. John Locke was granted dispensation from taking holy orders in 1666 explicitly to have more time to prosecute his studies "without that obligation"; see H. R. Fox Bourne, *The Life of John Locke*, 2 vols. (London, 1876), 1:131–32.

16. The Tenison anecdote (from 1700) occurs in variant forms at Keynes Mss. 130.6 Bk. 2 and 130.7 fol. 1^r.

17. Collins to Gregory, 1 May 1675, 29 June 1675, and 19 October 1675, Newton to J. Smith, 8 May 1675, in H.W.Turnbull et al., *Correspondence*, 1:341, 342–45, and 356.

18. Newton owned the 1672 edition of Mede's *Works*; see J. Harrison, *Library*, H1053.

19. Newton's experience is discussed in S. Mandelbrote, "Becoming Heterodox in Seventeenth-Century Cambridge: The Case of Isaac Newton" (forthcoming). I am grateful to the author for providing me with a prepublication version of his paper.

20. I infer that much of his citation was done from memory from the fact that Newton occasionally left blank the exact reference to which he was alluding; he often copied down such lists from earlier drafts when he was rewriting a piece of text.

21. National Library of Israel,Yahuda Ms. 11 fols. 6^r–7^r.

22. F. Manuel, *Portrait* (Cambridge, Mass., 1968), 28–29; for Jewish sources in Newton's work, see M. Goldish, *Judaism in the Theology of Isaac Newton* (Dordrecht, 1998), 30–31, 85–97.

23. For Clerke, see H.W.Turnbull et al., *Correspondence*, 2:485–500. For Socinianism in seventeenth-century England, see H. J. McLachlan, *Socinianism in Seventeenth-Century England* (Cambridge, 1951); S. Mortimer, *Reason and Religion in the English Revolution: The Challenge of Socinianism* (Cambridge, 2010); and P. Lim, *Mystery Unveiled: The Crisis of the Trinity in Early Modern England* (Oxford, 2012).

For Arianism, see M. Wiles, *Archetypal Heresy: Arianism through the Centuries* (Oxford, 2001).

24. See M. Wiles, *Archetypal Heresy*, esp. 10–26; and R. Williams, *Arius: Heresy and Tradition* (London, 1981), 1–26.

25. D. Petau, *Dogmata Theologica*, 5 vols. (Paris, 1644–50). See in particular Keynes Ms. 2, Part 2, and especially Keynes Ms. 4, which is a lengthy series of notes from Petau. Newton owned the expanded edition, the work that was edited by Jean le Clerc; D. Petau, *Opus de theologicis dogmatibus, auctius in hac nova editione… notulis T. Alethini [i.e., J. Le Clerc]*, 6 vols. (Antwerp, 1700); J. Harrison, *Library*, H1285.

26. C. Sand, *Nucleus Historiæ Ecclesiasticæ, exhibitus in Historia Arianorum*, 2 vols. (Amsterdam, 1669; 2nd ed., Amsterdam, 1676); G. Bull, *Defensio Fidei Nicænæ…* (Oxford, 1685). Newton owned the 1669 version of the *Nucleus* as well as Bull's *Defensio*; J. Harrison, *Library*, H1444, H307. See further S. Mandelbrote, "'Than This Nothing Can Be Plainer': Newton Reads the Fathers," in *Die Patristik in der Frühen Neuzeit*, ed. G. Frank, T. Leinkauf, and M. Wriedt (Stuttgart, 2006), 277–97; J.-L. Quantin, *The Church of England and Christian Antiquity: The Construction of a Confessional Identity in the Seventeenth Century* (Oxford, 2009), 345–49, 374–92; and D. W. Dockrill, "The Authority of the Fathers in the Great Trinitarian Debates of the Sixteen Nineties," *Studia Patristica* 18 (1990): 335–47.

27. R. Cudworth, *The True Intellectual System of the Universe* (London, 1678), 546–632, esp. 547–48. See M. Wiles, *Archetypal Heresy*, 62–69.

28. "Hypostasis" had various meanings in the early church but its core meaning is derived from the Greek roots "under" and "standing" or "status." To refer to a hypostatical unity of the Godhead implied something that was common or substructural to all three elements of the Trinity. For many, this appeared to differentiate inadequately between the parts of the Godhead and, to counter this difficulty, some proffered a notion of three *hypostases* though this view was held to commit the opposite offence and was susceptible to the accusation of tritheism.

29. R. Cudworth, *The True Intellectual System*, 555–60, 579–83, 589–90, 605, 608; T. Gale, *Court of the Gentiles, pt III, The Vanity of Pagan Philosophy Demonstrated* (London, 1677). See also S. Hutton, "The Neoplatonic Roots of Arianism: Ralph Cudworth and Theophilus Gale," in *Socinianism and Its Role in the Culture of the XVIth to XVIIIth Centuries*, ed. L. Szczucki (Warsaw, 1983), 139–45; and D. D. Wallace, *Shapers of English Calvinism, 1660–1714: Variety, Persistence and Transformation* (Oxford, 2011), ch. 3.

30. The literature on early modern views on idolatry is huge, but among the most pertinent are J. H. Leith, "John Calvin's Polemic Against Idolatry," in *Soli Deo Gloria: New Testament Studies in Honour of William Childe Robinson*, ed. J. M. Richards (Richmond, Va., 1968), 114; C. M. N. Eire, *War Against the Idols* (Cambridge, 1986), esp. 195–99, 201–10; M. Aston, *England's Iconoclasts: Laws Against Images*

(Oxford, 1988); L. P. Wandel, *Voracious Idols and Violent Hands: Iconoclasm in Reformation Zurich, Strasbourg, and Basel* (Cambridge, 1995); G. Stroumsa, "John Spencer and the Roots of Idolatry," *History of Religions* 41 (2001), 1–23; and J. Sheehan, "Sacred and Profane: Idolatry, Antiquarianism and the Polemics of Distinction in the Seventeenth Century," *Past and Present* (2006): 35–65, esp. 48–56.

31. Yahuda Ms. 14 fol. 9^{r-v}; J. Sheehan, "Sacred and Profane," 40–44. For Newton's critique of the distinction between dulia and latria (found in Augustine's *City of God*, Bk. 10, ch. 1), see Yahuda Mss. 2.3 fol. 4^r, 9^r and 2.5b fol. 18^r.

32. Yahuda Ms. 21 fols. 2^r–3^r, 13^v–14^v. There are three texts that comprise the analysis of 2 Kings 17:15–16, viz., Harry Ransom Research Institute, University of Texas, Ms. 130; Yahuda Ms. 21; and Huntington Library, Babson Ms. 437. The Babson document is a short draft of Yahuda 21, with three "queries" instead of the six particulars or propositions in the later text, while the short HRI text appears to be a second part of the earlier exposition in Yahuda 21 (but also refers to a further, presumably lost text).

33. Keynes Ms. 2, Part 1, fol. 11^r and Part 2 (from reverse end) 8^r. For a good analysis of Newton's later account of the Son, see M. Wiles, *Archetypal Heresy*, 81–85.

34. Yahuda Ms. 14 fol. 25^r.

35. Newton's books provide substantial evidence that he was immersed in the history of the early church in the early 1680s. His copy of Hilary, *Quotquot extant opera, nostro fere seculo literatorum quorundam non mediocri labore conquisita...* (Paris, 1652) is marked "1680 pret. 14^s. 6^d" in Newton's hand on flyleaf and has signs of dog-earing; his copy of E. Richer, *Historia Conciliorum Generalium, in quatuor libros distributa* (Cologne, 1680) is inscribed "1682 pret. 6s 6d, valet 10s" in Newton's hand on the flyleaf; and his edition of J. C. Suicerus, *Thesaurus ecclesiasticus, e Patribus Græcis ordine alphabetico...* (2 vols. [Amsterdam, 1682]) has "Isaac Newton. pret £1.s 12 Oct 3. 1682" on the flyleaf; see J. Harrison, *Library*, H764 and 1579; and also S. Mandelbrote, "Newton Reads the Fathers," 278–81.

36. See, e.g., Keynes Ms. 2, Part 2, fol. 13^r. De la Bigne's *Magna Bibliotheca Veterum Patrum et Antiquorum Scriptorum Ecclesiasticorum* appeared in a number of editions though Newton probably used the seventeen-volume edition published in Paris in 1644. An expanded version in twenty-seven volumes, titled the *Maxima Bibliotheca Veterum Patrum...*, appeared at Lyons in 1677 and was edited by Philippe Despont.

37. Yahuda Ms. 14 fols. 191^v–192^v (for Arnobius and cf. comments on 171^r); 193^r (for Tertullian), 193^v (for Eusebius), and 199^{r-v} (from the Shepherd of Hermas). See S. Mandelbrote, "Newton Reads the Fathers," 288–89n48.

38. Yahuda Ms. 14 fols 13^{r-v}, 15^v–16^v, and 116^r. For the significance of Justin for Arians, see M. Wiles, *Archetypal Heresy*, 18–20.

39. Yahuda Ms. 14 fols. 83^r–84^v.

40. See J. N. D. Kelly, *Early Christian Creeds*, 3rd ed. (Harlow, 1985), 205–332; and for the demise of Arianism in the second half of the fourth century, see M. Wiles, *Archetypal Heresy*, 27–46.

41. Newton composed a lengthy and detailed account of the Arian controversy in Yahuda Mss. 11 and 19; a shorter version is at Yahuda Ms. 2.5b fols. 38^v–47^r. See also Newton, *Historia Ecclesiastica (de Origine Schismatico Ecclesiae Papisticae Bicornis)*, ed. P. Toribio Pérez (Madrid, 2013).

42. Yahuda Mss. 11 fols. 1^r–2^r, 12 fols. 3^v, 12^r–13^r, 16^r, 18^r–20^r (for Constantine's statement of his desire for a settlement between Alexander and Arius), and 21^r–24^r, esp. 23^v. There is a longer version of the background to the Alexandrian controversy at Yahuda Ms. 19 fols. 13^r–43^r.

43. There are various accounts of the Nicene deliberations at Yahuda Mss. 19 fols. 24^r–51^r; 12 fols. 24^v, 25^r–27^r, 27^v (for Constantine's affability) and 2.5b fols. 40^r–41^r. Newton justified using the term "Athanasians" for the supporters of Alexander at Yahuda Ms. 2.3 fol. 29^v.

44. Yahuda Mss. 19 fols. 29^r–30^r (for Athanasius's control over Alexander), 30^v–43^r (esp. 34^r–43^r for a detailed account of various positions at Nicaea on the nature of the *logos*) and 43^v–47^r (for the claims of a Eusebian conspiracy), 2.5b fols. 41^v–42^r and 12 fol. 29^r (based on the testimony of Eusebius of Caesarea). Philostorgius's views were available in Jacques Godefroy [Jacob Gothofredus], ed., *Philostorgii Cappadocis, veteris sub Theodosio Iuniore scriptoris, Ecclesiasticæ historiæ, …* (Geneva, 1642); see Yahuda Ms. 14 fols. 51^v, 91^r, 99^r, 100^r, 125^v, 206^{r-v} and especially 75^r. P. R. Amidon, trans. and ed., *Philostorgius: A Church History* (Atlanta, 2007), is a modern edition of the work; for Philostorgius's own views see H. Leppin, "Heretical historiography: Philostorgius," in *Studia Patristica*, 34 (2001), 111–24.

45. William Andrews Clark Memorial Library, Los Angeles (hereafter WACL) Ms. N563M3 P222, "Paradoxical Questions Concerning the Morals and Actions of Athanasius," fols. 39^r–42^r, 79^r. Keynes Ms. 10 is a later and more polished version of the first half of this document. See also Yahuda Mss. 19 fols. 35^r–45^r; 12 fols. 29^r–31^r, and 5.3 fols. 13^r, 15^r–17^r.

46. Yahuda Mss. 19 fols. 29^r; 2.5b fols. 40^{r-v}, 42^{r-v}, and 11 fol. 2^r; for Constantia's influence and the return of Arius to Constantinople, see Yahuda Mss. 19 fol. 72^r and 2.3 fols. 25^r–27^r; for Alexandrian ecclesiastical politics in the 320s, see ibid., fols. 28^r–31^r; and for the Meletians, see ibid., fols. 31^r–34^r.

47. Newton's view of Constantine's murderous dealings with his close family is described at Yahuda Mss. 19 fols. 56^r–61^r (esp. 59^r–60^r); 12 fols. 31^r–34^r, esp. 34^r (for God's judgement), and a closely related version at Yahuda 2.3 fols. 34^r–36^r.

48. For Hobbes, see D. H. J. Warner, "Hobbes's Interpretation of the Doctrine of the Trinity," *The Journal of Religious History* 5 (1969): 299–313; F. Lessay, "Christologie de Hobbes: Le soupçon de Socinianisme," in *L'interpretazione nei secoli XVI e XVII*, ed. G. Canziani and Y. Zarka (Milan, 1993), 549–64, and Hobbes,

ed. N. Malcolm (Oxford, 2012) *Leviathan*, ed. N. Malcolm (Oxford, 2012), 3:778, 1196–98, 1210, 1230–4. For the *Historia Ecclesiastica*, see T. Hobbes, *Historia Ecclesiastica: Critical Edition, including Text, Translation, Introduction, Commentary and Notes*, ed. P. Springborg, P. Stablein, and P. Wilson (Paris, 2008) and J. Collins, "Thomas Hobbes's Ecclesiastical History," in *The Oxford Handbook of Hobbes*, ed. A. P. Martinich and K. Hoekstra (Oxford, 2016), 520–44.

49. Yahuda Ms. 2.5b fols. 42^v–43^r; see more broadly Yahuda Ms. 19 fols. 62^r–116^r.

50. Yahuda Ms. 11 fols. 2^r–3^r; Yahuda Ms. 2.5b fols. 42^v–43^v. Following Socrates and Sozomen, Newton held that the Council of Serdica took place in 347.

51. Yahuda Ms. 11 fols. 4^r–5^r; WACL Ms. N563M3 P222 fols. 5^v–6^r, 35^r–36^r; and Yahuda 19 fol. 13^r. Four councils were held at Sirmium between 357 and 359, and the offending council in question was the third. At the Council of Ariminum, a minority group led by Ursacius of Singidunum and Valens of Mursa sought to exclude the divisive term *ousia* and pushed instead for the so-called homoian position, that the Son was "like" the Father "according to the Scriptures."

52. Keynes Ms. 10 fols. 28^v–29^r; WACL Ms. N563M3 P222 fols. 34^r–35^r.

53. Keynes Ms. 10 fols. 29^{r-v} and 30^r–31^r; WACL Ms. N563M3 P222 fols. 35^r, 36^{r-v}, 37^r.

54. Keynes Ms. 10 fols. 30^v–31^r; WACL Ms. N563M3 P222 fol. 37^v.

55. For Philostorgius see Yahuda Mss 1.6 fols 1^v, 3^v, 7^v, 11^v; 19 passim and 2–5b passim. For a modern account of the way Athanasius framed his opposition to Arianism, see D. Gwynn, *The Eusebians: The Polemic of Athanasius of Alexandria and the Construction of the Arian Controversy* (Oxford, 2007).

56. Yahuda Ms. 5.3 fols. 1^r and 2^v.

57. Yahuda Ms. 5.3 fols. 3^r, 4^v–6^r, 7^v, 10^r, 13^r–14^r; compare with Yahuda Ms. 2.5b fols. 28^r–30^v. For modern discussion, see R. P. C. Hanson, *The Search for the Christian Doctrine of God: The Arian Controversy, 318–381* (Edinburgh, 1988), ch. 7, esp. 193–95.

58. Yahuda Ms. 5.3 fols. 17^v–20^r.

CHAPTER 5

★ Keynes Ms. 2, Part 2, fol. 67^r.

1. See inter alia C. Dugmore, *The Mass and the English Reformers* (London, 1958); J. Barish, *The Anti-Theatrical Prejudice* (London, 1981); M. Aston, *England's Iconoclasts*, vol. 1, *Laws Against Images* (Oxford, 1988); R. Clifton, "Fear of Popery," in *The Origins of the English Civil War*, ed. C. Russell (London, 1973), 144–67; C. M. N. Eire, *War Against the Idols: The Reformation of Worship from Erasmus to Calvin* (Cambridge, 1986); P. Lake, "Anti-popery: The Structure of a Prejudice," in *Conflicts in Early Stuart England: Studies in Religion and Politics, 1603–1642*, ed. R. Cust and A. Hughes (London, 1989), 72–106; A. Milton, *Catholic and Reformed: The Roman and Protestant Churches in English Protestant Thought, 1600–1640* (Cambridge, 1995), esp. ch. 4; and H. L. Parish, *Monks, Miracles and Magic: Reformation Representations of the Medieval Church* (London, 2005).

2. See J. Miller, *Popery and Politics in England, 1660–1688* (Cambridge, 1973). "Popish" recusants were Catholics who refused to take communion in the Church of England.

3. J. Miller, *Popery and Politics*, 154–95; and T. Harris, *London Crowds in the Reign of Charles II: Propaganda from the Restoration Until the Exclusion Crisis* (Cambridge, 1987).

4. Newton purchased Stillingfleet's *A Discourse Concerning the Idolatry Practised in the Church of Rome, and the Danger of Salvation in the Communion of It* (London, 1671) and his *An Answer to Several Late Treatises, Occasioned by a Book Entituled a Discourse Concerning the Idolatry Practised in the Church of Rome...Pt 1.* (London, 1673), each for £2s 6d; see J. Harrison, *Library*, H1561, 1562.

5. Pardies to Oldenburg, 30 March 1672, Oldenburg to Newton, 9 April 1672, Newton to Oldenburg for Pardies, 13 April 1672 and 10 June 1672, Pardies to Oldenburg, 11 May 1672, in H. W. Turnbull et al., *Correspondence*, 1:130–33, 135, 136, 142–44, 146–47.

6. Linus to Oldenburg, 26 September 1674, Newton to Oldenburg, 5 December 1674, in ibid., 1:318–19. See also *Philosophical Transactions*, 110 (25 January 1674/75): 217–19 (the anonymity had been requested by Newton). The second letter to Pardies had been published in *Philosophical Transactions* 7 (1672): 5014–18.

7. Linus to Oldenburg, 15 February 1674/75 and 11 September 1675 (N.S.), and Newton to Oldenburg, 13 November 1675, in H. W. Turnbull et al., *Correspondence*, 1:334–36, 356–58. Linus reminded Oldenburg of the October letter on 13 November 1675 (O.S.); see A. R. Hall and M. B. Hall, eds., *The Correspondence of Henry Oldenburg*, 13 vols. (Madison and London, 1965–86), 11:124, and 146–47 for Oldenburg to Linus, 17 December 1674 (O.S.). Linus's "second" letter appeared in *Philosophical Transactions* 121 (1675): 499–501.

8. Newton to Oldenburg, 13 November 1675, and Gascoigne to Oldenburg, 15 December 1675, in H. W. Turnbull et al., *Correspondence*, 1:356–59, 393–95; Oldenburg received it on December 28 (O.S.) and merely summarised it in the margins of the published version of Newton's letter of 10 January 1676; see *Philosophical Transactions* 121 (1676): 501–2, 503.

9. Newton to Oldenburg, 21 December 1675 and 10 January 1676, in H. W. Turnbull et al., *Correspondence*, 1:404–6, 407–11; part of the latter appeared in *Philosophical Transactions* 121 (1676): 503–4.

10. Newton to Oldenburg, 29 February 1676 and 26 April 1676, in H. W. Turnbull et al., *Correspondence*, 1:421–25; 2:1, 2n1. In the *Philosophical Transactions*, Linus's second letter was immediately followed by Newton's reply of 13 November 1675 and then by his 10 January 1676 response to Gascoigne; Newton's letter of 29 February 1676 appeared in *Philosophical Transactions* 123 (1676): 556–61.

11. Newton to Oldenburg, 11 May 1676; Lucas to Oldenburg, 17 May 1676, in H. W. Turnbull et al., *Correspondence*, 2:6–12, 79. Lucas's letter was published in

Philosophical Transactions 128 (1676): 692–98; Newton's reply of August followed at 698–705. See also S. Schaffer, "Glass Works," 88–91.

12. Newton to Oldenburg, 18 August 1676 and 22 August 1676, in H. W. Turnbull et al., *Correspondence*, 2:76–80, 81, 83, 94.

13. Lucas to Oldenburg, 13 October 1676, in ibid., 2:104–8, 246–47.

14. Newton to Oldenburg, 18 November 1676 and 28 November 1676, in ibid., 2:182–85.

15. Lucas to Oldenburg, 23 January 1677, in ibid., 2:189–92.

16. Newton to Hooke, 18 December 1677, Hooke to Newton, 24 December 1677, Collins to Newton, 5 March 1676/77, Collins to Wallis, late 1677; ibid., 2:200–201, 239–40, 242–43; R. S. Westfall, *Never at Rest*, 276–77; I. B. Cohen, "Versions of Isaac Newton's First Published Paper," *Archives Internationales d'Histoire des Sciences* 11 (1958): 357–75.

17. Newton to Lucas, 2 February 1677/78, Lucas to Hooke for Newton, late February 1677/78, Lucas to Newton, 4 March 1677/78; Newton to Hooke, 5 March 1677/78, in H. W. Turnbull et al., *Correspondence*, 2:246–53, 256–58, 262–63. There was a copy of Lucas's original letter of 13 October 1676, which had been made by Oldenburg and which was in the R.S. register (and which the editors of the Correspondence print at 2:104–8). The offending text is at ibid., 2:247 (and compare with the original at ibid., 2:104). Newton alluded to the differences in a further letter of c. June 1678, implying that they were between the copy and what he remembered of the first; see ibid., 2:267. For the fire, see A. R. Hall, "Newton's First Book (I)," *Archives Internationales d'Histoire des Sciences* 13 (1960): 39–60; and R. S. Westfall, *Never at Rest*, 277.

18. Newton to Lucas, 5 March 1677/78, in H. W. Turnbull et al., *Correspondence*, 2:259–60.

19. Newton to Lucas, 5 March 1677/78, in ibid., 2:262–63.

20. Hooke to Newton, 25 May 1678, Newton to Aubrey, ? June 1678, in ibid., 2:265–69.

21. For the background to the Popish Plot, which was hatched by Titus Oates and Israel Tonge in the late summer of 1678, see J. Kenyon, *The Popish Plot* (New York, 1972); and M. Knights, *Politics and Opinion in Crisis, 1678–81* (Cambridge, 1994).

22. Aside from his copy of Barrow's *A Treatise of the Pope's Supremacy*, Newton also owned Barrow's copy of John Cosin's *Historia transubstantiationis papalis. Cui præmittitur, atque opponitur, tùm S. Scripturæ, tùm Veterum Patrum, & Reformatarum Ecclesiarum doctrina Catholica...* (London, 1675); see J. Harrison, *Library*, H124, H444.

23. Yahuda Ms. 14 fol. 19^{r-v}.

24. Ibid., fols. 19^v–20^r.

25. Ibid., fols. 20^r–22^r.

26. Ibid., fols. 38^r–40^r, esp. 38^v.

27. Yahuda Ms. 2.3 fols. 68ʳ–70ʳ (esp. fol. 68ʳ for reference to another, presumably prophetic work) and 76ʳ–77ʳ. For Catholic clergy as the leading vanguard of the two-headed beast, see ibid. fols. 79ʳ–81ʳ (for the monks as first the body and then the entirety of the two-horned beast) and in particular Yahuda Ms. 2.2. For another, separate treatment of Athanasius's role in propagating "monkery," see WACL Ms. N563M3 P222 fols. 80ʳ–81ʳ, 76ʳ–78ʳ, 66ʳ–67Aʳ, 75ʳ–76ʳ (in that order). On occasion, e.g. ibid. fol. 67Aʳ, Newton deliberately removed any references to a prophetic framework for understanding the splitting of the order into Egyptian and Syrian components.

28. Yahuda Ms. 2.2 fol. 5ʳ.

29. Yahuda Ms. 2.2 fols. 1ʳ, 2ʳ–3ʳ, 6ʳ–9ʳ (for the purpose of the cult); 9ʳ, 23ᵛ–24ᵛ (for the origin of the evil).

30. Yahuda Mss. 11 fols. 8ʳ–13ʳ; 14 fols. 135ʳ⁻ᵛ (notes from Jerome's *Life of Hilarion*), and 137ʳ–138ᵛ (notes on Antony). See also Yahuda Mss. 2.3 fols. 70ʳ–72ʳ (esp. fol. 72ʳ for Egypt and Italy); 2.2 fols. 13ʳ⁻ᵛ, 18ʳ–21ʳ.

31. WACL Ms. N563M3 P222 fols. 66ʳ, 80ᵛ (for the historians), 81ʳ (the prodigious stories); cf. Yahuda Ms. 2.5b fol. 49ʳ for Bellarmine's view.

32. WACL Ms. N563M3 P222 fols. 67ʳ–67Aʳ (for the success of the "Life"), 66ʳ–78ʳ (for the *Life* as the origin of "Ecclesiastical Romances"), and 80ʳ (Athanasius's sophistry). Rosweyde's ten-volume hagiography, the *Vitae Patrum*, was first published in 1615 (with a third edition in 1628), and contained an extensive collection, which Rosweyde translated into Latin, of the sayings and lives of the Egyptian and Syrian Desert Fathers and Mothers. The texts were incorporated into the *Acta Sanctorum*, the great project on the lives and writings of the saints continued after Rosweyde's death (in 1629) by Jean Bolland. The first two volumes of this immense undertaking appeared in 1643.

33. Yahuda Ms. 2.5b fol. 42ᵛ and 2.3 fols. 48ʳ–58ʳ (for the propensity to violence of Athanasius's followers), esp. 52ᵛ (for the leniency of the secular arm), and 53ᵛ–54ᵛ (for the character of the Egyptians). Uniquely, at Yahuda Ms. 2.5b fol. 43ʳ Newton claimed that over some issues Athanasius was "unjustly pressured by his accusers" at the Council of Tyre in 335.

34. Yahuda Mss. 2.3 fols. 59ʳ–60ʳ; 2.5b fols. 36ʳ–40ʳ; and see Yahuda Ms. 2.2 fols. 20ʳ–21ʳ, 23ᵛ–24ᵛ, 24ʳ–28ʳ (for the Italian cities). For the prosecution of Athanasius and the prohibition against the monks' disputing with their opponents, see WACL Ms N563M3 P222, fols. 61ʳ, 63ʳ. In a rare example of cross-referencing his own work (at Yahuda Ms. 2.3 fol. 1ʳ), Newton referred to another treatment of Hilary—this is possibly the brief treatment at Yahuda Ms. 2.2 fols. 23ᵛ–24ᵛ.

35. Yahuda Mss. 2.3 fols. 62ʳ–65ʳ; 2.2 fol. 6ʳ (an alternative account of the fate of the "bones" of John the Baptist) and 2.5b fols. 19ʳ–20ʳ and cf. 26ʳ (for the "cults" of saint-worship and homoousianism). The truncated analysis of early Christian burial practices is at Yahuda Ms. 2.5b fols. 22ᵛ–24ʳ.

36. Yahuda Ms. 2.3 fols. 10ʳ–15ʳ, esp. 11ʳ and 13ʳ; compare with Yahuda Ms. 2.5b fols. 24ʳ–26ʳ and WACL Ms N563M3 P222 fols. 64ᵛ–65ᵛ.

37. Yahuda Ms. 2.3 fols. 16^r–17^r.

38. Yahuda Ms. 2.3 fols. 17^r–22^r, esp. 21^r. and Yahuda Ms. 2.5b fols. 25^r–26^r. Newton's copy of Pope Damasus's *Opera quæ extant et vita ex codicibus MSS. cum notis M.M. Sarazanii* (Paris, 1672) is inscribed "Is. Newton Donum R^{ndi} amici D. Moor S.T.D." [presumably Henry More] in Newton's hand on flyleaf; see J. Harrison, *Library*, H485.

39. See, in general, P. Hadot, *Philosophy as a Way of Life* (Oxford, 1995).

40. A. Napier, *Works*, 3:345, 347, 355–56, 363–64, 406, 432, 434. For a more detailed account of scholarly asceticism, see R. Iliffe, "Isaac Newton: Lucatello Professor of Mathematics," in *Science Incarnate: Historical Embodiments of Natural Knowledge*, ed. C. Lawrence and S. Shapin (Chicago, 1998), 121–55.

41. A. Napier, *Works*, 3:359, 361–62, 372, 375, 380, 398–401, 413 (and cf. 379), 428–29.

42. Keynes Ms. 130 (7); R. North, *General Preface*, 98, 102–3, 108, 111. "Madame en travestie" means a woman in disguise, or female transvestite.

43. R. North, *General Preface*, 139, 141–42, 144–45, 150, 151–59.

44. G. Cheyne, *Natural Method of Curing Diseases of the Body and Disorders of Mind* (London, 1742), 81; Keynes Ms. 129.2 fol. 10^r; Keynes Ms. 137; J. Evelyn, *The Diary of John Evelyn*, 6 vols., ed. E. S. de Beer (Oxford, 1955), 3:146.

45. Humphrey to John Conduitt, 14 February 1727/28; Keynes Ms. 130.2; Keynes Ms. 130.7 fol. 8^v; W. Stukeley, "Memoirs," RS Ms. 142 fol. 62^r; R. North, *General Preface*, 108.

46. Humphrey Newton to Conduitt, 17 January 1727/28 and 17 February 1727/28; Keynes Ms. 135 fols. 3^r, 7^r. Stukeley told Richard Mead in July 1727 that Humphrey had informed him that Newton had sometimes donned his surplice to go to St. Mary's and that Newton's studies prevented him from going to chapel in the evenings; see Keynes Ms. 136.3 fol. 7^r. Humphrey's stories were reworked in Stukeley's "Memoirs"; see RS Ms. 142 fols. 57^v–58^r.

47. J. Glanvill, *Vanity*, 95–105, esp. 95, 103–5.

48. J. Calvin, *Institutes of the Christian Religion*, Bk. 1. ch. 11. §8; see E. Evans, "The Puritan Use of Imagination," *Reformation and Revival* 10 (2001): 47–84, esp. 51–52, 61–70; and P. Lake, "Anti-popery," 72–106, esp. 74–75, 99.

49. Yahuda Ms. 11 fols. 16^r–20^v. For modern accounts, see V. Burrus, *The Sex Lives of Saints: An Erotics of Ancient Hagiography* (Philadelphia, 2004); D. Brakke, *Demons and the Making of the Monk: Spiritual Combat in Early Christianity* (Cambridge, Mass., 2006); P. Brown, *The Body and Society: Men, Women, and Sexual Renunciation in Early Christianity* (New York, 2008); and M. Foucault, "The Battle for Chastity," in M. Foucault, *Ethics: Subjectivity and Truth*, ed. P. Rabinow (New York, 1997), 185–97.

50. Yahuda Ms. 11 fol. 21^r.

51. Yahuda Ms. 11 fol. 22^r.

52. Yahuda Ms. 11 fols. 22^r–28^r. Newton owned *Palladii Divi Evagrii Discipuli Lausiaca quæ dicitur historia, et Theodoreti Episcopi Cyri Θεοφιλὴς, id est religiosa historia* (Paris, 1555); J. Harrison, *Library*, H1233.

53. Yahuda Ms. 11 fols. 28^r–31^r. Hilarion, whose *Life* was written by Jerome, is not to be confused with Hilary (bishop of Poitiers), one of the chief architects of orthodox Trinitarianism, although their lives overlapped and both are saints according to the Roman Catholic tradition.

54. Yahuda Ms. 11 fols 31^r–32^r.

55. WACL N563M3 P222, fols. 67A^r, 75^r. Newton commended moderate fasting by private men in secret or by the whole church openly on set occasions at Yahuda Ms. 18 fol. 2^r.

56. Yahuda Ms. 11 fols. 34^r–38^r.

57. Yahuda Ms. 11 fols. 38^r–40^r.

CHAPTER 6

1. Earlier accounts of Newton's work in this area can be found in J. E. McGuire and P. Rattansi, "Newton and the Pipes of Pan," 108–43; P. Casini, "Newton: The Classical Scholia," *History of Science* 22 (1984): 1–59; R. S. Westfall, "Isaac Newton's *Theologiae Gentilis Origines Philosophicae*," in *The Secular Mind*, ed. W. Warren Wagar (New York, 1982), 15–34; J. Gascoigne, "The 'Wisdom of the Egyptians' and the Secularisation of History in the Age of Newton," in *The Uses of Antiquity: The Scientific Revolution and the Classical Tradition*, ed. S. Gaukroger (Springer, 1991), 171–212; R. Iliffe, "'Is He Like Other Men': The Meaning of the *Principia* and the Author as Idol," in *Culture and Society in the Stuart Restoration*, ed. G. Maclean (Cambridge, 1995), 159–78; J. Buchwald and M. Feingold, *Origin of Civilization*, 433–46.

2. See F. E. Manuel, *The Eighteenth Century Confronts the Gods* (Cambridge, 1959); F. Yates, *Giordano Bruno and the Hermetic Tradition* (Chicago, 1964); C. B. Schmitt, "Perennial Philosophy: From Agostino Steuco to Leibniz," *Journal of the History of Ideas* 27 (1966): 505–32; D. C. Allen, *The Legend of Noah: Renaissance Rationalism in Art, Science and Letters* (Champaign, 1963); D. C. Allen, *Mysteriously Meant* (Baltimore, 1970); D. P. Walker, *The Ancient Theology: Studies in Christian Platonism from the Fifteenth to the Eighteenth Century* (London, 1972); E. Wind, *Pagan Mysteries in the Renaissance*, 2nd ed. (Oxford, 1980); J. Seznec, *The Survival of the Pagan Gods: The Mythological Tradition and Its Place in Renaissance Humanism and Art* (Princeton, 1983); J. Assmann, *Moses the Egyptian: The Memory of Egypt in Western Monotheism* (London, 1997); W. Schmidt-Biggeman, *Philosophia Perennis: Historical Outlines of Western Spirituality in Ancient, Medieval and Early Modern Thought* (Dordrecht, 2004); and F. Ebeling, *The Secret History of Hermes Trismegistus: Hermeticism from Ancient to Modern Times* (Ithaca, N.Y., 2007).

3. See K. Dannenfeldt, "Egypt and Egyptian Antiquities in the Renaissance," *Studies in the Renaissance* 6 (1959): 7–27; F. Yates, *Bruno*; D. P. Walker, *Ancient Theology*; W. Schmidt-Biggeman, *Philosophia Perennis*, 32–35.

4. F. Yates, *Bruno*, 21–116, 211–15.

5. G. J. Vossius, *De Theologia Gentili, et physiologia Christiana, sive De Origine ac Progressu Idololatriae…liber I, et II* (III, et IV) (Amsterdam, 1641), which was published

alongside his son Dionysius's edition of Maimonides's *de Idololatria Liber, cum Interpretatione Latina, & Notis*. Newton's heavily dog-eared copy shows just how intensively he used Vossius's work; see J. Harrison, *Library*, H1697. For Vossius, see N. Wickenden, *G.J. Vossius and the Humanist Conception of History* (Assen, 1993); and C. S. M. Rademaker, *The Life and Work of Gerard Joannes Vossius 1577–1649* (Assen, 1981), 306–15.

6. Samuel Bochart, *Geographia Sacra, cujus pars prior Phaleg de dispersione gentium et terrarum, divisione facta in ædificatione turris Babel, etc. pars posterior Chanaan de coloniis & sermone Phœnicum agit* (Frankfurt, 1681; orig. Caen, 1646–51). Newton's massively dog-eared copy of the 1681 edition is in Trinity College Library; see J. Harrison, *Library*, H231. For Bochart's life, see W. Whittingham, "Essay on the Life and Writings of Samuel Bochart," in *Essays and Dissertations in Biblical Literature*, vol. 1 (New York, 1829), 105–68, esp. 144–48; and Z. Shalev, *Sacred Words and Worlds: Geography, Religion and Scholarship, 1500–1750* (Leiden, 2011), 141–204.

7. For Rheticus, see R. Hooykaas, *Rheticus' Treatise on Holy Scripture and the Motion of the Earth* (New York, 1984), 150–52, 158; and T. Przypskowski, "La gnomique de Nicolas Copernic et de Georges Joachim Rheticus," *Actes du VIIIe Congrès International d'Historie des Sciences...* (Paris, 1958), 400–409. See also T. Digges, "A PERFIT DESCRIPTION of the Caelestiall Orbes According to the Most Aunciente Doctrine of the PYTHAGOREANS, Latelye Revived by CO-PERNICUS and by Geometricall Demonstrations Approved," in L. Digges, *A Prognostication Everlasting: Corrected and Augmented by Thomas Digges* (London, 1576). For Kepler, see A. Grafton, "Johannes Kepler: The New Astronomer Reads the Ancients," in A. Grafton, *Commerce with the Classics: Ancient Books and Renaissance Readers* (Ann Arbor, 1997), 185–224. More generally, see P. Casini, "Il mito pitagorico e la rivoluzione astronomica," *Rivista di filosofia* 85 (1994): 7–33.

8. R. Boyle, *Excellency of Theology, Compared with Natural Philosophy* (London, 1674), in M. Hunter and E. B. Davis, *The Works of Robert Boyle*, 12 vols. (London, 2000), 8:74; see also D. Levitin, "The Experimentalist as Humanist: Robert Boyle on the History of Philosophy," *Annals of Science* 71 (2014): 149–82, esp. 159–63, and D. Levitin, *Ancient Wisdom in the Age of the New Science: Histories of Philosophy in England, c.1640–1700* (Cambridge, 2015)

9. R. Boyle, *A Free Enquiry into the Vulgarly Receiv'd Notion of Nature* (London, 1686), in M. Hunter and E. B. Davis, *Works*, 10:471–72, 475, 482–83. D. Levitin, "Experimentalist as Humanist" (180), identifies the source of Boyle's account of the Sabians as Samuel Parker's *Tentamina de Deo....*(London, 1665).

10. H. More, *Conjectura Cabbalistica, or, A CONJECTURAL ESSAY OF Interpreting the Minde of Moses According to a Threefold Cabbala: viz. Literal, Philosophical, Mystical, or Divinely Moral* (Cambridge, 1653), sig. A4ʳ, Bʳ, B2ʳ; H. More, *A Collection of Several Philosophical Writings* (London, 1662), xi, 1, 3, 82, 100–103.

11. R. Cudworth, *The True Intellectual System*, 12–19, 46–55, 60–81, 111–17, 174–75. See S. Hutton, "The Neoplatonic Roots of Arianism: Cudworth and Gale," in

Socinianism and Its Role in the Culture of the Sixteenth to the Eighteenth Centuries, ed. L. Szczucki (Warsaw, 1983), 139–46; and D. Levitin, *Ancient Wisdom,* 355–68.

12. See F. Yates, *Bruno,* 416–23; E. Iversen, *The Myth of Egypt and Its Hieroglyphs in the European Tradition* (Princeton, 1993); D. Stolzenberg, *Egyptian Oedipus: Athanasius Kircher and the Secrets of Antiquity* (Chicago, 2013), 129. For Maimonides, see J. Assmann, *Moses the Egyptian,* 57–77; and G. Stroumsa, *A New Science: The Discovery of Religion in the Age of Reason* (Cambridge, Mass., 2010), 91–94; and for Casaubon, see A. Grafton, *Defenders of the Text: The Traditions of Scholarship in an Age of Science, 1450–1800* (Cambridge, Mass., 1994), 145–77.

13. E. Stillingfleet, *Origines Sacrae: Or a Rational Account of the Grounds of Christian Faith, as to the Truth and Divine Authority of the Scriptures, and the Matters Therein Contained* (London, 1662), 32–33, 42, 58–60, 100–103. See S. Hutton, "Edward Stillingfleet, Henry More and the Decline of Moses Atticus: A Note on Seventeenth-century Anglican Apologetics," in *Philosophy, Science and Religion in England, 1640–1700,* ed. R. Kroll, R. Ashcraft, and P. Zagorin (Cambridge, 1992), 64–84. And in particular D. P. Walker, *Ancient Theology,* 22–41.

14. E. Stillingfleet, *Origines,* 124–28, 425–26, 595–96, 598. For similar claims, see S. Parker, *A Free and Impartial Censure of the Platonick Philosophie* (Oxford, 1666), 83, 92–97; T. Gale, *The Court of the Gentiles, or a Discourse Concerning the Original of Human Literature Both Philologie and Philosophie, from the Scriptures and Jewish Church,* 4 parts (Oxford, 1669–77), 1:13 and 4:sig. A4^r; and M. Hale, *The Primitive Origination of Mankind Considered and Examined According to the Light of Nature* (London, 1677), 106, 168.

15. R. Cudworth, *The True Intellectual System,* 129, 174–75, 310–15, 320–21, 323–30.

16. J. Marsham, *Canon Chronicus Ægypticus, Ebraicus, Graecus, et disquisitiones,...* (London, 1672) (Newton owned the 1676 Leipzig edition, now in the Linda Hall Library for Science, Engineering and Technology, Kansas City, Missouri); J. Spencer, *De Legibus Hebræorum ritualibus et earum rationibus, Libri III* (Cambridge, 1683–85); J. Harrison, *Library,* H1036, H1545. As one might expect, both works are heavily dog-eared. See G. Stroumsa, "John Spencer and the Roots of Idolatry," *History of Religions* 41 (2001): 1–23; J. Assmann, *Moses the Egyptian,* 56–78; and D. Stolzenberg, "John Spencer and the Perils of Sacred Philology," *Past and Present,* 214 (2012): 129–63, esp. 146–52; and D. Levitin, *Ancient Wisdom,* 164–71.

17. T. Burnet, *Archaeologiæ Philosophicæ: Sive Doctrina Antiqua de Rerum Originibus. Libri Duo* (London, 1692), 43, 71, 78, 99, 121, 193–95, and esp. 330–33; J. Woodward, "Of the Wisdom of the Ancient Egyptians," *Archaeologia* 4 (1777), 212–311, esp. 217, 219, 221, 256, 276–78.

18. Newton to Halley, 20 June 1686, in H. W. Turnbull et al., *Correspondence,* 2:437. The "liber secundus" is now CUL Add. Ms. 3990; at this stage Newton was still working on a two-book model of the *Principia.* For more details, see I. B. Cohen, *Introduction to Newton's Principia* (Cambridge, 1971), 109–16.

19. Yahuda Ms. 16.2 passim; Yahuda Ms. 17.2 fols. 4^v, 10^r, and 13^v are drafts of Yahuda Ms. 16.2 fols. 54^{r-v}, and 12^r, the last of which is a fair copy in Humphrey's hand. In Yahuda Ms. 16.2 Humphrey's hand (with the exception of small additions by Newton and an extended, later sequence in Newton's hand from fols. 19^r–27^v) continues to fol. 58^r; Newton continued the tract to the end at fol. 79^r.

20. I. Newton, *The Principia: Mathematical Principles of Natural Philosophy*, ed. I. B. Cohen and A. Whitman (Los Angeles, 1999), 793. The reference to smatterers occurs in a letter from William Derham to John Conduitt of July 1733; Keynes Ms. 133 fol. 10^r .

21. CUL Add. Ms. 3990 fol. 1^r.

22. Fatio to Huygens, 5 February 1692 and Huygens to Fatio, 19 February 1692, in H. W. Turnbull et al., *Correspondence*, 3:193, 196.

23. Ibid., 3:338, 384, 386 (for Gregory's request to have the notes published). The scholia appeared in the preface to Gregory's *Astronomiæ Physicæ et Geometricæ Elementa* (Oxford, 1702); see also W. G. Hiscock, ed., *David Gregory, Isaac Newton and Their Circle: Extracts from Gregory's Memoranda, 1677–1708* (Oxford, 1937), 3–4, 29–30. The notes given to Gregory by Newton are in the Royal Society, Gregory Ms. 247 fols. 6^r–14^r, and are reproduced in P. Casini, "Classical Scholia," 24–36, along with transcriptions of a proposed addition to corollary II of Prop. VII from CUL Ms. 3965 fols. 268^r–272^r. The reference to Plutarch and Galileo is on fol. 8^r, noted in connection with proposed additions to prop. IV. The original note from Galileo is at Yahuda Ms. 13.3 fol. 27^r. Newton discussed the meaning of his reference to Plato with Richard Bentley in early 1693; see H. W. Turnbull et al., *Correspondence*, 3:240, 251, 255.

24. Gregory Memoranda, in H. W. Turnbull et al., *Correspondence*, 3:191–92, 385. For the "Geometria," see *The Mathematical Papers of Isaac Newton*, 8 vols., ed. D. T. Whiteside (Cambridge, 1967–81), 7:185–561, esp. Whiteside's introduction at 7:185–99.

25. H. W. Turnbull et al., *Correspondence*, 3:338; WACL Ms. "Out of Cudworth," p1 (from *The True Intellectual System*, 13, 120–21, 212); CUL Add. Ms. 3965 fols. 270^r. See also CUL Adv.b.39.1, Ms. interleaved between pp. 412–13, fols. 1^r–3^r and RS. Gregory Ms. 247 passim. Cf. J. E. McGuire and P. Rattansi, "Pipes of Pan," 113–19. Newton's library contained two editions of Lucretius's *Opera*—a 1615 Paris version and a heavily dog-eared Amsterdam edition of 1687; J. Harrison, *Library*, H988, H989.

26. Yahuda Ms. 17.2 fols. 15^{r-v}, 18^{r-v}; "Out of Cudworth," 1–2 (from *The True Intellectual System*, 249, 296–99); CUL Adv.b.39.1 fols. 2^r–4^v .

27. Yahuda Mss. 16.2 fols. 3^{r-v}; 17.2 fols. 15^v, 18^r; 13.3 fol. 17^v. Compare with the Gregory Memorandum on Thoth as a Copernican of May 1694 (H. W. Turnbull et al., *Correspondence*, 3:38). Newton's original notes from Eusebius of Caesarea's *Praeparatio Evangelica* on the Phoenician and Egyptian theology are to be found at Yahuda Ms. 13.3 fols. 1^r–3^r.

28. Yahuda Ms. 17.2 fols. 6^{r-v}, 15^{r-v}, 18^r–19^r; cf. also Yahuda Ms. 17.3 fols. 9^v–10^r, 13^r, the last reference originally from notes at Yahuda 13.3 fol. 19^v. References to Pythagoras and his disciples are to be found in the draft scholia for Proposition VIII of Book 3 of the *Principia*; R. S. Gregory Ms. 247 fols. 11^v, 12^{r-v}, and CUL Add. Ms. 3965 fols. 268^r, 272^{r-v}. Cf. also CUL Add. Ms. 3970 fol. 619^r.

29. Yahuda Ms. 17.2 fols. 18^v–19^r. The account in Yahuda Ms. 17.2 fol. 19^r of Pythagoras's Egyptian injunction upon his disciples to "learn silence" is taken from the Ms. "Out of Cudworth," p2 (from R. Cudworth, *The True Intellectual System*, 316).

30. Yahuda Ms. 17.2 fols. 18^v–19^r; Newton also dealt with the Ancients' views on comets in Yahuda Ms. 17.3. fols. 11^v–12^r, a text later incorporated into "The Original of Religions." For Newton and cometary theory, see J. A. Ruffner, "The Background and Early Development of Newton's Theory of Comets" (Indiana University PhD thesis, 1966), chs. 7–9, esp. 308–44; S. J. Schaffer, "Newton's Comets and the Transformation of Astrology," in *Astrology, Science and Society*, ed. P. Curry (Woodbridge, 1987), 219–43, esp. 226–28, 239–43; and D. T. Whiteside, *Mathematical Papers*, 6:49–85.

31. R. S. Gregory Ms. 247 fols. 6^{r-v}, 9^r, 10^{r-v}, 11^{r-v} (Newton autograph); CUL Add. Ms. 3965 fol. 270^r (drawn from his notes upon Cudworth); Newton to Bentley, 10 December 1692, in H. W. Turnbull et al., Correspondence, 3, 234. Newton's own copy of Lucretius's *De Rerum Natura* (Trinity College Library, Tr/ NQ.9.73) contains dog-ears which correspond exactly to the passages used in these scholia.

32. R. S. Gregory Ms. 247 fols. 7^r–11^v, 12^{r-v}, and in particular the treatment at Yahuda Ms. 17.3 fols. 1^r–2^v.

33. R. S. Gregory Ms. 247 fol. 13^r; CUL Add. Ms. 3965 fol. 269^r.

34. His notes on the ancient philosophy (which he used for "The Original of Religions" as well as for some of the Classical Scholia) are in Yahuda Ms. 13.3. Among relevant secondary sources, he also possessed Thomas Godwyn's *Moses and Aaron: Civil and Ecclesiastical Rites, Used by the Ancient Hebrewes; Observed, and at Large Opened*...4th ed. (London, 1631); and Thomas Stanley's *Historia philosophiæ Orientalis. Recensuit, ex Anglica lingua in Latinam transtulit...* (Amsterdam, 1690); see J. Harrison, *Library*, H483, H1551.

35. Yahuda Ms. 16.2 fol. 1^{r-v} (in the hand of Humphrey Newton); there is a draft of early paragraphs at Yahuda Ms. 17.2 fols. 20^r–21^v. See also K. J. Knoespel, "Interpretive Strategies in Newton's Theologiae gentilis origines philosophiae," in *Newton and Religion: Context, Nature and Influence*, ed. J. E. Force and R. Popkin (Dordrecht, 1999), 179–202.

36. Yahuda Mss. 16.2 fols. 1^v–3^v and compare with 17.2 fols. 20^v–21^r. Original notes for this are to be found on Yahuda Ms. 13.3 fols. 1^r, 16^v, 17^{v-r} and 19^v.

37. Yahuda Ms. 16.2 esp. fols. 4^r–6^r, 7^v, 11^r (for Galileo, repeated at 15^r and 46^r), 43a^v (for the outline of remaining chapters), 51^r–52^r, 67^r–71^r (for an attempted summary of different accounts). Compare with Yahuda 17.2 fol. 14^{r-v}.

38. Yahuda Ms. 16.2 fols. 12^r–18^r, 29^r–43^r, 56^r (for the absence of slavery, labour, or private property); there are a number of original notes for this exposition in Yahuda 13.3. For the later expansion of his interest in the history of the ancient world, see J. Buchwald and M. Feingold, *Origin of Civilization*, 148–52.

39. Yahuda Ms. 17.3 fols. 9^{r-v}, 11^r; Yahuda Ms. 41 fols. 1^{r-v}, 3^v. For a fascinating later account, based on Hesiod, of what Newton called "The Earliest Times in Europe," see New College Ms. 361.2 fol. 115^v.

40. Yahuda Ms. 41 fol. 1^v–2^v, 3^{r-v}, with drafts at 17.3 fols. 9^v–10^r. The most accessible secondary source for Stonehenge was Walter Charleton, *Chorea Gigantum, or, The Most Famous Antiquity of Great Britain, Vulgarly Called Stone-heng, Standing on Salisbury Plain, Restored to the Danes* (London, 1663), a response to Inigo Jones, *The Most Notable Antiquity of Great Britain, Vulgarly Called Stone-heng on Salisbury Plain, Restored*, ed. J. Webb (London, 1655).

41. Yahuda Ms. 41 fol. 4^{r-v}; Latin draft (on clean and unclean sacrifices) at Yahuda Ms. 17.3 fols. 9^v–10^v, 12^r.

42. Yahuda Mss. 41 fol. 5^r and 17.3 fols. 9^v–11^r. For the political contexts of worship in the ancient world, see Keynes Ms. 146 ("The Original of Monarchies") fols. 8^r, 10^r, 12^r, 23^r, 24^r. The notion of a Vestal fire plays no role in Newton's extensive and erudite analysis of the dimensions of Solomon's Temple in Huntington Library, San Marino, Babson Ms. 434.

43. Yahuda Mss. 41 fols. 5^r–7^r; 17.3 fols. 9^v and 10^r–11^r. See also H. Fisch, "The Scientist as Priest," *Isis* 44 (1953): 252–65.

44. H. W. Turnbull et al., *Correspondence*, 3:185, 291–92; Yahuda Mss. 41 fol. 5^r and 17.3 fols. 10^r–12^r.

45. Yahuda Mss. 41, fols. 8^r, 9^{r-v}; 17.2 fols 5^r, 21^v; Keynes Ms. 146 fols. 23^r–24^r, and 16.2 fols. 3^r, and esp. 57^r. In a much later account, the worship of statues was partially attributed to the fact that men became highly skilled at carving; see New College Ms. 361.3 fol. 65^r.

46. Yahuda Ms. 41 fols. 9^{r-v}, 10^v; cf. Yahuda Ms. 17.3 fols. 8^r (cf. draft at 5^v) and 12^r (for the inveterate human tendency to superstition).

47. Yahuda Ms. 41, fols. 9^r, 10^{r-v}; compare with 17.3 fols. 5^v, 8^r, 9^r, 13^r–15^r. For the Egyptians' transfer of their heroes' names to the stars, see Yahuda Mss. 16.2 fol. 57^r and 17.2 fols. 14^r, 20^v.

48. Yahuda Ms. 41 fols. 10^r–11^r; New College Ms. 361.3 fols. 32^{r-v} and the remarks on the institution of "Colleges of Priests" for the promotion of this worship among the Canaanites and Chaldeans on New College Ms. 361.2 fol. 23^r.

49. Yahuda Ms. 17.3 fols. 5^v, 7^r–8^r, 14^{r-v}, 15^r; Yahuda Ms. 41 fol. 26^r (based on Ms. 17.3 fol. 10^r). Some of this analysis drew from his notes on Cudworth; Newton deleted Cudworth's English translation and added a Latin translation that is not in Cudworth; see Yahuda Ms. 17.3 fol. 14^v, drawn from WACL, "Out of Cudworth" (itself from Cudworth, *The True Intellectual System*, 593).

50. Yahuda Ms. 17.3 fols. 10^r, 11^v–12^r.

51. Gregory, notes from 5–7 May 1694, in H. W. Turnbull et al., *Correspondence*, 3:338, and Yahuda Ms. 16.2 fol. 43aᵛ.

52. *The Ancient Religion of the Gentiles, with the Causes of Their Errors* (London, 1705), 3, 12–13, 14, 21, 41–47; C. Blount, *Great Is Diana of the Ephesians* (London, 1680), 3; C. Blount, *The Oracles of Reason* (London, 1693), 133–35. See D. P. Walker, *Ancient Theology*, 164–93; M. M. Rossi, *La vita, le opere, i tempi di Edoardo Herbert di Chirbury*, 3 vols. (Florence, 1947), 3:47–55, 66–70, 120–33; R. Bedford, *In Defence of Truth* (Manchester, 1979); and J. Champion, *The Pillars of Priestcraft Shaken: The Church of England and Its Enemies, 1660–1730* (Cambridge, 1992), 142–48.

53. The location of Newton's copy of Howard is unknown—see J. Harrison, *Library*, H778. More generally, see Champion, *Pillars*, 137–38. In the seventeenth century, Sanchuniathon's writings were known only through the *Præparatio Evangelica* of Eusebius of Caesaria, which contained a summary of a Greek translation of Sanchuniathon's work by Philo of Byblos.

CHAPTER 7

1. The broad range of apocalyptic exegesis in the later seventeenth century is discussed in W. Johnston, *Revelation Restored: The Apocalypse in Later Seventeenth-Century England* (Woodbridge, 2011), while the older Protestant tradition is examined in K. Firth, *The Apocalyptic Tradition in Reformation Britain, 1530–1645* (Oxford, 1978), 7–30; B. S. Capp, *The Fifth-Monarchy Men: A Study in Seventeenth-Century English Millenarianism* (London, 1972); P. Christianson, *Reformers and Babylon: English Apocalyptic Visions from the Reformation to the Eve of the Civil War* (Toronto, 1975); B. W. Ball, *A Great Expectation: Eschatological Thought in English Protestantism to 1660* (Leiden, 1975); and R. Bauckham, *Tudor Apocalypse* (Oxford, 1978).

2. Potter's work was published as *An Interpretation of the Number 666, Wherein, Not Onely the Manner, How This Number Ought to Be Interpreted, Is Clearly Proved and Demonstrated...* (Oxford, 1642); see R. Iliffe, "Newton, God, and the Mathematics of the Two Books," in *Mathematicians and Their Gods*, ed. S. Lawrence and M. McCartney (Oxford, 2015), 121–55. For a modern account of Mede's life and work, see J. Jue, *Heaven*.

3. Alterations to sentences in Yahuda Ms. 9.1, which is in Humphrey's hand, indicate that they are later than their counterparts in Yahuda Ms. 1. Second, arguments in Yahuda 9.2 such as the claim that the woman in the wilderness became the Whore of Babylon are not found in Yahuda 1 but are a key tenet of his early eighteenth-century prophetic papers.

4. J. Foxe, *Acts and Monuments of These Latter and Perilous Days Touching Matters of the Churche, Wherein Are Comprehended and Described the Great Persecutions Horrible Troubles That Have Bene Wrought and Practised by the Romish Prelates, Speciallye in This Realme of England and Scotlande, from the Yeare of Our Lorde a Thousand, unto*

the Time Now Present (London, 1563); see K. Firth, *Apocalyptic Tradition*, 73–85, 89–90, 93–96.

5. K. Firth, *Apocalyptic Tradition*, 96–98, 102–3, 107. In koine or common Greek, letters were associated with numbers, in this case Λ=30; A=1; T=300; E=5; I=10; N=50; O=70; S=200, totalling 666.

6. R. Bellarmine, *Disputationes de Controversiis Christianae Fidei adversus hujus temporis Haereticos*, 3 vols. (1581–93); see K. Firth, *Apocalyptic Tradition*, 163, 172.

7. J. Napier, *A Plaine Discovery of the Whole Revelation of Saint John: Set Downe in Two Treatises: The One Searching and Proving the True Interpretation Thereof: The Other Applying the Same Paraphrastically and Historically to the Text* (London, 1645; orig. Edinburgh, 1593), sig. A2^{r-v}, 1–59; see also K. Firth, *Apocalyptic Tradition*, 133–43; and P. Christianson, *Reformers and Babylon*, 97–99. The first edition was published in Edinburgh in 1593 and a second edition appeared in London in 1611.

8. J. Napier, *Plaine Discovery*, 1, 2, 5, 9, 10, 17–18, 27, 29–44. For Alsted, see H. Hotson, *Paradise Postponed: Johann Heinrich Alsted and the Birth of Calvinist Millenarianism* (Dordrecht, 2001).

9. See J. Mede, *The Works of J. Mede: Corrected and Enlarged According to the Author's Own Manuscripts*, ed. J. Worthington (London, 1672), 1–35, 36–42 (for the "Life" and "Additionals to the Author's Life" of Mede), esp. 12–13; K. Firth, *Apocalyptic Tradition*, 213–26; B. W. Ball, *Great Expectation*, 116–19, 172–73; P. Christianson, *Reformers and Babylon*, 123–30; and J. Jue, *Heaven*, 119–21 (for anti-chiliasm).

10. J. Worthington, general preface to J. Mede, *Works*, sigs ★★2^v, ★★★★2^r, ★★★★4^v. For Mede and Christian Hebraism, see J. Jue, *Heaven*, 128–32.

11. J. Mede, *Works*, 419–23.

12. Ibid., 423–24.

13. Ibid., 425–26.

14. Ibid., 427–32 (and J. Worthington, general preface to ibid., sig. ★★★4^{r-v}); for Brightman, see K. Firth, *Apocalyptic Tradition*, 164–76.

15. Ibid., 451–53; and K. Haugen, "Apocalypse (a User's Manual): Joseph Mede, the Interpretation of Prophecy, and the Dream Book of Achmet," *The Seventeenth Century* 25 (2010): 215–39, esp. 216–22.

16. Hartlib to Mede, 24 January 1638 and Mede to Hartlib, 29 January 1638 in J. Mede, *Works*, 2:1075–76, 1076–77. See also D. Brady, *The Contribution of British Writers Between 1560 and 1830 to the Interpretation of Revelation 13.16–18 (the Number of the Beast): A Study in the History of Exegesis* (Tübingen, 1983), 111–19; and R. Iliffe, "Mathematics of the Two Books."

17. H. Hammond, *A Paraphrase and Annotation upon All the Books of the New Testament, Briefly Explaining All the Difficulties Thereof* (London, 1653). For Grotius, see J. Van Berg, "Grotius's Views on Antichrist and Apocalyptic Thought in England," in *Hugo Grotius, Theologian: Essays in Honour of G.H.M. Posthumus Meyjes*, ed. H. J. M. Nellen et al. (Leiden, 1992), 169–82; and for Hammond, see J. W. Packer, *The Transformation of Anglicanism, 1643–1660 with Special Reference to Henry Hammond* (Manchester, 1969), 89–94.

18. H. More, *An Explanation of the Grand Mystery of Godliness* (London, 1660), xii–xiii, xxiv–xxvi, 172, 175, 177–78, 182–99 (for his analysis of the most important of Mede's synchronisms), and 203; R. Ward, *The Life of Henry More* (London, 1710), 165–68. More noted bitter attacks on his views in letters to Anne Conway of 24 May 1664 and 10 July 1665; see M. H. Nicolson and S. Hutton, *Conway Letters*, 223, 243. See also W. Johnston, "The Anglican Apocalypse in Restoration England," *Journal of Ecclesiastical History.* 55 (2004): 467–501, esp. 479–83.

19. H. More, *A Modest Enquiry into the Mystery of Iniquity, The First Part, Containing a Careful and Impartial Delineation of the True Idea of Antichristianism…* (London, 1664), signature A4^r, 180.

20. H. More, *Synopsis Prophetica: The Second Part of the Enquiry into the Mystery of Iniquity* (London, 1664), 185, 187, 202, 207, 213–14. For Baxter, see the excellent analysis in W. Lamont, *Baxter and the Millennium.*

21. H. More, *Synopsis*, 215–25 (for the list of rhetorical techniques), 227–59 (the Alphabet), and 259–61 (the Rules). See also S. Hutton, "More, Newton and the Language of Biblical Prophecy," in *The Books of Nature and Scripture*, 39–53.

22. H. More, *Synopsis*, 193–204, esp. 193, 200–204.

23. H. More, *The Two Last Dialogues, Treating of the Kingdom of God Within Us and Without Us* (London, 1668), sigs. a4d^v and a6^r, 46–49, 67–68, 117–95, esp. 117–22, 125–26, 128–62, 164–86, 193–98; H. More, *An Exposition of the Seven Epistles to The Seven Churches; Together with a Brief Discourse of Idolatry, with Application to the Church of Rome* (London, 1669); H. More, *Visionum Apocalypticarum Ratio Synchronisticis*, in H. More, *Henrici Mori Cantabrigiensis Opera Theologica …* (London, 1675), 21–29. See also More to Anne Conway, 2 January 1672 and More to Anne Conway, 5 February 1672 in M. H. Nicolson and S. Hutton, *Conway Letters*, 522–25, 528–29.

24. Yahuda Ms. 1.1 fols. 1^r–2^r. For a classic account of the proper demeanour of an exegete, see J. Worthington, general preface to J. Mede, *Works*, sigs. ★★★★4^v–5^r.

25. Yahuda Ms. 1.1 fols. 1^r, 3^{r-v}, 7^r.

26. Yahuda Ms. 1.1 fols. 1^r–2^r, 5^r–6^r. See also S. Mandelbrote, "'A Duty of the Greatest Moment': Sir Isaac Newton and the Writing of Biblical Criticism," *British Journal for the History of Science* 26 (1993): 281–302.

27. Yahuda Mss. 1.1 fol. 8^r, 9.1 fols. 3^r–4^r, and 9.2; and Keynes Ms. 5. The essay in Yahuda Ms. 9.2 was entitled "The Second Book," though it deals with the topic of the third book in his general outline. The outline is in Newton's hand though nearly all the rest of the document is in the hand of Humphrey Newton. Yahuda Ms. 9.1 was substantially changed from the earlier version at Yahuda Ms. 1.1, but a number of explications of prophetic images remained in a revised form.

28. Yahuda Ms. 1.1a fols. 1^{r-v} (a subsequently deleted draft of Yahuda Ms. 1.1 fol. 28^r).

29. Yahuda Ms. 1.1 fols. 3^v–8^r, 12^{r-v}. For references to the degree to which one could achieve certainty in prophetic interpretations, and to Newton's wish to avoid disputes in religion, see Yahuda Mss 1.1 fols. 10^r, 12^r; 1.1a fols. 1^r–2^r; 1.4 fol. 42^v, and 1.6 fols. 9^v, 16^r.

30. Yahuda Ms. 1.1 fols. 15^r, 18^r; see R. Delgado-Moreira, "Newton's Treatise on Revelation: The Use of a Mathematical Discourse," *Historical Research* 79 (2006): 224–46. Newton's dismay at Richard Bentley's request that he offer a mathematical demonstration that prophetic days were real years is related in *Memoirs of the Life and Writings of William Whiston*, 2 vols. (London, 1749–50), 1:106–7.

31. Yahuda Ms. 1.1 fols. 10^r, 12^{r-v}, 13^r, and 16^r.

32. Yahuda Ms. 1.1 fols. 12^{r-v}, 13^r.

33. Yahuda Ms. 1.1 fols. 20^r–23^r, esp. 22^r (with the earlier version headed "Definitions" at ibid., fols. 24^r–27^r).

34. "The Proof" at Yahuda Ms. 1.1 fols. 28^r–55^r is a later draft of Yahuda 1.1a fols. 1^r–31^r, which originally followed immediately on from the earlier draft in Yahuda Ms. 1.1 headed "Definitions." For horns, see Yahuda Ms. 1.1 fols. 38^v–39^r; and for eyes, ibid., fols. 38^v–39^v.

35. Yahuda Mss. 9.2 fol. 63^r (for external visible actions); and 9.1. fols. 19^v–21^v. For pertinent comments on these passages, see S. Snobelen, "Lust, Pride and Ambition: Isaac Newton and the Devil," in *Newton and Newtonianism*, ed. J. E. Force and S. Hutton (Dordrecht, 2004), 155–81.

36. Hobbes, *Leviathan*, Yahuda Mss. 9.1 fol. 21^v and 15.7 fol. 133^v, and Newton to Locke, 3 May 1692, in H. W. Turnbull et al., *Correspondence*, 3:214. More generally, see D. P. Walker, *Unclean Spirits: Possession and Exorcism in France and England in the Late Sixteenth and Early Seventeenth Centuries* (London, 1981), ch. 3.

37. Burnet to Newton, 13 January 1681, in H. W. Turnbull et al., *Correspondence*, 2:323, 326. For accommodationism, see A. Funkenstein, *Theology and the Scientific Imagination from the Middle Ages to the Seventeenth Century* (Princeton, 1986), 213–43; and R. Westman, "The Copernicans and the Churches," in D. Lindberg and R. Numbers, eds, *God and Nature. Historical Essays on the Encounter between Christianity and Science* (Berkeley, 1986).

38. Newton to Burnet, c. 20 January 1681, in H. W. Turnbull et al., *Correspondence*, 2:331–32. See also S. Mandelbrote, "Isaac Newton and Thomas Burnet: Biblical Criticism and the Crisis of Late Seventeenth-Century England," in J. E. Force and R. Popkin, eds, *The Books of Nature and Scripture*, 149–78; and S. Snobelen, "'Not in the Language of the Astronomers': Isaac Newton, the Scriptures, and the Hermeneutics of Accommodation," in *Nature and Scripture in the Abrahamic Religions: Up to 1700*, ed. J. van der Meer and S. Mandelbrote (Leiden, 2008), 501–40.

39. Newton to Burnet, c. 20 January 1681, in H. W. Turnbull et al., *Correspondence*, 2:333–34.

40. CUL Add. Ms. 3965 fols. 23^r, 47^r; I. Newton, *Principia*, 408–15, esp. 411 and 413–14. Newton's use of accommodationism to explain geocentric passages is at CUL Add. Ms. 4005 fols. 39^r–42^r. For earlier remarks in "De Gravitatione" on the need to abstract thoughts from sensible qualities, see A. R. Hall and M. B. Hall, *Unpublished Scientific Papers of Isaac Newton* (Cambridge, 1962), 122, 132.

41. I. Newton, *Principia*, 414.

42. Ernan McMullin offers a clear exposition of the exegetical principles in Galileo's Letter in "Galileo on Science and Scripture," in *The Cambridge Companion to Galileo*, ed. P. Machamer (Cambridge, 1998), 271–347.

43. CUL Add. Ms. 3965 fol. 47ʳ; I. Newton, *Principia*, 414. For Newton's appeal to "*quam proxime*" arguments, see G. Smith, "The Methodology of the *Principia*," in *The Cambridge Companion to Newton*, ed. R. Iliffe and G. Smith, 2nd ed. (Cambridge, 2016), 187–228.

44. Yahuda Ms. 1.1 fols. 14ʳ (this is formally equivalent to Rule 12) and 15ʳ–16ʳ. For Bale, see P. Christianson, *Reformers and Babylon*, 15–16.

45. Yahuda Ms. 1.2 fol. 1ʳ; Keynes Ms. 5 fols. 25ʳ–26ʳ, 30ʳ; Yahuda Mss. 1.1 fol. 12ᵛ, 8.1 fol. 6ʳ (cf. New College Oxford Ms. 361.2 fol. 135ᵛ) and 1.4 fol. 6ʳ.

46. Yahuda Mss. 1.1 fol. 27ᵛ, 1.7 fol. 33ʳ; and Yahuda Ms. 1.4 fols. 62ʳ, 133ʳ–134ʳ (cf. Yahuda Ms. 1.6 fol. 11ʳ).

47. Yahuda Mss. 1.3 fol. 11ʳ and 1.2 fols. 9ʳ–10ʳ; Keynes Ms. 32ʳ. Compare with Yahuda Mss. 1.7 fol. 5ʳ⁻ᵛ, 1.6 fol. 11ʳ; and Keynes Ms. 5 fol. 29ʳ.

48. Yahuda Ms. 1.2 fols. 11ʳ, 17ʳ ("Position 4"), 22ʳ, 31ʳ, 36ʳ–41ʳ (for "Position 6," which examines the horns as kingdoms); 41ʳ–53ʳ (esp. 44ʳ for the equivalence of the two-horned beast and the Whore); cf. Yahuda Ms. 1.3 fols. 47ʳ–48ʳ, 51ʳ. Yahuda Ms. 1.2 fol. 9ʳ embellishes a main "Position" with a number of "Questions" and responses; compare with Keynes Ms. 5 fols. 11ʳ–23ʳ. At Yahuda Ms. 9.1 fols. 4ᵛ, 21ᵛ, Newton argued that the metamorphic discourse of Ovid and others was all of a piece with the ancient figurative language.

49. Yahuda Mss. 1.2 fols. 23ʳ–24ᵛ, 26ʳ–30ʳ (for the subject of the prophecy being depraved pseudo-Christians), and 53ʳ–56ʳ; 1.3 fols. 82ʳ–86ʳ; compare with Keynes Ms. 5 fol. 23ʳ⁻ᵛ.

50. Yahuda Mss. 1.2 fols. 57ʳ–63ᵛ (Pos. 9), esp. 60ʳ–62ʳ; 1.3 fols. 65ʳ–78ᵛ (Prop. 15), esp. 66ʳ, 68ʳ, 69ʳ, 72ʳ, 74ʳ, and 86ʳ, and 88ʳ (for a draft of passage concerning the notable times of the Apostasy); 9.2 fols. 97ʳ–122ʳ, esp. 105ʳ–106ʳ (for Grotius and the little horn). Compare with Keynes Ms. 5 fols. 29ʳ–30ʳ, 32ʳ, 34ʳ, 37ʳ, 48ʳ, 50ʳ.

51. Yahuda Mss. 1.2 fols. 57ʳ–63ʳ (esp. 61ʳ) and 9.2 fol. 113ʳ. In the introduction to his "guide," Newton made a rare reference to "the reformations which have hitherto been made from Roman errors first by Waldenses and Albigenses and then by the Protestants": Yahuda Ms. 1.1 fol. 3ᵛ; see ibid., fol. 16ʳ for a justification of his own divisions.

52. Yahuda Mss. 1.2 fols. 12ʳ, 57ʳ; 1.3 fols. 21ʳ–26ʳ (for the war in heaven), and 67ʳ (for the identification of the woman with the saints); a more detailed analysis of the woman, the dragon, and the manchild from the late 1680s occurs at Yahuda Ms. 9.2 fols. 35ʳ–38ʳ.

53. Yahuda Mss. 1.3 fols. 27ʳ–29ʳ, 69ʳ–74ʳ, (esp. 70ʳ), 78ʳ–82ʳ, 1.4 fols. 150ʳ–151ᵛ, and 1.5 fols. 8ʳ–9ʳ.

54. Yahuda Mss. 1.1 fols. 20ʳ, 25ʳ; 1.3 fols. 66ʳ–67ʳ; and 9.2 fols. 59ʳ–63ʳ (for the division of the kingdom), 64ʳ–65ʳ (for the pairs of true and false churches), and 73ʳ–80ʳ (for the remnant and the saints being the two witnesses).

55. Yahuda Ms. 9.2 fols. 65ʳ, 68ʳ–70ʳ, 72ʳ–73ʳ.

56. H. More, *Apocalypsis Apocalypseos (or the Revelation of St. John the Divine Unveiled)* (London, 1680), H. More, *A Plain and Continued Exposition of the Several Prophecies or Divine Visions of the Prophet Daniel ... Whereunto Is Annexed a Threefold Appendage, Touching Three Main Points, the First, Relating to Daniel, the Other Two, to the Apocalypse* (London, 1681), lv–lvi, lxiii–lxv, lxxx; More to Anne Conway, 27 January 1679, in M. H. Nicolson and S. Hutton, *Conway Letters*, xvi, 447–48, and More to Sancroft, 2 January 1680, Bodleian Library, Tanner Ms. 38 fol. 115ʳ. The political contexts are discussed in J. R. Jones, *The First Whigs: The Politics of the Exclusion Crisis, 1678–83* (London, 1961), 74–114; and M. Knights, *Politics and Opinion in Crisis, 1678–81* (Cambridge, 2006).

57. More to Lord Conway, 2 January 1680 and More to Sharp, 16 August 1680; M. H. Nicolson and S. Hutton, *Conway Letters*, 477–78, 478–79, with changes based on the original (BL. Add. Ms. 4276 fol. 41ʳ). More generally, see R. Iliffe, "Making a Shew: Apocalyptic Hermeneutics and Christian Idolatry in the Work of Isaac Newton and Henry More," in J. E. Force and R. Popkin, *The Books of Nature and Scripture*, 55–88.

58. Newton to Hooke, 28 November 1679, in H. W. Turnbull et al., *Correspondence*, 2:300, 303n2; More to Sharp, 16 August 1680, in M. H. Nicolson and S. Hutton, *Conway Letters*, 478.

59. M. H. Nicolson and S. Hutton, *Conway Letters*, 479, with my own variant readings from the original.

60. Ibid. Hayter's work was *The Meaning of the Revelation, or a Paraphrase with Questions on the Revelation of John: In Which the Synchronisms of J. Mede, and the Expositions of Other Interpreters Are Called into Question* (London, 1675). See in particular 98–102, 113, 128–29, 149–52, 215–16. The D. N. B. records that in April 1683, shortly before his death the following year, Hayter had his work *Errata Mori: The Errors of Henry More Contained in His Epilogue Annex'd to His Exposition of the Revelation of St. John* ready for the press, although it was never printed.

61. M. H. Nicolson and S. Hutton, *Conway Letters*, 479.

62. H. More, *A Plain and Continued Exposition*, 266–69. Newton's copy of More's work, inscribed as being a gift from the author, is now in the Bancroft Library, University of California, Berkeley, BS1556.M67 P5/1681. I am grateful to the library for providing me with images of pages with Newton's remarks.

63. Ibid., 272.

64. Ibid., 273–74.

65. Ibid., 273, 277.

CHAPTER 8

1. Yahuda Ms 1.7 fol. 66ʳ; see also S. Horsley, ed., *Opera Omnia*, 5 vols. (London, 1779–85), 5:449–50.

2. K. Firth, *Apocalyptic Tradition*, 91–107; P. Christianson, *Reformers and Babylon*; P. Collinson, *The Birthpangs of Protestant England: Religious and Cultural Change*

in the Sixteenth and Seventeenth Centuries (London: Macmillan, 1991), 1–27; G. H. Turnbull, *Hartlib, Dury and Comenius* (Liverpool, 1938), 371–72; C. Webster, *The Great Instauration* (London, 1975), 9–11, 32–34, 126–27, 144. For Antichrist, see C. Hill, *Antichrist in Seventeenth Century England*, rev. ed. (London, 1990); and P. Lake, "The Significance of the Elizabethan Identification of the Pope as Antichrist," *Journal of Ecclesiastical History* 31 (1980): 161–78.

3. J. Napier, *Plaine Discovery*, 4–9, 11–15, 54, 56–57, and esp. 58–59 (for the beginning of the reign of Antichrist in 313 or 316). See also K. Firth, *Apocalyptic Tradition*, 143–45; P. Christianson, *Reformers and Babylon*, 97–100, and A. Grafton, *Joseph Scaliger: A Study in the History of Classical Scholarship*, 2 vols. (Oxford; New York, 1983 and 1993). Totila died in 552.

4. K. Firth, *Apocalyptic Tradition*, 162–69, 172; P. Christianson, *Reformers and Babylon*, 93–94, 100–103.

5. K. Firth, *Apocalyptic Tradition*, 169–75; P. Christianson, *Reformers and Babylon*, 103–6.

6. J. Alsted, *Diatribe de Milleannis Apocalypticis* (Frankfurt, 1627); see K. Firth, *Apocalyptic Tradition*, 209–12; and H. Hotson, *Paradise Postponed: Johann Heinrich Alsted and the Birth of Calvinist Millenarianism* (Dordrecht, 2000).

7. J. Mede, *Works*, 491–97; J. Worthington, *Miscellanies . . .* (London, 1704), 49–54.

8. J. Mede, *Works*, 498–510.

9. Ibid., 442–62.

10. Ibid., 462–66.

11. J. Mede, *Works*, 526–30. After the Glorious Revolution of 1688–89, bishops Sancroft and Lloyd, when entering into a discussion of the relevance of Revelation to contemporary political events ("the final destruction of Antichrist"), claimed to "approve of Mr Mead's way of Interpretation"; see E. S. De Beer, ed., *The Diary of John Evelyn*, 6 vols. (London, 1955), 4:636.

12. J. Mede, *Works*, 530–34; K. Firth, *Apocalyptic Tradition*, 218–23; J. Jue, *Heaven upon Earth*, 179–80.

13. Yahuda Ms. 1.4 fols. 153^r–163^r, esp. 156^r–160^r.

14. Yahuda Mss. 1.4 fols. 160^r–163^r and 1.5 fol. 11^r; at Yahuda Ms. 1.4 fol. 163^r Newton stated that he had treated the relationship between the Son and the Father at more length in another place, although it is not clear what this text is.

15. Yahuda Ms. 1.4 fols. 167^r–197^r, esp. 168^r, 169^r, 174^r, 176^r, 181^r, 182^r, 183^r, 189^r, 194^r, 196^r; at Yahuda Ms. 10b fol. 3^r Newton gave his reasons for disagreeing with Mede on dating the end of the third seal. There are earlier drafts (in a propositional form) at Yahuda Mss. 1.4 fols. 20^r–26^r; cf. Yahuda Ms. 1.8 fols. 1^r–12^r and Keynes Ms. 5 fols. 64^r–71^r. For Gibbon's account of these events, see E. Gibbon, *The History of the Decline and Fall of the Roman Empire*, 3 vols., ed. D. Womersley (orig. 1776–88; London, 1995), 1:559–80.

16. Yahuda Ms. 1.4 fols. 30^r–33^r, esp. 31^r (for the opening of the sixth seal in 312); 197^r–209^r (esp. 197^r, 202^r–204^r), 148^r–152^r. For Licinius, see Gibbon, *History*, 1:431–44.

17. Yahuda Ms. 1.4 fols. 12^r–17^r, 202^r, 208^r–209^v; Keynes Ms. 5 fols. 71^r–75^r, esp. 72^r.

18. Yahuda Ms. 1.5 fols. 1^r–6^r, 10^r–11^r, 12^r, and the extensively redrafted account of the ten horns at 13^r–73^r. For Constans's support of Athanasius, see E. Gibbon, *History*, 1:802–5, and for Constantius II's victory over Magnentius and his support for homoianism, ibid., 1:678–83, 792–810.

19. Yahuda Mss. 1.4 fol. 109^v; 1.5 fols. 6^r–7^r, 12^r–13^r; and 2.2 fols. 7^r–10^r. On the various stratagems by which Christian idolatry was promoted, see Keynes Ms. 5 fols. 78^r–83^r; Yahuda Mss. 2.3 passim; 9.1 fols. 17^r–25^r; 9.2 fols. 99^r–104^r; 10.1 fols. 2^r, 5$^{r–v}$ (a draft of Yahuda Ms. 1.4 fols. 67^r–68^r), 9^r, and 12^v–19^v (fol. 15^v is a draft of Yahuda Ms. 1.4 fol. 109^v); Yahuda Ms. 18 passim and Yahuda Ms. 39.

20. Yahuda Mss. 1.4 fols. 151^v–163^r; 1.5 fols. 7^r, 11^r, 74^r–85^r (for the role of the two-horned beast and the rise to dominance of the pope); compare with Yahuda Ms. 1.4 fols. 47^r–48^r for Athanasius's "broaching" of a new religion in 363. For Arianism in the West in the fourth century, see D. Williams, *Ambrose of Milan and the End of the Nicene-Arian Conflicts* (Oxford, 1995).

21. Yahuda Mss. 1.4 fols. 50^r, 52^r, 53^r, 65^v–66^v; 9.3 fols. 1^r–11^r, esp. 7^r–9^r (Yahuda Ms. 9.3 is a later and expanded draft of Yahuda Ms. 18 fols. 1^r–2^v). See M. Wiles, *Archetypal Heresy*, 44.

22. Yahuda Mss. 1.7 fols. 1^r–3^v (for the activities of Gratian and Theodosius in the late 370s) and 1.4 fols. 34^v, 42^v (for not wishing to dispute about religion—and cf. Yahuda Ms. 1.6 fol. 9^v), 210$^{r–v}$.

23. Yahuda Ms. 1.4 fols. 47^r–48^r, 49^r–50^r. For Gibbon, Theodosius was the first of the emperors "baptised in the true faith of the Trinity [and] his religious opinions were never affected by the specious texts, the subtle arguments, and the ambiguous creeds of the Arian doctors"; see E. Gibbon, *History*, 2:26–27. For the Council at Constantinople and the Theodosian edicts against heretics, see ibid., 2:33–35, esp. 34n42, 36–40.

24. Yahuda Ms. 1.4 fols. 50^r, 52^r–54^r, from J. Mede, *Works*, 457; compare with the same passage at Yahuda 9.2 fol. 89^r–90^r (in Humphrey Newton's hand and thus from the mid-1680s to the late 1680s), where Mede is acknowledged.

25. Yahuda Ms. 1.4 fols. 109^v, 66^v, 67^r–68^r (for the attack on backsliders; note the draft of this passage at Yahuda Ms. 10c fols. 5^r–6^r), 68^r–69^r, 72^r, 79^r; compare ibid., 74^v, 99^r–100^r and Yahuda Ms. 2.5 fol. 55^r. For the heathen oracle, see Augustine, *City of God*, Book 18, chs. 53–54; Newton crossed out the "St" in "St Austin" on Yahuda 1.4 fol. 79^r. For Baronius, see Newton's notes on the Arian controversy from the *Annals* at Yahuda Ms. 14 fols. 104^r–105^r. These notes are followed by further excerpts from Salvian, Sand, and Machiavelli's *History of Florence*.

26. Yahuda Ms. 1.4 fols. 84^r, 92^r, 95^r–105^r (esp. 102^r, 104^r–105^r). Salvian, writing in the fifth century, was unable to understand why God would have let the Arianised barbarians overrun the Roman Empire and assumed that their Christianity was based on a faulty translation of Scripture; see M. Wiles, *Archetypal Heresy*, 46.

27. Yahuda Ms. 1.4 fol. 53^r. See E. Gibbon, *History*, 1:779n44, 2:32n40, and esp. 2:429–35; M. Wiles, *Archetypal Heresy*, 40–51; E. A. Thompson, "Christianity and

the Northern Barbarians," in *The Conflict Between Paganism and Christianity in the Fourth Century*, ed. A. Momigliano (Oxford, 1963); P. Heather, *Goths and Romans, 332–489* (Oxford, 1991); and P. Heather and J. Matthews, *The Goths in the Fourth Century* (Liverpool, 1991), 141–53.

28. Yahuda Ms. 1.4 fols. 58^r, 59^r, 60^r, 66^v. See also Yahuda Ms. 1.7 fols. 1^r–3^v, and E. Gibbon, *History*, 2:52. For insightful analysis of the situation facing Milanese homoians after the condemnation of Arian positions in the Council of Aquilea of 381, see D. Williams, *Ambrose of Milan*, ch. 7.

29. J. Mede, *Works*, 462–65.

30. Yahuda Ms. 1.6 fols. 1^r–2^r, 5^v, 8^r, 9^r, 12^r ("Marginall Notes") and note variants at Yahuda Mss. 1.4 fols. 107^r–138^r, esp. 127^r and 1.7 fols. 4^r–10^r and Keynes Ms. 5 fols. 76^r–78^r (and more generally 79^r–91^r). For drafts of the intricate analysis of the kingdoms corresponding to the ten horns of the beast, see Yahuda Ms. 1.5 fols. 12^r–74^r (esp. 22^r–24^r and 47^r for the irrelevance of modern authors).

31. Newton owned a copy of Grotius's edition of Procopius, Jordanes, Isidore of Seville, and Paul the Deacon's histories of the Goths and the gothic wars; Grotius, *Historia Gotthorum, Vandalorum, & Langobardorum . . .* (Amsterdam, 1655). See J. Harrison, *Library*, H722. For Gibbon's view, see his *History*, 2:68–69, 99–115, 121–64; F. M. Clover, *The Late Roman West and the Vandals* (Aldershot, 1993); and H. Wolfram, *The History of the Goths* (Berkeley, 1988). For Alaric, see E. Gibbon, *History*, 2:122–211 passim; and F. P. Stevens, *From Constantine to Alaric* (Liphook, 1984). Like Zosimus, Sozomen relied heavily on the pagan history of Olympiodorus for his account of the period after Theodosius.

32. Yahuda Ms. 1.6 fols. 17^r, 18^r, 19^r, 20^r–24^r; there is a draft at Yahuda Ms. 1.7 fols. 10^r–14^r and a later version at Yahuda 1.4 fols. 138^r–147^r; at 138^r the start of the trumpet is dated to 408. For detailed notes and drafts of a treatise on the ten kingdoms (viz., the Vandals, Suevians, Spanish Alans, Gallic Alans, Burgundians, Britons, Franks, Visigoths, Hunns, and the kingdom of Ravenna), see Yahuda 1.5 fols. 15^r–73^r, esp. 69^r. See also E. Gibbon, *History*, 2:156–211.

33. Yahuda Ms. 1.6 fols. 21^r–24^r and Yahuda Ms. 1.4 fol. 144^r. See also Keynes Ms. 5 fols. 92^r–97^r, esp. 96^r for the lamentations of Christians against God's treatment of them.

34. Yahuda Ms. 1.6 fols. 25^r–44^r, esp. 25^r–26^v, and 27^r; see also Yahuda Ms. 1.7 fols. 14^r–20^r; Keynes Ms. 5 fols. 98^r–110^r (esp. 98^r and 100^r); and E. Gibbon, *History*, 2:277–362.

35. Yahuda Ms. 1.6 fols. 28^r, 29^r, 30^{r-v}, 32^r, 33^r; Keynes Ms. 5 fols. 103^r–107^r. Victor was bishop of Vita at the end of the fifth century. For a modern translation, see Victor of Vita, *History of the Vandal Persecution*, ed. J. Moorhead (Liverpool, 1992).

36. Yahuda Ms. 1.6 fols. 33^r–34^r; Keynes Ms. 5 fols. 108^r–109^r.

37. Yahuda Ms. 1.6 fol. 35^r–36^r and note the more detailed commentary on Catholic persecution at Keynes Ms. 5 fols. 109^r–110^r. The analysis in Yahuda Ms. 39 is a vivid extension of Yahuda Ms. 1.4 fol. 104^r concerning the nature of persecutors.

38. Yahuda Ms. 1.6 fols. 35^r, 39^r–40^r; cf. Keynes Ms. 5 fols. 103^r–108^r. For Gibbon on the credulity and legends of the monks, see E. Gibbon, *History*, 2:428, 441–44.

39. Yahuda Ms. 1.6 fols. 35^v, 40^{r-v}.

40. Yahuda Ms. 1.6 fols. 40^r–41^r; compare with Yahuda 9.3 fols. 9^r–10^r. See also E. Gibbon, *History*, 2:436, 439–40.

41. Yahuda Ms. 1.6 fols. 41^r–44^r. In the context of the banishment of the cavilling priests, Gibbon also noted from Victor that "the practice of a conference, which the Catholics had so frequently used to insult and punish their obstinate antagonists, was retorted against themselves." See E. Gibbon, *History*, 2:437–38.

42. Yahuda Ms. 1.6 fols. 45^r, 47^r, and in the following order, 45^r, 48^v, 46^v, 49^r, 47^v. See also the earlier draft at Yahuda 1.7 fols. 21^r–30^v, esp. 28^r–30^r where there is a learned scholarly analysis of the ending of the period of the fourth trumpet. Compare this with Yahuda Ms. 1.6 fols. 45^r–49^r and the later treatment at Keynes Ms. 5 fols. 111^r–121^r. For Belisarius's entry into Rome and the effect of the Lombards, see E. Gibbon, *History*, 2:654–58, 853–66.

43. Keynes Ms. 5 fols. 115^r–118^r, 119^r.

44. J. Mede, *Works*, 466–71. In general, see G. J. Toomer, *Eastern Wisedome and Learning: The Study of Arabic in Seventeenth-Century England* (Oxford, 1996).

45. Yahuda Ms. 1.7 fols. 30^v–41^r, esp. 30^v, 31^r, 32^r, 34^r (for the repetition of Mede's claim), 35^r. There is a later treatment of the fifth trumpet and vial at Keynes Ms. 5 fols. 122^r–130^r. At Yahuda Ms. 1.7 fol. 36^v Newton noted information from Pococke's comments on the origins and mores of the Arabs in his *Specimen Historia Arabum, sive Gregorii Abul Farajii* (1650), and in a rare performance, he wrote a number of words in Arabic. See Yahuda Ms. 14 fols. 69^r–70^r for notes from Pococke, and fols. 157^r–158^r for notes "Ex Elmacino." Newton paid 9 shillings for his copy of Elmacinus, *Historia Saraceni … a Muhammede … usque ad initium imperij Atabacæi … Latinè reddita operâ ac studio T. Erpenii. Accedit & R. Ximenez Historia Arabum …* (Lugduni Batavorum, 1625), noting that it was worth a lot more; see J. Harrison, *Library*, H552.

46. Yahuda Ms. 1.7 fols. 32^r–37^r, 38^r–42^r, and Keynes Ms. 5 fols. 126^r–127^r; compare with J. Mede, *Works*, 470.

47. J. Mede, *Works*, 472–77.

48. Yahuda Ms. 1.7 fols. 42^r–66^r, esp. 44^r–46^r, 47^r–51^r, 56^r. There is a draft at Yahuda Ms. 1.8 fols. 13^r–24^r (the map is at fols. 17a^r–18^r) and note Yahuda Ms. 10c fols. 1^r–4^v; Mede's table is in his *Works*, 472. In 1672 Newton had edited Varenius's *Geography*, though there is no evidence that he contributed anything substantial to it. The second edition, *Geographia generalis … emendata, & … aucta & illustrata. Ab I. Newton. Ed 2ª auctior & emendatior* (Cambridge, 1681) was, despite the title, exactly the same as the previous version.

49. Yahuda Ms. 1.7 fols. 42^r–66^r, esp. 42^r, 44^r, 51^r–52^r, 53^r–54^r (for the action of the sixth vial), 62^r–63^r, 64^r–66^r. Compare with Yahuda Ms. 1.8 fol. 8^v and Keynes Ms. 5 fol. 133^r. The earlier draft at Yahuda Ms. 10c fols. 7^r–8^v dates the onset of the

sixth trumpet to 1260 or 1261; there is a later treatment of the same period at Keynes Ms. 5 fols. 130^r–135^r.

50. Yahuda Mss. 1.7 fols. 65^r–66^r and 1.4 fols. 3^r, 11^r–12^r.

51. For Newton's procedures in mathematical physics, see I. B. Cohen, *The Newtonian Revolution* (Cambridge, 1983); and G. Smith, "The Methodology of the *Principia*."

CHAPTER 9

1. See W. Johnston, "Revelation and the Revolution of 1688–1689," *Historical Journal* 48 (2005): 351–89.

2. J. P. Kenyon, "The Commission for Ecclesiastical Causes, 1686–1688: A Reconsideration," *Historical Journal* 34 (1991): 727–36; A. MacIntyre, "The College, King James II and the Revolution, 1687–8," in *Magdalen College and the Crown: Essays for the Tercentenary of the Restoration of the College 1688*, ed. L. Brockliss, G. Harris, and A. MacIntyre (Oxford, 1988), 31–82; G. V. Bennett, "Loyalist Oxford and the Revolution," in *The History of the University of Oxford*, 5 vols., ed. L. Sutherland and L. Mitchell (Oxford, 1988), 3:10–21. J. R. Bloxam, ed., *Magdalen College and James II, 1686–1688* (Oxford, 1886), contains most of the documents relevant to the affair. Anthony Wood reported on the events in his *Life and Times* (Oxford, 1892), 2:416–24, 431; 3:186, 214–18, 246–51.

3. H. W. Turnbull et al., *Correspondence*, 2:467–68. Basset was only officially admitted as master on 7 March. Secondary material on the episode is available in T. B. Howell and T. J. Howell, eds, *A Complete Collection of State Trials and proceedings for High Treason and other Crimes and Misdemeanours from the earliest Period to the Year 1783*. 21 vols. (London, 1809–28), 11:1315–39; C. H. Cooper, *Annals of the University of Cambridge*, 5 vols. (Cambridge, 1842–1908), 3:614–43, esp. 618–22; P. C. Vellacott, "The Struggle of James the Second with the University of Cambridge," in *A. W. Ward: In Memoriam*, ed. W. E. Barnes (Cambridge, 1924), 81–101; M. Goldie, "Joshua Basset, Popery and Revolution," in *Sidney Sussex College, Cambridge: Historical Essays*, ed. D. E. D. Beales and H. B. Nisbet (Woodbridge, 1996), 111–30.

4. See Charles Montagu to George Stepney, 6 November 1686, National Archives, SP 105/82^{r-v}; H. W. Turnbull et al., *Correspondence*, 2:467–68; Lynnet to Alexander Akehurst, 19 April 1687; Trinity College Library Ms. O.11a.1^r; Keynes Ms. 130.10, 2nd series of foliation, 2–3 (note of 31 August 1726).

5. Keynes Ms. 118 fol. 3^r. Other documents relevant to Newton's preparation for the case are Keynes Ms. 144A and B, Ms. 145 (Appendix B), and Ms. 149. Humphrey wrote out the text of the Commission for Newton (Keynes Ms. 122) and later copied out the "Account of ye Cambridge Case," now Keynes Ms. 113. This was published the following year as *An Account of the Cambridge Case* (London, 1689).

6. Keynes Ms. 121 fol. 1ʳ⁻ᵛ. *Godden v. Hales* involved a Roman Catholic defendant, Sir Edward Hales, who had already been found guilty at Rochester Assizes of holding military office under the Crown without having taken the required oaths. His coachman, Arthur Godden, sued Hales for the £500 to which he was entitled as informer under the Test Act. See T. Harris, *Revolution: The Great Crisis of the English Monarchy, 1685–1720* (London, 2006), 192–94; H. Nenner, *By Colour of Law: Legal Culture and Constitutional Politics in England, 1660–1689* (Chicago, 1977), 99–101; M. Landon, *The Triumph of the Lawyers: Their Role in English Politics, 1678–1689* (Tuscaloosa, Ala., 1970), 201–5; E. F. Churchill, "The Dispensing Power of the Crown in Ecclesiastical Affairs," *Law Quarterly Review* 151 (1922): 297–316 and 152 (1922): 420–34; and P. Birdsall, " 'Non Obstante': A Study of the Dispensing Power of English Kings," in *Essays on History and Politics in Honour of Charles Howard McIlwain* (Cambridge, 1934), 64–74. For the political use of necessity, see J. P. Somerville, *Politics and Ideology in England, 1603–1640* (London, 1986), 127–28, 157–59; and R. Tuck, *Philosophy and Government, 1572–1651* (Cambridge, 1993), 57–58, 88, 118–19, 219, 223–26.

7. T. B. Howell and T. J. Howell, *State Trials* 11:1330–32, 1337–38; P. C. Vellacott, "Struggle," 98–99; C. H. Cooper, *Annals*, 3:621–68; Keynes Ms. 116 fol. 2ʳ. A copy of the Answer to the commissioners' questions concerning the non-admittance of Francis, which was read at the meeting of 27 April, is now Keynes Ms. 115 (reproduced in the manuscript version of the "Cambridge Case"; Keynes Ms. 113 fols. 3ʳ⁻ᵛ).

8. John Laughton to Arthur Charlett, 16 April 1687 and 6 June 1687; Bodleian Library, Ms. Ballard 23 fols. 11ʳ⁻ᵛ, 22ʳ; J. R. Bloxam, *Magdalen College*, 53–66, 68–70, 72–76 (for the evidence against Farmer), 79–80. Newton possessed a copy of a contemporary account of Fairfax's performance in front of the Commission, along with the response of the fellows. These are now Magdalen College Library Oxford, Ms. 432.

9. J. Mede, *Works*, 765–68, 775–77.

10. Ibid., 593, 602–3, 765–68, 771–72, 775–77.

11. Ibid., 535–37 (esp. 535 for Kimchi), 603–5, 771, 773–76; J. Jue, *Heaven*, 132–36; and esp. R. Smolinski, "The Logic of Millennial Thought, Sir Isaac Newton among His Contemporaries," in J. E. Force and R. H. Popkin eds, *Newton and Religion: Context, Nature and Influence* (Dordrecht, 1999), 259–90, esp. 261–62, 276–81.

12. J. Mede, *Works*, 613–19; H. More, *Grand Mystery of Godliness* (London, 1660), 232–41; T. Burnet, *Telluris Theoria Sacra ... Libri Duo Posteriores de Conflagratione Mundi, et de Futuro Rerum Statu* (London, 1689), 197; T. Burnet, *The Sacred Theory of the Earth ... 4 books* (London, 1697) 3:35–43, 55–61; 4:151–52. See M. C. Jacob and W. A. Lockwood, "Political Millenarianism and Burnet's *Sacred Theory*," *Science Studies* 2 (1972): 265–79, esp. 270–75; and R. Smolinski, "Logic," 267–70.

13. D. Cressener, *The Judgments of God upon the Roman Catholick Church ...* (London, 1689); P. Jurieu, *L'Accomplissement des propheties ou la deliverance prochaine*

del'Eglise (Rotterdam, 1686), partially translated as *The Accomplishment of the Scripture Prophecies, or the Approaching Deliverance of the Church* (London, 1687); and P. Jurieu, *A Continuation of the Accomplishment of the Scripture Prophecies, or a Large Deduction of Historical Evidences, Proving, That the Papacy Is the Real Antichristian Kingdom* (London, 1688).

14. D. Cressener, *Judgments*, sigs. A4^{r-v}, b1^{r-v}, 28–33; see W. Lamont, *Baxter and the Millennium*, 60–61; and W. Johnston, *Revelation Restored*, 189–224.

15. CUL Add. Ms. 3996 fols. 26^v–30^v, 54^r–56^r, 90^v, 93^{r-v}, 115^r–116^v. See also J. E. McGuire and M. Tamny, "Newton's Astronomical Apprenticeship: Notes of 1664/5," *Isis* 76 (1985): 349–65.

16. CUL Add. Ms. 3996 fols. 93^v, 129^r.

17. CUL Add. Ms. 3996 fol. 101^r.

18. CUL Add. Ms. 3996 fol. 101^r. Mede's analysis of the physical and prophetic meanings of 2 Peter were published in J. Mede, *Works*, 613–17.

19. Yahuda Ms. 6 fols. 2^v–8^r (draft at ibid., fol. 3^v).

20. Yahuda Mss. 9.2 fols. 123^r–125^r and 6 fol. 3^v.

21. Yahuda Ms. 9.2 fols. 144^r–158^r (for the return of the Jews), esp. 147^r, 150^r, 157^r–158^r.

22. Yahuda Ms. 9.2 fols. 125^r–129^r.

23. Yahuda Ms. 9.2 fols. 128^r–129^r, 131^r–132^r (for the lake of fire as hell), 133^r–134^r, 162^r–164^r; Yahuda Ms. 6 fol. 3^r (for the dragon as the spirit of error).

24. Yahuda Mss. 6 fols. 8^r–10^r and 9.2 fols. 123^r and 135^r–136^r.

25. WACL Ms. fols. 54^r–56^r (for Athanasius's deceits) and 63^r–64^r; H. W. Turnbull et al., *Correspondence*, 3.39; Yahuda Mss. 6 fol. 2^v, 9.2 fols. 132^r–133^r. More generally, see N. Burns, *Christian Mortalism from Tyndale to Milton* (Cambridge, Mass., 1972), 17–24, 148–82; B. W. Ball, *Soul Sleepers: Christian Mortalism from Wycliffe to Priestley* (Cambridge, 2008), 97–126; and J. Force, "The God of Abraham and Isaac (Newton)," in J. E. Force and R. Popkin, *The Books of Nature and Scripture*, 179–200.

26. Yahuda Mss. 6 fols. 16^r–17^r and 9.2 fols. 140^r–141^r (for Noah). In the late 1680s treatise he followed Grotius and others in expressing some doubts about the status of the text, remarking that it was "commonly ascribed to Peter." If the text was by Peter, he concluded, then it could only be understood by the further comment that Christ's mission was one of restitution and not destruction; ibid., fol. 141^r. See Smolinski, "Logic," 263–64.

27. Yahuda Mss. 6 fols. 12^r–13^r and 9.2 fols. 134^r, 138^r–140^r, 168^r–169^r.

28. Yahuda Mss. 6 fols. 18^r–19^r and fols. 138^r–139^r; Keynes Ms. 130.11.

29. Yahuda Mss. 9.2 fols. 138^r, 139^r–140^r and 6 fols. 2^v, 16^r, 19^r (for the need to fill space with inhabitants). Newton would certainly have been aware of Mede's tentative discussions about the exact nature of saintly existence in his *Works*, e.g., 773–77, 812, and probably of More's speculations in *Grand Mystery*, 221–30.

30. R. Iliffe, *Early Biographies*, 1:241; Keynes Mss. 130.11; Newton to Bentley, 25 February 1693, in H. W. Turnbull et al., *Correspondence*, 3:253. For Newton's

history of chronology, see J. Z. Buchwald and M. Feingold, *Newton and the Origin of Civilization* (Princeton, 2013).

31. CUL Add. Ms. 3996 fol. 128ʳ; Newton to Briggs, 12 September 1682, and Newton to Bentley, 10 December 1692 and 17 January 1692/93, in *Correspondence*, 2:233–34; and I. Newton, *Principia*, 381.

32. Newton to Bentley, 10 December 1692 and Gregory Memorandum from May 1694, in H. W. Turnbull et al., *Correspondence*, 3:234, 384; R. Iliffe, *Early Biographies*, 1:240–41.

33. Newton to Bentley, 17 January 1693, in H. W. Turnbull et al., *Correspondence*, 3:239–40. For comments on Newton's reading of Galileo, and the latter's remarks on how the planets could have reached their current positions by falling from great heights, see A. Koyré, "Newton, Galileo and Plato," in Koyré, *Newtonian Studies* (Cambridge, Mass., 1965), 201–20.

34. Newton to Bentley, 10 December 1692; Gregory, Memorandum, in H. W. Turnbull et al., *Correspondence*, 3:234–35, 334; *Opticks*, 344, 378; Keynes Ms. 133. See more broadly D. C. Kubrin, "Cyclical Cosmos" and for relevant drafts of the passage in *Opticks*, see CUL Add. Ms. 3970 fols. 246ʳ–247ʳ, 295ʳ, 478ʳ.

35. I. Newton, *Principia*, 926; Keynes Ms. 130.11. Newton told Bentley that the Cartesian "hypothesis" according to which an exhausted sun turned into a comet, and this in turn into a planet was "plainly erroneous" since comets came into the solar system from outside and never stayed; see Newton to Bentley, 10 December 1692 in *The Correspondence of Isaac Newton*, 7 vols., ed. H. W. Turnbull et al. (Cambridge, 1959–81), 3:234. In the "Queries" to the *Opticks* he argued that the sun and the fixed stars were giant Earths, "vehemently hot"; see CUL Add. Ms. 3970 fols. 231ᵛ–232ʳ. See, also D. C. Kubrin, "Cyclical Cosmos," 325–46; S. Schaffer, "Comets and Idols: Newton's Cosmology and Political Theology," in *Action and Reaction: Proceedings of a Symposium to Commemorate the Tercentenary of Newton's Principia*, ed. P. Theerman and A. Seeff (Newark, 1993), 206–31; and S. Schechner, *Comets, Popular Culture, and the Birth of Modern Cosmology* (Princeton, 1997).

36. H. W. Turnbull et al., *Correspondence*, 3:334 and 4:402; Keynes Ms. 130.11 (Conduitt's emphasis); Newton, *Principia Mathematica* (London, 1726), 501, 525. See also A. Koyré and I. B. Cohen eds., with the assistance of A. Whitman, *Isaac Newton's Philosophiæ Naturalis Principia Mathematica*, 720–21, 757.

CHAPTER 10

1. For the various stages in the work that led from "De motu corporum in gyrum" to the *Principia*, see I. B. Cohen, *Introduction to Newton's Principia* (Cambridge, 1971). The account of Newton's meeting with Halley is recorded in the memorandum given by Abraham de Moivre to John Conduitt in November 1727; see University of Chicago Library, Joseph Halle Schaffner collection, Ms. 1075.7 fols. 3ʳ–3Aʳ.

2. In general, see S. Shapin and S. Schaffer, *Leviathan and the Air-Pump*; and R. Serjeantson, "Proof and Persuasion," in *The Cambridge History of Science*, vol. 3, *Early Modern Science*, ed. K. Park and L. Daston (Cambridge, 2006), 132–75.

3. See Lucas to Oldenburg, 13 October 1676, in H. W. Turnbull et al., *Correspondence*, 2:105. Newton's earliest attack on probabilism occurred in his Lucasian lectures of 1670; see A. Shapiro, *Optical Lectures*, 1:87–89. On the role of witnesses in English experimental philosophy, see S. Shapin, "Pump and Circumstance: Robert Boyle's Literary Technology," *Social Studies of Science* (1984): 481–520, esp. 495–97; S. Shapin and S. Schaffer, "Leviathan and the Air-Pump," 55–78, esp. 58–62; R.-M. Sargent, "Scientific Experiment and Legal Expertise: The Way of Experience in Seventeenth-Century England," *Studies in the History and Philosophy of Science* 20 (1989): 19–45, esp. 27–37; S. Shapin, *A Social History of Truth: Civility and Science in Seventeenth-Century England* (Chicago, 1994); and R. W. Serjeantson, "Testimony and Proof in Early-modern England," *Studies in History and Philosophy of Science* 30 (1999): 195–236.

4. For Newton's various views on hypotheses, see I. B. Cohen, "Newton's Conception of Hypotheses," *Physis* 8 (1966): 163–84; A. Shapiro, *Fits, Passions and Paroxysms: Physics, Method and Chemistry and Newton's Theories of Colored Bodies and Fits of Easy Reflection* (Cambridge, 1993), 12–18. For Boyle and hypotheses, see R. S. Westfall, "Unpublished Boyle Papers Relating to Scientific Method," *Annals of Science* 12 (1956): 63–73, 103–17; R.-M. Sargent, "Scientific Experiment," 34–44.

5. Hooke's initial (private) referee's report on Newton's paper was contained in Hooke to Oldenburg, 15 February 1672, and Newton's irate reply was his letter to Oldenburg for Hooke of 11 June 1672. Hooke's comment about Newton's reticence in stating what a ray of light was was mentioned in a letter to Lord Brouncker in June 1672; see H. W. Turnbull et al., *Correspondence*, 1:110–14, 171–88 (esp. 173–74, 187), 198–203 (esp. 201). On the evolution of the 'Hypotheses' of the 1687 edition of the *Principia* into the "Rules" and "Phenomena" of subsequent editions, see I. B. Cohen, *Introduction to Newton's Principia*, 24–27

6. For natural philosophy and print, see A. Johns, *The Nature of the Book: Print and Knowledge in the Making* (Chicago, 1998).

7. Humphrey Newton to John Conduit, 14 February 1727/28; Keynes Ms. 135.

8. National Archives C 6/239/29 and C 6/247/34; Newton to Todd, in H. W. Turnbull et al., *Correspondence*, 5:253–54. For litigiousness in the period, see C. Brooks, *Pettyfoggers and Vipers of the Commonwealth: The "Lower Branch" of the Legal Profession in Early Modern England* (Cambridge, 1986), 48–150.

9. Newton to a friend, 11 January 1687/88, in H. W. Turnbull et al., *Correspondence*, 2:502–4. The Storers in question were distantly related to the family with whom Newton lodged in the 1650s.

10. Linus to Oldenburg, 15 February 1675; Newton to Oldenburg, 10 January 1675/76, in ibid., 1:334, 410.

11. Newton to Oldenburg, 13 November 1675, in ibid., 1:357–58. See *The Diary of Robert Hooke, M.A., M.D., F.R.S., 1672–1680* (London, 1935), 148–49.

12. Newton to Oldenburg, 13 November 1675, 30 November 1675, and 7 December 1675, in H. W. Turnbull et al., *Correspondence*, 1:358, 359–61.

13. Gascoigne to Oldenburg, 15 December 1675, in ibid., 1:393–95. Oldenburg received it on 28 December (O.S.) and merely préçised it in the margins of the published version of Newton's letter of 10 January 1675/76; see *Philosophical Transactions*, 121 (1675/76), 503.

14. Newton to Oldenburg, 21 December 1675, in H. W. Turnbull et al., *Correspondence*, 1:404–6; T. Birch, ed., *The History of the Royal Society*, 4 vols. (London, 1756–57), 3:269; and R. Hooke, *Diary*, 199–200, 205–6. The entry for 11 December in Hooke's diary may mean that it was only Aubrey who talked about Newton's hypothesis at the club.

15. CUL Add. Ms. 3970 fol. 531^r.

16. CUL Add. Ms. 531^v; Newton to Oldenburg, 21 December 1675, in H. W. Turnbull et al., *Correspondence*, 1:405–6.

17. Newton to Oldenburg, 10 January 1675/76, in ibid., 1:407–11, esp. 408; part of this appeared in *Philosophical Transactions*, no. 121 (1675/76), 503–4. The reference to Digby did not appear in the printed version. For the priority dispute over the balance-spring watch, see R. Iliffe, "'In the Warehouse': Privacy, Property and Priority in the Early Royal Society," *History of Science* 30 (1992): 29–68.

18. Newton to Oldenburg, 10 January 1675/76; Oldenburg to Newton, 30 December 1675 (now lost), 15 January 1675/76 (now lost); Hooke to Newton, 20 January 1675/76, in H. W. Turnbull et al., *Correspondence*, 1, 406n1, 408–9, 411, 411n1. Hooke's response to the reading of Newton's letter on 20 January is recorded in *Diary*, 213. In 1672 he had perceptively noted Newton's agitation about appearing in public disputes and had told Brouncker that he would take it as a "great Injury" if anyone (he was presumably referring to Henry Oldenburg) made any of his private correspondence public. See H. W. Turnbull et al., *Correspondence*, 1:198.

19. Newton to Hooke, 5 February 1675/76 and to Oldenburg, 15 February 1675/76; ibid., 1:416–17, 420. Newton's accompanying "Discourse on Observations" concerning the optical phenomena associated with thin transparent plates was read out at the meeting of the Royal Society on 10 February 1675/76.

20. See B. Vickers, *In Defence of Rhetoric* (Oxford, 1989), 21–26; N. Jardine, *The Birth of the History and Philosophy of Science: Kepler's Defence of Tycho Versus Ursus* (Cambridge, 1986), 72–79; and U. Rublack, *The Astronomer and the Witch: Johannes Kepler's Fight for His Mother* (Oxford, 2015), 243–63. For the rhetorical tradition, see G. A. Kennedy, *Classical Rhetoric in Its Christian and Secular Tradition from Ancient to Modern Times* (Chapel Hill, 1980); and for the early modern period, see R. Schoeck, "Lawyers and Rhetoric in Sixteenth-Century England," in *Renaissance Eloquence*, ed. James Murphy (London, 1983), 274–91.

21. W. Cave, *Ecclesiastici: or, the History of the Lives, Acts, Death and Writings of the Most Eminent Fathers of the Church That Flourisht in the Fourth Century* (London, 1683); S. Parker, *Religion and Loyalty: or, a Demonstration of the Power of the Church Within Itself. The Supremacy of Sovereign Powers over It. The Duty of Passive Obedience, or Non-Resistance to All Their Commands* (London, 1684); "N.B.P.C Catholick" [Nathaniel Bacon], *The History of the Life and Actions of St. Athanasius, Together with the Rise, Growth and Down-fall of the Arian Heresie: Collected from Primitive Writers* (London, 1664). Sand's work was *Nucleus Historiæ Ecclesiasticæ*, 2 vols. (Amsterdam, 1669, 2nd ed., Cologne 1676).

22. N. Bacon, *Life and Actions*, 12–15, 23, 26–29. For modern accounts of the following episodes, see R. Williams, *Arius: Heresy and Tradition* (London, 1987); R. P. C. Hanson, *The Search for the Christian Doctrine of God: The Arian Controversy, 318–381* (Edinburgh, 1988); D. W.-H. Arnold, *The Early Episcopal Career of Athanasius of Alexandria* (Notre Dame, Ind., 1991); T. D. Barnes, *Athanasius and Constantius: Theology and Politics in the Constantinian Empire* (Cambridge, Mass., 1993), esp. 10–55.

23. W. Cave, *Ecclesiastici*, 62–64, 66–69; see R. Williams, *Arius*, 70–72. Eusebius of Nicomedia should not be confused with the historian Eusebius of Caesarea. More generally, see R. Iliffe, "Prosecuting Athanasius: Protestant Forensics and the Mirrors of Persecution," in *Newton and Newtonianism: New Studies*, ed. J. Force and S. Hutton (Kluwer, 2004), 43–72.

24. S. Parker, *Religion and Loyalty*, 349–59, 374–75, 413–14. Eutychius's work was edited and translated in two volumes by John Selden and Edward Pococke as *Contextia Gemmarum sive Eutychii Patriarchæ Alexandrini Annales* (Oxford, 1658–59).

25. S. Parker, *Religion and Loyalty*, 376–80, 400 (for more on the nature of plotting). Eusebius had subscribed to the Nicene Creed favouring the *homoousios* but had not subscribed to the anathemas against Arius. The Melitians were named after Melitius, bishop of Lycopolis, who had proposed an extensive term of exclusion before readmittance to the church for those who had lapsed into worshipping pagan idols under the persecution of 305–6. In this he disagreed with Peter, bishop of Alexandria, and a schism arose within the church.

26. W. Cave, *Ecclesiastici*, 73–77; see also R. Williams, *Arius*, 74–77; and R. P. C. Hanson, *Search*, 255–56.

27. S. Parker, *Religion and Loyalty*, 383–85. For a modern view, see R. P. C. Hanson, *Search*, 256–58.

28. W. Cave, *Ecclesiastici*, 81–83; N. Bacon, *Life and Actions*, 47–48; T. D. Barnes, *Athanasius and Constantius*, 22.

29. W. Cave, *Ecclesiastici*, 79–81; S. Parker, *Religion and Loyalty*, 385–87; compare with N. Bacon, *Life and Actions*, 45–47; R. P. C. Hanson, *Search*, 258–59; and T. D. Barnes, *Athanasius and Constantius*, 22.

30. S. Parker, *Religion and Loyalty*, 388–90, 396–97; W. Cave, *Ecclesiastici*, 82–83; N. Bacon, *Life and Actions*, 48–49; R. P. C. Hanson, *Search*, 260–61; T. D. Barnes, *Athanasius and Constantius*, 22.

31. There are two different accounts of the trial of Athanasius at the Council of Tyre and his alleged subsequent rewriting of the events that took place both at the trial and in the immediate aftermath; see WACL Ms. N563M3 P222 (and the copy of part of the document at Keynes Ms. 10), and the much longer version at Yahuda Ms. 19, fols. 80^v–143^r.

32. WACL Ms. N563M3 P222 fols. 19^{r-v}; Keynes Ms. 10 fol. 12^r. and esp. Yahuda Ms. 19, fols. 99^r–100^r.

33. WACL Ms. N563M3 P222 fol. 15^r; Keynes Ms. 10 fol. 9^r. Under the leadership of Julius, the Council of Rome in 341 had cleared Athanasius of any wrongdoing and had reinstated him to his bishopric. This decision, which effectively annulled the verdict at Tyre (implying that it was not a full council), led to major division between the Eastern and Western churches. See S. Parker, *Religion and Loyalty*, 415–16, 422–26, 433–35, 439–40; see R. P. C. Hanson, *Search*, 266–68.

34. Keynes Ms. 10 fols. 9^r–11^r; WACL Ms. N563M3 P222 fols. 15^r–17^r.

35. Keynes Ms. 10 fol. 11^r; WACL Ms. N563M3 P222 fols. 8^r–9^v. For a different analysis of the episode, see Yahuda Ms. 19 fols. 92^r–96^r.

36. WACL Ms. N563M3 P222 fol. 9^v; Keynes Ms. 10 fol. 11^v. The reference to the role of monks in spreading the story is at Yahuda Ms. 19 fol. 103^r.

37. W. Cave, *Ecclesiastici*, 74–77, 83–84; N. Bacon, *Life and Actions*, 37–46, esp. 39; see also T. D. Barnes, *Athanasius and Constantius*, 20–21.

38. Keynes Ms. 10 fols. 14^v–15^r; WACL Ms. N563M3 P222 fols. 21^r–22^r; Yahuda Ms. 19 fols. 104^r–117^r, esp. 109^r–115^r.

39. Keynes Ms. 10 fol. 15^r; WACL Ms. N563M3 P222 fol. 22^r; Yahuda Ms. 19 fol. 114^r.

40. Keynes Ms. 10 fol. 16^{r-v}; WACL Ms. N563M3 P222 fol. 22^{r-v}.

41. To "lay or strew with gravel; perplex, puzzle, nonplus.

42. Keynes Ms. 10 fols. 18^v–19^r; WACL Ms. N563M3 P222 fols. 26^r–27^r.

43. WACL Ms. N563M3 P222 fols. 11^r, 14^r; Keynes Ms. 10 fol. 5^v.

44. Keynes Ms. 10 fols. 6^r, 7^r; WACL Ms. N563M3 P222 fols. 12^r–13^r. There is a brief later fragment at Yahuda Ms. 15.7 fol. 163^v.

45. Keynes Ms. 10 fol. 8^{r-v}; WACL Ms. N563M3 P222 fol. 13^{r-v}.

46. Hooke to Newton, 24 November 1679, in H. W. Turnbull et al., 2:297–98. Hooke's "programme" for analysing heavenly motions, which went back to the mid-1660s, is discussed in O. Gal, *Meanest Foundations and Nobler Superstructures: Hooke, Newton and the Compounding of the Celestiall Motions of Planets* (Boston, 2002).

47. Newton to Hooke, 28 November 1679, in H. W. Turnbull et al., *Correspondence*, 2:302–3.

48. Hooke to Newton, 9 December 1679; Newton to Hooke, 13 December 1679; Hooke to Newton, 6 January 1678/80 and 17 January 1679/80; Newton to Hooke, 3 December 1680, in ibid., 2:304–10, 312, 314.

49. Halley to Newton, 22 May 1686 and Newton to Halley, 27 May 1686, in ibid., 2:431, 433–34.

50. Newton to Halley, 20 June 1686, in ibid., 2:435–37.

51. Newton to Halley, 20 June 1686, in ibid., 2:437–39 (my italics).

52. Newton to Oldenburg for Huygens, 23 June 1673, in ibid., 1:290; Newton to Halley, 20 June 1686, in ibid., 2:436. The "Moon Test" calculation is at CUL Add. Ms. 3958.5 fol. 87^r.

53. Newton to Halley, 20 June 1686, in H. W. Turnbull et al., *Correspondence*, 2:439–40.

54. Halley to Newton, 29 June 1686, in ibid., 2:441–43.

55. Newton to Halley, 27 July 1686, in ibid., 2:446–47. For a noncommittal comment on the "remarkable" lack of the passage in Huygens's own copy of the letter, see ibid., 1:295n3. Determining whether Newton did or did not forge the letter will of course require the use of many of the same techniques that Newton himself used in his historical researches.

56. See J. Craig, "Newton and the Counterfeiters," *Notes and Records of the Royal Society* 18 (1963): 136–45; R. S. Westfall, *Never at Rest*, 567–70; T. Levenson, *Newton and the Counterfeiter: The Unknown Detective Career of the World's Greatest Scientist* (Boston, 2009).

57. Newton to the Treasury, c. July 1696, in H. W. Turnbull et al., *Correspondence*, 4:209–10; NA Mint Papers 19.1 fols. 430^r–34^r.

58. Petition of Chaloner, late 1697; Newton memo (early 1698), in H. W. Turnbull et al., *Correspondence*, 4:259–60, 261–62; J. Craig, "Counterfeiters"; R. S. Westfall, *Never at Rest*, 573–75; and T. Levenson, *Counterfeiter*, 204–16. The depositions are in NA Mint Papers 15/17. More broadly, see M. Gaskill, *Crime and Mentalities in Early Modern England* (Cambridge, 2000), esp. 123–199; and R. Weil, *A Plague of Informers: Conspiracy and Political Trust in William III's England* (New Haven, 2013), esp. 104–39.

59. The best general accounts of the calculus disputes are R. S. Westfall, *Never at Rest*, 698–780; and A. R. Hall, *Philosophers at War* (Cambridge, 1980).

60. See Keill to Newton, 3 April 1711, Newton to Sloane, c. 10 April 1711, Keill to Sloane (for Leibniz), May 1711, in H. W. Turnbull et al., *Correspondence*, 5:115, 117, 133–41; R. S. Westfall, *Never at Rest*, 715–18, 721–28. Newton's *de Quadratura Curvarum* was appended to the 1704 edition of *Opticks*, while William Jones edited Newton's "De Analysi" for publication in 1711.

61. R. S. Westfall, *Never at Rest*, 725–26; and in particular, F. Manuel, *Portrait*, 337–39. For Conti's viewing of the original papers, see R. Iliffe et al., *Early Biographies*, 1:237–38.

62. CUL Add. Ms. 3968 fols. 374^{r-v}, 378^v, with variants at fols. 377^r, 379^r; Leibniz to Conti, 29 March 1716, in H. W. Turnbull et al., *Correspondence*, 6:306. For Newton's savage attack on Bernoulli in 1717 for acting as a judge and a witness in

his own cause (the phrase alludes to John 5:31), see CUL Add. Ms. 3968 fol. 366^r; see also I. Newton, "An Account of the Commercium Epistolicum," *Philosophical Transactions* 342 (1715): 194; Keill to Newton, 17 May 1717, in H. W. Turnbull et al., *Correspondence*, 6:385–87; R. S. Westfall, *Never at Rest*, 782–83.

63. CUL Add. Ms. 3968 fols. 436^v, 437^v; compare with Add. Ms. 3970 fol. 480^v (for hypothetical philosophy as a "Rational Romance"); S. Clarke, *A Collection of Papers, Which Passed Between the Late Learned Mr. Leibnitz, and Dr. Clarke, in the Years 1715 and 1716* (London, 1717), 361.

64. Frank Manuel's insightful account of Newton's personality makes a broadly similar claim about Newton's need to govern his own tendency to anger; see F. Manuel, *Portrait*, 343–48.

65. Antonio Conti, *Réponse aux Observations sur la Chronologie de M. Newton, avec une letttre de M. l'Abbé Conti au sujet de ladite réponse* (Paris, 1726), cited in F. Manuel, *Portrait*, 355–56. The drafts of Newton's paper, along with variants of his attack on Conti, are at Yahuda Ms. 27.

CHAPTER 11

1. See J. R. Western, *Monarchy and Revolution: The English State in the 1680s* (London, 1972); J. R. Jones, *The Revolution of 1688 in England* (London, 1988); W. Speck, *Reluctant Revolutionaries: Englishmen and the Revolution of 1688* (Oxford, 1989); T. Harris, *Revolution: The Great Crisis of the British Monarchy 1685–1720* (London 2007); S. Pincus, *1688: The First Modern Revolution* (New Haven, 2009).

2. The "Immortal Seven" were the earls of Danby, Shrewsbury, and Devonshire, Viscount Lumley, Henry Compton (bishop of London but suspended since mid-1686 by the Court of High Commission), Edward Russell, and Henry Sidney (or Sydney; brother of the Republican "martyr" Algernon Sydney and Earl of Romney after 1694).

3. Yahuda Ms. 32; Trinity College Library Cambridge, Ms. R.16.38.442A, fol. 1^r, from the printed version of the letter "Translated from the French." For Petre, James, Louis, and the pope, see J. Miller, *Popery and Politics*, 229–38. Lot 294 of the 1936 Sotheby Sale comprised two copies in Latin of a letter written by a Jesuit in Liège to one in Freiburg; lot 31 contained other documents relating to William's impending arrival, none of which were apparently in Newton's hand.

4. See *The Entring Book of Roger Morrice*, 6 vols., ed. M. Goldie (Woodbridge, 2008), 4:308; Covel to Masters and Heads of Colleges, 15 December 1688, in H. W. Turnbull et al., *Correspondence*, 3:1; J. E. Foster, ed., *The Diary of Samuel Newton, Alderman of Cambridge* (Cambridge, 1890), 97; and R. Ashcraft, *Revolutionary Politicks and Locke's Two Treatises of Government* (Princeton, 1986), 541–43. For the wider context of James's departure, see R. Beddard, *A Kingdom Without a King: The Journal of the Provisional Government in the Revolution of 1688* (Oxford, 1988); J. R. Jones, *Revolution of 1688*; T. Harris, *Revolution*, 311–13.

5. Prince of Orange to the University of Cambridge, 29 December 1688, in H.W. Turnbull et al., *Correspondence*, 3:1–2; 3:8n1; P. Halliday, "Sir Robert Sawyer," New DNB; B. D. Henning, *The History of Parliament: The Commons, 1660–1690*, 3 vols. (London, 1983), 1:150.

6. Cambridge University Library Archives, O.III.8/2; for the elections at Oxford and Cambridge, see M. B. Rex, *University Representation in England, 1604–1690* (London, 1954), 296–348, esp. 301–2.

7. M. Goldie, "The Revolution of 1689 and the Structure of Political Argument: An Essay and an Annotated Bibliography of Pamphlets on the Allegiance Controversy," *Bulletin of Research in the Humanities* 33 (1980): 473–564; T. Harris, *Revolution*, 323–28; J. Kenyon, *Revolution Principles: The Politics of Party, 1689–1720* (Cambridge 1977), 7–14; R. Ashcraft, *Revolutionary Politicks*, 569–71.

8. Newton to Covel, 21 February 1688/89, in H.W. Turnbull et al., *Correspondence*, 3:12–13. The Declaration outlined the conditions under which the Convention was offering the Crown to William and Mary.

9. See R. Morrice, *Entring Book*, 5:42, 47–48, 53–56, 69–70, 79, 81; D. Lacey, *Dissent and Parliamentary Politics, 1660–89* (New Brunswick, N.J., 1969), 232–36; H. Horwitz, *Parliament, Policy and Politics in the Reign of William III* (Manchester, 1977), 22–29; Horwitz, *Revolution Politicks: The Career of Daniel Finch, Second Earl of Nottingham, 1647–1730* (Cambridge, 1968), 87–94; J. Spurr, "The Church of England, Comprehension and the Toleration Act of 1689," *English Historical Review* 104 (1989): 927–46, esp. 937–38; and R. Thomas, "Comprehension and Indulgence," in *From Uniformity to Unity, 1662–1962*, ed. O. Chadwick and G. Nuttall (London, 1962), 189–253, esp. 244–49.

10. For Hampden's attack on the Trinitarian clause, see A. Grey, *Debates in the House of Commons, from the Year 1667 to the Year 1694*, 10 vols. (London, 1769), 9:252–53. More broadly, see R. L. Greaves, *Secrets of the Kingdom: British Radicals from the Popish Plot to the Revolution of 1688–1689* (Stanford, 1992), 136–38, 169, 219, 236–39; R. Ashcraft, *Revolutionary Politicks*, 363, 595; J. Scott, *Algernon Sidney and the Restoration Crisis, 1677–1683* (Cambridge, 1991), 301–15; H. C. Foxcroft, ed., *The Life and Letters of Sir George Savile...First Marquis of Halifax*, 2 vols. (London, 1898), 2:204, 229; and D. Lacey, *Dissent*, 237–39, 401. For Morrice's surprise at the bill passing, see R. Morrice, *Entring Book*, 5:118.

11. CSPD 1689, 25 and 26 August 1689 (for Hampden's lobbying); "The Case of King's College" is now Keynes Ms. 117; Keynes Ms. 117A is a copy of John Reynolds's "An Account of King's College's Recovery of Their Right to Chuse Their Own Provost"; the recollection must postdate 1705 since Newton is referred to as "Sir Isaac Newton." Keynes Ms. 117B gives the college's own account for not electing Newton. For Newton's attitude to Boyle, see Newton to Fatio de Duillier, 10 October 1689, in H.W. Turnbull et al., *Correspondence*, 3:45, and for Boyle and alchemy, see L. Principe, *The Aspiring Adept: Robert Boyle and His Alchemical Quest* (Princeton, 2000).

12. Keynes Mss. 117 fols. 1^r–2^r and 117B fols. 1^r–2^r.

13. Keynes Ms. 117B fol. 2^r; A. Austen-Leigh, *King's College* (London, 1899), 153–58; CSPD, 1689–90, 280–81. Roderick was ordained by Thomas Sprat, who just over two decades earlier had written the famous *History of the Royal Society of London*. More recently Sprat had been a member of the Ecclesiastical Commission; detested by the radical Whigs, he had wisely refused to proceed against the Seven Bishops and took the oath of allegiance to William and Mary.

14. R. Morrice, *Entring Book*, 5:269–70, 324; Fatio to Newton, 24 February 1689/90, in H. W. Turnbull et al., *Correspondence*, 3:390; R. T. Gunther, ed., "The Diary of Robert Hooke," in *Early Science in Oxford*, ed. R. T. Gunther, 14 vols. (Oxford, 1921–45), 10:184. Hickman was rector of Farnham Royal and within months would be made chaplain-in-ordinary to William and Mary.

15. For the intellectual contexts of Locke's Dutch sojourn, see M. Cranston, *John Locke: A Biography* (London, 1957), 223–303; R. Woolhouse, *Locke: A Biography* (Cambridge, 2007), 197–265; and J. Marshall, *John Locke, Toleration and Enlightenment Culture* (Cambridge, 2007), 469–99.

16. See M. Cranston, *Locke*, 313–14, 321, 323, 333–34, 362–63, 376; R. Morrice, *Entring Book*, 5:335–36; M. Goldie, "The Roots of True Whiggism," *History of Political Thought* 1 (1980): 200–201, 226, and esp. 235n132; L. G. Schwoerer, *The Declaration of Rights, 1689* (Baltimore, 1981), 106, 109–10; Horwitz, *Parliament*, 60–62; R. Ashcraft, *Revolutionary Politicks*, 532–35, 537, 549–50, 595–96; and R. L. Greaves, *Secrets*, 314, 340–41.

17. See M. Cranston, *Locke*, 330–37, esp. 337; H. W. Turnbull et al., *Correspondence*, 3:71–78; and J. Locke, *Some Thoughts upon Education*, ed. John Yolton (Oxford, 1989), 245–46. For Newton's demonstration, dated "Mar 89/90," see J. Herivel, *The Background to Newton's Principia: A Study of Newton's Dynamical Researches in the Years 1664–84* (Oxford, 1965), 108–17, esp. 114. See also J. L. Axtell, "Locke's Review of the *Principia*," *Notes and Records of the Royal Society* 20 (1965): 152–61, esp. 154–57; L. Downing, "Locke's Newtonianism and Lockean Newtonianism," in *Perspectives on Science* 5 (1997): 285–310, esp. 292–93; and P. Anstey, *John Locke and Natural Philosophy* (Oxford, 2011), 148–57.

18. *Essay* (1690), IV.3.18 and IV.12.8–10; Locke to Tyrrell, 4 August 1690, Molyneux to Locke, 27 August 1692, and Locke to Molyneux, 20 September 1692; E. S. de Beer, *Locke Correspondence*, 4:110–12, 507–8, 523–24. See also P. Anstey, *Locke and Natural Philosophy*, 148–52.

19. Toland attacked anti-Trinitarian conceptions of Christ in his *Christianity Not Mysterious* (1696). In general, see P. Dixon, *Nice and Hot Disputes*; G. Reedy, *The Bible and Reason: Anglicans and Scripture in Late Seventeenth-Century England* (Philadelphia, 1985), 125–39; S. Trowell, "Unitarian and/or Anglican: The Relationship of Unitarianism to the Church from 1687–98," *Bulletin of the John Rylands Library* 78 (1996): 77–101; J. C. D. Clark, *English Society, 1688–1832: Ideology, Social Structure and Political Practice During the Ancien Regime*, 2nd ed. (Cambridge, 2000), 277–89; and R. Iliffe, "Friendly Criticism: Richard Simon, John Locke, Isaac Newton and the Johannine Comma," in *Scripture and Scholarship in*

Early Modern England, ed. A. Hessayon and N. Keene (Aldershot, 2006), 137–57. For Toland, see J. Champion, *Republican Learning: John Toland and the Crisis of Christian Culture, 1696–1722* (Manchester, 2004).

20. Anonymous [S. Nye], *A Brief History of the Unitarians, Called also Socinians. In Four Letters Written to a Friend* (London, 1687), 26–36, 67–68, 117–21, 137–38 (for 1 Tim. 3:16), 151–52 (for 1 John 5:7). Hedworth was the first to use the term "Unitarian" (in 1673); his letter is reproduced in Nye's work on 167–84. See also H. J. McLachlan, *Socinianism in Seventeenth-Century England* (Oxford, 1951), 299–316.

21. S. Nye, *Brief History*, 151–53, 137–39. In the King James Bible, 1 John 5:7–8 reads "For there are three that bear record in heaven, the Father, the Word, and the Holy Ghost: and these three are one. And there are three that bear witness in earth, the spirit, and the water, and the blood: and these three agree in one." The words in dispute run from "in heaven" to "in earth."

22. "A true Son of the Church of England" [Bury], *The Naked Gospel, etc.* (Oxford, 1690), 29, 31, 37–39, 41–43, 57–58.

23. [S. Nye], *Brief Notes on the Creed of St. Athanasius* (London, 1690); W. Sherlock, *A Vindication of the Doctrine of the Holy and Ever Blessed Trinity, and the Incarnation of the Son of God. Occasioned by the Brief Notes on the Creed of Athanasius, and the Brief History of the Unitarians, or Socinians* (London, 1690); [S. Nye], *The Acts of the Great Athanasius, with Notes, by Way of Illustration, on His Creed; and Observations on the Learned Vindication of the Trinity and Incarnation, by Dr. William Sherlock* (London, 1690), 4–5, 7–8, 9–10; See S. Trowell, "Unitarian and/or Anglican," 84–87; and P. Dixon, "Nice and Hot Disputes," 109–16.

24. See J. Marshall, *Resistance, Religion and Responsibility* (Cambridge, 1994), 218–65, 331–37; J. Marshall, "Locke, Socinianism, 'Socinianism' and Unitarianism," in *English Philosophy in the Age of Locke*, ed. A. Stewart (Oxford, 2000), 111–82; M. Firpo, "John Locke e il Socinianismo," *Rivista Storica Italiana* 92 (1980): 35–124; M. Cranston, *Locke*; D. Wootton, ed., *John Locke: Political Writings* (Harmondsworth, 1993), 49–87; and J. Higgins-Biddle, ed., *John Locke: The Reasonableness of Christianity* (Oxford, 1999), xliii–lxxi. For Le Clerc, see M. Klauber, "Between Protestant Orthodoxy and Rationalism: Fundamental Articles and the Early Career of Jean Le Clerc," *Journal of the History of Ideas* 54 (1993): 611–36.

25. Locke to Van Limborch, 12 June 1688, 12 March 1688/89, 12 April, 6 June, and 7 June 1689; Le Clerc to Locke, 9 April 1689 and 25 June 1689; Van Limborch to Locke 26 April, 5 June, and 8 July 1689; E. S. de Beer, *Locke Correspondence*, 3:473–75, 583–85, 595–98, 607–11, 630–35, 641–42, 646–50. For Locke's strategy of avoiding questions about his authorship of the *Epistola*, see Locke, *Epistola de Tolerantia: Letter on Toleration*, ed. R. Klibansky and J. W. Gough (Oxford, 1968), xx–xxvi, and on his extraordinary attention to preserving anonymity, see *Locke's Two Treatises on Government*, 2nd ed., ed. P. Laslett (Cambridge, 1970), 4–15, 79–80; M. Cranston, *Locke*, 320–21; and J. Higgins-Biddle, *Reasonableness*, xxxviii–xli.

26. Tyrrell to Locke, 18 February 1689/90, 5 March 1689/90, 18 March 1689/90, and 30 August 1690, Furly to Locke, 16 October 1690; E. S. de Beer, *Locke Correspondence*, 4:12, 22, 36, 144–47. For Locke's lodgings during 1690, see ibid., 4:83n3, 100, 116, 137, 148n2. Proast's attack on Locke was *The Argument of the Letter Concerning Toleration, Briefly Consider'd and Answer'd* (Oxford, 1690); Locke's *Second Letter Concerning Toleration* appeared under the name of "Philanthropus" and was licensed on 24 June. See M. Goldie, "John Locke, Jonas Proast, and Religious Toleration, 1688–1692," in *The Church of England 1689–1833: From Toleration to Tractarianism*, ed. J. Walsh, C. Haydon, and S. Taylor (Oxford, 1992), 143–71.

27. Le Clerc to Locke, 22 October 1690; E. S. de Beer, *Locke Correspondence*, 4:150–51 and 151–2n6. Le Clerc's defence of Bury was *An Historical Vindication of the Naked Gospel, Recommended to the University of Oxford* (London, 1691).

28. The "Third Letter" is reprinted in H. W. Turnbull et al., *Correspondence*, 3:129–42. The initial document sent to Locke in November 1690 was published (with the first few paragraphs missing) as *Two Letters of Sir Isaac Newton to Mr. Le Clerc, ... in Holland. The Former Containing a Dissertation upon ... I John, v. 7. The Latter upon ... I Timothy, iii. 16. Published from Authentick MSS ...* (London, 1754), and it was published in full in 1785 in *Isaaci Newtoni Opera quæ exstant omnia*, ed. S. Horsley, 5 vols. (London, 1779–85), 5:493–550. For later discussion of the text, see S. Mandelbrote, "Eighteenth-century Reactions to Newton's Anti-Trinitarianism," in *Newton and Newtonianism: New Studies*, ed. J. Force and S. Hutton (London, 2004), 93–111. For Haynes's translation of the analysis of 1 John 5:7, see W. Whiston, *A Collection of Authentick Records, Belonging to the Old and New Testament*, 2 vols. (London, 1727–28), 2:1077; it is currently Yahuda Ms. 20.

29. Newton to Locke and to "a Friend" [Locke], 28 October 1690 and 14 November 1690, in H. W. Turnbull et al., *Correspondence*, 3:79, 82, 83–129, esp. 83. In the initial letter to which the October missive was a response, Locke had remarked on his plans to travel to the Netherlands, possibly in the entourage of William III, which he also mentioned in other letters of early to mid-October; see E. S. de Beer, *Locke Correspondence*, 4:142, 148, 154, 156.

30. See Mill to Covel, 22 January 1686/87; BL Add. Ms. 22910 fol. 256^r; King's College, Cambridge, Keynes Ms. 135; Wotton to Bentley, 14 May 1689 and Bentley to Mill, 31 March 1691, in *The Correspondence of Richard Bentley*, 2 vols., ed. C. Wordsworth (London, 1842), 1:1–5. More broadly, see K. Haugen, "Transformations of the Trinity Doctrine in English Scholarship from the History of Beliefs to the History of Texts," *Archiv für Religionsgeschichte* 3 (2001): 149–68; and A. Fox, *Mill and Bentley: A Study of the Textual Criticism of the New Testament, 1675–1729* (Oxford, 1954), 61–62, 64–66, 145, 151, for the collation of Covel's mss. Newton mentioned consulting one of Laughton's books in the American Philosophical Library, Ms. Temp3. fol. 23^r. Mill and Laughton were both denounced by Thomas Hearne for their Whig political principles, Laughton in particular (in October 1705) for being "a rank Whig, a great Talker, and very

violent in his Aspersions of the True Ch. of England Men"; see *Remarks and Collections of Thomas Hearne . . .*, 11 vols., ed. C. E. Doble, D. W. Rannie, and H. E. Salter (Oxford, 1885–1921), 1:45, 53.

31. Keynes Ms. 2, Part 2, fol. 10^{r-v}. See B. Walton, *Biblia Sacra Polyglotta, complectentia Textus Originales, Hebraicum cum Pentateucho Samaritano, Chaldaicum, Græcum, Versionumque antiquarum, Samaritanæ, Græcæ LXXII. Interpretum, Chaldaicæ, Syriacæ, Arabicæ, Æthiopicæ, Vulgatæ Latinæ, quicquid comparari poterat, &c.*, 6 vols. (London, 1657), 5:922–93; [J. Fell], *Novi Testamenti Libri Omnes. Accesserunt Parallela Scripturæ Loca, necnon variantes Lectiones ex plus 100 MSS. Codicibus et antiquis versionibus collectæ* (Oxford, 1675), 600; Stephanus Curcellæus, *Novum Testamentum Græcum, cum variantibus lectionibus, tam ex MS. Quam impressis codicibus collectis* (Amsterdam, 1658; 2nd ed., 1675); C. Sand, *Interpretationes paradoxæ quatuor Evangeliorum: Quibus affixa est Dissertatio de Verbo, una cum appendice* (Amsterdam, 1670). See A. Fox, *Mill and Bentley*, 21, 32, 49–50; and K. Haugen, "Transformations," 156–61. For relevant texts in Newton's possession, see J. Harrison, *Library*, nos. H194, H198–205, H207–9, H215–17, H1514, and for a history of the anti-Trinitarian exegesis of these core texts, see S. Snobelen, " 'To Us There Is but One God, the Father': Antitrinitarian Textual Criticism in Seventeenth- and Early Eighteenth-Century England," in *Scripture and Scholarship in Early Modern England*, ed. A. Hessayon and N. Keene (Aldershot, 2006), 116–36.

32. Ussher and Grotius's variant readings and annotations were separately paginated in volume 6 of Walton's *Polyglot*; see also M. Poole, *Synopsis Criticorum aliorumque Sacrae Scripturae interpretum et commentatorum*, 5 vols. (London 1669–1676) 3: cols. 1623–25.

33. J. Lough, *Locke's Travels in France, 1675–9, as Related in His Journals, Correspondence and Other Papers* (Cambridge, 1953), 252–53; G. Burnet, *Dr. Burnet's Travels, or Letters, Containing an Account of What Seemed Most Remarkable in Travelling Through Switzerland, Italy, France, and Germany, &c. in the Years 1685 and 1686* (Amsterdam, 1687), 51–54; A. Barnes, *Jean Le Clerc, 1657–1736, et la République des Lettres* (Paris, 1938), 252. See M. Greig, "The Reasonableness of Christianity? Gilbert Burnet and the Trinitarian Controversy of the 1690s," *Journal of Ecclesiastical History* 44 (1993): 631–49, esp. 642–43. The Codex Vaticanus, is one of the four great uncial codices (composed in majuscule script, i.e., in capital letters) of the Bible, the others being the Codex Alexandrinus, the Codex Sinaiticus, and the Codex Ephraemi Rescriptus. The last two only became known in the middle of the nineteenth century and until recently, the Codex Bezae (discussed below) was considered a fifth member of this group.

34. Keynes Ms. 2, Part 1, cover sheet and part 2, fols. 10^{r-v}.

35. Keynes Ms. 2, Part 2, fol. 10^{r-v}; the information from Sand was repeated verbatim in the letter sent to Locke; H. W. Turnbull, et al., *Correspondence*, 3:89n"k." For the Erasmian controversies, see ibid., 3:100–104, and for evidence of Newton's use of Pearson, see ibid., 3:103n"b." More generally, see R. Coogan, *Erasmus, Lee and the Correction of the Vulgate: The Shaking of the Foundations*

(Geneva, 1992); J. H. Bentley, *Humanists and Holy Writ: New Testament Scholarship in the Renaissance* (Princeton, 1983); B. Metzger, *The Text of the New Testament: Its Transmission, Corruption and Restoration*, 3rd ed. (New York, 1992), 100–102, 255–56, 291n2; B. Ehrman, *The Orthodox Corruption of Scripture: The Effect of Early Christological Controversies on the Text of the New Testament* (Oxford, 1993); and J. Levine, "Erasmus and the Problem of the Johannine Comma," *Journal of the History of Ideas* (1997): 573–96, esp. 575–78, 591–94. The text cited against Erasmus by Lee is the Codex Montfortianus at Trinity College, Dublin.

36. Keynes Ms. 2, Part 2, fol. 10ᵛ; T. Smith, *A Sermon of the Credibility of the Mysteries of the Christian Religion Preached Before a Learned Audience* (London, 1675), 12, 15, 47–49.

37. L. Bredvold, *The Intellectual Milieu of John Dryden* (Ann Arbor, Mich., 1966), 98–105; H. Margival, *Essai sur Richard Simon et la Critique Biblique au XVIIᵉ Siècle* (Paris, 1900); P. Hazard, *The European Mind, 1680–1715* (New York, 2013); P. Auvray, *Richard Simon, 1638–1712: Étude Bio-bibliographique avec des Textes Inédits* (Paris, 1974); J. Champion, "'Acceptable to Inquisitive Men': Some Simonian Contexts for Newton's Biblical Criticism, 1680–92," in *Newton and Religion: Context, Nature and Influence*, ed. J. E. Force and R. Popkin (Kluwer, 1999), 77–96.

38. R. Simon, *Critical History of the Text of the New Testament; Wherein Is Firmly Established the Truth of Those Acts on Which the Foundation of the Christian Religion Is Laid*, 2 parts (London, 1689), 1:A2–A2ᵛ, A3ᵛ. For a clear statement on the meaning of the term "authentic" in Simon's analysis, see *Critical Enquiries into the Various Editions of the Bible* (London, 1684), 193–200.

39. R. Simon, *Critical History*, 1:10–12, 22–38, esp. 32–33. For Catholic admission of private interpretation, see R. Simon, *Critical Enquiries*, 186; and R. Simon, *A Critical History of the Versions of the New Testament: Part II* (licensed 22 November 1689), (London, 1692), 377–78.

40. R. Simon, *Critical History*, 2:128–37, 142–47, 156–57; and see B. Metzger, *Text of the New Testament*, 49–51 (the Claromontanus contains only the Pauline Epistles while the Bezae lacks them), 72–74 (for the Old Latin). For earlier comments on Jerome's Vulgate, see R. Simon, *Critical Enquiries*, 186–93.

41. R. Simon, *Critical History*, 2:141, 110, 122–24; 1:A3ʳ. Occasionally, he allowed that the Vulgate itself might need to be altered; see *Critical History*, 2:163 (re. the reinsertion of the words *without cause* in Matt. 5:22).

42. R. Simon, *Critical History*, 2:1–3.

43. Ibid., 2:5–8. Fell's edition was *Sancti Cæcilij Cypriani opera recognita & illustrata per Joannem Oxoniensem episcopum. Accedunt annales Cyprianici, sive tredecim annorum, quibus S. Cyprianus inter Christianos versatus est, brevis historia chronologice delineata per Joannem Cestriensem . . .* (Oxford, 1682).

44. R. Simon, *Critical History*, 2:9–10.

45. Ibid., 2:11–14.

46. H. W. Turnbull et al., *Correspondence*, 3:83. See D. Colclough, "Parrhesia: The Rhetoric of Free Speech in Early Modern England," *Rhetorica* 17 (1999): 177–212; and M. Foucault, *The Courage of Truth*, trans. G. Burchell (Basingstoke, 2011).

47. H. W. Turnbull et al., *Correspondence*, 3:84–86; C. Sand, *Interpretationes paradoxæ*, 380–81.

48. H. W. Turnbull et al., *Correspondence*, 3:88–89; see R. Simon, *Critical History*, 2:4; and C. Sand, *Interpretationes paradoxæ*, 386.

49. H. W. Turnbull et al., *Correspondence*, 3:90. For Sand's examination of the Armenian Codex, which he dated to before 400 C.E., see *Interpretationes paradoxæ*, 376; Newton had cited this in his theological notebook.

50. H. W. Turnbull et al., *Correspondence*, 3:90–92; compare, for example, with the list of patristic sources Sand gives in *Interpretationes paradoxæ*, 379–80.

51. H. W. Turnbull et al., *Correspondence*, 3:93; R. Simon, *Critical History*, 2:125.

52. H. W. Turnbull et al., *Correspondence*, 3:98–102.

53. Ibid., 3:108.

54. Newton to Locke, 7 February 1691, in ibid., 3:147–48. See also P. Anstey, "Newton and Locke," in *The Oxford Handbook of Isaac Newton* (forthcoming).

55. Newton to Locke, 14 November 1690; H. W. Turnbull et al., *Correspondence*, 3:82, 109–10. Preliminary notes on 1 Timothy 3:16 at Keynes Ms., Part 2, fol. 13^v, which are the seeds of the longer version in the second Locke "letter," were inserted next to a query about the identity of the Ancient of Days in Daniel 7:13. This topic was the subject of an exchange between Newton and Locke in February 1691, and appears to have been discussed at Oates at the start of that year; see H. W. Turnbull et al., *Correspondence*, 3:147.

56. See Keynes Ms. 2, Part 2, fol. 13^v (part of a lengthy series of passages from Scripture listed under the heading "Deus Filius"); B. Walton, *Polyglotta*, 5:826–27; J. Fell, *Novi Testamenti*, 530; and M. Poole, *Synopsis*, 3: cols. 1047–50. For the notes in the Racovian catechism, see Rees, *The Racovian Catechism, with Notes and Illustrations, translated from the Latin: to which is prefixed a sketch of the History of Unitarianism in Poland and the adjacent Countries* (London, 1818), 121–22, and for modern views, see B. Metzger, *The Text of the New Testament*, 187 (in a section entitled "Errors arising from Faulty eyesight") and B. Ehrman, *Orthodox Corruption*, 77–78.

57. H. W. Turnbull et al., *Correspondence*, 3:110–18. Grotius's variant readings are listed in the "Appendix" to Walton's *Polyglotta*, 6:54 (separately paginated).

58. H. W. Turnbull et al., *Correspondence*, 3:121–22; K. Haugen, "Transformations," 158–59 (and 161–63 for a slightly later analysis by Richard Bentley). From Morin[us], *Exercitationum ecclesiasticarum libri duo: De patriarcharum & primatum origine, primis orbis terrarum ecclesiasticis diuisionibus, atque antiqua & primigenia censurarum in clericos natura & praxi, etc.* (Paris, 1634).

59. H. W. Turnbull et al., *Correspondence*, 3:138–40.

60. J. Locke, "Of Study" in *The Educational Writings of John Locke*, ed. J. L. Axtell (Cambridge, 1968), 405–22, esp. 406–13. These ideas were expanded in "Of the

Conduct of Understanding," where Locke made the study of theology "every man's duty"; see F. Garforth, ed., *Of the Conduct of the Understanding* (New York, 1966), and in particular J. Marshall, *Resistance*, 76–77, 195–96, 363–65, 444–46. For Locke's view on the significance of friendship and of the virtues of Cicero, see J. Marshall, *Resistance*, 297n12, 299–310.

61. J. Locke, "Of Study," 416–17. See also the remarks on the duty to study Scripture in the short essay "Error" of 1698, in V. Nuovo, *John Locke: Writings on Religion* (Oxford, 2002), 81–83.

62. H. W. Turnbull et al., *Correspondence*, 3:122; more generally, see R. Iliffe, "Friendly Criticism."

63. For biblical study in the Republic of Letters, see M. C. Pitassi, "Le notion de communication dans l'exégèse biblique de la fin du XVIIe siècle," in *Commercium Litterarium: Forms of Communication in the Republic of Letters, 1600–1750*, ed. H. Bots and F. Waquet (Amsterdam, 1994), 35–50.

CHAPTER 12

1. Locke to Newton 7 February 1691, Le Clerc to Locke, 1 April 1691; Locke to Van Limborch, 18 June 1691; Newton to Locke, 30 June 1691, Le Clerc to Locke, 21 July 1691; E. S. de Beer, *Locke Correspondence*, 4:187n1, 197–98, 248, 277, 288–89, 302. The Trinity College Exit and Redit Book indicates that Newton was away from Trinity between 2 and 16 January 1691.

2. Gregory memorandum of 28 December 1691, in H. W. Turnbull et al., *Correspondence*, 2:191. See R. S. Westfall, *Never at Rest*, 499–500, 513–20.

3. Newton to Locke, 13 December 1691 (draft of letter), in H. W. Turnbull et al., *Correspondence*, 3:184, 185–86.

4. Pawling to Locke, 16 January 1692, in E. S. de Beer, *Locke Correspondence*, 4:364–65. The Trinity College Exit/Redit book indicates that Newton returned to his college on 21 January 1692. Fatio de Duillier told Newton in September 1691 that he would be staying with a French apothecary named Benoist, who lived on Suffolk Street, and this is almost certainly where Newton was found. See WACL Ms. 253L 1691 and E. S. de Beer, *Locke Correspondence*, 4:151.

5. Pawling to Locke, 16 January 1692 and Newton to Locke, 26 January 1691/92; E. S. de Beer, *Locke Correspondence*, 4:365–66, 376. Newton had been angling for a senior position at the Mint as early as May 1690; see R. S. Westfall, *Never at Rest*, 497.

6. Newton to Locke, 16 February 1692, 3 May 1692, Le Clerc to Locke, 1 April 1692, Locke to Clarke, 13 May 1692, and Locke to Newton, 26 July 1692; E. S. de Beer, *Locke Correspondence*, 4:387, 434, 450, 453, 485. Luke 22:16–20 is the Lucan account of the key moments during the Last Supper when Jesus broke the bread and told the apostles that it was his body, that they should do the same in remembrance of him and that they should likewise drink from his cup,

since it was "new testament in my blood, which is shed for you." On 12 March
1692 Furly asked Locke to inspect the passage in the Codex Bezæ and thanked
him for having done so on 31 August; see ibid., 4:415–18, 511. Fatio told Newton
on 18 May that he had just seen Locke, who confirmed that he had stopped the
publication of some letters in the nick of time; see WACL Ms. F253L 1692.

7. Newton to Locke, 7 July 1692, Locke to Newton, 26 July 1692, and Newton to
Locke, 2 August 1692, Fatio to Newton, 30 January 1693, Newton to Fatio, 14
February 1693, in H. W. Turnbull et al., *Correspondence*, 3:215, 216–19, 265–69.
The chemical composition of the red earth is unclear.

8. Fatio to Newton, 4 May 1693 and 18 May 1693, Hannah Barton to Newton, 24
August 1693, in H. W. Turnbull et al., *Correspondence*, 3:270–71, 278–79. The visit
to Timothy Langley at Bow Street is recorded at CUL Add. Ms. 3975 fol. 174^v
and the slightly later experiments are described at CUL Add. Ms. 3973 fol. 28^r.

9. Newton to Pepys, 13 September 1693, in H. W. Turnbull et al., *Correspondence*,
3:279. The Buttery Book at Trinity College suggests that he left Cambridge
sometime in the middle of the week between the eighth and fifteenth of September, probably on the tenth or eleventh, and returned not long after the twenty-
second; see J. Edleston, *Correspondence* (London, 1850), lxxxv, xc. For Pepys's
religious views, see K. Loveman, "Samuel Pepys and 'Discourses Touching Religion' Under James II," *English Historical Review* 127 (2012): 46–82, esp. 50–52.

10. Pepys to Millington, 26 September 1693 and 3 October 1693, Millington to
Pepys, 30 September 1693, in H. W. Turnbull et al., *Correspondence*, 3:281–83. See
also R. S. Westfall, *Never at Rest*, 536.

11. Newton to Locke, 16 September 1693, in H. W. Turnbull et al., *Correspondence*,
3:280. The Bull was the famous Bishopsgate terminus for carriages travelling to
and from Cambridge and its environs.

12. Locke to Newton, 5 October 1693, in ibid., 3:283–84. Locke's presentation
copy of *Opticks* is now in Trinity College, Cambridge. Newton dog-eared the
page on which Locke's account of good and evil appeared; see J. Harrison, *Library*, H967 (p. 157 of the *Essay*). For Locke's fear of being labelled a Hobbist,
see J. Dunn, *The Political Thought of John Locke: "An Historical Account of the Argument of the Two Treatises of Government"* (Cambridge, 1969), 81–82, and esp. 82n4.

13. Christiaan Huygens to Constantijn Huygens, 6 June 1693 (N.S.); C. Huygens,
Les Oeuvres Complètes de Christiaan Huygens, 22 vols. (The Hague, 1888–1951),
10:616; C. Jackson, ed., *The Diary of Abraham de la Pryme* (Durham, 1870), 23;
R. S. Westfall, *Never at Rest*, 277–78.

14. Newton to Locke, 15 October 1693, Newton to Leibniz, 16 October 1693, in
H. W. Turnbull et al., *Correspondence*, 3:280, 285–87; and R. S. Westfall, *Never at
Rest*, 518–20. For the mercury hypothesis, see P. E. Spargo and C. A. Pounds,
"Newton's 'Derangement of the Intellect': New Light on an Old Problem,"
Notes and Records of the Royal Society 34 (1970): 11–32. Newton had been engaging
in heavy experimentation with common mercury over the previous months.

15. Newton to Mencke, 30 May 1693, Mill to Newton, 7 November 1693 and 21 February 1694, Newton to Mill, 29 January 1694, in H. W. Turnbull et al., *Correspondence*, 3:270–71, 289–90, 303–4. The results of the theological project are now Yahuda Ms. 4; Mill referred to readings in part 1 of this document. The two Covel Mss. were bought by Robert Harley in 1715 and are now in the British Library.

16. "De motu sphæricorum Corporum in fluidis," CUL Add. Ms. 3965 fol. 47^r. Compare with comments on the inability of humans to grasp all the terms in infinite series expressed in his 1669 work "De Analysi"; D. T. Whiteside, *Mathematical Papers*, 2:242–43.

17. Millington to Pepys, 30 September 1693 and Pepys to Millington, 3 October 1693, in H. W. Turnbull et al., *Correspondence*, 3:282; Keynes Mss. 130.6, Book 2 and 130.5 fol. 2^r. Almost all of Conduitt's anecdotes about Newton's intellectual prowess seem to have originated with Newton.

18. Yahuda Ms. 1.1 fols. 2^r, 4^r, 7^r.

19. Keynes Ms. 2, Part 2, fol. A^v.

Bibliography

MANUSCRIPT SOURCES

Bancroft Library, University of California, Berkeley. BS1556.M67 P5/1681 (Newton's copy of More's *A Plain and Continued Exposition*).

Bodleian Library, Oxford. Tanner MS 54, fol. 77.

Cambridge University Library. Add. MS 6986 (James Duport, "Rules to Be Observed by Young Pupils and Schollers in the University").

Cambridge University Library. The "Waste Book" (CUL) Add. MS 4004.

Fitzwilliam Museum, Cambridge. Newton Notebook.

Grantham Hallbook, Grantham Public Library.

Harry Ransom Research Institute, University of Texas. MS130.

Huntington Library, San Marino, Calif. Babson MS 437.

King's College, Cambridge. Keynes MSS.

Magdalen College Library, Oxford. MS 432 (Fairfax's performance).

National Archives, London.

National Library of Israel. Yahuda MSS.

New College, Oxford. MS 361.2, fol. 135^v.

Pierpont Morgan Library, New York. Newton Notebook.

Royal Society Library, London. Stukeley MSS.

Smithsonian Institute. Dibner MSS.

Trinity College, Cambridge. MS 0.10A.33, p. 15 (James Duport, "Rules to Be Observed by Young Pupils and Schollers in the University").

Trinity College, Cambridge. Muniments, "Conclusions and Admonitions 1607–73," MS 184.

Trinity College, Dublin. MS 61.

University of Chicago Library. Joseph Halle Schaffner Collection.

Williams Andrews Clark Memorial Library, Los Angeles. Ms. N563M3 P222, "Paradoxical Questions Concerning the Morals and Actions of Athanasius."

ELECTRONIC RESOURCES

The Chemistry of Isaac Newton. Indiana University, http://webapp1.dlib.indiana.edu/newton/. *The Newton Project.* www.newtonproject.ox.ac.uk.

Commons Journal for 27 June 1642. http://www.british-history.ac.uk/report.aspx? compid= 3891.

William Clarke's Will. http://www.horry.org/clarke/williamclarke.html.

PRINTED PRIMARY SOURCES

Alsted, J. *Diatribe de Mille Annis Apocalypticis.* Frankfurt, 1627.

Amidon, P. R., trans. and ed. *Philostorgius: A Church History.* Atlanta, 2007.

Anon. *An Account of the Cambridge Case.* London, 1689.

Babington, H. *Mercy and Judgment: A Sermon.* London, 1678.

Bacon, N. *The History of the Life and Actions of St. Athanasius, Together with the Rise, Growth and Down-fall of the Arian Heresie: Collected from Primitive Writers.* London, 1664.

Barrow, I. *A Treatise of the Pope's Supremacy.* London, 1683.

Barrow, I. *The Usefulness of Mathematical Learning Explained and Demonstrated: Being Mathematical Lectures Read in the Publick Schools at the University of Cambridge.* London, 1734.

Bellamine, R. *Disputationes de Controversiis Christianæ Fidei adversus hujus temporis Hæreticos.* 3 vols. 1581–93.

Bentley, Richard. *The Correspondence of Richard Bentley.* Edited by C. Wordsworth. 2 vols.

Blount, C. *Great Is Diana of the Ephesians.* London, 1680.

Blount, C. *The Oracles of Reason.* London, 1683.

Bochart, S. *Geographia Sacra, cujus pars prior Phaleg de dispersione gentium et terrarum, divisione facta in ædificatione turris Babel, etc. pars posterior Chanaan de coloniis & sermone Phœnicum agit.* Frankfurt, 1681.

Bolland, J. *Acta Sanctorum.* Antwerp, 1629.

Boyle, R. *Experiments and Considerations Touching Colours.* London, 1664.

Boyle, R. *Of the Determinate Nature of Effluviums.* 1673.

Boyle, R. "New Pneumatical Experiments Concerning Respiration." *Philosophical Transactions* 5 (1670): 2011–31, 2035–56.

Boyle, R. *Excellency of Theology, Compared with Natural Philosophy.* London, 1674.

Boyle, R. *A Free Enquiry into the Vulgarly Receiv'd Notion of Nature.* London, 1686.

Boyle, R. *The Works of Robert Boyle.* Edited by M. Hunter and E. B. Davis. 12 vols. London, 2000.

Bull, G. *Defensio Fidei Nicænæ.* Oxford, 1685.

Burnet, T. *Dr. Burnet's Travels, or Letters, Containing an Account of What Seemed Most Remarkable in Travelling Through Switzerland, Italy, France, and Germany, &c. in the Years 1685 and 1686.* Amsterdam, 1687.

Burnet, T. *Telluris Theoria Sacra. . . . Libri Duo Posteriores de Conflagratione Mundi, et de Futuro Rerum Statu.* London, 1689.

Burnet, T. *Archaeologiæ Philosophicæ: Sive Doctrina Antiqua de Rerum Originibus. Libri Duo.* London, 1692.

Burnet, T. *The Sacred Theory of the Earth. . . .* London, 1697.

Bury, A. *The Naked Gospel, Etc.* Oxford, 1690.

Calamy, E. *An Account of the Ministers, Lecturers, Masters and Fellows of Colleges and Schoolmasters, Who Were Ejected or Silenced After the Restoration in 1660, by or Before the Act for Uniformity; Design'd for the Preserving to Posterity the Memory of Their Names, Characters, Writings and Sufferings.* 2 vols. 2nd ed. London, 1727.

Calamy, E. *A Continuation of the Account....* London, 1727.

Calvin, J. *Institutio Christianæ Religionis.* Geneva, 1561.

Cave, W. *Ecclesiastici: or, the History of the Lives, Acts, Death and Writings of the Most Eminent Fathers of the Church That Florisht in the Fourth Century.* London, 1683.

Charleton, W. *Chorea Gigantum, or, The Most Famous Antiquity of Great Britain, Vulgarly Called Stone-heng, Standing on Salisbury Plain, Restored to the Danes.* London, 1663.

Cherbury, E. Herbert of. *The Ancient Religion of the Gentiles, and Causes of Their Error Consider'd....* London 1705.

Cheyne, G. *The Natural Method of Curing Diseases of the Body and Disorders of Mind, Depending on the Body.* London, 1742.

Clarke, S. *A Collection of Papers, Which Passed Between the Late Learned Mr. Leibnitz, and Dr. Clarke, in the Years 1715 and 1716.* London, 1717.

Conti, A. *Réponse aux Observations sur la Chronologie de M. Newton, avec une lettre de M. l'Abbé Conti au sujet de ladite réponse.* Paris, 1726.

Cooper, C. H. *Annals of the University of Cambridge.* 5 vols. Cambridge, 1842–1908.

Cosin, J. *Historia transubstantiationis papalis. Cui præmittitur, atque opponitur, tum S. Scripturæ tum Veterum Patrum, & Reformatarum Ecclesiarum doctrina Catholica....* London, 1675.

Cressener, D. *The Judgments of God upon the Roman Catholick Church....* London, 1689.

Crossley, J. E., and R. C. Christie, eds. *The Diary and Correspondence of John Worthington.* 3 vols. Manchester, 1846–86.

Cudworth, R. *The True Intellectual System of the Universe.* London, 1678.

Curcellaeus, Stephanus. *Novum Testamentum Græcum, cum variantibus lectionibus, tam ex MS. Quam impressis codicibus collectis.* Amsterdam, 1658; 2nd ed., 1675.

Damasus. *Opera quæ extant et vita ex codicibus MSS, cum notis M. M. Sarazanii.* Paris, 1672.

de Beer, E. S. *The Diary of John Evelyn.* 6 vols. London, 1955.

de Beer, E. S., ed. *The Correspondence of John Locke.* 8 vols. Oxford, 1976–89.

De la Bigne, M., ed. *Magna Bibliotheca Veterum Patrum et Antiquorum Scriptorum Ecclesiasticorum.* 17 vols. Paris, 1644.

De la Bigne, M., and P. Despont, eds. *Maxima Bibliotheca Veterum Patrum.* 27 vols. Lyons, 1677.

Descartes, R. *Principia Philosophiæ.* Amsterdam, 1644.

Digges, T. *A Prognostication Everlasting: Corrected and Augmented by Thomas Digges.* London, 1576.

du Val, G., ed. *Aristotelis Opera Omnia, quæ extant, Græce et Latine.* Paris, 1654.

Edleston, J., ed. *Correspondence of Sir Isaac Newton and Professor Cotes.* London, 1850.

Elmacinus (al-Makin), G. *Historia Saracenica, qua Res Gestæ Muslimorum a Muhammede Arabe usque ad initium imperij Atabacæi....Latine reddita opera ac studio T. Erpenii.....* Lugduni Batavorum, 1625.

Eutychius. *Contextia Gemmarum sive Eutychii Patriarchæ Alexandrini Annales.* Edited and translated by J. Selden and E. Pococke. 2 vols. Oxford, 1658–59.

Feguernekinus, Isaac. *Enchiridii locorum communium theologicorum, rerum, exemplorum, atque phrasium sacrarum....*5th ed. Basel, 1604.

Fell, J. *Sancti Cæcilij Cypriani opera recognita & illustrate per Joannem Oxoniensem episcopum. Accedunt Annales Cyprianici....*Oxford, 1682.

Fell, J. *Tes Kaines Diathekes hapanta. Novi Testamenti Libri Omnes. Accesserunt Parallela Scripturæ Loca, necnon variantes Lectiones ex plus 100 MSS. Codicibus et antiquis versionibus collectæ.* Oxford, 1675.

Foster, J. E., ed. *The Diary of Samuel Newton, Alderman of Cambridge.* Cambridge, 1890.

Fourth Report from the Select Committee on Education. London, 1818.

Foxe, J. *Actes and Monuments of These Latter and Perillous Days Touching Matters of the Churche, Wherein Are Comprehended and Described the Great Persecutions....Practised by the Romishe Prelates.* London, 1563.

Gale, T. *Court of the Gentiles, or a Discourse Concerning the Original of Human Literature Both Philologie and Philosophie, from the Scriptures and Jewish Church, 4 parts.* Oxford, 1669–77.

Glanvill, J. *The Vanity of Dogmatizing: Or Confidence in Opinions Manifested in a Discourse of the Shortness and Uncertainty of Our Knowledge and Its Causes; with Some Reflexions on Peripateticism; and An Apology for Philosophy.* London, 1661.

Godefroy, Jacques [Jacob Gothofredus], ed. *Philostorgii Cappadocis, veteris sub Theodosio Iuniore scriptoris, Ecclesiaticæ historiæ, a Constantino M. Ariiq[ue] initiis ad sua vsque tempora, libri XII, a Photio Patriarcha Constantinopolitano, peculari (extra bibliothecam etius hactenus editam) opera, in epitomen contracti.* Geneva, 1642.

Godwyn, Thomas. *Moses and Aaron: Civil and Ecclesiastical Rites, Used by the Ancient Hebrewes: Observed, and at Large Opened....*4th ed. London, 1631.

Gregory, D. *Astronomiæ Physicæ et Geometricæ Elementa.* Oxford, 1702.

Gregory, F. *Onomastikon Brachu. Sive Nomenclatura brevis Anglo-Latino-Græca in usum scholæ Westmonasteriensis....*London, 1660.

Grotius, H. *Historia Gotthorum, Vandalorum, & Langobardorum....*Amsterdam, 1655.

Hale, M. *The Primitive Origination of Mankind Considered and Examined According to the Light of Nature.* London, 1677.

Hall, A. R., and M. B. Hall, eds. *The Correspondence of Henry Oldenburg.* 13 vols. Madison, 1965–86.

Halliwell, J. O., ed. *The Autobiography and Correspondence of Sir Simonds d'Ewes, Bart. During the Reigns of James I and Charles I.* 2 vols. London, 1845.

Hammond, H. *A Paraphrase and Annotation upon All the Books of the New Testament, Briefly Explaining All the Difficulties Thereof.* London, 1653.

Hayter, R. *The Meaning of the Revelation, or a Paraphrase with Questions on the Revelation of John: In Which the Synchronisms of J. Mede, and the Expositions of Other Interpreters Are Called into Question.* London, 1675.

Hearne, T. *Remarks and Collections of Thomas Hearne....*Edited by C. E. Doble, D. W. Rannie, and H. E. Salter. 11 vols. Oxford, 1885–1921.

Heywood, J., and T. Wright, eds. *Cambridge University Transactions During the Puritan Controversies of the Sixteenth and Seventeenth Centuries.* 2 vols. London, 1854.

St. Hilary, Bp of Poitiers, *Sancti Hilarij Pictauorum Episcopi, quotquot extant opera, nostro fere seculo literatorum quorundam non mediocri labore conquisita....*Paris, 1652.

Hill, T. *Six Sermons.* Cambridge, 1649.

Hiscock, W. G., ed. *David Gregory, Isaac Newton, and Their Circle: Extracts from David Gregory's Memoranda, 1677–1708.* Oxford, 1937.

Hobbes, T. *Historia Ecclesiastica, Critical Edition, Including Text, Translation, Introduction, Commentary and Notes.* Edited by P. Springborg, P. Stablein, and P. Wilson. Paris, 2008.

Hobbes, T. *Leviathan: Or the Matter, Forme and Power of a Commonwealth, Ecclesiastical and Civil.* Edited by N. Malcolm. 3 vols. Oxford, 2012; orig., London, 1651 and 1668.

The Holy Bible Containing the Old Testament and the New. London, 1660.

Hooke, R. *The Diary of Robert Hooke, M.A., M.D., F.R.S., 1672–1680.* Edited by W. Adams and H. W. Robinson. London, 1935.

Hoole, C. *He Kaine Diatheke, Novum Testamentum. Huic edition omnia difficiliorum vocabulorum themata, quæ in G. Pasoris Lexico grammatice resolvuntur, in margine apposuit C. Hoole.* London, 1653.

Hoole, C. *A New Discovery of the Old Art of Teaching Schoole in Four Small Treatises.* London, 1660.

Howard, L. *A Collection of Letters, from the Original Manuscripts of Many Princes, Great Personages and Statesmen.* London, 1753.

Howell, T. B., and T. J. Howell. *A Complete Collection of State Trials and Proceedings for High Treason and other Crimes and Misdemeanours from the Earliest Period to the Year 1783.* 21 vols. London, 1809–28.

Hunter, M., et al., eds. *The Correspondence of Robert Boyle.* 6 vols. London, 2001.

Jackson, C., ed. *The Diary of Abraham de la Pryme.* Durham, 1870.

Jacobson, W., ed. *The Works of Robert Sanderson.* 6 vols. Oxford, 1854.

Jansson, M., ed. *Proceedings in the Opening Session of the Long Parliament.* Vol. 1, "3 November–19 December 1640." Rochester, N.Y., 2000.

Johnson, R. *The Famous History of the Seven Champions of Christendom: Saint George of England, Saint Denis of France, Saint James of Spain, Saint Anthony of Italy, Saint Andrew of Scotland, Saint Patrick of Ireland, and Saint David of Wales. Shewing Their Honourable Battels by Sea and Land: Their Tilts, Justs, Turnaments for Ladies: Their Combats with Giants, Monsters and Dragons: Their Adventures in Forraign Nations; Their Inchantments in the Holy Land: Their Knight-hoods Prowess and Chivalry, in Europe, Africa, and Asia, with Their Victories Against the Enemies of Christ.* 2 parts. London, 1660; orig., 1596–97.

Jones, I. *The Most Notable Antiquity of Great Britain, Vulgarly Called Stone-heng on Salisbury Plain, Restored.* Edited by J. Webb. London, 1655.

Jurieu, P. *A Continuation of the Accomplishment of the Scripture Prophecies, or a Large Deduction of Historical Evidences, Proving, the Papacy Is the Real Antichristian Kingdom.* London, 1688.

Jurieu, P. *L'Accomplissement des propheties ou la deliverance prochaine del'Eglise*. Rotterdam, 1686. Partially trans. as *The Accomplishment of the Scripture Prophecies, or the Approaching Deliverance of the Church*. London, 1687.

Koyré, A., and I. B. Cohen, eds. *Isaac Newton's Philosophiæ Naturalis Principia Mathematica, the Third Edition (1726) with Variant Readings*. 2 vols. Cambridge, Mass., 1972.

Le Clerc, J. *An Historical Vindication of the Naked Gospel, Recommended to the University of Oxford*. London, 1691.

Locke, J. *Essai philosophique concernant l'entendement humain*. 3rd ed. Translated by P. Coste. Amsterdam, 1735.

Locke, J. *Of the Conduct of the Understanding*. Edited by F. Garforth. New York, 1966.

Locke, J. *Epistola de Tolerantia. Letter on Toleration*. Edited by R. Klibansky and J. W. Gough. Oxford, 1968.

Locke, J. "Of Study." In *The Educational Writings of John Locke*. Edited by J. L. Axtell. Cambridge, 1968.

Locke, J. *Locke's Two Treatises on Government*. 2nd ed. Edited by P. Laslett. Cambridge, 1970.

Locke, J. *An Essay Concerning Human Understanding*. Edited by P. Nidditch. Oxford, 1975.

Locke, J. *Some Thoughts upon Education*. Edited by John Yolton. Oxford, 1989.

Maimonides, M. *De Idololatria Liber*. Translated by D. Vossius. In *De Theologia Gentili...*, by G. J. Vossius. Amsterdam, 1641.

Marsham, J. *Canon Chronicus Ægyptiacus, Ebraicus, Græcus, et disquisitions....*London, 1672.

Mede, J. *The Works of J. Mede: Corrected and Enlarged According to the Author's Own Manuscripts*. Edited by J. Worthington. London, 1672.

Morcillo, S. Fox. *De naturæ philosophia, seu de Platonis, & Aristotelis consensione, libri V...*.Paris, 1560.

More, H. *Conjectura Cabbalistica, or, A Conjectural Essay of Interpreting the Minde of Moses According to a Threefold Cabbala: Viz. Literal, Philosophical, Mystical, or Divinely Moral*. Cambridge, 1653.

More, H. *The Immortality of the Soul, So Farre Forth as It Is Demonstrable from the Knowledge of Nature and the Light of Reason*. London, 1659.

More, H. *An Explanation of the Grand Mystery of Godliness*. London, 1660.

More, H. *A Collection of Several Philosophical Writings*. London, 1662.

More, H. *A Modest Enquiry into the Mystery of Iniquity, the First Part, Containing a Careful and Impartial Delineation of the True Idea of Antichristianism....*London, 1664.

More, H. *Synopsis Prophetica: The Second Part of the Enquiry into the Mystery of Iniquity*. London, 1664.

More, H. *Divine Dialogues. Containing Sundry Disquisitions & Instructions Concerning the Attributes of God and His Providence in the World*. London, 1668.

More, H. *An Exposition of the Seven Epistles to the Seven Churches, Together with a Brief Discourse of Idolatry, with Application to the Church of Rome*. London, 1669.

More, H. *Henrici Mori Cantabrigiensis Opera Theologica....*London, 1675.

More, H. *Apocalypsis Apocalypseos, (or the Revelation of St. John the Divine Unveiled)*. London, 1680.

More, H. *A Plain and Continued Exposition of the Several Prophecies or Divine Visions of the Prophet Daniel, Which Have or May Concern the People of God, Whether Jew or Christian: Whereunto Is Annexed a Threefold Appendage, Touching Three Main Points, the First, Relating to Daniel, the Other Two, to the Apocalypse*. London, 1681.

Morinus, J. *Exercitationum ecclesiasticarum libri duo: De patriarcharum & primatum origine, primis orbis terrarium ecclesiasticis diuisionibus, atque antiqua & primigenia censurarum in clericos natura & praxis, etc.* Paris, 1634.

Morrice, R. *The Entring Book of Roger Morrice (1677–1691)*. Edited by M. Goldie. 6 vols. Woodbridge, 2008.

Napier, J. *A Plaine Discovery of the Whole Revelation of Saint John: Set Downe in Two Treatises: The One Searching and Proving the True Interpretation Thereof: The Other Applying the Same Paraphrastically and Historically to the Text*. London, 1645; orig., Edinburgh, 1593.

Newton, I. "An Account of the Commercium Epistolicum." *Philosophical Transactions* 342 (1715): 194.

Newton, I. *The Chronology of Ancient Kingdoms Amended*. London, 1728.

Newton, I. *Observations on the Prophecies of Daniel and St. John*. London, 1733.

Newton, I. *Optice. Sive De Reflexionibus, Refractionibus, Inflexionibus & Coloribus Lucis, Libri Tres*. London, 1706.

Newton, I. *The Principia: Mathematical Principles of Natural Philosophy*. Edited by I. B. Cohen and A. Whitman. Los Angeles, 1999.

Nicolson, M. H., and S. Hutton, eds. *The Conway Letters: The Correspondence of Anne Finch, Countess of Conway, Henry More, and Their Friends*. Oxford, 1992.

Nye, S. *The Acts of the Great Athanasius, with Notes, by Way of Illustration, on His Creed; and Observations on the Learned Vindication of the Trinity and Incarnation, by William Sherlock*. London, 1690.

Nye, S. *A Brief History of the Unitarians, Called also Socinians. In Four Letters Written to a Friend*. London, 1687.

Nye, S. *Brief Notes on the Creed of St. Athanasius*. London, 1690.

Palladius, Bishop of Aspuna. *Palladii Divi Evagrii Discipuli Lausiaca quæ dicitur historia, et Theodoreti Episcopi Cyri, id est religiosa historia*....Paris, 1555.

Parker, S. *A Free and Impartial Censure of the Platonic Philosophie*. Oxford, 1666.

Parker, S. *Religion and Loyalty: or, a Demonstration of the Power of the Church Within Itself. The Supremacy of Sovereign Powers over It. The Duty of Passive Obedience, or Non-Resistance to All Their Commands*. London, 1684.

Pasor, G. *Lexicon Græco-Latinum in Novum Domini Nostri Jesu Christi Testamentum*.... 3 parts. London, 1649–50.

Petavius (Petau), D. *Opus de theologicis dogmatibus, auctius in hac nova editione notulis T. Alethini [i.e. J. Le Clerc]*. 6 vols. Antwerp, 1700.

Petavius (Petau), D. *Dogmata Theologica*. 5 vols. Paris, 1644–50.

Pococke, E. *Specimen Historiæ Arabum, sive Gregorii Abul Farajii Malatiensis, De origine & moribus Arabum succincta narratio*....Oxford, 1650.

Poole, M. *Synopsis Criticorum aliorumque Sacrae Scripturae interpretum et commentatorum*. 5 vols. London, 1669–76.

Potter, F. *An Interpretation of the Number 666*....Oxford, 1642.

Proast, J. *The Argument of the Letter Concerning Toleration, Briefly Consider'd and Answer'd*. Oxford, 1690.

Richer, E. *Historia Conciliorum Generalium, in quatuor libros distributa*. Cologne, 1680.

Rosweyde, H. *Vitae Patrum: De Vita et Verbis Seniorum sive Libri X, historiae eremeticae*. 10 vols. Antwerp, 1615, 2nd ed. 1628.

Sand, C. *Interpretationes paradoxæ quatuor Evangeliorum: Quibus affixa est Dissertatio de Verbo, una cum appendice*. Amsterdam, 1670.

Sand, C. *Nucleus Historiæ Ecclesiasticæ, exhibitus in Historia Arianorum*....2 vols. Amsterdam, 1669; 2nd ed., Amsterdam, 1676.

Schrevelius, C. *Lexicon Manuale Græco-Latinum et Latino-Græcum, Editio secunda auctior multo & emendatior*. Lugduni Batavorum, 1657.

Shapiro, A. E., ed. *The Optical Papers of Isaac Newton*. Vol. 1, *The Optical Lectures 1670–1672*. Cambridge, 1984.

Sherlock, W. *A Vindication of the Doctrine of the Holy and Ever Blessed Trinity, and the Incarnation of the Son of God. Occasioned by the Brief Notes on the Creed of Athanasius, and the Brief History of the Unitarians, or Socinians*. London, 1690.

Simon, R. *Critical Enquiries into the Various Editions of the Bible*. London, 1684.

Simon, R. *Critical History of the Text of the New Testament: Wherein Is Firmly Established the Truth of Those Acts on Which the Foundation of the Christian Religion Is Laid*. 2 parts. London, 1689.

Simon, R. *A Critical History of the Versions of the New Testament. Part 2*. London, 1692.

Smith, T. *A Sermon of the Credibility of the Mysteries of the Christian Religion Preached Before a Learned Audience*. London, 1675.

Snow, V. F., and A. S. Young, eds. *The Private Journals of the Long Parliament*. Vol. 3. New Haven, 1992.

Spencer, J. *De Legibus Hebræorum ritualibus et earum rationibus, Libri III*. Cambridge, 1683–85.

Stahl, D. *Axiomata Philosophica, sub titulis XX comprehensa*. 3rd ed. Cambridge, 1645.

Stillingfleet, E. *Origines Sacræ: Or a Rational Account of the Grounds of Christian Faith, as to the Truth and Divine Authority of the Scriptures, and the Matters Therein Contained*. London, 1662.

Stillingfleet, E. *A Discourse Concerning the Idolatry Practised in the Church of Rome, and the Danger of Salvation in the Communion of It*. London, 1671.

Stillingfleet, E. *An Answer to Several Late Treatises, Occasioned by a Book Entitled a Discourse Concerning the Idolatry Practised in the Church of Rome, Part 1*. London, 1673.

Stanley, T. *Historia philosophiæ Orientalis. Recensuit, ex Anglica lingua in Latinam Transtulit*....Amsterdam, 1690.

Suicerus, J. C. *Thesaurus ecclesiasticus, et Patribus Græcis ordine alphabetico*. 2 vols. Amsterdam, 1682.

Toland, J. *Christianity Not Mysterious*. London, 1696.

Trelcatius, L. *Locorum communium S. Theologiæ Instituto per epitome....*London, 1608.

Turnbull, H.W., et al., eds. *The Correspondence of Isaac Newton.* 7 vols. London, 1959–77.

Varenius, B. *Geographia generalis, in qua affectiones gēnerales telluris explicantur: Summa cura quam plurimis in locis emendata...ab I. Newton.* 2nd ed. Cambridge, 1681.

Victor of Vita. *History of the Vandal Persecution.* Edited by J. Moorhead. Liverpool, 1992.

Voltaire. *Letters Concerning the English Nation.* London, 1778.

Vossius, G. J. *Rhetorices Contractæ, sive partitionum oratorium, Libri V.* Oxford, 1631.

Vossius, G. J. *De theologia Gentili, et physiologia Christiana, sive De origine ac progressu Idololatriæ...liber I, et II (III et IV).* Amsterdam, 1641.

Walker, J. *An Attempt Towards Recovering an Account of the Numbers and Sufferings of the Clergy of the Church of England Etc.* London, 1714.

Walton, B. *Biblia Sacra Polyglotta, complectentia Textus Originales, Hebraicum cum Pentateucho Samaritano, Chaldaicum, Græcum, Versionumque antiquarum Samaritanæ, Græcæ LXXII. Interpretum, Chaldaicæ, Syriacæ, Arabicæ, Ethiopicæ, Vulgatæ, Latinæ, quicquid compari poterat, &c.* 6 vols. London, 1657.

Ward, R. *The Life of Henry More.* London, 1710.

Whiston, W. *A Collection of Authentick Records.* London, 1728.

Whiston, W. *Memoirs of the Life and Writings of William Whiston.* 2 vols. London, 1749–50.

Whiteside, D. T., ed. *The Mathematical Papers of Isaac Newton.* 8 vols. Cambridge, 1967–81.

Willis, T. *Cerebri Anatome: Cui accessit nervorum descriptio et usus.* 1664.

Willis, T. *Pathologiæ cerebri et nervosus generus specimen.* London, 1667.

Willis, T. *Affectionum quæ dicuntur hystericæ et hypochondriacæ pathologia spasmodica vindicate contra responsionem epistolarem Nathanael Highmori. M.D. Cui accesserunt exercitationes medico-physicæ duæ. 1. De sanguinis accensione. 2. De motu musculari.* London, 1670.

Willmoth, F., et al., eds. *The Correspondence of John Flamsteed, the First Astronomer Royal.* 3 vols. London, 1995.

Worthington, J. *Miscellanies....*London, 1704.

SECONDARY WORKS

Allen, D. C. *The Legend of Noah: Renaissance Rationalism in Art, Science, and Letters.* Champaign Ill., 1963.

Allen, D. C. *Mysteriously Meant.* Baltimore, 1970.

Anstey, P. *John Locke and Natural Philosophy.* Oxford, 2011.

Ariew, R. *Descartes Among the Scholastics.* Leiden, 2011.

Ariew, R. "The Infinite in Descartes's Conversation with Burman," *Archiv für Geschichte der Philosophie* 69 (1987): 140–63.

Arnold, D. W. H. *The Early Episcopal Career of Athanasius of Alexandria.* Notre Dame, 1991.

Ashcraft, R. *Revolutionary Politicks and Locke's Two Treatises of Government.* Princeton, 1986.

Ashworth, E. J. Introduction to the 1618 edition of *Logicæ Artis Compendium,* by Robert Sanderson. Bologna, 1985.

Assman, J. *Moses the Egyptian: The Memory of Egypt in Western Monotheism.* London 1997.

Aston, M. *England's Iconoclasts: Laws Against Images.* Oxford, 1988.

Austen-Leigh, A. *King's College.* London, 1899.

Auvray, P. *Richard Simon, 1638–1712: Étude Bio-bibliographique avec des Textes Inédits.* Paris, 1974.

Axtell, J. L. "Locke's Review of the Principia." *Notes and Records of the Royal Society* 20 (1965): 152–61.

Baird, K. "Some Influences upon the Young Isaac Newton." *Notes and Records of the Royal Society* 41 (1987): 169–79.

Ball, B. W. *A Great Expectation: Eschatological Thought in English Protestantism to 1660.* Leiden, 1975.

Ball, B. W. *Soul Sleepers: Christian Mortalism from Wycliffe to Priestley.* Cambridge, 2008.

Barish, J. *The Anti-Theatrical Prejudice.* London, 1981.

Barnes, A. *Jean Le Clerc (1657–1736), et la République des Lettres.* Paris, 1938.

Barnes, T. D. *Athanasius and Constantius: Theology and Politics in the Constantinian Empire.* Cambridge, Mass., 1993.

Bauckham, R. *Tudor Apocalypse.* Oxford, 1978.

Beddard, R. *A Kingdom without a King: The Journal of the Provisional Government in the Revolution of 1688.* Oxford, 1988.

Bedford, R. *In Defence of Truth.* Manchester, 1979.

Bennett, G. V. "Loyalist Oxford and the Revolution." In *The History of the University of Oxford.* Ed. L. Sutherland and L. Mitchell. 5 vols., 5:9–30. Oxford, 1988.

Bentley, J. H. *Humanists and Holy Writ: New Testament Scholarship in the Renaissance.* Princeton, 1983.

Birch, T., ed. *The History of the Royal Society.* 4 vols. London, 1756–57.

Birdsall, P. "'Non Obstante': A Study of the Dispensing Power of English Kings." In *Essays in History and Political Theory in Honour of Charles Howard McIlwain.* Edited by C. Wittke, 37–76. Cambridge, Mass., 1934.

Bloxam, J. R., ed. *Magdalen College and James II, 1686–1688.* Oxford, 1886.

Brady, D. *The Contribution of British Writers Between 1560 and 1830 to the Interpretation of Revelation 13.16–18 (the Number of the Beast): A Study in the History of Exegesis.* Tubingen, 1983.

Brakke, D. *Demons and the Making of the Monk: Spiritual Combat in Early Christianity.* Cambridge, Mass., 2006.

Bredvold, L. *The Intellectual Milieu of John Dryden.* Ann Arbor, Mich., 1966.

Broughton, P. "Arthur Storer of Maryland." *Journal for the History of Astronomy* 19 (1988): 77–96.

Brown, P. *The Body and Society: Men, Women, and Sexual Renunciation in Early Christianity.* New York, 2008.

Buchwald, J. Z., and M. Feingold. *Newton and the Origin of Civilization*. Princeton, 2013.

Burns, N. *Christian Mortalism from Tyndale to Milton*. Cambridge, Mass., 1972.

Burrus, V. *The Sex Lives of Saints: An Erotics of Ancient Hagiography*. Philadelphia, 2004.

Cambers, A. *Godly Reading: Print, Manuscript and Puritanism in England, 1580–1720*. Cambridge, 2011.

Cambers, A., ed. *The Life of John Rastrick, 1650–1727*. Cambridge, 2010.

Capp, B. S. *The Fifth-Monarchy Men: A Study in Seventeenth-Century English Millenarianism*. London, 1972.

Casini, P. " 'Acceptable to Inquisitive Men': Some Simonian Contexts for Newton's Biblical Criticism, 1680–92." In *Newton and Religion: Context, Nature and Influence*. Edited by J. E. Force and R. Popkin, 77–96. Kluwer, 1999.

Casini, P. "Il mito pitagorico e la rivoluzione astronomica." *Revista di filosofia* 85 (1994): 7–33.

Casini, P. "Newton: The Classical Scholia." *History of Science* 22 (1984): 1–59.

Casini, P. *Republican Learning: John Toland and the Crisis of Christian Culture, 1696–1722*. Manchester, 2003.

Champion, J. *The Pillars of Priestcraft Shaken: The Church of England and Its Enemies 1660–1730*. Cambridge, 1992.

Christianson, G. *In the Presence of the Creator: Isaac Newton and His Times*. New York, 1984.

Christianson, P. *Reformers and Babylon: English Apocalyptic Visions from the Reformation to the Eve of the Civil War*. Toronto, 1975.

Churchill, E. F. "The Dispensing Power of the Crown in Ecclesiastical Affairs." *Law Quarterly Review* 151 (1922): 297–316; and 152 (1922): 420–34.

Churton, E. "Memoir of Bishop Pearson." In *The Minor Theological Works of Bishop Pearson, D.D.* 2 vols. Edited by E. Churton. Oxford, 1844.

Clark, J. C. D. *English Society, 1688–1832: Ideology, Social Structure and Political Practice During the Ancien Regime*. 2nd ed. Cambridge, 2000.

Clifton, R. "Fear of Popery." In *The Origins of the English Civil War*. Edited by C. Russell, 144–67. London, 1973.

Clover, F. M. *The Late Roman West and the Vandals*. Aldershot, 1993.

Coffey, J. *Persecution and Toleration in Protestant England, 1558–1689*. London, 2000.

Coffey, J., and P. Lim, eds. *The Cambridge Companion to Puritanism*. Cambridge, 2008.

Cohen, I. B. *Introduction to Newton's "Principia."* Cambridge, Mass., 1971.

Cohen, I. B. *The Newtonian Revolution, with Illustrations of the Transformation of Scientific Ideas*. Cambridge, 1980.

Cohen, I. B. "Newton's Conception of Hypotheses." *Physis* 8 (1966): 163–84.

Cohen, I. B. "Versions of Isaac Newton's First Published Paper." *Archives Internationales d'Histoire des Sciences* 11 (1958): 357–75.

Colclough, D. "Parrhesia: The Rhetoric of Free Speech in Early Modern England." *Rhetorica* 17 (1999): 177–212.

Collins, J. "Thomas Hobbes' Ecclesiastical History." In *The Oxford Handbook of Hobbes*. Edited by A. P. Martinich and K. Hoekstra, 520–544. Oxford, 2016.

Collinson, P. *The Birthpangs of Protestant England: Religious and Cultural Change in the Sixteenth and Seventeenth Centuries.* London: Macmillan, 1991.

Collinson, P. *The English Puritan Movement.* Clarendon, 1990.

Coogan, R. *Erasmus, Lee and the Correction of the Vulgate: The Shaking of the Foundations.* Geneva, 1992.

Cooper, C. H. *Annals of Cambridge.* 5 vols. Cambridge, 1842–52.

Copenhaver, B. "Jewish Theologies of Space in the Scientific Revolution: Henry More, Joseph Raphson and Isaac Newton." *Annals of Science* 37 (1978): 489–548.

Corneanu, S. *Regimens of the Mind: Boyle, Locke, and the Early Modern Cultura Animi Tradition.* Chicago, 2011.

Corneanu, S., and K. Vermeir. "Idols of the Imagination: Francis Bacon on the Imagination and the Medicine of the Mind." *Perspectives on Science* 20 (2012): 183–206.

Costello, W. T. *The Scholastic Curriculum at Seventeenth-Century Cambridge.* Cambridge, Mass., 1958.

Cottingham, J., R. Stoothoff, and D. Murdoch, eds. *The Philosophical Writings of Descartes.* 3 vols. Cambridge, 1985.

Couth, B. *Crocadiles, French Flies and Other Animalls: Grantham at Peace and War 1633–1649.* Nottingham, 1995.

Couth, B. *Grantham During the Interregnum: The Hallbook, 1641–1649.* Woodbridge, 1995.

Craig, J. "Newton and the Counterfeiters." *Notes and Records of the Royal Society* 18 (1963): 136–45.

Cranston, M. *John Locke: A Biography.* London, 1957.

Crook, R. *Arthur Storer's World: Family, Medicine and Astronomy in Seventeenth-Century Lincolnshire and Maryland.* Grantham, 2014.

Curtis, M. *Oxford and Cambridge in Transition, 1558–1642.* Oxford, 1959.

Dannenfeldt, K. "Egypt and Egyptian Antiquities in the Renaissance." *Studies in the Renaissance* 6 (1959): 7–27.

Delgado-Moreira, R. "Newton's Treatise on Revelation: The Use of a Mathematical Discourse." *Historical Research* 79 (2006): 224–46.

Derham, W. "Select Remains and the Life of John Ray." In *Memorials of John Ray.* Edited by E. Lankester. London, 1846.

Des Chene, D. *Physiologia: Natural Philosophy in Late Aristotelian and Cartesian Thought.* Ithaca, N.Y., 1996.

Dixon, P. *Nice and Hot Disputes: The Doctrine of the Trinity in the Seventeenth Century.* London, 2003.

Dobbs, B. J. T. *The Janus Faces of Genius: The Role of Alchemy in Newton's Thoughts.* Cambridge, 1992.

Dockrill, D. W. "The Authority of the Fathers in the Great Trinitarian Debates of the Sixteen Nineties." *Studia Patristica* 18 (1990): 335–47.

Downing, L. "Locke's Newtonianism and Lockean Newtonianism." In *Perspectives on Science* 5 (1997): 285–310.

Dry, S. *The Newton Papers: The Strange and True Odyssey of Newton's Manuscripts*. New York, 2014.

Ducheyne, S. *The Main Business of Natural Philosophy: Isaac Newton's Natural Philosophical Methodology*. Dordrecht, 2012.

Dugmore, C. *The Mass and the English Reformers*. London, 1958.

Dunn, J. *The Political Thought of John Locke: An Historical Account of the Argument of the Two Treatises of Government*. Cambridge, 1969.

Ebeling, F. *The Secret History of Hermes Trismegistus: Hermeticism from Ancient to Modern Times*. Ithaca, N.Y., 2007.

Edleston, J. *The Correspondence of Sir Isaac Newton and Professor Cotes*. London, 1850.

Ehrman, B. *The Orthodox Corruption of Scripture: The Effect of Early Christological Controversies on the Text of the New Testament*. Oxford, 1993.

Eire, C. M. N. *War Against the Idols: The Reformation of Worship from Erasmus to Calvin*. Cambridge, 1986.

Evans, E. "The Puritan Use of Imagination." *Reformation and Revival* 10 (2001): 47–84.

Feingold, M. "The Humanities." In *The History of the University of Oxford*. Vol. 4, *Seventeenth-Century Oxford*. Edited by N. Tyacke, 211–357. Oxford, 1997.

Feingold, M. "Isaac Barrow: Divine, Scholar, Mathematician." In *Before Newton: The Life and Times of Isaac Barrow*. Edited by M. Feingold. Cambridge, 1990.

Feingold, M. "Science as a Calling? The Early Modern Dilemma." *Science in Context* 15 (2002): 79–119.

Fincham, K. " 'According to Ancient Custom': The Return of the Altars in the Restoration Church of England." In *Transactions of the Royal Historical Society*. 6th series, 13 (2003): 29–30.

Fincham, K., and N. Tyacke. *Altars Restored: The Changing Face of English Religious Worship, 1547–c.1700*. Oxford, 2007.

Firpo, M. "John Locke e il Socinianismo." *Rivista Storica Italiana* 92 (1980): 35–124.

Firth, K. *The Apocalyptic Tradition in Reformation Britain, 1530–1645*. Oxford, 1978.

Fletcher, H. F. *The Intellectual Development of John Milton*. 2 vols. Urbana, Ill., 1956–61.

Force, J. E. "Newton's God of Dominion: The Unity of Newton's Theological, Scientific and Political Thought." In *Essays on the Context, Nature and Influence of Isaac Newton's Theology*. Edited by J. E. Force and R. Popkin, 75–102. London, 1990.

Force, J. E. "The God of Abraham and Isaac (Newton)." In *The Books of Nature and Scripture*. Edited by J. E. Force and R. Popkin, 179–200. Dordrecht, 1994.

Force, J. E. " 'Children of the Resurrection' and 'Children of the Dust': Confronting Mortality and Immortality with Newton and Hume." In *Everything Connects: In Conference with Richard H. Popkin* 119–42. Leiden, 1999.

Foster, C. W. "Sir Isaac Newton's Family." *Reports and Papers of the Architectural Societies of the County of Lincoln etc.* 39, part 1 (1928): 4–56.

Foster, W. E. *The Committee of Plundered Ministers of Lincolnshire: Being Extracts from the Minutes of the Committee of Plundered Ministers*. Gilford, 1891.

Foucault, M. "The Battle for Chastity." In *Ethics: Subjectivity and Truth*. Edited by
P. Rabinow, 185–97. New York, 1997.

Foucault, M. *The Courage of Truth*. Translated by G. Burchell. Basingstoke, 2011.

Fox, A. *Mill and Bentley: A Study of the Textual Criticism of the New Testament, 1675–1729*.
Oxford, 1954.

Fox Bourne, H. R. *The Life of John Locke*. 2 vols. London, 1876.

Foxcroft, H. C., ed. *The Life and Letters of Sir George Savile…First Marquis of Halifax*.
2 vols. London, 1898.

Frisch, H. "The Scientist as Priest: A Note on Robert Boyle's Natural Theology." *Isis*
44 (1953): 252–65.

Funkenstein, A. *Theology and the Scientific Imagination from the Middle Ages to the Seventeenth Century*. Princeton, 1986.

Gabbey, A. "Philosophia Cartesiana Triumphata: Henry More (1646–71)." In *Problems of Cartesianism*. Edited by T. Lennon et al., 171–250. Kingston, Ontario, 1982.

Gal, O. *Meanest Foundations and Nobler Superstructures: Hooke, Newton and the Compounding of the Celestiall Motions of Planets*. Boston, 2002.

Garber, D. *Descartes' Metaphysical Physics*. Chicago, 1992.

Gascoigne, J. "Barrow's Academic Milieu." In *Before Newton: The Life and Times of Isaac Barrow*. Edited by M. Feingold, 250–90. Cambridge, 1990.

Gascoigne, J. "The Universities and the Scientific Revolution: The Case of Restoration Cambridge." *History of Science* 23 (1985): 391–434.

Gascoigne, J. "The Wisdom of the Egyptians and the Secularisation of History in the Age of Newton." In *The Uses of Antiquity: The Scientific Revolution and the Classical Tradition*. Edited by S. Gaukroger, 171–212. Dordrecht, 1991.

Gaskill, M. *Crime and Mentalities in Early Modern England*. Cambridge, 2000.

Gibbon, E. *The History of the Decline and Fall of the Roman Empire*. 3 vols. Edited by D. Womersley. London, 1995; orig., 1776–88.

Gibson, E. C. S. *The Thirty-Nine Articles of the Church of England*. 5th ed. London, 1906.

Goldie, M. "John Locke, Jonas Proast, and Religious Toleration, 1688–1692." In *The Church of England, 1689–1833: From Toleration to Tractarianism*. Edited by J. Walsh, C. Haydon, and S. Taylor, 143–72. Oxford, 1992.

Goldie, M. "Joshua Basset, Popery and Revolution." In *Sidney Sussex College, Cambridge: Historical Essays in Commemoration of the Quatercentenary*. Edited by D. E. D. Beales and H. B. Nisbet, 111–30. Woodbridge, 1996.

Goldie, M. "The Revolution of 1689 and the Structure of Political Argument: An Essay and an Annotated Bibliography of Pamphlets on the Allegiance Controversy." *Bulletin of Research in the Humanities* 33 (1980): 473–564.

Goldie, M. "The Roots of True Whiggism." *History of Political Thought* 1 (1980): 200–226.

Goldish, M. *Judaism in the Theology of Isaac Newton*. Dordrecht, 1998.

Grafton, A. *Commerce with the Classics: Ancient Books and Renaissance Readers*. Ann Arbor, 1997.

Grafton, A. *Defenders of the Text: The Traditions of Scholarship in an Age of Science, 1450–1800.* Cambridge, Mass., 1994.

Grafton, A. *Joseph Scaliger: A Study in the History of Classical Scholarship.* 2 vols. Oxford: Clarendon; New York: Oxford University Press, 1983 and 1993.

Grant, E. *Much Ado About Nothing: Theories of Space and Vacuum from the Middle Ages to the Scientific Revolution.* Cambridge, 1981.

Greaves, J. *John Bunyan and English Nonconformity.* London, 1992.

Greaves, J. *Secrets of the Kingdom: British Radicals from the Popish Plot to the Revolution of 1688–89.* Stanford, 1992.

Green, I. *The Christian's ABC: Catechisms and Catechizing in England, c. 1530–1740.* Oxford, 1996.

Greig, M. "The Reasonableness of Christianity? Gilbert Burnet and the Trinitarian Controversy of the 1690s." *Journal of Ecclesiastical History* 44 (1993): 631–49.

Grey, A. *Debates in the House of Commons, from the Year 1667 to the Year 1694.* 10 vols. London, 1769.

Guicciardini, N. *Isaac Newton on Mathematical Certainty and Method.* London, 2009.

Gunther, R. W. T. *The Further Correspondence of John Ray.* London, 1928.

Gwynn, D. *The Eusebians: The Polemic of Athanasius of Alexandria and the Construction of the Arian Controversy.* Oxford, 2007.

Hadot, P. *Philosophy as a Way of Life.* Oxford, 1995.

Hall, A. R. "Newton's First Book (I)." *Archives Internationales d'Histoire des Sciences* 13 (1960): 39–60.

Hall, A. R. *Philosophers at War.* Cambridge, 1980.

Hall, A. R., and M. B. Hall, eds. *Unpublished Scientific Papers of Isaac Newton.* Cambridge, 1962.

Hammond, P. "Dryden and Trinity." *Review of English Studies* 36 (1985): 35–57.

Hanson, R. P. C. *The Search for the Christian Doctrine of God: The Arian Controversy 318–381.* Edinburgh, 1988.

Harris, T. *London Crowds in the Reign of Charles II: Propaganda from the Restoration Until the Exclusion Crisis.* Cambridge, 1987.

Harris, T. *Revolution: The Great Crisis of the English Monarchy, 1685–1720.* London, 2006.

Harrison, J. *The Library of Isaac Newton.* Cambridge, 1978.

Hatfield, G. "The Cognitive Faculties." In *The Cambridge History of Seventeenth-Century Philosophy.* Vol. 2. Edited by D. Garber and M. Ayers. Cambridge, 1998.

Haugen, K. "Transformations of the Trinity Doctrine in English Scholarship: From the History of Beliefs to the History of Texts." *Archiv für Religionsgeschichte* 3 (2001): 149–68.

Haugen, K. "Apocalypse (a User's Manual): Joseph Mede, the Interpretation of Prophecy, and the Dream Book of Achmet." *The Seventeenth Century* 25 (2010): 215–39.

Hazard, P. *The Crisis of the European Mind, 1680–1715.* New York, 2013; orig., 1934.

Heather, P. *Goths and Romans, 332–489.* Oxford, 1991.

Heather, P., and J. Matthews. *The Goths in the Fourth Century*. Liverpool, 1991.

Henning, D. *The History of Parliament: The Commons, 1660–1690*. 3 vols. London, 1983.

Henry, J. "A Cambridge Platonist's Materialism: Henry More and the Concept of Soul." *Journal of the Warburg and Courtauld Institutes* 49 (1986): 172–95.

Herivel, J. *The Background to Newton's Principia: A Study of Newton's Dynamical Researches in the Years 1664–84*. Oxford, 1965.

Higgins-Biddle, J., ed. *John Locke: The Reasonableness of Christianity*. Oxford, 1999.

Hill, C. *Antichrist in Seventeenth-Century England*, rev. ed. London: Verso, 1990.

Holmes, C. *Seventeenth-Century Lincolnshire*. Lincoln, 1980.

Hooykaas, R. *Rheticus' Treatise on Holy Scripture and the Motion of the Earth*. New York, 1984.

Horsfall Turner, J., ed. *The Rev. Oliver Heywood B.A., 1630–1702: His Autobiography, Diaries, Anecdote and Event Books.…* 4 vols. Brighouse, 1881–85.

Horwitz, H. *Parliament, Policy and Politics in the Reign of William III*. Manchester, 1977.

Horwitz, H. *Revolution Politicks: The Career of Daniel Finch, Second Earl of Nottingham, 1647–1730*. Cambridge, 1968.

Hotson, H. *Paradise Postponed: Johann Heinrich Alsted and the Birth of Calvinist Millenarianism*. Dordrecht, 2001.

Howell, W. S. *Logic and Rhetoric in England, 1550–1700*. Princeton, 1956.

Huet, M. H. *Monstrous Imagination*. Cambridge, Mass., 1993.

Hunter, J. *The Rise of the Old Dissent Exemplified in the Life of Oliver Heywood*. London, 1842.

Hunter, M. *Robert Boyle: Scrupulosity and Science*. Woodbridge, 2000.

Hutton, S. "Edward Stillingfleet, Henry More and the Decline of Moses Atticus: A Note on Seventeenth-Century Anglican Apologetics." In *Philosophy, Science and Religion in England, 1640–1700*. Edited by R. Kroll, R. Ashcraft, and P. Zagorin, 68–84. Cambridge, 1992.

Hutton, S. "More, Newton and the Language of Biblical Prophecy." In *The Books of Nature and Scripture*. Edited by J. E. Force and R. Popkin. Dordrecht, 1994.

Hutton, S. "The Neoplatonic Roots of Arianism: Ralph Cudworth and Theophilus Gale." In *Socinianism and Its Role in the Culture of the XVIth to XVIIIth Centuries*. Edited by L. Szczucki, 139–45. Warsaw, 1983.

Huygens, C. *Les Oeuvres Complètes de Christiaan Huygens*. 22 vols. The Hague, 1888–1951.

Iliffe, R. "Friendly Criticism: Richard Simon, John Locke, Isaac Newton and the Johannine Comma." In *Scripture and Scholarship in Early Modern England*. Edited by A. Hessayon and N. Keene, 137–57. Aldershot, 2006.

Iliffe, R. "'In the Warehouse': Privacy, Property and Priority in the Early Royal Society." *History of Science* 30 (1992): 29–68.

Iliffe, R. "Is He Like Other Men? The Meaning of the *Principia Mathematica* and the Author as Idol." In *Culture and Society in the Stuart Restoration*. Edited by G. Maclean, 159–78. Cambridge, 1995.

Iliffe, R. "Isaac Newton: Lucatello Professor of Mathematics." In *Science Incarnate: Historical Embodiments of Natural Knowledge*. Edited by C. Lawrence and S. Shapin, 121–55. Chicago, 1998.

Iliffe, R. "'Making a Shew': Apocalyptic Hermeneutics and Christian Idolatry in the Work of Isaac Newton and Henry More." In *The Books of Nature and Scripture: Recent Essays on Natural Philosophy, Theology, and Biblical Criticism in the Netherlands of Spinoza's Time and the British Isles of Newton's Time.* Edited by J. E. Force and R. Popkin, 55–88. Dordrecht, 1994.

Iliffe, R. "Newton, God, and the Mathematics of the Two Books." In *Mathematicians and Their Gods.* Edited by S. Lawrence and M. McCartney, 121–55. Oxford, 2015

Iliffe, R. "'Prosecuting Athanasius': Protestant Forensics and the Mirrors of Persecution." In *Newton and Newtonianism: New Studies.* Edited by J. Force and S. Hutton, 113–54. Kluwer, 2004.

Iliffe, R. "The Religion of Isaac Newton." In *The Cambridge Companion to Newton.* 2nd ed. Edited by R. Iliffe and G. Smith, 485–523. Cambridge, 2016.

Iliffe, R., ed. *Early Biographies of Isaac Newton, 1660–1885.* Vol. 1 of *Early Biographies of Isaac Newton.* 2 vols. Edited by R. Higgitt, R. Iliffe, and M. Keynes. London, 2006.

Israel, J. *The Radical Enlightenment: Philosophy and the Making of Modernity.* New York, 2002.

Iverson, E. *The Myth of Egypt and Its Hieroglyphs in the European Tradition.* Princeton, 1993.

Jacob, M. C., and W. A. Lockwood. "Political Millenarianism and Burnet's *Sacred Theory.*" *Science Studies* 2 (1972): 265–79.

Janiak, A. *Newton as Philosopher.* Cambridge 2008.

Jardine, N. *The Birth of the History and Philosophy of Science: Kepler's Defence of Tycho Versus Ursus.* Cambridge, 1986.

Johns, A. *The Nature of the Book: Print and Knowledge in the Making.* Chicago, 1998.

Johnston, W. "The Anglican Apocalypse in Restoration England." *Journal of Ecclesiastical History* 55 (2004): 467–501.

Johnston, W. "Revelation and the Revolution of 1688–1689." *Historical Journal* 48 (2005): 351–89.

Johnston, W. *Revelation Restored: The Apocalypse in Later Seventeenth-Century England.* Woodbridge, 2011.

Jones, J. R. *The First Whigs: The Politics of the Exclusion Crisis, 1678–83.* London, 1961.

Jones, J. R. *The Revolution of 1688 in England.* London, 1988.

Jue, J. *Heaven upon Earth: Joseph Mede (1586–1638) and the Legacy of Millenarianism.* New York, 2006.

Kahn, V. *Wayward Contracts: The Crisis of Political Obligation in England, 1640–1674.* Princeton, 2004.

Kelly, J. N. D. *Early Christian Creeds.* 3rd ed. Harlow, 1985.

Kennedy, G. A. *Classical Rhetoric and Its Christian and Secular Tradition from Ancient to Modern Times.* Chapel Hill, 1980.

Kenyon, J. P. "The Commission for Ecclesiastical Causes, 1686–1688: A Reconsideration." *Historical Journal* 34 (1991): 727–36.

Kenyon, J. P. *The Popish Plot.* New York, 1972.

Kenyon, J. P. *Revolution Principles: The Politics of Party, 1689–1720.* Cambridge, 1977.

King, P. *The Life of John Locke.* London, 1858.

Klauber, M. "Between Protestant Orthodoxy and Rationalism: Fundamental Articles and the Early Career of Jean Le Clerc." *Journal of the History of Ideas* 54 (1993): 611–36.

Knights, M. *Politics and Opinion in Crisis, 1678–81.* Cambridge, 2006.

Knoespel, K. J. "Interpretive Strategies in Newton's Theologiae Gentilis Origines Philosophiae." In *Newton and Religion: Context, Nature and Influence.* Edited by J. E. Force and R. Popkin, 179–202. Dordrecht, 1999.

Koyré, A. *Newtonian Studies.* Chicago, 1965.

Kubrin, D. C. "Newton and the Cyclical Cosmos: Providence and the Mechanical Philosophy." *Journal of the History of Ideas* 28 (1967): 325–46.

Lacey, D. *Dissent and Parliamentary Politics, 1660–89.* New Brunswick, N.J., 1969.

Lake, P. "Anti-popery: The Structure of a Prejudice." In *Conflicts in Early Stuart England: Studies in Religion and Politics, 1603–1642.* Edited by R. Cust and A. Hughes, 72–106. London, 1989.

Lake, P. *The Boxmaker's Revenge: "Orthodoxy," "Heterodoxy," and the Politics of the Parish in Early Stuart London.* Stanford, 2002.

Lake, P. "Serving God and the Times: The Calvinist Conformity of Robert Sanderson." *Journal of British Studies* 27 (1988): 81–116.

Lake, P. "The Significance of the Elizabethan Identification of the Pope as Antichrist." *Journal of Ecclesiastical History* 31 (1980): 161–78.

Lamont, W. *Godly Rule, Politics and Religion, 1603–60.* London, 1969.

Lamont, W. *Richard Baxter and the Millennium: Protestant Imperialism and the English Revolution.* London, 1979.

Landon, M. *The Triumph of the Lawyers: Their Role in English Politics, 1678–1689.* Tuscaloosa, Ala., 1970.

Leith, J. H. "John Calvin's Polemic Against Idolatry." In *Soli Deo Gloria: New Testament Studies in Honour of William Childs Robinson.* Edited by J. M. Richards, 111–24. Richmond, Va., 1968.

Leppin, H. "Heretical Historiography: Philostorgius." *Studia Patristica* 34 (2001): 111–24.

Lessay, F. "Christologie de Hobbes: Le soupçon de Socinianisme." In *L'interpretazione nei secoli XVI e XVII.* Edited by G. Canziani and Y. C. Zarka, 549–64. Milan, 1993.

Levenson, T. *Newton and the Counterfeiter: The Unknown Detective Career of the World's Greatest Scientist.* Boston, 2009.

Levine, J. "Erasmus and the Problem of the Johannine Comma." *Journal of the History of Ideas* (1997): 573–96.

Levitin, D. *Ancient Wisdom in the Age of the New Science: Histories of Philosophy in England, c. 1640–1700.* Cambridge, 2015.

Levitin, D. "The Experimentalist as Humanist: Robert Boyle on the History of Philosophy." *Annals of Science* 71 (2014): 149–82.

Lim, P. *Mystery Unveiled: The Crisis of the Trinity in Early Modern England.* Oxford, 2012.

Lough, J. ed. *Locke's Travels in France, 1675–9, as Related in His Journals, Correspondence and Other Papers*. Cambridge, 1953.

Love, H. *Scribal Publication in Seventeenth-Century England*. Oxford, 1993.

Loveman, K. "Samuel Pepys and 'Discourses Touching Religion' Under James II." *English Historical Review* 127 (2012): 46–82.

Lucci, D. *Scripture and Deism: The Biblical Criticism of the Eighteenth-Century British Deists*. Bern, 2008.

Lund, R. *The Margins of Orthodoxy: Heterodox Writing and Cultural Response, 1660–1750*. Cambridge, 1995.

Lyon Turner, G. "Williamson's Spy Book." In *Transactions of the Congregational Historical Society* 5 (1912): 245–50.

MacIntyre, A. "The College, King James II and the Revolution, 1687–8." In *Magdalen College and the Crown: Essays for the Tercentenary of the Restoration of the College 1688*. Edited by L. Brockliss, G. Harris, and A. MacIntyre, 31–82. Oxford, 1988.

Mandelbrote, S. " 'A Duty of the Greatest Moment': Isaac Newton and the Writing of Biblical Criticism." *British Journal for the History of Science* 26 (1993): 281–302.

Mandelbrote, S. "Eighteenth-Century Reactions to Newton's Anti-Trinitarianism." In *Newton and Newtonianism: New Studies*. Edited by J. Force and S. Hutton, 93–111. London, 2004.

Mandelbrote, S. "Isaac Newton and the Book of Daniel." In *Die Geschichte der Daniel Auslegung in Judentum, Christentum und Islam*. Edited by K. Bracht and D. S. du Toit, 351–75. Berlin, 2007.

Mandelbrote, S. "Isaac Newton and Thomas Burnet: Biblical Criticism and the Crisis of Late Seventeenth-Century England." In *The Books of Nature and Scripture*. Edited by J. E. Force and R. Popkin, 149–78. Dordrecht, 1994.

Mandelbrote, S. "Than This Nothing Can Be Plainer": Newton Reads the Fathers." In *Die Patristik in de Frühen Neuzeit*. Edited by G. Frank, T. Leinkauf, and M. Wriedt, 277–97. Stuttgart, 2006.

Manuel, F. E. *The Eighteenth Century Confronts the Gods*. Cambridge, 1959.

Manuel, F. E. *Isaac Newton: Historian*. Cambridge, 1963.

Manuel, F. E. *A Portrait of Isaac Newton*. Cambridge, 1968.

Manuel, F. E. *The Religion of Isaac Newton*. Oxford, 1974.

Margival, H. *Essai sur Richard Simon et la Critique Biblique au XVIIe Siècle*. Paris, 1900.

Marshall, J. *John Locke, Toleration and Enlightenment Culture*. Cambridge, 2007.

Marshall, J. "Locke, Socinianism, 'Socinianism' and Unitarianism." In *English Philosophy in the Age of Locke*. Edited by A. Stewart, 111–82. Oxford, 2000.

Marshall, J. *Resistance, Religion and Responsibility*. Cambridge, 1994.

Matthews, A. G. *Calamy Revised: Being a Revision of Edward Calamy's Account of the Ministers and Others Ejected and Silenced, 1660–2*. Oxford, 1934.

Matthews, A. G. *Walker Revised: Being a Revision of John Walker's Sufferings of the Clergy During the Grand Rebellion 1642–60*. Oxford, 1948.

McGuire, J. E. "Newton on Space, Time and God: An Unpublished Source." *British Journal for the History of Science* 11 (1978): 115–28.

McGuire, J. E. "Space, Infinity and Indivisibility: Newton on the Creation of Matter." In *Contemporary Newtonian Research*. Edited by Z. Bechler. Cambridge, 1982.

McGuire, J. E., and P. Rattansi. "Newton and the Pipes of Pan." *Notes and Records of the Royal Society* 21 (1966): 108–43.

McGuire, J. E., and M. Tamny. *Certain Philosophical Questions: Newton's Trinity Notebook*. Cambridge, 1983.

McLachlan, H. *Sir Isaac Newton: Theological Manuscripts*. Liverpool, 1950.

McLachlan, H. J. *Socinianism in Seventeenth Century England*. Cambridge, 1951.

McMullin, E. "Galileo on Science and Scripture." In *The Cambridge Companion to Galileo*. Edited by P. Machamer, 271–347. Cambridge, 1998.

Metzger, B. *The Text of the New Testament: Its Transmission, Corruption and Restoration*. 3rd ed. New York, 1992.

Miller, J. *Popery and Politics in England, 1660–1688*. Cambridge, 1973.

Milton, A. *Catholic and Reformed: The Roman and Protestant Churches in English Protestant Thought, 1600–1640*. Cambridge, 1995.

Monk, J. H., ed. *The Life of Richard Bentley, D.D.* 2 vols. London, 1833.

Morgan, J. *Godly Learning: Puritan Attitudes Towards Reason, Learning and Education 1560–1640*. Cambridge, 1988.

Morrill, J. "The Church in England, 1642–9." In *Reactions to the English Civil War, 1642–9*. Edited by J. Morrill, 89–114. London, 1982.

Mortimer, S. *Reason and Religion in the English Revolution: The Challenge of Socinianism*. Cambridge, 2010.

Mullinger, J. B. *The University of Cambridge*. 3 vols. Cambridge, 1873–1911.

Napier, A., ed. *The Theological Works of Isaac Barrow*. 9 vols. Cambridge, 1859.

Nenner, H. *By Colour of Law: Legal Culture and Constitutional Politics in England, 1660–1689*. Chicago, 1977.

North, R. *General Preface and Life of Dr. John North*. Edited by P. Millard. Toronto, 1984.

North, R. *The Lives of the Norths*. 3 vols. Edited by A. Jessopp. London, 1890.

Nuovo, V. *John Locke: Writings on Religion*. Oxford, 2002.

O'Day, R. "James Duport." In *The New Dictionary of National Biography*. Edited by Colin Matthew and Brian Harrison. Oxford, 2004.

Packer, J. W. *The Transformation of Anglicanism, 1643–1660 with Special Reference to Henry Hammond*. Manchester, 1969.

Parish, H. L. *Monks, Miracles and Magic: Reformation Representations of the Medieval Church*. London, 2005.

Park, K. "Bacon's Enchanted Glass." *Isis* 75 (1984): 290–302.

Parkin, J. "Hobbism in the Later 1660s." *Historical Journal* (1999): 85–108.

Parkin, J. "Humphrey Babington." In *The New Dictionary of National Biography*. Edited by Colin Matthew and Brian Harrison. Oxford, 2004.

Peacock, G. *Observations on the Statutes of the University of Cambridge*. London, 1861.

Pincus, S. *1688: The First Modern Revolution*. New Haven, 2009.

Pitassi, M. C. "La notion de communication dans l'exégèse biblique de la fin du XVIIe siècle." In *Commercium Litterarium: Forms of Communication in the Republic of Letters, 1600–1750*. Edited by H. Bots and F. Waquet, 35–50. Amsterdam, 1994.

Pounds, C. A. "Newton's 'Derangement of the Intellect': New Light on an Old Problem." *Notes and Records of the Royal Society* 34 (1970): 11–32.

Prancic, T., and J. Doelman. "'Ora pro me, sancta Herberte': James Duport and the Reputation of George Herbert." *George Herbert Journal* 24 (2000/2001): 35–55.

Preston, A., and P. H. Oswald. "James Duport's Rules for His Tutorial Pupils: A Comparison of Two Surviving Manuscripts." *Transactions of the Cambridge Bibliographical Society* 14 (2011): 317–63.

Principe, L. *The Aspiring Adept: Robert Boyle and His Alchemical Quest*. Princeton, 2000.

Przypskowski, T. "La gnomique de Nicolas Copernic et de Georges Joachim Rheticus." In *Actes du VIIIe Congrès Internationale d'Histoire des Sciences....*, 400–409. Paris, 1958.

Quantin, J. L. *The Church of England and Christian Antiquity: The Construction of a Confessional Identity in the Seventeenth Century*. Oxford, 2009.

Quintrell, B. "Henry Ferne." In *The New Dictionary of National Biography*. Edited by Colin Matthew and Brian Harrison. Oxford, 2004.

Rademaker, C. S. M. *The Life and Work of Gerard Joannes Vossius, 1577–1649*. Assen, 1981.

Raven, C. *John Ray: Naturalist*. Cambridge, 1986.

Reedy, G. *The Bible and Reason: Anglicans and Scripture in Late Seventeenth-Century England*. Philadelphia, 1985.

Rees, T. *The Racovian Catechism, with Notes and Illustrations, Translated from the Latin: To Which Is Prefixed a Sketch of the History of Unitarianism in Poland and the Adjacent Countries*. London, 1818.

Rex, M. B. *University Representation in England, 1604–1690*. London, 1954.

Rossi, M. M. *La vita, le opera, I tempi di Edoardo Herbert di Chirbury*. 3 vols. Florence, 1947.

Rouse Ball, W. W. *Notes on the History of Trinity College, Cambridge*. London, 1899.

Rouse Ball, W. W. *Trinity College Cambridge*. London, 1906

Rouse Ball, W. W. *Cambridge Papers*. London, 1918.

Rublack, U. *The Astronomer and the Witch: Johannes Kepler's Fight for His Mother*. Oxford, 2015.

Ruffner, J. A. "The Background and Early Development of Newton's Theory of Comets." PhD diss., Indiana University, 1966.

Sargent, R. M. "Scientific Experiment and Legal Expertise: The Way of Experience in Seventeenth Century England." *Studies in the History and Philosophy of Science* 20 (1989): 19–45.

Schaffer, S. "Comets and Idols: Newton's Cosmology and Political Theology." In *Action and Reaction: Proceedings of a Symposium to Commemorate the Tercentenary of Newton's Principia*. Edited by P. Theerman and A. Seeff, 206–31. Newark, 1993.

Schaffer, S. "'Glass Works': Newton's Prisms and the Uses of Experiment." In *The Uses of Experiment: Studies in the Natural Sciences*. Edited by D. Gooding, T. Pinch, and S. Schaffer, 67–104. Cambridge, 1989.

Schaffer, S. "Newton's Comets and the Transformation of Astrology." In *Astrology, Science and Society*. Edited by P. Curry, 219–43. Woodbridge, 1987.

Schechner, S. *Comets, Popular Culture, and the Birth of Modern Cosmology*. Princeton, 1997.

Schmitt, C. B. "Perennial Philosophy: From Agostino Steuco to Leibniz." *Journal of the History of Ideas* 27 (1966): 505–32.

Schmitt-Biggeman, W. *Philosophia Perennis: Historical Outlines of Western Spirituality in Ancient, Medieval and Early Modern Thought*. Dordrecht, 2004.

Schoeck, R. "Lawyers and Rhetoric in Sixteenth-Century England." In *Renaissance Eloquence*. Edited by J. Murphy, 274–91. London, 1983.

Schwoerer, L. G. *The Declaration of Rights, 1689*. Baltimore, 1981.

Scott, J. *Algernon Sidney and the Restoration Crisis, 1677–1683*. Cambridge, 1991.

Seaver, P. *Wallington's World: A Puritan Artisan in Seventeenth-Century London*. Stanford, 1988.

Sepper, D. L. *Descartes's Imagination: Proportion, Images, and the Activity of Thinking* Berkeley, 1996.

Serjeantson, R. "The Education of Francis Willughby." In *Virtuoso by Nature: The Scientific Worlds of Francis Willughby FRS (1635–1672)*. Edited by T. Birkhead. Leiden, 2016.

Serjeantson, R. "Proof and Persuasion." In *The Cambridge History of Early Modern Science*. Edited by K. Park and L. Daston, 132–76. Cambridge, 2006.

Serjeantson, R. "Testimony and Proof in Early Modern England." *Studies in History and Philosophy of Science* 30 (1999): 195–236.

Seznec, J. *The Survival of the Pagan Gods: The Mythological Tradition and Its Place in Renaissance Humanism and Art*. Princeton, 1983.

Shalev, Z. *Sacred Words and Worlds: Geography, Religion and Scholarship, 1500–1750*. Leiden, 2011.

Shapin, S. "Pump and Circumstance: Robert Boyle's Literary Technology." *Social Studies of Science* (1984): 481–520.

Shapin, S. *A Social History of Truth: Civility and Science in Seventeenth-Century England*. Chicago, 1994.

Shapin, S., and S. Schaffer. *Leviathan and the Air-Pump: Hobbes, Boyle, and the Experimental Life*. Princeton, 1985.

Shapiro, A. E. "The Evolving Theory of Newton's Theory of White Light and Color." *Isis* 71 (1980): 211–35.

Shapiro, A. E. *Fits, Passions and Paroxysms: Physics, Method and Chemistry, and Newton's Theories of Colored Bodies and Fits of Easy Reflection*. Cambridge, 1993.

Shapiro, A. E. "The Gradual Acceptance of Newton's Theory of Light and Color, 1672–1727." *Perspectives in Science* 4 (1996): 59–139.

Sheehan, J. "Sacred and Profane: Idolatry, Antiquarianism and the Polemics of Distinction in the Seventeenth Century." *Past and Present* (2006): 35–65.

Skinner, Q. *Reason and Rhetoric in the Philosophy of Hobbes*. Cambridge, 1996.

Smith, G. "The Methodology of the *Principia*." In *The Cambridge Companion to Newton*. Edited by R. Iliffe and G. Smith, 187–228. 2nd ed. Cambridge, 2016.

Smolinski, R. "The Logic of Millennial Thought: Sir Isaac Newton Among His Contemporaries." In *Newton and Religion: Context, Nature and Influence*. Edited by J. E. Force and R. H. Popkin, 259–90. Dordrecht, 1999.

Snobelen, S. "Isaac Newton, Heretic: The Strategies of a Nicodemite." *British Journal for the History of Science* 32 (1999): 381–419.

Snobelen, S. "Isaac Newton, Socinianism and 'the One Supreme God.'" In *Socinianism and Cultural Exchange: The European Dimension of Antitrinitarian and Arminian Networks, 1650–1720*. Edited by M. Mulsow and J. Rohls, 241–93. Leiden, 2005.

Snobelen, S. "Lust, Pride and Ambition: Isaac Newton and the Devil." In *Newton and Newtonianism*. Edited by J. E. Force and S. Hutton, 155–81. Dordrecht, 2004.

Snobelen, S. " 'Not in the Language of the Astronomers': Isaac Newton, the Scriptures, and the Hermeneutics of Accommodation." In *Nature and Scripture in the Abrahamic Religions: Up to 1700*. Edited by J. van der Meer and S. Mandelbrote, 491–530. Leiden, 2008.

Snobelen, S. " 'To Us There Is but One God, the Father': Antitrinitarian Textual Criticism in Seventeenth- and Early Eighteenth-Century England." In *Scripture and Scholarship in Early Modern England*. Edited by A. Hessayon and N. Keene, 116–36. Aldershot, 2006.

Somerville, J. P. *Politics and Ideology in England, 1603–1640*. London, 1986.

Speak, G. " 'An Odd Kind of Melancholy': Reflections on the Glass Delusion in Europe (1440–1680)." *History of Psychiatry* 1 (1990): 191–206.

Speck, W. *Reluctant Revolutionaries: Englishmen and the Revolution of 1688*. Oxford, 1989.

Spurr, J. "The Church of England, Comprehension and the Toleration Act of 1689." *The English Historical Review* 104, no. 413 (1989): 927–46.

Spurr, J. " 'Rational Religion' in Restoration England." *Journal for the History of Ideas* 49 (1988): 563–85.

Spurr, J. *The Restoration Church of England 1646–1689*. New Haven, 1991.

Stevens, F. P. *From Constantine to Alaric*. Liphook, 1984.

Stewart, I. " 'Fleshy Books': Isaac Barrow and the Oratorical Critique of Cartesian Natural Philosophy." *History of the Universities* 16 (2000): 35–102.

Stewart, I. "The Statutes of the Lucasian Professorship: A Translation." In *From Newton to Hawking: A History of Cambridge University's Lucasian Professors of Mathematics*. Edited by K. Knox and R. Noakes, 461–74. Cambridge, 2003.

Stewart L. "Seeing Through the Scholium: Religion and Reading Newton in the Eighteenth Century." *History of Science* 34 (1996): 123–65.

Stolzenberg, D. "John Spencer and the Perils of Sacred Philology." *Past and Present* 214 (2012): 129–63.

Stolzenberg, D. *Egyptian Oedipus: Athanasius Kircher and the Secrets of Antiquity*. Chicago, 2013.

Stroumsa, G. "John Spencer and the Roots of Idolatry." *History of Religions* 41 (2001): 1–23.

Stroumsa, G. *A New Science: The Discovery of Religion in the Age of Reason.* Cambridge, Mass., 2010.

Tamny, M. "Newton, Creation, and Perception." *Isis* 70 (1979): 48–59.

Thomas, R. "Comprehension and Indulgence." In *From Uniformity to Unity, 1662–1962.* Edited by O. Chadwick and G. Nuttall, 191–253. London, 1962.

Thompson, E. A. "Christianity and the Northern Barbarians." In *The Conflict Between Paganism and Christianity in the Fourth Century.* Edited by A. Momigliano, 56–78. Oxford, 1963.

Thompson, R. "Some Newly Discovered Letters of John Ray." *Journal of Society of Bibliography of Natural History* 7 (1974): 111–23.

Todd, M. "Puritan Self-fashioning: The Diary of Samuel Ward." *Journal of British Studies* 31 (1992): 236–64.

Toomer, G. J. *Eastern Wisedome and Learning: The Study of Arabic in Seventeenth-Century England.* Oxford, 1996.

Toribio Pérez, P., ed. *Isaac Newton. Historia Ecclesiastica (De Origine Schismatico Ecclesiae Papisticae Bicornis). Editión Crítica, Traducción y Estudio.* Madrid, 2013.

Trabue, J. "Ann and Arthur Storer of Calvert County, Maryland, Friends of Sir Isaac Newton." *The American Genealogist* 79 (2004): 13–27.

Trowell, S. "Unitarian and/or Anglican: The Relationship of Unitarianism to the Church from 1687–98." *Bulletin of the John Rylands Library* 78 (1996): 77–101.

Tuck, R. *Philosophy and Government, 1572–1651.* Cambridge, 1993.

Turnbull, G. H. *Hartlib, Dury and Comenius.* Liverpool, 1938.

Turnor, E., ed. *Collections for the History of the Town and Soke of Grantham.* London, 1806.

Twigg, J. *The University of Cambridge in the English Revolution.* Cambridge, 1990.

Tyacke, N. *Anti-Calvinists: The Rise of English Arminianism, c. 1590–1640.* Oxford, 1987.

Vallance, E. *Revolutionary England and the National Covenant: State Oaths, Protestantism and the Political Nation, 1533–1682.* Woodbridge, 2005.

Van Berg, J. "Grotius' Views on Antichrist and Apocalyptic Thought in England." In *Hugo Grotius, Theologian: Essays in Honour of G. H. M. Posthumus Meyjes.* Edited by H. J. M. Nellen et al., 169–84. Leiden, 1992.

Vellacott, P. C. "The Struggle of James the Second with the University of Cambridge." In *In Memoriam: A. W. Ward.* Edited by W. E. Barnes, 81–101. Cambridge, 1924.

Venables, E. "The Altar Controversy at Grantham in the Seventeenth Century." *Associated Architectural Societies: Reports and Papers* 13 (1875–76): 46–60.

Venn, J., and J. A. Venn, eds. *Alumni Cantabrigienses: A Biographical List of All Known Students, Graduates and Holders of Office at the University of Cambridge, from the Earliest Times to 1900.* 4 vols. Cambridge, 1922–53.

Vickers, B. *In Defence of Rhetoric.* Oxford, 1989.

Walker, D. P. *The Ancient Theology: Studies in Christian Platonism from the Fifteenth to the Eighteenth Century.* London, 1972.

Walker, D. P. *Unclean Spirits: Possession and Exorcism in France and England in the Late Sixteenth and Early Seventeenth Centuries.* London, 1981.

Wallace, D. D. *Shapers of English Calvinism, 1660–1714: Variety, Persistence, and Transformation*. Oxford, 2011.

Wandel, L. P. *Voracious Idols and Violent Hands: Iconoclasm in Reformation Zurich, Strasbourg, and Basel*. Cambridge, 1995.

Ward, R. *Life of the Learned and Pious Henry More*. London, 1710.

Warner, D. H. J. "Hobbes' Interpretation of the Doctrine of the Trinity." *The Journal of Religious History* 5 (1969): 299–313.

Watson, F. *English Grammar Schools to 1660*. Cambridge, 1908.

Webster, C. *The Great Instauration*. London, 1975.

Webster, C. "Henry More and Descartes: Some New Sources." *British Journal of the History of Science* 4 (1969): 359–77.

Weil, R. *A Plague of Informers: Conspiracy and Political Trust in William III's England*. New Haven, 2013.

Western, J. R. *Monarchy and Revolution: The English State in the 1680s*. London, 1972.

Westfall, R. S. "Isaac Newton's Theologiæ Gentilis Origines Philosophicæ." In *The Secular Mind*. Edited by W. Warren Wagar, 15–34. New York, 1982.

Westfall, R. S. *Never at Rest: A Biography of Isaac Newton*. Cambridge, 1980.

Westfall, R. S. "Unpublished Boyle Papers Relating to Scientific Method." *Annals of Science* 12 (1956): 63–73, 103–17.

Westman, R. "The Copernicans and the Churches." In *God and Nature: Historical Essays on the Encounter Between Christianity and Science*. Edited by D. Lindberg and R. Numbers, 76–113. Los Angeles, 1986.

Whiteside, D. T., ed. *The Mathematical Papers of Isaac Newton*. 8 vols. Cambridge, 1967–81.

Whittingham, W. "Essay on the Life and Writings of Samuel Bochart." In *Essays and Dissertations in Biblical Literature*, vol. 1. New York, 1829, 107–68.

Wickenden, N. *G. J. Vossius and the Humanist Conception of History*. Assen, 1993.

Wiles, M. *Archetypal Heresy: Arianism through the Centuries*. Oxford, 2001.

Williams, D. *Ambrose of Milan and the End of the Nicene-Arian Conflicts*. Oxford, 1995.

Williams, G. H. *The Radical Reformation*. 3rd ed. Kirksville, 1992.

Williams, R. *Arius: Heresy and Tradition*. London, 1981.

Wind, E. *Pagan Mysteries in the Renaissance*. 2nd ed. Oxford, 1980.

Wolfram, H. *The History of the Goths*. Berkeley, 1988.

Wood, A. *The Life and Times of Anthony Wood, Antiquary at Oxford, 1632–95, Described by Himself*. Edited by A. Clark. 5 vols. Oxford, 1891–1900.

Woodward, J. "Of the Wisdom of the Ancient Egyptians." *Archaeologia* 4 (1777): 212–311.

Woolhouse, R. *Locke: A Biography*. Cambridge, 2007.

Wootton, D., ed. *John Locke: Political Writings*. Harmondsworth, 1993.

Woudhuysen, H. *Sir Philip Sidney and the Circulation of Manuscripts, 1548–1640*. Oxford, 1996.

Yates, F. *Giordano Bruno and the Hermetic Tradition*. Oxford, 1964.

Ziff, L. *The Career of John Cotton: Puritanism and the American Experience*. Princeton, 1962.

Index

512